Rules of Relief

Rules of Relief

Institutions of social security, and their impact

J.C. Vrooman

The Netherlands Institute for Social Research | SCP
The Hague, September 2009

The Netherlands Institute for Social Research | scp was established by Royal Decree of March 30, 1973 with the following terms of reference:
a. to carry out research designed to produce a coherent picture of the state of social and cultural welfare in the Netherlands and likely developments in this area;
b. to contribute to the appropriate selection of policy objectives and to provide an assessment of the advantages and disadvantages of the various means of achieving those ends;
c. to seek information on the way in which interdepartmental policy on social and cultural welfare is implemented with a view to assessing its implementation.

The work of the Netherlands Institute for Social Research focuses especially on problems coming under the responsibility of more than one Ministry. As Coordinating Minister for social and cultural welfare, the Minister for Health, Welfare and Sport is responsible for the policies pursued by the Netherlands Institute for Social Research. With regard to the main lines of such policies the Minister consults the Ministers of General Affairs; Justice; Interior and Kingdom Relations; Education, Culture and Science; Finance; Housing, Spatial Planning and the Environment; Economic Affairs; Agriculture, Nature and Food Quality; and Social Affairs and Employment

© J.C. Vrooman and The Netherlands Institute for Social Research | scp, The Hague 2009 - 2011
scp-publication 2009-11
DTP: Textcetera, The Hague
Figures: Information Design Studio, Amsterdam
Cover design: Bureau Stijlzorg, Utrecht

Cover illustration: *Relief Blues* (ca 1938), by O.L. Guglielmi (1906-1956). Tempera on fiberboard (61.1 by 76.2 cm); from the collection of the Smithsonian American Art Museum, Washington DC, usa.
With meticulous realism, Guglielmi shows a family gathered around a table in a small New York apartment during the Great Depression. A relief worker fills out forms to determine whether they qualify for a welfare benefit. Guglielmi portrays the unease and despair of those left unemployed, and their attempts to save face and maintain some dignity. The painter applied for relief himself during the early 1930s, before he managed to obtain a meagre stipend through the Works Progress Administration's 'Federal Art Project', a government-funded programme which at the time created 5,000 jobs for artists.

ISBN 978 90 377 0218 7 (paperback)
ISBN 978 90 377 0431 0 (hardcover)

NUR 740

Distribution in the usa, Canada and Mexico: Transaction Publishers, New Brunswick (usa)

The Netherlands Institute for Social Research | scp
Parnassusplein 5
2511 vx The Hague
The Netherlands
Tel.: +31 70 340 7000
Fax.: +31 70 340 7044
www.scp.nl
info@scp.nl

Contents

1		Introduction	9
2		Institutional theory	15
2.1		Institutions and the 'new institutionalism'	15
	2.1.1	Sociological institutionalism	18
	2.1.2	Rational choice institutionalism	20
	2.1.3	Historical institutionalism	23
2.2		North's economic-historical approach	25
	2.2.1	Institutions and transaction costs	25
	2.2.2	Formal and informal rules	26
	2.2.3	Enforcement	29
	2.2.4	Institutional change and path dependence	30
2.3		The evolvement and impact of institutions: a figural model	32
2.4		Institutions as socially constructed rules	39
2.5		Types of institution	48
2.6		Institutional hierarchy	53
	2.6.1	Constitutive and regulative rules?	53
	2.6.2	Core rights and derivative rights	54
	2.6.3	Hierarchies of formal rules	55
	2.6.4	Hierarchies of informal rules	56
	2.6.5	Correspondence between formal and informal rules	58
2.7		Actors, their relationships and their motivations	59
	2.7.1	Actors	60
	2.7.2	Relationships between actors	61
	2.7.3	Motivations of individual actors	63
	2.7.4	Motivations of corporate actors	71
2.8		Rule-driven interactions	72
	2.8.1	Institutions and interaction	73
	2.8.2	Interaction results and the context of rule application	75
	2.8.3	Rule acquisition	75
2.9		The rule generation process: creation and development of institutions	85
	2.9.1	The incentive to regulate	86
	2.9.2	Underlying causes of institutionalisation: the historical process	91
	2.9.3	The regulatory aspirations of actors	96
	2.9.4	Rule-interaction and institutionalisation	100
2.10		Conclusions	107

3	Social security and the institutional approach		111
3.1	Traditional definitions of social security		111
	3.1.1	The narrow approach	113
	3.1.2	The broad approach	118
	3.1.3	Criticism of the narrow and broad approaches	123
3.2	Social security in an institutional sense		126
3.3	Institutions and actors in social security		133
	3.3.1	Informal social security rules	133
	3.3.2	Informal social security systems	134
	3.3.3	Formal social security	136
	3.3.4	Informal elements in formal social security	137
	3.3.5	Social security actors	139
3.4	Undersocialised social security		141
3.5	Models of rule-driven social security interactions		143
	3.5.1	Familial social security	144
	3.5.2	Communal social security	148
	3.5.3	Informal occupational social security	152
	3.5.4	Formal demographic regulations	156
	3.5.5	Unemployment and social assistance benefit regulations	165
	3.5.6	Sick leave and disability regulations	174
3.6	The results of social security rules		182
	3.6.1	The historical background to rule application	183
	3.6.2	Consequences for actors	188
	3.6.3	Collective results	190
3.7	Institutional change: from informal to formal systems		200
3.8	Conclusions		203

4	Regimes of social security	209
4.1	Theoretical traits of social security regimes	210
4.2	An empirical typology	220
4.3	The generality of regime types	231
4.4	Conclusions	246

5	Benefit dependency		249
5.1	Regimes and benefit dependency: theoretical expectations		250
5.2	Measuring benefit dependency		261
5.3	The development of benefit dependency		264
	5.3.1	Relative volume	264
	5.3.2	Growth rates	271
	5.3.3	Volume composition	276
	5.3.4	Summary of the bivariate analyses	287

5.4	A causal model for benefit dependency growth		289
5.5	Country-specific models		302
	5.5.1	Impact of model variables	304
	5.5.2	Regime impact	311
5.6	Conclusions		326
6	Poverty		344
6.1	The theoretical poverty debate in political philosophy: some key elements		345
	6.1.1	Nature of the deficits: equality of what?	346
	6.1.2	Absolute or relative deficits	348
	6.1.3	Establishing thresholds	350
	6.1.4	The need for compensation	352
	6.1.5	Conditions for compensation	354
6.2	The meaning of poverty		357
	6.2.1	Basic principles	357
	6.2.2	A theoretical definition of poverty	360
	6.2.3	Poverty, inequality and social exclusion	362
6.3	Granting rights to the poor		364
	6.3.1	Compensatory rights	364
	6.3.2	The role of the government	365
	6.3.3	Conditioning	365
6.4	Operational poverty lines		366
	6.4.1	Notions on poverty among the population	367
	6.4.2	A typology of operational poverty lines	368
	6.4.3	Relative poverty lines	370
	6.4.4	Subjective poverty lines	375
	6.4.5	Objective absolute poverty lines	380
6.5	A generalised budget approach		383
	6.5.1	Reference budgets for a single person	384
	6.5.2	Initial poverty lines	385
	6.5.3	The indexation method	386
	6.5.4	Outcomes of the generalised budget approach in the Netherlands	387
6.6	The theoretical relationship between regime types and poverty		390
6.7	Empirical results		396
	6.7.1	Country-specific norm amounts for a single person	399
	6.7.2	Sensitivity analysis of equivalence scales	400
	6.7.3	The 'three I's of poverty' and the regime types	407
	6.7.4	Explaining the poverty incidence: multi-level models	412
6.8	Conclusions		418

7	The collective significance of social security institutions	427
7.1	Institutions and social security	428
7.2	Regimes, benefit dependency and poverty	440
7.3	The impact of social security regimes	449
7.4	Some implications	455

Acknowledgements 463

Notes 465

List of references 527

1 Introduction

Prior to the emergence of the modern welfare state, agencies taking care of the poor sometimes drew up 'rules of relief'. A Dutch written code dating from 1817 is exemplary in this respect. These 'Regulations governing the provision of care to the home-dwelling poor in the town of Den Bosch' established the conditions for local poor relief.[1] In order to obtain support, residents had to have been affected by certain specific events. The Regulations stated that a permanent need for municipal assistance could be due to "advanced age and physical defect, which either in whole or in part makes the person unsuitable for the performance of labour". Temporary need might arise in the event of "illness of short duration, cessation of work due to the season, women in times of confinement, and funeral expenses".

However, not everyone who became destitute due to such circumstances was entitled to poor relief. The local officials caring for the poor (*armverzorgers*) could only nominate people for support after they had ensured that the other conditions set out in the guidelines had been met as well. Above all, they had to ascertain the "virtuous conduct" of those requesting help; though interestingly enough, the Regulations failed to specify precisely what criteria should be applied in making such a judgement. In addition, to be eligible for help people had to have no ways of obtaining adequate means of subsistence from their blood relatives, from their town of birth if this was somewhere other than Den Bosch, or from other funds and subsidies. The *armverzorgers* also had to assess the degree of "industriousness" displayed by applicants in partially meeting their needs themselves, as well as whether their income could not be increased by "diligent labour".

Following the preliminary investigation by the officials, the poor were "sampled". Twice a year the regents of the municipal poor relief board, the auditors, and the masters of the ten local districts paid joint house calls to needy persons. Subsequently, the Council of Regents decided which individuals and families would receive support, and how much this would amount to each week in the coming summer or winter season. The *armverzorgers* were responsible for the distribution of weekly poor relief; and they were only allowed to increase the amounts set by the Council if unforeseen and exceptional costs arose. In their contacts with the poor, however, these local officials had considerably more latitude. They could restrict support as they saw fit, and largely at their own discretion. Poor relief could be withheld for one or more weeks if the recipients "display continuous bad behaviour, or show carelessness towards their children, or on other grounds which are deemed valid by the Lord Guardians of the Poor".

As time passed the protection against the consequences of old age, illness, unemployment and similar risks came more and more to be regarded as a national responsibility. The government was given a core task in safeguarding the living conditions of its citizens. In order to achieve this, the favours granted by municipal poor houses and church organisations to the deserving poor were gradually converted into the rights of the welfare state, and enshrined in national law. De Swaan (1988: 218-257) discusses this historical transition "from charity to social consciousness" extensively. In his view changing social circumstances – in particular the introduction of capitalist production methods, the ongoing "civilising process", the growth of the state apparatus, and innovations in administrative techniques – went hand-in-hand with changes in the configuration of influential social groups (the working class, the petty bourgeoisie, employers' organisations). The contesting elites went in search of new, stable ways to resolve the social issues of their age, building on what had already been achieved.

De Swaan stresses the importance of the increasingly long chains of interdependence in this regard. Economic markets were no longer local or regional, but acquired a national or even transnational character. On the social front, large-scale migratory movements, the erosion of the traditional structure of social estates (nobility, clergy, commoners), and the emergence of the nation-state meant that the mutual ties between individuals extended over greater geographical and social distances than previously. This growth of interdependence implied that solutions for the problems social security aimed to solve – especially the economic, political and health threats originating from a large group of urban poor – had to be sought at ever higher levels of abstraction. Initially the local parishes and guilds bore the brunt of this collective effort; later the burden shifted to the municipal authorities and national *mutualités*, before finally ending up with the modern welfare states, as yet the climax of the historical development.

Through this "collectivisation of care", the rules of relief became more comprehensive over the years. Not only did their number and complexity increase,[2] but above all their scope. As before, the government took responsibility for the alleviation of severe cases of indigence; but it also began guaranteeing its citizens rights to a certain level of income, medical assistance, employment counselling, social work, etc.

In essence, however, the main components of the rules have not changed. Just as in the Den Bosch Regulations from 1817, they indicate which events entitle people to a certain benefit or provision, and how far those rights extend. And the contemporary 'rules of relief' also still contain clauses on job search requirements, on means testing, on the administrative procedures to be followed, and on the sanctions that officials are empowered to impose. It is modern social security rules such as these that form the subject of this study.

To be more precise, the core focus is on the societal consequences of the *institutions* of modern social security. Institutions are regarded here as socially constructed rules which set out the rights and obligations of actors, and the associated conditions and sanctions. These rules may be formalised in laws or government regulations, or laid down in contracts between the different parties involved. They may also be more informal in nature and usually remain unwritten: people's mutual views on what constitute correct forms of behaviour in particular circumstances.

On the one hand, institutions are a collective *given*. People cannot choose the historically developed rules of the society into which they are born, and may find it difficult to extricate themselves from their controlling force – especially when they perceive the rules as self-evident. On the other hand, institutions are also a collective *product*. Rules are made by people, and often reflect the goals, interests, etc., of their compilers. Their continued existence depends on social recognition and acceptance: institutions which are not endorsed or observed do not achieve what they were intended to, and may easily become meaningless. Since they are socially constructed, institutions can in theory be revised, though in practice this may not be realised without a struggle. Institutional change generally requires complex negotiations between stakeholders, with the formal legislative process in political democracies being the characteristic example. Actors are moreover not always free to develop entirely different sets of rules. They often reason from the basis of existing institutions, which may appear to them as a natural order, the abolition of which could entail high material or social costs.

Since institutions lay down the rights and obligations of actors, they influence the interactions of people and organisations. This has consequences both for those directly involved (their social standing, professional career, income, profit, etc.) and for the community within which the rules apply (the relationships between social groups, crime rates, the education level of the population, etc.). Modern social security institutions are of particular importance for two reasons. First, current 'rules of relief' are large in number and control the behaviour of many actors: benefit claimants, contributors, benefits agencies and business organisations. For that reason, they may have far-reaching consequences for society. Social security institutions can exert a major influence on the economy, being reflected in the nation's wealth, the level of consumption and business investments. But there may be other implications, too: the degree of poverty and inequality, the health status of the population, the demographic profile, political relationships and the occurrence of social unrest can all be affected by the way in which the social security system is configured.

Secondly, modern social security rules are very deliberate social constructs. They are the outcome of an intensive and lengthy process of political decision-making which is aimed at realising certain collective goals that are perceived as desirable. That makes the field a suitable domain for investigating the nature of institutions and their social impact.

Research questions
There are two types of question at stake in this study. The first concerns the theoretical status of social security institutions, the second their empirical impact in modern societies. From a theoretical point of view it is essential to start by analysing in general terms what institutions are, how they may arise and influence people's behaviour, and what consequences they may have for the actors involved and their community. The obvious follow-up question concerns the applicability of such general notions to the domain of social security.

Once these theoretical questions have been dealt with, it is important to investigate what influence social security institutions actually have in practice. There are many ways to assess this, both in terms of potential causes (various social security rules) and possible effects (different types of outcome). The empirical analyses performed here home in on the causal relationship between coherent systems of formal social security institutions – or 'regimes' – and two macro-level outcome indicators: benefit dependency and poverty.

Chapter 2 looks at general theoretical issues, aiming to clarify the nature of institutions on the basis of the following questions:
- What does the notion 'institution' entail?
- What kinds of institutions can be distinguished, and how do they relate to each other?
- How do institutions give direction to social interaction, and which actors may be involved in this?
- What consequences can rule-driven interactions have?
- Under what conditions do institutions come into being, and what causes them to change?

Chapter 3 explores the main topic of this study, social security, once again from a theoretical perspective. First the meaning of the concept in the scientific literature is subjected to critical analysis, resulting in an institutional definition of social security. The same questions are then asked as in the preceding chapter, but this time specifically for social security rules. Attention focuses particularly on the 'interaction structure' of different types of social security schemes, and on the societal effects that social security can theoretically bring about.

The next three chapters concentrate on the empirical significance of modern social security regulations. The main question is consistently concerned with the collective results social security rules actually generate. The emphasis is on formal institutions: social security rules that are drawn up or ratified by governments. As De Swaan (1989: 11, 13) observes, such rules are currently structured largely at national level, and shielded from outside influences:

> Welfare states are national states, which are concerned with the care only of their own citizenry. [...] States erect borders between their territory and that of other states, and welfare states seal off their domain of care just as securely from foreign people. [...] The welfare state is by nature exclusive and anti-international.[3]

In view of this national structuring of formal social security schemes, the obvious procedure is to investigate their impact by means of a country comparison. The focus of interest here will not be the significance of separate rules or regulations, such as the benefit conditions in unemployment insurance or the level of early retirement pensions. Rather, the objective is to answer a more generic question: what results do the diverse formal national *systems* of social security achieve not in theory (*de jure*) but in practice (*de facto*)?

Chapter 4 first explores the existence of such systems empirically. The leading question is whether a quantitative analysis of a large number of formal social security institutions reveals any country clusters that are based on fundamentally diverging principles. If this is the case, we may speak of different *types of social security regimes*. Such regime types can be regarded as abstract models of institutional variety. Esping-Andersen's (1990) distinction between corporatist, social-democratic and liberal 'worlds of welfare' has become famous in recent years. The empirical adequacy of the typology has been tested previously by many authors, but often not in an entirely satisfactory way. One major problem is the limited number of formal institutions that are included in these analyses, which probably implies that the various national social security systems have been represented only partially. The main aim of the chapter is to provide a more elaborate empirical test, by investigating whether a wide selection of formal institutional traits shows any consistent clustering across 11 nations. Of these countries, the systems of Belgium, France, and Germany are regarded as corporatist regimes in Esping-Andersen's analysis. Denmark, Sweden, and Norway are examples of his social-democratic type; and the USA, Australia, Canada and the United Kingdom theoretically represent the liberal model. The Netherlands is also included in the empirical analysis, as an example of a social security system which is difficult to classify from a theoretical point of view.

In addition to this, several other interesting issues will also be examined in some degree. Are regime types stable over time? Are they mainly confined to social security, the labour market and the tax system, or are regimes more general, in the sense that national institutions in the fields of health, education etc. show a similar pattern of country clusters? And finally: to what extent do the formal regime types coincide empirically with informal institutions, or the prevailing notions on social security, labour and taxation among the population?

Attention then turns to whether social security regimes produce divergent collective outcomes. Chapter 5 introduces a very direct output indicator: the *volume of social security benefits* in various countries. The degree of 'benefit dependency' is an interesting dependent variable, as it is closely connected to the rights and duties attributed in social security regulations, and because it may affect economic growth, labour market behaviour, poverty, inequality, etc.

The key question is whether social security regimes differ in the number of benefit recipients they generate, in line with theoretical expectations. This issue will be explored for the same set of countries representing the various regime types (except Norway), on the basis of comparative benefit dependency data covering a twenty-year period (1980-1999). First, the theoretical relationship between regime types and the production of benefits is discussed and cast in a number of hypotheses. These refer to three aspects of benefit dependency: the relative volume (the share of the population receiving benefit); the annual rate of growth in the number of benefits; and the composition of the total benefit volume in terms of various social risks (old age, unemployment, disability etc.). The theoretical expectations are then submitted to an empirical test. The first issue at stake here is whether there is a direct link between the various regime types and the three forms of benefit dependency. After completing these descriptive analyses, and having discussed the implications in terms of the hypotheses, a stricter empirical test is performed. A multivariate model is developed, which makes it possible to assess empirically whether regime types contribute to the production of benefits after controlling for the influence of other factors, such as demographic differences between countries.

Chapter 6 looks at the relationship between regime types and another outcome indicator, the *degree of poverty* across countries. Combating poverty is a major objective of most social security systems; and the various regime types choose different strategies in order to realise this goal. Does this imply that the degree of poverty brought about by the three 'worlds' (plus the Netherlands) differs as one would theoretically expect?

Since poverty is a more complicated construct than the number of benefit recipients, the analysis starts with a demarcation of the phenomenon. How is poverty best conceived of from a theoretical point of view? Once this has been ascertained, various operational poverty lines are discussed and evaluated; and following this assessment a new criterion is proposed, which will be used for an empirical comparison of poverty in the same countries as in the previous chapters. The aim is to test a number of specific hypotheses on the relationship between social security regime types and poverty. Do the exponents of the corporatist, social-democratic and liberal regime types selected here vary in the degree of poverty they bring about, and do they do so in a way one would theoretically expect? Once again, this issue is first pursued in a descriptive manner, by inspecting the bivariate relationship between regime types and various poverty indicators. Subsequently the hypotheses are tested in a more rigorous way, by applying multi-level analysis to the data. Using this method enables the unique contribution of the regime types to the degree of poverty to be determined, controlling for the effects of other factors at the micro- and macro-level.

Chapter 7 brings together the main findings, and discusses some of the results and their implications for social science and policymaking. This overview attempts to elucidate the principal *motif* of the study: the collective significance of social security institutions.

2 Institutional theory

This chapter discusses institutions from a general conceptual and theoretical perspective, following the questions formulated in the Introduction. First a description is given of the way in which the concept is interpreted in the scientific literature, with an emphasis on the 'new institutionalism' in the social sciences (§2.1). Subsequently Douglass North's theory is considered, which views institutions mainly in a historical economic perspective (§2.2). Building on these insights, §2.3 outlines a general figural model of institutions and their social context. Its different elements are then treated in more detail in separate sections.

The idea that institutions should be seen as socially constructed rules is elaborated in §2.4. It will be argued that they encompass a social consensus on rights, duties, conditions and potential sanctions. The next two sections briefly describe the various types of formal and informal institutions (§2.5), as well as how they theoretically relate to each other (§2.6).

The actors for whom the social rules are intended, and their motivations and mutual relationships, are the focus of §2.7. Subsequently, §2.8 is concerned with the way in which institutions may influence the behavioural interchange of actors, and the results to which this leads. A special form of such rule-driven interaction is also discussed in this section, namely the way in which actors acquire rules.

Institutions are not unchangeable givens, but the product of the behaviour of actors in certain historic circumstances. The theoretical mechanisms underlying this rule generation process are the focus of §2.9. The chapter ends with a number of conclusions.

2.1 Institutions and the 'new institutionalism'

In everyday parlance the term 'institution' often refers to agencies with a social purpose. The Concise Oxford Dictionary defines the term *inter alia* as "a society or organization founded especially for the promotion of science, education, etc". In the social scientific counterpart to this, reference is often made to entities which fulfil core social tasks: marriage, family, the Church, voluntary associations, political parties, and so on. Zijderveld (2000: 33) gives an example based on anthropological functionalism, and also indicates the limitations of this teleological approach:[1]

> There are basic biological and social needs which are satisfied through actions. These actions are permanently needed for the satisfaction of the needs, and will in time become schematic. That is, they gradually grow into collective habits and patterns of behavior. There is, for example, the biological need for sexual intercourse. The behavior that satisfies this need, grows into a regular pattern – the institution of marriage.
> This is, of course, a rather a-historical and instrumental explanation of the origin of institutions. The original motive of this institution may have been the societal regulation of sexual intercourse, but when the institution exists as an objective and autonomous structure, it will trigger and then regulate other, possibly quite different needs – such as, for instance, the need to stabilize emotions of love and affection, and the need to dispose of a stable parenting facility. Solidly objectified and autonomous institutions may even liberate individuals from their

primary needs, set them free to design motives and aims which in turn may create or trigger new needs. For instance, the goal of a formal dinner party is usually not the satisfaction of the need for food. [...] It is, in a sense, a *Leerform*, an empty form which is filled with other motives and aims, such as networking, flirting, gossiping, forging political compromises, and making Mafia deals.

In the lemma that Eisenstadt (1968: 409) wrote for the *International Encyclopaedia of the Social Sciences*, he first discusses the standard functionalist interpretation of institutions:

> Social institutions are usually conceived of as the basic focuses of social organization, common to all societies and dealing with some of the basic social problems of ordered social life. Three basic aspects of institutions are emphasized. First, the patterns of behavior which are regulated by institutions ... deal with some perennial, basic problems of any society. Second, institutions involve the regulation of behaviour of individuals in society according to some definite, continuous, and organized patterns. Finally, these patterns involve a definite normative ordering and regulation; that is, regulation is upheld by norms and by sanctions which are legitimized by these norms.

In this approach the institutional domain of *family and kinship* provides the solution for the social tasks of reproduction and the initial socialisation of children. The institution of *education* is the answer to the social problems associated with the transformation from children to adults and with the transfer of cultural heritage. The institutions of the *economy* regulate the production, distribution and consumption of goods and services. *Political* institutions control the use of force, maintain internal and external order on a society's borders, and take responsibility for the achievement of collective goals (viz., the definition of those objectives, as well as the mobilisation and allocation of the necessary resources for their achievement). *Cultural* institutions are concerned with the creation and preservation of religious, scientific and artistic products ('artefacts'), and with their dissemination. Finally, there is a separate institution focusing on *stratification*: the distribution of positions, rewards and resources among individuals and social groups.

Eisenstadt then distances himself from this functionalist approach, however. In his view institutions do not exist because they meet the needs of individuals or societies, or because they reflect universal psychological or ecological tendencies. Such an approach too easily assumes that needs are homogenous, rather than acknowledging that they can differ or even conflict between groups, or between individuals and society as a whole. In addition, little attention is given to the socially optimal degree of the fulfilment of needs, and to alternative institutional solutions which may be effective in similar historical circumstances. Finally, functionalist theories have difficulty in explaining institutional change. All too often it is assumed that the same conditions that lead to the creation of certain institutions also ensure that they will continue to exist *ad infinitum*. This need not be the case, however: changes in the nature of the needs, or in the historical and structural context, can cause institutions to become dysfunctional. The theoretical task is to indicate under which circumstances they survive, change or vanish; but this question is frequently not asked in functionalist approaches.

According to Eisenstadt, institutions are not "given, constant, self-contained entities"; he prefers to speak of a dynamic process of *institutionalisation*. This is not an expression of abstract social functionality, but refers to the sustained regulation of exchange between actors. Institutionalisation can be seen as (Eisenstadt, 1968: 414)

> A process of continuous crystallization of different types of norms, organizations, and frameworks which regulate the process of exchange of different commodities.

The exchange relates to different goods in the various institutional domains: in the economy, for example, it refers to the strengthening or loss of market positions; in the political field it has to do with the power that people acquire, the support they generate and the compromises they are able to achieve. Institutionalisation of social exchange is expressed among other things in legislation, communications systems, the administrative organisation, and the regulation of economic and political markets.

In Eisenstadt's vision institutional change is not a blind, unfocused process. It is instead one which constantly builds on existing institutions (Eisenstadt, 1968: 415):

> The concrete organizational structures in the preceding situation [...] create the conditions for their own change.

Exchange theory states that 'institutional entrepreneurs' play a key role in the process of institutionalisation. These are people with a particular ability to articulate new goals and norms, to set up new organisations and to mobilise the resources needed to ensure their functioning. Their institutionalising capability is related to the control they have over key positions and resources; however, having a high degree of control does not automatically mean that they are influential in shaping institutions. Of crucial importance is whether they are sensitive to societal needs, and that they are able to ensure that their own solutions to those needs prevail. Institutional entrepreneurs attempt to achieve this through a mix of coercion, manipulation and persuasion. They are not entirely free in the choice of their goals and behaviours; the interests, the possibilities offered by their social position and those of their rivals (power, money, contacts, communication channels), their own views and those of their supporters, etc., limit the nature of the changes they can seek to bring about. However, their course of action is not entirely predetermined: entrepreneurs have some latitude, which in this approach is considered to be the most important driver of institutional change.

In Eisenstadt's definition, institutions comprise both the social rules for exchange, and the organisational configuration which effectuate these. From an analytical point of view it seems useful to separate these two aspects more explicitly. There are societal rules, and the extent to which they effectively regulate human behaviour depends among other things on collective organisational forms. However, these are two different things, which do not necessarily lie on the same line. Rigorous norms may be accompanied by a low level of collective organisation: e.g., the behaviour of scientists is governed by fairly strict professional rules, which are supported by a loose (and partly anonymous) network of peers throughout the world. It would be hard to maintain the argument that this weak organisation implies institutions are nonexistent in such a case.

Throughout this study the concept therefore does not refer to key organisational forms or to the deployment of social resources,[2] but exclusively to the applicable social rules. This fits in with a second everyday meaning of the term: "an established law, custom, or practice" (*Concise Oxford Dictionary*). It also aligns with the interpretation of the classical sociologist Durkheim, who saw institutions as manifestations of 'social facts', or collective ways of acting, thinking and feeling. According to him, this supra-individual, objectified reality is the quintessential object of study for sociology (Durkheim, 1901: XXIII):

> On peut en effet, sans dénaturer le sens de cette expression, appeler *institution*, toutes les croyances et tous les modes de conduite institués par la collectivité; la sociologie peut alors être définie: la science des institutions, de leur genèse et de leur fonctionnement.

In Durkheim's view, institutions offer a historically rooted pre-structuring of social reality and are therefore a means of avoiding anomia (lack of norms, social chaos). Starting from a different theoretical perspective, G.H. Mead (1934: 167, 211) arrives at a similar definition of institutions:

> What we mean by [an institutional form] is that the whole community acts toward the individual in an identical way ... An institution is, after all, nothing but an organization of attitudes which we all carry in us, the organized attitudes of the others that control and determine conduct.

A definition of institutions in terms of collectively rooted convictions which influence the behaviour of actors returns in a recent theoretical approach known as 'new institutionalism'. Hall and Taylor (1996) distinguish three variants of this: sociological, rational choice and historical institutionalism.

2.1.1 Sociological institutionalism

Adherents of sociological institutionalism defy the functionalist approach, in which the normative force of rules provides for social order. By contrast, the *cognitive significance* of institutions is emphasised. In line with social constructivism, of which the work of Berger & Luckman (1966) is a well-known exponent, sociological institutionalism posits that institutions do not consist exclusively of rules, procedures and norms. Above all they offer symbol systems, cognitive interpretation frames, and moral templates which guide behaviour: "Institutions influence behaviour not simply by specifying what one should do, but also by specifying what one can imagine oneself doing in a given context" (Hall & Taylor, 1996: 948). According to these authors, this has a number of implications. In the first place it blurs the distinction between bureaucratic rationality and 'culture'. Following on from Weber, organisational sociologists for a long time argued that the central role accorded to formal, rational rules and procedures in government agencies and companies is an efficient adaptation to the tasks that they fulfil in modern societies.

In this line of reasoning, culture – in the sense of shared beliefs or values – was often placed outside the arena of formal organisations. A *Wertrationalität* ('value rationality') was only considered important to explain the behaviour of voluntary associations, ideological movements and religious sects; but the actions of modern, formal organisations were driven in principle by *Zweckrationalität* ('ends and means rationality'). Sociological institutionalists counter this with the argument that all institutions have both formal and informal aspects (Hall & Taylor, 1996: 946-947):

> Many of the institutional forms and procedures used by modern organizations were not adopted simply because they were most efficient for the tasks at hand, in line with some transcendent 'rationality'. Instead [... many of these] should be seen as culturally-specific practices, akin to the myths and ceremonies devised by many societies, and assimilated into organizations, not necessarily to enhance their formal means-ends efficiency, but as a result of the kind of processes associated with the transmission of cultural practices more generally [...] Even the most seemingly bureaucratic of practices have to be explained in cultural terms.

Secondly, in contrast to the rational choice institutionalist view (see below), in this approach the individual is not an autonomous *homo economicus*. Sociological institutionalists have a dialectic perspective on the relationship between man and society. In the words of Berger & Luckman (1966: 79):

> Society is a human product. Society is an objective reality. Man is a social product [...] An analysis of the social world that leaves out any one of these three moments will be distortive.

Thus, cognitive frames of interpretation are created by people, but eventually acquire universal applicability. The transfer of these 'ways of seeing' in the socialisation process ensures that new generations are familiar with the rules. And when those generations apply the institutions, they confirm to both the social prescript itself and their membership of social entities. Hall & Taylor (1996: 948) therefore designate the sociological-institutionalist perception of the relationship between institutions and individual behaviour as interactive and mutually constitutive.

Thirdly, according to this view the process of creating and changing institutions cannot be explained entirely by the efficiency with which these achieve the instrumental goals of actors. Rather, institutional change is often induced by the appropriateness of certain types of rules (Hall & Taylor, 1996: 949):

> Organizations often adopt a new institutional practice, not because it advances the means-end efficiency of the organization, but because it enhances the social legitimacy of the organization or its participants. In other words, organizations embrace specific institutional forms or practices because the latter are widely valued within a broader cultural environment. In some cases, these practices may actually be dysfunctional with regard to achieving the organization's formal goals [...] This picture [may be captured] by describing it as a 'logic of social appropriateness' in contrast to a 'logic of instrumentality'.

Finally, the legitimacy of institutional arrangements is not self-evident. The fact that some institutions are regarded as socially appropriate while others are not has to do with the organisation of cultural authority. Sociological institutionalism recognises different sources of authority. The state and the political process can lend public authority to certain institutional arrangements through legislation or official recognition. In addition, the growing number of experts (technicians, lawyers, physicians, economists, sociologists) can use their professional authority as a basis for imposing standards on their peers and for influencing public policy relating to their field. Furthermore, institutions may be the result of an interactive decision-making process by actors in certain influential networks. Through peer group discussions they can reach a consensus on what are considered legitimate interpretations and solutions to social problems. Such an 'interactive legitimacy' can occur, for example, in international organisations which issue more or less mandatory recommendations as to which rules countries should follow in order to achieve a balanced government budget, economic growth, educational reform, technological innovation, etc. (Hall & Taylor, 1996: 949-950).

2.1.2 Rational choice institutionalism

The second variant, rational choice institutionalism, posits that individuals behave instrumentally and strategically. They determine their choices independently on the basis of their own preferences or tastes. These preferences are given, and individuals try to achieve them to the maximum through strategic behaviour based on a meticulous consideration of the possible costs and benefits of various alternatives. In this approach, institutions are rules which provide confidence in people's current and expected behaviour; in doing so, they lower the risks of commercial and social exchange. Institutions provide information about what normal behaviour is, limit the number of choice options, ratify contracts and agreements, impose sanctions when people defect, etc. Rules continue to exist as long as a substantial group of people believe they would be worse off not conforming with the prescribed behavioural pattern than by conforming to it. If this social support dwindles, institutions will change if a more efficient alternative is available (see Hall & Taylor, 1996: 942-946; Brinton & Nee, 1998).

Rational choice theory has been widely used in studies on the problems associated with collective action, such as political decision-making. Hardin's *Tragedy of the commons* (1968) is the exemplary portrayal of the 'social dilemma'.[3] In this article he referred to the predicaments that arise in farming villages with common grazing land when the latter becomes scarce. For each individual farmer it serves his self-interest to place as many animals as possible on the collective farmland; but if all farmers do this, the commons will eventually perish due to over-grazing. This is the essence of a social dilemma: behaviour that is rational for the individual has negative consequences for the community as a whole, and is therefore irrational from the point of view of the collective interest. A literary example of this mechanism can be found in Ian McEwan's novel *Enduring Love*.[4]

Social dilemmas are difficult to avoid when it comes to collective goods to which everyone has access, and from which many people derive utility. The conceivable solutions often bring their own disadvantages. In a *hierarchical* approach the desired behaviour is imposed by a strong central organisation (usually the national government). However, this tends to be at odds with the individual freedom of action. In democratic societies, a hierarchical solution is therefore only viable when the undesirable behaviour has consequences for other parties which are generally deemed unacceptable.

Contractual solutions seek to avoid people acting as free-riders through agreements between the direct stakeholders, with sanctions being imposed for infringement of the contractual stipulations and compliance rewarded. However, this becomes a complex matter if many actors are involved, if the consequences of the behaviour only become apparent after a long period, or if the individual costs and benefits are difficult to establish.

If a solution is sought for social dilemmas via the *market*, an attempt is made to change the costs/benefits ratio in such a way that it becomes rational for a critical mass of people to focus on the common interest. Market-based solutions may relate to the immediate costs and benefits of people's actions (price interventions, prevention of cartel-formation), or to the transparency and accessibility of information (e.g. by prescribing that companies must produce an annual report, and stipulating what they have to make public in it), and the required control mechanisms (e.g. external approval by independent auditors). However, the pricing of collective goods can meet with resistance, as for example with the introduction of road tolls during peak hours, which are regarded by many as a selective infringement of the right to mobility. Determining the optimum incentive structure in such a case is also often difficult, and introducing the regulation will involve costs (e.g. for the technical infrastructure needed to enable tolls to be levied).

Finally, solutions sought via the *community* try to make the general interest prevail through stimulating shared standards of conduct, promoting awareness of the disagreeable social outcomes of defection, more intensive social control, and establishing overt moral commitment. Examples include the promulgation of an official 'catalogue' of values and norms by the authorities; information campaigns targeted at the prevention of the collective bad; the visible naming and shaming of defectors; and making people take a public vow to behave as desired (no smoking, drugs or alcohol; abstaining from sexual intercourse before marriage; respecting the environment). The main problem here is that it tends to be difficult to impose shared standards, awareness, sanctioning and commitment 'from above': ultimately, the members of the community themselves must support such solutions and see them as self-evident. Where communal ties are weak or on the wane, it is not easy for third parties (such as policy-makers) to assure compliance through the community.

Schuyt (see Vrooman, 1999) stresses that the rational choice approach is attractive because of its simple structure, which offers an explanation for much of the behaviour of individual and collective actors. Many variants of the theoretical principles have been studied in empirical research (e.g. single-person and multiple-person dilemmas, zero and non-zero-sum games,[5] situations with complete and incomplete information on the implications of the choice process), and the theory has therefore been validated in all manner of fields. The theoretical model is applied in sociology to explain relationships between individuals (the selection of spouses, friendship relations), between organisations (cooperation and competition of firms), between individuals and organisations (hiring and firing of employees), between individuals and society (collective impoverishment due to individual rational behaviour, as posited by Hardin), and between collectivities (e.g. tax policy competition by states).

However, Schuyt also points to a number of methodological and theoretical objections, which make it doubtful whether rational choice theory can be regarded as the "quantum leap of the social sciences". In the first place the notion of 'rationality' is often interpreted very broadly in this approach, so that for example altruistic behaviour (giving money to a beggar) becomes explainable as a rational choice (because of the moral satisfaction derived from it). The theory then tends towards tautology, with all behaviour being rational in the final instance. In Schuyt's view, it is more common that behaviour is determined by a mix of rational choice and other motives, such as trust. He also questions whether the opposition between the individual and the collectivity is not over-emphasised in rational choice theory. For example, the right to Dutch citizenship does have individual bearers, but would be hard to imagine without a shared collective historical background; in reality, individual and society are often co-constitutive. Finally, he comments that in a rationalising society, rational choice theory may become something of a self-fulfilling prophecy. The greater the extent to which actions are rationally driven, the more types of behaviour can be explained by rational choice theory.

In the economic sciences a variant of rational choice institutionalism became in vogue in the 1990s, namely the 'new institutional economics' (NIE), or the economics of transaction costs (cf. Williamson, 1985, 1998; Williamson & Winter, 1991). This harks back to the classic work by Coase (1937, 1960), from which the proponents of the NIE derive their basic theoretical principle: *when it is costly to transact, institutions matter.* According to this approach, institutions are more or less efficient solutions for economic coordination problems, since they lower transaction costs. Unlike neo-classical economic theory, there is no assumption of actors behaving in a fully rational way, but rather of their 'bounded rationality', to quote Simon (1986). People do not necessarily wish to maximise their utility; and in everyday situations their opportunities for rational action are often limited. In certain conditions actors may settle for 'satisficing' instead of maximising utility: they try to achieve a level which they consider sufficient. Aiming for the satisfactory theoretically prevails when choices relate to aspects that are less central to the actor. For instance, a person may wish to maximise his income or happiness, but in purchasing specific consumer goods (such as washing-powder) many different brands probably will be good enough.

Perhaps even more important, the bounded rationality view stresses that people are not always able to make rational choices. Actual behavioural choices are often based on a simplified view of reality. Actors tend to take only a limited number of factors into account, which they think are most relevant or crucial to them; and in the process, they are prone to make misjudgements. In some cases they may not be able to acquire all the information that is relevant for making a rational choice; or they may not want to seek this, since it requires too much time or money. In other instances, information may be so abundant that people cannot process it adequately. Moreover, people are not always able to determine the consequences of their behaviour accurately in advance, and their preferences and interests may not be stable or clear. And finally, their decisions may be influenced by situational and personal factors (the degree of shade in the room, their serotonin level, their predisposition to calculate, their abilities to do so).

However, in the bounded rationality perspective actors *intend* to make rational choices, in the sense that they opt for actions which they regard as effective means to accomplish their ends (interests or preferences). Schmidtz (1995: 12-13) points out that people may act rational even if they 'objectively' make the wrong choices. What matters is that an actor is aware of his ends; that his behaviour is directed towards these goals; and that he has good reason to believe his particular line of action is effective enough.

2.1.3 Historical institutionalism

In the third approach institutions are fairly strongly allied to formal organisations, and their creation in a given socio-historical context is emphasised. As Hall & Taylor (1996: 938) point out, institutions are then regarded as

> Formal or informal procedures, routines, norms and conventions embedded in the organizational structure. [...] They can range from the rules of a constitutional order or the standard operating procedures of a bureaucracy to the conventions governing trade union behaviour or bank-firm relations.

Historical institutionalists generally share their view of the relationship between people and institutions with one of the other two schools mentioned above, sociological and rational choice institutionalism (Hall & Taylor, 1996: 939-940). In some other respects, however, their approach is a unique one. It is centred in the first place around the historical restraints of social evolution, as expressed in the notion of *path dependence*. Historical institutionalists distance themselves from the traditional view that similar developments – e.g. technological innovations – will lead to the same results everywhere. On the contrary, they argue that the existing historical context operates in an intermediating way: whether or not a given innovation is implemented, and the extent to which it catches on, depends greatly on the characteristics of the society concerned. Institutions play an important intervening role here: if the formal and informal rules are at variance with the innovations, the latter will not be implemented as a matter of course.

A textbook example of technological path dependence is the survival of the QWERTY standard for the keyboard layout in typing and word processing (David, 1985). In the 1860s, the first typewriters had the disadvantage that the impression made by the type bars on the paper was not immediately visible. If one of the keys got stuck, this caused the same letter to be typed over and over again, something which only became apparent when the carriage was lifted. The inventor of QWERTY, Richard Sholes, tried to minimise the number of collisions between the type bars by placing widely used letter combinations in English a long way apart. At the time this was a technological improvement, which was patented in 1868 and included in Remington's first 'Type-Writer' in 1872.

Already in the 1890s an alternative for QWERTY was available: Blickensderfer's 'scientific keyboard', which used the DHIATENSOR-arrangement, and enabled 70% of English words to be typed using the keys on the bottom row of the keyboard. According to David QWERTY nevertheless prevailed, mainly because users had already invested in the method: during the period that the market for typewriters was growing rapidly, touch-typing on QWERTY keyboards had become the standard. The costs of switching to a different system would have been relatively high for users; while for typewriter manufacturers it required a fairly small investment to incorporate QWERTY keyboards into their existing models (by soldering the type to different bars and changing the keys on the levers). The continued existence of this 'institution' can be seen as an example of path dependence: every new keyboard layout first had to demonstrate that the advantages of its introduction outweighed the drawbacks of abolishing the QWERTY standard (breaking through existing habits, the time and costs of retraining users). Later superior alternatives like the Dvorak or Velotype keyboards supposedly[6] did not succeed due to path dependence, which leads David (1985: 336) to conclude that

> Competition [...] drove the industry prematurely into standardization *on the wrong system* – where decentralized decision making subsequently has sufficed to hold it.

Of course, path dependence becomes more complicated when applied to the analysis of social processes. In historical institutionalism the theory has been developed mainly in comparative studies of government policy and collective decision-making. Countries may respond entirely differently to similar policy problems because the existing institutions make some solutions appear more obvious than others. There may be several reasons for this. The prevailing legislation and related informal rules can promote change, but can also hinder it. For example, whereas unprofitable farms go bankrupt in free market countries, they may be kept alive elsewhere via state subsidies, a practice that is often legitimised by referring to the national interest of an independent food supply, or by pointing to the need to protect farm products that are considered unique. Similar developments may also lead to different results if the shared views of policymakers (the 'policy culture') or the configurations of interests (e.g. strong or weak trade unions) vary among countries. A factor of prime importance is that countries have invested in their current institutions. This means that changing the formal rules can entail higher costs in some countries than in others. Moreover, if the informal views in a country oppose such a change of the formal institutions, it may prove difficult to implement it.

Hall & Taylor (1996: 941-942) conclude that the notion of path dependence implies that institutions are not always functional:

> Historical institutionalists stress the unintended consequences and inefficiencies generated by existing institutions, in contrast to images of institutions as more purposive and efficient.

A second characteristic of historical institutionalism is the attention for the *distribution of power and the existence of conflicts over scarce goods between rival groups*. Institutions are not neutral rules (Hall & Taylor, 1996: 941), but

[...] give some groups or interests disproportionate access to the decision-making process; and, rather than emphasize the degree to which an outcome makes everyone better off, [historical institutionalists] tend to stress how some groups lose while others win.

In the third place, this school of thought sees institutions as being *not the only cause of social change*. Although the formal and informal rules determine the direction and scope of changes in society, they do so in combination with other factors, such as demographic and socio-economic trends, scientific and technological developments, etc. As a result, society is "more complex than the world of tastes and institutions often postulated by rational choice institutionalists" (Hall & Taylor, 1996: 942).

2.2 North's economic-historical approach

In his theoretical analysis *Institutions, institutional change and economic performance* (1990), Douglass North combined several of the above insights, though he integrated the economic and historical perspectives better than the sociological aspects. North (1990: 3) defines institutions as

... the rules of the game in a society, or, more formally, *humanly devised constraints that shape human interaction*.

Institutions may be formal (laws, regulations) or informal (social norms, customs, behavioural codes). Infringing such rules incurs sanctions; this implies that the price of establishing defections and the severity of the punishment is an important part of the functioning of institutions.

Institutions have to be conceptually separated from organisations. North considers the former as "the rules of the game", while the latter are among the players. There is a dialectic connection between organisations and institutions. On the one hand the existing rules help determine which organisations are formed and how they develop; organisational forms are a response to the incentive structure offered by institutions. On the other hand, organisations also influence the development of institutions: they seek to change the opportunity structure in such a way that they derive more benefit from it.

2.2.1 Institutions and transaction costs

Institutions regulate human behaviour, and North assumes that actors behave on the basis of the bounded rationality perspective described earlier. He believes that transaction costs play a key role in the regulation of behaviour. These expenses are the sum of the costs of:
a) defining and protecting property rights, and monitoring and enforcing agreements;
b) measuring the valued attributes of goods and services.

Economists have traditionally focused mainly not on transaction expenses, but on transformation costs: the investment of land, labour and capital that is needed to change the physical characteristics of a good in such a way as to create added value. North, however, points out that transaction costs in modern economies are considerable – for the United States he estimates that they account for 45% of GDP – and therefore have a substantial influence on the economic process as well. And because institutions provide a framework for economic exchange, they are important determinants of the level of transaction costs.

First and foremost, institutions regulate the way in which *ownership* of a good is acquired, how it may be used or how its use may be denied to others, and how the contract can be observed. For example, the property rights to a dwelling are generally highly regulated in modern societies. There are formal rules dictating the content of the sales contract, the entry in the land register, agreements with the mortgage provider, the taxable status of home ownership and the tax deductibility of housing and maintenance costs, the inheritance laws, the possibilities to evict and prosecute squatters, etc. These rules are often reinforced by the self-evident mutual expectations of buyers and sellers on what is a reasonable margin between asking price and bid, the role of estate agents, etc. Institutionalisation needs not be that high, however. In a society where tracts of *terra nullius* are available, it may be that property rights are created by simply fencing off or inhabiting such areas and defending that land against any competitors.[7] But in both cases establishing the property right involves transaction costs: the fees for the notary, the mortgage provider and the tax office in the highly regulated society, and the costs of defending one's home in the other variant.

In addition, every economic exchange involves *measurement costs*. The value of an exchange commodity is the sum of the characteristics which are involved in the good or the service for both parties. If someone buys a house, they purchase a number of attributes: a certain number of square metres, a particular building style, the solidity of the construction, the attractiveness of the neighbourhood, the distance from central amenities, etc. To determine whether the desired characteristics are included in the sale and whether the asking price is in line with the market, it is necessary to make inquiries: comparing houses and neighbourhoods, carrying out architectural research, etc. This takes time and money, and in complex exchange it is often not feasible to obtain all relevant information. Moreover, information asymmetries often occur in practice: the vendor of the house generally knows more than the buyer, and either one may have an interest in hiding or revealing certain traits.

The costs of establishing property rights and measuring valued attributes may vary depending on how efficient the rules are. In general, total transaction costs increase as the type of exchange and the socio-economic setting become more complex; and as the ability of the actors to understand the context, and to enforce compliance with the rules, declines.

2.2.2 Formal and informal rules

North draws a distinction between formal and informal institutions. He suggests that the difference is a gradual one: it may be regarded as a continuum of institutionalisation, with customs, traditions and taboos at one extreme, and a written constitution at the other.

Formal rules are created in order to make exchange (in a political or economic sense) possible, and are based on the initial negotiating power of decision-making parties. Formal rules need not necessarily be efficient: in principle they are designed more to foster the interests of those in power than to optimise the general interest. North identifies three types of formal institutions: political and judicial rules, economic rules and contracts.

1. *Political and judicial rules.* These reflect the hierarchy of the various policy issues, as well as the key points of the decision-making procedure and the method of agenda formation. Political and judicial rules have a certain primacy because they shape the playing field for economic rules and contracts. This primacy is incomplete, however, because there is also a feedback mechanism in which actors attempt to influence the political and judicial rules.

In the simple case there is one dominant ruler, who in exchange for tax revenues dispenses justice, provides safety (or at least prevents chaos) and protects property rights. As different factions have different opportunity costs and negotiating power, they enter into individual contracts with the dominant ruler.

In a slightly more complicated model there is a representative body which acts in behalf of the interests of a limited number of groups (such as the Spanish *Cortes*, originally a parliament of the three estates). This enables the ruler to generate more tax revenues in exchange for the granting of privileges to the interest groups and their agents. This creates a hierarchical structure and an extensive bureaucracy.

In modern representative democracies there is a multitude of interest groups and a much more complex institutional structure designed to foster the exchanges between the various groups. There is also not just a single legislator, but a legislative assembly. All representatives (MPs) have to satisfy their own constituencies, each of which has its own characteristics. This cannot be achieved through a simple exchange of votes; often it is a matter of making prior agreements on voting cooperation, or of granting each other influence on certain closely defined topics and on the agenda (e.g. the chairmanship of committees).

2. *Economic rules.* These mainly establish property rights. In the simplest model property rights are a function of changes in economic costs and revenues: they arise when changes in relative prices and/or scarcity are such that they counterbalance the costs of granting or enforcing the rights. There are however also many inefficient rights, the monitoring of which is not economically viable. North explains this on the basis of the inefficiency of the political markets: rule makers do not wish to upset their influential supporters, or it may be that the costs of establishing and collecting levies are so high that a less efficient allocation of rights leads to higher revenues. An efficient distribution of property rights arises where the political transaction costs are low and the political actors have adequate subjective perceptions. In practice this is often not achieved.

3. *Contracts.* These contain the conditions governing specific exchange agreements. In traditional economic settings contracts often referred to the trading of a single good at a single moment. Modern contracts cover several goods and extend over a longer period. They are by definition incomplete and therefore stipulate which matters will be decided through arbitration by a third party or the courts.

According to North informal institutions, such as codes of conduct, norms and conventions, are often embedded in the formal institutions. In many respects, however, they are more important, as formal rules contain few instructions for everyday behaviour. Their influence is evident from the fact that the same formal rules can lead to different results in a different social and historical context, and from the persistence of informal rules long after a radical amendment of the formal institutions and their related organisational forms (e.g. the Japanese culture after the US administration following World War II; the Jewish and Kurdish culture in the Diaspora, the Orthodox Russian Church after 70 years of Communism).

North (1990: 37) broadly equates informal institutions to culture:

> Informal constraints [...] are part of the heritage that we call culture, [... which] can be defined as the transmission from one generation to the next, via teaching and imitation, of knowledge, values, and other factors that influence behavior.

A sociologist would probably be more inclined to refer to this latter aspect as socialisation or cultural transfer (see §2.8.3). North's view of culture is however closely connected to that of sociological institutionalism, because he stresses its cognitive significance: "Culture provides a language-based conceptual framework for encoding and interpreting the information that the senses are presenting to the brain" (North, 1990: 37).

The transmission of culture ensures that informal solutions for exchange problems survive; social change may occur, but in the long run it will be accompanied by a persisting undercurrent.

Informal institutions arise to coordinate repeated social interaction. Here again, North distinguishes three variants:

1. First there may be *extensions, elaborations and amendments of formal rules*. These are the 'unwritten laws' or conventions that arise as a result of repeated interaction between actors.
2. Then there are *socially sanctioned norms of behaviour*. North cites the example of a gentleman who is challenged to a duel to the death. The evening before he draws up a long list of reasons for not taking part in the duel, with at the top the strong argument that there is a fair risk that he will lose his life. Yet he still decides to participate in the duel: a gentleman would suffer a serious loss of reputation if he avoids what in his circles is a traditional manner of settling conflicts.
3. Finally, North points to the existence of internalised *standards of conduct*: ideas, ideologies and convictions which cannot always be reconciled with rational choice. Although he does not mention him by name, Weber's[8] classical analysis in *Die Protestantische Ethik und der Geist des Kapitalismus* (1905) clearly resonates in North's argument: "Effective traditions of hard work, honesty, and integrity simply lower the cost of transacting and make possible complex, productive exchange" (North, 1990: 138).

In North's view, in modern democratic societies informal institutions are important for two reasons. In such a context the formal rules (political and judicial rules, economic rules and contracts) usually are numerous and complex, but can never cover all possible circumstances. The rights established in the formal institutions therefore have to be strengthened by informal constraints: conventions, social norms and internalised standards of conduct that regulate the latitude of interpretation and action implied in the formal rules.

In addition, the costs of expressing opinions in democracies are often low, because freedom of speech is a constitutional right which is ratified by the prevailing views of the population, and because information is relatively freely available. These low costs mean that the subjective preferences of individuals are more important determinants of behaviour than is the case under an authoritarian regime, where the preferences expressed in public life have to toe the official line. The costs of expressing one's opinion in such a regime may be considerable: some statements are unlawful, those uttering them are regarded as social outcasts and moral reprobates, and censorship means a great deal of effort is needed if individuals wish to make their views known to others.

2.2.3 Enforcement

North (1990: 32-33) points to the importance of the ability to enforce desired behaviour for both formal and informal institutions. This enforcement can be achieved through direct reprisal by the injured party, through internalised codes of conduct, through sanctions imposed by the community, or through the actions of a third party (often the state). In complex exchanges where no complete information is available, enforcement is needed to achieve cooperative behaviour; without it the individual interests of the various actors would predominate. The costs of enforcement form part of the transaction costs, and reflect the uncertainties of the contract. They are a risk premium, whose amount depends on the likelihood that the other party will fail to meet their obligations, and the costs that this would entail for the first party. North comments that contracts in a profit-maximising situation are 'self-enforcing' when the rewards of complying with contracts are greater than the costs. In his view this occurs in tribal societies and small communities, where people have lots of information about each other and repeatedly engage in exchanges. Here, the measurement costs of contracts are low, but the costs of cheating, avoiding responsibility and opportunism are considerable. Formal contracts are not necessary; norms of behaviour govern the exchange. Modern societies, however, are characterised by large-scale impersonal exchanges. There are many valued attributes, the exchange often extends over a long period and is not repeated in the same form between the same actors. In this situation the measurement costs are high, and without enforcement the advantages of cheating would be much greater than the rewards of cooperative behaviour.

North clarifies this by calling on game theory. In the classic prisoner's dilemma a sub-optimum solution is often chosen because the collective payoff is much lower if one person cooperates (snitches his fellow prisoner) while the other does not. In a repeated or iterative game, however, cooperation is a more evident choice, provided a number of conditions are met: the information must be complete, and the exchange must continue indefinitely (if people suspect that the game is finite, the anticipated final moment will partly determine their choices). In reality, such conditions are often not met: the duration of the exchange is unknown, it involves several individuals who are not very well acquainted, and the information possessed by the various parties differs widely. In this situation enforcement – and, in the case of non-compliance, punishment – by a third party is necessary.

It is possible that voluntary organisations are the sole enforcement agent. However, North points out that in the context of impersonal exchanges in modern, mutually dependent economies, the transaction costs for information acquisition and sanctioning will quickly become too high. If the state acts as the enforcement agent, by contrast, it can generate huge economies of scale. This then creates a new dilemma, however. On the one hand a modern society cannot operate without formal 'third-party enforcement' by the state; but on the other hand those who represent the state are also agents who seek to maximise their utility: "Put simply, if the state has coercive force, then those who run the state will use that force in their own interest at the expense of the rest of society" (North, 1990: 59). This means that the state is not necessarily a neutral third party, which can assess the value of attributes at little or no expense, and which will automatically ensure that those who break the rules pay so much compensation to injured parties that defection is more costly than complying with agreements.

2.2.4 Institutional change and path dependence

North's view of institutional change is an interesting mix of the rational choice, sociological and historical institutionalism discussed earlier. He sees two driving forces: both mutations in relative prices and altered actor's preferences can lead to rule amendment. He regards the former as the most important. This involves changes in the ratio of factor costs (land/labour; labour/capital; land/capital), in the costs of information, and in civil and military technology. According to North, relative prices may change due to exogenous shocks, such as the plague epidemic in Europe in the late Middle Ages, which radically changed the price ratio between labour and land. However, he considers relative price changes largely as a process driven by endogenous developments. The role fulfilled by entrepreneurs is crucial in this respect. Over time they gain knowledge and experience, and as a result their transaction costs fall, in line with the notion that a game proceeds differently when it is played by professionals rather than amateurs. Therefore, if the professionals gain the upper hand relative prices will change, and this will create pressure to refine the rules of the game. Or to put it more precisely,

> The process by which the entrepreneur acquires skills and knowledge is going to change relative prices by changing perceived costs of measurement and enforcement, and by altering perceived costs and benefits of new bargains and contracts (North, 1990: 84).

If the relative prices change, this means it becomes attractive for some parties to reconsider existing contracts. Since these are embedded in the hierarchy of rules, this is often not possible without breaking higher rules or norms of behaviour. A disadvantaged party may then decide to attempt to change the formal rules. This subsequently distorts the equilibrium in the informal institutions, which are by nature embedded in the old formal structure. A change in the relative prices thus may change the formal rules with the result that behavioural norms, customs or traditions are gradually eroded and replaced by others, which better match the new formal institutions.

But North suggests that institutional change comes about not just because of changes in relative prices. Changes in the preferences or ideas of actors are a second potential source of change – in North's view often less important, but relatively autonomous nonetheless. He illustrates this by pointing out that the abolition of slavery in the United States cannot be explained on the basis of changes in relative prices. At the time of the American Civil War, slavery was still profitable in the Southern states, so there was no economic need for abolition. North attributes the institutional change that took place after the end of the Civil War in 1865 among other things to the strong intellectual force of the anti-slavery movement, combined with political democracy which enabled opponents of slavery to express their ideas at little personal cost. By contrast, the Southern slave masters had no means at that time and in that structure to persuade the entire electorate to back their point of view (North, 1990: 85). North argues that the causes of such changes in preferences, or 'cultural evolution', lie in random processes, learning mechanisms, and natural selection. It is however also possible that preferences adapt in response to relative price changes. To illustrate the latter North refers to the evolvement of family relationships in response to changing relative prices of work and leisure time and the introduction of contraceptives.

North stresses that it is ultimately the actors who make and recreate the rules. The existing institutions define an opportunity structure for individuals, to which they will gear their behaviour; and if their social success is too low according to the standards they apply, they will try to change the formal or informal rules. North allocates a key role here to political and economic entrepreneurs, an idea which corresponds with the view of Eisenstadt cited earlier. To what extent they succeed in this depends on their cognitions (formal knowledge, tacit knowledge and experience), their subjective norms and expectations, their interests and negotiating power, and the degree to which they succeed in competing with other interested parties in shaping the policy agenda and formal rules to their own wishes. As their rationality is by definition bounded, this can lead to socially sub-optimum solutions. Their bounded rationality also explains why entrepreneurs may react differently to economic, social or technological changes.

As he also attaches importance to informal rules and to the perceptions and accumulation of knowledge of entrepreneurs, for North institutional change theoretically is not a linear process. Changes in preferences may lead to modification of informal institutions, which in turn can prompt changes in the formal rules. There is also frequently interference between the two: if formal institutions are changed radically, the informal rules often offer resistance to excessive reforms, because they still offer a solution to the exchange problems of the actors. In these cases a new equilibrium may eventually emerge, in which the formal institutions move in the direction of the *ancien régime*, and the informal rules are modernised.

If the two driving forces – changes in prices and preferences – are combined, this offers a certain explanation for institutional variation in the short term, but still leaves unclear why inefficient institutions are able to survive. After all, if certain countries or organisations record lower achievements than others, the expectation would be that they eventually succumb to the competition. They would necessarily have to opt for the more efficient rules in the end, in order to prevent the best qualified part of the population leaving the country or the business going bankrupt. The survival of sub-optimal institutions can be explained by a third mechanism in North's theory: the notion of path dependence, which was discussed earlier under historical institutionalism. According to North, path dependence arises as a result of the increasing added value of institutions – as a result of high initial investments, learning effects, coordination effects and adaptive expectations – in combination with imperfect markets. It is, however, not an automatic or linear process (North, 1990: 98-99):

> [There is no question of] a story of inevitability in which the past neatly predicts the future. [...] Path dependence is a way to narrow conceptually the choice set and link decision-making through time. [...] Once a development path is set on a particular course, the network externalities, the learning process of the organizations, and the historically derived subjective modeling of the issues reinforce the course.

Path dependence is also one of the reasons that formal rules, when adopted by other countries or organisations, do not function in the same way or may generate different effects. German reunification provides an interesting example of this: the labour market and social security institutions of the old *Bundesländer* were 'exported' to the new federal states in the 1990s, but led to somewhat different results there (see Mars et al., 2002).

The foregoing makes clear that formal and informal institutions theoretically determine the behaviour of actors, and thus influence the economic and social performance of countries and organisations. For sociologists, the tenet 'institutions matter' is more self-evident than for neo-classical economists, whose paradigm adherents of the economic variant of rational choice institutionalism (NIE) oppose. The intellectual challenge is rather to establish *empirically* the magnitude of the socio-economic impact of institutions in diverging contexts. In this study this issue will be explored for specific types of rule sets: those pertaining to systems of social security. Before tackling this empirical question, however, it will be useful to elaborate the meaning of institutions more precisely, and to specify what such a demarcation implies for social security. The first is covered below, while the second is the subject of chapter 3.

2.3 The evolvement and impact of institutions: a figural model

It is not simple to integrate the three variants of 'new institutionalism' discussed above, partly because they have developed relatively autonomously. Here, building on the work of North, an attempt is made to synthesise them into a general figural model. This is not intended as a formal theoretical model, but rather as a heuristic aid, a flow chart of hypothetical relationships that may be translated into empirical statements (cf. Lindenberg, 1983: 21-22). The model seeks to indicate what institutions are, how they come into being, in what way they regulate interaction, and what consequences this has for both the actors involved and society at large. Figure 2.1 illustrates the main outlines; the individual elements will be discussed in more detail in the following paragraphs.

The model distinguishes between factors at the collective and actor levels. *Institutions* are the collectively defined rights and duties that aim to regulate behaviour, and their attached conditions and possible sanctions. Formal institutions are rules promulgated or recognised by the government; informal institutions are borne by groups or communities. In the hierarchy of formal institutions, the *meta-rules* which establish the method of decision-making are situated at the top. They give direction to the *rules for government production*: goods and services provided by the government (e.g. defence, education). They also influence the third type of formal rules, namely enforcement by the government, as a party above the parties, of the rights, duties and mutual relations of private actors. This *third-party recognition* forms the framework for *formal contracts* between private parties, the fourth type of formal institution. The contracts entered into by the government with private parties in its role as a producer (tenders for public works, etc.) are a specific variant of this.

Among the informal institutions, *values* theoretically give direction to *social norms*. The former consist of general principles of action, the latter of specific behavioural rules for actual situations. Unlike values, norms also contain the possibility of sanctions. *Conventions* differ from social norms in that they do not have an explicit value component; they specify correct behaviour in a neutral way. The content of such rules is arbitrary: the main thing is that conventions coordinate the interaction within a group or community, and confirm membership of it. *Informal contracts* are a fourth variant: contracts between private parties that are not enforced by the government. Informal contracts are theoretically directed by social norms and conventions.

Formal and informal institutions are interrelated and therefore correspond to a certain extent. In principle, however, they do not determine each other in full: informal rules do not automatically derive from formal rules, and the converse is equally untrue. This also applies within the formal and informal rule hierarchies: the lower-level rules bear a certain relationship to the higher-level rules, but do not automatically ensue from them. Rather, the translation process is a matter of social consensus.

Institutions try to regulate action, and at this level two types of *actors* are distinguished. In addition to individuals (natural persons) there are also corporate actors. These exist where the rights and duties of such organisations (companies, associations, government agencies) are separate from the individuals that form part of them; they are recognised as independent legal body in their own right. Corporate actors are the result of the organising behaviour of other actors. They arise when individual or existing corporate actors wish to achieve certain goals which they are unable to achieve by themselves. 'Organising' implies that existing actors accord a mandate and resources to a new or modified corporate actor in order to realise such aims.

Figure 2.1
The evolvement and impact of institutions (figural model)

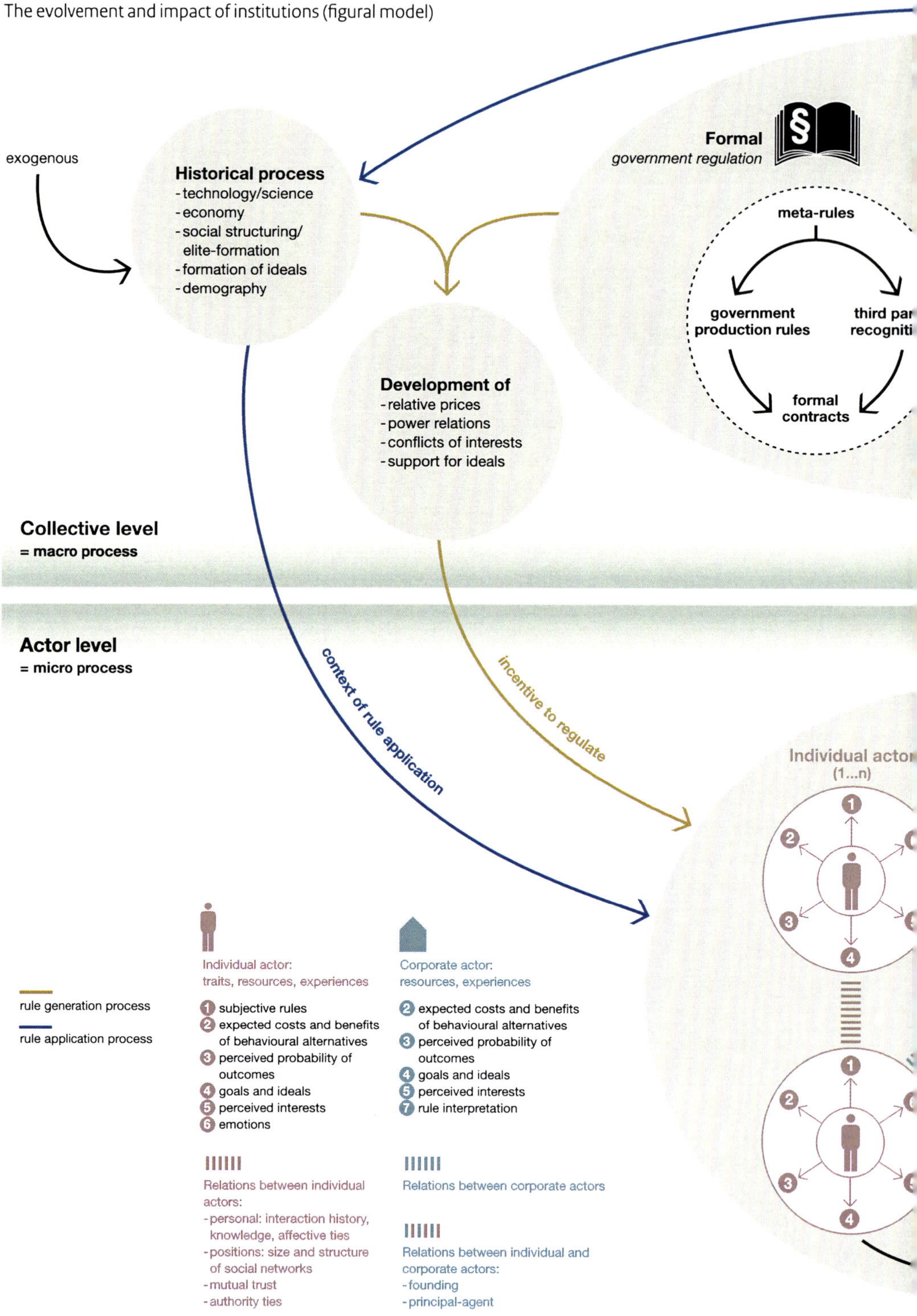

exogenous

Historical process
- technology/science
- economy
- social structuring/ elite-formation
- formation of ideals
- demography

Formal *government regulation*

meta-rules

government production rules

third par recogniti

formal contracts

Development of
- relative prices
- power relations
- conflicts of interests
- support for ideals

Collective level
= macro process

Actor level
= micro process

context of rule application

incentive to regulate

Individual actor (1...n)

— rule generation process
— rule application process

Individual actor: traits, resources, experiences
① subjective rules
② expected costs and benefits of behavioural alternatives
③ perceived probability of outcomes
④ goals and ideals
⑤ perceived interests
⑥ emotions

Corporate actor: resources, experiences
② expected costs and benefits of behavioural alternatives
③ perceived probability of outcomes
④ goals and ideals
⑤ perceived interests
⑦ rule interpretation

|||||
Relations between individual actors:
- personal: interaction history, knowledge, affective ties
- positions: size and structure of social networks
- mutual trust
- authority ties

|||||
Relations between corporate actors

|||||
Relations between individual and corporate actors:
- founding
- principal-agent

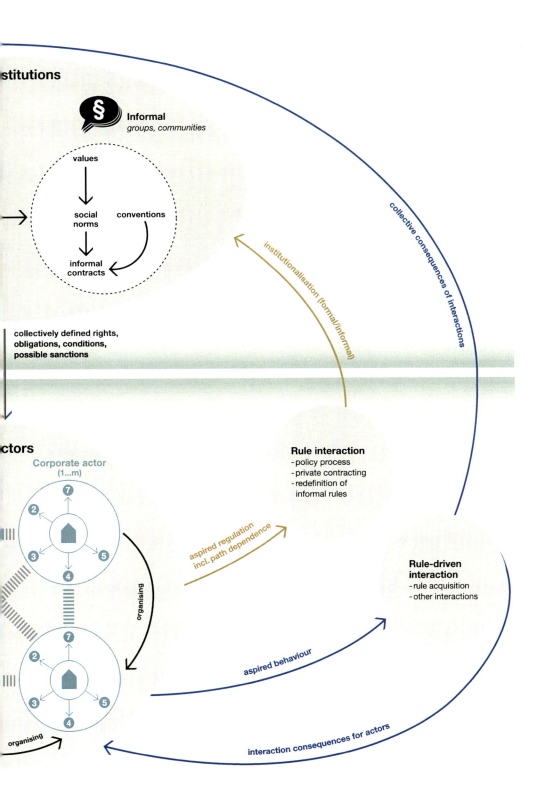

INSTITUTIONAL THEORY

Notwithstanding the autonomous rights of corporate actors, their acts are realised by individuals. These individuals are deemed not to act as natural persons in their own right, but as representatives of the corporate actor. The behaviour of such 'agents' can however deviate from the intentions of their patron (or 'principal'): they may put personal gain before the organisational interest.

In this model, the *motivations* of individual actors consist of subjective rule interpretations, the individual perception of interests, goals and ideals, the expected costs and benefits of behavioural alternatives, and the perceived probability of certain outcomes. Emotions may also be linked to particular forms of behaviour. The motivations of corporate actors are theoretically largely the same, but emotions are lacking because these are tied to natural persons. Of course, emotions can play a role for the individuals acting on behalf of corporate legal bodies.

The motives of actors are theoretically influenced by the institutions, the historical process and the consequences of earlier acts. Specific actor characteristics (personality traits, health status, available resources) and the relations with other actors can also prompt particular forms of behaviour. Relationships between individual actors are guided by their respective traits and interaction history; their positions in social networks; mutual trust; and authority ties. In relations between individual and corporate actors two particular mechanisms are at work: the 'founding fathers' of a new organisation to a large extent shape its goals and mode of operation; and once established, it may be difficult to ensure that individuals comply with the intentions and interest of the corporate actor. In the corporate context, motivations become theoretically more complex, because the agents can interpret the aspired behaviour of the principal in different ways (disagreements on the board, between departments, between employee representatives and management, etc.).

The model distinguishes between a *rule application process* and a *rule generation process*. The former indicates how a given institutional structure influences certain interactions and what results this brings about. The latter specifies the conditions that lead actors to change the rules, or leave them intact.

In the rule application process the weighting of motivations result in certain *behavioural aspirations* of the actor. These aspirations are not a carbon copy of socially constructed rules. There are several reasons for this: the rules are often incomplete or unclear; subjective rule interpretations may differ from what was collectively envisaged; and other motivations (e.g. the costs/benefits perception, emotions) may weigh more heavily than the allocated rights and duties. The course of interaction may also cause actual behaviour to deviate from the collective goals or the actor's aspirations. In principle, actors are not robotic rule-followers; though they can become so in certain circumstances, for example if the costs of defection are very high (e.g. because of severe physical sanctions), or where there are very strict behavioural expectations which the individual actors have internalised (for example, in a caste-based society or sect). Since the degree to which rules govern behaviour is an empirical question, it is important to establish to what extent the behaviour of actors is in line with the formal and informal expectations (indicating compliance) or are in conflict with them (indicating defection). Theoretically, the likelihood of defection is high in certain types of interactions. This holds in particular for the one-off, impersonal economic exchange of a single good between market parties, and in the case of collective provisions where no adequate solution has been found for the free rider problem.

The behavioural aspirations influence the *rule-driven interactions* between actors. Rule acquisition is a special variant of this, which relates to the way in which new actors learn about the existing formal and informal rules. The 'other interactions' in the model refer to all the remaining behavioural exchanges between actors in the private sphere (as members of households, families, associations or other groups), their economic transactions (as consumers, employees or employers), their political behaviour (as electors, candidates or party members), and so on. The various forms of interaction relating to social security, which are discussed in detail in chapter 3, also belong here.

If the rules are a given, the *results* they bring about depend on the historical circumstances in which they are applied. The economic climate, the demographic situation, social and technological developments and changes in aspired futures (ideologies) define a current *context of rule application* for individual and corporate actors. In the sphere of social security this is manifested for example in the likelihood that actors will be affected by certain events (e.g. unemployment due to dismissal). The context of rule application may also be reflected in their perceptions: whether the unemployed deem it worthwhile to seek work, the expected costs and yields of benefit fraud, the priorities set by the agents of social security organisations, etc.

First of all, institutions have *consequences at the actor level*. In social security, for example, the rule-driven interactions of an unemployed person with a benefits agency will influence his income level, it may lead to the requirement to follow a training course, etc. But there are also *collective effects* of rules, shown in figure 2.1 as a feedback to the historical process. The development of a community or society is influenced by the outcome of rule-driven interactions; and institutions are often also devised to achieve such collective results, especially as regards economic prosperity and the continuity of the social structure and ideology. This can again be illustrated using social security. The existence of social security rules may create new social categories (poorhouse inhabitants, state pensioners, single mothers living on welfare), influence the position of contributors and benefit recipients on the various stratification ladders, and affect the power of elite groups if they are a key issue in parliamentary elections. Social security institutions also impact on the collective wealth and its distribution, and they may influence technological development (for example via the level of investment in physical and human capital) and promote certain demographic changes (e.g. denatalistic and pronatalistic effects of child support, the influence of the relative levels of social assistance and pensions on migration flows) (see also §3.6).

The rule generation process shown in figure 2.1 suggests that it is not inevitable that collective rules will come into being or change. Institutions arise and develop through the rule-creating activities of actors in response to historical developments and the existing rule structure. The historical process relates to changes in the fields of technology and science, the economy, the social structure, the ideals that are formed, and demographic trends. Depending on the existing institutions, such trends confront actors with a certain incentive to regulate. This is a weighted sum of changes in four factors: developments in relative prices, power relations, conflicts of interest and support for certain ideals within a social system (community, society).

Alterations in these domains can lead actors to aspire different rules. This is possibly, but not necessarily the case; it depends on the way actors process the incentive to regulate. There may be alternatives to rule amendment they prefer: actors may adapt their behaviour within the applicable rules, accept their loss and gains under the prevailing institutions, or break the rules without changing them. It is also may be that the four factors do not point in the same direction, or are not strong enough in the perception of the actors concerned to necessitate rule change. Finally, rule change brings economic and social costs. The new rule has to be formulated, support has to be found for it, after its acceptance it has to be implemented, and after the rule has been changed the net collective yields must be positive. The perceived economic and social costs will be reflected in the inclinations of actors to regulate, and that is a source of path dependence. Such a 'brake on rule aspirations' may also result from the tendency of actors to perceive reality in terms of the existing rules (cognitive framing, moral templates).

The fact that actors consider certain rules desirable does not automatically mean that they will be created: that hinges on a process of *rule-interaction* by rule-making actors. The model distinguishes three variants of this interaction process. First there is the policy process in which the formal government rules are defined. In addition, private parties can enter into formal and informal contracts. Finally there is the possibility that actors will attempt to redefine the values, norms and conventions within their community. The three types of rule-interaction can result in a certain *institutionalisation*. Of course, the newly made rules need not correspond with the aspirations of all actors who were involved in their constitution.

Theoretically, institutional changes are set in motion primarily by *new actors*: individual 'normative entrepreneurs', new corporate actors, the members of a new generation, or a counter-elite challenging the position and views of the dominant elite of rule guardians. For several reasons, such new actors are more sensitive to changes in the incentive to regulate: they have invested less in the existing institutions, derive less benefit from them, and are less inclined to see reality in terms of the prevailing rules. As a consequence, they are more likely to see the shortcomings of the existing institutional structure and the advantages of rule changes.

Following this general overview, the figural model will be described in more detail in the remainder of this chapter. First we will elaborate the meaning of institutions (§2.4), the various types of institutions (§2.5), and how these may relate to one another (§2.6). Attention then turns to the actors (§2.7), the specifics of what rule-driven interaction entails, and the results to which it can lead (§2.8). The way in which actors acquire rules

– a special form of rule-driven interaction – will also be a topic here. Finally, §2.9 looks more closely at the rule generation process.

2.4 Institutions as socially constructed rules

Given their central position in the figural model, it is important to clarify the meaning of the term 'institutions'. As stated earlier, North (1990: 3) defines them as "humanly devised constraints that shape human interaction". The last two elements in this definition, in particular, raise questions. Do institutions necessarily imply behavioural constraints? And as a corollary to this: do institutions always relate to human interaction?

Applied to, e.g., social security, a positive answer to these questions would make the analysis more difficult. In the first place, many social security institutions tend to increase rather than limit people's behavioural options. They are 'rules of relief', which give people the right to benefit, to help in finding a job, to a safe and healthy working environment, etc. G.H. Mead (1934: 260-262) already pointed out this potential emancipating aspect of social institutions:

> There is no necessary or inevitable reason why social institutions should be oppressive or rigidly conservative, or why they should not be, as many are, flexible and progressive, fostering individuality rather than discouraging it.

This is difficult to reconcile with a definition in terms of constraints dictating what actors must or must not do. In addition social security comprises many rules that do not impact directly on the behavioural interchanges between people. For example, social security benefit is usually only paid if applicants have certain characteristics (e.g. a certain age), or after a certain event has taken place (e.g. the death of a partner). Such regulations have virtually no influence on the interaction between the applicants and the social security organisation, and can sometimes not be influenced by the actors concerned. However, they still belong to the 'rules of the game', and in that sense are institutional.

To remove these objections a slightly different delineation is adopted here, in which institutions are understood as *socially constructed rules which indicate the rights and duties of actors*. The rules may contain *conditions* for the granting of rights and imposition of duties, and also establish the positive and negative *sanctions* that may be applied. The various elements of this definition deserve some explanation.

Socially constructed rules

In line with North, the definition emphasises the social nature of institutions. They are prescripts constructed by groups, communities or governments of what people may and must do, the shared standards which separate the right ways of acting from the wrong ones. This excludes some rules. If they describe non-social natural laws – the sun rises each day, a formula[9] such as $P_D = log_{10}(1+(1/D))$ – then rules are in principle not institutional. Guidelines that are purely personal – the self-devised life principles of a hermit without followers, the inimitable yet often very compulsive rules of someone going through a psychosis – fall outside the definition as well. An absolute normative philosophy, which poses universal standards for ethically good behaviour, in itself is also not institutional. It may become so, however, if there are people who recognise and observe the life rules, such as a group of moral philosophers who support the specific deontology and put it into practice.[10]

By contrast, the laws enacted by a government, the rules of a monastic order (such as the *Rule of St. Benedict*), or the unwritten mores of a society or company are socially constructed, and are therefore examples of institutions. Although it is not unusual for institutions to have a certain stability, rules need not necessarily become embedded and unchangeable. Social rules may also consist of one-off arrangements between actors; the more tangible form they assume (e.g. in the form of implementation decrees), the more likely it is that they will have to be adjusted regularly in response to changes in the socio-economic environment and unforeseen or undesired consequences.

In contrast to the functionalist approach discussed by Eisenstadt (see §2.1), the production of 'cultural artefacts' is not regarded as an institution here. Undoubtedly, developments in the field of technology, science or art, and new ideas, can impact on the social construction of rules. Moreover, this form of culture is also often driven by rules: the standards adopted by scientists, artists and philosophers on what constitutes acceptable scientific knowledge, permissible artistic expressions, technical procedures to be followed, etc. The broad cultural domain as such is however not an institution in itself according to the definition applied here, because it does not indicate the rights and duties of the actors concerned.

In a looser formulation, North regards institutions as "the rules of the game", with individual actors and organisations as the players. Are social rules similar to the way *games* are regulated? North is in any event not alone in his use of this metaphor. The neo-realistic philosopher Searle (1995: 103), for example, states:

> Games are especially useful objects of study [...] because they provide a microcosm of larger social phenomena. Famously, Wittgenstein argued that there is no essence marked by the word 'game'. But all the same, there are certain common features possessed by paradigmatic games such as those in competitive sports – baseball, football, tennis, etc. In each case the game consists of a series of attempts to overcome certain obstacles that have been created for the purpose of trying to overcome them. Each side in the game tries to overcome the obstacles and prevent the other side from overcoming them. The rules of the game specify what the obstacles are and what can be done to overcome them, as well as what must and what must not be done. Thus in baseball the rules allow the batter to swing at the ball, but they do not require him to swing. However, after he gets three strikes he must leave the batter's box and leave someone else to bat. Most of the rules of the game have to do with rights and duties, [...] the overall aim is winning, and many of the intervening steps are procedural.

Others cast doubt on the game metaphor, however. Giddens (1984: 17-18) points out that social rules differ fundamentally from rules of a game in a number of respects. Social rules can be challenged by the actors, whereas the rules of the game are in principle incontestable – if they are questioned this leads to interruption or ending of the game.

Moreover, social rules often form an integrated complex, whereas the rules of a game usually stand alone. Partly because of this, social rules are much less uniform then the rules of a game; the tenet 'three strikes and you're out' leaves little scope for interpretation, whereas social rules are generally more vague and may compete or even conflict with each other, even if they are coded in formal legislation. Prevailing social rules also generally reflect the existing social differentiation, which they are therefore inclined to reproduce. The rules of a game, by contrast, are aimed at guaranteeing fair competition. Finally, Giddens comments that social rules are interwoven with the perceptions of the actors and their mutual behaviour. Often they do not so much dictate their acts directly – in the sense of prescribing what people must do or not do in particular cases – but are instead procedures for social interaction that are regarded as self-evident (or, to use the terminology of Garfinkel (1967), aspects of an 'ethnomethodology').

Giddens' objections to the metaphor perhaps fail to do full justice to the thriving of game theory in recent decades, and can be partially accommodated within more sophisticated games, especially in computer-based simulations. For example, network alliances and iterations of games can be allowed, the application of rules can be based on fuzzy logic, unequal power relations can be imposed as a restriction, etc. However, his assertion that social rules differ in essence from the simple rules of baseball or football is convincing, and in that sense the metaphor is not quite appropriate.

If rights and duties are social constructs, this begs the question of whether *ethical relativism* is theoretically unavoidable. This is the standpoint adopted by Coleman (1990: 49-53, 384-387) in his analysis of action rights, in which he opposes normative moral philosophy that attempts to identify theoretical codes of conduct which under certain conditions ought to be followed by all rational actors.[11] Coleman denies the existence of such a "right division of rights", arguing that rights are the result of a power-weighted consensus about the interests of actors, and that they cannot continue to exist without such a social consensus. He illustrates this by referring to the social construction of changes in the right to smoke in public, and to the ethical aspects of the collective suicides of 900 sect members in Jonestown (Guyana) in 1978. He regards acts as the latter as possibly justifiable if certain conditions have been met (knowledge of the consequences, a deliberate weighing up of the pros and cons, voluntary nature of the decision).[12] In Coleman's view, rights are always determined *endogenously*, within a given system of action. While it is possible to adopt different moral views from an *exogenous* standpoint – from another community, a certain philosophical ethic, etc. – this is no more than an outsider's opinion which does not constitute a higher judgement: "There is no absolute observation point, outside any social system, from which a moral judgment may be made" (Coleman, 1990: 387). This statement has far-reaching consequences. Frank (1991: 167) for example points out that in a political dictatorship the ruler determines the consensus, which means that, if one follows Coleman's reasoning, all that dictator's whims would become legitimate; and it would also imply that child abuse is a right as soon as it is approved by the power-weighted consensus of a community.

In principle, however, Coleman is correct. From a sociological perspective a certain definition of rights and duties can only be described; it cannot be regarded as universally applicable. If there is sufficient consensus in a community about the rule that the gods must regularly be offered human sacrifices, or that certain groups are pariahs, then this is legitimate according to the prevailing standard. Three qualifying comments need to be made here, however. The fact that there are no universal institutions does not imply that actors are free to interpret or ignore the rules as they see fit – or, as in the politico-philosophical assertions of Stirner (1971 [1845]) and of individualistic anarchism, that it is actually a requirement that they do so.[13] Even though institutions are socially constructed and therefore 'relative' in that sense, for actors they can still be coercive – because the rules generate shared advantages for all parties, because there may be severe sanctions for non-compliance, and above all because people grow up and live within a certain historical and social context. As result of this latter point, they will often be inclined to perceive reality in terms of the *ex ante* established rules, as the natural and inevitable convictions about what is right and wrong.

Furthermore, some acts, such as murder and theft within one's own community, have such negative consequences for others (externalities) that they are regarded in most social systems as unacceptable. In this sense these are fairly general rules – although even within advanced legal systems exceptions are sometimes made, for example by regarding killing someone as permissible where it is committed as an act of love or vengeance (*crimes passionnels*, blood feud), or is intended as a deterrent (imposition of the death penalty for certain crimes), or is in a perceived general interest (the execution of deserters and traitors in times of war).

Finally, it follows logically from the principle that rights and duties are defined within social systems that they can *acquire* a universal character in global social relations. This can occur more or less as a natural process, due to economic, social and cultural exchange and competition between communities and countries, whereby the granting of certain rights and the imposition of particular duties is generally regarded as beneficial or inspirational. It can also result from the active dissemination of general notions about rights and duties, to which governments and citizens are committed. This occurred after both the First and Second World Wars, and is crystallised for example in the *Universal Declaration of Human Rights* (1948), the *European Convention* (1950), the *European Social Charter* (1961), and a number of specific UN treaties.[14] Now these are relatively abstract rights, which sometimes represent no more than a requirement on the government to make some effort, with weak or unclear potential sanctions in the case of default. They are however a first step towards a constructed universal granting of basic rights, which is given direction by more or less rational principles (the protection of every individual's key interests, the expected economic and social yields). Once such rights and duties become historically recognised, it may become difficult to abolish them, as they have become self-evident in the expectations of citizens, and because governments prefer not to suffer loss of reputation in the international community.

Coleman ignores nuances such as these rather too easily. However, this does not alter the fact that even rules that are generally accepted by the actors concerned, which seek to impose curbs on behaviour with negative externalities, or which are supported by the international community, are ultimately social constructs. In certain circumstances (famine, ethnic cleansing, civil unrest, in the power vacuum following a revolution or lost war) or in certain groups (sects, subcultures), it is possible that they may not be recognised; and in this sense Coleman's relativist position is theoretically correct.

Rights and duties

Since the definition of institutions given here – in contrast to North's approach[15] – accords a central place to the rights and duties of actors, it is important to say something more about their nature and origin. The conceptual framework developed by Raz offers a useful starting point. Provided a person is able to possess rights,[16] according to this legal philosopher he or she has a right if "an aspect of [his] well-being (his interest) is a sufficient reason for holding some other person(s) under a duty" (Raz, 1986: 166). Duties can mean that others have to do something to safeguard the right of an entitled person, but also that they may not hinder the latter in exercising his right.[17] Although Raz deliberately gives a very general definition, he acknowledges that all manner of different rights can be distinguished. For example, there may be undivided or shared rights to a particular good (*object rights*). Rights can also relate to the provision of certain services (*service rights*) or to the performance of certain actions (*action rights*). The property rights that are central to the 'new institutional economics' approach may be regarded as a subset of various types of rights.[18]

Raz's definition of rights and duties has a number of implications. In the first place, according to his view a right is always based on the interests of actors: the core of a right is that someone is permitted to do, to possess or to obtain something, and that others may not hinder him in the exercise of that right, because his interests are at stake. Secondly, duties are not simply correlates of rights, in the sense that there is a single duty for every right. In Raz's view, rights prevail, because it is here that interests are recognised. Duties are legitimised as a result and derived from those rights: "rights are grounds of duties in others" (Raz, 1986: 167). In other words, rights justify and establish obligations; imposing duties on others is a means of safeguarding the rights of actors. Thus, according to this view rights and duties are not two sides of the same coin, as in the 'will theory of rights'.[19]

Raz points out that several duties may ensue from a single right. For example, someone's right to personal freedom imposes many duties on others: they may not forbid him from being somewhere, may not attack him, molest him, lock him up, etc., unless there are good reasons for doing so – as in the case of the imposition of a street ban on a stalker who infringes the personal liberty of someone else through the specific way in which he exercises his right to freedom of movement. According to Raz, duties are also more dynamic than rights: if the circumstances change an existing right can give rise to new duties. Finally, a right may also exist if there are no – or unclear – associated duties. Children's right to education, for example, may be established in law, but this does not make clear what duties this imposes on the various actors. The responsibility for realising this right may lie with the parents, the local community or central government. Raz argues that the precise allocation of obligations requires supplementary premises or rules, for example stipulating that parents must send their children to school, that the community must build the school, that central government must reimburse the staff and equipment costs and monitor the quality of the education. Conversely, duties can exist without any underlying rights. Raz (1986: 166) refers to notions such as 'chastity', 'honour' and 'chivalry', which are difficult to incorporate in his theory of statutory rights.

A final conclusion that can be drawn from Raz's definition is that rights and duties ultimately rest on consensus: there must be sufficient reason to recognise certain rights and to impose the ensuing duties on others. That consensus may be based on the weighing of the interests of several parties.

While Raz regards *interests* as the main source of rights and the associated duties, this need not mean that they are the only source. He sees interests as 'aspects of well-being' of actors, or as utilities. If actors have clear and unambiguous interests, which they adequately perceive, two complications arise: actors may have rights which in practice go against their interests; and it is also not uncommon for some interested parties to have weak rights. Raz (1986: 180) acknowledges the first of these: someone may for example inherit an estate that consists entirely of debts. His explanation for this is that people are usually allocated rights because they belong to a certain type of actors (citizens of their country, homeowners, relatives), who generally have an interest in the right in that capacity but where in individual cases the outcome can be less favourable.

Raz virtually ignores the second point. He seems to assume that the interest-related nature of rights also means that they are granted on the basis of a balanced weighing of interests. While that should perhaps be the case theoretically, historically it is more the exception than the rule.[20] Coleman (1990) also regards interests as the main grounds for granting rights, but emphasises that they are weighted with the *power* of the actors concerned. Rights are defined in a social context, and the interests of those with power weigh more heavily than those of the powerless. Raz's starting point that rights and the derived duties can be based on the interests of the actors is correct; but in the case of unequal power relations their constitution will frequently reflect a systematic bias in favour of the dominant actors. The definition of rights then reproduces the social differentiation at that moment, with the interests of the strong counting for more than those of the weak.

Coleman's view in turn raises the objection that the allocation of rights and obligations in this way appears to ensue mainly from the limited self-interest of the powerful actors involved in the constitution: *might makes right*. This, too, is not unusual historically, but in practice in a democratic society the collective consensus on certain *ideals* helps shape the allocation of rights and duties. Beliefs on how the society or community should function in the future are theoretically a third source for the allocation of rights and duties. They can ensure that rights do not reflect merely the interests of the actors holding power.

Interests, power and ideals are however not the only reasons for making or changing rules. The *costs and benefits* of rules and rule enforcement also play a role, an idea which is central to the 'new institutional economics' approach discussed earlier. A new or different rule makes little sense if its collective cost is greater than its benefit in economic and social terms, if it causes excessive expenditure for the actors involved, or if it is accompanied by high costs for measuring rights and applying sanctions. The material and social costs involved in the vesting of new rules (e.g. the possible fall of a coalition government) are relevant as well, as these may stand in the way of change.

Raz's definition focuses mainly on formal statutory rights and duties, which he regards as being of a different order from moral requirements ('oughts'), whereby it is expected that a person does what he is supposed to do without reasons being given. This would contrast with statutory rights, which are typified by the fact that they are justified on the basis of the utility or well-being of the stakeholders (Raz, 1986: 180). This imparts substantiated and coercive force to the resultant duties: they are not mere favours; there are good grounds on which actors are obliged to respect the rights of others.

However, it is not quite evident why statutory and moral rights and duties have to be as strictly separated as Raz proposes. In the classic definition by John Stuart Mill (1998 [1861]: 97), the difference is regarded as irrelevant:

> When we call anything a person's right, we mean that he has a valid claim on society to protect him in the possession of it, *either by the force of the law, or by that of education and opinion*. If he has what we consider a sufficient claim, *on whatever account*, to have something guaranteed to him by society, we say that he has a right to it.

There is a great deal to be said for this standpoint: moral rights and duties can be very detailed and extensively substantiated even where that motivation – as in the *Rule of St. Benedict* cited earlier – is religious, for example, not utilitarian. Conversely, codified rights may be only vaguely substantiated and not always based on a balanced weighing of interests, but for example on a consensus of Supreme Court judges appointed on political grounds.

Nevertheless, it is useful to draw a distinction between 'formal' and 'informal' rights and duties, because theoretically they influence the behaviour of actors in different ways. Formal rights and duties are defined or recognised by the government; informal rights and duties are based on the consensus within a given group or community. It naturally follows from this that the medium within which the rights and duties are contained makes no difference: the distinction between formal and informal does not correspond to whether or not rules are written down. Within a juridical system verbal agreement may be declared legally valid by the government, and the rights and duties contained within them will then have a formal character. By contrast, detailed written rules such as those of the Benedictine monastic order, which are based solely on the views of a particular religious community and are not enforced by any government, contain informal rights and obligations: a person leaving that community will not be forced by the secular authorities to continue complying with the rules. In fact enforceability is not, as Raz claims, a feature that separates formal from informal rights and duties. Rules that are officially defined or recognised by the government are not always enforceable, for example if a large part of the population do not endorse them or are insensitive to the envisaged negative sanctions. Moreover, in practice the government may have only limited scope for actually imposing sanctions, for instance if the sanctioning agents have little manpower, or because application of sanctions is considered too expensive. On the other hand, actors living in a very closed community, such as a sect, may have virtually no way to evade the socially imposed rules.

One final qualification concerns the relationship between rules and behaviour. The direct behavioural regulation that emanates from a given allocation of rights and duties lies at the heart of Raz's approach. The sociological institutionalism discussed earlier focuses attention on the role of actor perceptions. Rules generally leave a degree of discretionary scope, and their influence therefore also depends on their interpretation by the actors: rights and duties coordinate behaviour through the way they are perceived and processed. This can be a more or less deliberate assessment of behavioural alternatives, but it may also be that actors perceive reality entirely in terms of the existing rules. In that case they will regard certain modes of thought and action to be natural while being unable even to consider others. This subjective filter can have a major influence on the relationship between rights, duties and behaviour.

Conditions

A socially constructed rule may include conditions for the granting of rights and the imposition of duties. With regard to rights, a distinction can be made between *general* conditions (of the type: if C, A is entitled to R) and *current* conditions (A is entitled, if C, to R). The first must have applied at one time – for example, having Dutch forebears as a condition for obtaining Dutch nationality – whereas the latter must be met now (e.g. having a sufficient command of Dutch as a condition for obtaining a work permit for people who are not EU nationals). Such conditions can of course also be formulated negatively (if not C...).

Conditions for a right can relate to certain *events*, to *qualifying characteristics* of the interested party, and to *behavioural requirements*. For example, following a house burglary an insurance company will only meet the policyholder's right to compensation if a recognised crime took place during the period of validity of the policy, if the policyholder was the lawful owner of the stolen items at the time of the theft, and if the policyholder has reported the theft to the police and did not invite theft by leaving the door unlocked.

Duties may also be conditional. They may not apply to everyone, and those who are in principle duty-bound may not be so all the time or under all circumstances. If countries operate a system of national military service, this generally applies only for able-bodied men of a certain age; children, women and disabled and older men are then exempt. In labour relations the employee is generally obliged to follow the instructions of his employer. However, except in cases of total slavery, his duties will be conditional: they apply only during working hours and in as far as the directives are work-related.

Possible sanctions

Sanctions are an important element of institutions. They enforce the behavioural expectations embodied in the rule: the acts that are expected of the (potential) holders of the rights, and the duties of those whose task it is to secure those rights. Sanctions systems are based on the simple premise that compliance with the rules (fulfilling the conditions, meeting one's obligations) brings reward, while breaking the rules (defection: not meeting the conditions, neglecting one's duties) brings punishment. An institution sets out the *possible* sanctions; their actual application depends on the behaviour of actors and is based on the interpretation of the rules in the specific setting.

The legal anthropologist Hoebel (1954: 15) once gave an apposite summary of possible sanctions:

> The positive sanctions step up all the way from the lollipop, the smile, the pat on the back, applause, to honorific positions, bonuses, medals and citations, to posthumous enshrinement. The negative sanctions range from the curled lip, the raised eyebrow, the word of scorn and ridicule, the rap on the knuckle, and refusal to invite back to dinner; through economic deprivation, physical hurt, prolonged social ostracism, through imprisonment or exile to the ultimate [sanction ...] – execution.

This summing up shows that sanctions are not only positive or negative, but may also be informal or formal. Informal sanctions are rooted in groups or communities; they consist of all rewards and punishments regarded as appropriate within such social systems. Formal sanctions are imposed or supported by the government; they are often written down as a corollary to the definition of formal rights and obligations. Formal sanctions include the conferring of distinctions by the head of state and the imposition of punishments by judicial bodies (fines, court orders, detention), but also the public recognition of sanctions imposed within private-law structures, such as declaring legitimate the dismissal of employees who have stolen from their employer. Sanctions can also assume the form of new, 'remedial' rights and duties (indemnity, vindictive damages, community service orders). Formal and informal sanctions may lie on the same continuum – a person who is decorated can be admired – but this is not necessary (others may regard him as someone who allows himself to be appeased by the ruling class).

Coleman (1990: 278-282) points out that sanctions can also be awarded as a concerted effort. In addition to the 'heroic' sanctions described above, he also distinguishes 'incremental' sanctions. Heroic sanctions occur when a single actor may bring about the desired behaviour through the one-off imposition of a sanction (e.g. by threatening physical violence). The drawback is that the costs for the sanctioning actor are higher than if the behavioural enforcement would be imposed by several actors or take place over time, incrementally. To this it may be added that formal sanctions tend to be more expensive than informal ones, because of the higher transaction costs associated with establishing compliance and defection and sustaining the sanctioning organisations (the investigation and prosecution apparatus, the administration of the honours system). By contrast, gossip is a cheap informal method of applying sanctions. A continual process of reinforcement is at work here, which costs the generally large group of sanctioning actors no more than time and saliva, but which can have far-reaching consequences for the object of the sanctioning (isolation, loss of reputation). However, gossip is only usa-ble and effective in certain social circumstances. There must be a stable, morally homogenous group with sufficient opportunities for mutual contact; and the sanctioned party must be sensitive to the gossip, because he regards himself as part of the group and does not wish to become marginalised.

It is important to stress that it is not always necessary to incorporate exogenous sanctions in the rules. Where institutions are internalised by actors, this may also apply to the sanction mechanisms; the actors then feel guilty or embarrassed if they break the rules, and experience a sense of moral superiority when complying with them. If actors have a well-developed conscience, external sanctions are less important. From the perspective of the social system, this is a cheap solution, provided the costs needed to realise the formation of the required sense of right and wrong are tolerable.

The fact that a rule provides for sanctions does not mean that those sanctions will be applied in all cases. Imposition of sanctions may in practice incur high material and non-material costs (economic transaction costs, social resistance) or lead to undesirable side-effects (stigmatisation of certain groups). In such cases preference may be given to benign neglect: tolerance of defection.

Sanctions are moreover dynamic. Punishments that were once usual may at a later time be out of line with people's sense of justice and law (cutting off a hand for minor theft; locking up debtors in a debtors' prison until they have met their obligations). Even where such sanctions still exist formally, it is possible that in practice they are hardly if ever imposed.

2.5 Types of institution

After this discussion of the definition, it is important to look at what kind of institutions there are, and how they relate to each other. The figural model in graph 2.1 contains four formal and four informal types of institution. The formal institutions consist of meta-rules; rules for government production; rules where the government acts as a third party and establishes the rights and duties of private actors; and formal private contracts. With regard to the informal social rules, a distinction is made between values, social norms, conventions and informal private contracts.

Meta-rules
It was noted earlier that the distinctive feature of formal rights and duties is that they are defined or recognised by a government. In the meta-rules, the rights and duties associated with making or changing such rules are laid down. In the first place these indicate the areas with which the government must or may concern itself: the goals and objects of governmental rule-making. Often these are laid down in legislature in very general and perpetual terms, such as "It shall be the concern of the authorities to secure the means of subsistence of the population and to achieve the distribution of wealth" (Article 20 of the Dutch Constitution). Meta-rules may be given tangible form for a certain period in the form of a policy agenda, for example a government coalition agreement. The priorities of

the various objectives can be indicated in such a concord, as well as the measures to be taken to achieve the goals, what funds are available for this and what the envisaged result will be.

The meta-rules also specify which actors are involved in the legislative process. They create certain formal positions (monarch or president, government ministers, parliament, mayors, municipal councils, advisory councils, committees, etc.), lay down the rights and duties attached to such offices, and define the mutual relationships between them. The meta-rules also lay down how individuals can acquire such formal positions, for example through heredity, election or appointment by a higher authority.

Finally, the meta-rules contain process regulations. Those provisions place demands on the procedure of legislation: the form in which the rules are laid down, the need to hear the interested parties, the method of submitting, discussing and voting in the legislative assembly, the right to submit amendments, etc.

In principle, the meta-rules are formal in nature, but they may be elaborated in the informal rules of political actors, who may for example – explicitly or tacitly – agree that the largest political party may supply the chairman for the legislative assembly, that the next largest party may provide a chair for the most influential committee (e.g. the Treasury Committee), and so on.

Rules for government production

In a modern society a large part of formal institutions are concerned with regulating government production. These are formal rules that indicate which services the government provides (funding defence, the police, the judicial apparatus, the physical infrastructure, income transfers, education), and which rights and obligations arise from them for other actors (receipt of benefits, payment of tax and social insurance contributions, military service). Here, the government is in an asymmetrical exchange relationship with private legal persons (citizens, companies), and draws up rules which serve a cross-section of the goals and interests, with a certain weighting. Collective social security forms part of the government production.

Third-party recognition

Then there are the formal laws and rules that the government draws up by way of third-party recognition. These are rules which imply the acknowledgement by the government – as an authority standing above the parties involved – of the rights, obligations and the mutual relationships of private legal persons (citizens, companies). In this role, the government also acts as a 'third party of enforcement', for example by imposing prison sentences on individual actors who commit forgery, or by granting subsidies to companies which undertake recommended business activities (e.g. ecologically sound ways of production). Normally the third-party role of the government is codified in the Constitution, civil law, mercantile law and criminal law.

These are the types of formal institution that are central to the 'new institutional economics': rules such as these establish property rights, create the legislative framework for contracts between private actors, and thus influence relative prices. However, third-party recognition also embraces rules that are not strictly economic: it relates to all government regulation of the rights and duties of private actors. Third-party recognition is not concerned exclusively with property rights and rights to transact, but it also extends to the acknowledgement of the individuals' full legal capacity, the age at which persons are obliged to go to school, may legally marry or enter into sexual relationships, the right to abortion or euthanasia, etc.

The laws on public decency and morality are a particular form of third-party recognition. They are characterised by the fact that the government attempts to promote a specific moral order by forbidding certain behaviours by law (the use of contraception, carrying out abortion or euthanasia), not legitimising others (marriage between people of the same sex), or prescribing certain behaviours (observing the Sabbath as a day of rest). In this type of legislation, the interests and freedoms of direct stakeholders are often *not* recognised by the government. This marks a difference with ordinary law, where there are usually demonstrable injured parties the government tries to protect (victims of crimes of violence and theft, firms whose trading partners fail to meet their contractual obligations). Public decency and morality laws often reflect the informal rules of reigning elites, who use the government apparatus to declare the morality they deem desirable to be the general standard.[21]

Formal contracts

Contracts between private parties are formal if they are enforced by the government. They play an important role especially in economic trading relationships. Commercial contracts are formalised if they comply with the governmental rules on third-party recognition. As noted earlier, this does not necessarily mean everything has to be laid down in writing. It is sufficient if contracts are in line with the general competences and obligations specified by the government in such cases. Mercantile law, for example, may stipulate that within a given trade sector a certain body is responsible for arbitration. There is no need to record this role at great length in each specific private agreement then; tacit acknowledgement or a simple reference to it will be sufficient.

Formal contracts are generally less central in social exchange relationships (friendships, marriages, etc) than in economic ones. In social exchanges the value of the trading good is often unclear, because it is directly linked to the individuals concerned; if someone receives a ring as a present, its perceived worth for the recipient depends on whether the giver is a new lover, her own child or a distant relative. The required reciprocity is also often ambiguous: both the nature of the quid pro quo and the period within which it must be returned is unclear. Finally, social exchanges are not always voluntary. Differences such as these mean that social exchange relationships are less easy to capture in contracts. To the extent that government regulation plays a role, it mainly covers the legal and economic aspects, such as the rights and obligations imposed by the government on people who enter into a civil marriage.

A variant of formal contracting is where the government, based on its role as a producer, acts as a principal (and less frequently, as a contractor) and enters into commitments with private actors for this purpose. This occurs when public works are put out to tender, for example for the construction of physical infrastructure (roads, telecommunications), government buildings, the purchase of computers and software for the civil service, the police, schools, etc. In such cases the government itself is a second party to the contract, and special forms of third-party recognition generally apply: behavioural guidelines for civil servants and those with political responsibility, detailed tender regulations, and stipulations that are laid down in administrative law.

Values

North (1990) counts conventions, social norms and internalised behavioural standards among informal institutions. He is not very explicit regarding the meaning of the latter two types of social rules, nor on the points on which they differ; for example, he counts all "ideas" as internalised behavioural standards. In this study, the more usual sociological distinction between norms and values is applied. Both concepts refer to collectively shared notions about what actors should do. Values can be regarded as abstract collective guidelines for preferred current behaviour. They reflect what is regarded as good, true and beautiful. For example, people should be industrious, honest, social, devout, courageous, eloquent, chaste or polite. Or, in more modern variants: people should aim in their behaviour above all for material wealth, assertiveness and hedonism, or should strive for personal development, authenticity, self-awareness and independence. Values may differ or conflict between different groups and communities, as for example shows in religious conflicts and problems with the social integration of immigrants.

Values provide a general indication of rights and obligations. For example, the value 'solidarity' implies that a person in distress has a right to the support of other members of his group or community. Some values comprise mainly generic duties, with no corresponding rights. Owing to their abstract nature values cannot be contravened, and as a result there are no sanctions associated with them.

What constitutes 'courageous behaviour', for example, may vary depending on social position and time.[22] For instance, a middle-class person may demonstrate courage by catching a thief, while a convicted criminal will perhaps not implicate a 'considerate burglar' who complies with the informal rules of his trade. And what once constituted courage may at a different time in history be regarded as irresponsible. If thieves become increasingly organised in vengeful and heavily armed gangs, the behavioural expectations will change: the costs of the behaviour that in the past was courageous have become too high. An ordinary citizen may then already have displayed courage by calling the police and being willing to make a non-anonymous witness statement.

Social norms

It follows from this that social norms flesh out the abstract rights and duties encapsulated in values. They are specific behavioural prescripts for actual situations, which do carry the possibility of sanctions. It is not the done thing to read a book during a party, people are expected to help victims of a robbery, and it is manners to allow others to finish speaking – and if persons do not comply with the norm, they run the risk of being punished. Their linkage with values means that social norms are not arbitrary within a community, but meaningful.

Norms may also conflict between different groups and communities. This can arise from a conflict of values, but also from a shared value, to which differing social norms are attached. It is possible for norms to conflict exclusively in certain situations. For example, in the communal domain (public spaces, the labour market, education) the expected behaviour may be the same for everyone, whereas in the private sphere the 'house rules' diverge markedly and can give rise to clashes.

Conventions

Conventions differ from social norms in that they are not linked to specific values; they simply indicate what is correct, without elaborating the details of what is regarded as good, true or beautiful.[23] They coordinate the interaction within the group or community, and confirm membership of it. They are fairly neutral behavioural expectations, which impinge on the interests of all members of the communality and which apply for everyone in the same circumstances. The rights and obligations embedded within them are arbitrary in nature: a different distribution or design could have been chosen; the most important thing is that there is a clear rule. In principle, conventions arise informally, but they may be entirely or partly codified, as in the case of traffic rules, the official allocation of street and place names, and statutory rules for the spelling of a language.[24]

Symbolic behavioural expectations, whose meaning lies in collective expressions of unity or distinction (following the latest fashion, the adornment of football supporters, presenting the national flag, wearing logos), also have a conventional character. Although they are arbitrary, conventions may well carry the possibility of sanctions, often in the form of marginalisation or exclusion of groups or community members who do not adhere to them. Such conventions are not mere 'regulative rules' as described by Searle (1995). While it is true that they steer group interaction (for example by making the supporters of a particular football club recognisable as such), at the same time they confirm the shared identity (a true supporter at the very least wears something which expresses the club colours), and they therefore also create meaning.

Informal contracts

Informal contracts are promises and agreements concerning the rights and duties of actors which are not enforced by the government, but are based entirely on what is customary within the community. They may be trading agreements which operate in accordance with the norms of an international business community, or the behavioural rights and obligations which are allotted by the community when a child makes the status transition into adulthood. Here again the agreements may be laid down in writing, but they may also be verbal promises or behavioural expectations which are tacitly assumed. Informal contracts are often supportive in trading transactions, but play a central role in social exchanges. A church marriage – provided it is not endorsed by the government – is an example of this. The ceremony has no significance for the legal and economic status of the marital partners, but can be a meaningful *rite de passage* from which moral and symbolic rights and duties ensue. The government will however not enforce the latter: supervision of compliance with the terms of this informal contract, and the imposition of any sanctions in the event of defection, will have to come entirely from the community.

2.6 Institutional hierarchy

Institutions have now been defined as the social rules that determine which formal and informal rights, obligations, conditions and sanctions apply for actors. North (1990) points out that there is often a specific hierarchy between such rules. For example, two companies cannot draw up mutual contracts which contravene the higher rules imposed by official mercantile law. Although North does not regard institutions as a deductive system – there are also feedback mechanisms, and the relationship between formal and informal rules is a complex one – it is useful to say something more about the relationship between the various types of rules.

2.6.1 Constitutive and regulative rules?

Searle (1995) adopts a very definite standpoint. He argues that 'institutional facts'[25] can only exist within a system of rules which make possible certain activities. Such 'constitutive rules', he asserts, are of a higher order than 'regulative rules', which merely fulfil a coordinating role. Thus the rules of chess make possible the moves made during the game (Searle, 1995: 27-28):

> Some rules do not merely regulate, they also create the very possibility of certain activities. Thus the rules of chess do not regulate an antecedently existing activity. It is not the case that there were a lot of people pushing bits of wood around on boards, and in order to prevent them from bumping into each other all the time and creating traffic jams, we had to regulate the activity. Rather, the rules of chess create the very possibility of playing chess.

Giddens (1984) argues against such a strict division. He rightly points out that these are not different types of rules, but simply variant aspects of them. One facet is concerned with the ability of rules to assign meaning, while another is concerned with the behavioural regulation which ensues from it (Giddens, 1984: 19-20):

> Consider the following possible instances of what rules are:
> – 'The rule defining checkmate in chess is ...' [...]
> – 'It is a rule that all workers must clock in at 8.00 a.m.'
>
> [... These] have seemed to many to represent two types of rule, constitutive and regulative. To explain the rule governing checkmate in chess is to say something about what goes into the very making of chess as a game. The rule that workers must clock in at a certain hour, on the other hand, does not help define what work is: it specifies how work is to be carried on [...] That there is something suspect in this distinction, as referring to two types of rule, is indicated by the etymological clumsiness of the term 'regulative rule'. After all, the word 'regulative' already implies rules: its dictionary definition is 'control by rules'. I would say [...] that they express two aspects of rules rather than two variant types of rule. [The first rule] is certainly part of what chess

is, but for those who play chess it has sanctioning or 'regulative' properties: it refers to aspects of play that must be observed. But [the second rule] also has constitutive aspects. It does not perhaps enter into the definition of what 'work' is, but it does enter into that of a concept like 'industrial bureaucracy'. What [they] direct our attention to are two aspects of rules: their role in the constitution of meaning, and their close connection with sanctions.

2.6.2 Core rights and derivative rights

Another possible form of institutional hierarchy is the distinction that is drawn in the philosophy of rights between rules that accord core rights and those that accord derivative rights. Raz (1986) describes core rights as being linked directly to the interests of actors, and as a source of other rights. Derivative rights stem from core rights and are less immediately connected with actor interests. Raz regards this distinction as necessary mainly in order to explain the fact that in practice rights may occur which are not clearly related to interests. For example, the right to move about freely on Regent Street on a particular Wednesday morning does not ensue directly from any specific interest of the persons actually walking around at that moment. Its source lies in a core right to personal freedom and mobility, to move at will, and the interest that actors generally have in this freedom.

In the theory of rights, on the basis of such notions attempts have been made to compile natural hierarchies of rights and obligations. Raz adopts a less simplistic approach: according to him there is no universal deductive system, in which one right necessarily flows from another ('logical entailment'). At most there is a certain sequence of justification. Raz supports his argument by pointing out that the same right can be both a core right and a derivative right. He cites the example of someone who owns all the houses in a street. If he bought them one by one, there is a 'right to the street' as a derivative of the rights to the individual buildings, the core rights that are encapsulated in the individual purchase contracts. But if he inherits the whole street at once, there is then a core right to the street, from which the rights to the individual buildings ensue. Equally, it is possible to assert a 'core right' of freedom of expression, from which other rights, such as the right to make political statements that are contrary to government policy, ensue. But freedom of expression can also be a derivative right (Raz, 1986: 169-170):

> If [...] separate independent considerations justify freedom of commercial speech, and others still freedom of artistic expression, scientific and academic communications, etc., [and] there are no general considerations which apply to all of the protected areas of speech, then the general right to freedom of expression is a derivative right. It is the mere generalization from the existence of several independent core rights.

A second qualification made by Raz is that core rights can also be limited in their operation. However central they may be, they can be restricted if they impinge on other interests (Raz, 1986: 170):

> A general right statement does not entail those statements of particular rights which are instances of it. I may have a right to free speech without having a right to libel people. In mat-

ters of libel, the right to free expression may be completely defeated by the interests of people in their reputation.

Raz's qualifications are appropriate, but also beg the question of whether the distinction between core rights and derivative rights is an entirely useful one. Ultimately, according to his argument it is the method of codification that determines what is a core right and which rights are derived from it. The contrast then loses much of its persuasiveness. If there is no logical entailment, it is doubtful whether a strict division into these two types of rights will increase our understanding of actual institutional hierarchies. It may then be more sensible to describe the relationship between different empirical social rules directly. In many cases, a dichotomy between core rights and derivative rights will be too coarse for this.

2.6.3 Hierarchies of formal rules

The figural model in graph 2.1 shows much looser hierarchical rankings. The different types of formal and informal institutions are arranged according to their degree of abstraction, and their mutual relationships are not necessarily fixed for all eternity, but are socially and historically variable.

A first form of hierarchy can occur within formal institutions. As the name suggests, the meta-rules of government legislation and regulations are of a higher order than the rules concerning government production and the role of the government as a 'third party enforcer'. This does not mean that the meta-rules directly determine the content of other government rules, but it does imply that the lower institutions are not to be in conflict with, say, the general objectives of the government coalition agreement, and that the prevailing rules of procedure must be taken into consideration. Laws and regulations relating to third party recognition (and, if the government assigns contracts, the government production) also steer formal private contracts, without entirely determining their content.

Jurisprudence is a specific form of rule derivation. It consists of earlier interpretations of rules by the judiciary, which serve as a guide in the application of the rules in new cases. Jurisprudence creates a certain consistency of rule interpretation. This is however never complete: because different cases will seldom correspond entirely, the consistency always depends on the subjective interpretation of judges.

It is usual to find a certain hierarchy within formal institutions of one particular type. For example, it may be laid down in the Constitution that the government is responsible for an adequate defence of the nation's territory. Laws of a lower order (for example governing the actions of the Navy, Air Force, Army, etc.) can be established to stipulate how the military apparatus is built up, what competences and duties of action the various elements of the armed forces have, how far political responsibility for military actions extends, under what conditions compulsory military service can be imposed, etc. In turn, specific regulations governing the government production in this field can be linked to these laws, for example laying down the budgets for the purchase of aircraft, tanks, naval vessels, and so on. This in turn may lead to tendering procedures, which culminate in specific contracts with private suppliers. The entire national hierarchy can be influenced by supra-national rules: agreements between allies to make a certain defence contribution, to specialise in certain military tasks, etc. A hierarchy such as this is however also not a logical deductive system where lower-level rights and obligations can be derived from the general principle in only one way: it does not follow from the obligation to defend the nation that a government must spend a certain amount on a particular type of tank or cruise missile. Such derivations are not inevitable or eternal, but are consensual, and can therefore differ according to the socio-historical context (economic recession or boom, a pacifist or war-mongering political coalition in power, the presence or absence of mighty enemies on the national borders, the influence of arms manufacturers, and so on).

A special form of hierarchically arranged formal rules are welfare and social security regimes; the latter are the main focus of chapters 4 to 6 of this book. The regime notion refers to qualitatively different, cohesive systems of national formal rules which are aimed at achieving certain goals concerning the welfare and social security of the population, which are regarded collectively as desirable. The typology adopted by Esping-Andersen (1990) is the best-known example of this. He contrasts the liberal welfare regimes of the Anglo-Saxon countries with the corporatist systems of the Western European mainland and the social-democratic regimes prevailing in Scandinavia (see chapter 4).

2.6.4 Hierarchies of informal rules

There are also no inevitable derivations between informal institutions. It is possible for the most general institutions – values – to have a particular hierarchical ranking at a certain time and place. Some are regarded as being of a lower order then others: 'politeness' may then for example be seen as a less critical value than 'justice'. Over time, however, such a value hierarchy can change. In Western societies 'striving for salvation of the soul by doing good during one's earthly life' was once a central behavioural directive, but in recent decades, with secularisation and growing wealth, this has become a fairly peripheral value for many people. In its place, materialistic values (achieving financial success and a particular consumption pattern, being famous, having a young and healthy appearance) and post-materialistic values (ideas and self-development are more important than money, one's individual behaviour must not have harmful ecological effects) have come more to the fore.

Social norms are based on values; this implies a certain hierarchy, though the boundary between social norms and values is sometimes a relative one. Take these two examples of a ranking of informal rules:
(1.1) There is a consensus that it is generally desirable for people to respect each other;
(1.2) Politeness is a form of respect;
(1.3) Politeness demands that someone wanting to buy something in a shop waits their turn. If they do not, the bystanders suffering from the impolite behaviour can call the offending party to account; the latter must then apologise and refrain from verbal or physical aggression.

(2.1) There is a consensus that in trading parties generally should aim for good business practice;
(2.2) Good business practice requires that a purveyor fully respects the rights of the customer and the obligations entered into;
(2.3) Good business practice implies that a customer has a right to expect that goods purchased are received in good condition, and that a purveyor has an obligation to ensure that this is so. A customer may return faulty goods, and has a right to compensation for all loss suffered. A purveyor has a duty to eliminate defects and compensate for any loss. In cases which are not clear-cut, the customer is given the benefit of the doubt.

In both cases the highest rule can be regarded as a value and the lowest as a social norm. In the present formulation, the middle rule is a lower value; however, if it included the possibility of general sanctions, it could also be regarded as a higher social norm.

Both the individual rules and the derivations between higher and lower informal institutions are consensual: the consensus could also have taken a different form. Another group or community may not share the value of 'good business practice', or may interpret it differently. In the latter case, there may for example be consensus on the rule that a good businessman does everything in his power to maximise his profits, as long as he does not break the law in doing so; or, even more broadly, that he is prepared to break the law as long as the likelihood of being caught is negligible. The acceptable sanction methods may also be defined differently. For example, the rule that people should wait their turn in a shop may be recognised, but only the shop owner is allowed to sanction infringements of this duty. In that case it is conceivable that it would be regarded as an insult if the rule-breaker were called to account by other customers, and that the defector should react aggressively in order to protect his honour.

In some contexts it is clear for the actors concerned which concrete behavioural prescripts ensue from the general guidelines; in other contexts this is not the case. If a group or society is very closed (e.g. a religious sect, a clan, a class-based society, the 'pillarised' Dutch society around the middle of the 20th century), there will be a cohesive system of norms and values, from which clear behavioural dictates are derived, and the possible sanctions will be evident to all concerned in advance. Zijderveld (2000: 122-127) uses the term 'thick institutions' for this. However, in modern, more open societies it is often less evident which concrete behavioural rules ensue from the core values, and whether certain norms weigh more heavily than others. The lower informal rules can fragment, or the degree to which people endorse them may become more heterogeneous. It is also possible that although the institutions are clear and known to most members of the community, certain behavioural rules are treated as subsidiary or are considered by certain members no longer to apply to them. In such 'thin institutions', the likelihood of conflicting norms is greater, for example as regards the admissibility of abortion, euthanasia or the use of certain drugs. Thus a modern-day doctor whose patient announces that she would like an abortion has to ask him or herself whether the right to life of the unborn child should weigh more heavily than the patient's right to medical treatment, and how this relates to the norms as laid down in government laws and in the ethical code governing the medical profession.

A moral dilemma is a special case of conflicting norms. According to McConnel (2002), such a dilemma exists if an actor is confronted with two (or more) behavioural rules, both of which he can in principle comply with, but not at the same time. Moreover, it must not be possible to resolve the dilemma by ranking the behavioural rules hierarchically in a rational or socially accepted manner; Styron's novel *Sophie's Choice* offers a sad example of this.[26]

Social norms can also vary depending on the context and the actors to which they relate. This occurs, for example, if the rules governing public life differ markedly from those in the private sphere; when there is a 'double moral standard' in which different rules apply for men and women, immigrants and natives, the poor and the social elite, etc.; or when various social groups have highly diverging views on the work ethic, the need to pay taxes, or the admissibility of criminal activities (subcultures).

As stated, conventions are not theoretically derived from other institutions. Since changing conventions consequently does not in principle entail an infringement of higher rules, they can be very fluid. This is apparent, for example, from the rapid succession of clothing fashions and consumer hypes. However, a specific content or appearance of a convention can also have high symbolic or material value, and because of this can be very stable. Thus football supporters attach a great deal of importance to their club colours, and any attempt to change them radically will lead to loud protests and a reduction in fan loyalty. Something similar applies to the faith shown by consumers in certain brands, which can therefore have considerable market value. If conventions have been partially formalised via third-party recognition, there is a greater chance that changes will be accompanied by higher costs, and this fosters their stability. As an example, it is rare for a country to decide voluntarily to switch from driving on the left to driving on the right, or vice versa.[27]

Informal contracts are generally shaped by the social norms and conventions that prevail in the community, without their content being fully determined by those customs. The contracting parties have a certain freedom of action, but also know that they can expect negative sanctions if they infringe the accepted norms and conventions of their community.

2.6.5 Correspondence between formal and informal rules

A last possible form of ranking is the relationship between formal and informal institutions. As North rightly remarks, the two types of social rules may correspond with each other to a certain extent. He emphasises that informal rules often elaborate the freedom of action offered by the formal rules. However, the converse can also be defended: formal rights and duties can be regarded as a codification of the consensus between the actors involved. Some correspondence between formal and informal institutions is likely, because they are generated and evolve in the same historical circumstances. To what extent formal rules dominate over informal ones or vice versa is an open empirical question. This is most evident in times of institutional change. If the formal stipulations do not or no longer adequately reflect the interests of certain groups, they may be regarded by them as illegitimate. The formal rules can then come under pressure from the basis of the informal rules. The converse is also possible; as North states, informal institutions may adapt to changes in the formal institutions, possibly leading to a new equilibrium after a certain time.

As mentioned before, contracts between private parties may be formal (enforced by the government) or informal (enforced by a group or community, e.g. a business community).[28] It is also not uncommon for contracts to contain both informal and formal elements. The informal rules then give direction to the aims of the formal contract (e.g. maximising profit in an acceptable way), while at the same time providing an elaboration of the formal contract, in which it is not possible to define all eventualities.

The right to vote in a democracy offers an example of the complex and dynamic relationships between formal and informal rights and obligations. Often this right is based on an *informal* consensus regarding the desirability of popular sovereignty and the definition of full citizenship. At a certain point these are codified in statutory elections for representative bodies, and in the granting of active and passive *formal voting rights* (i.e. the right both to vote and to stand for election) to private citizens – possibly to the exclusion of certain groups (minors, ethnic minorities, the poor, criminals, women). Formal rights may also carry *formal obligations*, as in Belgium, where there is not only a system of compulsory voting but where people, if summoned, also have a statutory duty to sit on the electoral committees in polling stations. On the other hand, formal rights can also give rise to *informal obligations*. If there is no compulsory voting it may be that a good citizen is expected to go and vote – if only out of respect for the struggle by previous generations to win suffrage. The informal obligation can of course also operate in the other direction: in certain groups or communities there may be a prevailing norm that people should not vote because this would be tantamount to giving support to the unjust decisions of a closed political ruling class. Some informal enforcement might be expected in both cases, in the form of social approval where the rule is obeyed and disparagement if the norm is infringed.

2.7 Actors, their relationships and their motivations

Institutions are reflected in the behaviour of actors because they specify their rights and obligations. However, from the foregoing it has not yet become apparent how this happens. It will therefore be useful to give an indication of which actors can be influenced by rules, what mutual relations can be theoretically observed, and what motivations may dictate their behaviour. This section seeks to shed more light on this.

2.7.1 Actors

Actors are the bearers of rights and obligations, and can perform behaviour. The figural model distinguishes between two types of actor: natural persons and corporate actors. The first are individuals, the latter organisations or bodies which form an independently acting legal persona. Sometimes certain individual actors play a key role in the definition and interpretation of social rules; they can then be regarded as political, economic or social entrepreneurs.

Corporate actors include companies, the Armed Forces, government departments, social security organisations, schools, churches, voluntary associations, clubs, pressure groups, trade unions, etc. They arise as a result of organising: the process whereby individual or corporate actors transfer their rights and obligations to a new corporate actor in order to achieve a certain goal, and supply the necessary resources for this. Corporate actors are deliberately constructed, generally have a certain hierarchical structure (departments, operating companies), and are usually purposeful: the acts of all stakeholders are coordinated in such a way that the predefined objective is brought closer. If the exogenous circumstances change, this may require adaptations to the goals or modes of operation of the corporate actor – although these are often less flexible and innovative than is assumed by some economists.

The government is a special corporate actor, which is expected to fulfil certain core tasks on the basis of the prevailing societal consensus (government production) and to act as a neutral third party which monitors relations between private legal persons from a general perspective (third-party recognition). If that societal consensus changes, this can have consequences for the structuring of the government apparatus: the central government tasks may be reviewed, and the budgets for government organisations reallocated. The government is not a homogeneous actor; there are several territorial and functional administrative layers, with variable relations between rule-definers, dispensers of justice, politically responsible administrators, and the civil service apparatus. Individual actors from these groups constitute a rich mix of agents of the government, and they to do not always serve the interests of their principal.

Supranational organisations, such as the UN and the EU can be independent corporate actors, focusing on supranational government production and third-party recognition, not only for private legal persons but also for national governments. The latter applies when certain powers are transferred from the national level to the supranational organisation, which is also given resources (in the form of direct payments by the member states, or via supranational levies). In that case the relationship between supranational organisation and national government does not differ essentially from that between central government and the lower layers of administration in the participating countries: they have well-defined tasks, responsibilities and resources, and they represent the collective interests that have priority at the various levels. It is however also possible for the supranational organisation to act as a corporate agent of the national governments. Its main task then is to achieve a form of common coordination, within margins laid down by the member states. In an even lighter form the supranational organisation is neither a corporate actor nor an agent, but is merely a discussion platform. In practice, hybrid forms occur. The mutual consultation function may form the basis; in certain areas supranational organisations try to promote harmonisation (such as in the 'open method of coordination' in the EU's social policy); and in a few carefully delineated domains they act as independent corporate actors (the regulation of economic competition, monetary policy).

Groups and communities are not regarded as actors here. The difference between the two is that a group is usually smaller than a community and is characterised by shared activities.[29] Both social contexts are important, because they are the carriers of informal rules. In the figural model, groups and communities are exogenous to the actors. Through rule-setting and enforcement procedures, they may influence actor perceptions, motivations and behaviour; groups and communities, however, cannot act themselves. This view logically implies that 'collective behaviour', in which large numbers of people act in the same way, is not considered here as group or communal action.[30]

Theoretically, a corporate actor can consist of one group, and in that case they may coincide (e.g. a commercial partnership of a limited number of like-minded associates). Once a certain size is reached, however, one or more groups or communities will quickly form within the corporate actor. The fact that the members of those groups or communities develop joint activities (a lunch club, tennis club, etc.) does not make them into actors. They may, however, be carriers of the so-called 'corporate culture'. In the terminology used here this is a collection of informal rules of the groups or communities occurring within a corporate actor, not of the organisation.

2.7.2 Relationships between actors

In figure 2.1 the mutual relations between individual actors are divided into four aspects. The interaction history, the associated knowledge that actors have about each other and their affective ties are relational aspects that are linked to the *persona* of the actors. If the actors change, those relationships also change and the interactions may take a different course.

On the other hand, much of the research into social networks stresses the importance of the relative *positions* of actors, separate from the persons. Reference is made for example to the influence that actors can acquire by entering into strategic relationships with others, or by deliberately using the 'structural gaps' which appear in their social network (see e.g. Burt, 1992; Wasserman & Faust, 1994; Snijders, 2001).

Trust is a central concept in sociological rational choice models, as a key mediating variable. A rationally behaving actor will allow his actions to be determined in part by the trustworthiness of the actors with whom he is dealing. His perception of the outcome of behavioural alternatives is weighed against the chance that others will comply with or default on their obligations. In such approaches the concept is also sometimes regarded as a characteristic of certain social networks, groups or communities: the social capital consists among other things in the amount of trust in such social systems (see e.g. Coleman, 1990: 91-116, 300-321).[31] Trust is seen here as a feature of the relationship between individual actors, which may be embedded in wider social bonds. This distinction is a useful one, among other things because even in communities with a large amount of social capital the trust between some actors can be low.

Authority ties describe the accepted hierarchical relations between individual actors, in line with the familiar definition by Weber (1988 [1922]: 28), who defines *Herrschaft* as "die Chance, für einen Befehl bestimmten Inhalts bei angebbaren Personen Gehorsam zu finden".[32] Authority is power or influence that in the mutual relationships of actors is accepted as proper, because it has been legitimised in some way. It is never absolute, but is a relational probability: in the final instance authority rests on mutual recognition, as even in the most despotic regimes a subordinate may elect to deny the authority and accept the negative consequences of doing so. A characteristic of authority is that it confers a right to demand obedience on the party holding the authority and a duty to obey on those of subordinate rank. In his analysis Weber (1988 [1922]: 122-176) also posits a relationship with the institutional structure, although he does not denote this as such. The legitimisation of power may result entirely from informal rules: the *traditional* authority that ensues from a belief in and loyalty to customs, as in the relationship between monarch and subject, between landowner and serf, between paterfamilias and progeny. It can also be a *rational* authority, where formal rules grant authority to particular individuals (bearers of office in government and business). A distinction is often made here between legal and functional authority; the former is derived purely from the dignity of the office, while the second is based on the expertise of the incumbent and is therefore more unstable: a functional holder of authority must maintain and continually prove their qualities, on penalty of loss of authority. Weber's third type of authority is less clearly linked to prevailing social rules. *Charismatic* authority is mostly based on the affective ties between followers and their leader, to whom they attribute exceptional personal gifts. This is theoretically the least stable form of authority, because its basis disappears once the followers lose their faith in the messianic qualities of their leader. Weber (1988 [1922]: 142-148) sees the "Veralltäglichung des Charisma" as a common threat to this type of authority: the need for stable patterns of behaviour, the failure to meet the high expectations that have been raised, and practical matters that have to be arranged all contribute to the erosion of the original élan. Charismatic authority can however play an important role in processes of social change if it manifests itself at the right time and place, by arousing an enthusiastic belief among the followers in the desired future, in addition to a strong willingness to act. Traditional, rational and charismatic authority are ideal types, which in practice occur in hybrid forms: a political leader whose rational authority is strengthened by a charismatic relationship with his followers; inherited charisma that is passed on through tradition to the progeny of the original prophet, etc.

Theoretically, there are two types of relationships between individuals and corporate actors (cf. Coleman 1990: 325-370). On the one hand, certain individuals may be regarded as the founding fathers of new organisations and thus give direction to their aims and functioning. The constitution of new corporate actors – the formulation of objectives, the allocation of resources – is therefore usually distorted towards the individual perceptions and interests of their initiators. This also occurs if the establishment of the new organisation is a decision at the corporate level: e.g., the managers of merging companies cannot step outside their own cognitive frames, and generally guard their interests carefully in constituting the new entity.

On the other hand, individuals often act as agents of their organisation, in which case they are expected to strive to achieve the aims of this principal using the permitted methods. This relationship is governed by institutions, in particular the formal stipulations of the employment contract and the informal conventions, norms and agreements that are shared by groups within the organisation. Despite this regulation, the agents may also try to exploit the organisation as a vehicle for their own ambitions, interests and self-enrichment: the core of the 'principal-agent' problem.

Obviously, there may also be relations between corporate actors and individuals who are no agents of the organisation (clients, auditors, supervisors, shareholders), and various relations between corporate actors (co-operative societies, holding companies and their affiliates, oligopolies) are possible.

2.7.3 Motivations of individual actors

The central question in this section is what theoretically motivates actors to follow or break rules. The question will first be examined for individuals – without the aim to develop a complete theory of the self,[33] however – and then for corporate actors.

In the case of individual actors, a first possible assumption could be that in principle they simply follow rules and will only break them – i.e. act contrary to the intentions of the rule-designers – if the prescriptions are unclear. As in practice rules can generally not be defined in such a way that they can never be misinterpreted, non-compliance cannot always be avoided: imperfect rule specification provides scope to act, and this will sometimes lead to defection. Jones & Sergot (1993) illustrate this when they state how difficult it is to achieve "regimentation", even in relatively simple systems. This term refers to unavoidable, enforced compliance: the behavioural options are so strictly defined that compliance with the rule is inevitable. If there are two actors with asymmetrical rights and obligations, the rights of A will always be guaranteed in this case, whereas B cannot do otherwise than comply with his obligations. This occurs, for example, if the lending system of a library is set up in such a way that a member can borrow certain books, the librarian is obliged to provide them, and the loan is automatically cancelled once the lending period has elapsed. In theory, such a system could be designed by making the books available exclusively in electronic read-only format, without the possibility of printing them. Even then, however, design faults which are not removed, and external circumstances (such as a power cut) can mean that the envisaged behaviour is not realised.

It is undoubtedly the case that the specification of rules theoretically influences the degree of compliance with them. However, this cannot explain intentional defection by actors who know and understand the rules; nor can it explain group-related behavioural differences. The limits of the simple 'epistemological' view on compliance and defection can be illustrated by the act of suicide, which in most societies is regarded as breaking the collective rules. Thus the Bible, for example, in addition to the general prohibition "Thou shalt not kill" (Exodus 20: 13), which can be applied to suicide, also contains a number of passages in which the human body is equated to God's holy temple, which may not be violated on penalty of retribution.[34] The exegesis is generally added here that the human body belongs to God and that it is therefore not for man to end his life himself. The principle has often also been expressed in formal legislation in countries with a Christian tradition.[35] If the explanation for suicide is sought solely in the clarity or ambiguity of rules, it should be almost non-existent in practising Protestant and Roman Catholic communities: both the informal and formal rules are generally well known in these communities, and are rarely seen as ambiguous. Yet suicide also occurs among practising Christians; and between different religious communities suicide rates may vary significantly.

The rational choice institutionalism discussed earlier explains rule-conformity and rule-breaking from a different perspective. In this approach, rules exist because they offer collective advantages. They lower the costs of economic and social transactions by making behaviour predictable: the number of choices is limited, contracts can be enforced in a simple and standardised way, and breaking the rules carries an appropriate punishment. However, the behaviour of individual actors is not led by the collective benefits, but by an attempt to maximise their personal gain from their actions. Their choices are determined by the relative advantages and drawbacks of compliance and defection, the risk of being found out and caught in the event of infringements, and the severity of the likely positive and negative sanctions; in other words, by incentives, which are partly determined by the rules.

The rational choice approach does not offer a satisfactory explanation for situations in which people obey or break rules when this appears to be clearly against their personal interests. It also leaves unclear why comparable individuals make different choices under the same set of rules, and why behavioural variation between groups and communities occurs if the incentive structure is similar. These problems are usually addressed by referring to the unspecified tastes or preferences of individual actors.

Once again, suicide is an interesting case here, because in principle it would appear to be against the individual's personal interests. From a rational choice perspective, actors make an individual judgement of the pros and cons of staying alive, and will commit suicide if the drawbacks clearly prevail. The decision by the besieged Jews of Masada to end their lives is an example of this.[36] The concept of 'contemplated suicide' also fits in with the theory: isolated elderly people and the terminally ill will end their lives if they no longer see any point in extending it, and if they find the costs of suicide acceptable (access to the means of a painless death, no fear that next of kin will suffer too greatly emotionally, socially or materially, etc.). However, contemplated suicides account for only a small proportion of all suicides.[37] The remainder are difficult to understand from the perspective of rational choice institutionalism, as are two other points: similar individuals in the same circumstances who decide to continue living, and differences in the suicide rates of various social groups and countries.

A bounded rationality variant can partially remove some of these objections. According to this view, the weighing-up process by actors will necessarily be limited, because they do not possess all information (or have too much), because their interests and preferences may be unclear or contradictory, and because they cannot always see in advance the full consequences of their behaviour. They do however continue to strive for maximisation of their personal utility, and will therefore follow or break rules depending on their subjective perception of the advantage of doing so. This view is more realistic empirically because variations in behaviour can be linked to differences in information and perceptions, and are not attributed simply to the black box of individual tastes and preferences. From this perspective, suicide can occur not only as a result of a lengthy and reasoned process of consideration, in which the individual weighs up the pros and cons of continued existence. In certain situations people may have incorrect perceptions: they may end their lives because of mental illness, loss of a loved one or the influence of drugs, whereas in reality this does not serve their interests. However, this does not offer an adequate explanation for why comparable actors under the same circumstances do not act in this way. It also offers no explanation of why suicide is relatively more common among, for example, adolescents, atheists and the Japanese.

In sociological approaches compliance and defection are usually explained on the basis of how the rules are embedded in social systems and the historical process. In a simple functionalist variant, people in principle obey rules because they have internalised then during a process of early socialisation. Defection can then only occur if something has gone wrong during the training for people's social roles – imperfect socialisation creates sociopaths. Such an "oversocialized conception of man" (cf. Wrong, 1961) is however too straightforward. It ignores ambiguities in the rules, contradictions between institutions and between the rules in different groups, and the possibility that not every rule is the object of socialisation or becomes definitively imprinted in actors (see also §2.8). Moreover, it is difficult to understand in this theoretical scheme how social rules could ever change: 'normal' people are by definition conformist and will not be able to perceive rule amendments as a result of the imprinting, while sociopaths are generally not seen as suitable institutional entrepreneurs. Equally unclear is how actors deal with the internalised rules if the social circumstances change radically.

Other sociological theories emphasise the variations that can occur between social systems in the content and ranking of rules, the influence of changing social conditions, and the passive and active rule interpretation by actors. The latter aspect means that they are able to question the rules, though this will be difficult for highly significant institutions. The symbolic aspects of key informal rules often make it hard for actors to recognise behavioural alternatives, because they are unable to step outside the prevailing cognitive interpretation frames and moral templates. Such a perspective leads to other explanations for committing suicide. Durkheim's *Le suicide* (1897) is of course the classic study of the social conditions surrounding this phenomenon. In terms of the figural model in §2.3, his familiar types can be denoted as follows. 'Anomic' suicides are the result of radical exogenous events (occupation of the country, long-term economic crisis), which weaken the prevailing informal institutions across the board. 'Egoistic' suicides ensue from the weak development of rules in certain groups. This is a result of low group cohesion and a high degree of individualism, so that actors are not deterred from defective choices. In Durkheim's approach this explains why suicide occurs more frequently among Protestants and people living alone than among the better integrated Catholics and married people. 'Altruistic' suicides are inspired by the ideals of a particular group, which are not dominant in society at large. They are focused on the establishment of new rules, and the individual actor sacrifices him or herself for the superior goal. In Durkheim's fourth type, 'fatalistic' suicide, there is no such future objective, but highly imperative norms and conventions apply within the group, with heavy sanctions for defection. An example are the soldiers in the First World War who took part in the battles in Flanders and Northern France, losing huge numbers of men for little territorial gain. They could not evade this, because of their military training, solidarity with their fellow warriors, and the death sentence they would face on desertion. Interestingly, Durkheim's latter two types make clear that in some social circumstances suicide is not rule-breaking but is rather the rule.

Building on Durkheim's typology, sociologists have pointed to other social causes of suicide: the isolation and exclusion of certain groups, lack of integration in certain phases of life (adolescents, old age) or following certain life events (loss of a partner or children), weakness of the social network, a decline in social status, frustration about future expectations, culturally defined loss of face, etc. Such sociological explanations can help us to understand the differences in suicide rates between various social groups. Ultimately, however, they permit nothing more than probabilistic statements: the social conditions referred to increase the likelihood that someone will take their own life, but not everyone living under those same conditions will commit suicide.

It should be added that the behavioural aspirations of actors also may depend on their individual characteristics. Even when the rules are unambiguous, the incentives are unidirectional for rational-minded persons, and the social conditions are homogeneous, it is still possible that some actors will obey the rules while others break them. This individual variety is obviously the object of psychology, where behavioural motivations are regarded in terms of fairly stable personality characteristics, which are the product of the interaction between congenital characteristics and environmental influences. Because cognitive development differs between individuals and between domains, not all actors will regard the same choice as rational in comparable circumstances. In addition, the tenets of this discipline point to the influence of specific personality traits. These include extraversion, agreeableness, conscientiousness, neuroticism, openness to experience and intelligence, but also dominance, authoritarianism, conformism, risk aversion, etc.

Besides this, people may have developed a certain behavioural pattern that does not serve their interests directly because of their personal experiences, traumatic or otherwise. Furthermore, behaviour can be driven to a great extent by emotions, and there may be considerable variation here between actors and situations. Frijda (1986, 2007) regards emotions mainly as changes in 'action readiness', or action tendency. He stresses the importance of appraisal, which implies that emotions are not related to objective situations, but rather to the way actors evaluate these[38] (Frijda, 1986: 2-4, 474):

> Emotion [...] appears to be a hypothesis to explain behaviour that has neither sufficient nor adequate purpose or reason; the explanation, then, is sought 'within' the subject. Emotions are linked to certain physiological changes (sweating, trembling, blushing, faster heartbeat), to subjective valuations (good/bad, beautiful/ugly, etc.) and to self-references ('I feel...'). Finally, emotions are evoked by external stimuli which the actor considers significant.

Other branches of psychology accentuate the influence of developmental stages (infant behaviour is mostly non-reflective), physical and mental health status, the eliciting of behavioural reactions by external stimuli, and presumed needs (physical safety, self-fulfilment) which people try to achieve through their actions. Without seeking to integrate all these psychological schools here, it must be acknowledged that individual causes can be important in determining whether people obey or break rules. An attempt can also be made to explain suicide on the basis of individual characteristics (depression, limited cognitive faculties, low resistance to stress, intense emotionality) and experiences, such as earlier suicides in their immediate environment. The intended purpose of a person committing suicidal acts also plays a role: some people genuinely regard life as unbearable; others above all try to make clear that they need help or want their relatives to change behaviour.

The reasoned action models from social and economic psychology combine a number of these insights. They are widely used in research that seeks to explain the behaviour of consumers, voters, etc. Behaviour is seen in this approach as the result of the attitudes and subjective norms of individuals. Attitudes are positive or negative appraisals of behavioural alternatives. They depend on the belief that the behaviour will lead to certain outcomes, and the evaluation of those results. Subjective norms are the judgments that an individual expects of significant others if he opts for a particular course of behaviour. They follow from the beliefs that specific persons think the actor should perform the behaviour, and the actor's motivation to comply with his referents. Attitudes and subjective norms do not lead directly to behaviour, but are weighted and then result in a certain behavioural intention. It is this intention that forms the basis for individual actions.

Sometimes reasoned action models are expanded to include other determinants, such as personality traits and socio-demographic characteristics. These are then exogenous factors which impinge on the attitudes and subjective norms via the beliefs, evaluations and motivations. They also influence the relative weight of attitudes and norms in the behavioural intention. Attitudes to certain rules are sometimes put forward as explanatory background characteristics as well (see e.g. Ajzen & Fishbein, 1980).

If the reasoned action perspective is applied to suicide, this phenomenon is theoretically first of all the result of a positive attitude to the ending of life. Death is evaluated more positively than survival, and the person concerned expects the attempt to be successful and not too painful. In contrast to the rational choice approach, the actor's attitude is not necessarily the result of an elaborate weighing of the pros and cons of suicide; it need not be based on rational argument. Consequently, the model is in principle not limited to explaining contemplated suicides. A second difference compared with the rational choice perspective is that a strong subjective norm can imply that a positive attitude to suicide will not translate into a behavioural intention. Theoretically, this is driven by the actor's belief that his group of referents will disapprove of suicide (they will be sad, their memory of the actor will be besmirched), combined with a sufficiently strong inclination to care about their views.

A strong point in reasoned action models is the focus on the intra-psychological, subjective processing of social expectations, and the significance of the anticipated results in behavioural choices. At the same time, the treatment of rules is fairly limited and one-sided: to the extent that behaviour is institutionally determined, this applies mainly to the perception of social norms. Values, conventions and formal rules are largely left out of consideration. In addition, attention for the social aspects is limited to the immediate significant others, with little consideration of the wider social environment and the historical process. Finally, actors are above all regarded as rule-processing subjects; their active, rule-creating role remains in the shadows.

The position of individual actors in the figural model (graph 2.1) reconciles a number of the theoretical approaches outlined above. At the centre are the more or less stable characteristics of the actor: physical and psychological traits, the individual biography with a particular set of experiences, and the personal resources which they have at their disposal (knowledge, capacity for work, capital). These are surrounded by a shell of perceptions and emotions, which impinge on the assessment of behavioural alternatives in an actual situation. These include:
- The subjective rules. This is the personal translation of the exogenous behavioural rules, in which the actor makes his own interpretation and weighing of formal and informal institutions, focusing on the behavioural alternatives. If the rules are internalised or the actor has developed a certain *habitus*, subjective rules may be pre-reflexive;
- The expected costs and benefits of the behavioural alternatives. These relate both to material gains and losses and to the perceived influence of the behavioural options on the actor's reputation, esteem, etc;
- The probability of outcomes. This is the subjective assessment by the actor that his acts will produce the desired consequences: the amount of gain from compliance and defection, the chance that rule-breaking will be discovered and that sanctions of a given severity will be imposed, etc;
- The goals which the actor strives for, partly fed by the ideals he supports;
- The perception that the actor has of his interests (self-interest or wider interests);
- The emotions the actor associates with various modes of behaviour.

In this approach, these perceptions and emotions depend on the one hand on the stable characteristics of the actor, and on the other on the institutional structure and the historical circumstances in which the rules are applied. The results of earlier interactions (learning effects) and the relations maintained with other actors (e.g. authority, trust) also have an influence. The combination of subjective perceptions and emotions results in a certain behavioural aspiration.

From this sketch of the motivations of actors, it is possible to deduce when defection will be attractive for actors. This is the case in the first place if the *institutions* encourage this, which occurs if:
- Defection is more profitable than complying. This particularly happens when breaking a rule generates great material or immaterial benefits, and is simple to achieve because it costs little money, effort and time;
- The rule does not specify clearly the rights, obligations, conditions and possible sanctions;
- The sanction for defection is lower; if rule-breaking carries a severe material, physical or social penalty, rules will less often be broken, even if the cost/benefit equation is favourable; but if the sanction is mild, rules will be broken even if this generates little profit;
- Rule-breaking is less visible, so that the chance of being caught is smaller; if defective behaviour brings a positive result and can be kept completely secret, actors will opt to break rules even where sanctions are severe;
- Sanctions are not applied in practice; severe sanctions have little effect if they are not actually imposed.

In addition, however, the *context* is also important: the object of interaction, and the historical situation in which it takes place, influence the behavioural aspirations of actors. The more the interaction resembles an impersonal exchange, the more important rational motivations become. In that case, behavioural choices can follow fairly directly from the perception of costs and benefits, which correlates with the historical circumstances and the 'opportunity structure' that is defined by the formal and informal rules. This applies even more strongly if this impersonal exchange is non-recurring in nature, relates to a single costly good, and takes place between no more than two actors. *Ceteris paribus*, well-reasoned defection is therefore more likely to occur in the purchase of an expensive consumer article on an open market than in a long-term collaborative business project involving several participants.

The likelihood of non-compliance is also high where the interaction relates to a (semi-)collective good. In that case, the benefits of defection (use of common meadowland, smoking in public) usually fall to the individual actors in the short term, and they are inclined to regard their behaviour as a personal, one-off decision. It is only with the passage of time that the collective losses manifest themselves (overgrazing, higher incidence of lung cancer), and these cannot be traced back to the behaviour of individual actors at a specific moment. Interactions where the market character is less dominant

– for example leisure activities, behaviour within love relationships, artistic expressions, religious acts, sport, voluntary work – are in principle determined to a lesser extent by the weighing up of costs and benefits. Nevertheless, these behavioural modes, too, can become 'commodified' if much worth is attached to market principles and consumption by a certain group or society.

However, even in highly commodified or social dilemmatic contexts, in which the rules and historical circumstances foster rational defection, not every actor will be non-cooperative. This is because of the *subjective filtering* of institutions and historical circumstances. Relevant factors in this connection are:
- Incomplete information or erroneous understanding of the rules and historical circumstances. For example, if the information on the costs and benefits is not transparent, or is contradictory or excessive, the actor cannot easily oversee the consequences of his behaviour in advance. This ambiguity increases his freedom of action, but can also lead to unintended or undesirable consequences;
- The existence of powerful pre-reflexive subjective rules directed towards compliance. As stated, this occurs in the case of internalised rules and habit formation. Relationships of trust and authority with other actors may also play a role;
- Certain emotions (such as feeling uncomfortable if one breaks the rules) and stable personality characteristics (authoritarianism, altruism, risk-aversion, limited cognitive faculties, psychological and physical handicaps) which stand in the way of rule-breaking.

This perspective on individual actors in theory offers a more complete understanding of the suicide example. If under certain circumstances the rule applies that life should be taken, suicide is rule-compliant behaviour, a variant that could be described as *normative suicide*. Examples include the mass suicides by the Jonestown sect[39] and the practice of *sati* (lit.: 'devotion') whereby Hindu widows in India demonstrated their devotion to their deceased husband by voluntarily being burned alive on their husband's funeral pyre – a practice which still occurs occasionally. In suicides of this type, rule-compliance is often enforced: one of the reasons that the British Governor-General Lord William Bentinck declared *sati* to be illegal in 1829 was that in many cases it boiled down to nothing more than community-sanctioned execution.[40]

In other instances, suicide is an example of rule-defection. This non-compliance theoretically rests on certain combinations of perceptions and emotions, which are driven by institutions, actor characteristics, historical circumstances and the actor's relationships. In *contemplated suicides* particular actor traits (illness, limited cognitive faculties) lead individuals to regard the disadvantages of remaining alive as too high, to believe there is a sufficient chance of the suicide attempt succeeding, and to allow their own perceived interests to prevail. These motivations weigh so heavily that the actor is not diverted from his well-reasoned choice by any subjective rules, personal goals and ideals, or relationships with other actors.

Socially induced suicides differ from normative suicides because in principle they are defective. They mainly result from weak subjective rules, which can arise either from feeble or ambiguous group norms or from clear rules that have not (yet) been properly internalised. The relational network of the actor is limited and not directed at the prevention of rule-defection. These suicides are not based on an extensive weighing up of personal costs and benefits. They occur more often among actors (young adults, lonely elderly persons) and communities that are undergoing transitions.

Emotional suicides are determined mainly by personal circumstances. Intense individual emotions (such as grief) and delusions (because of illness, drug abuse, etc.) dominate; rational judgements and social circumstances play a subordinate role.

2.7.4 Motivations of corporate actors

In figure 2.1 the forces driving corporate actors are largely the same. They too have certain characteristics: the resources they have available and the collective experience that organisations have built up. They are embedded in certain actor networks as well, and react to the historical circumstances. Corporate actors also interpret the rules and social context, have goals and ideals (the 'mission'), define the interests of the organisation in a certain way, and base their acts partly on the probable outcomes of behavioural alternatives. The difference, of course, is that corporate actors are not people.[41] This implies they do not have emotions, and that all perceptions ensue from their dominant agents. However, the behaviour of corporate actors cannot simply be reduced to the motivations of the individuals of which they are comprised. Three elements are of particular importance here:

- The goals and future ideals of the corporate actor. If these are aimed at profit maximisation, as is the case with a commercial firm, the rational weighing up of the economic costs and benefits will play a decisive role in the assessment of behavioural options (product development, investment, mergers, business expansion, recruitment and dismissal of staff, etc.). If, as in a political organisation, the achievement of consensus on future policy is important, then it is not only the economic costs and benefits that are important, but also the possible political gains and losses. In this broader rationality, choices that are politically meaningful or expedient are the prime aim, even though in economic terms they may well be sub-optimal. In organisations with an idealistic or social aim (recreation, animal protection, religious conversion, combating diseases) this is even more the case; here, realisation of the object is the main concern, and the financial balance is of secondary importance (maximum fundraising, minimum implementation costs).
- The strength of the organisation's formal rules, and of the informal rules of the organisational community or groups within it. If these institutions are very compelling and are based on a high degree of socialisation or a well-developed *habitus*, the perceptions and emotions of the agents can to a large extent be forced into line. Traditional government bureaucracies, the army and police are textbook examples of this, but in

organisational sociology reference is also made to the strict formal procedures and informal expectations in manufacturing industries, the offices of commercial firms, and religious sects. In these circumstances it is less important who fulfils a function, because the rules largely establish required behaviour. There are however also organisations where the formal and informal rules are fairly loose (e.g. in creative and scientific institutions), and where individual agents have considerable latitude in steering the actions of the organisation.
- The corporate hierarchies. Certain actors as a result of their function, their network or their informal power may shape the behaviour of the organisation more strongly than others. This applies especially in organisations with a pyramidal structure, which is linked to strictly enforced hierarchical values, norms and conventions.

2.8 Rule-driven interactions

Although the meaning of the notion 'act' is an obvious one in everyday language use, it is not a simple concept to define precisely. *Acts* can be regarded as the *events*[42] that an actor brings about, i.e. that which he does or achieves. They are a subtype of the more general notion *actions*, which can also be performed by machines or tools. However, those appliances are themselves not actors: they perform actions, but not acts.[43] The definition of the term acts leaves unresolved the issue of what 'do' and 'achieve' actually entail. Here a fairly pragmatic approach is adopted to this topic, with no attempt at an exhaustive reflection on the philosophical discussion (see e.g. Mele, 1997).[44] First and foremost, acts are taken to include the physically observable movements made by an actor (an individual moves his leg) or manipulations of objects (the actor kicks a ball). However, the notion also includes the symbolic or social meaning of such observable acts (a football player scores a goal). Acts need not be observable: they can also include certain mental activities. For example, an actor who thinks through his best mode of operation in a given situation is displaying problem-solving behaviour. Not all intra-psychological sensations are however acts: the emotions felt by an actor are not acts, though any physical expressions of those emotions are. The fact that the footballer weighs up which corner of the goal to choose before shooting is an act; his personal feelings of triumph or failure after the attempt on goal are not. However, his public expressions that refer to those emotions – cheering, putting his head in his hands – are acts (even if they are over-acted).

Acts may be intentional, but also unwitting. To stay with the example of football: the player preparing to shoot will bend his knee more or less consciously to steer the ball in the right direction, but when the physiotherapist tests his knee reflexes this act is unintended. In practice, this distinction is sometimes difficult to establish.[45]

Interaction[46] consists of a series of acts that involve several actors. These actors are all focused on the same goal or physical objects, and can respond to each other's acts. The form of these behavioural exchanges varies. Interactions may be simultaneous or sequential – the difference between a football match in which all the players try to control the ball at the same time, and the chess game in which moves are made in turn. They may also be non-recurring or lasting – an immediate economic exchange on the basis of a one-off agreement, compared with repeated bartering within the context of an indefinite cooperation agreement. And of course, they can take place between two actors, or in an interaction structure with a large number of participants in a network where the physical distances are great. While each actor makes their contribution to the interaction, its total may comprise more than the sum of the individual acts.[47]

2.8.1 Institutions and interaction

To a certain degree all interaction is influenced by rules, because language and implicit expectations play an important role in it. On the other hand, in the discussion of actors (§2.7) it became clear that institutions generally do not determine behaviour completely: 'regimentation' (unavoidable compliance with the rules) is difficult to achieve in practice. Rules leave the actors some latitude of acting because they are unclear or not specific enough, and they are always interpreted subjectively. In addition, actors are not always led by institutions; theoretically, other motivations are also important: their emotions, their perceptions of the costs and benefits of behavioural alternatives, the probability of outcomes, their goals and interests, and their ideals. And finally, it is possible for actors to respond differently to the same rules because of their diverse characteristics, resources, experiences and relationships.

Here, rule-driven interaction is understood as behavioural exchanges between actors that depend on *specific* socially acknowledged rights and duties, with the related conditions and possible sanctions. This is the case, for example, for the interaction between a GP and their patient, in so far as this is regulated by the formal protocols and informal expectations that exist regarding the proper treatment of a medical problem (intake, diagnosis, treatment, referral, etc.). Whether or not the two actors adhere to more general norms and conventions – the doctor who adopts a sympathetic or aloof stance, the patient who verbalises his problem in good or poor English – does not form part of the specific rules that govern this interaction, though the encounter can be influenced by them. Evidently, the fact that an interaction is rule-driven does not imply that the applicable social rules are the sole factors determining its course: specific rules are usually embedded in the general institutional context, and the motivations of actors do not ensue directly from behavioural prescripts (see §2.7).

The economic behaviour of individuals and corporate actors provides examples of rule-driven interaction: the series of acts within a company; the mutual actions between companies; the exchanges between consumers and sellers; the permanent negotiations between trade unions and employers' representatives; and also the coordinated economic interactions between nations (e.g. the supporting purchase of certain currencies by National Banks in order to influence exchange rates). But interactions that are generally not included in the economic arena are also rule-driven: the relationships between friends or marital partners; family contacts; the exchanges within groups and associations; political behaviour (by voters, candidates, party members), and so on. The behavioural exchanges between actors which are governed by social security rules also fit into this category. These will be discussed in more detail in chapter 3, on the basis of a number of theoretical interaction models for the different types of social security schemes.

The extent to which interaction is rule-driven can vary. If two strangers meet by chance in a setting that is unknown to both of them and where their behaviour cannot be observed, it may be assumed that the interaction will not be greatly influenced by social rules concerning specific rights and obligations. Simmel (1971a [1908]) referred in this connection to the 'objectivity of the stranger'.[48] Set against this are certain rituals and ceremonies, in which the successive acts of the participants are strictly prescribed and heavily sanctioned by the community.

If interaction is rule-driven, the behaviour of the actors concerned can in principle be assessed in terms of compliance or defection, but it cannot be taken for granted that this will actually occur. In the first place, it may be difficult to establish whether rules are being broken or observed, because they are often fairly unspecific. This applies especially for the more abstract institutions (values and formal meta-rules). It was noted earlier that values cannot be contravened: whether or not actors infringe them can only be measured using the social norms and formal rules that are actually linked to these general guiding principles. Institutions at a lower level of abstraction do contain behavioural prescriptions, but these can often be interpreted in several different ways in actual interaction processes. The rights and obligations are frequently fairly general, with ill-specified conditions, and some uncertainty about the applicable sanctions and their imposers in the situation at hand. This ambiguity of the rules means that compliance and defection in rule-driven interactions can depend greatly on the interpretations of the actors concerned.

In the second place, establishing defection and compliance requires that the stakeholders keep a record of this during the interaction, and impose sanctions where necessary. As stated, North (1990) does not regard this monitoring and enforcement as something that will happen automatically. Both lead to transaction costs, which are not always acceptable to the actors in economic or social terms; thus, certain rules may not be put into effect because the price of monitoring and sanctioning is too high. Following the figural model in §2.3 this can be stated in slightly more general terms. Establishing compliance or defection and applying sanctions requires an interaction process, which is not self-evident and which does not automatically proceed in the correct way; it has to be socially organised in some way or other. In the case of informal rules there must be a certain relationship between the stakeholders in the community, and there must be an accepted method for identifying and punishing defection (e.g. gossip, verbal reprimands, ostracism, pillory, etc.) or rewarding compliance (status or monetary returns, admiration). In the case of formal rules, government officials entrusted with monitoring and sanctioning generally have to follow a specified chain of acts, or procedure, with closely defined tasks for the police and judiciary (investigation, instigating charges, prosecution, sentencing, rehabilitation, etc.).

2.8.2 Interaction results and the context of rule application

All rule-driven interaction is aimed at achieving certain results. In the figural model in graph 2.1 these outputs relate to the actors involved and to the collective the rules apply to. The results for the actors may concern changes in their resources and experience (wealth, knowledge) and alterations of their perceptions (including the subjective rule interpretation), their emotions, and their relationships with other actors.

The consequences at the collective level refer to the impact of rule-driven interactions on the evolution of a community or society. Often these are to a certain degree intended: institutions are usually aimed at achieving certain collective outcomes. In figure 2.1 these collective outcomes are shown as a feedback from the interactions at the actor level to the historical process. This implies behavioural exchanges are not only important for the immediate stakeholders, but also influence technological developments (such as innovations in production techniques), the economy (growth of collective wealth, labour market development), the social structure (differentials in income, status, elite-formation), the prevailing ideals (the future that a community wants for itself) and demographic trends (birth rates, mortality, migration). On the other hand, the historical process is also theoretically a determinant of the collective results: the outcomes of the rules depend in part on the circumstances under which actors implement them, the context of rule application.

Consumer behaviour offers a simple illustration of this two-way causal relationship. The existing institutions influence the purchase of certain goods: agreements between market players, government rules on VAT, income tax and compulsory social security contributions, certification and inspection of production processes, levies on imported goods, etc. However, to what extent consumers actually buy such goods, given these institutions, also depends on the historical background against which these rules are applied, in particular the economic climate and its impact on people's perceptions of their disposable income. Keynesian economic theory stresses that their actual spending behaviour in turn influences economic growth. In §3.6.3 this line of thought is developed further for the collective results that can be achieved by social security rules.

The historical process is discussed in more depth in §2.9, since it is also the engine driving the creation of institutions. First, however, a special form of rule-driven interaction deserves some attention: the way in which actors acquire rules.

2.8.3 Rule acquisition

As institutions are social constructs, it follows that actors cannot know them instinctively. Logically, certain acts or interactions must take place which allow the actors to learn and internalise the rules. This begs a number of obvious questions. Which actors are involved in the process of rule acquisition, and under what conditions are they prompted to act? Which rules do the actors learn, when and how? What is the result of rule-acquiring acts and interactions? Without discussing these questions exhaustively, a number of theoretical notions will be considered here concerning individual[49] rule acquisition (for a more detailed discussion see e.g. White, 1977; Klaassen, 1981; Hurrelmann, 2002; Hurrelmann & Ulich, 2002).

In the field of sociology, these topics are key to theories on the 'social order problem'. If every society or community is confronted with a permanent "barbarian invasion of new-born infants" (Parsons, 1951: 208), how is it possible that such social systems survive? The classic sociological answer assumes a certain method of socialisation. This is often interpreted as a process of one-sided transfer of existing rules to new socialisees. Thus, the system's prevailing culture is passed on to the new generation and the problem of social order is in principle solved. White (1977: 2) illustrates this with "die-stamping" definitions such as the following:

> The process by which society moulds its offspring into the pattern prescribed by its culture is termed socialisation. [...] Socialisation is the process which converts individuals to people. [...] We may define socialisation as the process by which someone learns the way of a given society or social group so that he can function within it.

Sociological theories on socialisation mostly share the assumption that people are initially malleable (see Klaassen, 1981: 206-207). For example Durkheim (1922: 50-51) states:

> L'enfant, en entrant dans la vie, n'y apporte que sa nature d'individu. La société se trouve donc, à chaque génération nouvelle, en présence d'une *table presque rase* sur laquelle il lui faut construire à nouveaux frais.

The egoistical individual being of the newborn child, which has only organic needs, must be remodelled to create a social being, according to Durkheim. Parsons (1951, 1964) also regards newborn children as organisms which in addition to biological urges have only predispositions for social learning, i.e. plasticity, sensitivity and dependence. The individual reconciles such organic characteristics with the personality that he or she develops during the socialisation process that makes them part of the social system. Structural-functionalist theories refer in this connection to the role-less status of newborn children. The critical, Marxist-oriented sociology also regards human beings as highly malleable: the ideas and convictions that are imparted to new actors bear a direct relationship to the social position of their socialisers and are, in fact, an ideology. For social constructivists, finally, the starting point is generally man's 'world-openness' (Berger & Luckman, 1966). They emphasise that *homo sapiens*, unlike most higher animal species, possesses virtually no instincts. As result he may develop a varied behavioural repertoire, but this requires a lengthy period of socialisation.

In sociological theories, socialisation is often seen as inevitable, especially at the start of a human life. *Functionalists* emphasise that new actors have to be trained because otherwise they would not be able to exist in their society, thus jeopardising the survival of that social order. Socialisation is therefore promoted collectively, and consists primarily of processes of identification, direct instruction and the providing and training of behavioural models in the socialisees. Pedagogic role expectations are attributed to parents, teachers and other socialising actors. Failure to fulfil those roles evokes negative sanctions, leading in the most extreme cases to the possible acquittal of their educational tasks (removal from the parental home in cases of child neglect, dismissal of unsuitable teachers, closure of poorly performing schools). The method of socialisation varies from one society to another, and within those societies between the different social milieus. In general, the early socialisation takes place within the family. It proceeds largely via identification with the parent, so that the characteristics acquired in this way develop a high degree of stability, becoming imprinted in the personality. In modern societies the school is theoretically also an important socialiser. That is where the socialisees acquire the detailed knowledge needed because of the highly advanced division of labour; and that is where they learn generally applicable norms and values, which can offer some correction for the particularistic – and possibly deviating – rules learned in the home setting. With this in mind an elaborate educational infrastructure is maintained, a detailed educational curriculum established, and the take-up of educational facilities by the socialisees encouraged (financial support, compulsory education, etc.). The socialisation process enables the socialisees to learn the rules and skills they will need in the future, as members of the community, and for the specific social roles they have to fulfil within it. After learning them, the socialisees know what is expected of them, and what the consequences will be if they fail to meet those expectations. The emphasis in this approach lies mainly on the *integrative* function of socialisation.

Critical *Marxist sociology* essentially follows this same functionalist line of thought, but place greater emphasis on the *allocative* function of socialisation. By this they mean the reproduction and legitimisation of existing social inequality or, in their specific jargon, the *Einübung in die Klassengesellschaft* (Huch, 1972). The socialisation process is differentiated: the lower social classes, girls and ethnic minorities are taught different rules, language codes and skills from the higher social echelons, boys and indigenous citizens. This transfers the existing social positions and stratification principles to new actors and ensures that these are not called into doubt by them. Education plays a key role in this allocation; it imposes the social views of the dominant groups on the lower strata, and selects and qualifies pupils in accordance with the existing social distinctions. A variant within this approach does not regard reproduction as an automatic process; evidently, complete reproduction would make any social change impossible, which does not tally with the empirical evolution of most societies. From this more optimistic social-democratic perspective, emancipatory potential is often attributed to education. Extra attention and resources aimed at deprived children could offer compensation for the inequalities that arise in the pre-school phase, allowing social allocation to take place on more meritocratic grounds. Such a compensatory policy has in fact been implemented in many Western countries in recent decades, though often with modest results.[50]

Rational choice socialisation theories generally accord a central role to the *qualifying* function of socialisation, which is mainly achieved via education. The training of 'human capital' is a collective interest because it benefits labour productivity, innovative capacity and the economic development of the community, although the return on investing in education is not always easy to determine. Individual socialisers and socialisees strive to optimise the qualification level (the number of years' schooling, the diplomas attained, skills that can be used on the labour market), because they have a personal interest in doing so. A rational parent who does not teach his child to behave and does not ensure that he receives sufficient formal training, endangers the child's future and will later suffer the consequences (loss of reputation, a child who does not care for him when he is in need). And a rational socialisee who does not attain the right diplomas (but also a certain use of language, a network, an interesting cv, etc.) has little chance of obtaining a good or well-paid job, high social status or an attractive partner. Thus, from this theoretical perspective some degree of socialisation is inevitable as well; although the specific learning route chosen by those concerned will depend on the prevailing relative costs and benefits.[51]

Social constructivists take a broader view of socialisation, which includes its *symbolic* implications as well. For them, socialisation is not exclusively about the – position-specific or otherwise – deliberate transfer of concrete behavioural rules, the training of skills, and getting the right credentials. It also involves the imparting of cognitive frames, moral templates, desirable affects and social identities. Socialisation is ineluctable in the first phase of life in particular, because of the symbolic power that parents have over their children during that period. This was expressed aptly by Berger & Luckman (1966: 151):

> Every individual is born into an objective social structure within which he encounters the significant others who are in charge of his socialization. [...] Their definitions of his situation are posited for him as objective reality. [...] They select aspects of (this world) in accordance with their own location in the social structure, and also by virtue of their individual, biographically rooted idiosyncrasies. The social world is 'filtered' to the individual through this double selectivity. Thus the lower-class child not only absorbs a lower-class perspective on the social world, he absorbs it in the idiosyncratic coloration given it by his parents [...] Consequently, the lower-class child will not only come to inhabit a world greatly different from that of an upper-class child, but may do so in a manner quite different from the lower-class child next door.

According to this view, the child cannot do otherwise during the 'primary socialisation phase' than identify with its socialisers (Berger & Luckman, 1966: 154-155):

> The child does not internalize the world of his significant others as one of many other possible worlds. He internalizes it as *the* world, the only existent and only conceivable world, the world *tout court* [...] However much the original sense of inevitability may be weakened in subsequent disenchantments, the recollection of a never-to-be-repeated certainty [...] still adheres to the first world of childhood. Primary socialization thus accomplishes what (in hindsight, of course) may be seen as the most important confidence trick that society plays on the individual – to make appear a necessity what is in fact a bundle of contingencies, and thus to make meaningful the accident of his birth.

Primary socialisation is chiefly a task of the parents. Building on the insights presented by Mead, in social constructivism this is not regarded as a one-sided transfer, but as a process of interaction which is partly involuntary and pre-reflexive. Initially by imitating the behaviour of its 'significant others', and later by identifying with them, the child learns to recognise the attitudes of others, to understand their purpose and to acquire them. Because the socially recognised denotations are set down in language, the procurement of language skills plays a central role in this process. Play is an important aid: it allows the child to experiment with meanings, to learn to place itself in the position of others and to role-play. Primary socialisation can be regarded as successfully completed when the socialisee generalises the attitudes and roles of its significant others. They are no longer the views of the child's parents, but have become everyone's normal ideas, the notions of the 'generalised other'.

In this approach, primary socialisation is concentrated on a central but fairly limited domain: the acquisition of general linguistic and social roles in the first phase of life. However, much of the transfer takes place later, when the ability of reflection is more developed in the new actors and the identification is less inevitable: "Put crudely, it is necessary to love one's mother, but not one's teacher" (Berger & Luckmann, 1966: 161). In this phase there is more scope for a conscious transfer of knowledge and skills, and the socialisee has a more independent, more considered contribution to the learning process. This is defined as secondary socialisation: the initiation of actors who have already completed the primary socialisation process into new elements of the society of which they will become part. The transfer of behavioural prescriptions is often an important subsidiary aim in this phase: the secondary socialisation process also makes clear the rules by which a new batch of actors (such as future police officers, civil servants, businessmen or scientists) should shape their professional lives. On the one hand there are the official codes of conduct for police officers and civil servants, the accounting and statutory conditions which must be observed by a business employer, and the written professional code of the scientist. On the other hand there are the core values of the profession (maintaining order, serving the public good, making profit in a legitimate fashion, the verifiable pursuit of truth) and the associated norms, conventions and informal agreements.

Secondary socialisation is a more extensive process in societies with an elaborate division of labour, with the associated more differentiated distribution of knowledge and roles. Its universalistic nature means it is by definition somewhat at odds with the idiosyncratic, though perceived as natural, outcomes of primary socialisation.

One objection to the classic sociological approach to rule acquisition is that relatively little attention is generally paid to the development of individual competences, something that is denoted using terms such as 'personalisation' or 'ontogenesis'. In *developmental psychology*, by contrast, this concept plays a central role. These theories do not start from the premise that a newborn child is a malleable barbarian, an unwritten page that can be filled in at will by those around it. Rather, it is assumed that there is a succession of qualitatively different developmental stages which have to be gone through by every human being. This is not a universal ground plan which fixes the fate of the individual. Only the sequence is general; the precise timing and the way in which the individual goes through the phases can vary, depending on individual characteristics, the social background of the children concerned, and the society in which they grow up. Moreover, the acquiring of new competences depends on the development achieved by the individual in earlier phases.

The phase theory put forward by Piaget is an example of such an approach, focused mainly on cognitive development. In his approach, the 'sensorimotor' phase (0-2 years) is concerned primarily with the acquisition of mental representations of simple goal-directed motor actions (sucking, grasping, kicking, and throwing). This is followed by the pre-operational stage (2-7 years) and the period of 'concrete operations' (7-11 years), in which the child acquires symbolic functions such as language and play, the ability to conceptualise and the ability to enter into interpersonal relationships. Around the 11th year a fourth, qualitatively different phase begins, the period of formal operations (abstract thought, logical proof, values). In this approach, a child develops its competences as part of his organic growth process (especially brain development), through practice and experience, through social interaction and direct transfer, and by seeking new equilibria through self-regulation. The social setting often plays a facilitating role in this process, providing the stimuli on the basis of which the child forms itself (Piaget & Inhelder, 1969: 152-159). Such a view is diametrically opposed to the classical sociological perspective, in which socialisers impart the social rules unilaterally to socialisees. Such direct transfer does have a place in developmental psychology theories, but is always dependent on the way in which new actors perceive and receive it (Piaget & Inhelder, 1969: 156):

> Even in the case of transmissions in which the subject appears most passive, such as school teaching, social action is ineffective without an active assimilation by the child.

Another objection is that many sociological theories pay scant attention to the potentially conflicting nature of the socialisation process, and often do not acknowledge that a socialisation that is regarded as successful from a collective point of view need not be so for the person concerned. Wrong (1961: 186-188) illustrated this point in his classical critique of the structural-functionalist view of socialisation:

> Freud's theory of the superego has become the source and model for the conception of the internalisation of social norms [...] in sociological thinking. [...] What has happened is that internalisation has imperceptibly been equated with 'learning' or even 'habit-formation' in the simplest sense. Thus when a norm is said to have been 'internalised' by an individual, what is frequently meant is that he habitually both affirms it and conforms to it in his conduct. The whole stress on inner conflict, on the tension between powerful impulses and superego controls the behavioral outcome of which cannot be prejudged, drops out of the picture [...] What is overlooked here is that the person who conforms may be even more 'bothered', that is, subject to guilt and neurosis, than the person who violates what are not only society's norms but his own as well. [...] To Freud, it is precisely the man with the strictest superego, he who has most thoroughly internalised and conformed to the norms of his society, who is most wrecked with guilt and anxiety [...] Sociologists have appropriated the superego concept, but have separated it from any equivalent of the Freudian id [...;] the presence in man of motivational forces bucking against the hold social discipline has over him is denied.

Psychological theories which build on the Freudian body of thought are more sensitive to these tensions, but here the controlling force of society at large, and the need to prepare the individual for the social roles he has to fulfil, are often under-stressed.[52]

More *recent sociological theories* emphasise that socialisation processes need not by definition lead to the unilateral imprinting of strict, permanent behavioural rules. The transmission of standards of conduct may vary, depending on the nature of the rules (e.g. parents may be more inclined to socialise their religious or political convictions than the value of self-determination, which could ultimately threaten family cohesion), and on characteristics of the socialiser (authoritarian or lower class parents may have other rules and rely more on disciplining and punishment than individualistic or middle class parents) and the socialisee (e.g. different standards and socialisation methods being applied for girls and boys). Moreover, as children grow of age socialisation in the reverse direction may also occur, with parents adopting elements of the world view of their mature offspring (cf. Kohn, 1983). In more general terms, life course sociology stresses that individuals continue to adapt their convictions over the years, in response to changes in their environment. In modern societies this is in fact inevitable: communities are complex and volatile, the rules are more vague and fluid than in the past, and the traditional socialising actors (family, neighbours, church, political party, trade union) have lost significance in recent decades. The standardised, predictable life course of the past – a succession of social roles – has been replaced by singular personal biographies, with many transitions in social relationships and on the labour market. Individuals can no longer be equipped in their early years with a stable body of rules which can guide them through the rest of their lives. Instead they are forced to make choices and to give direction to their lives themselves. In doing so they compile their own life course; and to the extent that socialisation takes place it assumes the form of a self-governed *éducation permanente* (Beck & Beck-Gersheim, 1994; Kohli, 2002; Geulen, 2002: 50-54).

Yet the question can be asked as to whether life-course sociology, in its tendency to set its face against the classic socialisation perspective, does not overestimate the 'compulsory autonomy' of the modern citizen. Even in modern societies, the behaviour of individuals is still guided by institutions. It is plausible that formal rules, made or ratified by the government, have over time become more important than informal rules. The role of the traditional socialising actors is however by no means played out, though in some areas they may have become less uniform and more fragmented, less 'thick'. Even if the traditional nuclear family has become less stable, this does not necessarily mean that modern families no longer provide an effective socialisation context. If anything, the primary socialisation process seems to have intensified in recent decades: in Western countries many parents, especially in the growing middle classes, try more actively than in the past to foster the development of language, personality and morality in their children. Naturally, this is called for by the increased complexity of society, but other factors promote it as well: the greater prosperity, higher education level and ambitions of many parents, the falling number of children and the more democratic relationships in modern families. Socialisation through formal education also appears to become more rather than less important. Indications for this are the growing participation and longer duration of schooling, the rising final qualification levels and the broadening of educational aims in the curriculum (such as the imparting of social skills). Certain traditional socialising actors (e.g. churches) have perhaps become less important, but it is plausible that their role has partly been taken over by others (peers, the media, Internet communities), whose behavioural expectations need not necessarily be less compelling. The life-course sociology approach rightly focuses attention on the permanent and dynamic nature of socialisation processes in modern societies, but may misjudge the degree to which the behavioural choices of individual actors are in fact predetermined.

It would be desirable to formulate a more integrated socialisation theory, which among other things adequately covers the various aspects of social integration and personalisation, the tension between the two, and the relative influence of the different socialisers in various phases and socio-historical circumstances (for an initial attempt, see: Hurrelmann, 2002). This theoretically interesting challenge goes beyond the scope of this study, however. Here we merely identify a number of possible basic principles:

1) Social rules are acquired by new actors within a process of *socialisation*. This not only imparts the existing knowledge and mores to them, but also entails a degree of individual development (skills, aspects of identity). Newborn children are not completely malleable; they have their own developmental potential, which comes to fruition to some degree during the socialisation process. In reaching this point they pass through a number of general phases of development: a baby does not know what its mother approves and disapproves of; a four year-old can generally not understand algebra; and few adolescents are able to appreciate the beauty of the Goldberg Variations. The developmental process mirrors organic changes and is cumulative: each phase builds on the achievements in earlier stages, so that there is a form of path dependence in the personal development of individual actors. There is a fundamental tension between the transfer of the socio-historical institutions and the 'personalisation' of the individual (development of identity, competences).[53]

2) Socialisation is not a one-sided act on the part of socialisers, but an *interaction process* which requires the socialisees to play an active role. Socialising acts by parents, teachers, friends, colleagues, etc. are only effective if the new actors are receptive to them and actually take them on board – i.e., understand their purpose and are able to incorporate them in ideas, competences and aspects of identity that they have already developed. Beyond early infancy, socialisation is therefore to a considerable degree a matter of self-regulation.

3) To a certain extent socialisation is a process of *rule-driven interaction*. Parents often want to meet the demands placed on 'good' mothers and fathers in their community; teachers generally try to comply with the statutory requirements (completion of the curriculum, achievement of certain attainment targets), as well as the expectations of their colleagues and the standards of their profession. The socialisees are expected to listen to their parents, to learn what they are taught at school, etc. On the other hand, the rules that govern socialisation are also often fairly vague, which means they offer little in the way of direction. They are also socially and historically variable: views on the best way to bring up and educate children change in response to developments in society, the dominant pedagogic views, political objectives, etc.

4) Socialisation is *not always intentional*. In particular, primary socialisation does not involve the deliberate imprinting of generally applicable social rules. To a large extent it is based on the affective relations of socialisers and socialisees, and arises as a result, almost a side-effect, of their day-to-day interaction.
5) For a variety of reasons, *socialisation is not self-evident*. The envisaged socialisees may not respond to socialising attempts if they consider them contrary to their short-term interests (playing, watching TV, lounging) or to the development of competences that they personally value highly, such as practising sport or performing music. Socialisers also do not automatically meet general social expectations. Parents, teachers, etc. are not by definition agents of society at large, but often have their own views on the socialisation process (goals, priorities, methods) and on what is good for the socialisees. Moreover, socialisers may not be familiar with dominant rules or may consciously reject them; they can also be unwilling or unable to carry out socialising acts because these do not match their skills, priorities or interests. For example, a parent may decide not to teach their child to swim because they do not know that this is expected of them; because they consider swimming unnecessary, unclean, improper or dangerous; because they themselves are not good enough swimmers; or because, set against the expected return, taking their child to swim will cost too much in terms of time, money or trouble.

In addition, the rules of different socialisers may conflict, for example if the rules on 'cleanliness' or 'honesty' differ greatly at home and at school. It is also possible that the resources are inadequate. Children who fail to complete their education because there is too little money to buy teaching materials or because they have to contribute to the household income are the classic example of this. Finally, the mutual relations between socialisers and socialisees may be sparse or poor (no 'connectedness'), so that there is no basis for socialising interactions.
6) The socialisation process is not uniform. Socialisees differ in their developmental potential and their method of self-regulation; their socialisers are not the same, and they may go through identical socialisation pathways in different ways. As a result, the socialisation process in theory generates a *heterogeneous outcome*, even with regard to characteristics that have become more or less anchored in individual actors at an early age. For example, individuals do not all acquire the same work ethic; they will attain a certain orientation towards this dominant value, depending on their competences and the specific slant placed on it in their family life, at school and in their circle of friends. It is not necessarily stable, but can change along with the labour market opportunities people perceive over time.
7) The process by which new actors acquire rules is socially and historically variable, both in terms of the phasing, the socialisers involved and their relative strengths. Tentatively, and allowing for variation, in modern Western societies the following *general pattern of rule acquisition* can be assumed:
    – In the first socialisation period very general informal rules are acquired, mainly in the family. This takes place more or less *en passant*: through the identification with significant others, through play, through listening to stories, etc. This is related to the understanding of language, symbolic actions, etc.

- Everyday conventions, concrete social norms and practical competences then follow. As well as the family, the school plays a key role here. Instruction and sanctioning become more important, but depend on the way in which the socialisee processes them. For example, the socialisee learns to read and write, the rules of politeness, basic skills such as swimming, how to behave in traffic, etc.
- The next stage involves the development of higher values, personal identity and more theoretical knowledge. This involves a focus on abstract questions about the reasons for, the essence and the legitimacy of the societal rules. The family occupies a less central position, while peers, church organisations, associations, etc. become more important. Schools focus on preparing the socialisee for working life or further education. The knowledge, skills and concrete behavioural rules that are needed for this move to centre stage, while the general training fades more into the background.
- The latter phase also involves a global familiarisation with the formal rules that apply in the socialisee's own community. Mainly through education, the socialisee receives an impression of the existing distribution of rights and obligations and their legitimacy, as laid down by the government: the basic principles of the meta-rules, third-party recognition and government production (politics, civil law, criminal law). This is knowledge in outline: the extent and complexity of the formal institutions means it is not efficient to bring the socialisees into contact with all details, all the more so because the rules can change rapidly. Only the formal rules which are very general (the Constitution) or important for their later working life (e.g. the statutory regulations governing bakery work) are discussed in more detail.[54] Beyond this, given the advanced division of labour, the socialisation of formal institutions mainly concerns 'rule experts': civil servant officials who draft laws, judges and lawyers who apply them, supervisory authorities, etc.

8) However, a number of comments can be made to qualify this presumed general pattern. In the first place, the precise phasing can vary depending on the socialisees concerned, the socialisers with which they come into contact, and the social circumstances in which both exist. Secondly, the socialisation process is not complete once socially recognised adulthood has been reached. Rule acquisition continues in later life, and the perception of rules, required behaviour and social opportunities by individual actors may change. This requires a less static view of socialisation processes, mainly by analysing them in terms of the life course of actors. A final comment is that even highly socialised rules cannot fully determine future behaviour. Many rules are general in nature, and if the behaviour of actors is not blatantly in conflict with them, they can partly choose their mode of action. For example, in open democratic societies adult persons sharing a household can determine for themselves how they want to treat each other socially and economically, as long as they do not manifestly contravene the limits laid down by the government and their social community.[55] Here, the actors themselves may draw up many of the rules of their own particular relationship, without there being any question of direct socialising interactions involving others.

2.9 The rule generation process: creation and development of institutions

The emphasis in the foregoing section was on the way in which existing institutions influence actors and bring about certain results. What was not discussed was how social rules arise and change; that is the focus of this section. Some supporters of the 'new institutional economics' discussed earlier have an unambiguous opinion on this. In their view, institutions and the associated enforcement mechanisms offer coordination gains in economic transactions. Rules such as these establish property rights, which can be understood as "an actor's rights, which are recognized and enforced by other members of society, to use and control valuable resources" (Alston et al., 1996: 34). In this approach price mechanisms play a decisive role in the genesis and development of institutions. However, the prime cause is often sought in exogenous changes,[56] which are mostly technological in nature. The development of new farming methods, industrial production processes, communication facilities, etc. can alter the relative prices of labour, land and capital, and can also influence the transaction costs (measuring the value of goods, application of sanctions).

According to this line of reasoning, a certain distribution of *property rights* in society reflects the *interests* of the actors, their *negotiating power* and the *relative prices*. These issues are often incorporated in the NIE as a sort of four-part entity. Rights and interests are in principle correlated, based on the idea that it is efficient to attribute rights on the basis of interests: interested parties will generally ensure that rules are not contravened, because of the personal disadvantage they would suffer. Rational rule-makers will thus ensure that the allocation of property rights corresponds with the distribution of interests. Property rights and power are also theoretically strongly interrelated in the NIE. The latter concept refers to the negotiating strength of contracting parties, and this form of power is often directly linked to the distribution of property rights. Thus Eggertsson (1996: 14) argues that:

> The system of property rights [...] refers to the effective control, by individuals and groups, of valuable assets, including human capital. In other words, the system of property rights describes the distribution of power in society.

The relationship between the establishment of property rights and relative prices is rather more complex, but is also a very close one. On the one hand the existing rules influence the relative prices, mainly via the transaction costs. On the other hand, changes in relative prices may lead to the creation of new rules or the amendment of existing ones. Two types of explanation are generally given for institutional innovation in the NIE. The first is direct: institutional change will take place when certain sources become so valuable or scarce as a result of exogenous developments that the transaction costs involved in measuring and enforcing property rights are no longer prohibitive, in other words are lower than the benefits that the actors concerned can expect from them in economic exchange. The second explanation reinforces the first. If exogenous developments lead to changes in the relative prices, it may be that the existing allocation of property rights no longer reflects the interests and negotiating power of the actors. Those who regard themselves as disadvantaged after a price change will attempt to adjust the rules in such a way that justice is done to their interests and negotiating power. Those who have gained advantage will seek to maintain their position by insisting on rights acquired earlier and demanding new protective measures, for example via import levies and certification requirements.

The institutional structure created by such a process of change is sometimes regarded in the NIE as a new and efficient optimum equilibrium. Some, such as North, follow a rather more sophisticated line of reasoning in which old rules that have become inefficient can survive and new or revised institutions may be sub-optimal. This is a consequence of the mechanism of path dependence, of the historically developed perceptions and preferences of rule-making actors, and of the disproportionate influence of certain actors on the rule definition – for example because they control the state apparatus.

In the NIE paradigm, rules arise and change via negotiations between rational actors. Entrepreneurs and corporate actors play a key role in this process: they are often regarded as the carriers of institutional change. The importance that North attaches to entrepreneurs has already been discussed; elsewhere he stresses the innovative role of organisations: "It is the interaction between institutions and organizations that shape the institutional evolution of an economy" (North, 1998: 249). A similar notion is found in Coleman's (1990: 531-552) related sociological approach. In his view, the growth in the number of corporate actors has meant that they increasingly determine the development of society; not only through the accumulation of capital and knowledge within organisations, but also because much social interaction is linked to corporate actors. The number of exchanges between organisations has increased greatly, and natural persons spend a large part of their lives acting as agents for the companies, government institutes and associations of which they form part.

2.9.1 The incentive to regulate

The NIE's view on institutional change can be criticised and complemented in a number of respects. Firstly, its direct cause is attributed to changes in *relative prices*. In figure 2.1 price mutations were also presented as an incentive that may lead to rule amendments. This means that actors will desire new or different institutions if price changes imply that the proceeds of social interaction (discounting the transaction costs of measurement and rule-enforcing) after the introduction or revision of the rules are expected to be higher than previously.

In the figural model presented in §2.3, however, price changes are not the only cause of institutional change. This has to do in the first place with a slightly different theoretical view of *power*. In the NIE, the distribution of power and the structure of property rights largely coincide – a standpoint in which, interestingly, some 'neo-capitalist' institutional economists find themselves on the same side as the authors of the *Manifesto of the Com-*

munist Party.[57] In this approach, power is reduced to the capacity for control of what are regarded as valuable goods or events. Coleman (1990: 133) applies a similar definition of power, albeit a more subtle one:

> The power of an actor resides in his control of valuable events; the value of an event lies in the interests powerful actors have in that event.[58]

Many sociologists consider such a view of power to be too limited. They argue that threatening to apply coercion and the ability to arouse feelings of anxiety or fear in other actors are central aspects of the notion of power, without which phenomena such as suppression in man-woman relationships or the geopolitical relations between states cannot easily be understood (see e.g. Collins, 1991). Power is more than negotiating power, more than control over goods or events that are regarded as valuable. For this reason the classic Weberian definition, in which the emphasis lies on the ability to impose one's own will on others, may be more accurate (Weber, 1988 [1922]: 28):

> Macht bedeutet jede Chance, innerhalb einer sozialen Beziehung den eignen Willen auch gegen Widerstreben durchzusetzen, gleichviel worauf diese Chance beruht.[59]

This sociological notion of power attaches central importance to coercion, or the threat of coercion. Its binding nature distinguishes power from influence, which implies more in the way of argumentation or suggestion, and in the final analysis cannot be enforced; and also from authority, in which certain power relations are regarded as legitimate by actors.

If power is defined in this broader sense, the connection with relative prices is theoretically looser than advocates of the NIE assume. The power relations between actors can then also change if relative prices remain constant – think of political coups where one corrupt political regime is replaced by another. And this in turn implies that changes in the relative power of actors are in theory an independent source of institutional change.

Something similar holds for *interests*. In the NIE this notion is taken mainly to represent the self-interest of rational actors, understood as the maximisation of the individual profit of certain actions for given preferences. Such an interpretation makes the role of interests in the process of institutional change relatively unproblematic. If a price change reduces the relative profit of economic exchanges, the self-interest of some actors will suffer. Assuming preferences remain unchanged they will then modify their behaviour or, if it is more profitable, seek to change the rules. They will succeed in this if they are able to generate sufficient negotiating power, for example by working together with other interested parties.

Theoretically, however, interests are not quite as uniform as the advocates of institutional economics presume. Interests can be defined as everything that serves the well-being or utility of actors, and what those actors therefore wish to see assured. This embraces more than individual self-interest. Actors may also attach importance to interests that they share with others: the collective interests of the family, the firm, the social class and the nation-state. It is moreover a dialectic concept: interests become most sharply defined when they come into conflict with others, and it is doubtful whether they can be truly general.[60] Such conflicts of interest can occur between persons, organisations, and corporate actors and their agents. However, a single actor may also experience conflicting interests, for example double-earners who have to try and reconcile the interests of their personal career, the interests of their employer and those of their family. Finally, the temporal perspective of the actor is also important: short and long-term interests can differ markedly.

If interests can be so diverse, they can play a role in the process of institutional change that goes beyond the intermediating reflex of *homo economicus* to price changes. What weighs most heavily in the diversity of interests and potential conflicts of interest is not known *a priori*, but can vary according to the social system, the historical circumstances and the perceptions of the actors. Competitive markets are strongly driven by individual or corporate self-interests, and in those circumstances such interests can indeed play an important role in the definition of rules. In other social systems, such as families, the collective interests are likely to weigh more heavily, and the rules will be drawn up and amended in that light. Moreover, the conflicts of interest can change within a given social system. Historical developments can lead to the emergence or decline of certain types of actor that share specific interests. At the level of a society, for example, this may concern an increase in the number of workers due to industrialisation, of older people due to population ageing, of benefit claimants due to the growth of social security; or in the demise of maidservants or casual workers in agriculture. In the economic subsystem this can be translated into the rise and fall of corporate actors, for example due to technological developments or changed competitive relations (e.g. the emergence of Internet companies, the declining importance of farms in the economic process of Western countries). In the micro socio-economic systems this also plays a role: if families grow in size or dwindle, the conflicts of interest within them will become different.

Actor interests need also not be stable. If the share of women in the potential labour force does not change but they wish to work more often, this group of actors will attach more importance to good childcare facilities. If actors share certain interests, or if their priorities change, the societal conflicts of interest will also change. This can result in some actors desiring different rules, and this is therefore also a potential source of institutional change.

Figure 2.1 also includes a direct cause of institutional change which is absent in the standard NIE theory: the support for certain ideals. Reference was made earlier to the autonomous role that North attributes in the process of rule-making to the ideas or preferences of actors, citing the example of the impact of the American movement to abolish slavery.[61] Here this factor is presented more specifically as *support for ideals*, or the backing that exists among actors for plans to structure social systems differently. This is conceptually distinct from the historical development of such ideals, and also from the informal institutions. The latter consist of rules that have already been accepted: values, norms, conventions and informal contracts may well have an idealistic charge, but they are behavioural guidelines that have already been recognised and which by definition cannot be a source of institutional change.

Support for ideals can in the first place be thought of as 'the feelings of the common people' in an autocracy, or as 'public opinion' in a democracy. However, it encompasses more than this: it is also about ideas for change as advocated by those in power, views regarding the desired structure of the social system which prevail among professional advisors (civil servants, philosophers, priests, scientists), and the ideas for the future propounded by influential corporate actors (companies, administrators, idealistic organisations). At issue here is the support for change ideals. These are not necessarily progressive or emancipatory, but may also be directed towards the restoration of institutions that have been lost, or towards assumed traditions of the community or nation which never existed in reality.

A fundamental question is whether ideals really play an independent role in institutional change. From a strict rational choice perspective this is not the case. For example, following Coleman's analysis of revolutions,[62] it may be expected that actors will desire a new rule or a rule change if they believe that:
- They have a key interest in this, i.e. they believe that the new rule will promote a form of well-being or utility to which the actor attaches importance;
- An attempt to change a rule has a sufficient chance of succeeding at acceptable cost. Put differently, the present power relations mean that the change is likely to be attainable, and the costs to the actor of the change process will probably not be excessive;
- The rule change may fail, but in that case will probably result in acceptable costs (negative sanctions).

In such an approach, an actor will never wish to see rules drawn up that do not mirror his interests, are not attainable or which carry too high a penalty in the event of failure. In a bounded rationality variant, there are a number of obvious exceptions to this scheme of thought. Desires for rules that go against key interests are then for example possible if the interests, power relations and gains of the behaviour are unclear in advance, or when actors are manipulated or bribed, base their preferences on the authority of others, are ill, etc.

In taking this line, however, the rational choice approach fails to acknowledge the role that convictions can play in the process of institutional change. People may want different rules simply because they feel that they are better, even though the change goes against their main interests. Radical rule changes are sometimes only possible if people ignore their current personal or collective interests[63] and are prepared to accept the heavy negative sanctions that come with failure as the price of their convictions. In the process leading to the independence of India and Pakistan, the conflicts of interest between the British administrators and the Hindu, Muslim and Sikh elites and the other population groups played a central role; but the support that Gandhi managed to engender for his convictions helped to determine the institutional path that was ultimately taken.

This does not mean that changes in the support for ideals *always* provide a stimulus for institutional change. This factor, too, may be of subordinate significance in certain social systems and historical circumstances (the rules for a trade fair, an autocratic regime that is in firm control). In other contexts, however, they will be decisive for the process of rule change. This applies above all for the drafting of formal rules in a democratic society, where power relations are instable and the costs for expressing dissent are low. In such a situation public opinion may be of decisive importance; and the success of politicians and policymakers then largely depends on the support they are able to generate for their own ideals, for example by controlling or manipulating the mass media.

Summarising, institutional change theoretically occurs when new or different rules are more profitable as a result of relative price mutations, are opportune because of changed power relations, are in line with changing conflicts of interest, or are desirable on account of a wider distribution of certain wishes for the future. The socially weighted sum of changes in these four factors possibly provides an incentive to regulate, but there is no fixed connection or causal arrangement, as in the NIE theory discussed earlier. Some of the logical possibilities are:

(1) *Direct incentive:* $\Delta(A) \rightarrow \Delta(i)$, with B,C,D (x_1)
(2) *Blocked incentive:* $\Delta(A) \rightarrow \sim\Delta(i)$, with B,C,D (x_1)
(3) *Indirect incentive:* $\Delta(A) \rightarrow \Delta(B,C,D) \rightarrow \Delta(i)$

where:

A, B, C, D: relative prices, power relations, conflicting interests, support for ideals (in random order)
i : incentive to regulate
x_1 : initial level
Δ : change
$\sim$: not
$\rightarrow$: induces

In the case of a *direct incentive* (1), a change in one of the four factors (A) offers a stimulus for change because the other factors (B, C and D) do not prevent this at that moment. This occurs, for example, when a relative price change makes another rule more efficient, and the existing conflicts of interest, power relations and support for ideals do not in principle impede a rule change. The latter is the case, by contrast, with a *blocked incentive* (2). Rule changes which would be efficient following price changes may for example be blocked by those in power, the vested interests or dominant ideals. With an *indirect incentive* (3), a change in A does not in itself provide a sufficient stimulus, but it does facilitate changes in B, C, and/or D, leading to an incentive for rule change. It may for example be the case that changes in the conflict of interests between pensioners and those in work do not lead directly to a redefinition of the social rules, but do indirectly promote such institutional change because they work through into support for certain ideals among the electorate.

    All manner of variations on these basic schemes are possible; for example, simultaneous unrelated changes may take place in the incentive factors, which reinforce or impede each other. Of course, the magnitude of such changes is also crucial for the stimulus for rule amendments. Whether or not a given incentive is translated into new rules depends, moreover, on the perception that actors have of that incentive (their desire for new rules), the degree to which those perceptions work through into concrete rule-setting activities, and the result thereof. Before going into this in more detail, however, it is necessary to look briefly at the underlying causes of institutional change.

2.9.2 Underlying causes of institutionalisation: the historical process

If an incentive to regulate ensues from changes in relative prices, power relations, conflicts of interests and support for ideals, the obvious follow-up question is how such mutations are brought about. Theoretically, the underlying causes of institutionalisation are related to the historical process at the collective level.

According to advocates of the NIE, *technological and scientific developments* are an important driving force in the historical process. These may concern material production, with the most prominent examples being major breakthroughs such as the agricultural and industrial revolutions, developments in military technology (weapons, logistics), the growing importance of biotechnology and information technology, etc. Changes in immaterial knowledge, such as different methods of funding and actuarial calculations in commercial dealings, as well as scientific insights into the functioning of the economy and society, can however also be included here. Such developments increase the labour participation rate and change the relative prices, making them a driver of the economic process.

In figure 2.1, technological and scientific developments are also a potentially important underlying cause of institutional change. However, three comments need to be made here. First, their influence does not operate only via relative prices: technological developments can also influence the power relations, conflicts of interests and support for ideals. Examples might include changing relations between those who have and do not have access to new military technology, alterations in the conflicts of interest between workers and capital-holders after the introduction of a new production method, and the impact on public opinion of scientifically presented ideas on environmental policy.

Second, the development of knowledge and technology also may depend on the existing institutions. North (1990) argues in this connection that the institutional framework determines what knowledge and skills actors will acquire, and that this is decisive for the direction the evolution of a society will take.[64] Or in terms of the figural model used here: not only can institutional changes ensue from developments in technology and knowledge, which work through in the incentive to regulate; but the existing rules also determine the form of knowledge accumulation that is attractive for the actors. This steers their knowledge-driven actions, and thus influences technological and scientific development.

Thirdly, technological and scientific developments are theoretically not the only underlying cause of institutional change. In figure 2.1, several types of historical determinants are distinguished. This point will be examined in more detail below.

The *economic process* is presented in the figural model as an independent underlying cause of institutionalisation. This mainly refers to changes in the collective wealth and its distribution. These are the result of the economic actions of actors at micro-level: the way in which, given a certain rule structure, they employ production factors. The development of the national (or regional, or supranational) product is the core variable in the economic process. Theoretically, many other economic factors lie at the basis of this process: changes in private consumption and savings, investments by government and industry, imports and exports, the monetary, trade and redistributive policy pursued by the government, and so on. And the degree of growth of the collective wealth also has economic consequences: it works through into the development of wages, profits, benefits and the degree of capacity utilisation of the production apparatus. This in turn has implications for supply and demand on the labour market (and thus for the unemployment rate), and for the distribution of national income. Feedback mechanisms – in particular via consumption, savings and investments – mean that this in turn influences collective production.

The precise relationship between all these aspects of the economic process is of less importance here (for an overview of the most important relationships see e.g. De Kam et al., 1989: 104; Douben, 1986: 80-95). What does need to be pointed out is that the development of the core variable, the national product or national income, can be influenced in the long term by technological change, but is not entirely determined by it. For shorter economic cycles the above endogenous determinants, and factors that lie outside national economic systems (such as prices on the world market, international economic developments), may be more important in explaining changes in the level and distribution of collective wealth.

This implies that the inherent dynamic of the economic process can also bring about changes in the incentive to regulate, independently of technological developments. Changes in the collective wealth and its distribution are reflected mainly in mutations in relative prices, the exacerbation or easing of the conflicts of interest between economic actors (companies, trade unions, employers' organisations), and changes in their relative negotiating power. This becomes evident, for example, during deep economic recessions; these can cause firms and governments to want to redefine the prevailing rights and obligations of employees, trading partners and citizens, often under the motto of 'necessity knows no law'.

The concept of *social structuring* refers to two constituent processes. The first is social differentiation, i.e. the development of recognisable groups of actors within a social system. Examples include the rise and fall of the nobility, the citizenry, the working class, rich and poor groups, single-parent families, etc. The second process is social stratification. This relates to mutations in the position of such groups of actors in the social rankings, or changes in the social strata.[65] Social stratification can imply that the position of certain groups on a given social ladder changes, for example if the prestige of teachers declines. It is however also possible for changes to occur in the ladders themselves, i.e. the principles of social ranking that apply within a given society. The actors' descent (social class, caste, racial or ethnic origin) may be the dominant stratification criterion, but so may their economic position or opportunities (economic classes, income groups, profession), their social status (prestige, fame) or their capacities and achievements (meritocratic principles).

The two processes of social structuring are allied to the allocation of social positions and the distribution of scarce goods, or in other words social inequality (see e.g. Dronkers & Ultee, 1995). This means that there is also a certain relationship with the economic process, especially in class-based societies, where economic differentials define the hierarchy of the various groups. However, contrary to what is assumed in the Marxist tradition, social structuring is not by definition an epiphenomenon of the economic process; at most this may be the case in specific historical circumstances.

If the groups, their position in the ranking, or the stratification criteria change, this can impact on the incentive to regulate. The conflicts of interest can take on another guise (e.g. from status groups to economic classes), the support for certain ideals that are linked to new criteria or strata may increase (e.g. backing of universal suffrage instead of voting rights based on property ownership), the relative prices may be influenced (e.g. because a growing group of workers are collectively able to negotiate higher wages), and the existing distribution of power may be contested (e.g. by new groups demanding representatives to be appointed in strategic government functions).

According to the figural model social structuring does not however determine the rules of society, as is sometimes assumed in Marxist theory. The relationship between the social structure and institutions is dialectic. On the one hand institutions are partly the result of social structuring, because dominant groups will always try to shape those rules for their own benefit. It is not automatically the case that they will succeed, however, because the existing social rankings are not the only engine driving the process of institutionalisation. In the historical process the other factors mentioned above also are a driving force; and the actual rule outcomes also depend on how actors incorporate the changed incentive in their rule-creating activities. Thus, institutionalisation is certainly not a simple carbon copy of the existing social order.

Conversely, the formal and informal rules also theoretically influence the social structuring. They direct the behaviour of actors; and the collective results of these acts can confirm or change social differentiation and stratification. Thus, for example, social security rules may reproduce the relationships between social classes, if the collective rules guarantee more extensive rights to the higher than to the lower strata. It is however also possible that they will promote the emancipation of backward groups, by assuring everyone of a relatively high subsistence minimum.

Elite-formation is a special aspect of social stratification. Elites are more than the highest strata in a social system: they are groups that give direction to the institutional development. This is reflected in a definition such as that given by Thoenes (1962: 5), who sees a social elite as
> A constituent group, which claims the role of knowing, realising and enforcing the precepts which determine the structure, functions or development of the wider society or a section of it.

This implies that elites can act as rule-prophets, rule-innovators and rule-protectors. Thoenes sees these as different stages in the process of elite-formation, in which the message is first announced, the plan it entails is then realised, and the order achieved after the implementation of the scheme is maintained.

The actual influence of elites on the process of institutional development depends on a number of factors. First, of course, is their perception and appreciation of the prevailing social rules. Also important is the extent to which they are able to secure key social positions or, in the terms used by Pareto (1968 [1901], 1935 [1916]), the extent to which they belong to the 'governing elite': monarchs, ministers, MPs, senior civil servants, policy advisors, military personnel, captains of industry, and spiritual leaders. This depends not only on their own power and insights, but also on the selection behaviour of other actors, within the formal and informal rules that apply (the political institutions:[66] the electoral laws, traditions on the succession of rulers, etc.). Finally, a number of structural features of elites are also important. To what extent is the ruling elite internally homogenous or heterogeneous, and to what extent does it enjoy the loyalty of the lower strata (voters, the middle classes, workers, farmers)? And above all: are the governing elites open or closed? In the former case members of the lowest strata can penetrate the ruling social groups. This may provide a stimulus for gradual changes to the rules, because the perceptions of these newcomers often diverge; they have been raised with different ideals, represent other interests, do not seek to use power solely at the benefit of the traditionally dominant groups, and may be more sensitive to changes in relative prices. In the case of a closed elite, however, the leaders form a stable group with homogenous interests and a common social background (going to the same schools, shared networks, norms and values, distinctive language and behavioural conventions), who recruit successors from their own circles and progeny. A governing elite such as this will not readily set in motion institutional changes, even when economic or social circumstances make this desirable. In such a case, the succession of generations will not provide an impulse to amend the social rules, since the members of this elite are largely interchangeable: 'the King is dead, long live the King'. Institutional renewal can then only take place as a result of elite circulation: the rise of counter-elites that advocate rule-innovation, compete with the governing elite and are able to completely or partially replace it.

The societal role of elites is often associated with undemocratic relationships and social stagnation: the inevitable, seemingly natural rule of an autocratic minority over the majority, which reinforces the status quo. Elite-formation can however also play an important role in a democratic context, and in theory can lead both to institutional stability and rule change. This argument has been elaborated by Thoenes (1962: 187-228) in his analysis of the role of elites in modern welfare states. He contrasts a closed 'elite of officials', which puts itself forward as the protector of the existing order on the basis of quasi scientific knowledge, with an 'open sociology', which acts as an intellectual vanguard, and among other things criticises the foundations of society and delineates the political problems of the future. Whether certain elites wish to preserve or change the prevailing rules is ultimately an empirical question, not a matter of natural or historical inevitability. The *Enarques* in France provide an example of this: created with the aim to select the best people for key social positions in an open process, in practice they increasingly form a closed and fairly conservative elite.[67]

The *formation of ideals* is a process that is concerned with the development of new ideas about the future design of a social system. In essence, ideals are subjective constructs, although they can be underpinned by scientific insights. They may be vague ideas for the future – the desirability of a strong military apparatus, public transport, the long-term 'mission' of an organisation – but cohesive and elaborate sets of ideals are also possible. If these are constructed around one or a limited number of fundamental future goals, it is possible to speak of an ideology. Ideologies can be supported by elites and social groups with an interest in achieving the future aims they espouse; in figure 2.1, however, they are not equated with their supporters or the social stratification process.[68] Political idea systems (such as liberalism, socialism, fascism), religious *Weltanschauungen* and policy doctrines (e.g. imperialism) are the most pronounced examples. In these ideologies individual freedom, equality, a powerful nation surrounding a strong leader, living in accordance with religious principles, and expansion of the territorial or economic domination are respectively the core objectives.

To some extent the development of ideals has its own dynamic. The process is often based on the insights of a vanguard of intellectual and social entrepreneurs. Personal qualities, experiences and sensitivity to the *Zeitgeist*, or what moves the people, all play a role here. On the other hand, the formation of ideals is not an entirely autonomous process; it is controlled in part by other aspects of the historical process: technological innovations, economic developments, and changing social oppositions can lead to the identification of new problems that require a solution. Communication facilities and the existing rule structure are theoretically also important. In a restrictive setting they make it impossible to express certain ideals: the technology to communicate with other interested parties does not exist or is not accessible, or the rules attach severe negative sanctions to the dissemination of certain ideals. In an open society there are ample opportunities for communication and there is a free, independent and highly diversified media, fostering the formation of new and competing ideals through open public debate.

New ideals can have a direct influence on institutional development if they engender support among (part of) the ruling elite, a counter-elite or the lower strata, so that their rule wishes change. Theoretically, however, they can also influence the rule structure via the other incentives, if the formation of different ideas concerning the desirable future design of a social system means that actors begin interpreting the conflicts of interest, power relations and relative prices differently.

The *demographic process* relates to changes in the size and composition of a social system due to births, mortality, household formation and internal/external migration. This can have consequences for the economic process (e.g. the size of the potential labour force, the ageing of the population) and certain forms of social stratification, such as the emergence of oppositions between the existing lower class and new immigrants who compete with them on the housing or labour market. However, demographic developments may also be significant apart from their influence on the collective wealth and social hierarchy. If the relative size of demographic groups changes, the conflicts of interest, power relations, relative prices and support for certain ideals within a given social system can also evolve. *Ceteris paribus*, this may cause the distribution of rule wishes in the population to change, and especially in a democratic society this can impact on institutional development.

The figural model also contains a reference to *exogenous factors* that can influence the historical process. These are developments that take place outside the social system in question, such as natural disasters, developments abroad, and so on. Finally, it should be mentioned that the influence of the historical process on the incentive to regulate can be either evolutionary or take place in sudden jolts. The latter can occur, for example, when a governing elite is replaced at a stroke as a result of a revolution or occupation by a foreign power.

2.9.3 The regulatory aspirations of actors

On the assumption that the underlying historical developments do actually provide an incentive to regulate, under what conditions will actors desire new or different rules? According to the proponents of the NIE, this is a fairly linear process: if relative prices change structurally, rational actors will want to amend the existing rules or establish new ones, if they believe they will profit from this and expect that they can realise the envisaged change. However, a number of comments can be made to qualify this idea of an automatic reflex.

In the first place, it is not so much the objective changes that are important, but above all the subjective perception of those changes by the stakeholders. North (1990: 85) states the following in this connection:

> Changing relative prices are filtered through pre-existing mental constructs that shape our understanding of those price changes. Clearly ideas, and the way they take hold, play a role here.

This means that the perceptions of actors, as discussed in §2.7, help to determine the conversion of the incentive to regulate into rule wishes. It is not enough that prices, power relations, conflicts of interest or ideals change. Actors must also become aware of this – the transparency of information is an intermediating factor – and regard it as worthwhile to create new rules. These new rules must match their personal objectives, interests and ideals more closely, and must appear likely to generate higher returns than if the rules were left unchanged. In their perception, creating new rules must also be a better solution than the alternatives that are possible within the existing rules. A relative price change need not lead to rule amendments: actors may consider it better to accept their loss, modify their behaviour within the prevailing prescripts, or break the existing rules.

Furthermore, actors are often not free to desire entirely new rules. The historical institutionalism discussed earlier refers to the intermediating role of current rules, or the path dependence. The existing institutional framework forms a socio-historical filter, through which, for example, technological innovations in different social systems can lead to divergent results. This is because of the investment in the existing rules, which means that abolishing them would entail costs; and it is also because the subjective perceptions and evaluations of actors, especially policymakers, are often an extension of the existing rules, so that for them certain changes are inconceivable. North (1990) is even more explicit; he explains the self-reinforcing operation of rules on the basis of their increasing returns (in the case of existing institutions the high initial investments need no longer be made), the favourable effect on economic and social interaction (the coordination gains), learning effects, and the apprehension of reality in terms of the existing rules by actors. In a perfect market path dependence is theoretically inconceivable, because the most efficient solution will always be chosen. Because markets are generally not perfect in practice, North argues that exogenous changes often result in adaptations of the rules that fit in with the historical developments to that point. In fact, as stated, he sees path dependence not as a linear process in which the past determines the future, but rather as a guiding principle.

Based on this it may be assumed that existing institutions will have a stronger influence on the direction of changes in the rules as:
- The initial material and social costs of new rules are higher;
- The coordination gains of the existing rules in the economic and social arena is higher;
- The existing institutions are more strongly embedded in other rules (high/low, formal/informal);
- The existing institutions correspond with the subjective rules of actors.

In figure 2.1 path dependence is not shown as an abstract socio-historical principle, but as an intersubjective brake on the rule wishes of actors at the micro/level. The reason for this is that path dependence occurs only when actors acknowledge the significance of the existing rules, and endorse them either consciously or pre-reflexively. Theoretically, therefore, an existing rule with objectively high coordination returns can be abolished if the rule-making actors do not acknowledge or no longer want its social benefits – for example in times of political revolution.

The nature of rule wishes
It is of course impossible in general to predict what kind of rules actors will desire. This depends on the characteristics of the actors concerned, the nature and strength of the incentive to regulate and the historical circumstances: which rules already exist, how strong is the resultant path dependence, and what is the nature of the community and government that has to support the institutions? Yet a number of theoretical observations can be made concerning the nature of the regulatory aspirations.

Clearly, in determining their wishes actors will take account of the possibilities offered by the community and the government to establish rules. It is attractive to seek regulation by the government where a community does not share any higher values and social norms, where communication is defective, where the members distrust each other or are not willing to sanction defective behaviour. Similarly, if the government is weak, fails to keep its promises, is corrupt or is dominated by a limited number of actors, it will be better to seek to establish informal rules. Logically, there is little point in seeking regulation if neither the community nor the government provides a sufficient basis for this.

If effective institutions can in principle be created both via the community and via the government, informal rules have certain advantages. Once they are established they are cheap, and at the lower levels (mutual agreements, conventions) are fairly flexible, so that they can be adapted quickly to changed circumstances. Formal rules may turn out to be more expensive: establishing them can be a lengthy process, and because the enforcement is entirely external the social and economic transaction costs can be higher because of the need for monitoring and sanctioning. On the other hand, they have the advantage of being easier to control, in contrast to values and higher social norms which are difficult for individual actors to influence and which can develop largely autonomously.

Since formal and informal institutions can generally not be seen in isolation from each other, wise rule-making actors do not lose sight of the prevailing informal practices when framing new formal rules, and vice versa. If the discrepancy between institutions is too great, the new rule may turn out to be ineffective and become undermined after a certain time – for example because breaking of the new formal rules has to be tolerated due to persistent informal traditions.

Finally, actors will generally try to establish rules at the lowest hierarchical level that can achieve the intended coordination. One does not change the Constitution in order to accomplish something that can be attained by amending an obscure implementation decree.

If wishes for new rules emerge, the envisaged rule components – rights, duties, conditions and possible sanctions – need to be specified. Existing higher institutions – values, higher social norms, meta-rules and existing government regulations – can serve as a guide here, without the new rules being derived directly from them. If, by contrast, the aspired regulation targets existing institutions, the question is which rule components will be given central importance. Theoretically it is plausible that actors will first wish to modify the sanctions associated with an existing institution, then the conditions, subsequently the duties, and finally the rights. Adapting the available sanctions is the least drastic measure in terms of the original aim of the rule. It leaves the claims and commitments intact, and is focused primarily on the correct application of the existing rule. Changing the conditions attached to rights and duties theoretically constitutes a greater adaptation of the rule, since it influences directly the number and composition of the beneficiaries and those held under obligation. However, the core of the rule, the rights and duties as such, remains intact when the conditions are amended. The next logical step is to change the duties, because this is less fundamental than redefining the rights. This follows on from the view by Raz cited earlier, namely that duties are usually derived from rights, and can therefore be adapted more readily to changed social circumstances. Following this line of reasoning, changing rights is theoretically the most radical option.

In practice, however, it cannot be taken as read that actors will always focus their rule wishes on changing the sanction mechanisms, and will as far as possible seek to leave the rights unchanged. Considerations of proportionality can play a role: if something is perceived by actors as a major collective problem, this may require radical changes which cannot be achieved simply by changing the possible sanctions. The outcome of earlier change attempts may also influence actors' rule wishes. For example, if it has already been tried to achieve a given result by tightening up the negative sanctions, and if this has failed, there will in time be a move to review the higher rule components. In addition, the expected costs of rule change will also play a role. Increasing the sanction possibilities may require more resources, and limited adaptation of the conditions, duties or rights may then be cheaper. Finally, pragmatic considerations – the expected ability to achieve the particular amendments during the rule interaction – can be decisive in shaping the rule wishes that actors put forward in practice.

Innovating actors

A final point here is the question of which actors articulate the rule wishes. In other words, who are the carriers of institutional change? As stated, proponents of the NIE accord a central role to entrepreneurs and corporate actors. However, both invite some qualification. With regard to entrepreneurs, it first has to be noted that the NIE economists are inclined to *define* them as people who bring about fundamental changes in the rules, so that it is not clear why precisely these individuals carry institutional change. Furthermore, the term is sometimes used ambiguously, which can create the impression that every businessman is potentially an entrepreneur. In reality, of course, they are specific actors, often with controversial ideas about business and society. They need not be businessmen at all; it can just as easily be visionary scientists or politicians that play a key role in the process of institutional renewal. Thirdly, it is sometimes made insufficiently clear that entrepreneurs are also a historical product. Not only must they have innovative ideas, but they must also be the right person at the right place and time. Institutional renewal occurs when entrepreneurial qualities coincide with historical opportunities; in other words, when certain social developments foster the rule changes proposed by innovative actors, and the prevailing rules are not so strict that they exclude any possibility of change. Ultimately, proponents of the NIE often see entrepreneurs too much as gifted loners, ignoring their social background. In reality entrepreneurs can also fulfil their innovative role as members of a counter-elite, with a commitment to certain ideals and protecting the interests of particular social groups. They are not by definition isolated geniuses, but often people who are rooted in specific forms of social stratification.

There is also more that can be said about the innovative role of corporate actors. Ingram (1998: 259), for example, points out that economists are inclined to overestimate the innovation potential of organisations. They are not infinitely adaptable entities that continuously gather knowledge and use it to enable them to respond flexibly to changing circumstances. Rather, many organisations tend towards inertia, both for internal reasons (investments made, the raising of precedents to normative standards) and because of external factors, such as statutory constraints on changing business activities, the desire to protect existing exchange relationships with other organisations, and the risk of loss of legitimacy and reputation after radical changes. Ingram's reasoning applies *a fortiori* for government actors: these often have a long history, their goals are sometimes vague and unstable, and they have to reconcile a diversity of interests from the perspective of what is collectively acceptable.

The best assumption is probably that institutional change is borne mainly by relatively *new actors*, with the capacity to cast doubt on the adequacy of the existing rules. They may be individual normative entrepreneurs, who are not affiliated with the *ancien régime*; they may be members of a new generation; they may be a counter-elite on the rise; or they may be new organisations. Such actors have three key advantages: they have invested less in the existing institutions, they often benefit less from them, and they perceive reality less strongly in terms of the prevailing rules. This makes them more sensitive to the shortcomings of the existing rules and the advantages of institutional renewal.

2.9.4 Rule-interaction and institutionalisation

The fact that central actors wish to change the rules in response to changed incentives does not automatically mean that this will actually happen. Much depends on the inherent dynamic of the social process in which rules are constructed (negotiations, competing issues, short-term and long-term objectives). The creation of rules usually requires interaction between interested parties. Even in the most asymmetrical relationship imaginable – the relationship between slaves and their masters – rules cannot be imposed entirely one-sidedly, but are to a certain degree negotiable.[69] Rule-interactions generate a certain amount of (re-) institutionalisation: the adaptation of existing rules, the introduction of new ones. In figure 2.1 three types of rule-interaction are presented: the drawing up of formal and informal contracts between actors (private contracting); the policy process in which the government rules are defined; and the evolution of informal rules.

Private contracting

To the extent that proponents of the NIE analyse rule-interaction, they have in mind mainly private contracting. The simplest example of this is an agreement between two individual businessmen on a direct exchange of goods. This agreement may come about through extensive negotiations resulting in the drawing up of a formal contract; but it can also take shape as a result of traditional bartering methods, in which the bargain is sealed with a handshake or a symbolic statement. As already noted, such forms of rule-interaction always take place within the framework of higher rules. In the former case the formal embedding of the agreement within prevailing mercantile law is important, while in the latter case it is the shared informal behavioural expectations of the actors (including the sanctions in the event of non-compliance) that are decisive. Institutional change is given form here via the renegotiation of existing agreements and by including different stipulations when entering into new commitments. As stated earlier, private economic contracts can incorporate much more: the economic exchange may extend over a longer period, may take place between corporate actors, may include several contracting partners, and may proceed via third parties. The negotiations on the rules then become more complex and lengthy, because intricate interests can be involved and more provisions have to be made for the conflicts that are more likely to occur.

In the case of social exchanges at micro-level, such as entering into affective relationships, the interaction on the rules to be followed is often less explicit. Sometimes concrete promises and agreements are made which define the mutual rights and obligations of the actors. A ceremony or ritual act may be linked to this, whereby the government formalises the union, or the community ratifies it. More frequently, however, the rule-interaction in social exchanges is dynamic. It is a process in which people gradually develop tacit expectations about the mutual rights and obligations, and adapt them as the circumstances change. This is governed by subjective derivations from the prevailing social norms and conventions, the past and recent experiences of the actors concerned, and their knowledge and present appraisal of their partner.

Defining government rules

The policy process that gives rise to the meta-rules, rules on government production and third-party recognition is the core of historical institutionalism (see §2.1). In this approach it is mainly the formal decision-making in representative democracies that is analysed. This is a long-lasting exchange of rule wishes between groups with diverging interests. The legislative assembly is the platform for rule-interaction, though the latter is also influenced by the executive and judiciary powers. The relationship between the various administrative layers of the government plays a role as well. The civil service can be an influential link: officially bound to loyalty to those with political responsibility, but in practice often an 'officials' elite' which is inclined to impede institutional change. This tendency is related to their sensitivity to the collective and personal costs of rule change, and this is often reinforced by their knowledge of the policy dossiers and the informal codes of the civil service, which are directed towards continuity of the policy process.

Single actors, such as private citizens and firms, generally do not have a direct say in the terms of the government rules, unless they form part of the administrative elite. They can seek to exert an influence through lobbying, protest actions, public hearings and objection procedures, and through participation in interactive decision-making. Corporate actors who are organised around certain interests (trade unions, employers' organisations, quangos, idealistic single-issue organisations) are more likely to play a central role in the policy process. This is especially true when their following is large, when they maintain intensive contacts with the government or certain political parties, or when their cooperation is required to enable rule change to be implemented successfully.

Rule-makers cannot act entirely as they see fit. They are after all bound by the mandate of their rank and file (their interests, the ideals they support) and by the meta-rules (e.g. the party manifesto, the government coalition agreement), and have to take this into account when formulating new or different rules. If they step outside this mandate they run the risk of being voted out at a subsequent election. In serious cases they may be forced to step down in a vote of no-confidence, a recall campaign or, in the case of major offences, an impeachment procedure.

The course of the policy process is not predictable, and does not always produce the results that the actors envisage. If the rule-wishes of policymakers are a given, the outcome of the rule-interaction depends in the first place on the degree to which these wishes conflict. And if they diverge, on whether they can be reconciled through compromise or long-term trade-off of rule wishes, in a way that fits within the formal procedural rules of the regulatory assembly and the informal norms and conventions of the rulemakers (the 'policy culture'). The feasibility of such proposals depends on the power relations in the legislative assembly, and on the influence that policymakers believe the rule change will have on their esteem and on the future voting behaviour of the electorate. Even if this leads to renewed rules, institutionalisation may still not produce the desired outcome, or may prove to be inefficient. Through the historical process, this can in turn work through into a further new incentive to modify the rules.

The evolution of informal rules

The way in which the informal rules of groups or communities arise and change is more difficult to understand. For some economists there is no problem here, because they regard informal institutions as irrelevant. In the words of Frank (1992: 149):

> Economists have largely ignored the existence of [social] norms; and when they have addressed them specifically, it has usually been to assert that rational agents would never follow them.

Sometimes they acknowledge the existence of social norms, but place them in the rational choice paradigm. Informal rules then arise when individual actors derive utility from them, and change or disappear when this is no longer the case. The 'signalling theory' put forward by Posner (2000) is an example of this.[70]

Economic institutionalists often attach more importance to the informal rules. They do not explain their creation on the basis of the profit of individual actors, but in terms of their significance for the coordination of economic exchange. According to this reasoning, informal institutions generally change as a consequence of mutations in relative costs and adaptations to the formal rules. Often an evolutionary selection process is assumed here, in which only the most efficient behavioural standards survive. North (1990: 84-85) finds this reasoning too simple, however. He comments that

> Fundamental changes in relative prices over time will alter the behavioral pattern of people and their rationalization of what constitutes standards of behaviour. [...] To account for the complex changes in norms of behavior [...] in terms of relative price changes alone, however, is a vast oversimplification of a complex and still little understood aspect of human behavior.

In reaction to this North stresses the interaction between changes in the informal and formal rules, with a new equilibrium arising after a certain time. However, he leaves unanswered the question of what the precise reason is for the creation and evolution of informal institutions.

Sociologists often regard informal rules as highly central determinants of behaviour, but have a different blind spot: they often treat them as exogenous factors which require no further explanation. This is fairly unsatisfactory from a theoretical point of view, as rightly remarked by Coleman (1990: 248):

> Much sociological theory takes social norms as given and proceeds to examine individual behavior or the behavior of social systems when norms exist. Yet to do this without raising at some point the question of why and how norms come into being is to forsake the more important sociological problem in order to address the less important.

In the sociological approach, an explanation is often sought in terms of the *rule hierarchy*: social norms will be modified if the guiding values change. This of course only shifts the problem to a higher level, because theoretically it becomes necessary to specify why those values alter. Moreover, it is not likely that key values change so frequently that this offers an adequate explanation for the many modifications in lower-level social norms and conventions that can occur in practice.

A further possibility is that informal rules are the product of groups of actors who deliberately *influence the socialisation context*. To do this they must ensure that the structure and content of in-school education and out-of-school upbringing are tailored as far as possible to their own preferences and world view, and they must preferably be capable of maintaining this indoctrination for several decades. Such a scenario may be feasible in a stable totalitarian society – though even here those in power can never fully control the exogenous factors that affect people (disasters, economic adversity). However, in a democratic society, where the socialising acts of parents and teachers are fairly autonomous, such a 'regimentation of rule acquisition' is far more difficult to achieve. One possibility is to establish relatively closed communities, which aim to create a new, better type of person and society. Apart from religious sects one can also point to communities based on idealistic rules for life and learning, such as Israel's *kibbutzim*. These, however, often are short-lived or lose their initial zeal.[71]

In Coleman's view, social norms arise if two conditions are met: there must be a demand for them, and the relationships between actors must be such that there are incentives to fulfil this demand. A demand for norms arises in his view when a certain action brings positive or negative consequences for others (externalities), so that there is an interest in regulating behaviour. However, not every externality leads to the creation of norms; in some cases those put at a disadvantage simply accept their loss, or the potential beneficiaries waive their gain. According to Coleman, the potential for founding social norms occurs only in special circumstances. The costs of imposing sanctions must be acceptable to those who benefit from the creation of the norm, and the number of free-riders must remain within limits; in other words, unintended beneficiaries must not be able to avoid the imposition of sanctions. According to Coleman, such circumstances only arise in certain social settings. There must be a relationship between those who create the externalities and those who experience than ('connectedness'), and the members of the latter group must also be in mutual contact ('closure of the network'). If this is not the case, it is not possible to apply positive or negative sanctions. For this reason, social norms are more likely to arise in communities with high levels of connectedness and closure, a high degree of mutual trust and substantial social capital, than in the anonymity of the metropolis (Coleman, 1990: 241-299).

Coleman is right to regard the genesis of norms as problematic, but his explanatory scheme also begs questions. In the first place, it seems plausible that the creation of social norms is fostered not so much by the presence of existing externalities, but rather by the perception that actors have of changes in such external behavioural implications. In addition, in Coleman's analysis the externalities are treated too much as a static premise. The theoretical challenge is of course to indicate what can cause the externalities, or the perceptions of them, to change and lead to the creation of social norms. A further point is that Coleman (1990: 243-244, 265), though pointing out that informal rules are often embedded in structures or systems of norms, analyses those mainly at the level of individual actors. This creates the impression that actors who benefit from a rule and who live in a community with a high degree of connectedness and network closure are free to regulate behaviour by agreeing norms. In reality, however, they can often not establish or change informal rules without taking into account higher values and norms and the formal government rules, and path dependence may also play a role – primarily because the members of the community have difficulty imagining other informal guidelines than those which they have already internalised. Finally, Coleman depicts the creation of such informal institutions as a more or less conscious and natural act by rational actors whose interests are being harmed or served, without making clear precisely how this occurs. This ignores the complex, slow and partially unintended evolution of such informal rules.

In figure 2.1, a slightly different mechanism lies at the basis of the development of informal rules. Actors may wish to change values, norms and conventions if the historical process gives rise to new relative prices, power relations, conflicts of interests and support for ideals which provide an incentive. New rules of this kind need not be related to possible externalities; Coleman already noted that not every informal institution can be regarded as a regulation of behaviour that has undesirable consequences for others.[72]

Informal rules can only be created or changed in a social system if there is a sufficient consensus on the desirability of doing so. Informal institutions cease to exist if people no longer recognise and observe them, and they come into being where actors articulate them and begin acting in accordance with them. Such changes can arise from a different constitution of the community (its demographic size and composition, its social structure), but may also be related to other changes in the historical process (new ideals, an economic crisis, technological innovation) which lead to the social coordination achieved earlier being regarded by the members of the community as no longer adequate.

In contrast to the policy process, this type of institutional change is not a matter of a more or less rational exchange of arguments on a platform for rule interaction. People do not generally get together in a meeting under the motto of 'let us agree values, norms and conventions' – and even if someone believes that a new consensus can be deliberately cultivated or imposed, the result will often be different from what they had envisaged.[73] What is involved here is a change in the *communis opinio* as to what is right or proper and what is not; a change that becomes entrenched in everyday conversations, contacts and observations, and in which people affirm each other in their dissent on the prevailing institutionalisation. The number of actors who openly cast doubt on existing norms and conventions increases, more and more cases of defection occur, and the willingness in the community to impose sanctions falls. At the same time, the belief may arise that different rules could be more effective in solving current problems, part of the community may begin acting in accordance with those new standards, and some will begin sanctioning defection and compliance from the amended attitude. This redefinition of collective rules is very much a social process: individual actors determine the extent to which they themselves confirm or undermine the rules, but the informal institutions will only be changed if the consensus of the community regarding the rules has altered.

The process may be illustrated by the evolution of social norms on extramarital sexual relations. The changing historical context (a technological innovation, such as the introduction of the contraceptive pill) alters the rule-making incentive: the material and social costs of extramarital sex fall as the risk of unwanted pregnancy declines. This can work through into the perceptions of actors (the number of people who accept the norm that 'sex outside marriage is not permissible' reduces) and lead to defection that is no longer sanctioned (more people have sex without being married and, in contrast to the past, are not widely criticised or ostracised). If behavioural regulation is still desirable in order to prevent the negative collective consequences (such as the spread of sexually transmitted diseases), a new informal rule may arise over time, provided a critical mass within the community shares a consensus on this (for example, 'sexual contact outside marriage is permissible as long as people practise safe sex').

This shows that individuals cannot achieve such a redefinition on their own, although it is possible for certain actors to play a leading role in this process. Exemplary in this respect are 'normative entrepreneurs' who are sensitive to the needs of the community and articulate those; or members of a counter-elite who present an alternative to the social rules of the governing elite.

The communal process of redefinition relates mainly to informal rules of which the actors are aware. Lower-level norms and conventions can often be modified relatively simply, because the actors have not internalised them and are therefore able to question them. In the case of conventions this is made even easier by the fact that the content of such rules is arbitrary. In principle, rule-making actors are often bound by the higher behavioural standards here, which may not be contravened too explicitly. Since the derivation of the rules is often ambiguous – several different lower-level norms and conventions may be derived from the same higher institution – this limitation is however often not very restrictive.

Values and higher norms are sometimes internalised, and this makes them relatively stable and less sensitive to external changes. At the level of individual actors, the elasticity of such higher informal rules is low, and if changes occur they are often tied to forceful path dependence. This does not however mean that they are inert. Since informal institutions are social constructs at the macro-level, or features of the society in which they exist, individual actors cannot strictly speaking 'have' norms and values. At most they have a certain orientation or subjective interpretation vis-à-vis the informal rules of their community, which may be more or less self-evident to them. This interpretation is not by definition constant, but can change if the personal circumstances alter markedly. For example, long-term incapacity for work can undermine the motivation to work of those affected, even if they previously had a strong work ethic. If the incentive to regulate at the macro-level changes strongly – i.e. relative prices, power relations, interests or the support for ideals alter considerably – it may be that the value orientations of virtually every individual actor changes. This can be the outcome of structural historical developments (e.g. if a society becomes more egalitarian, many actors may uphold the value 'respect', but will be less inclined to respect superiors and inferiors differently) or of incidents with lasting consequences (such as a war or revolution).

Cohort replacement may be another way to explain changes in higher behavioural guidelines theoretically. Assuming that core values and higher norms are internalised during the formative years, every new cohort may place a slightly different interpretation on these, as a result of their specific socialisation context (greater or lesser material wealth, changes in the education system and curriculum, historical events such as wars, famine, epidemics, economic crises which can scar the new actors). If the contrasts between the formative years of different clusters of birth cohorts are large, it is appropriate to refer to them as different generations (the War generation, the baby-boomers, etc.). Presuming cohorts thus have acquired a different orientation to the higher informal rules, it is logical to assume that the mechanism of cohort replacement at collective level will lead to a gradual change in core values and higher norms. When new cohorts or generations grow into adulthood and take over the central social positions from their predecessors as these age and die off, the dominant informal rules gradually may for example become more post-materialistic (see e.g. Inglehart, 1977, 1990; Becker, 1992). The 'culture shift' accomplished through cohort replacement will generally be slow: there is forceful path dependence, as a result of the persisting role of the older generations and their influence on the socialisation of the newborn.

The theory is attractive because it offers an explanation for both the change and continuity in high-level informal institutions. However, it is questionable whether its core assumptions actually hold water (see also §2.8.3). For example, it is doubtful whether the result of the socialisation that people go through in their formative years is always as stable as is assumed, or that the socialisee adopts such a passive, receptive role. The number of unchangeable, deeply anchored rules may be limited, and even those are always dependent on the meaning that actors give to them at a later point in their lives. It is also plausible that the socialisation context of a cohort is usually less uniform then the theory supposes, on account of the wide differences between social backgrounds, genders, regions, etc. If the socialisation within cohorts is usually heterogeneous, it follows from this that its results will also be diversified. Evidently, the replacement of one heterogeneous cohort with another will not constitute a major driving force in the evolution of values and higher norms. This may explain the rather limited empirical evidence (see e.g. Dekker & Ester, 1995; Van den Broek, 1996) for the mechanism of differential cohort-socialisation and their impact on values and social norms through the succession of generations.

2.10 Conclusions

In chapter 1 the following general conceptual and theoretical questions were formulated:
- What does the notion 'institutions' entail?
- What kinds of institutions can be distinguished, and how do they relate to each other?
- How do institutions give direction to social interactions, and which actors may be involved in this?
- What consequences can rule-driven interactions have?
- Under what conditions do institutions come into being, and what causes them to change?

All these questions have been discussed at length in this chapter, with the figural model presented in §2.3 acting as a guide. Here it may be useful to recap some of the answers that have emerged from the conceptual and theoretical analysis.

The nature of institutions
Institutions are socially constructed rules that indicate the rights and duties of actors. They also specify the conditions attaching to the granting of those rights and the imposition of those duties, and what positive and negative sanctions are possible.

The fact that institutions are social constructs excludes the contents of natural laws and absolute normative philosophies from the definition. It also implies a certain degree of ethical relativism; there is no 'right division of rights', a specific attribution of rights and duties can be described but not be regarded as universally applicable.

The core of a right is that someone is permitted to do, to possess or to obtain something, and that others may not hinder him in exercising that right. Rights usually imply that someone else is held under a duty. Object rights relate to particular goods, service rights to the provision of specific facilities, and action rights to the performance of behaviour. Rights theoretically reflect the interests of actors, but also their power, shared ideals, and the relative costs and benefits of rules (including their vesting, monitoring and enforcement).

Rights and duties ultimately rest on a social consensus; and both the granting of rights and the imposition of duties may be subjected to various conditions. In order to gain a right, it may be necessary for specific events to occur, that the interested parties have certain qualifying characteristics, or that they show specific forms of behaviour. Duties may not apply to all actors; and those who are in principle duty-bound may not be so all the time or under all circumstances.

Sanctions are rewards in case of compliance with the rules, and punishments associated with defection. Institutions specify the possible sanctions. These may be positive or negative, and be enforced by authorities or at the level of groups and communities. Sanctions may also be awarded in a 'heroic' way (a single actor imposing a one-off reward or punishment), or collectively and incrementally. They need not be exogenous, but in the case of individual actors may also be internalised, in the form of feelings of guilt, embarrassment and superiority associated with defection and compliance.

Types and hierarchy of institutions

There are two main kinds of institutions. Formal institutions are promulgated or enforced by the government; informal institutions are based entirely on the social consensus within groups or communities. Formal institutions can be subdivided into meta-rules (e.g. the Constitution, election laws), describing the rights and duties regarding the establishment of formal regulations; rules for the production of goods and services by the government (such as defence, education); third-party recognition by the government of the rights, obligations and relationships of citizens and companies (e.g. civil law, mercantile law); and contracts between private parties that are enforced by the government (e.g. commercial contracts complying with mercantile law). Informal institutions can be subdivided into values, which are general behavioural guidelines; social norms, or specific behavioural prescripts for actual situations, which carry the possibility of sanctions being imposed; conventions, which are arbitrary and neutral expectations, mainly serving to coordinate behaviour efficiently; and informal contracts between private parties that are not endorsed by government.

There is no fixed hierarchy either between formal and informal rules or within these two main types. Informal rules may be a specification of formal ones, but the latter can also be regarded as a codification of the informal consensus. To what extent either one dominates the other is an open empirical question.

Within sets of formal or informal institutions, it is a common general principle that rules at a lower level of abstraction (e.g. laws on government production or third party enforcement, social norms) may not contravene the more abstract institutions (such as formal meta-rules, values). This hierarchical ranking is rather loose, however. Lower rules cannot be derived from higher ones by logical deduction: various lower-level attributions of rights, obligations, conditions and possible sanctions may correspond with the same higher principles. The relationships between different types of rules are based on social consensus, and can therefore diverge both historically and socially.

Actors and rule-driven interaction

A distinction can be made between natural persons and corporate actors (organisations which form an independently acting legal persona). Actors do not necessarily accept the rules as givens, but create a representation of them. Institutions therefore do not influence behaviour directly, but only after being filtered by actors. These are led not only by their interpretations of the rules, but also by their resources, experiences and a number of motivations: their goals, ideals and interests; their assessments of the costs and benefits of behavioural alternatives; the probability of outcomes; and emotions. With corporate actors there is theoretically an additional 'principal-agent' problem. How can an organisation assure itself that the individuals acting on their behalf (employees, management, etc.) do not seek to serve their own interests and preferences, but behave as loyal representatives of the wishes of their principal?

Several forms of rule-driven interaction are possible: economic exchange between persons and organisations; relations between friends; political choices at elections; and so on. Rule acquisition is a specific variant of this. Because institutions are social constructs, new actors do not know them instinctively, and must learn them. The socialisation of new actors is not a process that can be taken for granted, and is not a matter of an automatic and one-sided imprinting of behavioural precepts. Rather, it is a continuous interaction process, in which the transfer of existing rules may be at odds with the need for personal development. The outcome of the process is heterogeneous, depending on the socio-historical context in which it takes place and on the individual characteristics and experiences of the socialisers and socialisees.

Individual and collective impact of institutions

Rule-driven interactions produce results for the actors involved which may lead to changes in their resources (wealth, knowledge and experiences) and their perceptions. Theoretically the outcomes at the collective level are more interesting. In principle rules are drawn up in order to achieve certain shared objectives. Rule-driven interactions can therefore influence technological and scientific innovation, the economic process, the social structuring (including the emergence and decline of elites), the formation of ideals and demographic trends. However, rules not only determine this historical process; their operation also depends on the prevailing context of rule application, for example the economic climate.

The rule generation process

Institutions are actor-made. The socially weighted sum of changes in relative prices, power relations, conflicts of interest and the support for certain ideals may provide actors with an incentive to formulate new rules or change existing ones. Mutations in these factors, and thus in the incentive to regulate, arise theoretically from the interaction of the existing rules with technological innovations, economic and socio-cultural changes, demographic trends and the emergence of new ideals.

Depending on the way actors process the incentive to regulate, they may come to desire new or different institutions. However, such aspired regulation does not automatically lead to new forms of institutionalisation. Path dependence acts as a brake on rule change, and also implies that an identical change incentive may lead to diverging rule amendments in different socio-historical circumstances. Moreover, the actual institutionalisation is determined by the course of the rule-interaction. This is quite evident in the policy process by which the meta-rules, the rules on government production and third-party recognition are established. This clearly has its own dynamic, the results of which may not coincide with the rule aspirations of the actors concerned.

Because institutions at a lower level of abstraction (implementation decrees, informal contracts) are often more elastic than higher-level ones (the Constitution, certain core values), the costs of rule change are usually lower in the former case.

New actors often play a decisive role in institutional change. These may be members of an up-and-coming generation, emerging counter-elites, new organisations or individual normative entrepreneurs. New actors are more sensitive to the limitations of the existing rules and the benefits of new ones. They have also invested less in the old institutions, they derive less benefit from them, and they perceive reality less from the basis of the existing rules.

In the next chapter the insights discussed here will be used for a theoretical exploration of the institutions of social security, the main topic of the rest of this study.

3 Social security and the institutional approach

In this chapter the main object of this study, social security, is delineated from a theoretical perspective. A number of questions on this issue were formulated in the Introduction, and the topics to be discussed here derive from these. In §3.1 some traditional definitions of social security as a theoretical notion are discussed and compared. Subsequently the main elements of the theoretical analysis of institutions in the previous chapter are applied to social security. §3.2 demarcates the concept from this institutional perspective. A number of specific types of social security rules are then described, as well as the actors to which they apply (§3.3). The way in which actors generally acquire formal and informal institutions was discussed extensively in the previous chapter. This is elaborated in §3.4, which focuses on the rather 'undersocialised' character of social security rules. §3.5 sketches various models of rule-driven interaction that may occur in social security. A discussion follows of the theoretical results of such behavioural exchanges, with the emphasis on the collective consequences (§3.6). The process through which social security rules arise and change is elucidated on the basis of a historical example: the transition from largely informal to predominantly formal systems (§3.7). The final section sets out the main conclusions.

3.1 Traditional definitions of social security[1]

While several of the institutions to which the concept refers have a long history (especially in poor relief), the notion of 'social security' itself is a fairly recent one. The earliest examples of use of the term date from the 19th century. In a speech to mark the independence of Venezuela, Simón Bolívar (1819) pronounced that:[2]

> El sistema de gobierno más perfecto es aquel que produce mayor suma de felicidad posible, mayor suma de *seguridad social* y mayor suma de estabilidad política.

The concept was also used in the proclamation of the first national congress of the Italian Labour Party (1894) and in a decree issued by the Council of People's Commissioners of the Soviet Socialist Republic (1918) (see Veldkamp, 1978: 1-2). However, the actual starting point lay in the US *Social Security Act* of 1935. This scheme, introduced as part of President Roosevelt's *New Deal*, was initially called the Economic Security Act, but following a number of amendments during the passage of the bill through Congress it was proposed that the name be changed. The term 'social security' referred simply to all issues covered by the scheme, and reflected the fact that through the Act *society* was providing some degree of *economic security* to its citizens. The Act aimed to protect insured workers in industry and commerce against the major "hazards and vicissitudes of life"; and, in the midst of the Great Depression, to guard society against the widespread poverty and social unrest that could result from mass unemployment.

The *Atlantic Charter* (1941), in which Roosevelt and Churchill set out the USA's and Britain's shared objectives of post-World War II policy, also used the concept. Its fifth principle aims

> [...] to bring about the fullest collaboration between all nations in the economic field with the object of securing, for all, improved labour standards, economic advancement and *social security*.

In the *Beveridge Report* the term is used as an overarching concept to describe the three collective methods of covering the economic risks of households: "social insurance for basic needs; national assistance for special cases; voluntary insurance for additions to the basic provision". In the report, social security refers in particular to the body of income regulations, but it also implies care and reinsertion (Beveridge, 1942: 120):

> The term 'social security' is used here to denote the securing of an income to take the place of earnings when they are interrupted by unemployment, sickness or accident, to provide for retirement through age, to provide against loss of support by the death of another person, and to meet exceptional expenditures, such as those connected with birth, death and marriage. Primarily social security means security of income up to a minimum, but the provision of an income should be associated with treatment designed to bring the interruption of earnings to an end as soon as possible.

In 1944 the International Labour Organisation, which had been charged with working out the detail of the social objectives of the *Atlantic Charter,* published a report entitled *Approaches to Social Security*. It contains one of the oldest substantive definitions of the concept (ILO, 1944: 80):

> Social security is the security that society furnishes, through appropriate organisation, against certain risks to which its members are exposed. These risks are essentially contingencies against which the individual of small means cannot effectively provide by his own ability or foresight alone or even in private combination with his fellows. It is characteristic of these contingencies that they imperil the ability of the working man to support himself and his dependants in health and decency. Accordingly, as the State is an association of citizens which exists for the sake of their general well-being, it is a proper function of the State to promote social security. While all State policy has some bearing on social security, it is convenient to regard as social security services only such schemes as provide the citizen with benefits designed to prevent or cure disease, to support him when unable to earn and to restore him to gainful activity. Not all such measures, however, can be considered as affording security. For security is a state of mind as well as an objective fact. To enjoy security, one must have confidence that the benefits will be available when required, and, in order to afford security, the protection must be adequate in quality and quantity.

Following these publications 'social security' became the umbrella term used to denote both the post-WWII national provisions and the older social insurances and poor relief arrangements.[3] The European Union, in particular, uses the related concept of 'social protection', which has a similar meaning.[4]

In current scientific literature social security is delineated in various ways. The more common approach equates social security to the collective instruments which under certain circumstances offer income protection in the form of benefits and provisions. There is also a broader approach in which social security serves other ends as well, is not limited to what the government provides, and is not confined to awarding income entitlements in cash or in kind. The main elements of both traditions will be discussed below.

3.1.1 The narrow approach

When interpreted *in sensu strictu*, social security is often regarded as the entire body of government provisions aimed at providing a cushion for private households which as a result of specific events or circumstances have ended up in a weak income position. The following elements characterise this interpretation:
- The *objective* of social security is to offer a certain degree of income protection;
- The *instruments* used to achieve this goal comprise social insurance and national provisions regulated by law;
- The main *intervention* implied in these instruments is to provide benefits in money or in kind;
- Social security focuses on specific, clearly defined *risks*.

These four aspects of the narrow approach of social security are discussed in more detail in the rest of this section.

Income protection as an objective
According to Deleeck (1991: 18), modern social security has a dual income protection purpose: it has to guarantee a minimum income for everyone, and in addition it has to maintain the existing standard of living to a certain degree. Historically, the 'universal minimum income' goal supplanted the 'income continuity' objective. The main purpose of the pre-WWII system of social insurances was to maintain the standard of living of the working population to a certain extent. Some later authors still regard income continuity as the primary objective of social security, arguing that this should be assured as far as possible for all citizens. This is expressed for example in Laroque's (1966: 84) definition of the concept:
> A guarantee by the whole community to all its members of the maintenance of their standard of living, or at least of tolerable living conditions, by means of a redistribution of incomes based upon national solidarity.

In the wake of the Second World War, however, the goal of assuring a minimum level of income for all became predominant. In the *Atlantic Charter* the hope was expressed that after the War, "all the men in all the lands may live out their lives in freedom from fear and want". In the Beveridge Report, the universalistic principle was given shape in the form of a blueprint for post-war social security, which was intended to guarantee "the abolition of want" for the entire British population[5] (Beveridge, 1942: 7-9). The Van Rhijn Commission (1945/1946: part I, 13), which was charged with drawing up general guidelines for the Dutch system after the War had ended, defined social security as

> A body of rules whose intended purpose is (a) to compensate wholly or partly loss of income arising from certain specifically defined risks (such as illness, old age, etc.) or the additional expenses brought on by certain events (e.g. an increase in family size); and (b) to provide medical and nursing care as well as the opportunity for rehabilitation.

On reading further it becomes apparent that social security is intended primarily to meet situations of financial uncertainty and, in line with international developments at the time, should focus on "providing indemnity against want", or providing protection against poverty for all inhabitants.

Deleeck's 'dual objective' was present in many of the collective social security systems that actually emerged after the Second World War. In spite of their marked structural differences (which will be discussed in chapter 4), the modern schemes often guaranteed both a minimum income to the most vulnerable groups, and some kind of income continuity to the working population.

The instruments: social insurance and national provision

The social security systems which evolved in the 20th century were generally a hybrid form of the 'pure' models of social insurance and national provision (cf. table 3.1). *Social insurance* is also referred to as the 'Bismarckian' model of social security, which developed in the later part of the 19th century in Germany. Historically, this system represented an important change: certain risks – initially mainly old age, illness and occupational accidents – that had previously been the responsibility of the individual or the local and church community were now covered by collectively funded arrangements. The need for this state interference was argued in both negative and positive terms. On the one hand a stronger government role was regarded as indispensable for combating certain social ills (poverty, social unrest), while on the other it was considered as a means of supporting the process of nation building. For the rising working classes and the poorer sections of the bourgeoisie (such as the Protestant *kleine luyden* in the Netherlands), state intervention was moreover one of the instruments for achieving their emancipation. In Western Europe, the struggle to achieve statutory protection for socio-economic risks ran largely parallel to the controversies on universal suffrage and the right to education for all children.

The primary objective of social insurance is to ensure continuity of income, to maintain the existing standard of living at a certain level. It is aimed at a limited target group, generally employees in a specific sector. The coverage provided by social insurance is limited to events that are actuarially insurable; selection of risks is unavoidable, which means for example that someone who is already ill can be excluded from a disability benefit insurance scheme.

Social insurance entitlements (either in the form of cash benefits of benefits in kind) depend on two things: the contributions made by the insured parties – without payment of contributions there is no entitlement to benefit – and the extent of the loss suffered. The principle of equivalence means that there is a causal link between contribution, potential and actual risk, and benefit level, sometimes referred to in the literature as the

Table 3.1
Social insurance and national provision: pure models

	Pure model of:	
	Social insurance	**National provision**
Target group	selective (employees in various sectors)	universal (all citizens)
Covered risks	individual insurable risks (individual risk selection)	risks considered to be a collective responsibility (no individual risk selection)
Benefit level	dependent on own contributions and extent of loss suffered (equivalence)	dependent on neediness of applicants; possibly means-tested
Funding source	earmarked contributions from employers and employees	general revenue or earmarked contributions from entire taxable population
Contribution level	based on actuarial risk (contribution differentiation)	based on ability to pay (solidarity principle)
Funding method	capital fund or pay-as-you-go among employers and employees	pay-as-you-go (apportionment) among taxable population
Organisational structure	autonomous organisations per sector, non-governmental (with official recognition); one body for benefit payments and collection of contributions	limited number of (semi-)government organisations; benefit payments and collection of contributions may be split
Responsibility for benefit and contributions levels	autonomous fixing of premiums and benefits by administration	central government sets contribution and benefit levels
Administration perspective	mainly endogenous (insurance principles)	mainly exogenous (general interest, clients)
Relation with other policy sectors	self-contained, no connection with other policy areas	explicit ties with health care, education, etc.
Supervision	self-regulation, insurance autonomy	independent supervision by separate (semi-)government agency

Sources: Veldkamp (1984); Geleijnse, Vrooman & Muffels (1993); adapted

'causality triptych'.[6] Social insurance is funded by the collection of contributions (premiums) from the employers and employees concerned. The amount of the premiums is geared to the actuarial insurance risk, and can therefore differ from one sector of industry to another, between age groups, etc. The total premium required may be apportioned among the individual participants of the scheme so that current contributions are used to pay current benefits (pay-as-you-go schemes), or reserves may be built up to cover future financial obligations (funded schemes). The administration of social insurance regulations is placed in the hands of autonomous organisations for each branch of insurance. These organisations collect the premiums and distribute the benefits. This process takes place purely from an endogenous insurance perspective: benefits are paid in accordance with the policy conditions, without considering the general interest or social position of the insured parties.

Social insurance is regulated by law, but need not be administered directly by the government. This 'insurance autonomy' is reflected among other things in the autonomous fixing of the contribution level by the agency concerned, and the absence of independent supervision. To the extent that supervision does take place, it is regulated by the sector itself, or possibly by a separate body with a limited mandate.

National provision is an exponent of the 'Beveridgean' perspective, after the influential report drafted during the Second World War at the request of the British government. This too marks a turning point in thinking on social security. After the economic crisis in the 1930s, the misery that the War visited on the people and the threat emanating from rising Communism, it was considered desirable to increase government responsibility for the welfare of the population. State intervention to ameliorate acute social ills was no longer enough; what was needed now was to establish the principle of government responsibility to offer all citizens security of income, regardless of the contribution they had made to society in the form of their labour and social insurance premiums.[7]

The system of national provision focuses on the minimum income goal, and therefore seeks to guarantee a certain threshold amount, usually graded by various household types. The entitlements are universal in nature: all citizens who fall within the terms may apply for it. There is no risk selection because the minimum income guarantee applies to risks that cannot be borne by every individual, and therefore is a collective responsibility. The amount of the benefit does not depend on the contribution paid or the extent of the loss suffered, but on the neediness of the applicants. The right to benefit is accordingly sometimes made dependent on an assessment of actual need through means testing. The scheme may be financed either out of the general revenue (taxation) or through earmarked contributions from the entire taxable population. Where contributions are levied, a key difference compared with the social insurance model is that the amount of the contribution is not based on the insurance risk, but on the ability of the contributors to pay, the 'solidarity principle'. Generally an apportionment method is used to determine the contribution levels: the estimated amount needed in order to pay benefits in a given year is divided among the entire taxable population. A contribution-based provision without means testing is regarded as a form of *national insurance*; a means-tested scheme that is funded from general revenue is designated as *national (social) assistance*.

Organisationally, national provisions are administered by a limited number of government or semi-government agencies. Collection of contributions and payment of benefits may be kept separate, for example split between the tax authorities and a benefits agency.

The exogenous perspective of the collective interest and the clients drives the administration of national provisions; it is also regarded as desirable to establish a connection with other policy sectors, such as health care and education. There is powerful independent supervision and close financial control (e.g. by an Audit Chamber). Government and Parliament play an important role in the national provision model: the level of contributions and taxes, as well as the amount of the guaranteed minimum income, are fixed at the national level.

In practice these models do not occur in their pure forms. Many social insurances have acquired provision-like features over time, for example due to a broadening of the target group, the introduction of need elements in determining the level of benefits, and more attention for the social implications of awarding benefits and collecting contributions. Conversely, insurance elements often crept into national provisions; the covered population may be limited (e.g. by restricting survivor's benefits to older widows or widows with young children), benefit levels may be made dependent on the number of years resided in the country, etc.

Providing benefits as the main intervention

In its narrow sense social security consists mainly of transfers in the form of money or in kind. The income security which is the aim of the statutory systems of social insurance and national provision is achieved primarily by providing households with financial support and compensations when they have difficulty in meeting certain costs. This emphasis on the 'benefits' side of social security is illustrated by the definition formulated by Halberstadt (1976: 22-24), who characterises it as

> The entire body of discretionary or automatic individual, financially appraisable entitlements to a certain standard of living.

This is in fact a fairly broad definition, since it refers to entitlements which can occur both in the form of generic transfers (old age pensions, unemployment benefit, social assistance) and of earmarked retributions (student grants, housing subsidies, health care, subsidies for utilising public transport, sports facilities, libraries, museums etc). However, the focus on the standard of living suggests the monetary, compensatory character of social security is its central feature; other possible interventions, such as preventing someone from becoming unemployed or incapacitated for work, or promoting reintegration into employment, play a subordinate role. In this view, social security is above all a monetary issue, a system that converts financial contributions into benefits and compensations.

Coverage of a limited number of risks

In the narrow approach social security only offers income protection when certain events or emergencies occur, also referred to as 'social risks'. Generally, the events covered are those referred to in Convention No. 102 of the International Labour Organisation (ILO) (the *Social Security (Minimum Standards) Convention*, 1952). This is a limitative summary; social security incorporates the provisions that come into effect when households have insufficient income or have difficulty in meeting costs as a result of specific events.[8] These 'contingencies' are:
– Survival beyond a prescribed age, to be covered by *old age benefit*;
– The loss of support suffered by a widow or child as the result of the death of the breadwinner (*survivor's benefit*);
– Responsibility for the maintenance of children (*family benefit*);
– The treatment of any morbid condition (including pregnancy), whatever its cause (*medical care*);
– A suspension of earnings due to pregnancy and confinement and their consequences (*maternity benefit*);
– A suspension of earnings due to an inability to obtain suitable employment for protected persons who are capable of, and available for, work (*unemployment benefit*);

- A suspension of earnings due to an incapacity for work resulting from a morbid condition (*sickness leave benefit*);
- A permanent or persistent inability to engage in any gainful activity (*disability benefit*);
- The costs and losses involved in medical care, sickness leave, invalidity and death of the breadwinner due to an occupational accident or disease (*employment injuries*).

For each of these risks the convention lays down what part of the population at least has to be covered, the minimum level and duration of benefits, and the basic conditions for entitlement. It also stipulates this can be achieved through social insurances or national provisions (including social assistance; 'indigence' is not considered a separate risk). However, the limitative summary excludes a number of risks from the domain of social security. Events such as divorce, excessive housing costs, high transport costs, etc., are not covered as independent items, and neither are the costs which relate to prevention and restoration.

3.1.2 The broad approach

In recent decades wider views on social security have emerged in the literature. In this broad approach, all the features mentioned above are extended. The objective of social security is not only to provide income protection, but also security of work, health, and social participation. In addition, social security instruments are not limited to collective insurance and provisions regulated by law, and payment of benefits is not by definition predominant; interventions aimed at prevention and restoration theoretically play a key role. And according to this view, social security relates to more than just the traditional social risks.

These elements of social security *in sensu largo* also require some explanation.

Limiting 'human damage' instead of income protection

In the broad approach, the object of social security is not restricted to guaranteeing a minimum subsistence income or assuring a certain continuity of the acquired living standard. A definition used by Berghman (1990: 6) is illustrative here;[9] he characterises social security as

> A state of complete (or optimum) protection against human damage.

The notion of 'human damage' is given central prominence in the Flemish social security literature (cf. Viaene et al., 1990: 61-65). Human damage means the loss of certain capacities by an individual which disrupts the relation with their social and natural environment. From this perspective, Viaene et al. (1976) define social security as

> A permanent evolution towards offering the highest possible level of protection against human damage for the highest possible number of people.

According to this view, social security should be focused on two theoretical forms of damage: loss of income and loss of health. In order to achieve these aims social security has three theoretical ways of intervening, or 'modes of operation' (Viaene et al., 1990: 65):

> This evolution is sought in the first place through the prevention of health damage; secondly, where damage occurs, through its rapid and complete restoration; and, in last and subordinate place, through a policy of compensation of labour income losses, which underpins the prevention and restoration policy.

In this definition, social security is not regarded as a complex of provisions, but as a process of societal evolution, aimed at maximising protection levels for as many people as possible. Combating human damage is the primary objective: the goal of social security is to counter an actual or potential loss of income and health (the latter is sometimes taken to include subjective well-being as well). The demarcation of human damage is a wide-ranging one, including not only the immediate 'utilitarian' losses, such as the direct income reduction suffered by an employee who is laid off, but also the long-term consequences, the implications for the social and natural environment, and the repercussions that cannot be expressed directly in economic terms (such as a decrease of happiness). Health is therefore defined very broadly, as a state of optimum physical, psychological, social and ecological well-being. Characteristic of this approach is also the fact that the aims of social security are interpreted in a dynamic and forward-looking way. Human damage is not seen as a one-off risk that can be compensated by a single benefit payment (income substitution based on limited causality), but as an event which can continue to have an impact into the future, and will continue to demand attention ('finality').

Because the notion of 'damage' thus tends to become all-embracing, some authors advocating a broad approach reduce the objectives of social security to a limited number of theoretical dimensions (see e.g. Muffels, 1993; Berghman & Verhalle, 2003). The purpose of social security is then to correct losses in terms of:
a) income,
b) employment, and
c) health and social participation.

As a consequence, social security cannot focus solely on the traditional income protection functions, but also has to seek to increase labour market participation and to achieve an optimum state of health and social integration. In principle these dimensions are not independent of each other. People who become medically unfit to work not only suffer a deterioration of their health but also lose their job, part of their income, their social contacts at work, and the social status and social integration that being in employment brings.

However, the various objectives may be difficult to achieve simultaneously in practice. Geleijnse et al. (1993: 28-38) refer in this context to 'policy contradictions', implying that seeking to achieve one objective cannot always be reconciled with realising another:

- If the income security objective is maximised and benefit levels are high, the incentive for beneficiaries to look for work may be limited, and it may become too expensive for employers to take on low-skilled workers. In addition, some groups of recipients may not be regarded as meriting such high benefits; they then risk being stereotyped as scroungers and lazybones, and they may consequently become isolated from mainstream society. Maximising the income security objective can thus lead to an inadequate fulfilment of the objectives of securing employment and social integration;
- If on the other hand policy efforts are directed towards maximising participation in employment, for example by keeping benefit levels very low and regarding all work as in principle appropriate for everyone, this can undermine the objectives of guaranteeing income security, health and social participation. Groups which find themselves unable to acquire work are then in danger of ending up in structural poverty (because of the low benefit levels), while people may also feel compelled to accept jobs that could harm their health or social life (hazardous or strenuous work, occupations that do not reflect their training and capacities, night shifts);
- And finally: maximising health and social participation can undermine the income and employment objectives. An example might be a medical examiner who too readily declares someone unfit for work because this is the best solution given their current health status. Such people thus lose their position on the labour market and may have considerable difficulty finding work again at a later date. The disability benefit in most cases will be less than the previous earnings, and in the long run the income loss may become even greater, due to missed career opportunities and, possibly, as a result of the limited indexing of benefits.

This implies that social security can at best aim for a simultaneous optimisation of the objectives of income security, security of employment, and security of health and social participation. Precisely where this optimum lies is socially and historically variable, bearing in mind Coleman's view that there is no such thing as a universal "right division of rights" (see §2.4).

Not only social insurance and national provisions

Veldkamp (1978, 1984) has argued that social security should not be equated with the existing systems of social insurance and national provisions. In his view all schemes and arrangements – both collective and individual – aimed at securing the continuity of an existing standard of living form part of social security. He uses the following extensive definition (Veldkamp, 1978: 4):

> Social security [comprises] the whole complex of institutions and provisions aimed at guaranteeing a certain standard of living [...] by substituting income as far as possible where the existing source of income disappears and by compensating directly or indirectly for costs which are difficult to bear [... as well as the institutions and provisions] aimed at removing as far as possible the causes of the inadequacy or loss of income. [It thus includes] not only the traditional social insurance and other social provisions, such as social assistance schemes, but for example also the system of housing subsidies, employment policy, student grants, and so on. Wherever a system of income guarantees, income substitution and income complementarity exists, this must be regarded as social security.

In Veldkamp's vision, social security in a broad sense consists first of all of arrangements to which people can turn if they lose their work or income, or when they face health-related costs that are difficult to meet. This includes the traditional social insurances and national provisions, but also extends to housing benefit and student grants.

A second type of social security consists of arrangements that are intended to prevent people from losing their job or income, and therefore having to make use of benefit schemes. Veldkamp includes among these preventative instruments sickness and accident prevention, the regulation of working conditions, measures designed to promote employment, the notification and assessment of proposed mass redundancies, the disclosure of merger negotiations between firms, and the minimum wage.

In the third place social security in a broad sense consists of more than the arrangements that are enforced by the government and formalised in national law. This idea has been elaborated by Berghman (1986: 13-16), who refers to the 'invisible' forms of social security. In doing so he builds on the 'social division of welfare' proposed by Titmuss (1958), who identified three complementary methods for configuring welfare arrangements in a modern society:

> In the first group Titmuss includes social benefits and services which constitute the visible heart of the welfare state and which he brings together under the term *social welfare*. In addition he refers to *fiscal welfare*: the body of tax exemptions and reductions which increase the disposable income in the same way that benefits do. Finally, he speaks of *occupational welfare*, as the body of employment-related fringe benefits which are funded wholly or partly by the employer.

Although Titmuss did not define his threefold division explicitly for the analysis of social security, according to Berghman it can serve this purpose well. Berghman does however state two additions are needed to Titmuss's typology. The *private welfare* category consists of arrangements people make by themselves (savings, supplementary private pensions, annuities). Provisions emanating from the civil society (e.g. church charity, mutual societies) could constitute a further type of social security; Berghman suggests the term *voluntary welfare* for this.

In its broad interpretation, therefore, social security is not limited to the traditional system of statutory social insurance and national provisions. It includes all government provisions aimed at ensuring security of income, work, health and social participation: not only social insurance and provisions, but all arrangements sustaining social and fiscal welfare. Moreover, it is not limited to schemes in which the government plays a decisive role. The same objectives can in principle be achieved by occupational, private and voluntary arrangements.

More interventions

It is already apparent from the definition used by Viaene et al. that the objectives of social security can be achieved not only through the payment of benefits. There are various theoretical 'modes of operation' of social security, and these are often arranged hierarchically. In this line of reasoning, top priority should then be given to measures aimed at *prevention*;[10] if this is not achievable, efforts must be directed towards *restoration* of the loss of income, employment and health/social participation as soon as possible. Only when restoration is not feasible consideration should be given to (partial) *compensation* for the damage suffered. In the narrow approach of social security, by contrast, it is precisely this latter function that is key: the damage suffered is 'bought off' and relatively little attention is given to prevention and restoration.

Viaene et al. regard it as characteristic of the forthcoming 'third phase' of social security – after the emergence of the Bismarckian (social insurance) and Beveridgean (national provision) principles – that the main emphasis should in future be placed on prevention. Other authors consider this a less self-evident development. Van Langendonck (1992) points out three obstacles to prevention:

– It is not always economically viable. Prevention may require high absolute investments for a limited and often uncertain return; and companies or societies investing in prevention are in a relatively unfavourable position vis-à-vis competitors economising on such costs;
– It is not always socially acceptable. Prevention of alcoholism or sporting injuries can theoretically be achieved by prohibiting alcohol or banning the more dangerous sports (boxing, alpinism, motor racing). However, such drastic measures probably will not be supported by economic stakeholders and the public at large, and may elicit unintended behavioural reactions (e.g. bootlegging, illegal fighting competitions);
– The usefulness of preventive operations cannot always be readily objectified. Prevention refers to a negative fact (ensuring a risk does not manifest itself) which is hard to ascertain; and the longer nothing happens, the more difficult it becomes to maintain a high degree of preventive measures. Apart from that, there is also often no one single clear cause on which preventive interventions can focus (multiple causality of loss).

To this can be added the comment that a social security policy focused on prevention is not always *possible*. Demographic risks, such as old age, are hardly subject to influence by preventive measures: the risk manifests itself fairly independently of the policy, which can at most regulate the take-up of the various arrangements (for example by raising the statutory retirement age). For older persons, but also for other groups such as the seriously ill and 'non-employables' (socially dysfunctional persons, the homeless), the compensation function of social security will remain crucial and the opportunities for prevention are limited. While prevention may assume a more prominent role in future social security, for reasons such as these it is doubtful whether it can ever be its main intervention.

Generalising this statement, it may be useful to widen the range of interventions available to social security, but it does not seem self-evident that the various modes of operation theoretically have to be applied in a hierarchic fashion. While acknowledging that social security in a broad sense is not confined to compensation, in specific circumstances it very well may be that it is cheaper or socially more acceptable to award benefits than to put much effort in prevention or restoration. This is in line with the analysis of institutional hierarchy in the previous chapter, which stated that there are no inevitable or eternal links between higher and lower rules (cf. §2.6); such derivations always reflect the prevailing social consensus.

Moreover, the interventions of social security are not mutually exclusive. For example, it may be that disabled persons return to work for their old employer at a lower wage, with the government topping up their income to its original level, and funding adaptations to the workplace which help to carry out the current job and avert renewed or different complaints arising. In such a case the interventions are mixed: there is a partial restoration of the employment loss suffered, a compensation for the structural loss of income, while the adaptation of working conditions serves the prevention of future disability.

Broadening and blurring of the risk definition

In the broad approach, social security therefore has to achieve more (not only income protection, but combating all forms of human damage), comprises more than just social insurance and provisions, and is not focused exclusively on compensation. It is therefore not surprising that the risk covered is also interpreted more widely. Social security not only has to offer protection against the financial consequences of unemployment, illness, old age, disability, etc.; it also has to help prevent or eliminate benefit dependency, prevent loss of health and promote (re)integration into employment and society. The envisaged social protection thus encompasses much more than simply cushioning the income consequences of the social risks set out in the ILO list. Irrespective of the cause and nature of the loss suffered, social security should seek to provide a maximum or optimum level of protection against human damage. The method used to achieve this is of secondary importance.

Consequently the broad approach of social security also implies a certain 'blurring of risk': if someone has suffered damage (in terms of income, employment, and health/social participation), social security must try to meet that loss, no matter whether it is caused by long-term unemployment, an accident at work, ageing, divorce or something else.

The broad interpretation of the instruments of social security implies that it is not necessarily a government task to provide coverage for this wide and blurred set of risks; this may also be attained via occupational, voluntary and private provisions.

3.1.3 Criticism of the narrow and broad approaches

The differences between the narrow and broad approaches of social security are summarised in table 3.2 in terms of the objectives, instruments, interventions and risks covered. In the narrow approach the primary objective is to provide income protection, in the sense of a minimum income guarantee for all and a certain degree of income continuity for the working population. The main instruments for achieving this objective are statutory social insurance and national provision. These compensate for a lack or deterioration of income, provided that the shortage is the result of one or more of a number of closely defined risks.

Table 3.2
The narrow and broad approaches of social security

	Narrow approach	Broad approach
Objectives	**Income protection** 1 guarantee of a minimum income to all citizens based on need 2 continuity of existing standard of living, especially among the working population	**Protection against human damage** not only income protection, but also security of (paid) employment, health, and social participation
Instruments	**Statutory social insurance and national provision**	**All provisions** focused on security of income, employment, health, and social participation; social, fiscal, occupational, private and voluntary provisions
Interventions	**Compensation** (through benefits and provisions) has priority	If possible, **prevention** should precede **restoration**; **compensation** is the final resort
Risks covered	**Limited number of risks** (ILO list) - old age - death of the breadwinner - maintenance of children - treatment of illness - maternity - unemployment - sickness leave - disability - occupational accidents and diseases	**Risk broadening and blurring** all events that can lead to human damage, regardless of the precise cause

In the broad approach, social security targets all forms of human damage, thus aiming to provide security of income, employment, health, and social participation. Social insurance and national provision are one means of doing this, but fiscal, occupational, private and voluntary arrangements can equally well be used. Compensation of losses is the final resort; if possible, interventions aimed at prevention and restoration should take precedence. The covered risks not only include the standard calamities, but all events that have led to human damage, regardless of their precise cause. Consequently, the risk definition is widened and blurred.

Both views on social security have their advantages and disadvantages. One strength of the narrow approach is that it makes absolutely clear that the design of the social security system is important. Historically, political battles are often waged over the concrete structuring of schemes, over the specific institutionalisation of general principles. This is in line with the theory set out in the previous chapter; the proposition that 'institutions matter' implies that the design of a social security system largely determines its outcomes. At the same time, the major weakness of this approach is that social security is equated to its compensatory mechanism with regard to specific 'ossified' risks. This is not very satisfactory theoretically, since it reduces social security to nothing more than a collection of income arrangements.

There are several reasons for preferring the broad approach. Here social security is not equated to specific historical instruments of income protection, but is defined in terms of its general objective (combating human damage) and their achievement. In this perspective the arrangements offered are above all a means of realising the goals, with the useful extension that the modes of operation are interpreted more widely: they not only include compensation, but also instruments aimed at prevention and restoration.

However, the broad approach also has disadvantages. In the first place it is understandable that, in reaction to the traditional perspective, the broad approach emphasises that social security is not only about statutory arrangements. Yet this should not lead to the conclusion that the *design* of a social security system is not a key feature; the body of schemes and arrangements is important because it establishes the rights and duties of actors and therefore gives direction to their behaviour.

A second problem is that the objectives of social security are defined in a very *comprehensive* way. The interpretation of human damage may be so wide that there are few events that are not covered, thus limiting the heuristic value of a separate 'social security' concept – it more or less becomes equivalent to the notion of the welfare state.

Furthermore, the broad approach is often rather *a-sociological*, since it accords virtually no role to people's behaviour and their subjective perceptions of social security. In terms of the institutional theory discussed in the previous chapter, however, these constitute an important intermediary factor. Social security rules steer the perceptions and behaviour of actors (benefit recipients, contributors, case managers etc.); and their reaction to those rules largely determines the impact of the social security system.

Equally, the objectives and design of the social security rules are human products; they are created in a process of rule interaction by specific actors, on the basis of their perception of the communities' need to create such institutions. Social security does not evolve by itself, but is the result of human interactions that are linked to a certain consensus among 'social security entrepreneurs' on the best way to respond to actual changes. The broad approach of social security tends to neglect this, and is therefore somewhat *a-historical*. The view of Viaene et al. (1990), which interprets social security as an unconstrained evolution towards ever higher levels, is illustrative in this respect. The emergence of the first social insurance arrangements, followed by national provisions and the expansion of the risks covered, can undoubtedly all be seen retrospectively as an evolution. However, this does not mean that such a course of development is inevitable or that it can be extrapolated *ad infinitum*. In fact, recent decades have seen a retrograde movement in many modern welfare states, in which the collectively funded social security system has been curbed considerably (cf. Leibfried & Mau, 2008). This makes it clear that evolution towards ever higher levels of protection is not an automatic process. The way in which social security develops is not a theoretical given but is historically determined, as demonstrated by the variety of social security regimes in different countries (see chapter 4).

The *collective significance* of social security also tends to be rather neglected in the broad approach. By according central importance to the concept of human damage, social security is measured primarily by its influence on individuals and households. This ignores its more general role: an essential characteristic of social security is that it serves common goals or shared interests, such as the desire to limit poverty, inequality and avoidable benefit dependency. For example, the efficient combating of poverty theoretically reduces the likelihood that certain forms of collective damage will occur ('public bads': theft, social unrest, illness), and also creates collective profits ('public gains': e.g. instead of having to work in order to supplement their family's income, children are able to attend school, which serves the long-term development of human capital and economic prosperity). This public impact of social security can be a sufficient reason for the government to be accorded a key role.

3.2 Social security in an institutional sense

In view of the shortcomings highlighted above, a different approach is preferred here, in which social security is regarded as the entire body of rules which offer people economic protection for the benefit of society. Stated in a more precise way, social security consists of the *collectively defined rights, duties, conditions and potential sanctions which aim to generate positive social outcomes by protecting individual actors against economic deficits*.

A set of institutions

Three aspects characterise the definition proposed here. In the first place it implies that social security is a set of socially constructed rules, or institutions. Social security is a body of rights, duties, conditions and potential sanctions devised by actors, which works through into their motivations and expectations, and consequently may influence their behaviour. The form in which the rules are cast makes no difference: they may be laid down in written form in laws and government decrees, but may also be based on tacit agreements within a community. Thus for example the right to an adequate income for older persons forms part of social security, regardless of whether it is guaranteed by a statutory state pension or by the informal expectations of the elderly vis-à-vis their children and the local community.

In line with §2.4, the elements of social security institutions can be regarded as variations on the following logical fundamental structure:[11]

(1) *Social consensus*   On the basis of prevailing relative prices, powers, interests and ideals there is a sufficient shared understanding that society gains if:
(2) *Conditioned rights*   – A is entitled to R if (E happens to A); (A=Q); (A does C)
(3) *Conditioned duties*   – B must fulfil O to secure R, or not interfere with A in exercising R, if (B=Q)
(4) *Potential sanctions*   – S- is possible if (A induces (E or Q)), (A ~does C), (B ~fulfils O), or (B interferes with A)
   – S+ is possible if (A ~induces (E or Q)), (A does C), (B fulfils O), or (B ~interferes with A)
where: A: potential beneficiaries
B: duty-bound contributors and intermediaries
R: rights of A
O: obligations of B
E: conditions: eventualities
Q: conditions: qualifying properties
C: conditions: conduct
S-: negative potential sanctions
S+: positive potential sanctions
~: not

The first statement expresses the consensual nature of social security institutions. They rest on a social agreement that it is beneficial for society to establish social security rules which reflect the current relative prices, power relations, dominant interests and support for ideals. These collective purposes are not elements of the rules as such, but constitute their vindication, an issue which will be elaborated below.

The second proposition relates to the rights: those who can claim them, the nature of the rights to be granted, and the conditions attached to them. Category A comprises the actors which are potential beneficiaries of social security,[12] the bearers of the rights R. The latter are the core of the 'rules of relief'. R consists primarily of the entitlements to prevention, restoration and compensation (monetary or in kind) which may be offered by the government or community. However, procedural entitlements, such as the right to appeal to higher agencies if someone believes they have not received that to which they are entitled, also forms part of the rights structure.

The rights are usually defined in a hierarchical way; e.g. the constitutional right to a minimum standard of living translates into specific rights to social assistance of a certain level and duration. Such a hierarchy is consensual, in line with the position taken by Raz (1986) that there is no 'logical entailment' between core rights and derivative rights (cf. §2.6.2).

Social security rights are generally conditioned. Three types of conditions can be identified. The first, E, relate to the specific eventualities that confer the right: the 'operational definitions' of, for instance, old age (e.g. reaching one's 65th birthday), indigence (e.g. having a net disposable income below EUR 800 a month), unemployment (e.g. loss of at least four hours of paid labour), or disability (e.g. not being able to earn 15% of previous earnings due to an illness or impairment). E-type conditions theoretically refer to particular actor states, to which the government or community in principle attaches rights.[13] The eventualities in social security usually pertain to certain types of economic protection (cf. below). E-type criteria are often defined as prerequisites, or necessary conditions for R; yet meeting them may not be sufficient to award entitlements to the A-group, as additional criteria may apply.

Conditions of the Q-type are an example of these. They refer to supplementary qualifying characteristics of an applicant, such as a certain employment history, or an income or personal wealth that is not above a certain limit. C-type requirements, on the other hand, are 'conduct conditions': behavioural demands that have to be met by the potential beneficiaries, such as expecting them to seek work or to do something in return for their benefit.

The three types of conditions may be general or current in nature. General conditions always apply, as in the stipulation that sufficient contributions must have been paid, that a certain employment history has been built up, etc. A current condition would be the stipulation that benefit recipients must presently be willing to accept work involving a number of hours of travel.

Though not necessary, it is possible for all types of conditions to be attached to social security rights simultaneously. For instance, the right to unemployment benefit may carry the conditions that the unemployed person has lost a minimum number of working hours, is willing and able to perform labour, and makes serious efforts to find a new job.

The consensus extends further to include the duties imposed on others in order to secure the rights of the potential beneficiaries (statement 3). Group B consists of the duty-bound contributors and intermediaries. Its members may have a direct personal relationship with the beneficiaries (children who support their parents financially), but there may also be a large pool of contributors who generally do not know the beneficiaries. Group B is delineated by qualifying properties, or Q-type conditions;[14] e.g. a person has to pay a contribution to the hospitality industry unemployment fund if he is gainfully employed in a hotel or restaurant for at least 12 hours weekly. Q-type conditions may be very generic (all resident adults have to contribute), but may also target specific groups (the young, the better-off, those working in high-risk jobs).

Intermediate actors – benefits agencies, supervisory authorities, magistrates, advisors – may also be subject to duties and therefore belong to B. They often have some leeway to determine independently how they treat their clients, how they interpret the rules in actual cases, etc. This latitude should not be regarded as a right of the duty-bound. Rather, it is the result of an unclear specification of their duties, or in other words, it is the discretionary scope of B within O.

In informal social security systems, the specific obligations O of group B consist in extending the socially expected aid and assistance. In formal systems the obligations of the contributors imply the duty to pay levies in order to finance benefits and interventions aimed at prevention and restoration. The duties of intermediary organisations mostly relate to assessing the entitlements and actually providing these, but also to the collection of contributions, the auditing of the legitimacy and impact of the administrative process, judging cases of appeal, etc.

Obligations in social security are often focused on securing claim rights, such as benefits. However, non-interference duties may also be imposed. This occurs, for instance, if an employment agency is not allowed to force an unemployed person into accepting a low-skilled job if he or she has not yet completed a training course which would enhance his job prospects.

The collective consensus also relates to the potential sanctions in the event of defection and compliance (statement 4). The rules may provide for negative sanctions such as banishment from the community, 'naming and shaming', suspension of rights, demanding repayments, fines, and imprisonment. These may be imposed upon potential beneficiaries if they attempt to induce their rights or do not behave as required. They may try to acquire entitlements by bringing about or giving a false account of events and qualifying characteristics (e.g. resigning from one's job, pretending to be seriously ill; changing one's household situation and failing to disclose this) or they may not meet the conduct conditions imposed on them (e.g. not seeking employment). Social security rules may also provide for positive sanctions in case of compliance with the rules, for example by making it possible for beneficiaries to be paid a financial reward on accepting a job.

Sanctions such as these are usually imposed externally by duty-bound actors, for instance a benefits agency. Sanctioning is not an autonomous right of B, but a consequence of B's obligation to secure the right of A. If the benefits agency hands out a fine this does not ensue from its fundamental prerogative to do so; it is a consequence of its duty to limit the granting of rights to actors who meet the conditions.

The duty-bound group can also be the subject of sanctions if they default in the fulfilment of their obligations. This situation arises in cases of social insurance premium fraud and tax evasion by contributors, social security agencies which do not pay benefits properly or which achieve insufficient reintegration, etc.

Serving collective purposes

The definition also stipulates that social security reflects collective purposes. The rules provide some persons with rights and oblige others to perform duties, but that is not their final objective. Social security institutions protect some members of a community or nation at the expense of others not out of benevolence, but because there is a shared conviction that the collectivity will be served by doing so. Every social security arrangement reflects a dominant view that it is socially beneficial to cover economic risks in a specific way. Through the institutions, rule-making actors expect to achieve results which are considered desirable for the community or society at large; and in the final analysis that is the *raison d'être* for any set of social security rules.

In contrast to the perspective of the human damage theory, the structure of rights and duties implied in social security is not regarded here as an autonomous reality which can and should continue to evolve *ad infinitum*. Social security is a historical construct; its course of development correlates with the evolution of the perception of what serves the community or nation best. The consensus on the collectively desirable outcomes can reflect various motives of rule-making actors. As noted in the previous chapter, institutional change is generally a weighted product of changes with respect to four factors, none of which logically prevails. Social security rules may therefore emerge or be amended because this is considered to be profitable; e.g. when the social and economic disruption brought about by a growing discontented urban proletariat is considered more costly than providing them with basic protection in terms of income, health and working conditions. It is also possible that new or amended forms of social security are deemed to be more in line with changing power relations and conflicts of interest, for instance because they aim to pacify the emerging working class. The motives of the actors in establishing or changing the social security rules may be largely ideological as well. This occurs for example when they regard it as an expression of the value of Christian charity or of general principles of justice and fairness. It is possible for these changes in relative prices, power relations, interests and the support for ideals to occur simultaneously and to be mutually reinforcing, thus leading to new forms of social security. Yet theoretically this is not necessary; they may also occur in isolation or oppose each other (cf. §2.9.1).

The expected result of social security rules may relate to the attainment of collective gains, but also to combating communal disadvantages. The first category includes shared views on the promotion of prosperity and the social cohesion of the community; improving the functioning of the labour market and the economy; and stimulating the emancipation of certain social groups or, by contrast, reproducing the natural order of estates and classes. The second category embraces the consensus that social security rules may prevent or limit famine, poverty, widespread disease, class conflicts or labour disputes.

The particular social security institutions on which rule-making actors agree can vary according to time and place; and the opportunities to establish or change the rules depend on the routines, interests and investments encapsulated within the existing institutions. The consensus may also fluctuate across different sections of the community. For example, for groups such as the elderly, the disabled and single-parent families the employment dimension is sometimes subordinated in favour of income protection. Finally, the consensus need not be unanimous: what is important is that there is sufficient common understanding. In a democratic system, formal social security rules must generally be approved by a qualified majority of the legislative assembly. In the case of informal social security institutions it is important that dominant actors within the community consider the rules beneficial for the whole.

Protecting individual actors against economic deficits

A third aspect of the definition stipulates that social security tries to protect individual actors against certain economic deficits. The deficits theoretically refer to a lack or loss of income, labour, health and social participation. Their economic nature has to be understood in the sense that the lacks or losses can be appraised in financial terms: a low or diminished income, a decrease in working hours or hourly wages, the costs of medical care and social participation (e.g. visiting one's next of kin). Social security rights may compensate for such lacks and losses, but also include the financial cost of measures aiming at prevention and restoration.

A further restriction is that social security is by definition aimed at persons or households: it is the coverage of the economic deficits of individual actors that is at stake, not those of large corporations, voluntary associations, etc. The obvious reason for this limitation is that the theoretical objectives of social security are concerned with the prevention, restoration and compensation of deficits in terms of income, labour, health and social participation. Such shortages in principle only occur in natural persons – for instance, organisations can experience poor health only in a metaphorical sense.[15]

Restricting social security to the economic protection of individuals is in line with the historical roots of the concept (cf. §3.1). It also has the merit that social security, thus conceived, does not become a catch-all phrase for any kind of collective intervention, or an equivalent of the more general notion of the welfare state. While it is still fairly wide, a demarcation of social security in terms of the monetary equivalent of lacks and losses of income, labour participation, health and social participation is more restrictive than one in terms of 'any form of human damage'. For instance, measures which attempt to mitigate the ecological damage humankind may suffer because certain species are threatened by extinction generally do not belong to social security as it is understood here; that damage bears no direct relation to the individual economic lacks and losses referred to in the definition. Yet the regulation of the long-term consequences of, for instance, occupational diseases is part of social security – ideas of finality surely enter into the definition.

The notion of risk – to be understood as the eventualities which bring about lacks or losses – is not included in the definition. This is because theoretically social security may be provided without taking the causes of economic deficits into account, as the example of the full unconditional basic income shows. Such a scheme periodically grants an amount of money to all citizens, irrespective of whether they are working or not, are ill, old, needy, etc. By awarding a basic income society seeks to shield its members from the undesirable situation of not having enough money to live in an acceptable way, no matter what the cause of the income deficit is.[16]

Nonetheless, in most actual social security systems there are specific attributions of rights, duties, conditions and potential sanctions to cover the eventuality of unemployment, disability, old age and the like. In practice, social security institutions usually include the causes of economic deficits, specified in E-type conditions, because this has a number of potential advantages.[17] If there is a consensus that the causality triptych of social insurance (cf. §3.1.1) is important in any way, the rules necessarily provide an explicit demarcation of the risk involved.

What social security is

On the basis of the definition no universally applicable list of social security institutions can be given. This is because the contents of the rules always reflect the prevailing consensus in specific socio-historical circumstances. Suppose that in a given community bearded persons are not allowed to work for religious or hygienic reasons; this could lead to high unemployment among men who cannot afford to shave. If a legal rule stipulates that the local authorities, in order to counter the negative collective repercussions, must reimburse daily visits to the barber for a shave, this is a form of social security. It is an entitlement protecting a considerable part of the population against economic losses, to which conditions may be attached (exclusion of women and pre-adolescents, means testing), and which specifies the obligations that have to be fulfilled (e.g. the duty to pay contributions to a local 'shaving fund'),[18] and the sanctions that may be applied (e.g. imposing a fine on bearded persons walking in public areas).

Obviously, the definition does not allow for any *deontological* demarcation of the content of the rules, as sociologically speaking there can be no such thing as a 'right division of social security rights'. However, following the definition there are some *logical* curtailments. The premise that social security is a set of institutions implies that everything which does not refer to rights and duties, with their associated conditions and possible sanctions, does not belong to it. The concept therefore does not relate to social insurance or national provision as such, as in the traditional narrow interpretation; but to the rights, duties, conditions and sanctions incorporated in these regulations.

Similarly, based on the institutional criterion the organisations responsible for the rule elements – benefit and employment agencies, social security funds – are not part of social security proper either; rather, they are corporate social security actors (cf. below).

As a consequence of the stipulation on the collective purposes of social security, arrangements that are not considered to serve a shared objective at the macro-level are to be excluded from the definition as well. This usually[19] applies to things such as private fire and theft insurance policies. Although these are embedded in the formal institutions of civil and contract law and target the economic position of households, coverage of the latter is not commonly regarded as serving a collective purpose. Even so, this does not mean that what has been denoted by Berghman (1986) as 'private welfare' should never be regarded as social security. Where private arrangements are deemed to benefit society in some way or another, and are therefore collectively enforced, they unquestionably enter into the definition. Thus, saving for one's old age is not social security if it merely reflects the preferences of a few individuals to retire early; but it certainly is if the community expects people to provide their own pension and applies negative sanctions in the event of defection (for example by showing disapproval to elderly people who are dependent on social assistance).

Provisions that are not aimed at individual actors do not belong to social security as defined here either. This is the case, for example, for the rules on state aid to large businesses facing insolvency. Such measures may clearly influence the take-up of social security arrangements (by preventing job redundancies) and thus the economic position of potential beneficiaries and contributors; but as there are no direct individual entitlements and duties involved, such arrangements are too generic to be counted as a form of social security.

Institutions which affect individual actors but do not have a direct bearing on their economic protection also fall outside the definition. The example of 'ecological risks' has already been mentioned; but the rules governing higher education, the housing market or the sentencing of criminal offenders generally are not part of social security either. However, the components of such rule systems which explicitly refer to economic risks of persons (such as student grants, housing benefit, or preparing convicts for return to employment after their release) do fall within the scope of the definition.

Apart from these logical restrictions, the contents of social security rules implied in the definition can only be ascertained in a *descriptive* way, for instance by trying to recount the shared consensus in a given historical context; e.g. the common denominator prevailing in affluent modern democracies at the beginning of the 21st century. Such a descriptive list could include rules aiming at:
– The classic income risks of social security, viz. the contingencies in the ILO list (old age, unemployment, surviving dependants, the maintenance of children, illness, disability, sickness leave and occupational diseases and accidents). While their coverage through national legislature is comparatively recent, many of these risks were already regarded as a ground for local poor relief in pre-industrial times. Thus the early 19th-century *Regulations* in the town of Den Bosch mentioned in the Introduction contain – albeit in

rudimentary form – most of the events mentioned in ILO Convention no. 102, with the exception of employment injuries;[20]
- New income risks, such as parental leave, divorce and income fluctuations as a result of freelance labour. Unavoidable one-off expenditures that cannot be borne by the individual or household may also fall into this category (e.g. breakdown of domestic appliances);
- Labour risks: minimum labour standards (e.g. working hours, working conditions); child care facilities for working parents; and measures which aim to prevent disability, restore labour capacity or reintegrate individuals into the employment process (including subsidised employment and workfare);
- Health risks: the costs of medical treatment, including prevention, rehabilitation and formal or informal care;
- Social participation risks: the costs of socially required activities that the actor cannot afford (visiting one's relatives, sports club membership for children, minimum transport facilities).

Yet the actual shape social security takes may diverge widely over time and between communities or nations. Currently new risks, such as paternity leave and divorce, are only considered a collective responsibility in the more extensive social security systems, especially those in Scandinavia. Similarly, guaranteeing a minimum level of social participation remains a rather insignificant element of most modern social security systems. And even the coverage of the classic risks of social security at a low level is not taken for granted in all affluent modern democracies. This is illustrated by the fact that ILO Convention no. 102 has not been ratified by several OECD countries, including Australia, Canada and the USA. There remains a considerable empirical variation between national social security systems, a topic which will be explored further in the next chapter. However, now that the concept has been defined, it is useful to look first in more detail at the institutional approach to social security.

3.3 Institutions and actors in social security

Social security institutions can appear in an informal or formal guise; i.e. the accreditation of rights, conditions, duties, and sanctions may rest directly on the prevailing consensus in a community or they may be defined or recognised by the government. The theoretical nature of formal and informal social security rules and the relationships between them will be outlined here, as an elaboration of what has been said in the previous chapter about various institutions in a general sense. The types of actors that may be involved in social security will also be defined more precisely in this section.

3.3.1 Informal social security rules

Every social security system contains informal elements. The *values* of solidarity and fairness as perceived in a community or society shape the definition of specific rights, duties and potential sanctions. Within the general hierarchy of values, the position of such notions is not fixed. If solidarity and fairness values are considered subordinate to 'individual freedom should not be interfered with', for example, this can limit the attribution of social security entitlements.

Social security *norms* are the rights and duties that are actually recognised by members of a group or community: Which risks are economic, and should these be a collective responsibility? Which entitlements are justified, and to what extent should the community provide for them? Who is required to make contributions in order to secure the general rights? Which penalties can beneficiaries, contributors and intermediary actors expect if they default?

Conventions relate to routines in social security interactions between beneficiaries and duty-bound. For instance, custom may prescribe that the contributions of the community are collected at a certain moment in time (e.g. via a weekly church collection), or that poor relief recipients can report at a certain time to an issue point for food, water, fuel or financial support.

Informal social security *contracts* may consist of tangible agreements between private actors; for example, someone who borrows money from a relative to help them out in a time of need and promises to pay it back within a certain period.

3.3.2 Informal social security systems

As the Den Bosch *Regulations* discussed in the Introduction show, it is possible for social security schemes or systems to be completely informal. Berghman (1986), as noted earlier, speaks in that case of 'voluntary' social security. This term is somewhat unfortunate, because informal social security schemes can be very compelling. The beneficiaries may have to accept burdensome duties: a show of submissiveness, shame and gratitude towards the group or community; a highly demanding quid pro quo, for example having to perform heavy labour in the workhouse; or the moral obligation to display loyalty to their benefactors. They often also face negative informal sanctions. Merely by making use of the informal arrangements it is possible that beneficiaries end up at the bottom of the social hierarchy; and their reputation may be so badly damaged that their chances – and those of their children – of climbing back up the social ladder will be severely compromised for many years to come. If the community thinks beneficiaries have to blame themselves for their dependency (because they have not done enough to avoid being in a situation of need, did not save when they were able to do so, have ignored the religious prescripts, or have led a bad life in some other way), they can be regarded as undeserving, and consequently may be the subject of moral rejection, taunting or exclusion.

Similarly, the contributors in informal systems may find it difficult to shirk the acts of benevolence they are supposed to perform. Even if the decision whether or not to contribute is discretionary, in reality the duty-bound often have to take account of their social position and the disapproval they will face if their contribution does not meet the expectations (e.g. losing their place on the front row at church). The single 'voluntary' element in schemes of this type is that there is no enforcement by the government: such systems are based entirely on the norm that individual actors have a certain right to support from the members of their group or community if certain risks occur and they meet the habitual conditions.

Informal social security systems may consist of *familial*, *communal* or *occupational* arrangements. Familial social security is based on relationships between blood relatives (nuclear and extended family, clan). It includes, for instance, the expectation that children will sustain and care for their parents when they are too old to work and no longer have sufficient means of their own. Such an arrangement may incorporate a form of informal reciprocity, in that grown-up descendants repay what they received from their parents in their childhood.

Communal social security is based on local community organisations, and is generally associated with church charity and works of mercy by affluent members of society. Direct support through the donation of money, food, fuel, clothing and medical help is the best-known form of communal social security. Other examples include providing shelter for certain categories of the needy (older persons, the disabled, widows and orphans, foundlings, beggars) in communal care homes, mental homes, orphanages or workhouses; or placing such groups in private lodging with paid caretakers. 'Patronage' can also be included under communal social security. In this form of care, attempts are made to ensure that paupers become moral and religious citizens by arranging for the well-to-do to personally oversee their lifestyles, among other things through home visits (see for examples in the Netherlands: Van Loo, 1987: 35-46).

Informal occupational social security is built around labour relationships. The guild funds are an historical example of such a system: the entitlements were limited to guild members and their dependent relatives. Currently, employers still may offer provisions which are no part of the formal contractual employment relationship, but in most affluent societies this is a rather marginal phenomenon (e.g. the right of employees in a bakery to take home left-over bread).

These informal social security arrangements can exist alongside each other, in a complementary or nested form. The duty to provide help then may rest in the first instance on the next of kin; if they are absent or default on their obligations, these may pass to the extended family or clan; and if that provides insufficient remedy, the responsibility could shift to the community organisations (such as the church) or the municipality.

Informal social security systems can only exist where there is a recognisable group or community which shares the informal rules (values, norms, conventions and informal contracts) to a sufficient degree. An informal social security system can fulfil a number of functions for a group or community. Of course, its primary aim is to combat the most serious social ills (hunger, illness, child mortality), thus improving the collective welfare and future prospects of the community as a whole. Apart from that, it may serve the emancipation of disadvantaged groups within the community. Furthermore, by complying with the normative expectations of social security rules solidarity is expressed in a very tangible way, and perpetuation of the collectivity is enhanced. Informal social security can moreover offer a means of demarcating internal and external hierarchies. Within the group or community the mutual dependence relationships and social relations are confirmed, while at the same time social integration is fostered by excluding outsiders from the protection provided.

3.3.3 Formal social security

Modern social security systems are generally highly formalised; they are created or ratified by the government through legislation and regulations. In the narrow approach discussed earlier, social security is even equated to such government arrangements. Three main types of formal social security can be distinguished:

a. Collective social security, also referred to in the literature as the 'first pillar'. Following the line of argument of Titmuss and Berghman, a distinction can be made here between social security produced by the government in the form of social insurance and national provisions (social welfare or 'visible social security'), and the tax breaks and subsidies that the government grants to individuals or households (fiscal welfare). The latter can be further subdivided into provisions that are comparable to benefits or a partial basic income (such as tax credits) and reimbursement of the costs that people actually incur (tax relief for pension contributions, annuities, medical expenses).

b. Occupational social security enforced by the government, or 'second pillar' arrangements. This occurs for example when the law stipulates that employer and employee representatives are responsible for implementing an unemployment benefit scheme; that employers are responsible for supervising the sickness absence of their employees; that collective labour agreements apply for all firms within a given sector, and so on. Occupational social security can also exist without government enforcement, but is then informal in nature (cf. above).

c. Government-enforced private social security contracts, or 'third pillar' provisions. These include private pension and health insurance plans, for example, in which the relationship between the insurer and the insured is steered by government rules. This is the case for example when the government compels people to enter into such a contract with a certified insurance company. As stated earlier, any tax relief awarded by the government for the costs incurred do not form part of this system; that is collective social security in the form of fiscal welfare. Where such arrangements are not enforced by the government but by the community (for example, a widely shared expectation that people will save up for their retirement themselves), such private contracts have an informal character. If they are based entirely on personal preferences, they are not included under social security as defined here at all.

Formal social security institutions can theoretically be ranked in an infinite number of ways. As indicated before, it is usual for the rules to exist in a certain hierarchy, though without one inevitably deriving from another; there is a top-down ranking of formal institutions, but no logical entailment. Constitutional recognition of the right to social security may force the government to formulate certain specific laws on the right to, e.g., social assistance benefit, unemployment benefit, collective old-age pension and so on. These laws will generally be elaborated in specific regulations, administrative decrees and jurisprudence. The entire national body of formal institutions can be influenced by supranational rules, such as European Union regulations, directives and decisions,[21] UN and ILO conventions, etc. All these rules, and the derivations between them, stand in a certain hierarchical relationship to each other. This hierarchy is based on consensual interpretations. The awarding of social assistance benefit in specific cases at a certain level and for a particular period of time does not ensue inevitably from the basic right to social security, but is the result of an accumulation of political and administrative choices. Equally, the hierarchy does not imply that the higher rules are more important. The rules which define specific rights, duties, conditions or sanctions (such as benefit levels, contribution rates, work incentives, fines in case of defection) may weigh more heavily in the motivations and behaviour of actors – and in the social outcomes achieved – than the abstract intentions at the top of the institutional hierarchy.

A second ranking option concerns the relationship between the three types of institutions in formal social security: collective, occupational and government-enforced private rules. The term *pillars*, which is frequently used in the literature, suggests a parallel hierarchy with a vertical division of responsibilities. For instance, the government may restrict its first pillar role to a social safety net in the form of social assistance benefit. Unemployment and disability benefit arrangements and old age pensions can then be regarded as a statutory responsibility of employers and trade unions in the second pillar. In such a system, households could be expected to take steps themselves to cover other risks (such as survivor pensions and arranging childcare facilities) in the third pillar, with the government possibly reimbursing some of the costs through the tax system.

Yet a horizontal distribution of responsibilities is also possible, in which the three types of institutions are arranged in *layers*. This occurs, for example, when old age benefit consists of a first pillar national pension with uniform amounts, which is topped up to a certain percentage of the previous earnings via occupational pension schemes, in addition to which people may draw on provisions that they have built up themselves in the past with the help of the government. This layered variant is sometimes described as the 'cappuccino model'. In such an arrangement, the three types of social security can operate as communicating vessels: if the state pension is only partially adjusted for inflation, for example, this puts pressure on the funding or level of occupational and private pensions.

3.3.4 Informal elements in formal social security

Even though modern social security systems are typically highly formalised, informal institutions can theoretically still play an important role in them. This applies in particular to the role of complementary informal arrangements, the public support for formal rules, and the possible existence of deviating norms in some sections of the community.

Modern societies with extensive formal systems still can contain informal social security arrangements which play a supplementary role. Communal social security is not entirely without importance, although it is often invisible in the statistics. Examples might include activities such as those of the Salvation Army, Food Banks, and other organisations which combat the more severe forms of poverty on the basis of their moral or social conviction. Reference can also be made to companies which provide student grants to certain groups; to mutual non-profit arrangements (e.g. cooperative insurance schemes for trade union members, which can be regarded as the successors to the funds maintained by the guilds to support poor, sick or old guild members); and to provisions outside the monetary economy, such as the entitlements and duties contained in Local Exchange and Trading Schemes (LETS; cf. Seyfang, 2001; Williams et al., 2001).

It has already been mentioned that informal occupational social security is rather marginal in highly developed modern welfare states. Familial social security has undoubtedly lost much of its key role as well, but it has not been eradicated, as borne out by the following current examples:
- familial assistance where the collective provisions are absent or demand a high contribution from the recipient, for example the provision of childcare services by grandparents or other relatives when both parents are working;
- informal care, or help provided by people to their sick or needy relatives;
- financing children's higher education; this may take the form of the complete funding of education courses and living expenses by the parents, or the provision of extra resources by the extended family;
- incidental gifts and legacies;
- support in the event of acute financial problems, such as the replacement of consumer goods that are deemed necessary, paying off debts, acting as guarantor;
- migrants who provide financial support for relatives in their country of origin. This concerns, for instance, about a quarter of the Dutch households with roots in Morocco.[22]

The public support aspect relates to the question of how well the actual or proposed configuration of formal social security matches the views that prevail in the population. General notions on solidarity and fairness work through into – not always abundantly clear – opinions about the social risks that should be covered, the groups that ought to be eligible for that cover, the rights (benefit levels, duration, etc.) and duties that are considered appropriate, the desired sanction possibilities, and the strictness with which sanctions should be applied. There are two possible areas of tension here. In the first place, a part of the community may feel that government should produce more or different social security, while others think it should stay equal or be minimised. These differences of opinion were very prominent in the political struggle surrounding the construction of collective social security at the end of the 19th and early 20th century in many Western countries (cf. §3.7). In the second place, policymakers who are responsible for the government rules may believe that the collective interest is best served with a wider, narrower or different social security system, while the community may disagree. This antagonism arises particularly in times of government cutbacks, such as attempts to curb collective (pre-)pension arrangements, which in some countries have led to mass social protests. However, a situation can also arise where policymakers presume that the population needs different forms of social security (such as flexible collective arrangements with more individual freedom of choice), whereas public support for this turns out in practice not to be very extensive or to be highly specific (see e.g. Hoff & Vrooman, 2002).

Informal social security rules should ideally complement and support the formal rules. For instance, the conditions on job search requirements should in principle be endorsed by unemployment benefit recipients and those around them. In practice, however, certain groups may apply informal rules which are at odds with the formal social security rules. This idea is developed particularly in the research tradition that builds on the 'culture of poverty' which Lewis (1959, 1968, 1969) believed he observed in poor slums in Mexico, Puerto Rico and the USA. In his view, people living in such neighbourhoods are forced by the economic constraints to develop a particular strategy or philosophy for coping with their poverty, which is perpetuated in new generations (Lewis, 1969: 188):
> By the time slum children are age six or seven, they have usually absorbed the basic values and attitudes of their subculture and are not psychologically geared to take full advantage of changing conditions or increased opportunities which may occur in their lifetime.

Wilson (1987) stressed that a deviant culture such as this does indeed occur among the underclass in the large American cities, but that this cannot be seen in isolation from their structural position, in particular their weak connection to the labour market. In his view, the new urban poverty is so problematic primarily because the residents of poor inner-city neighbourhoods are predominantly unemployed, whereas in the past the working poor dominated; this is giving rise to 'jobless ghettos' (Wilson, 1997: 3-24).

This theme has been explored in the Netherlands in several qualitative studies focusing on the coping strategies of benefit recipients (cf. Kroft et al., 1989; Engbersen, 1989, 1990; Engbersen et al., 1993; Engbersen & Staring, 2000). This line of research mainly revealed that in many cases the reaction to benefit dependency was a traditional one, and was in line with formal rules and the norms and values that are considered dominant in Dutch society. A number of smaller groups, however, had deviating views on the acceptability of breaking rules, on the government, and on the advantages and disadvantages of working. This was reflected in rational strategic behaviour: even when their entitlements were doubtful, these groups were more inclined to apply for benefits and to continue drawing them.

3.3.5 Social security actors

The picture that was outlined in §2.7 in principle also applies for the actors in social security, their mutual relationships and their motivations. The actors here can be theoretically divided into current and potential beneficiaries (people in need of help, benefit claimants, insured parties), contributors (taxpayers and social insurance contributors), intermediating social security organisations (a local poor relief fund, a national social security administration) and other corporate actors (such as firms). Social security actors may have both corporate and individual agents. For instance, a board of trustees may be the corporate representative of a municipal poor relief fund, with local care officials acting as their individual agents; or a medical benefits institute may be the corporate agent of the national social security administration, and employ medical assessors as individual agents. Individual benefit recipients may have agents as well, e.g. trade unions and individual lawyers who represent their interests in legal procedures.

The actors do differ theoretically according to the type of system, as will become apparent in the description of social security interaction models in §3.5. Informal social security systems are generally based on fairly direct, local and personal exchanges between beneficiaries (those in need of help) and contributors (family, church, community, guild). The rules often allow for a fair amount of discretionary power, in that the rights and duties are defined in fairly vague terms. Sanctioning is largely informal (gossip, scandal) and the intermediate actors are often weakly developed.

In modern, formal social security systems, by contrast, these corporate actors and their agents occupy a central role, in the form of the massive social security bureaucracies. Firms are also important corporate actors, because their behaviour (hiring and firing, dealing with sickness) partly determines how many people need to fall back on social security. In formal social security systems the direct relationship between beneficiaries (claimants and recipients) and contributors (those paying taxes and social insurance premiums) is often broken; the exchange relationships are manifold, national and impersonal. Rights, duties, conditions and potential sanctions are laid down in detail in formal laws, regulations and administrative decrees. Informal sanctioning is of subordinate importance, although certain groups of benefit claimants may be regarded as less deserving than others, and for that reason be treated condescendingly.

There are several reasons why it is theoretically plausible to assume that actors in formal social security systems will be more inclined to defect than those in informal systems. The potential group of people with an entitlement is large, while the benefits of rule-breaking are relatively high and the plethora of rules offers a generous opportunity structure. The looser connection with the rules of communities and groups means the informal monitoring and sanctioning are weak. In combination with the low visibility of modern benefit dependency, this may result in a low risk of being caught in the event of defection. Finally, the collective nature of formal systems implies that the social dilemma inherent in social security comes to the fore explicitly. As the exchange is impersonal, in the short term defection does not affect anyone in particular; while in the longer term it only harms the government, which 'belongs to everyone and no one'. The way in which various models of rule-driven social security interaction can foster defection is discussed in more detail later. First, however, the question will be addressed of how actors acquire social security rules.

3.4 Undersocialised social security

In the previous chapter a number of principles were formulated concerning rule acquisition (see §2.8.3). This section develops the proposition that, following these principles, it is plausible that social security institutions are typically transferred to new actors rather late and not very intensively.

Generally speaking, people do not need social security rules at an early stage of life in order to be able to function in their social setting. Social security rules therefore do not usually form part of the primary socialisation process. Typically, this hiatus is only partly filled in adult life, as most actors do not apply social security rules on a day-to-day basis. Secondary socialisation consequently also occurs to only a limited extent. The exception to this is the rather small group of professional rule experts: policy officials who draft laws and regulations, administrators, judges and lawyers specialising in social security. In formal systems they usually go through an extensive and permanent process of socialisation in order to be able to continue practising their specialist profession properly. Furthermore, certain benefit recipients may acquire a detailed knowledge of the rules, becoming 'experts through experience' with regard to the rules that matter to them.

In informal social security systems a child may become broadly acquainted with the rules as a result of the actual and idiosyncratic experiences he and his family or community go through. The application of such rules of relief can leave a deep and lasting impression on children, as borne out by the frequent discussion of the theme 'growing up in poverty' in autobiographically tinted novels, from Charles Dickens' *Oliver Twist* (1837) to Frank McCourt's *Angela's Ashes* (1996). Also, in familial systems the socialisers have an interest in instilling some basic principles or expectations, as they are likely to become dependent on their children in old age. Yet this does not imply that the socialisees will understand the details of the rules: typically, children have only a dim notion of the specific informal social security rights, duties, conditions and sanctions their parents are faced with.

Formal social security rules are less likely to form part of the everyday experience of young socialisees. These institutions are often complex, abstract and ambiguous, so that it is difficult to acquire knowledge of their content, especially at an early age; this demands the cognitive ability to see the logic behind them, and a degree of moral awareness. Since parents normally have no direct interest in whether or not the socialisees are familiar with the formal rules – as the risks are covered at the impersonal level of the nation state – they have no strong inclination to undertake socialising acts in this domain. This is not made up for in the secondary socialisation process: in the educational curriculum formal social security rules often are covered only in very broad terms, if at all.

The foregoing makes it theoretically plausible that social security tends to be imprinted on the new generations in a very limited fashion; and that this 'undersocialised character of social security' is expressed more emphatically in formal than in informal systems.

The lack of internalisation implies that rational actors are likely to break the rules. There is no internal incentive which prevents contributors from keeping their payments to a minimum, or beneficiaries from striving to derive the greatest possible gains from social security arrangements. This can only be avoided if individual actors can be incited to behave in a way that would not seem rational in the short term, or through the establishment of an effective external monitoring and sanctioning system.

In familial social security systems, a number of factors work against defection. As stated, such rules may be socialised to some degree, partly because the socialisers have an interest in this. Even more important is the fact that the rules are based on long-term, highly affective relationships, in which reciprocity can also play a major role. As a result, it may indeed be 'unthinkable' for children not to support their elderly parents. But if the mutual relationships have become distorted, or if the resources of the adult children are too meagre, this is anything but self-evident.

In communal and occupational social security systems the affective ties between the stakeholders are generally less strong. Here, the obvious way to resolve the problem of the undersocialised nature of social security is to make the rules explicit, carefully monitoring compliance with them, and sanctioning infringements publicly. The risk of defective behaviour can be reduced further by keeping contributions at a reasonable level and restricting the rights as far as possible.

As the undersocialisation is theoretically greatest in formal social security systems, the risk of rule-breaking is highest here. This rapidly leads to a social dilemma: there is nothing to deter actors from seeking to maximise their personal utility, and in the long run this can make it impossible to keep the collective provisions intact. There are several ways of addressing this from a theoretical perspective, but they offer no fundamental solution to the problem of defection.

One way of attempting to tackle it might be by embedding the formal rules in informal ones and relying upon monitoring and sanctioning processes within the community. For instance, policymakers may try to link specific formal social security institutions (a certain duration of social assistance, the taxation level) to abstract values and norms in an attempt to justify them ('we have to look after the weaker members of society'; 'every citizen must stand on his own two feet'; 'we need to ensure that the money goes to those who genuinely need it'). Yet for various reasons it is likely that the embedding of formal rules in informal institutions will often be difficult to achieve. The translation of such abstracts into actual formal social security rules is an arbitrary process and cannot be imposed from above. An individual actor who does not share the general informal notions and their specific derivation in formal rules, and who is not put under any pressure to comply, can easily disregard them. Moreover, formal social security institutions often emerge precisely because communities are unable to sustain their informal systems based on shared values and norms, and on the affects and relationships of trust and authority between actors prevailing in well-defined social networks (cf. below). This makes it unlikely that such 'old solutions' can underpin specific formal attributions of rights and duties to any great extent.[23]

Legislators may also attempt to define formal social security rights, duties, conditions and sanctions in very strict terms, leaving as little room for manoeuvre as possible for the actors concerned; however, as stated earlier, a complete 'regimentation' is difficult to achieve in practice.

Alternatively, the government can increase its monitoring activities, and consistently mete out severe punishments for infringements. But this leads to high transaction costs; and as many infringements may be hard to detect, this strategy is in danger of becoming both ineffective and inefficient.

Finally, an attempt can be made to arrange the financial incentives in such a way that a rational actor will be encouraged to observe the rules which are regarded as collectively desirable. If the aim is to encourage benefit claimants to go to work, for example, one approach might be to maximise the difference between the total income transfers and the wages from employment. Yet there is often a practical limit to what is considered possible here. Increasing net wages costs employers or the government money, possibly with negative consequences for the economy as a whole (reduced investments, labour demand); cutting benefit levels in turn hits the spending power of households, potentially generating more poverty and other undesirable social effects. Quite apart from this, theoretically the behaviour of actors is not determined solely by financial incentives.

These considerations make it unlikely that the social dilemma inherent in formal social security systems can be entirely resolved. Even so, much depends on the structure of interaction among the parties concerned, and the particular course taken in actual behavioural exchange.

3.5 Models of rule-driven social security interactions

If social security rules exist, how do they influence the interactions between actors? To answer this question, a number of theoretical interaction models are explored in more detail in this section, building on the analysis in §2.8.

All social security interactions start with the *granting of certain rights* to beneficiaries by individual benefactors or corporate actors (e.g., the local administration), in accordance with the prevailing stipulations. The rights relate to the three theoretical interventions introduced above: the behavioural interactions which aim at the *prevention, restoration* or *compensation* of a lack or loss of income, labour, health and social participation. Logically, the *imposition* and *collection of the contributions* needed to fund the interventions also form part of the rule-driven interactions of social security. If there is no direct transaction between beneficiaries and benefactors, this requires exchanges between the duty-bound collectors and a collecting intermediary authority (a revenue officer, a fund). Further common types of interaction relate to *monitoring* and *sanctioning*: checking whether actors are sticking to the rules and imposing rewards and punishments accordingly.

The way in which these eight types of interaction are applied in practice, and which actors are involved, is not fixed. The actual interactions in social security can differ widely between, e.g., systems in which family relationships are at the core, and systems that are built mainly around government rules. The former lack an intermediating corporate actor, while in formal systems there is generally a social security organisation acting as the 'spider in the web'. In familial systems the rights and duties tend to be less clearly specified, and certain interventions (e.g. prevention) are rare. Monitoring often is close, but the expected sanctions in case of defection tend to be unpredictable.

Within one and the same type of social security system the interaction pattern may vary with the specific risk covered. For example, in cases of unemployment and retirement the behavioural interactions governed by formal social security regulations are often different. Unemployment benefit recipients usually are expected to look for a job, and old age pensioners are not. And even if the risk and social security type are the same, a great deal of variety in the behavioural exchanges is possible. For example, the interaction pattern linked to formal unemployment benefit schemes may differ widely between two countries, owing to differences in national legislation and in the informal expectations of the actors concerned.

This great variation makes it difficult to pin down the interaction patterns in social security unambiguously. Six theoretical models are developed in this section. These should be regarded as stylised types, which in practice may be subject to many empirical variations and exceptions. First, an indication is given of how the behavioural interactions between actors can be structured in three models of informal social security: familial, communal and occupational systems (§3.5.1-3.5.3). This is followed by a discussion of three interaction types of formal social security (§3.5.4-3.5.6). These relate respectively to systems designed to cover demographic risks (old age, surviving dependants, costs of children); unemployment and social assistance; and sickness absence and disability. In the discussion of each theoretical interaction model three central questions are at stake:
1. What is the interaction structure; or, which actors are involved in which types of interaction?
2. To what extent are the interactions rule-driven?
3. What is the theoretical likelihood of rule-compliance and defection?

3.5.1 Familial social security

Actors and interactions
Figure 3.1 presents a relatively simple interaction model of familial social security. Like all graphs in this section, this is an enlargement of a segment of the figural model presented in §2.3; it zooms in on the actors and the types of interaction[24] that are driven by social security rules.

Each family (1 ...n) is depicted as an individual subsystem of social security, which is embedded in a wider community. In this variant there are no support relationships between families. The interactions between the generations of blood relatives lie at the heart of the system: within one family the *parents*, *grandparents* and *children* provide mutual material support. In principle, most of the support in the three-generation family is provided by the parents. As they are in a productive phase of life they have the means to support family members, and it is logical that the duty of assuring the rights of younger and older family members rests on them. However, this obligation is not inevitable. If the earning capacity of the parents disappears partly or completely (e.g. due to death, illness or unemployment), the rights and duties may come to lie elsewhere. The younger generation might then for example have to interrupt their education in order to earn money for the family, or grandparents may be expected to make a financial or material contribution, e.g. by selling their house.

Other family members may also be involved in this form of social security: brothers/sisters, uncle/aunts, nephews/nieces and distant relatives. In the variant presented here their role is a subsidiary one; they may be enlisted if it proves impossible to obtain the support needed within the three generations. However, it is also possible for this type of system to be based on the wider family network, as in clan-based systems.

In familial social security systems such as that portrayed in figure 3.1, the relationships between the actors are direct: there is no intermediating agent who collects and redistributes the means. There are also no corporate actors, but only directly involved individuals. These two structural features mean that this type of interaction model is in principle free of the principal-agent problem described in the previous chapter (see §2.3, §2.7). In addition, all relationships are reciprocal: each member of the family system can be both a beneficiary and a contributor. The interactions are also repeated and sequential. The exchange does not take place immediately, but extends over the entire life of the family members concerned, with earlier duties only leading to rights much later, and vice versa. Finally, in the familial social security model there is no clear relationship between the individual contributions and returns. People are generally expected to offer and receive support at the moment that a need arises. For some this works out advantageously, for others disadvantageously (e.g. depending on whether needy grandparents are short or long-lived). At the system level – viewed across all families – it may be assumed that the costs and benefits in the long term are roughly in balance, since otherwise the sustainability of this social security model is jeopardised.

The central mode of interaction in the model is the provision of material support in money or in kind (board, lodgings, care) to family members. The entitling eventuality is the indigence, or material want, of any of the family members, which often manifests itself as a sudden situation of need (loss of a breadwinner, grandparents becoming too weak to continue working). The risks are relatively unspecified: the cause of the need and its culpability are not relevant. The family member requiring help generally has to ask for it. The support provided reinforces the implicit agreements within the family: the person providing it strengthens his entitlement to future help if he should ever suffer acute material want. For those receiving the support the reverse applies: their duty to provide support in the future to family members needing help is heightened.

In addition, the social security interactions consist mainly of monitoring the informal rights and duties and applying sanctions in the event of defection. Gossip and the threat of squandering the right to future family support play an important role here. The sanctioning can also be reinforced by the wider community to which the family belongs. The other theoretical types of interaction are less important in this model. It is mainly

Figure 3.1
Interaction model I: familial social security

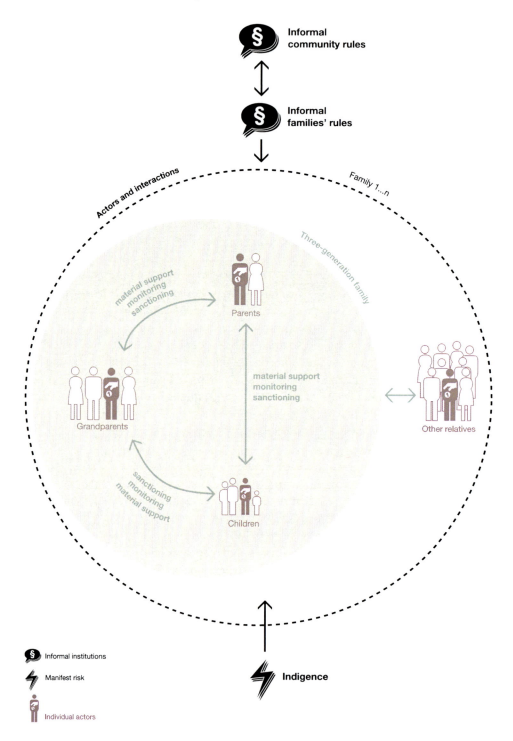

concerned with immediate provision; interventions geared to prevention and restoration of those in need are almost nonexistent. There is also usually no clear collecting function: support is generally provided on the basis of the directly mobilisable resources within the family.

Familial social security institutions

Figure 3.1 shows that the interaction is mainly driven by the informal rules of the family, which are embedded in the wider community of which the family forms part. The behavioural expectations regarding cases of indigence are socialised only moderately, but more so than in formal social security systems. They relate to general values such as 'it is right if family members help each other' and derived norms such as 'someone who is able to do so should support their parents when they are in need'. At the family level, this translates into specific norms and conventions governing the entitlements and obligations between the members: a certain consensus within the family on the applicable rights and duties, and the willingness to monitor compliance and punish defection.

This demands a reasonably homogeneous structure of views and sufficient 'connectedness' within the family. Even then, the informal institutions and the derivations between them often are vague: the norm cited above leaves unanswered the question of the degree to which people should support their parents, for how long, and in what way; and within a family, the applicable rights and obligations may remain implicit until an emergency arises. In this model, therefore, although the interaction is driven by informal rules, the actors concerned retain a great deal of latitude in interpreting their rights and duties.

There are a number of disadvantages to social security systems driven by the informal rules of the family. People with a limited network (widows and orphans without relatives, elderly persons without children) have few duties, but also virtually no rights if they find themselves in need of help. Moreover, the risks within a family need not be independent. Where a community has closed social structure, with little social mobility and homogeneous strata (classes, estates, castes), risks such as unemployment, disability and having a large number of children often weigh disproportionately on certain families at the lower end of the social scale. If someone from the bottom strata loses their job during an economic crisis, the likelihood that their family members will suffer the same fate is high. Even where there is an extensive network and a great willingness to provide mutual support, families from the lower strata often see the support capacity become insufficient at the moment that the need for such aid increases.

Finally, there is usually a degree of asymmetry within the family between the providers and recipients of support: it is generally the relatively wealthy family members who pay and the poorer ones who receive. For the wealthier family members this may present a problem if the need for support by their relatives is so great that it limits their behavioural alternatives. They may for example not be able to invest the money that is spent on the family in things that produce a greater return (such as business activities, education for themselves or their children). On the other hand, poorer family members who will probably never be able to repay their material debt may feel obliged to provide some form of non-material compensation. They may try to accomplish this by adopting a subservient attitude towards their benefactors, by bestowing honour on them, or by granting them authority; but this of course restricts their own options of behaviour.

Compliance and defection in familial social security
The freedom of action allowed to the family members has consequences for the extent to which defective behaviour theoretically occurs. The vagueness of the rules means that infringements are difficult to establish. This can give rise to family arguments about the correct rule interpretation, for example on the question of who should take the widowed grandfather who can no longer look after himself into their home, and what the hosts should receive in return for this.

In the second place, the rights and duties are determined not only by the degree of need, but also by chance, arbitrariness and the existing affective relationships. The apple of the family's eye, the one who meets all the expectations of the family, or to whom a high earning capacity is ascribed, can often count on more support and fewer duties than the black sheep, those who marry beneath their station, or those who are not expected ever to bring in any money. Familial social security systems can thus readily be perceived as unfair.

Defective behaviour is also made more likely by the fact that the rules are only moderately socialised and there is no government to enforce them. Actors can therefore always decide not to comply with the rules. The likelihood of this increases as the burdens become heavier to bear and the expected future gains more uncertain. This occurs in particular where there is an accumulation of risks (mass unemployment, large numbers of children and elderly relatives to care for); when the connectedness or homogeneity of views within the family declines; or when the wider community no longer enforces the family rules.

3.5.2 Communal social security

Actors and interactions
In the Introduction to this study, an example was given of an interaction pattern that is characteristic of communal social security. The 'Regulations governing the provision of care to the home-dwelling poor' (*Reglement op de verzorging der Huisarmen*) in the town of Den Bosch express in a nutshell what kind of behaviour is expected of the actors in such a system. In figure 3.2 an interaction structure of this type is elaborated more systematically. The central acts are applying for poor relief; the assessment of the applicant's entitlement and the actual distribution of monetary or material support to the families; monitoring and sanctioning; and the collecting of the necessary funds. Where they occur at all, interventions focused on prevention, restoration and (re)integration are of secondary importance.

The *potential beneficiaries* are members of the local community. To be eligible for social security there must be a recognised want, or case of indigence, and the potential beneficiary must ask for help. The applicants must meet certain qualifying and behavioural conditions (no help available from family, good moral conduct, doing something in return).

In this type of system there is an intermediating corporate actor: a *local social security organisation*, for example in the form of a communal poor relief institute. The *board* is the most powerful corporate agent in the communal social security organisation, with their members acting as individual agents. They define and interpret the 'rules of relief', supervise the attendants and collectors, and manage the funds. Sometimes they also have final responsibility for the awarding of rights and imposition of duties. In the Regulations from Den Bosch, the Council of Regents fulfilled this central role. Colleges such as these were often more than a management board, being closely connected with the administration and often acting as defenders of the rules of the community. They verified the nominations put forward by the local poor relief officials by making home visits and thereafter establishing the entitlement of the party concerned. They also ensured that the written rules of relief and their implementation corresponded with the rules that applied within the community, at least among the dominant groups. These boards generally did not accurately reflect the composition of the local population, but were constituted through co-option from the better-off members of the community.[25]

The *attendants* are the most visible individual agents of the communal organisation. They are charged with the intake and with the administration of the system. In discharging this administrative task, they are first of all responsible for distributing benefits that have been awarded, for example to the needy poor. However, they are also responsible for permanent monitoring (to establish whether the need still exists, that there is no evidence of "continuous bad behaviour", etc.) and for the imposition of negative sanctions (e.g. temporarily withholding benefit). They normally have fairly wide-ranging discretionary authority. In the example given in the Introduction, the local officials caring for the poor acted as the attendants.

The *collectors* also play a key role, being responsible for collecting contributions, for example by means of home visits or a church collection, which they must then pay to the fund manager in the board.

The *contributors* in such a system generally come from the more well-to-do ranks of the local community. They raise the funds of the communal social security system through voluntary gifts (including church collections) and legacies. However, the corporate actors may also have access to their own resources. For example, the church poor relief boards in the past sometimes had significant income from the possession of land, property and securities. In addition, a part of the proceeds of the municipal tax levies was sometimes earmarked for communal social security. It was also possible that local taxes on certain articles (e.g. bread, beer) were used to fund the social security system, so that the beneficiaries of this form of social security also helped to fund it partially (for the Netherlands see: Van Loo, 1987: 35).

Figure 3.2
Interaction model II: communal social security

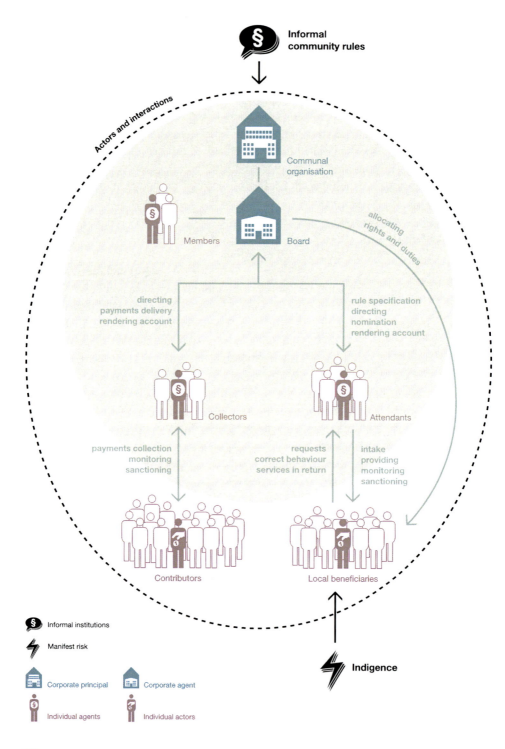

Communal social security institutions

Communal social security is based chiefly on the informal rules of the community concerned. Sometimes those rules are laid down in writing by the board of the communal organisation, in the form of regulations such as those in Den Bosch, which can then be seen as a codification of the informal institutions. A typical feature of this form of social security is that the entitlements of the beneficiaries are constrained considerably. In order to minimise the costs for the community as well as free-rider behaviour, their rights are meagre and the conditions the applicants have to fulfil are strongly emphasised. However, those conditions are defined only vaguely, with the criteria for measuring 'virtuous conduct', 'industriousness displayed in meeting one's own needs', and so on, not being specified.

By contrast, the behaviour of the intermediary actors is generally less rule-driven. The Den Bosch example shows that the attendants had a high degree of autonomy in determining how the rights, conditions and duties should be interpreted, in the assessment of defective behaviour, and in the imposition of sanctions. In communal social security the payments made by the contributors often are voluntary as well. These discretionary elements in the system are only constrained through the general informal rules of the community. Reciprocal expectations may in fact have mandatory force if the intermediary actors regard them as self-evident, given their position within the community and their convictions. Yet this need not necessarily be the case. Because there is no power residing above the parties, the beneficiaries cannot enforce their rights; ultimately, they are dependent on the mercy of the attendants and the favours that the well-to-do are willing to bestow on them. Communal systems of social security therefore often tend towards reproduction of the existing social hierarchy.

Compliance and defection in communal social security

Defection by the beneficiaries can theoretically occur in this system if they bring about their own indigence. The possibility of such inducements is implied in the graph by the relationship between the manifest risk and the local beneficiaries. However, there are several factors that make it unlikely that this type of intentional rule-breaking will occur very frequently in communal social security systems. The target group is usually limited to the 'deserving poor', and the support offered is fairly unappealing: it is meagre, the application test is severe and often humiliating, and being on poor relief often entails a considerable loss of social status. Moreover, strict checks are carried out to ensure that the beneficiaries continue to meet the conditions, and the negative sanctions of rule-breaking are generally heavy. In addition, monitoring and sanctioning are not only carried out by those who are officially charged to do so (the attendants), but are also often reinforced by the wider community through gossip and heaping disgrace on rule-breakers. The beneficiaries are generally people who have no alternative and who cannot afford to lose the communal support. All these factors mean that the costs of defection are generally higher than the gains, and compliance is a rational course of action for people relying on poor relief. This is not to say that defection never occurs: households that are no longer in need may still try to continue receiving support in order to build up a reserve, and families which do not meet the moral standards (for example because of alcoholism, unplanned pregnancies) may attempt to hide the facts. But the likelihood of these attempts succeeding is not very high, because of the regular checks carried out to assess the rights (as in the Den Bosch example, where support was meted out on a seasonal basis), and the intensive official and informal monitoring and sanctioning processes that occur. Still, in extreme situations groups of beneficiaries may defect, for example in the form of food riots and foraying in times of famine.

Theoretically, the defection problem is greater among the individual agents of the corporate actor. Their wide discretionary powers can quickly lead to arbitrary and capricious decisions. In contrast to the previous interaction model, the principal-agent problem emerges clearly from figure 3.2. It is by no means a given that the individual members of the board will serve the interests of the community in specifying the rules and supervising the collectors and attendants, as numerous historical examples indicate.[26] The subordinate individual agents do not automatically act as their board wishes either. Attendants may for example give preferential treatment to friends and family, collectors may run off with the cash.

There is also a real chance of defection on the part of the contributors. As their contributions are generally voluntary and not highly visible, they can in principle neglect their duty. Compliance can be stimulated if the informal rules make the required contribution explicit, and if the collectors and the community reinforce this by means of strict monitoring and consistent imposition of sanctions. Yet this is not always possible: there may be no consensus on the contribution level, the transaction costs that would be involved may be considered too high, and heterogeneous, 'unconnected' communities may not be capable of strict enforcement.

3.5.3 Informal occupational social security

Actors and interactions
Informal occupational social security occurs where rights and duties are founded in the employment relationship without being enforced by the government. They may for example consist of a company scheme for childcare or the reimbursement of medical expenses, company study grants for employees' children, or an emergency fund for employees. Generally speaking, such provisions are aimed at maintaining or improving the labour productivity of the employees, as a means of supporting the usual business activities. Yet they need not be additional: it is also possible to establish an entire system of informal social security on the employment relationship, as in the social support provided by the European guilds in the pre-industrial age. Although the employment history plays a key role in the pure model of social insurance (cf. table 3.1) and in 'second pillar' provisions as well, it should be pointed out that the latter are not specimens of informal occupational social security. Social insurance and mandatory occupational schemes are formal arrangements: the government lays down the social security rights and duties

of employees and employers in national law, or publicly acknowledges the contracts between these private parties.

Theoretically many variants on the interaction structure of informal occupational social security are possible.[27] Figure 3.3 shows a fairly simple example which relates to a small firm with a single owner-director. There is no involvement by the government, trade unions, employers or external supervisors, and administration of the system takes place within the firm. There are three types of individual actor: the owner-director of the firm; the bookkeeper; and the employees. The *owner-director* is an individual principal and sets aside a budget from the company funds, instructs the bookkeeper and, as the person with the ultimate responsibility, takes the final decision on the rules in cases of doubt. The *bookkeeper* is an individual agent of the owner and is accountable to him. He is responsible for the practical aspects of administration: the intake, the allocation of rights and duties (possibly backed by the signature of the owner), the actual distribution and the processing of relevant mutations. Finally, he has to monitor the correctness of the awarded rights and duties, and must where necessary impose sanctions.

The *employees* may be required to register voluntarily as participants in the occupational scheme, although this may also take place tacitly or be mandatory. In some cases they have to apply for help, and when it is granted the beneficiaries can be obliged to report any mutations that could affect their right to it (e.g. the composition of the household, number of hours worked, additional sources of income). In the model it is assumed that the company acts as the contributor, but it is also possible that the employees are required to make a contribution and thus to fund the system themselves to some extent.

Occupational social security institutions

The rights and duties, their conditions and the potential sanctions associated with such an occupational social security system may be laid down in a written firm statute, but may also be based on a firm practice that has developed over the years, with wide discretionary powers for the owner-director and the bookkeeper. Such informal company rules to some extent reflect the values, norms and conventions of the community in which the firm operates, and of groups within the firm. Sometimes they may also be related to a certain professional ethic, especially in organisations dominated by highly trained professionals (such as a law firm).

Compliance and defection in occupational social security

From a theoretical point of view, the main form of defection in such an occupational social security system lies with the employees. They may apply while they are not entitled, or, if they have been granted entitlements, they may not report relevant changes in their situation. Certain factors make employee defection more likely. In the first place, the employees' relationship with their company may primarily be market-based, as specified in their employment contract. They sell their labour capacity to the organisation in return for a certain wage, and the company uses the labour input to try and achieve its

Figure 3.3
Interaction model III: informal occupational social security

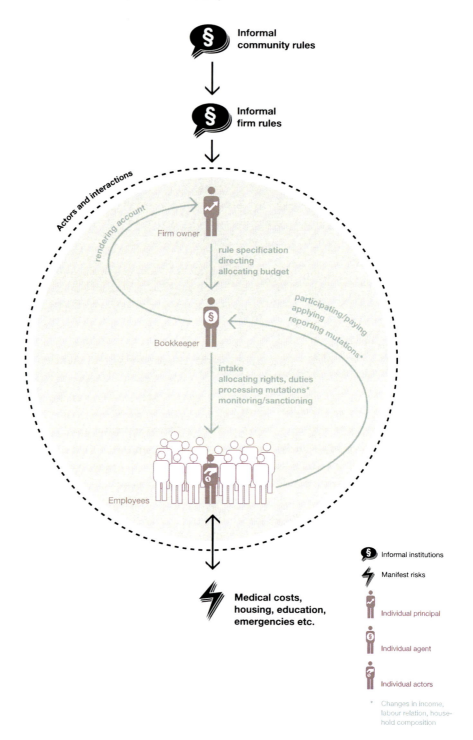

corporate aims (making a profit, serving the public). It was noted earlier that in such commodified circumstances rational defection is theoretically more likely to occur than in situations where affective relationships dominate: stealing from the boss is often considered less reprehensible than breaking the rules shared with family or friends. However, there can be wide differences between organisations on this point: in non-profit associations that pursue a certain ideal the everyday conduct of management and workers may be driven less by costs and benefits than in commercial enterprises, which may reduce the likelihood of rule-breaking.

Defection is also fostered by the fact that company rules are generally socialised relatively late. People only become familiar with them during their training and when they work at the company concerned, and actors can ignore such recent behavioural guidelines more easily than the norms, values and conventions that they have known for years. This is particularly true when the occupational institutions differ markedly from the rules that apply in the wider community. However, there are also organisations with a powerful integrated culture, which is transferred via an intensive process of secondary socialisation. This may reduce the risk of defection, though it is plausible that a 'company moral' is never fully internalised.

Another factor that tends to increase the chance of defection is that monitoring and sanctioning are often poorly developed in occupational social security systems. For the bookkeeper this is a secondary task, and the number of cases of fraud uncovered and the amounts of money involved may not justify the high costs of monitoring and sanctioning. The imposition of sanctions is often limited to demanding the return of the surplus that was provided, possibly supplemented by a negative entry in the personnel file. Very serious cases (involving large amounts, repeated and sustained fraud) may lead to dismissal (either immediate or following a legal procedure) and criminal prosecution, but this is often the exception rather than the rule. Close monitoring and consistent imposition of sanctions can have a negative effect on the motivation of staff and on the external image of the company, and a certain degree of defection may therefore be tolerated, as a form of 'slack'.

On the other hand, there are also factors which make compliance in occupational systems likely. There is frequently a complex exchange which extends over a long period. Utilisation of occupational social security constitutes only one element of the employment relationship, and defective behaviour may have wider consequences. An employee who is caught breaking the rules may not only face direct sanctions (demands for repayment) but may also no longer be regarded as reliable or trustworthy, may be assigned different duties, be passed over for promotion, etc. The gains that are set against these potentially heavy indirect costs may sometimes be considered too small. Many of these provisions are supplementary in nature, and as long as the chance of being caught is not negligible rational actors will not be willing to risk their position in the long term for a relatively small short-term advantage. People are less inclined to commit fraud with a small medical expenses claim if there is a fair chance that they will lose their job if they are discovered.

In addition, defective behaviour is sometimes quite visible because the company holds a large amount of information on the employees and because of the daily contacts with colleagues. That applies in particular if the conditions that confer entitlement are verifiable, as in the case of an occupational pre-pension scheme (age, contributions paid).

It can be deduced from the foregoing under which circumstances employee rule-breaking becomes more likely in occupational social security systems. The chance of defection is greater in commercial companies with a high staff turnover (large numbers of short-term contracts, temporary agency staff, casual labour) and where the contacts between employees are not very intensive. A weak corporate culture with many unsocialised new employees also exacerbates the defection problem. Generous provisions can make the potential gains of defection substantial, especially where the beneficiaries include a relatively large number of low-paid workers. If this is combined with a low risk of discovery (because infringements are not easy to discover, or because monitoring and sanctioning are not practised very intensively), defection may become an attractive option.

It is also possible that the other actors in informal occupational social security systems do not comply. There is a principal-agent problem in the relationship between the owner-director and the bookkeeper. The latter may neglect his administrative tasks or fail to apply his discretionary powers consistently (nepotism, requiring something in return, running off with the money).

Defection by the owner-director is not altogether unlikely either. For instance, he may refuse to make available sufficient funds, or may specify the rules in an arbitrary or patronising way. The owner-director can be especially inclined to do so if he regards the business as his autocratic possession and the negotiating power of the employees is limited. On the other hand, the likelihood of defection by the principal theoretically is curtailed due to the high costs it may incur: a negative impact on the firm's reputation, and on the motivation and social climate within the firm.

3.5.4 Formal demographic regulations

Actors and interactions
The fourth interaction model concerns the formal systems designed to cover demographic risks: collective old age and surviving dependants' pensions, and governmental arrangements designed to help meet the costs of raising children (e.g. through child benefit). The group of *potential beneficiaries* in figure 3.4 is no longer limited to members of the family, the local community or employees within a single company, but generally extends to all people covered by the law (residents, employees, certain sectors of industry). The *contributors* in this system may be employees, employers or the residents who pay direct or indirect taxes (VAT, customs duty) or social security contributions. It is also possible that contributions are not earmarked, but that the government sets aside a certain budget from the general tax revenue.

Beneficiaries and contributors are not in a direct relationship with each other in this model and generally do not know each other. A fairly complex social security organisation functions as an intermediary. The *board* of directors is the key corporate agent of the organisation and is responsible for the general strategy. It also acts as a principal, as it is responsible for running the various organisational units. The members of the board are their individual agents.

In the model there are three corporate agents who have to render account to the board; each of these fulfils a specific theoretical function. There is a *fund*, which is responsible for imposing and collecting contributions and administering the monies collected. In an insurance system this fund may also be charged with advising on the level of premiums on the basis of actuarial principles. Where the system is funded from general means the fixing of premiums is a political responsibility. In that case, policymakers may not act in an actuarially correct manner, but may also take into account the consequences for the income position of beneficiaries and contributors, and weigh the allocation of funds to the demographic social security systems against other budgetary items.

Benefits and provisions are delivered by a *benefits agency* in this model. The agency is responsible for the intake, and establishes whether the covered eventuality has occurred, i.e. whether applicants have reached a certain age, whether their partner or parent has died, or whether they are responsible for looking after children. The benefits agency also verifies whether potential beneficiaries meet the applicable qualifying conditions, such as having paid the required premiums over a certain length of time, having fulfilled the minimum number of years of employment, being residents, being in a particular type of household, etc. The third component of the social security organisation, the *monitoring/ sanctioning agency*, verifies that the payments collected and benefits paid are correct and imposes sanctions where necessary.

These three entities are borne by the *officials* who take care of the actual administrative process. They are individual agents of the benefits agency, the monitoring and sanctioning agency, and the fund. The processing of mutations is also part of their task. Among beneficiaries, this mainly relates to changes in the household situation and, if their right depends on it, the level and sources of income. On the side of the contributors, changes in all factors that affect the level of contributions (income, type of employment relationship, age, tax bracket) are important.

Compensation is the central type of intervention in formal demographic regulations. The interactions of the social security organisation with potential beneficiaries and contributors generally relate to the provision of benefits or pensions, and the collection of the payments required to fund those. Typically, prevention and restoration of losses are not at stake in this kind of regulation: ageing, the death of an earning partner or parent, and the costs of child-rearing usually to a large extent are unavoidable events, and it is impossible or undesirable to restore the prior situation. It may be that a social support task is attributed to the social security organisation, for example the aim to combat loneliness among the elderly. Since such activities tend to be rather limited, they have been allocated to the benefits agency in this model, rather than to an independent unit of the social security organisation.

Naturally, the structure of the social security organisation may be different in practice. For example, the three entities may each have its own board, or they may not be as strictly

Figure 3.4
Interaction model IV:
formal demographic social security regulations

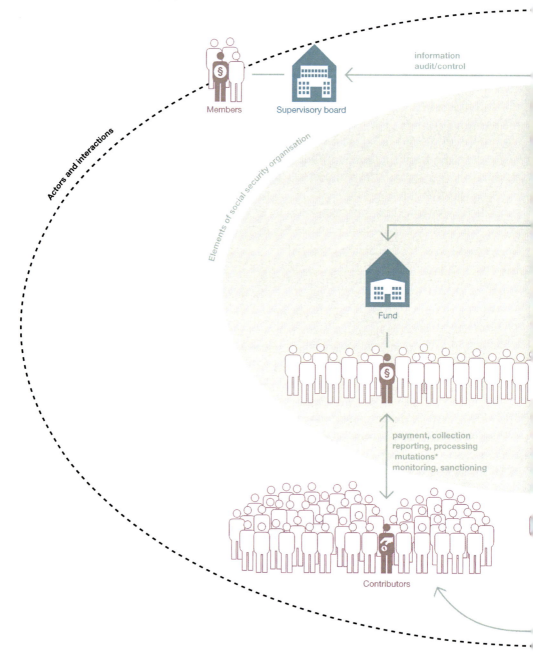

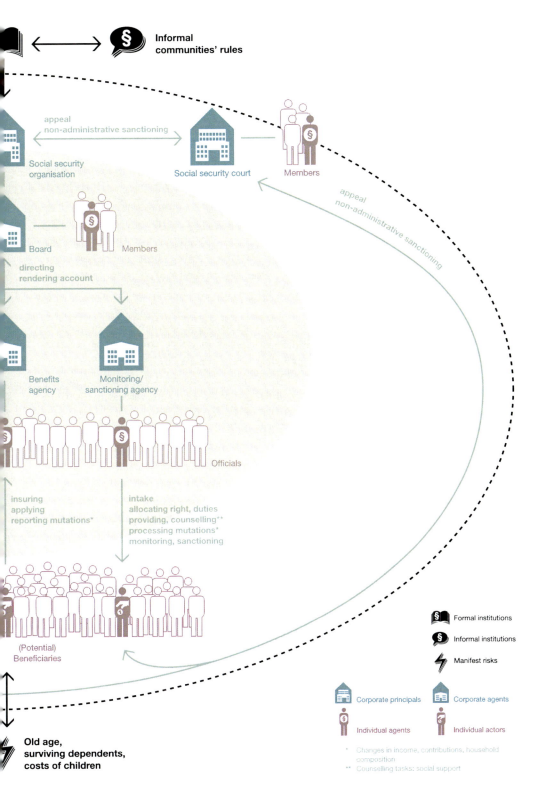

segregated as they are shown here. The number of actors may also be greater, for example if each scheme is operated by a separate social security organisation (e.g. for child benefit, pensions in certain sectors of industry), each with its own board, fund, administrative apparatus and monitoring/sanctioning mechanisms. There may also be greater differentiation within each function, for example with separate departments for carrying out investigations and imposing sanctions. In this (and the next) model of formal social security it is assumed that the government (country, region, municipality) has direct responsibility for the 'output': in other words, the social security organisation is a government agency. It is however also possible for the administration to be left to an autonomous body, to community-based organisations (such as churches, trade unions, employers or their representatives, patient associations, or combinations of these), the potential beneficiaries (mutual societies or associations) or to commercial companies. If the government gives their interventions a statutory basis and supervises their activities, this is still a formal social security system. Evidently, the growing number of actors, each with their own, partially differing interests, does theoretically increase the principal-agent problem in the social security organisation.

A further two corporate principals are shown outside the social security organisation in the model. There is a *social security court* in which beneficiaries, contributors and the units of the social security organisation can all appear as both plaintiffs and defendants. Administrative decisions may be argued or ratified here, and sanctions can be imposed which do not normally form part of the competence of the social security organisation (e.g. custodial sentences). The social security court is often hierarchically differentiated, in that decisions by the lower judges can sometimes be overruled by higher magistrates (a Court of Appeal, a Supreme Court, rulings by the European Court of Justice). There may also be various courts for separate social security arrangements (a Pensions Court). It is also possible that some social security issues are placed within the general legal system (civil or criminal courts), e.g. benefit fraud exceeding a certain amount.

The final actor is the *supervisory board*, which audits and controls the social security organisation. It may be a separate organisation with independent members or, on the contrary, representatives of the various interest groups or factions within the community. It may also be an inspectorate within the government. Obviously, the members of the social security court and the supervisory boards are individual agents of their organisation.

Institutions of formal demographic social security

In figure 3.4 the behaviour of the actors is driven primarily by the content of the formal demographic social security systems. These often define the rights and duties of beneficiaries and contributors in great detail, and also establish the specific interpretation of events and qualifying conditions by means of protocols, administrative decrees, etc. The decisions of the social security court additionally lead to the creation of detailed jurisprudence, which serves as a guide for the handling of future cases – a source of path dependence in the rule specification. The precise duties and powers of the social security organisation, and the relations between the board and the individual entities, are often laid down in separate organisational laws.

The content of formal demographic systems and informal institutions may be expected to correspond to a certain extent. The rights, duties, conditions and potential sanctions contained in the demographic regulations will reflect the wishes and ideas of dominant groups in the community to some degree, and the existence of such arrangements evokes expectations among the population.

Theoretically, however, the correlation is weaker than in the earlier informal interaction models. As mentioned before, it is difficult to embed formal systems in informal institutions. The relationships between actors are typically national, impersonal and indirect; their abstract nature implies they are no part of everyday life within the family, the local community or specific firms. Furthermore, it should be noted that in a democratic society formal systems are the result of a complicated policy process. The continuous exchange of rule wishes between representatives of various groups has its own dynamic (cf. the discussion of rule-interaction in §2.9). The filter of the policy process means that the formal rules do not automatically reflect the informal rule wishes, even where the latter are fairly uniform.

On the other hand, it is difficult to imagine that the gap between the formal regulations and the informal rules will be extremely wide, at least on rule elements which a large majority of the population consider important. If this were the case, in a democratic society the responsible policymakers are in danger of being dismissed.

Compliance and defection in formal demographic regulations

There is a greater risk of defection in this interaction model than in the previous ones. A first reason is existence of a complex *social security organisation*. The board does not automatically do what is in the interests of the organisation, and the individual members of the board may allow personal motives to weigh more heavily than their official administrative responsibilities. The three corporate agents – fund, benefits agency and monitoring/sanctioning agency – may not act in accordance with the wishes of the board, and may fail in their duty of accountability. This may occur because the interests of the entity (e.g. keeping as many officials as possible employed) are in conflict with those of the organisation as a whole (paying benefits correctly and with as few staff as possible). Individual officials may also allow their own interests to prevail over those of their organisational entity and their clients, or may become embroiled in internal battles about tasks and priorities. Comparable problems of defection can occur in the relationship between the supervisory board and the social security court on the one hand and the social security organisation on the other (inadequate supervision, non-impartial court rulings), and between the members of those external bodies and the corporate actor they are supposed to represent (a supervisor that defends particular interests, an alcoholic judge rendering erratic verdicts).

Finally, the influence of external stakeholders (political parties, trade unions, employers) may imply that the actual administration of the demographic social security regulations neglects the original objectives laid down by the legislator. They may for example advocate levies which are too low from an actuarial point of view, in order to bring about a reduction in the tax burden, or to compensate employers and households for the negative income consequences of other government measures. Or they may be in favour of a more lenient or stricter monitoring and sanctioning policy than the legislator intended, depending on their ideological preferences and their perception of the wishes of their supporters and electorate. If these political entrepreneurs have formal powers (e.g. via budgetary or appointment rights), or exercise a strong influence on the board via their network, it may be difficult for the social security organisation to ignore such wishes.

In summary, the principal-agent problem is theoretically considerable in this interaction model, because of the large number of parties with partially conflicting interests, and the possibility of intervention by external stakeholders. The likelihood that intermediary actors will not pursue their duties is exacerbated by the considerable financial flows and the complexity of administration and supervision; the benefits of defection may be high, the risk of discovery negligible.

Yet there are also factors which may help limit defection of this type. A first one has to do with the specific nature of demographic social security regulations. As the main focus is on the compensation of income lacks or losses, the social security organisation does not have to set priorities relative to other types of intervention (such as risk prevention or employment placement). Since both the events that give an entitlement to provisions and the contributions structure are fairly simple, the latitude allowed to the social security organisation is smaller than in, say, the administration of an unemployment or disability benefit regulation. The range of tasks to be carried out is also less complex in some respects. Typically, a large majority of applicants are entitled, and the selection of beneficiaries 'at the gate' is therefore less complicated in demographic systems. The fact that rights of this type often are rather stable reduces the likelihood of administrative errors in processing mutations. Retirement pension is usually paid until the death of the recipient; surviving dependants' pension generally lasts until the recipient becomes eligible for retirement pension or finds a new partner; and parents commonly are entitled to family benefit until the children reach a certain age or start working.

In addition, there are also ways of actively limiting defection in the social security organisation. A first way is to specify the powers of the board, the various entities and the officials in great detail, for example in an organisational law. If the interests and competences are laid down clearly, if the actors concerned have a strong incentive to carry out their tasks properly (e.g. through financial and reputation incentives), and if there is efficient and impartial auditing and control by the supervisory board, the risk of defection can be reduced.

The culture within the social security organisation may also prove to be decisive. It is not a company seeking to maximise profit, but a government agency whose task is to serve the public interest. If the officials and their superiors regard themselves as civil servants in a literal sense, this can keep defection within bounds. But it is not self-evident this will occur; it demands intensive secondary socialisation of the formal rules and a certain *esprit de corps*, together with an appropriate remuneration policy (salary, responsibilities, social esteem).

The most visible forms of defection by *beneficiaries* in demographic regulations consist of obtaining benefits without being entitled or failure to report changes. In a notorious fraud case dating from 1999, for example, a Dutch claimant obtained EUR 4,500 net per month in benefits, among other things by claiming child allowance for seven minors belonging to other family members residing in the UK – including a top-up amount because the children were 'living away from home'.[28] And in the administration of pensions and surviving dependants' benefit schemes, variations on Gogol's *Dead Souls* crop up with some regularity.[29]

Several factors encourage such types of defection. The amounts involved are considerable, and this of course is attractive for the low income groups in particular. The interaction between beneficiaries and the social security organisation is much less intensive and frequent than in the previous interaction models, and partly takes place through written correspondence. This makes defective behaviour less visible, a problem exacerbated by the fact that those close to the beneficiaries are not responsible for monitoring and sanctioning, and do not experience any individual disadvantage if their relatives break the rules; the costs of defection are spread among all contributors. If defection is discovered the consequences are moreover often limited: the culprits generally have to pay back the unlawfully received benefit plus a fine, but they are not in danger of being expelled from their family or community or of harming their job or career, as in the informal interaction models discussed earlier. Finally, defective behaviour is encouraged by the relatively undersocialised nature of formal social security rules (cf. the previous section).

On the other hand, there are also factors which make defection by beneficiaries less likely, at least compared with the formal systems that will be discussed later in this chapter. The nature of the criteria conferring entitlement is the most important of these. The central E-type conditions in the demographic systems – old age, death, having custody over children – are not easily to influence by those concerned, at least not unless they commit criminal acts (forgery, murder). As the eventualities can be determined rather objectively on the basis of official figures, it is not easy to submit a credible unauthorised application: the chance of being caught through administrative detection, for example on the basis of the population register, is fairly high (provided the registration system is reliable and contains the required information for the entire group of potential beneficiaries). Consequently, the moral hazard[30] is theoretically smaller in demographic schemes than in unemployment, social assistance and sick pay and disability benefit regulations.

The profile of the client group limits the likelihood of defection by beneficiaries even further. Older people, recipients of surviving dependants' pension and parents of young children do not meet the theoretical profile of the 'calculating' benefit claimant: young, highly educated, without ties and amoral. Still, the more specific qualifying conditions – such as the rules that allocate pension entitlements to younger partners, provisions on the remarriage of widows, benefits that are linked to the household situation or to need – can create a certain 'user latitude' in demographic systems (cf. for the Netherlands: De Voogd & Van Schooneveld, 1991).

Defection by the *contributors* (employers, employees, taxpayers) can take several forms, especially shirking: the legal avoidance or illegal evasion of their contributions.[31] Avoidance refers to calculating behaviour which is not in conflict with the legal rules, but at most with the intent or tenor of them. Examples are where employers avoid social security contributions by formally having activities carried out abroad, or where they pay a large proportion of staff salaries untaxed (for example in the form of expenses, payments to employees who are officially registered as self-employed or freelance). By contrast, evasion does involve rule-breaking. It arises when the duty-bound fail to disclose or to disclose correctly the base of their contributions: lower wages, shorter working times, or fewer employment relationships than they actually have; or where they do not pay social insurance contributions that are due and make their recovery impossible. Both forms of defection reduce the total financial revenue, which in time can make it necessary to raise the contributions or reduce the entitlements.

For the contributors defection is theoretically attractive. A rational actor will be inclined to minimise his contributions, because these increase the wage bill for companies and reduce the disposable income of households. Defection has a positive return in the short term, while the disadvantages manifest themselves only in the long run, probably with limited consequences for the rule-breakers personally. Avoidance and evasion of contributions in formal social security does not hit anyone in particular; it relates to the funding of a collective good, and any negative future consequences cannot be traced back to individual actors.

The main way of combating defection by contributors[32] in formal social security schemes regulations implies an attempt at regimentation, or automatic compliance, in combination with strict monitoring and sanctioning by the administration. As mentioned before regimentation can never be complete; but the establishment of certain collection procedures can make rule-breaking troublesome for the contributors. The most general measure is of course to make contributions mandatory by national law. In addition to this, defection by duty-bound employees can be limited by obliging employers to withhold the contributions from gross wages and to transfer them directly to the social security fund or the tax inspector. If employers are obliged to contribute, they may be required to report new employment contracts and wage mutations to the social security organisation, to have their administration carried out or approved by an external auditor, and to inform employees about the contributions paid (including the gross/net breakdown on pay slips).

In its monitoring role, the social security organisation can have a key instrument in the verification of identities, mutations and employment relationships though the use of national registers and personal social security numbers. The monitoring/sanctioning agency can also devote special attention to sectors where the risk of contribution defection is high because of the large flows of money and the low-paid, transitory workforce (the hospitality industry, the agricultural sector, the construction industry). Deterrence through a consistent and severe punishment of infringements can reduce the likelihood of defection by contributors as well, but such strict sanctioning may not always be regarded as proportional by the community or the actors concerned.

The latter points to a final factor of importance: the informal rules prevailing among the contributors of formal demographic regulations, or their 'fiscal ethics'. They may incline towards defection because in formal schemes the duty to contribute is highly undersocialised, and the social pressure to pay the dues is less marked than in informal systems. On the other hand, theoretically the willingness to contribute is greater in demographic regulations than in the two other formal schemes discussed below. The solidarity with the 'deserving clients' of this type of scheme tends to be stronger than with, e.g. people on social assistance. Older persons, widows and orphans and children are vulnerable social groups, who cannot be blamed for their benefit dependency, and who have no viable alternative, as they are not considered capable of work. Moreover, it is likely that the contributors themselves, or people close to them, will at some point make use of the demographic schemes. Thus they have some personal interest in paying their dues; but this will not stop all the duty-bound contributors from free-riding.

3.5.5 Unemployment and social assistance benefit regulations

Actors and interactions

The interaction model for the formal unemployment and social assistance benefit regulations (figure 3.5) resembles the previous one, but there are a number of structural differences. An additional corporate actor has appeared, namely *firms*. These play a key role in that the number of beneficiaries partly depends on the firms' recruitment and dismissal policy. As demanders of labour, firms maintain relations both with the potential beneficiaries and the social security organisation. In the graph the firms have been depicted as a corporate principal, because of the key hierarchical relationship they maintain with their employees; but if they deduct contributions from the wages and transfer these to the fund, firms may also be regarded as a corporate agent of the latter.

Some aspects of the position of the *social security organisation* are different as well. In contrast to the demographic schemes the central risks in this model, unemployment and indigence, are sometimes avoidable; and if it does arise it is in principle reversible. This opens the way to other types of intervention. Theoretically, in the unemployment and social assistance schemes the social security organisation does not focus exclusively on compensation, but also aims at prevention and restoration. In the model these tasks are attributed to a separate corporate agent, a *prevention/reinsertion agency* within the social security organisation.[33] For the short-term unemployed the emphasis in its tasks is usually on job-placement, with the agency trying to match the pool of job-seekers to the labour demand of firms. This may be supplemented with training courses and work experience projects (retraining, job application training, apprenticeships, day/block release programmes, etc.). The tasks regarding the long-term unemployed and social assistance benefit recipients may also include offering sheltered employment to people who are considered insufficiently productive in the mainstream labour market. In addition this group may require extensive social support: in order to secure their place on the labour market and in society, it is often necessary to provide financial and social aid (debt rescheduling, budgeting

Figure 3.5
Interaction model V:
formal unemployment and social assistance regulations

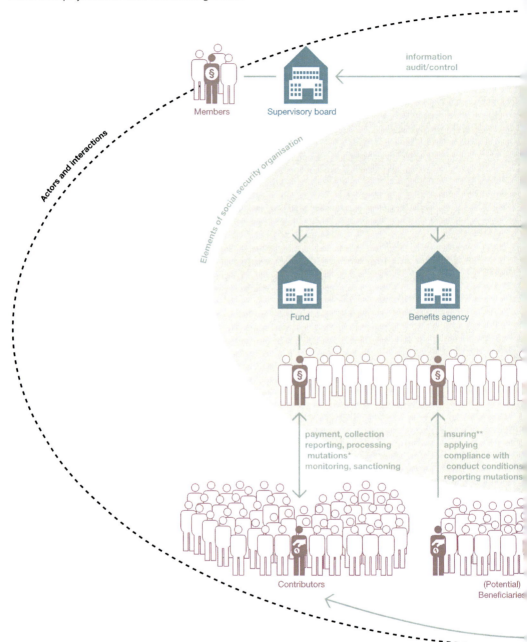

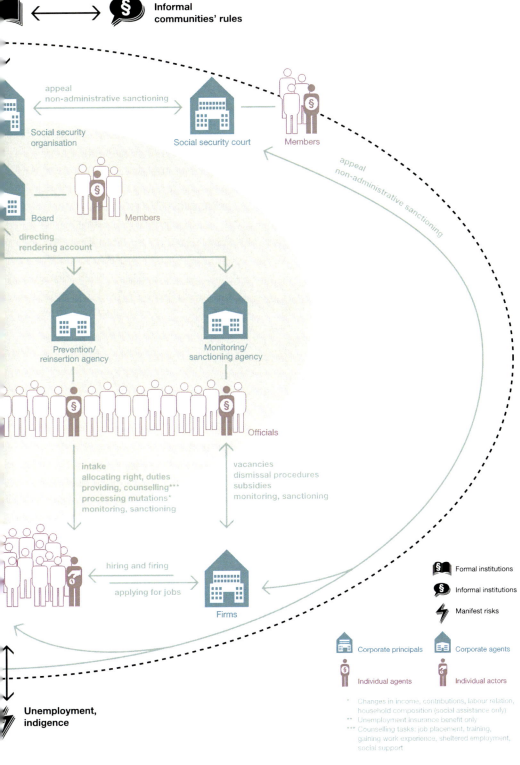

SOCIAL SECURITY AND THE INSTITUTIONAL APPROACH 167

assistance, securing suitable accommodation, medical help, finding day-care facilities). Interventions aimed at increasing the coping abilities of benefit recipients and countering their social exclusion are also among the tasks of the prevention/reinsertion agency.

In this model, the social security organisation is also a party to the relationship between (potential) beneficiaries and firms. It has to supervise the efforts of the unemployed to find work, verify that firms follow the correct dismissal procedures, assess how the reintegration process operates in practice, etc. This makes the tasks of the *monitoring/sanctioning agency* more comprehensive and more complex. This agency may also be authorised to apply positive sanctions, such as incentive bonuses for unemployed people who find work, or temporary wage cost subsidies for employers. Employment-related interventions such as these play no role in the demographic systems.

A number of tasks of the *benefits agency* have changed too. The occurrence of an entitling eventuality E is less easy to establish than in the demographic schemes because unemployment and indigence are vaguer concepts than, say, reaching the age of 65. This is often solved by incorporating a large number of Q-type conditions in the rule-set, for example relating to the number of hours or the income that a person must have lost before being regarded as unemployed, the specification of what may be regarded as 'suitable employment' for a job-seeker, or to the means that are to be included in determining the degree of indigence (incidental earnings, assets, the incomes of the partner, other household members and relatives). Of course such detailed stipulations place stricter demands on the benefits agency than in the previous model.

In addition, unlike the demographic schemes, benefit entitlements may be linked to conditions of behaviour. Examples of such C-type conditions are that applicants must not have induced their lacks and losses of work and income themselves (no voluntary unemployment, excessive spending patterns, etc.), they must make themselves available for work, and they must be actively seeking a job. However, in unemployment benefit and social assistance schemes the behavioural prerequisites tend to be not as far-reaching as in the informal forms of social security discussed earlier. For instance, they set no strict criteria with regard to ethically correct behaviour. It is also not unusual for certain groups – older and long-term unemployed, single mothers with young children – to be completely, partially or temporarily exempted from the conduct conditions.

The processing of mutations is an aspect of administration that is more intensive than in the previous model. The number of criteria is larger: changes in income, the employment relationship and (for social assistance benefit) household situation may influence the entitlements and the contribution level. In addition the population of benefit recipients is more volatile. While the demographic risks discussed earlier are relatively stable and predictable, the stock of unemployment and social assistance benefit recipients is far more likely to change. Beneficiaries may find work or begin living with someone who provides for them; but the job or the relationship may prove to be instable, forcing them to fall back on social security again, etc. Among seasonal workers, commuting between employment and benefit dependency is in fact the standard pattern. It is also possible for beneficiaries to combine their benefit with work or a different benefit, for example because of partial incapacity for work. Incorporating changes in such cases of accumulation can demand a great deal from the benefits agency.

The *contributors* to unemployment benefit schemes are generally the employers and employees, possibly augmented by benefit recipients.[34] The required contributions fluctuate much more than in the demographic schemes and therefore are more difficult to predict in the long term. This is because the demand placed on the schemes depends on the economic cycle and on structural changes in labour supply and demand (developments in technology, immigration, work preferences of women and older persons), the extent and consequences of which are difficult to predict. This creates more insecurity for the *fund* than in the previous interaction model. The problem is less apparent in social assistance schemes, as these are usually funded from the general coffers, raised through national or local taxation.

Beneficiaries have a different relationship with the social security organisation than in demographic regulations. There the objective is simple and is shared by all actors: the benefit is generally awarded, and provided it is distributed correctly both sides will usually be satisfied. The scope for conflicts is greater with unemployment and social assistance benefits. Benefit applications are more frequently rejected, and it is possible that one actor will stress the importance of the resumption of work while another regards the benefit entitlements as the key goal of the interaction. The nature of the entitling events further increases the likelihood of disputes: there is usually little room for discussion about the age of a retired person, but an unemployed person may fundamentally disagree with the administration officials on the assessment of his or her attempts to find work and the reasons that those attempts have failed. The contact is moreover generally rather more intensive than in the demographic systems. The interaction involves more than mere correspondence; normally, a number of intake, monitoring and supervisory interviews are mandatory. This makes it less impersonal, sporadic and indirect than in the previous formal model – though the contacts are not as intensive as in informal social security systems. Conflicts in unemployment and social assistance schemes can therefore emerge in the interview room, and the actors may not by definition behave reasonably (aggression and threats by benefit claimants, arbitrary decisions by officials, clinging to the letter of the law, driving applicants from pillar to post). In social assistance systems, conflicts are made even more likely by the fact that the provisions often are a last resort. If the allowance is not granted (or if it is cut off owing to a limit on duration or the imposition of a sanction) clients who fail to find work will not have an adequate regular income. This may have serious consequences for them (dependence on relatives or illegal activities, increasing debt problems, disconnection of gas and electricity, eviction) and is likely to evoke protests. Given these opposing interests the beneficiaries may decide to organise themselves, for example into client councils, but the influence of these on the administrative process tends to be limited.[35]

Owing to the complexity of the administrative process and the ambiguity of the entitling criteria, it is more likely than in the previous interaction model that clients and firms will contest decisions taken by the social security organisation and will appeal to the *social security court*. The wide-ranging task of the social security organisation also means that the *board of directors* is in principle more important than in demographic systems. It has to coordinate more agencies, control a more complicated administrative process and give more elaborate instructions on the precise interpretation of the legal rules. Of particular importance is that the board must allocate priorities and resources to the various tasks of the social security organisation, which as stated may to some extent be in conflict with each other. It is not only important that the benefits are paid correctly and on time by the social security organisation, but also that unemployed people are offered a job or the prospect of work, that the counselling programme set up to achieve this is adequate and not too expensive, that preventive interventions are made where possible, and so on. To conciliate all these aims, the management has to make judgements within the framework of the applicable rules. Evidently, the auditing and control tasks of the *supervisory board* are more comprehensive in this model as well.

Institutions of formal unemployment and social assistance regulations

As in the previous model, the behaviour of the actors in the unemployment and social assistance and benefits systems is steered largely by formal rules which lay down the rights, duties, conditions and potential sanctions. However, since the entitling events are less clear-cut and there are more qualifying and conduct conditions, the latitude of actors is greater.

In this type of scheme the official rules will be embedded to some extent in the informal institutions; even so, and similar to the demographic regulations, this may not go very deep. Theoretically it is quite possible that the informal norms, values and conventions of certain groups of beneficiaries are diametrically opposed to the content of the formal institutions. For example, they may not share the prevailing work ethic, may not regard it as a problem to abuse social security, may be strongly focused on their own direct gains, etc. The emergence of such a deviating 'benefit culture' among unemployment and social assistance beneficiaries is theoretically fostered by the fact that they are often more geographically concentrated than, say, pensioners, and because they tend to be more homogeneous in terms of education level and social background. If they are dependent on benefit for a long period, in particular, they may develop informal institutions which deviate from the formal rules.

Compliance and defection in formal unemployment and social assistance regulations

On all points the likelihood of defection in unemployment and social assistance benefit schemes is greater than in the previous interaction model. In the *social security organisation* the principal-agent problem is magnified because there are more agents with partially conflicting objectives (income compensation, restoration of work, social support). In addition, in all departments of the organisation the administration is more complex, as a result of the less definite nature of the entitling eventualities, the more elaborate qualifying criteria, the introduction of conduct conditions and the higher volatility of entitlements and contributions. This complexity increases the officials' latitude and the likelihood of errors. The larger principal-agent problem and the more intricate administrative process make the management tasks of the board far more demanding.

Defection within the social security organisation may imply certain key functions are neglected; for instance, the main focus may be on providing income support, with limited attention for prevention and restoration. This can be due to the way officials and the board of directors perceive their interest. If their job or salary depends on the number of clients of the organisation, they have no incentive to prevent unemployment or social assistance dependency, and may not be inclined to stimulate a fast reinsertion of benefit recipients into the labour market. The problem may be reinforced if representatives of group interests (trade unions, employers' organisations) sit on the management or supervisory board of the social security organisation. This is rather common in corporatist unemployment insurance systems. It is often justified by arguing that these actors are experts on labour market issues, represent the contributors, and are key actors in implementing labour market policy at the local level. Even so, it stands to reason that the two sides will try to exert their influence on the social security organisation in order to achieve their own objectives: job security, low contributions and socially acceptable redundancy schemes for less productive workers. This can lead to an inefficient and, from a societal point of view, suboptimal method of administration.

The principal-agent problem and the complexity of the administrative process are difficult to overcome. Regimentation is harder to accomplish than in the previous model, and may in fact prove to be counterproductive. The Dutch unemployment insurance system provides an interesting example (cf. Van der Veen, 1990). In the 1980s it was administered by industrial insurance associations under the responsibility of organisations of employers and trade unions. The organisations sought to constrain the policy freedom of the officials as far as possible via strict administrative guidelines, bureaucratic procedures and direct intervention in administration decisions (via the so-called 'small committees', consisting of trade union and employers representatives). This led to a fixation on the timely distribution of the correct benefit amounts, in accordance with the rigid process rules. In doing so, the boards and officials neglected their tasks of labour market reinsertion and social support, which at that time probably led to a higher number and a longer duration of unemployment benefits than necessary.

The risk of defection by *beneficiaries* is theoretically greater than in the demographic systems as well. It may take the form of improper applications, undeclared working whilst receiving benefit, failure to report changes in their situation and non-compliance with the imposed behavioural obligations. Unemployment benefit claimants, for example, may (cf. Verheul, 1989: 65-67, 73-75):
- not report that their unemployment is their own fault,
- incorrectly state wage amounts and employment history, for example via forged documents,
- not report that they have resumed work,

- fail to mention or reject without reason offers of work,
- make insufficient efforts to find work and submit incorrect reports on this,
- fail to participate in reintegration activities (job application training, following training programmes, carrying out sheltered employment), and
- frustrate the monitoring attempts by the social security organisation, for example by not appearing after being summoned by an official.

Such types of defection also can occur among social assistance beneficiaries, but in addition this group may:
- conceal the fact that they have assets and extra earnings (including income of a partner),
- present the household situation incorrectly (failing to mention cohabitation, wrongly stating that they have children living at home),
- fail to cooperate with initiatives for social integration, such as debt rescheduling.

To some extent beneficiaries' defection is fostered by the same factors as in the demographic systems. Here again the amounts involved are considerable, the interaction with the social security organisation is relatively large in scale and anonymous, and the formal rules are only weakly socialised. However, other elements also play a role. The ambiguous criteria, the complex rules and the high volatility mean that, other things being equal, the opportunities for defection are greater, monitoring is more difficult and the chance of being caught is smaller than in demographic regulations. The moral hazard is also greater in unemployment and social assistance benefit schemes: it is easier for beneficiaries to create or preserve their entitlements themselves. An obvious example is failure to seek work actively, but there are also more ingenious forms of 'inducing' behaviour. If, for example, receipt of unemployment benefit carries conditions relating to employment history, it is not surprising that some working people will try to meet the requirement and then withdraw from the labour market for some time. And if the social assistance benefit for two single persons is higher than for a couple living together, some couples will gear their behaviour to this by officially living at different addresses or formally entering into a different type of relationship (e.g. tenant/subtenant, main resident/lodger).

This does not mean that every recipient of unemployment or social assistance benefit will defect wherever possible. The costs and benefits of rule-breaking may not be favourable enough in their perception (low returns, high sanctions, too risky), or the informal rules in their immediate social network may strongly frown upon defective behaviour (norms of family and friends, religious prescripts). The personal characteristics and experiences of the recipients can also be an obstacle to rule-breaking: a cooperative attitude, respect for authority, having access to sufficient funds elsewhere, earlier experiences with work and unemployment, etc. The risk of defection need not moreover be constant. New benefit claimants may have different views about how to deal with formal rules, and a change in the economic climate can change the incentive to defect. Benefit recipients may be less inclined to look for a regular job intensively in periods of economic downturn, if they think the probability they will succeed is very small. Instead, they may prefer to top up their income by working in the black or shadow economy.

Once again, the defection problem among *contributors* is greater in some respects than in the previous interaction model. People often assume that they themselves are not at great risk of being affected by unemployment or indigence. That is an essential difference compared with the much more predictable risk of old age, where every healthy individual contributor expects to live long enough to draw a pension. Due to the low anticipated personal gains actors will be more inclined to minimise their contributions: subjectively contributors often feel as if they finance the unemployment and social assistance benefits of others. Put differently, the lower subjective utility of contributions theoretically increases the inclination of the contributors to engage in avoidance and evasion. This is exacerbated by the fact that unemployment and social assistance benefit recipients are often seen as less deserving than pensioners and families with children. Beneficiaries tend to be regarded as less weak and as capable of work, and it may be considered partly their own fault that they are unemployed or needy. As a result of this perception, contributors may be less inclined to pay for them than for needy old persons, widows and children. Here again, however, a specific negative ethics can only emerge if the contributions are earmarked.

The introduction of *firms* in this model obviously creates new opportunities for defection as well. From the perspective of the collectivity, it is desirable that firms cause as few people as possible to move on to these benefits; and that where possible they engage unemployment and social assistance beneficiaries. However, the corporate interest often demands that, in their hiring and firing behaviour, firms select people who they expect to make the biggest contribution to the corporate goals, or productivity. As this is difficult to determine in advance, rational employers will use proxy criteria: age, past performance, the suitability and currency of training, health, seniority or length of unemployment, command of the native language, social skills, etc. Subjective perceptions that are not directly related to productivity can also weigh heavily in the recruitment and dismissal policy: a dislike of certain groups, the physical attractiveness of the employee, and the sharing of a certain background, social network or particular activities.[36] Both the proxy criteria and the subjective appraisal by employers tend to work to the disadvantage of the weakest groups on the labour market. As a result older persons, the low-skilled, sick employees and members of ethnic minorities are more readily dismissed, while unemployed persons from these groups are often no match for other candidates, such as school-leavers and mothers re-entering the labour market. Such 'bounded rational' selection behaviour by employers may have negative consequences for the community. People who are regarded as less productive or as a bad risk tend to be overrepresented in the stock of unemployment and social assistance beneficiaries; they may experience prolonged periods of benefit dependency, which further reduces their labour market prospects.

There are several ways to combat rational defection in the hiring and firing behaviour of firms. It may be outlawed by drawing up legal rules which forbid non-recruitment and dismissal based on criteria that are considered unacceptable, such as health, age, gender or ethnic origin. Firms may also be required to employ fixed quotas of people from specific vulnerable groups, such as the disabled and certain ethnic minorities. Attempts to change the cost-benefit ratio are another example. The costs of people entering the social security system may be charged to individual companies via a system of premium differentiation, fines or deductibles. Conversely, firms can be encouraged to hire benefit recipients by (temporarily) boosting productivity via wage cost subsidies, contribution discounts or the use of risk-free trial placements. Finally, attempts may be made to influence the informal rules, by making companies aware of their broader role in the community ('corporate social responsibility'), to eliminate the unfavourable perceptions that employers have of certain groups, and to play on the reputation of firms by praising good employers in public and chastising defectors.

Such strategies not necessarily resolve the social dilemma of 'selective selection' by employers. Discrimination of specific groups is often difficult to prove; quota regulations require an intensive and costly process of monitoring and sanctioning; changing the cost-benefit ratio may require considerable financial means; and firms operating on highly competitive markets tend to be rather unsusceptible to moral appeals. Moreover, if such measures are effective but have a negative impact on the profitability or functioning of the companies concerned, this may have undesirable collective second order consequences as well (substitution of labour by capital, lower investments, job redundancies, etc.).

3.5.6 Sick leave and disability regulations

Actors and interactions

The interaction model for formal sick leave and disability regulations (figure 3.6) has the most complicated structure. Sickness absence occurs when people employed by a firm have medical reasons preventing them from working. It often precedes cases of disability, or work incapacity. Here, illness or impairments make gainful employment wholly or partially impossible, and the employment relationship generally has been terminated or the conditions of the labour contract have become more unfavourable (less hours, lower salary). Disability, however, can also affect those who formerly were not in salaried employment (e.g. people incapacitated from an early age, the self-employed, students, housewives).

Characteristic of these systems is that medical experts to a large extent determine whether the entitling eventualities have occurred. The onset of old age, unemployment or indigence can be determined by officials using a set of decision criteria. Whether or not someone is unable to work because of illness or disability is however a matter for the judgement of medical experts. They make a diagnosis, indicate the degree to which the observed medical limitations make a person too ill to work, and give an indication of when and how the patient is likely to be able to resume his activities. Assessing the central risk thus requires medical approval: without an official medical opinion entitlements cannot be ascertained, and the benefits agency is not able to pay or reject applications for sickness or disability benefit, for aids or support, etc. In cases of short term sickness (e.g. as a result of influenza) the applicant may be given the benefit of the doubt, and a self-report to the employer or social security organisation may entitle him to sick leave; or a simple certificate from the GP will do. Sickness of longer duration, and especially the assessment of disability, usually involves an extensive medical examination procedure by specialists, possibly in consultation with labour experts. The latter investigate the work-related risks and strain, the residual earnings capacity, the possibility of using aids and adaptation of the workplace or organisation on reintegration, etc.

The assessment to what extent sickness and disability make working impossible can be problematic. Doctors do not always arrive at the same diagnosis and may also evaluate the recovery prognosis and required socio-medical interventions differently. An unequivocal medical diagnosis still may imply that one person is able to work while another is judged as sick or disabled. This has to do with factors such as the nature of the work to be performed (an office worker can continue working with a leg injury, while a bus driver cannot), the loss of earning capacity, the degree of support available in the client's social network, and the personal resilience of the patient. The subjective opinions of the medical experts can also play a decisive role in determining the degree of illness and incapacity for work. In addition, the applicants sometimes disagree with the medical opinion, possibly leading to demands for second opinions.

As regards the other theoretical conditions for entitlements, benefit recipients may be required to work or seek a job to the extent of their residual capacity; and if they do not do so, be regarded as partly unemployed. The household situation and additional means generally play no role. Sick leave and disability regulations are often individualised, with benefits (or continuation of salary payments) set at a certain percentage of the most recent earnings. Some form of means testing, however, may be applied in non-employee schemes and in the guaranteed minimum amounts payable under employee insurances.

Because of the crucial role of the health evaluation in the model this task has been allocated to a separate corporate agent within the social security organisation, a highly professionalised medical assessment agency. However, the review of illness and impairments may also be attributed to the benefits agency or be integrated with the functions of prevention and reinsertion; or it may be placed outside the social security organisation, with GPs, specialists or private sick leave and disability assessment institutes acting as the medical gatekeepers.

The other interactions are largely comparable with those in the previous model, but there are some differences. Because illnesses and disabilities can frequently be avoided or treated, theoretically there is a greater role for preventive or restorative actions by the *social security organisation* than in the previous interaction models (e.g. counselling on working with hazardous substances, issuing medical aids at the workplace). This of course makes the prioritisation of interventions more complex; apart from income protection and job security, the health of the client also has to be considered. A one-sided focus on the latter is natural from a medical/professional perspective, but is not in the interests of

Figure 3.6
Interaction model VI:
formal sick leave and disability regulations

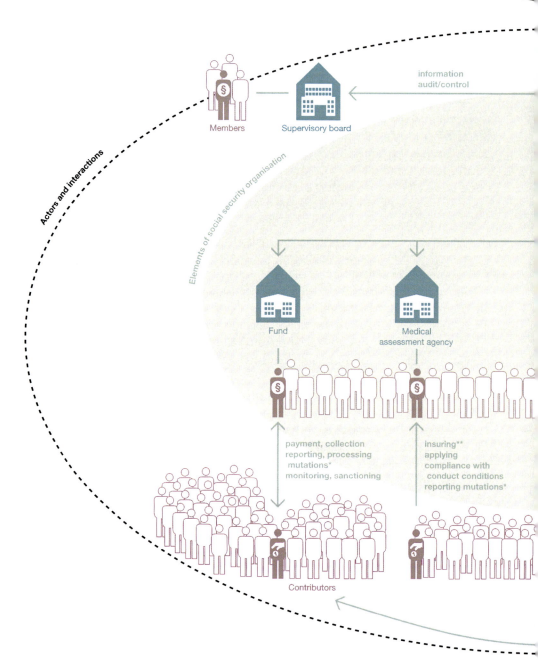

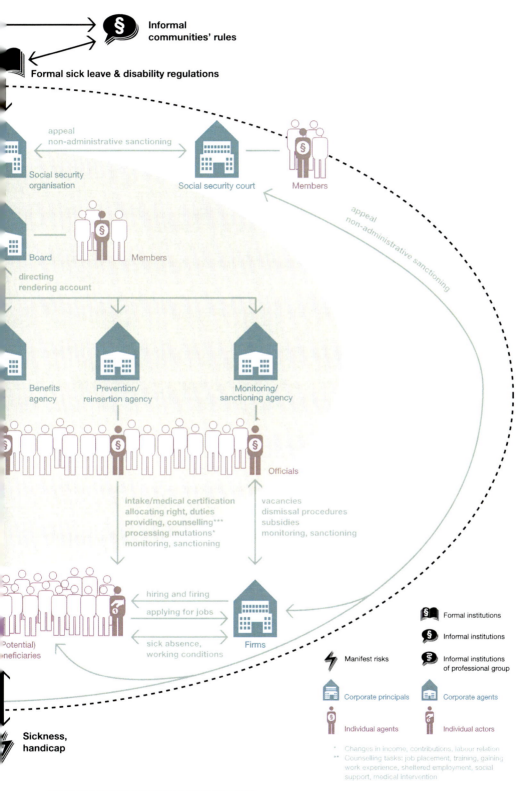

SOCIAL SECURITY AND THE INSTITUTIONAL APPROACH

the contributors. By contrast, if the emphasis is placed on guiding clients back into work, this may be at odds with their preferences: beneficiaries generally consider their health to be the most important thing, and do not wish to see this jeopardised by the imposition of activities that are a physical or mental burden to them.

Owing to the health aspects, the support tasks of the social security organisation are more extensive than in the previous models, as these may include targeted medical interventions. The employment placement activities and the offering of subsidised employment are constrained by the need to find work that takes into account the client's impairments. The social support function may include measures which enable the client to cope with their disorders or disabilities in everyday life.

The inclusion of the medical assessment function, the difficulties involved in the evaluation of work incapacity, and the more elaborate support tasks make the administration of the schemes more complex. This increases the risk of contestable decisions, and makes appeal procedures more likely. The risk of errors is mitigated somewhat by the fact that sickness and disability generally are less volatile than unemployment and indigence; their duration often is predictable, or, in the case of chronic disorders, indefinite. This means that the entitlements of the beneficiaries theoretically have to be reviewed less often than in unemployment and social assistance schemes, but more frequently than in demographic schemes.

The task of the *board* is evidently more wide-ranging than in the previous model, as the medical aspects of administration create greater complexity and a more complicated prioritisation process. In view of their specialised and professional background, the medical assessment agency may be difficult to control.

In the model the interactions between *firms* and *potential beneficiaries* (employees) are more complex as well. Both are obliged to observe the rules relating to working conditions (prohibition of hazardous activities, compliance with safety instructions) and to sick absence (requirements for reporting sick, handling absenteeism). The social security organisation has to monitor and sanction this via the labour inspectorate – one of the oldest forms of formal regulation and organisation in this domain.[37]

In disability benefit schemes organisations representing beneficiaries often play a more active role than in unemployment and social assistance regulations. This is mostly because dependency tends to last longer in case of invalidity, which implies there is a less volatile supply of candidates, with a higher interest in organising. Even so their influence on the administrative process need not be very great, for reasons similar to those pertaining to other client councils (cf. above). This will especially occur when the client organisations are fragmented, for example with several groups representing people with different disorders.

Institutions of formal sick leave and disability regulations
In the model, the behaviour of the actors is driven not only by the provisions of the sick leave and disability regulations and the informal rules of communities; the rules that generally prevail among medical professionals also play a role, and the three types of

institution are not necessarily extensions of each other. Formal benefit rules and professional rules may diverge in two respects. First, there may be differences in the professional and formal demarcation of illnesses and impairments. Typically, the sickness and invalidity concept may be broader in the medical profession than the conditions that qualify for the benefit. This discrepancy is exacerbated by technological developments (medical research, better diagnostic techniques, more extensive range of treatments) and the growth in medical specialisms, which to some extent create their own demand. In addition, medical assessors within the social security organisation may be confronted with conflicting rules: the expectations of their masters do not always correspond with the informal values, norms, and conventions that they have internalised as professionals during their medical training.

Informal rules relating to illness and work incapacity may deviate from the statutory definition and the professional criteria as well. People sometimes experience impairments that are not recognised by physicians as ailments (e.g. subjective complaints with no scientifically demonstrable cause) or for which the benefits agency does not confer an entitlement (e.g. injuries caused by dangerous leisure activities, partial incapacity below a certain threshold, insufficient loss of income). This gulf can be wider in some parts of society than in others, owing to deviant views about illness and its treatment. Examples are a culture of absenteeism in certain companies and trade sectors, where employees consider taking sick leave as the normal thing to do when the weather is bad or when a child is in need of care; or the benefit culture which long-term disabled persons may develop if they live in geographical concentrations (for instance, in areas which have traditionally had a large share of high-risk employment, such as heavy industry or mining).

Compliance and defection in formal sick leave and disability regulations

In many respects the incentives to comply and defect are comparable with those in the previous interaction model. However, there are some points that are specific to the collective arrangements for sick leave and incapacity for work.

In the *social security organisation* the principal-agent problem is theoretically greater, partly for the obvious reasons relating to the complexity of the organisational structure, the prioritisation of the various interventions, and the nature of the entitlements and conditions laid down in the formal rules. However, there is also a specific defection issue here, which can be described as 'the doctor's dilemma'. This is not, as in G.B. Shaw's play, a reference to the conflicts of interests and of conscience in individual physicians, but to a special manifestation of the principal-agent problem. On the one hand the social security organisation needs a medical assessment agency in order to establish the entitling events, and from this perspective the social security organisation has an interest in acquiring sufficient medical expertise. On the other hand, in doing so it is bringing in an assertive professional group, which has gone through a lengthy process of secondary socialisation; and as a result, they may feel more committed to the rules of the medical profession than to the formal institutions the social security organisation has to comply with. This increases the likelihood that the medical assessors who act on behalf of the social security organisation will go their own way; they may ignore the instructions and objectives of the board, and may allow the health interests of the beneficiaries and their own professional code (not doing anything that may harm the patient)[38] to weigh more heavily than the letter of the law and the organisational interests. The existence of a third set of rules guiding the behaviour of the medical assessors makes the principal-agent problem between the board of directors and the medical assessment agency, in comparison with the other structural relationships within the organisation, qualitatively different and more urgent. Of course, theoretically the problem becomes even greater if the medical assessors are independent advisors who are not on the administration's payroll.

This type of defection can be tackled in several ways. Regimentation may be pursued by drawing up detailed medical examination protocols linked to strict supervision of the doctors. Alternatively, the medical assessment can be made less dependent on the opinion of a single doctor, for example by including a second opinion in the examination procedure as standard; or by establishing the entitlements in an intensive collaborative process with labour experts, benefit officials and reinsertion consultants. It is also possible to try and link the medical professionals more to the organisational interest, for example by basing their pay to the number of rejected applications and the number of recovery declarations. A contractual solution could consist of specific agreements made with the national medical association, setting out the rules of conduct for professionals working in social security. Finally, the doctor's dilemma can be addressed by creating a separate profession specifically for the purpose of carrying out medical assessments. Apart from the required medical skills and knowledge, such 'social security physicians' must be imbued with explicit professional norms, which take into account the interests of the social security organisation and the wider community.

However, there are disadvantages to all the above strategies. It may be hard to attain a high degree of regimentation, because the required expertise is very specific, and the professionals therefore have an edge in knowledge and information. Financial incentives may be at odds with the professional rules, possibly causing doctors working in social security to acquire a bad reputation among their colleagues and making it difficult to recruit qualified professionals. Co-assessment with other disciplines may increase the transaction costs of the administration process, and contractual solutions may not be viable, because the national medical association has no strong interest in stretching its own rules to suit the social security organisation. The normative force of detailed rules imparted in the training of a specific group of social security physicians should not be overestimated. This often will involve a relatively late, not overly penetrative form of socialisation, as a corollary to the standard medical curriculum. In practice, all these solutions may turn out to be rather ineffective or inappropriate. The doctor's dilemma is therefore theoretically one of the major defection problems in administering sickness and disability benefit schemes.

For the *beneficiaries* the sickness or disability schemes are often more attractive than unemployment or social assistance regulations. Benefits are high and exempted from means testing, and in most cases last until recovery has occurred. The rights to support are generally more extensive as well. The duty to accept work is less pressing; the fully incapacitated need not search for a job, while for the remainder the condition generally applies that accepting work must not harm their health any further. In cases of sickness and disability the social 'legitimacy of idleness' is also often greater. The beneficiary can in principle not help the fact that he has been struck by illness; it could happen to anyone, and he has demonstrable, medically certified impairments. In the view of many this may justify the rights he has been granted.

In theory, the attractiveness of this type of benefit fosters rule-breaking on the part of the recipients. The possible types of beneficiaries' defection are to some extent the same as those for unemployment and social assistance benefits: incorrectly claimed benefit amounts, inaccurate presentation of employment relationships, failure to report mutations in their income or household situation, etc. Others relate to the specific E-, Q- and C-type conditions of sickness and disability benefit schemes. For instance, potential beneficiaries may (see also Verheul, 1989: 67-70):

- deliberately cause the illness themselves, or simulate the symptoms and manipulate the doctor's opinion in the consultation room (inducement),
- prolong their illness by refusing medical examination and help (obstruction),
- present the illness as worse than it is (aggravation),
- submit false declarations of unfitness for work, e.g. via doctors' certificates purchased abroad,
- report sick for a single day if they have insufficient days of leave or a lack of motivation ('pulling a sickie'),
- report sick for a long period as a result of labour conflicts or in connection with reorganisations, and
- fail to report, or report on time, the fact that they have recovered and are able to resume work.

The likelihood that such defective behaviour will occur depends on many factors, many of them the same as with unemployment and social assistance benefits (the amounts involved, complex and ambiguous formal rules which are weakly socialised, impersonal contacts with the social security organisation, conflicting interests). The formal definition of illness and incapacity for work, however, is a specific factor. A short and exhaustive account of entitling occupational illnesses offers less scope for defection than a broadly defined eventuality condition such as 'being able to earn less, due to illness or impairments, than a similar but healthy person'. But the likelihood of rule-breaking by the beneficiaries also depends on the assessment procedure, the embedding of the medical assessment agency in the social security organisation, and the informal rules of relatives, neighbourhood and firm. The state of the economy can play a role as well; for instance, during a recession employees tend to be less inclined to report sick on questionable grounds, because they are afraid of becoming unemployed if they were to be caught.

The willingness of the *contributors* to comply with their funding duties cannot be taken for granted either. *Ceteris paribus* it may be assumed that the likelihood of contributor's defection is higher than in pension schemes, but lower than in unemployment or social assistance arrangements. While everyone expects to retire, and many people consider themselves as immune to the risks of unemployment and indigence, the perceived probability of falling ill or becoming disabled generally lies somewhere in between: everyone can be struck by illness or incapacity for work at some point of their career. A moderate subjective utility of contributing can therefore be expected. The duty-bound may also be rather inclined to contribute because the perceived deservingness of the recipients, or the legitimacy of idleness (cf. above), tends to be greater than in cases of unemployment or indigence (though smaller than where elderly, survivors or children are concerned).

A common type of defection by *firms* occurs when they base their selection and dismissal policy on the perceived likelihood of sickness and disablement. When dismissing incumbent personnel they possess information about their sickness history; and the bad risks may be placed at the top of the list of potential dismissals. Firms do not possess this information when taking on new staff. In that case they may seek to select against bad risks by requiring candidates to undergo medical examinations; but these do not cover all illnesses and their predictive value is limited. Moreover, they are sometimes illegal or only permitted if impairments make it difficult to do a particular job (e.g. poor eyesight in people who want to become train drivers). In practice, this quickly leads to selection by proxy: job opportunities are then poor for groups which firms perceive as being at high risk of illness or incapacity, such as older persons, women or people who have previously claimed disability benefit.

A special form of firm defection is the presentation of unemployment as disability. Employers and employees may have a common interest in regarding people who are to be dismissed (e.g. because of reorganisation) as unfit for work. The employers are able to rid themselves in a social manner of employees they regard as less productive, whilst transferring a large share of the costs of dismissal (redundancy schemes, social plans) to the collectivity. The employees, for their part, end up in a relatively more favourable benefit system than if they would have been forced to rely on unemployment or social assistance benefit. Hiding unemployment in this way requires some degree of collaboration between employers and employees; in other words, the defection is tacitly or explicitly a joint undertaking. A shared intention on the part of these actors may not be enough, however. The likelihood that attempts to disguise unemployment as disability will succeed also depends on the possibilities offered by the formal institutions, the willingness of the benefits agency to interpret those rules in a lenient fashion, the priority given to this type of defection by the monitoring/sanctioning agency, and whether or not the supervisory board and the social security court regard this as acceptable. In the Dutch disability benefit system 'discounting unemployment' was an officially approved practice in medical assessments between 1973 and 1987 (see for instance scp, 1998: 432).

3.6 The results of social security rules

Social security institutions are designed to achieve results that are regarded as collectively desirable. They are focused on the realisation of communal gains, within the prevailing relative prices, power relations, dominant interests and support for ideals. If the institutions are constant, then according to the figural model outlined in graph 2.1 the results to be achieved depend among other things on the circumstances within which actors apply the rules. Before discussing the theoretical results of social security rules in more detail, it will be useful to explore the influence of this historical context.

3.6.1 The historical background to rule application

Changes in the context of rule application, as discussed in §2.8, theoretically influence the results of social security rules in two ways. The first is direct: it may impact on the number of entitling events, and this works through into the interactions considered in the previous section. Historical developments can lead to an increase or decrease in the manifest risks – in all models discussed in the previous section the main condition for entitlements, and a driving factor for social security interactions. The second relates to changes in the perceptions of individual actors or agents, which can alter their aspirations and may lead to more or less defection.

Demographic trends are one historical factor that can have a strong influence on the number of entitling events. Of course this is most pronounced in the formal demographic schemes discussed earlier: the number of older persons, surviving dependants and families with children who are theoretically eligible for collective support correlates with the birth and mortality rates, the average age of marriage, fertility rates, migration processes, etc. State pensions, where every resident has a right to retirement benefit on reaching a certain age, are an extreme example. Presuming no entitled persons refuse their pension, every change in the balance between the influx of newly eligible elderly and the outflow of deceased persons will translate fully into the number of benefit recipients.

Obviously, in formal social security schemes an increase in the entitling events will affect the complicated interaction structure and the interdependent network of actors involved in it. The number of claims rises, and the social security organisation therefore has to establish rights and duties more frequently and deliver the entitlements accordingly: distribution of more benefits and provisions, and possibly more actions geared to prevention, reintegration and medical assessment. All things being equal, the swelling of the client base also leads to a rise in the number of mutations that have to be processed and an increase in the required monitoring and sanctioning activities. Of course there is also a greater need for funding. If the reserves are inadequate to cover the growth in entitlements, this implies that the contributions by employers, employees or taxpayers will have to rise; at least, as long as the institutional framework remains intact. Given the limited resources and the rising workload of the organisation, the board has a more difficult task in determining where the administration priorities should lie: on correct distribution of benefits, placement in paid work (if applicable, as in the case of young widows), promoting the well-being and social participation of benefit recipients, tackling fraud, and so on. The strain on the supervisory board and the social security court increases as well: as the number of entitlements rises, shortcomings in the administration will also be more frequent and more contestable decisions will be made.

However, informal familial, communal and occupational systems may also come under pressure if the number of needy older persons, surviving dependants and families with children grows substantially. For instance, if the prevalence of indigence among such groups rises in a familial social security system and the rules remain unchanged, the demands placed on the network of relatives will be intensified.

And even formal schemes which are not generally regarded as 'demographic' can be sensitive to certain population developments. For example, the take-up of sickness and disability benefit may increase if the share of elderly persons in the labour force grows, as a result of the rising average probability of becoming ill or incapacitated. The number of people in receipt of social assistance benefit correlates partly with migratory movements: if the number of needy immigrants exceeds the number of poor emigrants, the benefit volume will rise. Similarly, changes in the age at which people marry and have children can impact on the number of entitlements; the sooner they do so, the more child benefit has to be paid out at the national level, as the average number of children tends to increase. The prevalence of divorce is another example: the more frequent it becomes, the more social assistance benefit will have to be paid to single-parent families.

Demographic developments are often gradual, influencing the number of events over a protracted period of time. Yet demographic shocks can also occur, and these may knock the social security system off balance. The number of people dependent on benefit can increase sharply in times of famine, natural disasters, high refugee flows, or an expansion of the national territory and population (e.g. as a result of acts of war, colonisation or federalisation). Even if the latter process takes place peacefully, the consequences for social security can be significant. An example is the influence that German reunification had on benefit volumes and the distribution of entitled persons across various schemes (see chapter 5). The effects of such radical demographic changes moreover sometimes continue to be felt for a long time. If the birth rate or mortality rate in certain cohorts was high, this can still have an impact on the take-up of social security many years later. Examples include the easing of the pressure on German, French and British pension schemes in the 1950s which emanated from influx of the small 1886-1895 birth cohorts (mass deaths of young men in the trenches of the First World War) and again in the first half of the 1980s from the people born between 1915 and 1919 (low birth rates as the military were engaged in warfare). The anticipated growth in the number of retirement benefits as the post-Second World War baby-boomers will retire is another example.[39] Because comparatively small or large cohorts generally spawn proportionate numbers of offspring, demographic shocks such as these continue to influence the take-up of benefits in the even longer term, with a further delay of 25-30 years.

Although the demographic process exerts its influence primarily via the events, it can also affect the perceptions of actors. This applies, for instance, to the possible future decline of the solidarity between generations with regard to pension schemes that are funded by the apportionment (pay-as-you-go) method. One assumption is that the rising financial burden of contributing (growing numbers of pensions, fewer contributors) expected in the years to come will in the long run inevitably erode the willingness to fund the pensions, as the required contributions would swallow up too large a share of income, and would no longer be in fair proportion to the entitlements the current contributors may expect when they themselves retire. Whether this form of solidarity will actually decrease in the near future is doubtful, however. Empirical research suggests that in many countries currently the vast majority of the population believe that the government must ensure a decent standard of living for the elderly (see chapter 4).

The *economic process* is a second important context for the application of social security rules. It relates both to the course of the economic cycle and the more structural trends such as the long-term development in labour productivity, the substitution of labour by capital, or the declining importance of agriculture and industry in favour of the services sector.

If many people fall out of work during a period of recession, and the institutions remain stable, this will lead to an increase in the number of beneficiaries and to longer periods of dependency. In informal social security systems, more unemployed persons fall back on support provided by the rules of relief prevailing in their family, community or occupation. In formal systems the number of people taking up unemployment and social assistance benefits rises, though the number of entitled persons in schemes with a 'hidden' unemployment component – early retirement pension, disability benefit – can also increase. The volume growth in such circumstances has both an inflow and an outflow component. On the one hand the economic downturn leads to more people being laid off and declared unfit for work; on the other hand, the likelihood that benefit claimants will find work declines because of the smaller number of jobs available and the increased competition with other groups (such as school-leavers, who are cheaper and have more up-to-date training). The growth in the total benefit volume can be dampened somewhat because the number of 'work-related' benefits declines during a recession: if there are fewer people in work, the number of people entitled to sick pay, childcare facilities, etc., also tends to fall.

The social security organisation must accommodate fluctuations in the benefit volume resulting from the economic cycle. In principle the fund reserves ought to be adequate to cope with a temporary increase or decrease, and the other agencies should also be able to respond in a flexible way to cyclical changes in their workload (more or less intake, prevention, reinsertion, monitoring, sanctioning, support tasks, etc.). Yet in practice the resources of these corporate agents may not always be sufficient to enable it to absorb economic fluctuations. For instance, during an economic recession a government is likely to set limits to the organisation's budget in order to avoid sharp rises in spending. Under these circumstances acute deficits may arise, also because the average costs of many interventions mount up: it becomes more difficult for benefit claimants to find work, and as long-term unemployment rises so does the need for social support, etc.

Where an increase in unemployment has structural causes (and the rules do not change), this logically implies that the number of events increases permanently. This raises the theoretical minimum of the benefit volume, the required funding and the workload of the social security organisation. It is also possible that unemployment neither rises nor falls as a result of structural economic changes, but becomes concentrated in different groups.[40] As a corollary to this, the composition of the unemployed population will change as well, which may require adaptations in the administrative procedures.

The economic process theoretically also influences the perceptions of actors. People who are unemployed or unfit for work may regard their chances of finding work as poorer during a recession, making them less inclined to seek work intensively. The social security organisation may tolerate this to a certain extent. The administering officials, in view of their rising workload, may regard it as efficient and justified that benefit claimants who are difficult to place are not forced to look for jobs which they have little chance of getting anyway. The perceptions of firms also depend on the economic context; if they believe the economy is about to improve, they will be less inclined to dismiss people than when they anticipate a lengthy recession. Evidently, high unemployment rates are likely to impact on the recruitment and pay policy of companies as well. Since they have more choice when there is plenty of labour available, employers can impose strict selection criteria and lower the wages and fringe benefits they offer. On the supply side, some groups may decide under these circumstances to withdraw from the labour market altogether. Women who choose not to work and concentrate on their family care tasks instead, and young people who prolong their educational careers, are examples of such 'discouraged workers'.

One point for conjecture is whether formal social security systems can become permanently out of balance as a result of economic shocks. Van Praag et al. (1982) make this assumption when they refer to the 'flywheel effect' in social security. According to this theory, the shock of a sudden rise in unemployment such as occurred at the start of the 1980s can create a vicious circle of rising benefit dependency and rising contributions. This will ultimately lead to the demise of the social security schemes as the required contributions become unaffordable.[41] Others cast doubt on this assertion: the effect of such economic shocks has proved difficult to demonstrate in quantitative empirical research. The sharp rise in the number of benefit claimants in the Netherlands in the 1980s did for example lead to an increase in wage costs, but was not translated into a further rise in unemployment. The reason is probably that employees and trade unions were afraid to make high pay demands under those conditions: "in recent decades the effect of high unemployment on wage restraint was much greater than that of higher average costs in driving up pay" (De Beer, 2001: 108). According to this latter analysis, the rise in Dutch unemployment benefit volumes in the 1980s must be ascribed to the after-effects of the expansion of the social security system and to rather autonomous social and cultural trends (such as individualisation).

This illustrates the relevance of other historical developments to the application of social security rules. The number of entitling events can also be influenced by changes in the *social stratification*. If, for example, the percentage of people voluntarily living alone increases, this theoretically leads to a higher take-up of social assistance. Not only does the number of potentially entitled households grow, but the likelihood of their being in need of support also rises because there are fewer households with a partner's income to fall back on. Changes in the relative size of various socio-economic groups can also impact on the entitlements. As the share of self-employed people rises, the percentage of the labour force in receipt of unemployment insurance benefit tends to fall. Similarly, if the proportion of full-time breadwinners among couples declines and the proportion of double-earner households increases, this is likely to boost the number of entitling events in employee insurance schemes (because more people are insured), while the take-up of means-tested assistance may decline (because the partner's incomes imply that households are not poor enough to qualify if one member loses their job).

A changing social stratification can also alter the perceptions of actors; for instance, if the long-term unemployed become highly concentrated in specific neighbourhoods, the social security organisation may decide to regard them as a new target group for its social interventions.

Technological and scientific developments influence the number of entitling events primarily through changes in the production process. Innovative technologies may invoke new forms of economic activity and can boost total labour demand; but it is also possible that changed production methods raise efficiency and therefore depress employment. Both trends affect the take-up of benefits which are driven by the unemployment risk. It is also possible that they impact mainly on the composition of employment (greater demand for IT specialists, smaller demand for typists), thereby altering the risk of unemployment for specific groups on the labour market.

Technological and scientific innovations can also impinge on the risks covered by sick leave and disability benefit schemes. If the proportion of post-industrial employment increases, it is obvious to expect the number of occupational accidents to decline (due to the reduction in hazardous and physically strenuous industrial labour), whereas work incapacity as a result of psychological disorders may become more frequent. Advances in medical technology and knowledge (more specialisms, improved diagnostic methods and techniques) imply that somatic and mental diseases are recognised more frequently and sooner. This tends to increase the risk that people will be declared unfit for work, although the success of improved medical treatments may partly offset this.

It was argued earlier that the *ideals* that are dominant in a community can shape the rule generation process, in particular where formal rules are being drafted in a democratic society with unstable power relations, divided interests and low costs of expressing deviant opinions. However, in principle, ideals have little influence on the occurrence of risks during the rule application process. If the dominant view of the future changes – and the rules do not – the number of people who become old, unemployed, unfit for work, etc. does not increase or decrease. Even so, if new ideas about the desired future become accepted, this may lead to alterations in the subjective perceptions of actors and the way in which they apply the rules. The possible impact of changing policy doctrines illustrates this. In the Dutch social security policy up to the 1990s the 'entitlements doctrine' dominated, based on the principle that the first priority in the administrative process should lie in guaranteeing the income rights of those affected by social risks. In 1976, for example, the explanatory memorandum to the budget of the Ministry of Social Affairs stated that closures and reorganisations of firms often led to psychological incapacity to work among the employees, and that "it is good that these people can be accommodated in the disability benefits scheme" (TK, 1976/1977: 14). Looking back, policy makers were inclined to conclude that this was tantamount to approval of hiding unemployment in the disability benefits in order to limit the social consequences of mass redundancies. Over the next fifteen years the official policy line underwent a sea change, with the emphasis shifting to an 'activation doctrine'. In 1991 the same Ministry (TK, 1991/1992a: 21; TK, 1991/1992b: 1) announced its vision of the future by stating that

> it should [...] be a characteristic of a good social security system that not too many people need to make use of it, and that unavoidable use should not last any longer than necessary. [...] Increasing participation in gainful employment is the goal to which (the Ministry) will devote the highest priority. [...] This means that not only the employment policy, but also the income policy, the social security policy and the policy to improve the quality of work will as far as possible be geared to promoting labour participation.

If such contrasting policy visions are endorsed by the board and the officials – something which is by no means certain – the discretionary scope available to the social security organisation in applying the rules is likely to be used differently. Under the first doctrine, the most important thing will be to provide income and social support to the beneficiaries, whereas the second set of policy ideals will lead to the promotion of active job-seeking behaviour where possible, including strict monitoring and sanctioning.

3.6.2 Consequences for actors

The model in figure 2.1 indicates that rule-driven interactions have an impact on the actors. Since social security rules are in the first place designed to secure the rights of the beneficiaries, the results for these actors are in theory the most important. For them, the consequences may be partly intentional and positive. The application of the social security rules can – in comparison to the case where no such rights are granted – improve their income position, their labour potential, and their health and social participation. Thus they may be better off in terms of key resources, existential actor traits and the social relations they maintain within the community. Through preventive, restorative and compensatory interventions, social security allows the beneficiaries to make ends meet more easily or to preserve their standard of living to some extent; it helps them to find a job or to enhance their labour market prospects; and it creates the conditions for social integration and physical and mental health.

In addition there are a number of unintended positive consequences of the interaction process for the beneficiaries. They have more leisure time, and they are not exposed to the burdens and inconveniences of work: the physical and psychological effort required, the risk of becoming ill through working, hierarchical relationships and labour conflicts, travel time, etc.

Yet social security may also have negative effects for the beneficiaries. First of all, although they may be in a better position than they would be without social security, they still tend to be worse off than they were in the past. The rules offer relief, but generally do not provide *complete* prevention, restoration or compensation of the loss or lacks experienced by the recipients. From a collective point of view this is understandable; the costs of social security should be kept at an acceptable level, and the incentive to perform productive labour must not become too weak.

Even more important is that while social security rights are granted with positive intentions, having to depend on them may still have a negative impact on the recipients. This is a topic which goes back to studies on the attitudinal and behavioural repercussions of unemployment in the 1930s (Lazarsfeld-Jahoda & Zeisl, 1933; Eisenberg & Lazarsfeld, 1938; Jahoda, 1982). As a result of losing their job and becoming dependent on social security, people may experience a deterioration in their health and psychological well-being (more anxiety, depression, feelings of uncertainty and worthlessness; cf. McKee-Ryan et al., 2005). Unemployment can also lead to less – and less meaningful – time structuring, a pessimistic view of the future and a reduction in social contacts. A person's social position can be affected as well: their social prestige may decline, they may be stigmatised for being in receipt of benefit, and they may feel marginalised.

Taking the argument a step further, social security institutions and the interaction process in which the rights are granted may also directly evoke negative personal consequences for recipients. At the heart of the neo-conservative criticism of the welfare state is the allegation that social security does not help to emancipate people, but makes them dependent and inactive instead. The incentive for people to shape their own lives is taken away; the social security organisation tells beneficiaries what to do, and has an interest in sustaining the passive attitude of its clients (see e.g. Murray, 1984). A similar conclusion, albeit from an entirely different theoretical starting point, is drawn in critical sociology. Here the central focus is on the role of social security in imposing duties and discipline. In exchange for the rights they have been granted, beneficiaries must act in a loyal and morally correct manner, seek work intensively, participate in reintegration programmes, etc. The anonymous social security bureaucracy carries out strict monitoring of these duties and clamps down hard on rule-breakers. This can lead to feelings of being trapped, of powerlessness and of dependency vis-à-vis the social security organisation or the wider community. Or, in the frequently used terminology of Habermas (1981), the obligations imposed on the beneficiaries by social security schemes generally result in a *Kolonialisierung ihrer Lebenswelt*.[42]

The extent to which such positive and negative consequences actually emerge depends on the scope of the rules. For instance, if the rights in a formal system are generous and the duties light, if the social security organisation interprets the rules leniently and the informal rules emphasise solidarity, many of the negative repercussions referred to above may in fact be limited. The consequences experienced at the micro-level also tend to be linked to the duration of benefit dependency (the longer it lasts, the more negative the impact) and to the behavioural alternatives: the likelihood of finding employment, and the working conditions if people do so. Ultimately, therefore, the outcomes of social security interactions for the entitled persons have to be established empirically. In the fairly extensive Dutch social security system around 1995, the extent to which being out of work was voluntary proved to be an important intervening factor. Unemployed and disabled people reported lower well-being, poorer health, more stress, greater social isolation and less active use of their leisure time. People who had retired early and had therefore chosen voluntarily to be out of work were much less troubled by these phenomena. Their subjective feeling of well-being (satisfaction, happiness) was in fact even greater than that of those in work (De Beer, 2001: 115-201).

The micro-consequences of the interactions for the other actors are theoretically of secondary importance, and mostly are fairly obvious ones. For instance, individual contributors see their spending power constrained as a result of the duties imposed, and firms may be affected in terms of labour costs, and in the size, composition and quality of their workforce. Within the social security organisation, the various agents will realise the aims of their principals to a certain extent. For this they may be rewarded or punished in terms of salaries, budget and staff allocations, and the granting and withdrawal of privileges. Similarly, the social security organisation as a whole, the social security court, the supervisory board, etc. will be judged by their stakeholders in terms of the attainment of external goals, which may have repercussions on their budget, reputation or power.

3.6.3 Collective results

Following the figural model in §2.3, the collective results of rule-driven social security interactions feed back into the historical process. The institutions are especially likely to affect the degree of social structuring and the economic process, as social security rules typically intend to intervene in those areas. Before discussing the significance of this in more detail it is important to point out once more that the collective outcomes of social security need not be stable; for instance, the degree of benefit dependency, poverty and inequality generated by the same set of rules can vary within and between countries, depending on historical circumstances and the course taken in the interaction process. The instability theoretically is reinforced by the fact that the feedback creates the possibility of its own dynamic. As the results of rule-driven social security interactions work through into the historical process, the rule incentives may change and new rule wishes possibly emerge among the actors. Through the rule interaction on government production, typically in the legislative assembly (cf. §2.9.4), this can translate into institutional change. The latter implies that social security interactions are no longer driven by the same allocation of rights and duties, which can lead to changes in the collective results, and so on.

It may not be simple to assess to what extent certain collective outcomes imply the realisation of the communal goals social security sets out to achieve, because those aims tend to be fluid as well. As stated before, all institutional arrangements of this type reflect a prevailing conviction that it is socially beneficial to cover economic risks in a specific way. This of course means that the macro-objectives of social security are not theoretically fixed, but vary with the perceptions of dominant actors. It is therefore not always clear whether specific collective results are intended or unintended. To assess this, one has to recall the intentions that the rule-makers had when constituting the rules, and to describe the re-interpretation of those intentions at later moments. For instance, the founders of a disability regulation originally may have aimed at an extensive protection against the loss of income, while their successors may stress that disabled persons should utilise their remaining capacity for gainful employment as much as possible. Evidently, this will influence the way the collective outcomes of the disability scheme will be appreciated in terms of goal attainment.

Impact on social structuring

The first collective outcome in terms of social structuring is a rather obvious one. Social security rules lead directly to forms of social differentiation which would not arise without these institutions. The introduction of social security arrangements tends to create recognisable social categories: the children from the poorhouse, people on the dole, the long-term unemployed (or 'UB-40s'), single welfare mothers, OAPs, and so on. They may be aware of their shared social position, and may organise themselves on those grounds, for example in client organisations. Social differentiation and organisation can also occur among the contributors and agents of the social security organisation: discontented tax payers may unite and form a single issue political party, the doctors of the medical assessment agency may join in a professional association, and so on.

Social security also influences the process of social stratification, which, as mentioned in chapter 2, refers to changes in both the position of social groups on various social ladders (criteria for social distinction, such as income, descent, prestige, achievements), and the dominant ranking principles (the relative importance of the social ladders). Theoretically, social security mainly aims at influencing the rankings. Through awarding rights, and diverting the funds gathered from the contributors to the beneficiaries, the rules try to uphold the income, labour market position, health and social integration of the vulnerable strata of the population to some degree. This may prevent the beneficiaries from displaying behaviour that the community regards as undesirable (criminality, prostitution, vagrancy, emigration). This is not to say that the rules by definition reduce the oppositions between different groups considerably; the influence of social security on distribution ladders is an empirical question. Social security is usually accompanied by redistribution: the taxes and premiums paid by the contributors are used to secure the income, employment, health and social participation of the recipients. Depending on the way of institutionalisation, this can both reinforce and reduce the differences between social groups. If systems are set up along Bismarckian lines, the emphasis is on reproduction of the existing social hierarchy, mainly in terms of the differentials between status groups. Evidently, if every social or occupational group has its own social security schemes, the solidarity principle only applies within the existing social strata, and the differences between them remain intact. Universalist forms of social security, by contrast, may reduce social polarisation because here there is more solidarity between higher and lower strata.

The impact of social security interactions on the dominant ranking principles is theoretically less marked. Generally, social security rules tend to reflect the prevailing stratification criteria rather than determine their relative weight. Yet the latter is not entirely impossible. If a closed, class-based society suddenly has solidary social security rules imposed upon it – for example following a revolution or after losing a war – this can lead to a decay of the traditional stratification ladders. Since the resources are no longer allocated in accordance with the old class distinctions, the different social strata become less recognisable and the status-specific standards of conduct (such as showing respect to benefactors) may no longer be respected in interactions. Other hierarchical principles may then eventually come to dominate, for example the oppositions between occupational classes or educational groups.

Elite-formation, the fourth aspect of social structuring identified earlier, can also theoretically correlate with the prevailing social security rules. This applies particularly in democratic societies. Here the selection of the political elite may be determined by the importance that voters attach to current social security issues (indexation of benefits, maintaining the level of pensions) and by the number and composition of the beneficiary population (the 'beneficiaries' vote'). The 'median voter hypothesis' (Black, 1948, 1987; Downs, 1957) goes a step further. Its basic assumption is that rule-makers necessarily optimise the utility of persons holding the middle ground in the electorate, as this is the surest way to gain a democratic majority. This implies, among other things, that it does not really matter which elite is in charge: all public services, including the system of social security transfers and contributions, will always have to reflect the preferences of the electorate around the median income, age, education, expectations, etc., because their vote is decisive. If those median values change, the institutions will have to follow; e.g. an ageing population will imply that median voters favour higher, wage-indexed pensions, and any political candidate must accommodate those preferences in order to be supported by a majority of the electorate.[43]

The establishment and survival of government coalitions can also depend on political compromises on social security issues. If the power of the political elites hinges on this, it is likely that the rule generation process will be affected as well. This can imply that only expedient amendments to the formal social security rules will be made, while changes that violate the coalition agreement or endanger the public favour are likely to be suspended or reversed.

Impact on the economic process

The central question with regard to the economic consequences of social security is whether the prevailing rules increase or reduce the prosperity of a community. By way of introduction, a few qualifying comments can be made here. In the first place, the influence of social security institutions should not be overstated. Collective wealth depends primarily on the natural resources, infrastructure, technology, knowledge and human capital which a community possesses. Some of these factors may be influenced by social security rules, but in principle they are by no means determined by them. Moreover, collective prosperity may depend to a large extent on developments outside the community, regardless of the local or national institutions. For example, the output of the relatively open Dutch economy is determined to a considerable extent by developments in world trade and its main trading partners, movements in interest rates on the international capital markets, the exchange rate of the euro, the monetary policy of the European Central Bank, and so on. Besides this, the economic effects of social security are theoretically complex. This can be seen very clearly in economic models which depict the many interactions between social security institutions, labour market characteristics and economic growth.[44]

Different economic schools paint a different picture of the influence of social security on communal prosperity.[45] First and foremost, the influence depends on the definition of wealth. If it is perceived in subjective terms, the prosperity of a community can be defined as the sum of the utility, satisfaction, or happiness that actors derive from the individual and collective goods they possess (cf. Van Praag & Ferrer-i-Carbonell, 2004; Layard, 2005). With such a definition social security rules increase communal wealth to the extent that actors derive direct advantage from it (the personal rights they acquire), save on transaction costs (because they do not need to weigh up which individual insurance will suit them best), and value the certainty that the community offers them (as they may have to fall back on social security themselves). It is also possible that people are sensitive to the prosperity of others, or to the inequality of the distribution, and for that reason experience a higher subjective utility as a result of social security transfers. The fact that others are no longer poor or deprived can be appreciated as a token of civilisation or connectedness of the community to which one belongs.

For the beneficiaries, the subjective contribution to prosperity by social security will generally be positive on balance; otherwise they would probably make no use of the scheme.[46] In order to assess the total, this has to be balanced against the way other actors assess the costs and benefits of the institutions. The contributors, for instance, will tend to experience a negative subjective utility as a result of the fall in their net income (although this may be mitigated by their possible future entitlements and a positive appraisal of lower poverty and inequality rates).

Generally, however, economists prefer a more objectified approach to prosperity, defining it as the degree to which scarcity has been eliminated, or the extent to which needs are met through the use of scarce resources. As this is difficult to determine at the collective level, the total income of a community or its total output is often used as a proxy. Here again, the definition is debatable. For example, should the monetary value of domestic work and the shadow economy (crime, undeclared employment) be included in calculating the wealth of the community? And should the social costs of the production process, such as environmental damage, also be taken into account?

By convention, the yardstick used to measure national wealth is per capita gross domestic product (GDP), or the added value of the output of industry and the government which is realised per head of the population.[47] Theoretically this is determined by many different economic variables (cf. §2.9.2). In order to assess the effects of social security on collective prosperity, it is necessary to investigate how the rules affect such factors, and how this translates into actual output.[48]

One potential positive economic effect of social security institutions is that they may enhance or maintain productivity. As noted earlier, the promotion of public gains and the prevention of public bad were very important motives in the creation of the first formal social security schemes. The collective provisions can directly increase the productive capacity of the community; by making people generally healthier, happier, better integrated etc. they enable more or better goods and services to be produced. It is also possible that social security systems contribute to the prevention of serious social problems such as crime, labour conflicts and epidemics, or help to maintain the productive capacity when a community is hit by mass unemployment or disasters.

A variant of this line of reasoning stresses the positive effects achieved through the education of the population. In an imperfect capital market and with declining returns on education, people with a low income will not invest to the maximum in education for themselves or their children (cf. Aghion et al., 1999: 1630). An adequate basic level of social security, linked to compulsory schooling and a generally accessible education system can correct for this. The community then acquires a better educated labour force than would be the case without the institutions; and such an increase in 'human capital' theoretically leads to higher economic growth.[49]

Social security can also have a positive influence on prosperity by boosting consumption. Income transfers influence consumption expenditure because poor beneficiaries spend a greater proportion of their income than the better off; they also more frequently purchase local goods and services, thus reducing imports. In an unfavourable economic climate, social security can help to counter a collapse in demand and a downturn in production. When the economy is booming the expenditures of benefit recipients may give GDP growth an additional boost, and a larger amount can be redistributed without the disposable incomes of the contributors falling in real terms.[50]

Fourthly, the cushion of certainty provided by social security implies that actors can afford to take more financial risks. This may lead to changes in behaviour which increase the communal wealth. For example, if the risks of occupational disease and impairment are covered, this may make more people inclined to look for work, leading to a higher labour supply and more, or cheaper, production. Social security institutions can also make it easier for people to change jobs; and greater job mobility may imply that the available productive capacity is utilised more effectively. Social security can increase the propensity to invest as well; it is less risky to set up or expand a business when there is a social safety net to fall back on.

A final potential positive contribution to collective output consists of the employment created in the administration of social security. In modern welfare states a substantial number of people are employed in the various parts of the social security organisation. Between 1980 and 2000, for example, this sector accounted for approximately 80,000 employment years on average in the Netherlands, roughly 1.5% of the total employment volume.[51]

The assumed direct positive effects on productivity underlie the creation of the first modern social security schemes, which in most Western countries occurred between 1875 and 1930. The influence exerted through consumer spending was a key element in Keynesian economic theory, which drove the development of the social security systems after the economic crisis in the 1930s and the Second World War. The policy pursued at that time was based among other things on the belief that economic growth and the creation of more extensive formal social security arrangements go hand in hand.

In the wake of the recession in the 1980s, policy in many Western countries fell under the influence of the neoclassical theory. This economic school mainly stressed the negative side-effects of social security. The chief proposition is that public provisions do not offer compensation for imperfections in the capital and labour markets, but on the contrary that the involved redistribution distorts the market mechanism. According to this view, social security regulations give economic actors (firms, employees, beneficiaries) fewer or the wrong incentives, and this ultimately has a negative effect on collective wealth. It is therefore argued that state intervention should be kept to a minimum, that the number of rules should be reduced and that existing social security arrangements should be largely privatised. This standpoint follows inexorably from the theoretical framework adopted by many neoclassical economists: rational actors operating in perfectly competitive, self-regulating, and continuously clearing[52] markets. From this premise most aspects of formal social security tend to imply a loss of economic efficiency. The positive functions of this kind of rules – the expected collective gains for which they were created in the first place – are absent; the potential contribution of social security to the wealth of the community is ignored. Put differently (Atkinson, 1999: 8),

> The theoretical framework incorporates none of the contingencies for which the welfare state exists. There is no uninsured uncertainty in the model, nor involuntary unemployment, nor is the future introduced in any meaningful way. The whole purpose of welfare state provision is missing from the theoretical model.

Despite this qualifying comment, it is of course possible that the economic disadvantages of social security schemes actually outweigh the gains. The neoclassical criticism of social security focuses on four points.

First it is emphasised that formal social security systems reduce the need to save, since private households need to set aside less to cover the eventualities of becoming old, unemployed, unfit for work, sick, etc. This implies that less money is available to invest in the means of production and that the interest rate will go up. Ultimately, the capital stock will fall, and in a closed economy the level of national wealth then by definition drops as well. Theoretically, this wealth-reducing aspect especially applies to pay-as-you-go schemes.[53] Mason (2005: 557) notes that the empirical evidence on the issue is rather mixed: a few studies report a large impact on saving rates, while others find weak effects or conclude that the size of social security transfers does not depress saving at all.

A second criticism from the neoclassical perspective concerns the effect of social security contributions on labour costs. An extension of social security dependency may lead to increasing employer contributions, or push up labour costs indirectly if rising employee contributions translate into higher wage demands. Because this would lead to a decrease in the expected profit, firms may decide to increase their prices, to invest less, to substitute labour by capital,[54] or to relocate their activities ('outsourcing') to a cheaper town, region, or country. All of these reactions theoretically have a negative impact on collective prosperity: less demand for goods and services, a decrease in production, more unemployment, etc. In addition, higher contributions may affect labour supply, although the net impact of this on collective prosperity theoretically is unclear.[55]

The third element of the neoclassical critique concerns the influence of social security on the unemployment rate through the labour market behaviour of benefit recipients and employers. Unemployment and social assistance benefits (and other schemes with a 'hidden' unemployment component) may reduce the need for recipients to go to work and can make employers more inclined to lay off surplus personnel. Since higher unemployment means that the production capacity is not being used to the optimum, this reduces the collective wealth. Benefit levels are a first factor here; in theory, unemployment rises more the closer average benefit levels are to average wage levels, i.e. as the replacement rate rises. The duration of benefit also plays a role; the longer the maximum level of benefit is paid, the higher unemployment will be in theory. Finally, the so-called poverty trap implied in additional income-related benefits (such as housing benefit) may make it unattractive for benefit recipients to start working.

According to the influential study by Layard et al. (1991), an increase in the replacement rate of 10 percentage points means that unemployment will rise over time by 1.7 percentage points, while increasing the duration of the benefits by one year pushes up unemployment by 0.9 percentage points. These findings contradicted the results of earlier research (cf. e.g. OECD, 1994), in which the generosity of benefits was found to have a non-significant or very limited effect on the labour supply; and the conclusion is in fact still not entirely without controversy (for a critical discussion see Atkinson, 1999: 43-48). A later study moreover pointed out that the negative effect on unemployment is partially offset by the fact that more generous social security benefits increase the willingness to go to work (Nickell, 1997: 67-68):

> While high benefits lead to high unemployment, they also lead to high participation because they make participation in the labor market more attractive ... the higher unemployment effect and the higher labor market participation effect tend to cancel out.

There are several reasons why it is plausible that the effects of social security benefits on unemployment are less uniform than the neoclassical theory assumes, especially the effect on job-seeking behaviour. Looking for and finding a job does not always depend on the short-term relative financial attractiveness of working and being dependent on benefit. The main reason Dutch benefit recipients give for not working are their health condition and their bad labour market prospects, not the limited material gains of employment. Almost all benefit recipients want to work if they are able to, and they often accept jobs that are no more lucrative than their initial benefit. The nature of the job is a decisive factor: attractive jobs are accepted by a wide majority of the job-seekers, regardless of the pay; while unattractive work is often refused, even when the rewards are higher (Hoff & Jehoel-Gijsbers, 2003; Van Echtelt & Hoff, 2008).

The neoclassical approach also ignores the many labour incentives that are typically included in social security regulations. For example, most benefit entitlements apply for only a limited period, and there are often all kinds of administrative constraints which seek to reduce the period of benefit dependency (duty to apply for work, intensive job counselling, monitoring and control, positive and negative sanctions).[56] Informal social security rules may also run counter to the neoclassical assumptions; e.g., even those not in work often believe that people should earn their own keep where possible. In a Dutch survey jobless men and women actually scored higher on a work ethic scale than their working peers[57] (De Beer, 2001: 168-170).

A fourth mechanism by which social security in the neoclassical perspective may limit economic growth regards the competition of transfer incomes with government investments which would produce a higher return. If social security costs rise there is less money available for, e.g. the transport infrastructure, education, and funding scientific research. This, too, in the long run may reduce the collective wealth, as there is less mobility, human capital and technological innovation than would be the case without social security.

As this overview shows, the effects of social security on the prosperity of the community are complex, and it is not possible to make a final statement on theoretical grounds as to their direction or extent. Whether the positive or negative economic effects of social security dominate has to be determined empirically, for real benefit systems and the actual circumstances prevailing in a specific context of rule application. However, the available empirical research on this topic also fails to produce any uniform conclusions. The effect of specific social security rules often proves to be slight. In their classical meta-analysis, Danziger et al. (1981: 1019) concluded that income transfer programmes had only a limited impact in reducing the labour supply and private savings. Set against this was a sharp reduction in poverty and income inequality (see also e.g. Moffitt, 1992). The picture does not become any clearer if the combined effect of many social security institutions is examined. Atkinson (1999) discusses ten studies in which the influence of the total raft of social transfers is incorporated in models which seek to explain economic growth. Most of the studies relate to OECD countries and cover periods ranging from 12 to 25 years. In two of these studies the result was not significant. Four mentioned a positive effect of social security transfers: an increase of five percentage points in welfare spending led to an increase in the annual GDP growth of between 0.3 and 0.9 percentage points. In the other four studies the situation was reversed: the same increase in spending caused GDP to fall on an annual basis by 0.3-1 percentage points. One study concluded that "social security expenditures ... show positive and significant relationships with economic growth", another that "social security transfers reduce growth rates rather strongly" (see Atkinson, 1999: 34-35). In a more recent empirical study which focused on old age pensions in 64 countries, Zhang & Zhang (2004) found a positive impact of social security on economic growth. According to these authors, an increase in pension expenditure does not affect relative savings; it does however lead people to have fewer children, while they simultaneously invest more in the education of their offspring. The latter 'human capital' effect of social security would be the dominating one (Zhang & Zhang, 2004: 473, 494, 496):

> The empirical evidence suggests that social security tends to stimulate per capita growth by reducing fertility and increasing human capital investment without affecting the savings rate. [...] Social security may be conducive to growth through tipping the trade-off between the number and quality of children toward the latter. [... This] differs from the popular view in the literature that regards social security as harmful to economic growth [... and from the outcomes of] recent related work, and further investigation of this issue is still highly needed.

All in all, the empirical material offers no help in pronouncing a final verdict on the impact of transfers on collective prosperity. As mentioned earlier, this is to be expected: theoretically the economic effects of social security institutions depend on the precise nature of these rules, the historical context in which they are applied, and the perceptions and rule-driven behaviour of the actors involved.

Social security not only influences the level and growth of collective prosperity, but also its distribution. This type of institution by definition involves a redistribution of money or goods from contributors to beneficiaries; thus, it impacts on the personal[58] distribution of income after taxes and transfers. In this way it reduces the economic differentials between individual actors; the latter are often correlated to the prevailing social rankings (status groups, caste, social classes, ethnic origin), but the correspondence need not be perfect.

In principle the redistributive part of the economic process can take three forms. Incomes may be transferred from higher to lower income groups (vertical redistribution, from rich to poor), between different types of households within the same income group (horizontal redistribution, for example from single persons to married couples), and between generations (intergenerational redistribution, typically from younger to older generations).

To some extent, the degree of redistribution and the economic differentials depend directly on the social security institutions. These rules establish the duties of the contributors, the means by which the contributions are raised (taxing the incomes of all residents, employee and employer contributions, consumption taxes), and the contributions structure (the level and degree of progressiveness of the contribution rates, contribution-free allowances, tax relief). The rules also determine the rights of the beneficiaries: the level of benefits and provisions, the duration of the entitlements, the restrictions on access. Theoretically, the more generous the rights, the further the duties extend, and the more redistribution will occur. Yet the actual degree of redistribution and income inequality is also affected by the context in which the rules are applied and by the behaviour of actors. Economic, demographic and social trends can all have a marked effect on benefit volumes, and the number of recipients codetermines the amount of redistribution. The way in which actors apply the rules is also relevant: the extent to which beneficiaries abuse social security and contributors avoid or evade their duties, the intensity of monitoring and sanctioning by the social security organisation.

The empirical research on this topic concentrates on the national distribution of annual incomes from employment. In Western welfare states the extent of redistribution brought about by social security and the degree of income inequality following the collective transfers are found to diverge, both between countries and over time (see e.g. Ervik, 1998; Gottschalk & Smeeding, 2000; Ferrarini & Nelson, 2002; Förster & Mira d'Ercole, 2005; OECD, 2008).[59]

It may be important to reiterate the difference between social structuring and income inequality briefly here. As stated, the former refers to the differentiation of social groups, their positions on social stratification ladders, the dominant stratification criteria and the process of elite-formation. Income inequality is one of the outcomes of the economic process; it tends to reflect the prevailing social structure, but need not coincide with it. The same degree of income inequality (e.g. equal Gini coefficients) can apply to divergent social distinctions. For instance, in similar distributions the composition of low-income groups may vary: in a predominantly agricultural society the lowest deciles will contain large numbers of unskilled casual farm workers, whereas in a modern welfare state benefit recipients and students will dominate. And although groups with a high status or prestige tend to have high incomes as well (because they have better access to education and well-paid jobs, and more opportunities to influence the rules in such a way that they legitimately acquire a high income), the correlation is not complete. An elected government leader does not always receive a top income; the voluntary poor (monks who have taken a vow of poverty, ascetics) may carry high esteem; the *nouveaux riches* are often regarded with disdain.

Other collective results

Social security arrangements are often set up in order to achieve certain social and economic results. This does not mean that they cannot influence the other elements of the historical process depicted in figure 2.1. The potential influence on technological developments (promoting innovation through the certainty offered by social security, fewer investments) has already been discussed above. Social security rules generally do not lead directly to the formation of new ideals. At most they do so via the social and economic results which are (or are not) regarded as fair or efficient. As stated, in that case the desire for different rules, or for the maintenance of the existing social security system, can play a key role in the rule generation process.

The effects of the institutions on the demographic process are theoretically greater. In the first place, they can have a direct influence on birth and death rates. If a social security system fails to prevent poverty to a sufficient degree and people cannot afford adequate medical provisions, this can in the long run work through into the population statistics. Thus, social assistance and specific arrangements for child benefit, old-age pension and exceptional medical expenses can have a direct influence on child mortality and life expectancy. Mortality rates may increase where the state pension system pays very low benefits or where health provisions are too expensive or not universally available. The presence or absence of social regulations may also affect the need to reproduce, something that is an issue of debate especially in countries where the fertility rate is considered too low (typically, less than the average of 1.7-1.9 births per woman required for a stable population size). Introducing an extensive system of old-age pensions may have a denatalist effect: people no longer need children to look after them in their old age and will therefore be less inclined to reproduce, especially if birth control is both available and culturally accepted. The negative impact of old age pension expenditure on fertility has been corroborated by, e.g., Zhang & Zhang (2004, cf. above). Yet it may be partly offset by the pronatalist impact of generous family provisions (McDonald, 2002): child benefits, lump-sum payments (e.g. 'baby bonuses' at birth), general or earmarked tax rebates or credits (e.g. for additional costs of childcare, housing), and subsidised goods and services for children (e.g. medical and dental care). The effects of such schemes tend to be rather limited, however: based on an econometric model covering 22 industrialised countries, Gauthier & Hatzius (1997) estimated that a 25 percent increase in family allowances in the long run raises the average fertility rate by 0.07 children per woman.

Social security institutions may also influence household formation. If, say, widows lose their right to surviving dependants' benefit if they remarry, this can dissuade them from embarking on a new relationship. Conversely, people's prime motive for changing their household position may be to acquire certain rights; single-parent families may be established partly as a result of the opportunity structure offered by social assistance schemes, child benefit, specific tax advantages, etc.

A final demographic process which may theoretically be affected by social security rules concerns migratory movements. Attractive social security schemes may pull in foreigners (immigration), whereas a low level of provisions may push people into emigration. Such 'social security tourism' is theoretically fostered if the discrepancies between countries in the formal systems are considerable, the differences in language and informal rules are surmountable, and migration cannot be regulated effectively, e.g. by imposing legal settlement requirements or a system of work permits.

3.7 Institutional change: from informal to formal systems

This section looks briefly at the rule generation process in social security. The perspective on institutional change that was outlined in the previous chapter (see figure 2.1 and §2.9) theoretically also applies to the genesis of social security rules. This will be demonstrated here on the basis of one of the greatest changes in social security: the transition from largely informal arrangements to predominantly state systems, which took place in Western Europe mainly between 1875 and 1930 (see also the analysis by De Swaan (1988), as discussed in chapter 1). Naturally, this transition did not occur in precisely the same way in each different country: both the content and the phasing of the transition varied. However, the broad outlines of the transition can be described adequately in terms of the theoretical rule generation process in figure 2.1: changes in the historical process lead to a different incentive to regulate, which brings about changes in the perceptions of actors; this in turn, primarily via the policy process, results in new forms of institutionalisation.

In the historical process a number of elements coincided. First demographic, technological and economic developments changed the nature and scale of the risks. The population was growing rapidly, among other things due to better medical care which led to falling infant mortality and longer average life expectancy. This increased the labour supply as well as the number of dependants. In the Netherlands, for example, the number of people aged 60 and above rose by 86% in the second half of the 19th century, while the number of 0-19 year-olds climbed by 69%. There was large-scale mechanisation of the production process in this period, coupled with a growing supply of low-skilled labour. The latter were in a dependent position with respect to the owners of the capital goods. Under these historical circumstances the number of needy elderly persons increased, the number of accidents at work rose, wages were barely above the subsistence minimum, labourers had to work very long hours, and economic recessions prompted mass unemployment. Low family incomes fostered socially undesirable behaviour such as child labour, prostitution and crime.

On the other hand, in principle the economic growth was sufficient to finance collective provisions via redistribution or insurance. The necessary accounting techniques (probability calculus, actuarial mathematics) and data (e.g. mortality tables) were available, and the legal system was sufficiently developed to enable the rights and duties of the citizens to be defined. As a result of the transition from local to national economies and labour markets, the vesting of formal institutions enabled economies of scale to be realised in the administration process.

In terms of social structuring, the oppositions between the classes became more important. The traditional, often more or less aristocratic elite found itself competing with representatives of the well-to-do liberal bourgeoisie, or was even replaced by it.[60] This new ruling group was in turn challenged by competing counter-elites: socialists, communists, feminists, anarchists and representatives of various religious minority groups, some of them linked to the petty bourgeoisie. These opposing forces to some extent promoted equality and emancipation ideals which took their inspiration from the Enlightenment, but became much more radical in the 19th-century ideologies. The counter-elites also harked back to the Christian traditions of charity, mutual care and striving for eternal salvation, ideals which were not easy to reconcile with the growing social ills of the time.

Thus, the historical process impacted on all factors which theoretically drive institutionalisation: the relative prices were altered (mainly because of the low wages and high risk of factory workers becoming needy); the conflicts of interest shifted (mainly because of the more pronounced class differences); the power relations changed (due to the rise of the bourgeoisie as a dominant or competing elite, and the formation of various counter-elites in reaction to this); and the ideals propagated by the counter-elites gained ground in society.

The consensus on the formalisation of social security did not come about without a struggle. In many countries there was a heated debate on 'the social question' and the need for government intervention. The fact that a form of consensus was ultimately achieved in most Western countries had to do with three changing perceptions, which increasingly led the actors concerned to aspire formal regulation. In the first place a different view of causality began to gain influence. The occurrence of mass unemployment, poverty, poor working conditions, etc., was no longer ascribed purely to the moral shortcomings of individuals or the lower echelons of society, nor to any form of divine predestination, but increasingly came to be regarded as a consequence of the way in which industrial production was organised and embedded in society. This turned these phenomena into social risks in need of a collective solution.

In the second place there was a growing awareness that the existing informal social security arrangements were unable to provide an adequate answer to the scale and nature of these risks. The scope for family support was limited, because relatives of needy individuals tended to be unemployed or indigent as well. The benefits provided by charitable institutions became more meagre due to dilution effects: the growth in the available resources failed to keep pace with the rising demand (for the Netherlands see e.g. Van Loo, 1992: 67). On top of this, demographic changes – especially mass migration from the countryside to the rapidly growing urban areas – meant that local communities had become unstable. As a result the systems of social norms on which these forms of familial and communal social security were based became less effective. The informal occupational social security arrangements common to traditional crafts and trades proved inadequate in the context of modern industrial production. And the large pool of labour supply meant that modern firm owners generally regarded occupational social security as needless cost increases (with the exception of a small minority of socially aware entrepreneurs).

Thirdly, many people felt there was no alternative to government regulation, and this increasingly came to be seen as advantageous. Formalisation of social security could meet the dual objective of promoting public gains and preventing public losses. The bourgeois elite frequently saw this as a means of ameliorating the greatest ills of the industrial production process: externalities such as strikes, health risks that might be transferred to them, etc. The desire among this group to vest a strong nation-state, which could compete economically and militarily with other countries, also played a role. That goal was more achievable with a healthy, fairly educated and loyal population, something which could be promoted via adequate social security arrangements. As this was a common interest of the ruling bourgeois elite, it was a natural presumption that these risks should be covered collectively and compulsory.

For the counter-elites, formalisation of social security was a means of promoting a decent standard of living and emancipation for their rank and file; here the redistribution motive was dominant. Government regulation would enable the oppressive strictures of the old charity system – based on favours and strongly focused on reproducing the existing social status quo – to be broken. Market-based solutions were regarded as less expedient, partly because of idealistic factors (the rejection of 'capitalist' solutions for social problems), and partly because the lower classes could expect risk selection. As 'bad risks', they would not be accepted by private insurers, or only at premiums that they could not afford; and although for some eventualities (such as funeral expenses) mutual nonprofit insurance companies could offer a solution, the counter-elites typically regarded state intervention as the only viable solution for the major industrial risks (unemployment, illness and incapacity for work, old age, medical expenses).

Such rule wishes ultimately resulted in formalised social security rules because the nature of the policy process also changed in the same period. The transition from suffrage based on property ownership or tax payments to a universal suffrage was important, since it altered the power relations in the legislative assembly. As a result, more account had to be taken of the interests and rule wishes of people who were not allied to the ruling elite. This was accompanied by the formation of political parties, which made the ties between electors and elected less personal. Parliaments also made frequent use of their non-legislative powers, for example by exercising the right to conduct inquiries in order to chart the situation with regard to social ills and thus to justify government intervention.

The institutionalisation that occurred in the policy process reflected the diverse rule wishes of the dominant bourgeoisie and of the counter-elites, who entered into an alliance. The content and form of the formal social security system was also determined in part by the decisions on competing issues in the political arena, such as the funding and demarcation of state and private education. The eventual compromise typically broke through the existing status quo less decisively than the counter-elite had aimed for. The regulations were often limited to a basic coverage for the most pressing risks (child labour, accidents at work, illness and old age), and the emphasis was generally placed on maintaining the existing social hierarchy, in line with the social insurance model.

3.8 Conclusions

In this part of the study, a number of conceptual and theoretical issues already discussed in chapter 2 have been explored for social security. What does this notion entail? What are social security institutions, what types can be discerned, and how do they relate to each other? How do people acquire such rules? In what way do social security institutions govern interactions, and which actors are involved in the process? What are the consequences of such interactions? How are social security institutions created, and what causes them to change? The answers given to these questions can be summarised as follows.

Social security
Current scientific literature yields both narrow and broad approaches to social security. The narrow approach focuses mainly on guaranteeing a minimum income for all inhabitants and maintaining the acquired standard of living for the working population if peo-

ple are affected by a limited number of specific risks. This is accomplished through statutory social insurances and national provisions. In the broad approach, social security is not confined to income protection. It seeks to compensate all 'human damage' (security of income, employment, health, and social participation), and is not limited to legal arrangements provided by the government. Compensation of losses through awarding benefits should in principle only occur if interventions aimed at prevention and restoration are not possible. The cover provided is not limited to traditional risks such as old age, unemployment or disability, but includes all eventualities leading to human damage, regardless of the cause.

Both approaches have some disadvantages. The first equates social security to a collection of formal income regulations for specific and conventional risks. The second appears to equate it to the entire welfare state and takes little account of the impact of specific rule arrangements. The broad approach is also a-historical in its presumption of a natural evolution towards ever higher levels of social security; and a-sociological in its scant attention for the importance of actors as rule-creators and rule-subjects, and in its focus on the individual impact of interventions, thereby neglecting the collective consequences of social security.

For these reasons, preference is given in this study to an institutional demarcation of the concept. In this view, social security comprises the collectively defined rights, duties, conditions and potential sanctions which aim to generate positive social outcomes by protecting individual actors against economic deficits. Thus conceived, social security is essentially a set of rules; these may be contained in traditional Bismarckian social insurances or Beveridgean national provisions, but other forms of institutionalisation are possible as well. Building on the institutional analysis in chapter 2, all social security rules can be presented in terms of a logical fundamental structure (see §3.2).

Institutions of social security

According to the definition, social security logically does not include arrangements without a collective purpose (such as theft insurance), or which are not aimed at individuals (e.g. state aid to large enterprises) or have no direct bearing on the economic deficits of persons or households (for instance, long-term ecological risks). Neither is it possible to make a positive identification of social security on deontological grounds; there is no such thing as a right division of social security rights which has to be applied universally. The content of social security institutions as defined here is always consensual and historical. The common denominator for affluent modern societies includes rules aiming at the classic contingencies of social security (old age, unemployment, surviving dependants, the maintenance of children, illness, disability, sickness leave, and occupational diseases and accidents); at new income risks (e.g. parental leave, divorce); at labour risks (minimum standards on working hours or conditions, child care facilities, subsidised employment, workfare); at health risks (medical costs, including prevention, informal care, etc.); and at the costs of socially required activities (e.g. sports club membership for children).

Social security systems always contain informal elements: values relating to solidarity and fairness, norms concerning the allocation of rights and duties that are recognised within a group or community, and conventions in relation to the operation of the schemes (such as application procedures). Social security may also be structured entirely informally, for example as a mutual care system.

Although informal regulations have not disappeared entirely, in modern societies formal social security arrangements at the national level prevail. In these formal systems a theoretical distinction can be made between collective social security, occupational social security that is enforced by the government, and private contracts that are regulated by the government (the first, second, and third pillars).

Regulations must always to some extent be supported by the consensus within the community; however, there is no compulsory or logical hierarchical ranking of informal and formal social security rules.

Acquiring social security rules

Social security institutions are theoretically weakly socialised. In childhood, people do not need these rules in order to be able to function; and in adulthood, most people do not apply them on a day-to-day basis either. Moreover, the rules are often complicated, abstract and ambiguous, making them difficult to internalise in both primary and secondary socialisation. Apart from a limited group of professional 'rule specialists', there is little explicit transfer of the social security institutions. The undersocialised nature of social security is theoretically greatest in formal systems; in informal systems, socialisers have an interest in instilling some basic principles of rights and duties, because they are likely to become dependent on the good will of their offspring in the future. As a consequence, the risk of rule-breaking is theoretically greatest in formal systems.

Actors and interactions

The main actors in social security include the beneficiaries, the contributors, social security organisations and other corporate actors, in particular firms and government agencies. Basic interactions are the granting of rights; interventions aiming at the prevention, restoration or compensation of lacks and losses; the imposition and collection of contributions; and monitoring and sanctioning. However, the actors, their mutual relations and interactions vary depending on the type of scheme. This was elaborated in six theoretical models of rule-driven interaction representing differing social security systems.

In informal interaction models a distinction can be made between familial, communal and occupational types. Familial schemes typically cover the risk of indigence through a direct and sequential exchange of material support among relatives. The interaction is driven by the informal rules of the family, which are embedded in the wider community. Even so, actors have considerable latitude in interpreting their rights and duties, as the rules are vague and only moderately socialised. This makes defection likely, especially where there is an accumulation of risks (e.g. mass unemployment), the connectedness within the family is low, or the family rules are not endorsed by the wider community.

Communal systems are governed by local informal rules and are aimed mainly at combating material want among residents. In the interaction structure, a local social security organisation mediates between contributors and beneficiaries. The rights of the latter are meagre and subject to strict qualifying and conduct conditions, and are monitored closely. However, the board, collectors and attendants of the communal organisation have great freedom of action. This introduces a 'principal-agent problem' which is absent in familial schemes.

Informal occupational schemes exist if rights and duties are tied to the employment relationship, but not enforced by government; for instance, the social security provided in the European guild system, a modern company scheme for the reimbursement of medical expenses, or an emergency fund for employees. The rules may be written down in a firm statute, but can also be traditional tacit agreements within the firm; they may cover a variety of risks. Defection on the part of the employees is especially likely in commercial companies with a high staff turnover, limited social control, monitoring and sanctioning, a weak corporate culture and generous entitlements.

In formal systems the interaction structure is theoretically different for demographic schemes, unemployment and social assistance benefits, and sick leave and disability benefit regulations. These not only cover diverging risks, but also relate to different actors and interactions. Demographic schemes (old age and survivor's pensions, child benefit) have a large social security organisation governed by a board and with different branches for the functions of collection (the fund), distribution (the benefits agency) and monitoring/sanctioning, enacted by the officials of the administration. In addition, a supervisory board oversees the administrative process, and a social security court passes judgments on appeals. The rules governing entitlements, duties, conditions and potential sanctions are codified in formal law or enforced by the government; they are generally supported by informal community rules. Rule-breaking within the social security organisation is encouraged by the extensive principal-agent problem; but defection by the beneficiaries may be limited as a result of the rather simple entitling conditions (age, death of breadwinner, having child custody) and the profile of the client group (elderly, surviving dependants and parents tend to be less 'calculating').

Unemployment and social assistance schemes have an additional type of actor (the firms who hire and fire personnel), and the social security organisation has extra tasks, mainly in the sphere of prevention, reintegration and social support. The entitling criteria are both more numerous and more complex, and some of the conditions are more susceptible to fraud. The 'moral hazard' is also greater: it is easier for clients to create or sustain the risk themselves. As a result, defection by the client and by the agents of the social security organisation is more likely to occur than in demographic schemes. The same applies to contributors, who may be less inclined to pay their dues. They do not expect to have to use these schemes themselves, and opinions on the unemployed and social assistance beneficiaries tend to be less positive than the views on recipients of pensions and child benefit.

Formal sick leave and disability regulations have the most complicated interaction structure. The social security organisation has an extra function to perform – assessing the medical incapacity to work – which is often attributed to an additional corporate agent. This also introduces a set of medical professional rules, which may be at odds with the formal institutions of these schemes. The 'doctor's dilemma' increases the principal-agent problem in the social security organisation.

The theoretical impact of social security institutions

In theory, social security rules have consequences both for the actors involved and for the collective context within which they apply. At the individual level, the effects for the beneficiaries are the most important, because the main purpose of social security is to safeguard their income, employment, health and social participation. However, theoretically the awarding of rights can also have negative consequences: reduced feelings of well-being, fewer social contacts, marginalisation within the community, feelings of purposelessness, or pessimism regarding the future. The neo-conservative critique of social security states that the rules needlessly create dependency and passiveness among benefit recipients; and critical sociology stresses the anti-emancipatory and disciplinarian elements of social security rules, which can have a major and intrusive impact on the lives of beneficiaries.

The collective results of social security rules manifest themselves first and foremost in the process of social structuring within the community. This refers both to the creation of new social categories (such as pensioners and welfare mothers), and to the influence of the rules on the position of social groups on the 'distribution ladders'. All social security systems involve some redistribution: the funds collected from the contributors are diverted to secure the income, employment, health and social participation of the beneficiaries. Whether and to what extent this redistribution heightens, reinforces or reduces the prevailing social hierarchy is ultimately an empirical question. The importance attached by electors to certain social security issues, and the influence of the 'beneficiaries' vote' mean that social security can also impact on the selection of the political elite: another social structuring effect.

In addition, social security also influences economic development by affecting the level and growth of collective prosperity. Theoretically the economic effects can be both positive and negative. Arguments for a positive influence can be based among other things on the contribution to economic efficiency and helping to stave off loss of demand. Examples that may be cited of the negative effects include the reduced inclination of households to save, the increase in labour costs and the disincentives among the labour supply that social security can bring about. Whether the positive or negative effects on prosperity dominate cannot be determined theoretically in advance; once more, this is an empirical question, the answer to which is related to the actual social security arrangements and social conditions that prevail in a given historical period.

Social security institutions not only affect wealth, but also its distribution, especially in the sphere of income inequality. Diverging sets of institutions can achieve different results in this respect.

Among the other collective effects of social security, the demographic impact is theoretically the most important. For instance, the way these rules are shaped may influence fertility and mortality rates, household-formation and migratory movements.

However, the consequences of social security rules always depend on the historical context in which they are applied. The latter concerns both the extent to which entitling events occur and work through into interactions, and the perceptions of the actors. For example, population ageing and economic recession have an impact on benefit volumes and the funding of pensions and unemployment benefits: the number of entitled persons increases, while the number of contributors falls. Such developments can influence views on the desirability of solidarity between generations, the opportunities that people believe they have on the labour market, etc.

The institutionalisation process

Social security institutions arise and undergo change in accordance with the rule generation process that was outlined in chapter 2 (see figure 2.1 and §2.9). Changes in the historical circumstances lead to different incentives to regulate, which cause the perceptions of key actors to change, and this leads to new forms of regulation; for formal systems, the policy process plays a key role. The applicability of the theoretical view on institutionalisation can be demonstrated by the sea-change from informal social security arrangements to predominantly state systems which occurred in many Western European countries between 1875 and 1930.

It has been stressed several times in this chapter that the effects of social security institutions are not fixed in stone for ever, but depend on the content of the rules and the specific circumstances in which they are applied. The theoretical analysis performed here is therefore no more than a launch pad. A key purpose of this study is to investigate the actual impact of different national systems of formal social security rules on some key variables at the macro-level. These empirical issues will be explored in the following chapters.

4 Regimes of social security

This chapter analyses the differences between the social security institutions of several countries.[1] The key question is whether the empirical variation in formal rules makes it possible to identify certain 'regimes' of social security. The regime concept offers an interesting starting point for analysing the social impact of formal institutions. Of course, an obvious way to study the issue would be to compare specific formal regulations in different countries. For the European Union member states, the EC's databases on social security schemes provide a wealth of material.[2] And for certain benefit schemes extensive comparisons of rule elements have been made in the past – see for instance Einerhand et al. (1995) on disability arrangements, Eardley et al. (1996) and OECD (1998a, 1998b, 1999) on social assistance schemes, and Bradshaw & Finch (2002) on child provisions. Such an approach also has several disadvantages, however. Single formal rules or regulations often contain arbitrary elements, reflecting policy compromises agreed upon at a specific moment. They may also be quite volatile, with certain rule elements changing in line with the perceived priorities on the political agenda.

Moreover, an isolated approach in terms of specific elements of national law may hamper the assessment of their social effects. The latter often requires examining the embeddedness of schemes in other relevant formal institutions. For instance, a meagre national welfare law may be at the root of widespread poverty, but that is not an inevitable causal nexus. Even if social assistance does not amount to anything much, poverty may be limited due to elaborate social insurances or an efficient 'welfare to work' programme.

And of course, the more countries one wants to compare, the more details of specific schemes one has to consider. These very details can make it hard to see the wood for the trees: it may become difficult to focus on the main points of variation between the formal rules prevailing in different countries.

Such drawbacks can be largely mitigated by studying social security *regimes*. The concept refers to different types of coherent formal institutions at the national level, which are designed to achieve distinct collective goals. In terms of the figural model outlined in §2.3 they constitute the core of the formal rules on 'government production' in the field of social security. Because regimes are historical constructs reflecting a long developmental process, path dependence (cf. chapter 2) makes it likely their essence is relatively stable. It is for this reason that the subsequent chapters of this study will be devoted to the collective effects of regimes, rather than the influence of specific regulations. Of course, the preliminary question then is to what extent different regime types actually exist. Are regimes theoretical ideal-types, or empirical phenomena? This is the central issue here.

As a first step, §4.1 delineates regimes and their theoretical traits, mainly by means of a systematic reconstruction of the characteristics that are central to Esping-Andersen's influential typology.

Subsequently, a multivariate scaling procedure is applied to empirical indicators for such traits (§4.2). This seeks to answer the main question of this chapter: can countries actually be placed in clusters which correspond to the theoretical regime typology? As a corollary to this, §4.3 examines how universal regimes are. Their stability over time will briefly be discussed, and their applicability to other domains of welfare, such as health, housing and education. Specific attention will be paid to the relationship with informal institutions: to what extent do formal regimes correspond to the notions on social security rights and obligations among the general public? The conclusions are summarised in §4.4.

4.1 Theoretical traits of social security regimes

Most western countries saw strong growth in their social security system during the post-ww II period. However, there still is considerable variation in the way nations structure their arrangements. Such differences theoretically reflect the interplay of several factors. Esping-Andersen (1990: 105-138) points to historical context variables such as:
- economic and demographic developments (growth, wealth distribution, unemployment, number of older people);
- the power of political actors (the labour classes, employers' organisations, farmers, religious groups, the new middle classes, pensioners);
- political alliances which have been possible or impossible at certain crucial moments, for example the Catholic-Socialist coalitions which created the national insurance system in the Netherlands in the 1950s;
- the extension of welfare arrangements according to the previously existing institutional structure (path dependence).

Several authors have tried to summarise the main differences between countries in the form of a typology of welfare states, or regimes. The scheme employed by Titmuss (1974) became a classic. He distinguishes three ideal-types: the residual welfare model, the industrial achievement-performance model and the institutional redistributive model. In the *residual welfare* model, the individual or the social network to which he belongs (household, family, community) bears primary responsibility for the financial consequences of social risks. Only when this private coverage proves inadequate does the government step in. Benefits function as a social safety net, and are therefore minimal, temporary and accompanied by a means test to ascertain the inadequacy of the individual's own income and assets.

In Titmuss's *industrial achievement-performance* model, greater weight is accorded to government responsibility for income protection. Risks are covered in proportion to the individual's contribution to the collective labour productivity. Social policy ensues from economic policy, in which the operation of the free market dominates. State social security arrangements are supplementary to the social protection that is arranged through collective bargaining between employers and trade unions. Rights often depend on labour performance, employment history and occupational status.

In the *institutional redistributive* model, social security is a means of expressing the collective responsibility for individual welfare. In a modern society the family and the market are no longer able to provide adequate and fair coverage of social risks. The government therefore has to adopt a redistributive approach. It provides benefits and provisions, with the needs of households as the key criterion for the attribution of rights and duties.

Esping-Andersen (1989, 1990, 1996, 1999) adopts a similar threefold division. His central tenet is that three divergent *welfare regimes* can be identified, which differ in terms of:
a) *de-commodification*; i.e. the degree to which individuals or families are able to achieve a socially acceptable living standard, independently of their participation in the market. The level, duration and accessibility of social provisions are important variables here;
b) *stratification*; in Esping-Andersen's theory this describes the way in which countries shape citizenship through the structuring of rights. Welfare states of the same size can aim at very different stratification effects. One system may try to sustain the existing hierarchy and status divisions; another may increase social differences, for instance through a polarisation of educational and labour market opportunities; while a third may aim to realise high minimum standards for every citizen, no matter what their background;
c) *the organisation of the labour market*; welfare regime types are interwoven with specific ways of regulating employment. They affect the supply of labour through the various work (dis)incentives they provide for women and elderly people (e.g. family programmes, child care, early exit schemes). The regime types also diverge in the labour demand they generate, for instance in the required number of social security officials, nurses and teachers; and more generally, in the size and nature of 'post-industrial' employment: social and personal services (government jobs, the 'fun industry' in catering and tourism, cleaning work, etc.), and other forms of employment not directly related to the production of actual goods (management, marketing, lawyers, information and computer experts).

Table 4.1 provides a summary of specific features of the three types identified by Esping-Andersen: the liberal,[3] the corporatist and the social-democratic welfare regime. The welfare regime concept is considered wider than the 'welfare state': "The basis for typology construction are welfare *regimes*, not welfare *states* nor individual social policies". It implies more than a certain mix of social insurances and national provisions (cf. chapter 3). Regimes are mainly defined in reference to "the ways in which welfare production is allocated between state, market, and households" (Esping-Andersen, 1999: 73).

The Anglo-Saxon countries are considered to be the main representatives of the *liberal* welfare regime. This regime type has limited collective provisions, comparable with Titmuss's residual model. Historically, these countries did not expand their social security schemes to any great extent because worker mobilisation was limited (weak trade unions and leftist parties), because social democrats did not enter into long-term political alliances (e.g. no 'red-green' coalitions with the rural classes), and because the new middle class of white-collar workers resisted income transfers and were not "wooed from the market to the state", as in Scandinavia (Esping-Andersen, 1990: 29-33).

In the liberal model the target group is limited to those in need, who are unable to meet their basic requirements in any other way. In order to keep this group small, strict access conditions are applied: benefit recipients must not be capable of work, and stringent means-testing is used to determine the level of need. The duration of benefits is limited to the period that the recipient is unable to work. The level of the benefit is meagre, tending to be more of a 'survival benefit' than an amount which would enable the recipient to play a full part in society. Apart from civil servant schemes, there are no separate collective provisions for specific occupational groups. Levies are low and the collective provision is funded from general resources (taxation). In contrast to this system, private provisions in the liberal welfare regime are relatively extensive – at least for those who have access to them. The middle and higher social classes have taken out separate insurance or enjoy employee benefits from their companies. The tax system generally encourages people to make private provision, through tax exemptions and tax allowances. Where a minimum wage exists at all it is low: so as not to interfere with the presumed operation of the pricing mechanism on the labour market, there is no interference in wage formation at the minimum level. The labour market participation rate of women, older people and disabled people is fairly high, because the low level of benefits and the absence of collective (early) retirement schemes do not create a disincentive – if anything, the reverse. There is little collectively guaranteed employment, even for groups with poor labour market prospects. Post-industrial employment is extensive and lies largely outside the government sphere. A dual structure prevails: good post-industrial jobs for a large group of business professionals (lawyers, consultants, personnel managers) and poor-quality 'junk jobs' which fall to the low-skilled (poorly paid jobs in catering, entertainment, cleaning, et cetera). In terms of stratification the liberal welfare regime leads, according to Esping-Andersen (1990: 65) to "a curious mix of individual self-responsibility and dualism": a group at the bottom which is primarily dependent on stigmatising, means-tested public assistance; a middle class which mainly depends on social insurance; and a privileged group which buys the main provisions on the market. There is the prospect of a future proletarianisation effect if the number of 'junk jobs' were to lead to a substantial group of working poor: "At the low end of the American service economy, wages are close to poverty level, and fringe benefits almost non-existent" (Esping-Andersen, 1990: 228). This proletarianisation could be concentrated in certain groups (ethnic minorities, single-parent families), but also might cross the traditional dividing lines, making the oppositions within these groups even more starkly apparent. In the American case: "As some women become yuppies and some Blacks become bourgeois, the women and Blacks left behind will experience more keenly the phenomenon of relative deprivation" (Esping-Andersen, 1990: 229). But it is also possible that proletarianisation will not occur. 'Junk jobs' could also mainly be filled by a floating population, and might serve as a springboard to better positions for most people.

The level of 'de-commodification' is low in the liberal welfare state: it is difficult for people to achieve an acceptable standard of living if they do not have qualities with sufficient market value (or – in the case of pensioners – have not utilised those qualities in the past). The precise degree of de-commodification varies with the stringency of the means-testing and the level of benefits, however.

The countries of continental Europe and Japan are characterised by Esping-Andersen as *corporatist* welfare regimes. These often have an autocratic tradition: in the past, social insurance schemes were established in order to generate direct loyalty on the part of the individual to the central state or monarchy. Under the auspices of the state, the system was designed to replicate the existing status and class differences, with an elevated position for civil servants personifying the state. Since the Catholic church was often jointly responsible for the development of the system, this type of welfare regime is often biased in favour of the traditional family structure, in line with the principles outlined in papal encyclicals.[4]

The coverage provided by collective provisions in these welfare regimes is selective and hierarchical. Separate collective insurance schemes attribute rights and obligations, in accordance with the individual's social position. The access conditions are fairly strict and are based on actuarial principles: there is an arithmetic relationship between the contributions paid (or the employment history) and the provisions to which the individual is entitled. Benefits may be paid for a long period, provided sufficient entitlement has been built up. The level of benefits is high and is generally a percentage of the previously earned income. The number of collective schemes is large, with civil servants enjoying a privileged position. The levies are fairly high, and schemes are usually funded through the payment of contributions. The 'familialism' of corporatist welfare regimes is reflected in the exclusion of non-working women from social insurance schemes, good family provisions which encourage full-time motherhood, and underdeveloped childcare facilities, which makes it hard to combine work and care tasks.

The predominance of collective social insurance schemes means the coverage offered by private provisions is limited. A high minimum wage operates on the labour market, which is fixed by law or laid down in government-sanctioned collective labour agreements. The prevailing incentive structure results in a low labour market participation of women. The participation rate of older and disabled people is also limited: early exits from the labour market are stimulated through collective early retirement schemes, sometimes in the guise of generous unemployment and disability regulations. There is little collectively guaranteed employment, with just a limited number of sheltered employment schemes, mainly reserved for (early) disabled people. For a number of reasons, post-industrial employment is fairly underdeveloped. Corporatist regimes try to reduce the labour supply of women; the government sector – which potentially offers much work of this type – remains relatively small; and the high levies make the creation of low-paid work in the areas of social and personal services difficult.

Table 4.1
Esping-Andersen's welfare regime types

Characteristics	Liberal	Corporatist	Social-democratic
Collective benefits			
- coverage (main target group)	limited - the poor without means	selective and hierarchical - professional groups	universal - all residents
- entry conditions	very strict - incapable of work - means-testing	fairly strict (actuarial) - employment history - contributions paid	only strict if work-related - residency for a certain number of years - job search behaviour - participation in training or workfare programmes
- limitation of duration	strict - benefit paid only as long as recipient cannot work	(quasi-)actuarial - long benefit duration if sufficient rights accrued	not too strict - benefit continues as long as risk is manifest
- level of benefit	meagre - subsistence minimum	high - wage related	high - adequate social minimum and/or wage related
- collective schemes for specific occupational groups	few - civil servants	many - status groups - civil servants (high level)	none
- level of contributions	low	fairly high	high
- method of funding	general taxation	mainly through contributions	general taxation
Private benefits			
- coverage	high (for middle classes) - stimulated through tax benefits/credits	low	low
Employment			
- minimum wage	absent or very low	high	high
- (dis)incentives to employment of women	no disincentives - low level of benefits → fairly high labour participation	many disincentives - breadwinner benefits - generous motherhood and child allowances - few childcare facilities → low labour participation	many incentives - individual benefit entitlement - elaborate leave arrangements for care tasks - extensive childcare facilities - high contributions force both partners to work → high labour participation
- (dis)incentives to employment of older people and disabled	no disincentives - no collective retirement schemes → high labour participation	many disincentives - collectively funded schemes for early retirement, disability and unemployment → low labour participation	few disincentives - use of collective retirement schemes is discouraged - active reintegration of disabled → high labour participation
- collectively guaranteed employment	virtually absent	limited - sheltered employment for handicapped persons	extensive
- post-industrial employment	extensive dual structure - good jobs in professional business services - low-skilled 'junk jobs'	few - mainly industrial employment	extensive government sector - welfare, care, social security, education - large share of middle-ranking posts occupied by women

(Table 4.1)

Characteristics	Welfare regime type		
	Liberal	**Corporatist**	**Social-democratic**
Stratification			
- differences between groups of citizens which are promoted by regime	reinforcing distinctions - welfare clients/working poor - middle class - privileged classes	reproduction of stratification - occupational groups - gender - household type	none - universalist
- expected future development	proletarianisation	insider/outsider problem - contrast between working/non-working	private/collective opposition - contrast between females working in collective sector and males employed in private firms
De-commodification			
- extent to which a regime promotes an acceptable living standard, independently of one's market value	**low**, depending on: - stringency of means-testing - minimum benefit level	**medium**, depending on: - replacement rates - stringency of actuarial principles - scope of social assistance	**high**, depending on: - benefit levels

Sources: Esping-Andersen (1989, 1990, 1996, 1999)

In terms of stratification, corporatist welfare regimes often tend to reinforce traditional differences based on occupational status, household composition and gender. As a possible future scenario, Esping-Andersen presents a division between insiders and outsiders, with working people on the one hand and non-working women, young people, the elderly and the disabled on the other. The collective negotiations between employees and employers are focused in this scenario entirely on the interests of those in work; pay demands are set high at the expense of job opportunities for less productive workers and non-workers. Combined with the lack of employment incentives for women, this results in "a diminishing yet highly productive workforce supporting a growing but unproductive outsider population" (Esping-Andersen, 1990: 227).

The degree of de-commodification is generally higher than in liberal welfare states, but is largely concentrated among professionals with an adequate employment history. The precise extent of 'market-independence' depends on the replacement rate (the benefit level as a percentage of previous earnings) and the flexibility with which the actuarial principles – the equivalence between contributions paid or employment history, and entitlements – are applied.

According to Esping-Andersen, the Scandinavian countries represent variants of the *social-democratic* welfare regime. In his analysis these systems emerged as a result of high worker mobilisation (strong trade unions), a broad alliance of social democrats and well-organised family farmers (who traded an extension of social security in return for farm-price subsidies), and a successful incorporation of the new middle classes in formal regulations (Esping-Andersen, 1990: 29-33).

The social-democratic regime aims to realise a high level of social protection for all inhabitants. Benefits and provisions are accredited at a level which corresponds to the wishes of the most critical among the new middle classes, and no distinction is drawn between the rights of the working class and those of the better-off. This is achieved through compulsory collective insurance schemes with earnings-related benefits. The most characteristic feature is the nexus between income protection and work: employment plays a crucial role in this regime. It is an expensive system, which can only be sustained if there is a consistent commitment to full employment for both men and women. In order to be able to pay for the generous provisions, the number of benefit claimants must be limited and the number of taxpayers maximised. This is quite different from the two other regime types, where economic inactivity by certain groups is accepted (housewives and early retirees in the corporatist welfare state; people who are unable to find a place in the market in the liberal variant).

The social-democratic variant is universalistic: all inhabitants have access to collective provisions for a large number of social risks. In line with this, the entry conditions for benefits that bear no relation with the labour market (especially old age pensions) are not very rigorous: having lived in the country for a limited number of years may be sufficient to gain entitlements. On the other hand, applicants of working age may be subjected to rather strict tests on their job search behaviour, and can be forced to participate in intensive training programmes and 'workfare' schemes, especially for unemployment and social assistance benefits.

There are no strict limitations on the duration of rights. Benefits and provisions may be granted for as long as the social risk continues to manifest itself. The level of collective benefits is high, often being linked to the most recently earned wage. Where this is not the case, a high statutory minimum income is available, which is adequate to permit full participation in society. The universalistic nature of the social-democratic type is reflected in the absence of separate collective provisions for specific occupational groups: everyone falls within the same schemes. Of course, financing this comprehensive welfare regime requires high contributions, which are usually collected through general taxation.

In the social-democratic regime the coverage offered by private provisions is low; the extensive collective arrangements make these unnecessary. In line with the elaborate social security schemes, the minimum wage is high as well. There is however a commitment to wage moderation at the higher wage levels, because otherwise employment in the extensive government sector would become too expensive. The labour market participation of women is promoted through specific provisions (individual benefit entitlements, leave arrangements for performing care tasks, extensive childcare facilities). The high contributions are also a work incentive: only when both partners are gainfully employed can an adequate household income be generated. Older people and disabled workers are discouraged from leaving the labour market, through activating labour market programmes and the restriction of early exit routes. This leads to rather high participation rates in these groups.

A large part of the labour market is collectivised, through a sizeable government sector and sheltered employment programmes. The lion's share of the post-industrial jobs is to be found in welfare, social security, care and childcare organisations. Esping-Andersen (1990: 222) refers to this as "a social-welfare led post-industrial employment structure". The majority of the large number of women in the labour market are absorbed by this extensive collective sector, where they occupy mainly middle-ranking positions. There are few post-industrial jobs outside the government sector: the high wages rule out the creation of 'junk jobs' (outside the informal circuit).

Given its universalistic approach, the social-democratic welfare regime is designed to eliminate differences between groups of citizens. In practice, however, stratification effects may arise, because the level of benefits and provisions is constrained by cost considerations. New forms of stratification are conceivable as well. If wage moderation cannot be sustained, government jobs and collective employment may become endangered, and conflicts of interest could arise between the mainly female employees in the collective sector and the predominantly male workforce of private enterprises. In such a case "social democracy can only hope that the bonds of marriage are strong enough to weather the storm of economic warfare" (Esping-Andersen, 1990: 227).

The same line of reasoning applies to de-commodification. In theory, the universalistic and generous design means the degree of market-independence under this system should be higher than in the corporate or liberal regimes. In practice, however, even within social-democratic regimes full de-commodification (e.g. through a high basic income for all inhabitants) is hard to achieve, because there are limits to the social security entitlements a nation can afford.

Esping-Andersen's regimes are ideal-types. He argues that none of them will occur in a pure form in the real 'worlds of welfare capitalism'. Corporatist countries, for example, usually have a safety net in the form of means-tested social assistance, covering those who are not, or no longer entitled to social insurance. Schemes that are mainly universalistic in a social-democratic fashion sometimes contain corporatist elements, with rights depending upon past labour experience or contributions; and countries adopting a 'residualist' approach may have collective pension schemes which exceed the subsistence level by quite a wide margin. This makes it important to analyse the empirical power of the typology, in terms of both the structure of formal social security institutions in different countries, and the collective results these generate. The actual existence of the typology will be dealt with in the next section, while the social outcomes of different regime types will be highlighted in the two chapters that follow.

Before turning to this, however, some reflection on the regime typology is appropriate. First of all, Esping-Andersen's demarcation of 'regimes' seems ambiguous in some respects. At the most abstract level he treats them as general *principles of rule generation*: the aspired kind and degree of stratification and de-commodification that guide the constitution of social security schemes. In other cases, Esping-Andersen stresses the *actual differences in formal social security*. Sometimes this is very general, as when he points to the responsibilities of the state, the market and households to secure certain risks (cf. the definition quoted earlier). In other instances, Esping-Andersen considers specific formal rules to be the core of his regime notion, as table 4.1 clearly shows. Finally, at times he seems inclined to let certain *social outcomes* enter into the definition. Although Esping-Andersen is right in stating that social security and labour market institutions are often very much interwoven, there is a hint of tautology in his presentation of the share of post-industrial employment as an indicator for the existence of different regime types. The same applies when he produces trends in labour-market exits and female labour force participation as circumstantial evidence for his typology (Esping-Andersen, 1990: 144-161), rather than concentrating on the actual institutions that brought about such outcomes.

In terms of the theoretical notions outlined in the previous chapters, *regimes* may be more adequately defined as diverging systems of coherent formal institutions at a national level, which aim to realise distinct collective goals.[5] Regime types represent qualitatively different collective agreements on the way rights, duties, conditions and potential sanctions are attributed by government, either through direct legislation or third-party enforcement. The concept of *social security regime* is suitable for describing the diverging institutional frameworks Esping-Andersen had in mind, and which are also the crux of this chapter. *Welfare regimes*, on the other hand, consist of qualitatively different, coherent systems of formal institutions which also include justice, housing, education, etc., in line with the 'wider' connotation of the welfare state concept discussed previously.

There are two reasons why regimes should not be equated with social outcomes. The institutional 'traits' form the quintessence of the typology; and while regime types may aim to achieve certain results, it is not a necessary condition for the identification of regimes that such outcomes are actually realised. Moreover, following the figural model of chapter 2, there is no direct link between formal institutions and collective results. It is of course quite possible distinct regime types enhance different social outcomes, but the latter also depend on other factors: the historical context of rule application (economic, demographic, social, technological and ideal developments), the degree of correspondence between formal and informal institutions, the perceptions of actors, and the actual course rule-driven interaction takes. This makes the relationship between regime types and collective results a specific topic of research, which requires close empirical inspection. The next two chapters will explore this issue for two types of social outcomes: benefit dependency and poverty.

Ever since its publication, Esping-Andersen's *The three worlds of welfare capitalism* has provoked heated debate on the number and character of welfare regimes. In their review of this literature, Arts & Gelissen (2002) point out that a number of authors believe there is a fourth regime type, which could be described as the 'Mediterranean' group or the 'Latin periphery'. A salient feature of this type would be the rudimentary nature of formal social security; for instance, there is no general safety net through national social assistance. Collective old age pensions, however, may be rather generous. The attribution of rights and duties in the Latin regime type would be concentrated on the family. The administration of social security is fragmented over a great number of non-state organisations, which encourages patronage (the protection or favouring of certain social groups by elites, in return for loyalty). It is contestable whether these features justify considering such configurations as a regime type in itself. Some maintain the systems prevailing in the Mediterranean countries are merely rudimentary and more informal versions of the corporatist type, with which it shares many basic principles (e.g. the key role of the family).

Japan is often presented as the textbook example of another kind of regime: the 'Eastern Asiatic' variant, also known as *welfare orientalism*. In this type, social protection is provided primarily through familial, communal and company-based occupational social security, with public social insurance schemes acquiring a supplementary and fairly residual character. Culturally, the system is often supposed to be rooted in Confucian traditions. Goodman (1998) points to several specific regime traits, especially in Japan's *minseiin* system of community care. However, he doubts whether the Japanese welfare type really is firmly rooted in the country's history.[6] White & Goodman (1998) note a number of characteristics that the social security systems of Japan, South Korea and Taiwan share with the corporatist regimes of Europe: an important role for non-state agencies, a strong emphasis on funded social insurance, and "a fragmented array of particular schemes for core social groups [...] which both reflects and reinforces differentials in power and status in society" (White & Goodman, 1998: 14). In line with this observation, Esping-Andersen (1990, 1999) is inclined to consider the Eastern Asiatic configuration as a variant of the corporatist regime type, just like the Latin periphery systems.

Siaroff (1994) suggests yet another type. He states that differences in *gender inequality* in different countries are neglected in Esping-Andersen's typology; the diverging labour market and social security positions of men and women would not weigh heavily enough. Siaroff proposes four regime types: the 'Protestant social-democratic' countries of Scandinavia, the 'Protestant-liberal' countries in the Anglo-Saxon tradition, the 'developed Christian democratic' countries of continental Europe, and countries with a 'late mobilisation of women' – a residual group comprising the Mediterranean countries of Europe, Japan, Ireland and Switzerland. Esping-Andersen (1999: 88) retorts that he has in no way neglected the gender dimension: it is a key point in his distinction between social-democratic and corporatist regimes. Moreover, Arts & Gelissen (2002) observe that Siaroff's classification, despite the differences in nomenclature, largely corresponds to Esping-Andersen's typology. Only the 'late mobilisation of women'-regime may be regarded as a new separate type, but this is rather a mixed bag, relating to countries which were not central to the original typology. To this may be added that it is not clear why gender-related aspects of regimes should outweigh other formal institutions, if the key question relates to the development of a general typology.

A further extra regime type could be the *Antipodes*. Some claim that Australia and New Zealand do not fit into the liberal category in which Esping-Andersen places them (cf. Castles, 1996, 1998). These countries operate a minimum income guarantee for all households, including those which could generate an income in the marketplace. While most benefit schemes have some kind of means test, this is only effective above a fairly high income threshold, leading to a substantial take-up. For instance, Eardley et al. (1996: 4-40) point out that roughly 80% of elderly Australians receive a means-tested collective old age pension. Such extensive protection by the state, it is argued, distinguishes the Antipodes from countries with a pure liberal regime. However, Esping-Andersen (1999: 74-77) is not convinced by the argument. He regards Australia and New Zealand as variants of the liberal type, with which they share much in common: the limited scope of formal social security, the predominance of means-tested schemes, and the individual responsibility to take out risk insurance.

Two final comments relating to Esping-Andersen's theory are its neglect of the international context of social security regulations, and the rather limited attention paid to institutional change. His regime types are stable, relatively closed and autonomous national systems, largely modelled at the *status quo* of the 1980s. This disregards developments such as the process of economic globalisation, the enlargement of the European Union, and the social security amendments that have taken place in most Western countries over the past decades. In his later work Esping-Andersen (1996, 1999) acknowledges that welfare states may be "in transition", but he sticks to the structural differences between his three regime types.

4.2 An empirical typology

This section empirically examines the differences between the social security regimes of eleven countries. The nations considered here have been selected because of their presumed institutional variety: they correspond to the different 'worlds' of Esping-Andersen's original typology. He places three of these countries in the corporatist group (Belgium, France, Germany), four in the liberal cluster (Australia, Canada, the United States and the United Kingdom), and three in the social-democratic group (Sweden, Norway and Denmark). The Netherlands theoretically holds a position somewhere between the corporatist and social-democratic countries.[7]

The empirical validity of Esping-Andersen's typology has been tested before, for instance by Kangas (1994), Ragin (1994), Shalev (1996, 2007), Bonoli (1997), Korpi & Palme (1998), Obinger & Wagschal (1998), Pitruzzello (1999), Gough (2001), Hicks & Kenworthy (2003), and Saint-Arnaud & Bernard (2003). These studies mainly rely on cluster or factor analysis, techniques which are far better suited to identify the similarities and differences between countries than the combination of tabulation and regression methods originally used by Esping-Andersen. In their meta-analysis Arts & Gelissen (2002: 153) summarise the results and conclude:

> Esping-Andersen's original three-worlds typology neither passes the empirical tests with flying colors, nor dismally fails them. The conclusion is, first, that his typology has at least some heuristic and descriptive value, but also that a case can be made for extending the number of welfare regimes to four, or even five. Second, these analyses show that a significant number of welfare states must be considered hybrid cases: no particular case can ever perfectly embody any particular ideal-type.

However, there are several reasons for doubting whether the previous empirical work provides an adequate test of Esping-Andersen's typology. First of all, the institutions that were included in the studies often did not cover all aspects of social security regimes. For instance, Ragin (1994) and Shalev (1996) analysed pension benefits, Gough (2001) social assistance schemes, and Kangas (1994) focused on health insurance regulations, which hardly play a role in the original typology. Such partial analyses may be quite interesting in their own right, but of course cannot fully corroborate or rebut Esping-Andersen's typology.

A second problem concerns the limited number of indicators in these empirical studies. Bonoli's classification (1997) is an extreme example: he tested the validity of Esping-Andersen's typology by merely plotting two variables, gross social expenditure as a proportion of GDP, and the share of contributions in social security funding. But in other cases too, often only six to ten variables were analysed, which hardly does justice to the wealth of attributes Esping-Andersen associates with his regime types. This is not only a matter of data restrictions, but there is also a methodological issue at stake. Country comparisons tend to suffer from the 'small-*N*'-problem. Goldthorpe (2000: 49) sketches it quite succinctly:

> Where individuals are the units, populations can be sampled so as to give Ns of several hundreds or thousands; but where nations are the units, N cannot rise much above one hundred even if all cases are taken, and is often far less. In applying techniques of multivariate analysis, serious difficulties therefore tend to be encountered in that N is not much greater than the total number of variables involved. Statistically, this means that there are too few degrees of freedom, that models become 'overdetermined', that intercorrelations among independent variables cannot be adequately dealt with, and that results may not be robust. Substantively, it means that competing explanations of the dependent variable may not be open to any decisive evaluation.

In a causal approach it may be possible to bypass the 'small-*N*'-problem through multilevel analysis, with individuals, regions or sectors as basic units, and a given classification of regime-types as explaining factors at the country level. However, if one tries to assess the internal coherence of regime types using traditional cluster or factor analysis, not too many variables can be included.

Shalev (2007) raises yet a third objection. Most empirical tests of the typology treat variables as if they were continuous phenomena: the size of the welfare state, the score on a de-commodification index (cf. Scruggs & Allan, 2006), etc. Theoretically, however, it is important to search for meaningful distinctions in the formal institutions of countries, and whether it is possible to identify underlying general principles. From a methodological point of view, Shalev (2007: 289-290) considers the empirical analyses in *The three worlds of welfare capitalism* rather unsatisfactory:[8]

> Esping-Andersen's first technique (tabular analysis) was unnecessarily 'soft', while the second (regression) is fundamentally in conflict with his analytical premises ... No systematic test was carried out of whether his ensemble of indicators of welfare state regimes actually do 'hang together'; and if they do, whether countries indeed cluster in three distinct subgroups on underlying policy dimensions ... These empirical results are of questionable value, being based on regressions with 5 or 6 explanatory variables and only 18 cases. The key difficulty, however, is that asking whether political effects 'matter' after 'controlling for' other causes

is a different and more banal question than what actually interested Esping-Andersen. [... The regression approach] treats both policy and politics as continuous variables scattered across the whole spectrum of potential variation – not as a limited number of qualitatively different configurations with distinctive historical roots. [... Esping-Andersen] applied multiple regression as a blunt instrument for tapping gross differences between groups of countries, differences that arguably could have been more effectively conveyed by the use of tables and charts without the implication of constant linear effects across different contexts.

Shalev (2007: 290) also questions the appropriateness of Qualitative Comparative Analysis (QCA), which applies formal criteria (based on Boolean algebra) in order to ascertain whether attributes are associated with particular outcomes. Kangas (1994) and Ragin (1994) used this technique in order to identify welfare regimes, but the results were not very convincing:

> [... Kangas's and Ragin's] creative efforts ran into serious difficulties. Kangas had trouble finding the Liberal countries and Ragin was placed in the awkward position of having to assign one third of his countries to a 'spare' category, which automatically excluded them from his analysis. In performing cluster analysis of countries both authors were forcing them to fit into a single regime, thereby predetermining an issue in need of empirical exploration.

And Goldthorpe (2000: 51-52) criticises QCA in a more fundamental way:

> The fact that QCA remains a logical technique means that its results are far more exposed to major distortion, both by difficulties in the selection of independent variables and by the occurrence of error in data than are results derived from statistical techniques.

Shalev therefore advocates a combination of multidimensional scaling and factor analysis as the appropriate way to analyse welfare regimes. Other experimental techniques that have been suggested include fuzzy set theory (Kvist, 1999; Ragin, 2000: 286-308; Vis, 2007) and neural networks (Hagfors & Kangas, 2004).

A more fitting trial of Esping-Andersen's regime typology would be to try and measure the empirical interdependence of key variables as indicated in table 4.1 as accurately as possible; and this is the aim of this section. In order to map out the actual correspondences and differences in the formal social security institutions of these countries, a categorical principal component analysis (CatPCA) was performed on 54 characteristics. In line with Shalev's recommendation, the technique applied here combines optimal scaling with principal components analysis.[9] As in classic PCA, variables are reduced to a limited number of uncorrelated dimensions. However, CatPCA deviates from this standard technique because it does not assume that variables are continuous; it can also handle indicators of rank or class (ordinal and nominal variables). In an alternating procedure, first for each variable category quantifications (and component loadings) are calculated from the initial scores of cases ('objects'). Subsequently new object scores are computed from the scaled categories, then again category quantifications from scaled cases, and so on, until a convergence criterion is reached. The scaling of cases and the variable categories occurs in line with the specified measurement level. The latter serves as a restriction: the average correlation of the variables with the dimensions is maximised, given the chosen level of measurement. Since CatPCA treats the rows and columns of the data matrix as equivalent alternatives, the technique is less sensitive to the 'small-N'-problem than standard factor analytic or PCA approaches.

The CatPCA technique is especially suitable for testing Esping-Andersen's typology, because the number of theoretical dimensions he uses is limited, and the indicators listed in table 4.1 mostly have an ordinal or nominal measurement level. If the underlying variables do indeed correlate as expected, it should be possible to represent the three regime types adequately in two-dimensional space. Because CatPCA produces optimal scaling of both countries and regime characteristics, countries and regime traits which share many features will obtain more or less the same scores on the dimensions, whereas cases and categories with little in common will be positioned a long way apart. This makes it possible to identify the degree to which formal institutions empirically coincide, and to ascertain whether countries actually form distinct clusters.

The variables[10] in the CatPCA that has been performed are largely based on quantitative international comparisons relating to the first half of the 1990s, and together present a fairly complete empirical operationalisation of the theoretical traits of Esping-Andersen's ideal regime types. This implies that the emphasis lies with formal social security rights (benefit levels, replacement rates, duration, coverage), duties (mainly contribution levels) and, to a lesser extent, conditions (means testing, disability thresholds); and the main focus is, in Titmuss's terminology, on social welfare, with some fiscal elements. Bearing in mind the social security definition and the interaction models of formal social security that have been outlined in the previous chapter, several other institutional traits theoretically could have been included as well;[11] but the aim of the current selection is to approximate empirically the elements of the original theoretical typology, as reconstructed in table 4.1, as closely as possible.

The institutional characteristics were generally scaled at an ordinal level. All variables have been categorised into distinct classes. Sometimes this discretisation is self-evident (e.g. whether survivor's pensions are means-tested or not), but especially for quantitative variables it may be more complicated. To classify these, cut-off points were chosen wherever natural gaps in the distribution occurred (cf. Wildeboer Schut et al., 2001: 35-39, where the data are reported in more detail). The large number of variables means that the scaling results are quite stable: sensitivity analyses showed that adding or deleting a few does not lead to different principal components or other clusters of variables and countries. The same applies if one looks at solutions across more dimensions, or with other scaling restrictions.[12]

Figure 4.1 displays the component loadings: the correlations of the ordinally scaled variables with the two principal components. Variables pointing in the same direction are highly correlated on both dimensions. The graph suggests three major clusters of regime features and a single outlying indicator.

The first group of variables shows high loadings on the first dimension, but low ones on the second (numbers 1-26 in figure 4.1). The horizontal axis is largely associated with variables measuring whether a regime is residual or extensive. Low scores generally indicate frugal benefits of limited duration, combined with strict entry regulation through means testing. As a corollary, the funding required is low. For high scores the opposite holds: more generous benefits which last longer, less means testing, and higher costs.

More specifically, a scaling on the negative side of the horizontal axis corresponds to low replacement rates (benefits as a percentage of former earnings) in the first and fifth year of unemployment. Child benefits are meagre, and earnings-related occupational pensions may substitute only a small part of previous employment income.[13] There is no link between the duration of the insurance period and the level of collective old age pensions. The limits on duration are manifest in earnings-related unemployment benefit, which is usually paid for a maximum of one year. A low score on the first dimension also indicates that means-tested social assistance makes up a large part of total social security spending, and that child benefits and collective old age and surviving dependants' pensions are means-tested as well.

Another entry restriction is the threshold in disability benefit schemes covering the *risque social* (a multiple-nominally scaled variable, not in the graph). A low score on the first dimension generally indicates an individual has to be almost fully incapacitated (80-100%) in order to be eligible for such a disability benefit. The *risque professionnel* is only covered for employees, not for the self-employed, trainees, interns, and so on.

A number of characteristics related to funding also score highly on the first dimension. A low score on the horizontal axis means a comparatively small part of GDP consists of tax and social security contributions. It also indicates low average contribution rates at the level of the OECD average production worker, and limited marginal contribution rates for single people and double-earners with an income one third above that reference income. A negative score on the first dimension also coincides with low employer's contributions.

On the labour market, the degree of residualism is reflected particularly in maternity and parental leave arrangements. A low score is associated with a limited proportion of working women being entitled to these schemes, a low level of maternity benefits and the absence of earnings-related leave arrangements. Tax breaks for work-related expenses are limited as well, which theoretically is a further disincentive to take up employment.

For two variables in this group the component loadings are somewhat contrary to expectations, although these are admittedly rather low (numbers 11 and 25 in the graph). A high statutory minimum wage is associated with otherwise residualist system characteristics, and vice versa.[14] Moreover, the existence of a separate orphan's pension was theoretically expected to be a trait of extensive regimes, especially of the corporatist type. However, this feature also turns out to load on the 'residualist' direction of the first dimension.[15]

The second major group of variables shows high negative component loadings on the vertical axis, and low to moderate[16] values on the horizontal one. It consists of features which are theoretically associated with corporatist regimes (numbers 27 to 39 in the graph). First of these is a high degree of occupationalism: the provisions for specific occupational groups aimed at maintaining their standard of living are extensive. Expenditure on social security for civil servants, for example, is high.

Occupationalism goes together with a tight link between employment or past labour experience and benefit entitlements. For instance, disability benefits are high when medical impediments are due to occupational activity, accidents or diseases (the *risque professionnel*). Sometimes employees who become incapacitated due to their work even continue to receive their full salary. On the other hand, the coverage of disability that is not related to salaried employment (the *risque social*) is limited. The early disabled, the self-employed, students, housewives and unemployed persons who become incapacitated, usually are not entitled to disability benefits.

These characteristics are associated with rather good (semi-)collective pensions for the surviving dependants of employees, without duration limits up to the pensionable age.[17] This contrasts sharply with widows, widowers and orphans of persons without an employment contract, who have to rely on their own means or on social assistance.

In the same category, child benefits are generally linked to family size, with no specific targeting of the low-income groups. This is reflected in the tendency to grant high child benefits to large families which cannot be considered poor; and in the fact that poor lone-parent families are not especially favoured.

A considerable share of funding is contribution-based, which implies a strong emphasis on compulsory solidarity between workers under the responsibility of the state.

On the labour market, employment contracts are largely covered by collective labour agreements, and specific incentives often coincide. Maternity and paternal leave lasts fairly long, but is largely unpaid. It is combined with a low coverage of formal child care facilities in the 0-3 years age bracket. The tax allowances for couples with children are high. However, the additional tax advantages a single-earner family receives (over single persons) that do *not* relate to children are limited. This suggests that fiscal work disincentives in this cluster of 'corporatist' traits are not linked to having a partner, but rather to the presence of children.

A third group of variables combines high positive component loadings on the second dimension with moderate loadings on the first.[18] These traits, numbered 40-49 in the graph, are theoretically associated with social-democratic regimes. In the sphere of pensions all inhabitants are entitled to a collective old age pension, and the minimum level is comparatively high. Most employees are covered by a compulsory, earnings-related pension scheme. The statutory retirement age for men is rather high (65 years or more), and full early retirement pensions are limited.[19] A threshold is applied when disability is related to occupation. After five consecutive years of unemployment, social assistance benefits for families with children are high. However, child benefits for poor families with many children are not especially generous. As regards funding, the marginal tax rates for couples with children are substantial.

Based on the category scores, two multiple-nominally scaled variables (not shown in graph) are also placed within this cluster in a consistent manner. Spending on active

Figure 4.1
Optimal scaling of 54 characteristics of social security regimes (CatPCA, component loadings)[a]

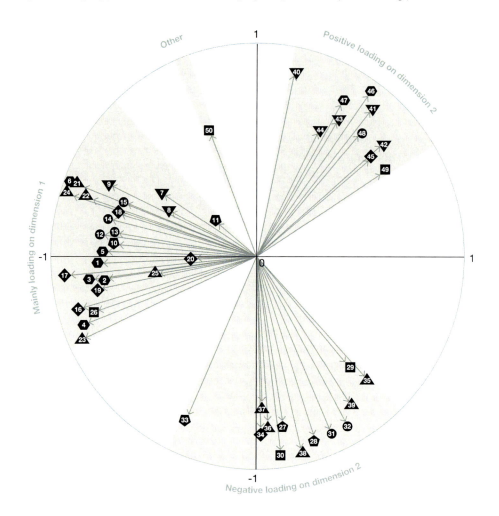

Markers and abbreviations of formal social security institutions

● Unemployment and social assistance schemes (UA)
▼ Old age retirement pensions (OA)
● Surviving dependants' pensions (SV)
● Costs of children (CH)
◆ Funding (FU)
▲ Labour market and participation (dis)incentives (LP)
■ Disability schemes (DA)
⬟ Occupational schemes (OC)

Sources: Bradshaw et al. (1993); DHHS (1991); Eardley et al. (1996); EC (1990); ILO (1992); de Kemp (1992); OECD (1988; 1993; 1994; 1995a; 1995b; 1997a; 1997b); SCP (1992); TK (1996/1997)

Groups of variables[b]

Mainly loading on dimension 1
1. UA: unemployment benefit level in first month, couple + children, 2/3 APW (net replacement rate*)
2. UA: unemployment benefit level in first month, couple + children, APW (net replacement rate*)
3. UA: social assistance level after 5 years unemployment, couple (net replacement rate*)
4. UA: social assistance level after 5 years unemployment, single person (net replacement rate*)
5. UA: means-tested social assistance as a % of total social security spending
6. UA: duration of earnings-related unemployment benefit (not means-tested)
7. OA: equivalence of insurance period and benefit level
8. OA: gross replacement rate* of earnings-related occupational pensions
9. OA: means testing of collective retirement pensions
10. SV: means testing widow's pensions
11. SV: separate orphan's pension
12. CH: child benefit level (average of 18 family types)
13. CH: child benefit level for non-poor lone-parent families (relative to average level)
14. CH: child benefit: income-related/universal
15. CH: total level of provisions for children
16. FU: average rate of direct taxation and social insurance contributions (single earner+children, APW*)
17. FU: direct/indirect taxes + contributions (% GNP)
18. FU: employer's contributions: average surcharge (%; single earner + children, APW*)
19. FU: marginal rate for single person (1.33 APW*, taxes + social insurance contributions)
20. FU: marginal rate for double earner + 2 children (1.33 APW*, taxes + social insurance contributions)
21. LP: tax exemptions for work-related expenses (as % of average income of single earner, APW*)
22. LP: coverage of maternity leave (entitled women as a % of working women)
23. LP: duration of paid and earnings-related maternity and parental leave
24. LP: level of maternity benefit
25. LP: statutory minimum wage
26. DA: disability coverage (risque professionnel*)

Negative loading on dimension 2
27. OC: separate schemes for occupational groups
28. OC: level of protection for civil servants
29. DA: disability benefit level (risque professionnel*)
30. DA: disability coverage (risque social*)
31. CH: child benefit level for non-poor couples + 4 children (relative to average level)
32. CH: child benefit level for poor lone-parent families (relative to average level)
33. SV: collective pension for widows of employees
34. FU: contribution-funded social security (% of total funding)
35. LP: additional tax advantages for one-earner couples (not related to children; as a % of gross income)
36. LP: additional tax deductions for couples with children
37. LP: children (0-3 years) in formal child care (% of total)
38. LP: coverage of collective labour agreements
39. LP: total duration of maternity and parental leave

Positive loading on dimension 2
40. OA: collective old age pension for all inhabitants
41. OA: minimum level of collective retirement pensions for non-employees
42. OA: coverage of earnings-related occupational pensions
43. OA: statutory retirement age (men)
44. OA: (semi-)collective schemes for full early retirement
45. FU: marginal rate for single earner + 2 children (1.33 APW*, taxes + social insurance contributions)
46. UA: social assistance level after 5 years unemployment, couple + 2 children (net replacement rate*)
47. UA: social assistance level after 5 years unemployment, lone-parent family + 2 children (net replacement rate*)
48. CH: child benefit level for poor couples + 4 children (relative to average level)
49. DA: disability threshold (risque professionnel*)

Other
50. DA: disability benefit level (risque social*)

a. Component loadings cannot be computed for 4 multiple-nominally scaled variables in the analysis
DA: disability threshold (risque social*)
LP: weeks of leave (statutory minimum)
LP: active labour market policy (% GNP)
SV: collective provision for widows of residents

b. Variables listed in grey run from high to low, or indicate a yes/no dichotomy

* risque professionnel = disability related to occupational activity, accidents or illnesses
risque social = disability not related to occupational activity
APW = average production worker (OECD-definition)
replacement rate = benefit income/previous income (gross = before taxes, net = after taxes)

labour market policy is relatively high (over 1.1% of GDP), as is the statutory minimum amount of annual leave (more than four weeks).

One variable (number 50 in the graph) does not belong to any of these three groups. In most countries, entitlements to disability schemes covering the *risque social* were earnings-related in the period considered here. However, two liberal and one social-democratic country had flat-rate benefits, which leads to a component loading in between these clusters.[20]

All in all, the component loadings indicate a clear interpretation of the two dimensions. On the horizontal axis, observations are ranked on a continuum stretching from residualist (negative scores) to extensive (positive scores) regime characteristics. This resembles what is sometimes referred to as the *scope* of social security, or the social security effort – although the first dimension reflects many variables, not just expenditure as a percentage of GDP, the commonly adopted effort indicator (see for instance Wilensky, 1975). On the vertical axis observations are scaled between two poles which may be termed 'particularistic' (negative scores) and 'universalistic' (positive scores); hence, this can be regarded as a dimension indicating the degree of *universalism*.

Figure 4.2 shows the object scores: the values attributed on these two dimensions to countries as a result of the optimal scaling procedure. Three distinct clusters and one mixed case may be discerned; the classification is corroborated by additional cluster analyses and by latent profile modelling of the object scores.[21] First, there is a *liberal* group of nations, which comprises the United States, Australia, Canada and the United Kingdom. Countries with a liberal social security regime score low on social security scope (the first dimension), and are scaled about average on the y-axis, mostly with a slight bias toward the universalistic side. Based on the characteristics studied here, the USA is far and away the most 'residual' country. It displays many traits which are typical of the liberal regime, and quite often these fall into the most extreme category. The USA is closely followed by Australia, which is therefore also a rather clear specimen of the liberal social security regime. Since Australia in no way falls outside the liberal group, the scaling results do not corroborate the 'Antipodes' thesis as proposed by Castles (1996, 1998). The discrepancy compared with the United States is caused mainly by the fact that Australian benefit levels and the required funding are somewhat higher. Contrary to the USA, the Australian collective old age pensions scheme covers all its residents. However, in Australia the gross replacement rate of the total old age pension (including occupational benefits) is the lowest of all countries analysed here, probably as a result of means testing.

Within this set of countries, Canada and the United Kingdom are less characteristic representatives of the liberal type. Their scores on the first dimension indicate that the formal institutions of these countries are more extensive than those of the USA and Australia. This applies particularly for the higher replacement rates in unemployment and social assistance schemes, better income provisions covering the cost of children, and higher minimum levels of the collective old age pension for persons with no past labour

Figure 4.2
Optimal scaling of 11 countries on formal regime traits (CatPCA, object scores)

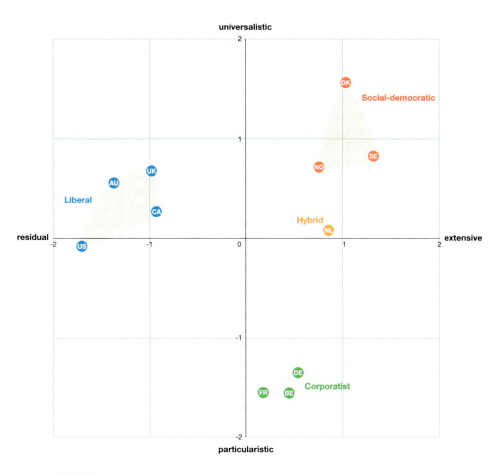

Sources: cf. figure 4.1

experience. Tax and contribution rates in Canada and the UK are correspondingly higher as well.

In a number of respects these two watered-down versions of the liberal regime differ, however. Replacement rates are generally slightly higher in the UK, but this is offset by the limited importance of means-testing in Canada, and its extensive coverage of maternity leave.[22] It should also be noted that the UK has the most universalistic regime within the liberal cluster. The above-average score on the second dimension suggests that some elements reflecting the Beveridgean heritage still prevail in the British social security system. Esping-Andersen (1999:87) regards Britain as "an example of regime-shifting or, perhaps, of stalled 'social democratization'..."[23]

The second cluster consists of three countries which Esping-Andersen designated as *corporatist*: Belgium, France and Germany. These countries do indeed achieve fairly extreme scores on the second dimension, tending towards the corporatist pole. However, they also fall on the positive side of the x-axis, which indicates a substantially higher social security scope than in the liberal group. Thus the exponents of the corporatist regime studied here also have rather extensive social security systems.

This cluster is the most homogeneous of all. However, there are slight differences between the three corporatist countries. The German system appears to be somewhat more extensive than Belgium; and France has the more residual social security arrangements within this group. On the second dimension Germany seems somewhat less corporatist than either Belgium or France. Moreover, each country has some specific peculiarities. In Belgium, unemployment benefit is not limited in duration, but its level is lower than is customary in corporatist countries. If one includes the benefits for specific target groups, France has fairly substantial social assistance regulations. And in a number of respects, the German disability benefit schemes are comparable to what one would expect in a social-democratic regime.

The Nordic nations of Europe form a third distinct group. On the first dimension these score higher than the corporatist countries, while on the second they surpass the liberal cluster. This means that the *social-democratic* regime, as was expected, is the most extensive and universalistic type. Countries belonging to this cluster are less homogeneous than the corporatist group. Sweden and Denmark are the purest representatives of the regime, but both have a specific bias: the Swedish social security system seems slightly more extensive, while the Danish system is more universalistic. The outlying position of Denmark reflects its scores on variables loading high on the second dimension. Far more often than in Sweden, Norway and the nations representing the liberal type, the scaled values of Denmark are the opposite of the corporatist countries' scores.

Norway comes out lower than Sweden on the first dimension and lags behind Denmark on the second, just below the Swedish score. This makes Norway a less characteristic example of the social-democratic regime. Compared with their Nordic counterparts, the scope is smaller, which is due mainly to slightly lower replacement rates and more modest contribution rates. Also, less money is spent in Norway on activating labour market policy. The limited coverage of earnings-related occupational pensions indicates a lower degree of universalism. This is a voluntary insurance in Norway, which reaches approximately 25% of employees. In Sweden and Denmark this insurance is compulsory for all.

These are all primarily differences of degree, however. The scope of the Norwegian social security system exceeds that of the three corporatist countries, and in terms of universalism the score is well above average. Norway may be a less typical example, but it certainly belongs to the social-democratic cluster.

The Netherlands, finally, is the only one of the countries analysed here which cannot be placed squarely in one of the three clusters. For the early 1990s the Dutch system emerges as a *hybrid* of social-democratic and corporatist traits. The first dimension indicates that the Netherlands is rather similar to the Nordic countries in terms of scope: slightly less extensive than the regimes of Denmark and Sweden, but comparable to Norway and outranking the corporatist countries. This stems especially from rather generous benefit conditions and correspondingly high costs of social security.

On the second axis, however, the Netherlands turns out to be not as universalistic as the social-democratic countries, although the Dutch score leans over to their side. Like in Sweden and Denmark, the target groups of social security tend to be comprehensive, most manifestly in social assistance and in the national insurance schemes for the elderly, surviving dependants and children. But in a number of other respects the Netherlands resembles a corporatist regime: the protection of the acquired standard of living in case of unemployment and disability, the large share of social insurance contributions in funding, the high level of protection for civil servants, and the disincentives to the labour supply of women and less productive workers. These empirical scaling results therefore confirm Esping-Andersen's (1999: 88) observation that "the Netherlands remains a Janus-headed welfare regime, combining both social-democratic and conservative attributes". However, in the period considered here the Dutch social security system also had a number of unique features. This concerns especially the absence of a distinction between *risque professionnel* and *risque social* in disability regulations; and the combination of a universal pay-as-you-go state pension with extensive funded occupational benefits in old age schemes.

4.3 The generality of regime types

Regime types are not eternal givens, but constructs of history. One hundred and fifty years ago the collective agreements on nationwide social security institutions were very rudimentary everywhere, falling well behind what would currently be considered a 'residual' regime. And there are no compelling reasons to assume that the social security regime types described in the previous section will continue to exist forever. Future political scientists may very well regard them as exemplary of a certain historical phase, reflecting the diverging social consensus prevailing in these countries in the second half of the 20th century. From the figural model in chapter 2 it follows that social security regimes may change. The consensus on the 'right attribution of social security rights' in a community can evolve in a different direction if historical developments fundamentally alter the incentive to regulate, and strategic actors respond to this in an effective way during the process of policy-making. In the near future, various factors could induce such divergences of the present institutional paths. The influence of globalisation on economic performance and labour markets could make certain revisions of social security systems efficient and inevitable. The ageing of populations may have a severe impact on the financial sustainability of the more elaborate social security systems, a pressure which may clash with the social stratification effects the electorate would prefer. Social trends towards individualisation and less gender inequality could make a different attribution of rights desirable. And the extension and economic integration of the European Union – coordinated by a Brussels policy apparatus which may be less inclined to act as an agent of the national principals – might lead to a convergence in the direction of a new 'European social model', blurring the distinctions between the social-democratic, corporatist and liberal regime types found here.

This makes it relevant to discuss the generality of regime types in some more detail. A first question that may be raised is their actual *stability over time*. Several empirical analyses suggest that the three welfare regime types are fairly continuous phenomena during the period that will be studied in the next chapters, the final decades of the 20th century. The analysis performed above confirms the existence of the three 'institutional worlds' at the beginning of the 1990s. Shalev (2007) carried out a secondary analysis of the 13 policy indicators in the original Esping-Andersen data, which relate to the late 1970s and early 1980s. A linear factor analysis resulted in two dimensions, labelled by him as 'institutionalism' and 'corporatism'. The clusters of nations found by Shalev correspond rather closely[24] to those in figure 4.2. Finally, we performed a similar CatPCA for the period 1998-2001 for a project which sought to map out the current regime types in the enlarged EU. Although a wider set of variables and countries was taken into consideration, very similar clusters of countries emerged (Soede et al., 2004).[25]

Taken together, these studies corroborate for the period 1980-2000 the existence of the 'worlds' as originally proposed by Esping-Andersen. Because both the underlying dimensions and the clustering of countries are fairly consistent over time, it may be assumed that the classification is empirically valid during these two decades. Of course, as was pointed out, this does not guarantee that the different regime types will continue to exist in the future. On the other hand, path dependence could play a decisive role. The material and social costs of complete regime shifts may be quite high, the cognitive frames and interests of policymakers could stand in the way, and the informal rules of the electorate may set limits to the direction and degree of change that is attainable.

A second issue is the applicability of the typology to *other domains of welfare*, such as health, housing policy and education. In their overview article Arts & Gelissen (2002: 153) conclude that "if one looks at other social programmes than the ones applied by Esping-Andersen, it becomes clear that they do not conform so easily – if at all – to his welfare regime patterns".

This is backed, for instance, by comparisons of the public sector in various countries. If it exists at all, the dividing line in the type of health system seems to lie between the Protestant countries of Northern and Western Europe, and the Catholic nations in the southern regions, especially where the higher medical consumption in the latter is concerned (SCP, 2001: 281-295). In housing policy the picture is even less clear:

> The typology of welfare states [...] offers little help in understanding the situation. One would expect to find a strong social rented sector in social democratic countries, but this applies only to Denmark. Austria is the only country were housing has clear corporatist elements [because] landlords in the fairly large social rented sector are affiliated to trade unions and political parties (SCP, 2001: 49).

In the design of the education system,[26] on the other hand, the three welfare regimes emerge rather clearly. The Scandinavian countries have a uniform school type for all children aged six to sixteen, with a strong focus on equal opportunities and aiming to attain the highest educational levels possible – although this does not necessarily imply that these goals will be achieved. In the UK, the government plays a rather weak regulatory role, and there is ample room for private initiatives, leaving a lot of freedom to schools and other educational actors – just as one would expect of a liberal welfare regime. Germany and Austria show a distinct corporatist pattern. Pupils "are divided among programmes with different labour market and social prospects at an early stage, with the dual system – in fact a continuation of the guilds – later training them for a particular occupation" (SCP, 2001: 496). The dual system requires close cooperation between the government, employers and employees, and has the effect that "youngsters have good job prospects on leaving school, [but] are closely tied to a particular occupation in their further career" (SCP, 2001: 496), thus replicating the existing social stratification. In France the corporatist structure is less clear, however. Here education is considered a key public responsibility, with an important role for the central government, which in theory advocates rigid meritocratic selection through a system of *concours*.[27]

All in all, wider welfare regimes do not necessarily coincide with the social security regimes of the previous section. Esping-Andersen's position is rooted in the 'power-resource theory', as summarised by Korpi (2003: 590): "Welfare regimes to a significant extent are the outcomes of distributive conflicts involving class-related interest groups and political parties, conflicts were the relative power of actors is significant". Such conflicts of course take place; but theoretically it is not evident that the outcome should be the same in every domain of welfare. Following the institutional analyses in chapters 2 and 3, it may very well be that social security, health care, housing policy and education have a specific history. New formal rules which shape these domains are generated and transformed during interaction processes among political actors. This may happen in diverging historical contexts (periods of economic boom or recession, pre- or post-war, etc.), with different stakeholders (political parties, social partners, specific interest groups, professionals) and a considerable variation in relative prices, the structure of power and interests, and ideals. From this theoretical point of view, welfare domains need not be fully interdependent. In certain historical circumstances they may even not correspond at all, with each 'province of policy' having different actors, a specific agenda of issues, and a separate path of institutional development. Esping-Andersen's notion of welfare regimes therefore seems rather wide, even if one considers it as an ideal-type in Weber's (1988 [1922]: 190-214) sense. The concept of social security regimes provides a more accurate demarcation of the phenomena he refers to theoretically.

A third, and from a theoretical point of view rather interesting, question relates to the *correspondence of formal regimes and informal institutions*. Research in this area has not produced conclusive results so far (see for instance, Papadakis & Bean, 1993; Gundelach, 1994; Kluegel & Miyano, 1995; Svallfors, 1997, 2003; Bonoli, 2000; CPB/SCP, 2003; Pfau-Effinger, 2005; van Oorschot & Arts, 2005; Larsen, 2006). An elaborate analysis was carried out by Arts & Gelissen (2001; see also Gelissen, 2002: 89-123). They stress the determining role of Esping-Andersen's regime types, as one of their key questions is: "does living under a specific welfare regime *cause* people to adhere to a particular conception of [a] moral community?" (my emphasis). Theoretically Arts & Gelissen treat welfare regimes as contextual factors at the macro-level. 'Cognitive factors' (learning, habit formation, and framing processes) are presumed to have certain individual effects: knowledge of the distributive rules in society, habituation to its distributive arrangements, and solidarity frames. Collectively this would translate into notions of solidarity and justice principles, shared by the populations of different countries.

In their empirical analysis Arts & Gelissen present several dependent variables to indicate such collective fundamentals. They use seven items from the *International Social Survey Programme 1996* (ISSP) on tasks the government should, or should not, perform, from which they construct a factor score for the preferred level of solidarity. The responses to three questions from the *European Values Study 1999* (EVS) are treated as separate indicators for preferred justice principles: to what degree should a just society strive for equality, take care of basic needs, and stimulate equity?[28] Arts & Gelissen subsequently build a number of multilevel models, through which they seek to assess the effects of welfare regimes (the macro-level) and several individual characteristics on the solidarity notions and preferred justice principles of people living in various countries. Their results are somewhat indeterminate. There is a significant relationship between welfare regime type and the preferred level of solidarity, but the correspondence is not very close. As Arts & Gelissen theoretically expected, the populations of social-democratic countries prefer a high degree of solidarity; but in countries belonging to the Mediterranean type this inclination is even stronger. All other nations come out much lower on the preferred degree of solidarity. The corporatist countries fall slightly below the liberal regimes, where one would theoretically expect the lowest level of preferred solidarity (Arts & Gelissen, 2001: 294). The remaining results are rather singular. On 'preferred equality' the inhabitants of countries with a social-democratic regime actually fall behind people living under a liberal welfare type; and the gap compared with the Mediterranean countries is even more striking (Arts & Gelissen, 2001: 295). The same happens with 'need': in order for their society to be just, the population of countries with a social-democratic regime think it less important that basic needs are met than people living in liberal welfare states. Only in terms of equity do the differences run in the direction one would expect, with the greatest adherence to a meritocratic justice principle in the liberal countries. The variance that could be attributed to the regime types turned out to be rather low, however[29] (Arts & Gelissen, 2001: 295).

Although Arts & Gelissen answer their question on the influence of regime types on public opinion with a qualified 'yes', the evidence they present for their causal hypothesis is not overwhelming. There may be theoretical reasons for this. Arts & Gelissen assume, essentially, that regimes determine opinions because they form a context of socialisation. Through learning, habit formation and framing, citizens would acquire certain notions of social security which reflect the regime type they live in. However, in chapter 3 it was stipulated that social security institutions are fundamentally *undersocialised*. Young people and their socialising agents do not need such rules in everyday life, which leads to a low incentive to pick up or install them at an early age. Moreover, modern social security regimes are often complicated and may be rather ambiguous. This makes them hard to learn or to become accustomed to at a later stage, even where people are willing to do so. Finally, educational curricula provide little explicit training in social security rules, with the exception of a small group of professionals (specialist lawyers, employees of benefit agencies). All of this makes an intensive and uniform 'socialisation of welfare regimes' rather unlikely – especially in the sense that these systems of formal rules are differentially internalised by the citizens of various countries. If there is a correspondence between formal regimes and informal institutions, socialisation does not seem a likely candidate to explain the nexus.

In the previous chapters it was pointed out that theoretically there is no evident causality. The adherents of the 'new institutional economics' often assume that formal institutions determine informal ones. From their point of view official regulations, such as state benefit schemes, are created because they are collectively efficient. However, formal rules cannot possibly cover all alternatives that may arise in actual economic and social interactions; and values, social norms and conventions serve to fill in these gaps. If formal regulations stay efficient over a longer period of time, informal institutions eventually will follow. Or, in North's more sophisticated version of this theory: formal and informal rules will in the end converge in a new efficient equilibrium. Sociologists, on the other hand, usually attach prime importance to informal institutions. They often take the existence of values and social norms for granted (cf. chapter 2, especially Coleman's criticism of this point). From there it is a small step to presume these give direction to the creation of public rules. In this line of reasoning formal institutions are the coagulum, or codification, of socially defined moral standards.

As was argued in chapter 2, the causal links between formal and informal institutions should be an empirical issue. In the case of social security regimes and their informal counterparts this would require an extensive analysis of the historical genesis of these different institutions in various countries. This goes beyond the more modest aim of this section, which seeks to explore the actual degree of correspondence between formal regimes and the informal social security rules of different nations – a matter of empirical coherence, not the testing of a certain causal order. However, previous empirical analyses of the relationship between regime types and informal rules are not convincing, because these often show one or more of the following shortcomings:

1) Inadequate regime classification. This may relate to both between-cluster and within-cluster variance. The first occurs when countries are assigned to regime types to which they do not actually belong. The latter may happen if clear examples of a certain regime type are lumped into one and the same category with less straightforward cases.[30] Of course, if the classification of formal institutions into regimes is partially invalid empirically, this will distort its correlation with informal institutions.

2) Inapt measurement of informal rules. Such institutions theoretically refer to the division of rights and obligations a community or society actually prefers. Following this definition attitudes towards government spending on welfare (e.g. Papadakis & Bean, 1993: 236) are, for instance, bad indicators for informal rules. These are not about the rights and obligations actors currently hold: spending preferences cannot be considered values, social norms or conventions, but refer to the aims policymakers should pursue in formal social security legislation. Moreover, they have no bearing on the actual situation, because they often relate to the course to be taken in the future. With such indicators, it is quite likely that *Standortsgebundenheit* will sometimes show effects that run opposite to the current design of social security. People living under a residual regime type may generally prefer a limited social security system, but it could be that they want to see the basic protection somewhat extended in the future. And it is conceivable that the population of a country with comprehensive social provisions largely supports such an extensive regime, but thinks the current system is 'over the top'.[31] If the informal rule indicators are ill-suited, it is evident the relationship with regime types will become blurred.

3) One-dimensional selection of informal institutions. Quite often indicators for informal institutions are chosen that theoretically correspond to the first dimension of figures 4.1 and 4.2. The preferred degree of collective responsibility for the coverage of certain risks, inequality aversion, meritocratic justice principles, and the like all theoretically reflect the 'scope' dimension. On the other hand, indicators of the second principal axis (universalism/particularism) are rare: informal pendants of occupationalism, the special position of civil servants, the labour disincentives for women and less productive workers, etc., are hardly ever included. This of course means that if one finds country clusters in terms of informal institutions, one can expect these to reflect the contrasts on the first dimension, with the main dividing line between countries with small (liberal, Mediterranean) and extended (corporatist and especially social-democratic) social security regimes. Whereas Esping-Andersen's typology is multi-dimensional, most research on the informal rules associated with regime types refers to the first component only.[32] This of course implies that the distinction between countries of the corporatist and social-democratic types tends to become unclear, as the difference is made mainly by the second dimension.

Owing to these limitations, it may be that much of the former work in this field was not wholly adequate to detect the actual correspondences between social security regimes on the one hand, and the informal rules held by the various populations on the other. To test this, an exploratory analysis was performed on data from the 1996-1999 waves of the *International Social Survey Programme*. The same countries were included as in the previous section, with the exception of Belgium, which did not take part in the ISSP-waves analysed here.[33] This leaves four nations belonging to the liberal regime type (the USA, Australia, Canada and Great Britain), three social-democratic ones (Sweden, Denmark and Norway), two corporatist examples (Germany and France) and one hybrid (the Netherlands).

Variables were selected on a number of grounds. First, they had to relate to social security, labour market orientations or taxes, thus excluding more general value orientations as analysed, for instance, by Gundelach (1994). Further, variables should refer to informal pendants of formal institutions: the rights and obligations of actors, the actual responsibilities the government should have in providing social security, the legitimacy of informal defection of formal rules, or sanctioning. Thirdly, they should be indicators of either scope or particularism/universalism. This was empirically validated by inspecting the bivariate correlations with the regime clusters. A few pragmatic considerations played a role in the selection process as well. Variables which were fairly similar in these four ISSP waves were left out, as were indicators with too many missing values. The procedure resulted in 16 items, which were used as input for yet another categorical principal components analysis.[34]

As the component loadings[35] in figure 4.3 make clear, there are three distinct groups of variables. The first dimension is dominated by five informal rules with negative loadings (items 1-5 in the graph). Theoretically these are mostly in line with a liberal regime. A low score on the x-axis indicates that a comparatively small part of the population think the government should be responsible for providing a decent standard of living for the elderly and the unemployed, for providing jobs and for reducing income differentials. This often coincides with less aversion to inequality at the top of the income distribution, measured over six typical occupations.[36]

The second cluster of variables combines high positive loadings on the second dimension with moderate positive ones on the first (items 6-10). This consists of informal rules that theoretically fit in well with the social-democratic regime type. Meritocratic wage criteria are considered less important than elsewhere, and the preferred earnings inequality between lower and higher occupations is comparatively low. Furthermore, a relatively large share of people would enjoy their jobs if they did not need the money. In line with this, the share of the respondents who think that a job should offer good career opportunities is comparatively limited. Finally, there is a female bias in the preferences for working in the collective sector. This indicator was chosen because, following Esping-Andersen, a high labour participation rate of women obliged to pay taxes is a precondition for the financial sustainability of the social-democratic regime. This is largely realised through a high labour demand in the sectors of welfare, care, education and social security.[37] A positive score on the y-axis therefore suggests more aversion to income inequality between the top and the bottom, a comparatively post-materialistic work ethic, and a rather strong inclination of women to work in (semi-)government jobs.

Figure 4.3
Optimal scaling of 16 indicators of informal social security rules (CatPCA, component loadings)

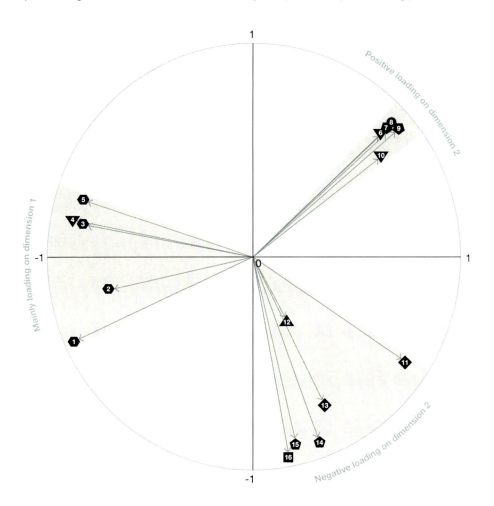

Markers and abbreviations of informal social security rules

● Governmental responsibility for decent standard of living, income redistribution, and providing jobs (GOV)
▼ Income inequality aversion (INA)
⬢ Postmaterialist work orientation (PMW)
● Female preference for collective sector (FEM)
◆ Prestige of state officials (PST)
▲ Wage criteria: seniority (SEN)
⬠ Lenient interpretation of formal rules (LEN)
■ Traditional gender roles (TGR)

Sources: International Social Survey Programme 1996-1999; Cultural Changes in the Netherlands 1999

Groups of variables[a]

Mainly loading on dimension 1

Response categories

❶ GOV: 'Should it be the government's responsibility to provide a decent standard of living for the unemployed?' — % definitely/probably should

❷ GOV: 'It is the responsibility of the government to reduce the differences in income between people with high incomes and those with low incomes.' — % (strongly) agree

❸ GOV: 'Should it be the government's responsibility to provide a decent standard of living for the old?' — % definitely/probably should

❹ INA: Dispersion measure based on: 'About how much should [6 higher occupations*] earn each year before taxes?' — Gini coefficient of respondents' preferred earnings of 6 higher occupations*

❺ GOV: 'Should it be the government's responsibility to provide a job for everyone who wants one?' — % definitely/probably should be

Positive loading on dimension 2

❻ INA: 'In deciding how much people ought to earn, how important should it be how well he or she does the job?' — % essential

❼ PMW: 'Good opportunities for advancement' (how important respondent thinks this is in a job?) — % (very) important

❽ FEM: 'I would choose: working in a private business – working for the government or civil service.' — % government/civil service (ratio female : male respondents)

❾ PMW: 'I would enjoy having a paid job even if I did not need the money.' — % (strongly) agree

❿ INA: Dispersion measure based on: 'About how much should [lower vs. higher occupations**] earn each year before taxes?' — Theil coefficient (between) of respondents' preferred earnings, 3 lower vs. 6 higher occupations**

Negative loading on dimension 2

⓫ PST: Ranking score: 'About how much should a cabinet minister in the national government earn each year before taxes?' — scale of mean preferred earnings of 9 occupations** in country (cabinet minister score)

⓬ SEN: 'In deciding on pay for two people doing the same kind of work, how important should (it) be how long the person has been with the firm?' — % essential/very important

⓭ PST: 'I would choose: working in a private business – working for the government or civil service' (males). — % government/civil service (male respondents)

⓮ LEN: 'A taxpayer does not report all of his income in order to pay less income taxes.' — % not/a bit wrong

⓯ LEN: 'A person gives the government incorrect information about himself to get government benefits he is not entitled to.' — % not/a bit wrong

⓰ TGR: 'All in all, family life suffers when the woman has a full-time job.' — % (strongly) agree

a. Variables listed in grey run from high to low.

* Preferred earnings for: lawyer; doctor in general practice; cabinet minister in the national government; Supreme Court Judge; owner-manager of a large factory; chairman of a large national corporation

** Preferred earnings for: unskilled factory worker; shop assistant; skilled factory worker; plus the 6 higher occupations above

[ ] Multiple items in questionnaire

The third group of items (numbers 11-16) has high negative loadings on the second dimension, and low or moderately positive ones on the first. Theoretically these features are mainly associated with the corporatist regime. A fairly high proportion of the population think that family life will suffer if mothers work full-time. More than in other countries, people think seniority should be a wage criterion. The high ranking of the cabinet minister in the distribution of preferred earnings suggests a considerable prestige of state officials. The latter is corroborated by the comparatively large proportion of men that would prefer to work in the collective sector. A high negative scale value on the second y-axis also indicates that a lenient interpretation of formal rules is more common than elsewhere: the percentage of respondents who think that tax evasion or obtaining social security rights through presenting false information is not wrong (or only slightly), is higher than in other countries.[38]

Summarising, the first dimension measures the degree to which the population supports or rejects liberal principles on government responsibility for living standards and employment. The second dimension mainly reflects a distinction between social-democratic and corporatist informal rules. Both of these are negatively correlated with the 'liberal' principles on the first dimension.

The scale values of the countries on these two axes are presented in figure 4.4. From this it can be concluded that the first cluster of variables (negative loadings on the x-axis) mainly indicates the differences between the USA, Canada, Great Britain and Australia on the one hand, and the remaining cases on the other. The second group of variables (positive loadings on the second dimension) mostly shows a distinction between Norway plus Sweden, and the other countries. The third group (negative loadings on the y-axis) largely measures the contrasts between Germany plus France, and the rest.

The resulting clustering of countries is quite similar to that of the regime types in the previous section. The first dimension shows a contrast between countries with liberal informal rules and the rest, while the second differentiates between countries having social-democratic and corporatist informal institutions. Once again the latter cluster is quite homogeneous (although it consists of only two countries here, due to the missing Belgian data), while within the liberal and social-democratic groups some dispersion occurs. The classification is supported by the outcomes of a cluster analysis of the object scores on the two dimensions.[39]

The USA, Canada and – to a lesser extent – Great Britain and Australia form a liberal cluster, with low scores on the first dimension. This implies that less than elsewhere the citizens of these countries think that the government should be responsible for ensuring a decent standard of living for the elderly and unemployed, for the provision of jobs and for reducing income inequality. They also show less aversion to income differentials at the top. Within this group of countries, the scale values of the United States and Great Britain are consistent with figure 4.2. The USA has the most residual social security regime, and this is backed up by the informal rules of its population, which are generally the most 'liberal' – or libertarian, as some Americans might prefer to say – of all the countries. The UK

Figure 4.4
Optimal scaling of 10 countries [a] on informal social security rules (CatPCA, object scores)

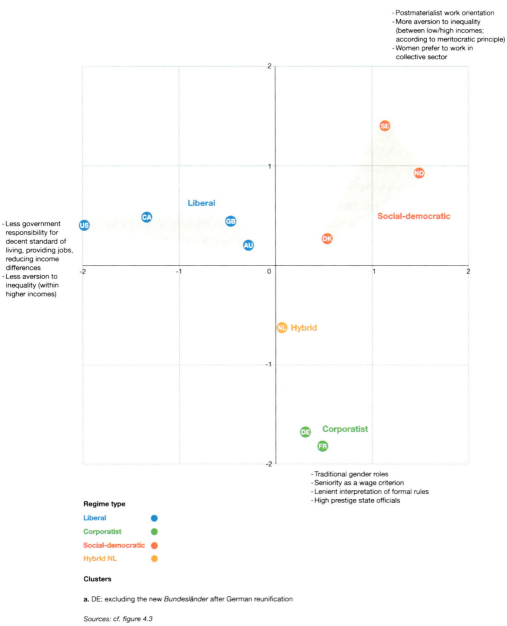

a. DE: excluding the new *Bundesländer* after German reunification

Sources: cf. figure 4.3

social security regime is a less pure specimen of the liberal type, and in line with this governmental interventions and smaller income differentials at the top are more favoured by the British than in the other liberal countries. The relative positions of Canada and Australia, however, are not wholly in line with the scaling of their regime types. Just as in the UK, the Canadian social security regime is by no means a perfect example of the liberal type; but the Canadian informal social security rules are fairly liberal, although they lag behind the USA level. In Australia the opposite occurs; here, the rather residual social security regime of figure 4.2 coincides with informal institutions that are considerably less liberal than in the USA. This can only partially be explained by missing data.[40]

Sweden and Norway are scaled close to each other, with high scores on the positive side of both the first and the second dimension – the direction of the social-democratic traits of figure 4.3. A high proportion of people have a strong aversion to inequality, and want the government actively to combat it. Governmental intervention to ensure work for all and a decent standard of living is considered desirable. To a lesser extent than elsewhere, people feel that job performance ought to be the central wage criterion. Postmaterialistic work orientations prevail, and females have a stronger preference for working for the government or the civil service than in other countries.

Although according to figure 4.2 Norway is a less pure representative of the social-democratic regime type, the informal rules of its population seem very similar to those prevailing in Sweden. Denmark shows the reverse pattern: a social security regime which is clearly social-democratic, but informal institutions that are on the verge of this cluster. On the first axis, the comparatively low Danish score may be explained by the fact that two high-loading variables are missing. If social-democratic responses are imputed for these data, Denmark moves closer to Norway and Sweden, but still remains a less typical case. On the postmaterialism items, Denmark scores considerably lower than Sweden and Norway, and the female preference for working in the government sector is less pronounced as well. On the second dimension, the Danish resemble the Swedes and Norwegians in their comparatively strong rejection of traditional family roles, benefit fraud and tax evasion, but they are corporatist in two other respects: many people think seniority should be a key wage criterion, and a fairly high proportion of men favour working in the government sector. Thus, Denmark seems decidedly less social-democratic in terms of informal rules than Norway and Sweden, whereas it is a rather pure type in its regime characteristics. This result is in line with findings from other sources. According to the *European Values Study 1999* and a *Eurobarometer* survey conducted in 2001, the Danish frequently score lower on such informal issues than Swedish and Finnish respondents (cf. CPB/SCP, 2003: 25, 27).

The third cluster comprises France and Germany. These countries attain high negative scores on the second dimension of figure 4.4, in the direction of the corporatist traits. Their populations have strong preferences for traditional gender roles and for seniority as a wage criterion, and show a rather lenient interpretation of formal rules. The desired earnings of a Cabinet minister are comparably high and males favour working for the government, suggesting that the prestige of civil servants is substantial.

Once again, the Netherlands may be considered a hybrid, with scale values rather close to the origin of figure 4.4. On the first dimension, the scores on the government's responsibility for providing jobs and reducing income differentials are relatively high, which sets the country apart from the liberal regimes. However, two other variables loading high on the first dimension (items 1 and 3) were missing in the data set, which reduces the scaling value. A sensitivity analysis showed that if 'social-democratic' or 'corporatist' responses are imputed for these variables, the Netherlands attain a higher value on the first dimension, close to the position of France.

The second dimension is a very mixed bag in the Dutch case. In some respects the Netherlands resembles Sweden and Norway, but in others it is more similar to France and Germany. The Dutch favour postmaterialism, but to a lesser degree than the Swedes and Norwegians; and the female preference for working in the collective sector lags far behind the Scandinavian level. The Dutch attain a 'corporatist' level on traditional gender roles and the acceptability of tax evasion. On the other hand, they record fairly low scores on the preference of males for working in the collective sector, on the importance of seniority as a wage principle, and on the acceptance of benefit fraud. Therefore, it is likely that the Netherlands has a truly hybrid score on the second dimension, and in fact occupies a higher position on the first than figure 4.4 suggests.

The hypothesis of correspondence between formal regimes and informal rules thus seems to be confirmed more clearly than in the previous work. The correlation of country scores on the first dimension of figures 4.2 and 4.4 is 0.84, that between the scale positions on the second dimension about the same (0.85). The support found here is a consequence of both the way regimes were scaled in the previous section, and of the informal institutions that were chosen here. The inclusion of indicators for the specific informal traits of the corporatist and social-democratic regimes seems especially important in this respect.

The question at issue was to what extent formal social security systems and informal institutions coincide: a matter of correlation, not one of causality. Having established this correspondence, some further remarks can be made in the light of the institutional theory addressed in the previous chapters.

Larsen (2006: 50) has suggested that cross-national differences in 'welfare attitudes' may be explained by the way regimes structure society in terms of job opportunities, generosity and selectivism. In his view, these subsequently shape peoples' perception of how social relationships should be, especially in terms of 'deservingness', in the sense that this concept was elaborated by Van Oorschot (2000, 2005). According to Larsen this would translate into cross-national differences in support for welfare policy.

Although there are interesting similarities with the analysis performed here, the theoretical line of reasoning Larsen proposes is somewhat different. A first distinction is that informal institutions refer to a wider concept than the notion of deservingness. In the previous section, the structural traits of formal social security regimes were reduced to their scope and the degree of universalism/particularism.[41] The current analysis showed these to be linked to their normative counterparts. The deservingness of social security recipients is one aspect of these; but the informal rules considered here also refer to other matters, such as the obligations of actors (e.g. paying contributions), the tolerability of breaking the rules (defection and sanctioning), the social status of government officials, etc.

A more fundamental difference is that Larsen (2006: 50) considers his deservingness and 'welfare attitudes' as dependent variables, which logically result from the structural features of regime types at the macro-level; while following the theoretical notions of the previous chapters, causality does not seem to be as straightforward as that. Let us briefly reiterate some of the main arguments that were put forward earlier:

- institutions are socially constructed rules indicating the rights and duties of actors, including conditions and sanctions. Formal institutions are based on legislation, or on public enforcement of private arrangements. Informal institutions refer to general values, social norms, conventions and agreements prevailing in the community;
- formal and informal institutions are theoretically correlated. This is not because either one determines the other, but is due to the fact that both types of institution aim to realise collective goals by steering behaviour through the allocation of rights and duties; and because both are vested and evolve in the same historical process. Their correspondence is not necessarily perfect, because several formal rules may fit in with a given informal rule (and vice versa); and because the outcomes of the formal and informal rule negotiations do not necessarily coincide (e.g. as a result of compromises in the policy process);
- modern social security institutions are largely formal in nature: the allocation of rights and duties is to a large extent codified in government regulations. Present-day 'voluntary' social security (communal or familial schemes) tends to be rather marginal. Informal rules are largely subsidiary to the official 'rules of the game', in the sense that they complement and support the formal institutions. However, certain groups may hold informal views which deviate from the standard ('benefit cultures' among the underclass in certain neighbourhoods);
- regime types refer to specific configurations of formal rules: diverging national sets of coherent formal social security institutions at national level, which are intended to bring about specific collective goals.

From this point of view, for a number of reasons the correspondence between formal social security regimes and the informal rules prevailing in the various countries is likely to be high. National social security laws can by definition not cover all individual circumstances, and informal institutions may specify the latitude allowed by the formal schemes. For example, the official job-search requirements of the unemployment laws may be elaborated and endorsed by local community norms. Conversely, all social security regimes require some degree of informal support: in a democratic society the different 'worlds' will not be able to survive if they are fundamentally at odds with voters' notions of what is a legitimate attribution of social security rights and obligations.

A third reason why regimes and informal rules may coincide is their common origin. As stressed by Esping-Andersen, regimes are products of history; in terms of the figural model in §2.3, they result from a specific configuration of relative prices, power relations, conflicts of interest and support for ideals. In the 20th century the corporatist, social-democratic and liberal systems of formal institutions generally emerged because they were regarded as more efficient solutions to the problems of mass unemployment, poverty, etc. than their predecessors. They also reflect the diverging group interests (industrial workers, farmers, new middle classes) that prevailed in the various countries at the time. These were traded off in the policy process, where the introduction of universal suffrage had made it possible to obtain a democratic majority for 'red-green' or Catholic-Socialist coalitions, for example. The ensuing social security legislation reflected elements of the ideals of their various founders. Thus, historically informal notions of justice, solidarity etc. among the population at large and the national elites were instrumental in the vesting of social security regimes. If these ideals are still echoed in the current informal rules on social security entitlements, duties etc. among the population, the shared history will imply a high correlation of informal rules and formal regimes.

A final aspect has to do with adaptation of informal rules as a result of the long-term exposure of the population to the various regime types. Once established, social security regimes tend to be rather stable as a result of path dependency. Changes in the formal regulations are often based on the principle of 'maximising regime consistency, minimising regime divergence' (cf. Soede et al., 2004: 59-64), because this incurs the lowest costs and electoral risks for the traditional governing elites and their supporters. This stability of the regime typology over time can have an impact on the informal rules. The mere fact that people have been exposed to the different regime types for several decades may have resulted in a growing correspondence of formal institutions and informal social security rules over the years. Within each type, it is possible that the general public have increasingly come to regard the existing attribution of entitlements as acquired rights, and the attached obligations of taxpayers as self-evident.

Yet each of these grounds may be disputed, and a high correlation of regime types and informal rules is therefore not inevitable. Informal institutions do not necessarily imply an elaboration and endorsement of the official rules; if 'benefit cultures' and tax-payers resistance are widespread, the opposite holds. Some public support for social security regulations may indeed be required; but informal notions of rights and obligations can be connected to formal institutions in many ways, and the link with the abstract level of regimes is particularly flexible. Although informal rules and formal regimes often have common roots, this does not mean they have to coincide. Historically ideals were only one of the factors in the vesting of the regimes, and at the time these may have been compromised in the process of rule negotiation. For instance, after the Second World War Dutch social democrats did not manage to introduce the universal old age state pension which was their aim, but had to accept a social minimum based on compulsory national insurance, which was topped up by earnings-related occupational pensions (cf. Roebroek & Hertogh, 1998: 289-306). It is also possible that the ideals which prevailed then are no longer shared by the present-day population; for example, in social-democratic regimes the decline of the traditional working class may imply that fewer people currently support the solidarity principle of national social insurance schemes.

Finally, the relevance of the 'exposure' argument – which is rather similar to the line of reasoning proposed by Larsen (2006) – should not be exaggerated. The regime types have existed for several decades, but perhaps not long enough to make a lasting impression on the informal rules of the general public, especially because, like all formal social security rules, the institutions expressing the different regime types tend to be undersocialised (cf. §3.5). As a result the regimes are probably not deeply rooted in the populace; and this implies that in a different historical context they may come to hold other views on the right attribution of social security rights and duties. If changes in the 'incentive to regulate' are sufficiently great – as a result of a war, a major recession, mass unemployment, marked ageing of the population, high migration, famine – the consensus is likely to alter, and even regime shifts may not be unthinkable.

4.4 Conclusions

The first part of this chapter described the theoretical traits of social security regimes: diverging systems of coherent formal social security institutions at a national level. Esping-Andersen (1990) identified 'three worlds of welfare capitalism'. His ideal-type of a liberal regime theoretically has residual collective social security schemes: low benefits of limited duration, strong targeting of the needy through means testing, low spending on activating labour market policy, no collective child care provisions, and so on. On the other hand the type has a rather well-developed private insurance system for the middle classes. De-commodification (the extent to which one can attain an acceptable standard of living, independently of one's market value) is low, and the liberal regime tends to sharpen social stratification into three layers: welfare clients and the working poor; the middle classes; and the privileged.

The social-democratic welfare regime is theoretically located at the other extreme. Here benefits are available for all, at a generous level, and may continue for as long as the social risk is apparent. The high collective costs this implies can only be afforded through an effective activating labour market policy. The participation rate of women is considerable, but they mainly work in the services sector. Private insurance is less important. This system aims at high de-commodification and a reduction in stratification.

Esping-Andersen's third type is the corporatist one. Such a regime is theoretically well-developed, but benefits have a more selective basis. Rights are often tied to paid contributions and past labour experience. Certain groups, such as civil servants, have benefit schemes of their own – often at a higher level, corresponding to their elevated social status. Families with children are well-protected through collective schemes, without striving for economic independence of both spouses. The labour market participation of women is therefore low, as is the participation rate of elderly men and disabled people. The degree of de-commodification is theoretically limited. In terms of stratification, corporatist regimes seek to reproduce the existing differences between status groups.

Empirical validity of the typology

Although Esping-Andersen's typology may be criticised – especially his equating of regime traits with certain social results – the concept is interesting if one wishes to analyse the variety of formal institutions. His regime types indicate general, qualitatively different and coherent systems of formal rules. However, their empirical status is open to debate, as the many alternative classifications of regime types published over the last decades prove. The main object of this chapter was to test the empirical validity of Esping-Andersen's theory. Previous empirical analyses in this field have often only covered a part of the social security regime (e.g. pensions or health insurance), which cannot be considered the core of the regime types. Moreover, the number of variables was generally rather limited, and the multivariate techniques applied often assumed linear relationships, while the essence of the typology consists in categorical differences on a limited number of underlying dimensions.

A categorical principal components analysis (CatPCA) was performed over 54 formal regime traits. These referred, firstly, to the main formal social security regulations: pension schemes, disability benefits, surviving dependants' pensions, unemployment and social assistance schemes, and provisions to accommodate the cost of children. The specific bias of corporatist countries was measured by the existence of separate schemes for occupational groups, and the level of social protection for civil servants. Besides this, a number of indicators for funding and labour market disincentives were included. For the scaling procedure a sample of countries was selected that would theoretically cover Esping-Andersen's three regime types. Sweden, Denmark and Norway were expected to be social-democratic, and Belgium, France and Germany to be corporatist. The USA, Canada, the United Kingdom and Australia were theoretically considered to be liberal, although some authors claim the latter country to be part of a separate 'Antipodean' type. The Netherlands was hypothesised to be a hybrid case, combining social-democratic and corporatist traits.

Generally speaking, the CatPCA results confirm the existence of Esping-Andersen's 'three worlds of welfare'. The component loadings of the variables fall into a number of consistent groups. They allow for a clear interpretation of two underlying dimensions, one referring to the scope of the rights and obligations implied (residual/extensive), the other to the degree of selectivity in social security (particularistic/universalistic). On these two principal components the clustering of countries largely corresponds to what was expected. Seven countries scale as characteristic exponents of the regime types: Sweden and Denmark for the social-democratic regime type, which is extensive and universalistic; Belgium, Germany and France for the corporatist model (extensive-particularistic), and the USA and Australia for the liberal group (residual, and neither clearly universalistic nor particularistic). Three countries are less clear specimens, although they belong to the clusters as expected. In the social-democratic group, Norway is less extensive than Sweden, and less universalistic than Denmark. The United Kingdom and Canada have social security regimes with a somewhat wider scope than the other liberal countries.

The Netherlands emerges as the only true hybrid, however, occupying the expected position between the social-democratic and corporatist countries.

Generality of regime types

Finally, the generality of the regime types was analysed. If the empirical findings presented here are combined with those of Shalev (1996, 2007) and Soede et al. (2004), the three 'worlds of social security' can be considered relatively stable phenomena during the final decades of the 20th century. However, they cannot be translated easily into more general welfare regime types. Esping-Andersen's trichotomy is not clearly manifest in other domains of welfare. Although there seems to be a fairly close match with the design of education systems, this is much less so in the health sector or in housing policy.

On the other hand the link between regime types and informal rules turned out to be rather straightforward. In countries with a liberal social security regime, a smaller proportion of the population wants the government to be responsible for reducing income inequality, and for providing jobs and a decent standard of living for people who are out of work than in countries belonging to the social-democratic and corporatist types. Also, in the liberal group there is generally less aversion to income differentials at the top. The social-democratic regime type comes with social-democratic informal rules: people are in favour of government intervention, they have a predilection for income equality, show postmaterialistic attitudes towards work, and women massively opt for (semi-)government jobs. In countries with a corporatist regime, the population also prefers a 'strong' government. Apart from that they favour traditional gender roles, attribute a rather elevated status to state officials, think seniority should be an important earnings criterion, and have a relatively lenient interpretation of formal rules. Finally, the Janus-headed Dutch social security regime is backed by a set of informal rules that resemble those of the corporatist countries in some respects, and the social-democratic regimes in others. Thus, the correlation between formal regime types and informal institutions is quite high. Small differences occur in Denmark and Australia on the one hand – which are informally less pure than their formal system – and Norway and Canada on the other (less pure specimens of their regime types, but quite typical examples in terms of the informal rules). The main finding, however, is that all countries belong squarely to the same clusters in figures 4.2 and 4.4.

The results presented in this chapter suggest that social security regimes are real phenomena, not mere ideal constructs invented in what Abrahamson (1999) called the "welfare modelling business" of political science – a trade which may incidentally not always be a particularly profitable one. The conclusions provide a good starting point for the issue that is at stake in the next two chapters: do the various regime types produce diverging collective outcomes?

5 Benefit dependency

The fact that a section of the population receive benefit is one of the most important collective outcomes of the institutions of social security. This 'benefit dependency' is a direct consequence of the attribution of rights that forms a key element of all social security rules. The number of people living on benefit not only impacts on public expenditure, but also has a broader historical significance: the degree of benefit dependency can influence the economic process and social structuring of a society considerably. Theoretically, relationships may be assumed in particular with the growth and distribution of collective prosperity, the differentiation of social groups and their position on central stratification ladders (cf. §3.6.3).

This chapter explores whether the empirical types of social security regimes discussed previously exhibit differences in the number of benefit recipients they produce. It examines to what extent developments in the benefit volume in ten countries in the period 1980-1999 can be linked to the social security regimes to which they belong: the social-democratic, corporatist and liberal types and the hybrid Dutch system. Regime types – clusters of countries with diverging systems of coherent formal institutions at a national level, which aim to realise distinct collective goals – can be regarded as sparse models of institutional variety, at a high level of abstraction. It is reasonable to assume that the production of benefit dependency in the various regime types will vary, precisely because they strive to achieve different collective objectives.

The scientific importance of an analysis of the relationship between regime types and benefit dependency is twofold. In the first place, empirical research in this field is scarce, primarily because of the limited availability of data on benefit dependency. Since the design of social security arrangements takes place at national level, data collection tends to be country-specific, often lacking in uniformity for the various benefit schemes. Thus, within each country, there may be a wide divergence in the registration methods and accuracy of the figures on the take-up of pensions, unemployment insurance, social assistance benefits, etc. This data problem is even more apparent when it comes to international comparisons of trends in benefit dependency. Until fairly recently there were virtually no cross-comparative volume figures available with any degree of reliability and consistency, and none at all for a time series of any length.

A second reason is related to a proposition that was put forward in the previous chapter: rather than defining regimes *a priori* in terms of the outcomes they generate, the relationship between such institutional configurations and their collective results should be a matter of empirical research.

The question explored here is also relevant from a policy perspective. Most Western governments have been attempting to curb the number of benefit recipients in recent decades. Several policy objectives underlie this drive. Apart from a desire to resolve short-term budgetary problems and concerns about the financial sustainability of social security schemes in the light of population ageing, it is also directed at increasing labour market participation and at targeting the available means on the neediest members of society. If a particular regime type facilitates better 'volume curtailment', this can guide the formulation of future policy – though it may be desirable to look not only at the trend in the number of benefits, but also at other factors such as the likely consequences for income differentials, labour market participation and the poverty rate (cf. chapter 6).

The terms 'number of benefits', 'benefit dependency' and 'benefit volume' are used here to refer to the same phenomenon. Three different aspects of this phenomenon are addressed in the empirical analyses: relative volume, volume growth and volume composition. First, in §5.1, the theoretical relationship between the different regime types and the benefit volume is discussed. This generates hypotheses concerning the influence of social security regimes on the three aspects referred to. Some of the problems in measuring the number of benefits are discussed in §5.2, where the data used here will also be explained briefly. Attention then turns to the question of whether there is a direct correlation between regime type and the three aspects of benefit dependency, and whether the differences operate in the expected direction (§5.3). The growth figures are then subjected to a multivariate analysis. In §5.4 a causal model is developed and tested for a pool of countries; this incorporates the most important exogenous factors (demographics, economy, labour market) and institutional changes. Country-specific versions of the model are presented in §5.5, where an attempt is made to establish whether there really is a relationship with the type of social security regimes after the impact of other factors has been discounted. The main conclusions of the chapter are set out in §5.6.

5.1 Regimes and benefit dependency: theoretical expectations

In his theory, Esping-Andersen devotes little attention to the theoretical relationship between regime types and the number of benefits. His original analysis is concerned mainly with the divergent policy strategies employed by countries in the 1980s, stressing the growing interconnectedness of the labour market and social security policy in that period (Esping-Andersen, 1990: 144-161). However, a number of observations on the development of the benefit volume in European welfare states are relevant. Esping-Andersen points out that many corporatist welfare states opted for a labour market exit strategy from 1980, which was aimed primarily at combating rising unemployment. In countries such as France and Germany, but also in the hybrid Netherlands, the labour supply was constrained by the policy of allowing older workers to exit from the labour market via fairly generous schemes for early retirement, disability benefits and long-term unemployment. Moreover, the entry of women to the labour market has traditionally been discouraged in this regime type by offering high child benefits, good surviving dependants' insurance and tax breaks for breadwinners with children. Both policy strategies tend to foster a relatively high benefit volume.

In the social-democratic regimes of Sweden and Denmark, by contrast, the main thrust of policy was to maximise labour supply. Unlike in the Western European welfare states, older workers were not pushed into early retirement schemes *en masse* in the 1980s.

Moreover, labour participation, especially by women, is actively promoted in this regime type by creating employment in the public services sector (typically in the fields of care, welfare and education). These factors in theory mean that benefit dependency in social-democratic regimes is lower than in corporatist regimes. Yet Esping-Andersen makes an important qualification in this respect. To promote labour participation, the Scandinavian welfare states have extensive provisions for working parents and sick employees: leave arrangements related to maternity, the caring for close relatives and the medical incapacity for performing one's job. This implies that there is a relatively high level of 'benefit dependency' *within* the employed population. In other words, the high labour participation in the social-democratic regimes is accompanied by high rates of absenteeism and large-scale take-up of legally guaranteed occupational social security benefits. In Sweden, for example, not only is the female participation rate very high, but it is also the case that "on any given day, more than 20 percent of employed women are absent with pay" (Esping-Andersen, 1990: 155).

Esping-Andersen does not however formulate a very explicit hypothesis on the relationship between regime types and the benefit volume. Based on his observations certain differences between the corporatist and social-democratic regimes may be assumed. The large-scale exits of elderly from the labour market may imply that the benefit volume in the first type of regime is higher, though this probably will be partly offset by the high absenteeism rates of employed persons in the second regime type. The composition of the total population of benefit recipients also is likely to differ between the two regime types. In the corporatist countries, arrangements for surviving dependants, child benefit and early retirement possibly account for a large proportion of total benefit volumes. By contrast, social-democratic countries may be expected to have a relatively high proportion of employee benefits, including sick leave. With regard to the liberal regime type it is not possible to derive any straightforward hypotheses on the size and composition of the benefit volume from Esping-Andersen's analysis. One could be inclined to suppose that the number of social security recipients will be lower in these systems (because of means testing, the less generous benefits, the more limited duration of benefits), and that a rather large share of benefit dependency will consist of social assistance provisions.

In principle, the outcomes of the analysis of social security regimes in the previous chapter could offer avenues for the development of more substantiated hypotheses. A first assumption that may be posited is that the scope of the system is the most important determinant of the number of benefits. Countries with a high score on the first dimension in figure 4.2 would then be expected to produce a high benefit volume, while countries with a limited scope would generate relatively few benefits. This assumed opposition between 'extensive' and 'residual' regimes can be supported by reference to the relative generosity of the benefits provided, the duration of entitlements, the role of means testing, and so on. However, an argument against this 'scope hypothesis' is that it is precisely the regime type with the broadest scope, the social-democratic system, which explicitly tries to limit benefit dependency, among other things by pursuing an activating labour market policy. If that policy is successful, then theoretically a wide scope need not by definition imply that the number of benefit recipients is high.

An alternative is to base the hypotheses on the second dimension of the typology from the previous chapter (universalism/particularism). For instance, the benefit volume might be expected to be greatest in the particularistic corporatist regimes, due to the high take-up in occupational social security and civil service schemes, the advanced age of statutory retirement, the extensive protection of widows and orphans, the low entry thresholds and high levels of employee disability benefits, and the lack of attention for activating labour market policy in such systems. On the other hand, it might also be assumed that the volume would be greatest in the universalistic social-democratic regimes, as a result of the large target group of public social security in this regime type. The contrasts on the second dimension are thus difficult to interpret in terms of the number of benefits they are likely to bring about.

This leads to the conclusion that it is not possible to link the benefit volume unequivocally to the ranking of countries on the two dimensions which emerged in the earlier typological analysis of formal institutions. A more focused approach is required in order to develop theoretically substantiated hypotheses.

Figure 5.1 shows the score on a theoretical 'benefit dependency boost index' for the same eleven countries which figured in chapter 4. The index was constructed by analysing the differences between countries for 60 formal institutions – partially overlapping with those in figure 4.1 – with regard to their potential impact on the number of benefits. In the first step, separate indices were constructed for the boosts ensuing from the formal rules on the risks of old age, unemployment, social assistance, etc., and from a number of labour market institutions (activating labour market policy, collective labour agreements, statutory minimum wage). The general index was obtained by adding up these scores, after weighting in accordance with the potential influence of the various schemes on the total number of benefits in the population. This weighting is necessary because there are, for example, far more people aged over 65 who are eligible for old age pension than there are parents with an entitlement to care leave. In the former case we are dealing with full year cohorts, who will make use of the provision until their death, while the second case concerns a group of working parents who will withdraw fully or partially from the labour market for a limited period. The index reflects the situation in around 1990; the details of the procedure followed are set out in Annex 1.

Based on this analysis, the four countries belonging to the liberal regime type theoretically have the lowest volume-boosting effect, with an average index score of -1.00. They score lowest on average on the arrangements for disability, unemployment and early retirement as well as on the statutory employee benefits (sickness benefit, maternity and parental leave arrangements). Higher index values are reached only for social assistance schemes and labour market institutions. The liberal countries theoretically have a relatively high social assistance benefit volume; not because this provision is more open or generous than elsewhere, but primarily because the other arrangements are less extensive so that, all other things being equal, more people are forced to rely on the social safety net. In the area of labour market institutions, the low spending on activating labour market policy theoretically pushes up the benefit volume. The retirement pension arrangements, which weigh heavily in the total index, score around the average in the liberal countries, mostly because the formal retirement age for men (65 years) is lower than in most social-democratic countries but higher than in the corporatist welfare states.

Figure 5.1
Theoretical benefit dependency boost index for 11 countries, by regime type (1989-1991)

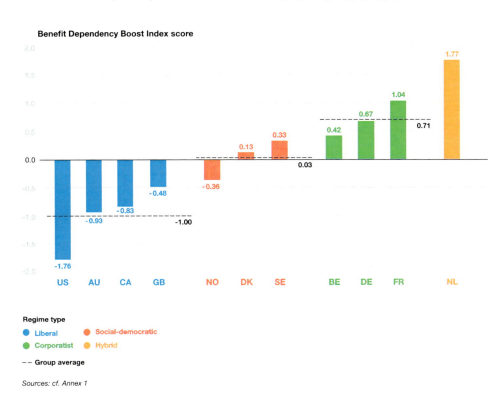

Sources: cf. Annex 1

There is a fairly wide dispersion within the liberal group, although their index score is in all cases lower than that of the representatives of the social-democratic and corporatist social security regimes. The *United States* has far and away the lowest score of all countries, and on the grounds of the formal institutional structure should therefore theoretically generate the lowest number of benefits. This is primarily a result of the limited scope of the social assistance and unemployment arrangements, the absence of mass early exit programmes and the lack of a lowered formal retirement age. In addition, the USA records the lowest score of all countries on collective employee benefits (sickness benefits and leave arrangements), though these do not carry much weight in the total index and the differences compared with the other liberal countries are not very great. It is remarkable that the USA achieves a much lower score on the constituent index for social assistance benefit than the other liberal countries, while it scores comparatively high on labour market institutions – mostly because activating labour market policy is limited – and survivor's benefits.

The benefit volume in *Australia* should theoretically be curtailed because retirement pensions are means tested. The same applies for survivor's pensions, though they carry less weight in the total volume. The benefit volume is further constrained by the absence of a collective unemployment insurance system. This implies that in principle unemployed persons have to rely on social assistance, on which Australia attains the highest boost score. The country also ends up high on the formal retirement age (which is low for women) and labour market institutions (little in the way of activating labour market policy).

The relative number of benefits paid in *Canada* is expected to be higher than in Australia, primarily because of Canada's score on unemployment insurance and survivor's benefits, which is more elevated than in the other liberal countries. The fact that the retirement age has not been lowered (65 years for both sexes) exerts some downward pressure on the benefit volume.

In the liberal group, the benefit volume in principle should be highest in *Great Britain*, among other things because there are more opportunities here for exiting the labour market early than in the other liberal countries. In addition, the low formal retirement age for women theoretically pushes up the volume of these benefits in Great Britain, though this is offset to some extent by the fact that people can also choose to retire after the age of 65. Great Britain also theoretically scores higher than the average for the liberal countries on social assistance, unemployment benefit and sickness benefit. However, the benefit volume is expected to be constrained by the flat rate disability benefits.

The three countries in the social-democratic regime cluster occupy a middle position, with an average index value of 0.03. Typically, they score low on some arrangements but high on others. Little benefit boost is expected in general from the pension and early retirement schemes (because of the fairly high formal retirement age and the limited opportunities for early exit), survivor's pensions and social assistance benefit. The extensive activating labour market policy also theoretically constrains the benefit volume in the social-democratic regimes. However, this is partly cancelled out by the expected high volumes of disability benefit, unemployment benefit, sickness benefit and employee leave arrangements.

The spread within the social-democratic cluster is smaller than in the liberal group. *Norway* theoretically has the lowest benefit dependency. This is due to the low scores on unemployment and social assistance benefits, the high standard retirement age (67 years) and the limited early exit opportunities. When it comes to disability benefit and survivor's pensions, however, the Norwegian score is higher. The activating labour market policy, which is more limited than in the two other social-democratic countries, also theoretically boosts the volume somewhat.

Denmark occupies a middle position, both within the social-democratic group and across all countries together. The number of benefits is in theory depressed fairly substantially by the high statutory retirement age (which until 2004 was 67 years; it has since been lowered to 65 years) and the lack of a separate arrangement for surviving dependants. The take-up of disability benefit is also theoretically lower than in Norway and Sweden because the entry thresholds (the required minimum percentage of incapacity for work) are higher and the benefit levels lower (a flat rate benefit is paid for non-occupational disability). Against this, however, Denmark theoretically achieves a fairly high score on the number of unemployment benefits, early exits, social assistance and employee benefits, so that ultimately it ends up in the middle.

Sweden comes out on top in the social-democratic cluster. Retirement pensions are decisive here: Sweden has a standard retirement age of 65 years, which generates additional benefits compared with Norway and Denmark. If this factor is left out of consideration when calculating the benefit dependency boost index, Sweden is overtaken by the other two countries.[1] Theoretically, Sweden has the lowest benefit volume boosting effect for early exits and labour market institutions (because of the high expenditure on activating labour market policy). However, in around 1990 Sweden scores the highest of all countries on sickness benefits and leave arrangements, while the volume of disability benefits, unemployment benefits[2] and survivor's pensions was also theoretically substantial.

Of the three regime types, the countries in the corporatist regime may be expected to generate the highest benefit volume (average index value 0.71). In theory, they bring about especially large numbers of retirement and early exit benefits, and also score highly on unemployment and survivor's benefits. The score is never low on the other arrangements, with the exception of the expected volume of social assistance benefits. This latter arrangement is less generous than in the social-democratic countries, and the extensive nature of the other provisions earlier in the 'benefit chain' imply that people less often have to rely on social assistance benefit.

Belgium theoretically has the lowest number of benefits in the corporatist group. Its score on the index is comparatively low because of the limited nature of disability benefits, social assistance benefits and sickness leave and the fairly high spending on activating labour market policy. However, the benefit volume in Belgium is theoretically driven up by the low statutory retirement age for women, the ample opportunities for early exit and the high expected take-up of survivor's pensions and unemployment insurance.

Germany records a slightly higher score on the benefit dependency boost index. The volume is expected to be fairly high for the relatively generous social assistance benefits, sickness benefits and survivor's pensions. The take-up of unemployment insurance and early exit arrangements is also theoretically rather high in Germany, though is somewhat lower than the expected volume in Belgium and France. Compared with those two countries, there is theoretically a substantial reduction in the benefit volume in Germany due to the higher formal statutory retirement age (65 years for both sexes).

It is largely this latter factor which ensures that *France* comes out highest in this cluster; the comparatively low retirement age for both men and women (60 years) is expected to lead to large numbers of additional benefits. France also achieves a higher dependency boost score than all other countries on early exits. In addition, a high volume of benefits is made more likely by the institutional traits of the disability schemes (especially the high benefit level and the low entry threshold for the *risque professionnel*) and the limited activating labour market policy. France scores lower than the other corporatist countries on unemployment insurance and social assistance, which at the time of this study had recently been introduced and which had a limited duration (three months, with a possibility of extension).

The Netherlands, with its hybrid system, achieves the highest score on the index (1.77). From the perspective of the benefit volume, the Dutch benefit arrangements in around 1990 can be theoretically characterised as 'the worst of three worlds'. As with the corporatist countries, a high volume may be expected in the early exit arrangements, survivor's benefits and unemployment insurance. The Netherlands theoretically shares a large number of benefits with the social-democratic cluster because of its sickness and disability benefits. And although the number of social assistance benefits is expected to be somewhat lower than in Australia, Canada and Great Britain, the Netherlands scores fairly high on this typically 'liberal' benefit, too. The only areas where this hybrid system did not score highly in around 1990 were the formal retirement age (65 years for both sexes), employee leave arrangements and the spending on activating labour market policy. On the two latter institutional characteristics, the Netherlands lags behind the social-democratic countries and tends more towards the corporatist level.

The constituent scores for disability and unemployment benefit are the highest in the Netherlands of all 11 countries. The fact that the disability benefit volume is expected to be so high is due to the extensive coverage, low entry threshold and high benefit levels for the *risque social*; the Dutch benefits for occupational disability are not in the top group. The number of unemployment benefits in around 1990 is theoretically considerable as well, because the benefit conditions in the Netherlands were almost as favourable as those in Sweden or Denmark, while activating labour market policy targeted at the unemployed (training for unemployed people, specific measures for unemployed and disadvantaged youth, support for unemployed people starting businesses) was much more limited than in those countries.

It is not surprising that this combination of institutional arrangements implies that the benefit volume in the Netherlands is likely to be the highest of all countries considered here – though the high score for this hybrid regime on the benefit dependency boost index may be inflated somewhat as a result of the substitutability of certain benefits.[3]

The ranking of the countries on the index thus suggests that there are clear differences between the regime types in the number and type of benefits they can be expected to generate on the basis of their formal institutions. The ranking found – the lowest benefit volume in countries in the liberal cluster, the highest in the corporatist group, with the social-democratic regime taking a middle position – is not consistent with the position of the regime types in the typological analysis in the previous chapter (the country scores on the first and second dimensions in figure 4.2). It can be expressed in a number of hypotheses about the three aspects of the benefit volume distinguished earlier: relative volume, volume growth rates and volume composition.

(1) Relative volume

The differences between the country clusters on the benefit dependency boost index lead to the following theoretical expectations with regard to the relative benefit volumes:

(1A) In the hybrid Dutch social security regime, the relative volume of benefits is higher than in countries with a corporatist regime;
(1B) In countries with a corporatist social security regime, the relative volume of benefits is higher than in countries with a social-democratic regime;
(1C) In countries with a social-democratic social security regime, the relative volume of benefits is higher than in countries with a liberal regime.

Thus, the *relative volume hypothesis* can be simply expressed as follows:

$$v_{HYB} > v_{CRP} > v_{SD} > v_{LIB}$$

where v = number of benefit years as a percentage of the population in the relevant age group
HYB = hybrid social security regime (NL)
CRP = representatives of the corporatist social security regime type (BE, DE, FR)
SD = representatives of the social-democratic social security regime type (SE, DK, NO)
LIB = representatives of the liberal social security regime type (US, AU, CA, GB)

By way of extension, it may also be interesting to look at the within-cluster ranking. Does the USA, as figure 5.1 theoretically suggests, rank much lower in the liberal cluster than Australia and Canada, which in turn rank lower than Great Britain? Is the relative benefit volume in Denmark larger than in Norway but smaller than in Sweden? And does France have more benefits than Germany, while Belgium comes lowest in the corporatist cluster? However, these are secondary hypotheses, which will be looked at only briefly.

(2) Growth rates

Similar expectations can be derived from the benefit dependency boost scores with regard to the annual percentage growth in the absolute number of benefits. The latter indicator differs from the relative volume in two respects: looking at the annual changes means that the differences between countries in the level of benefit dependency are left out of consideration; and there is no link with the relevant age group.

One advantage of using growth figures is that they provide a very direct measure of the number of benefits generated in a specific period, i.e. the difference between the number of people moving onto and off social security benefits within a given year, abstracting from the historically determined stock. If we wish to analyse the causes of benefit dependency, growth rates moreover offer a number of practical and technical advantages (these will be explored further in the discussion of the causal model in §5.4). There are however also a few potential problems. High growth figures may arise partly autonomously – if the size of the population increases, the benefit volume will expand for that reason alone – and they then say little about the performance of a specific social security regime. In addition, growth rates are sensitive to base rate and ceiling effects. If the initial benefit volume is very low, there is a strong chance that it will grow steeply in percentage terms over time, while in absolute terms the increase may be fairly small. Conversely, the higher the initial volume, the more likely it is that the number of benefits will not rise very sharply in percentage terms, whereas the increase in the size of the groups concerned may well be considerable.

This also implies that looking at growth rates can lead to different conclusions than when considering relative volumes. For example, welfare states that are 'late developers' may experience strong percentage growth in the number of benefit recipients, while benefit dependency expressed as a percentage of the total population may still be negligible. In comparative analyses they may then end up near the top of the country ranking in terms of the growth rates, whereas they remain at the bottom of the list in the relative volume figures.

Although the two indicators are of course related, it is therefore useful to formulate separate hypotheses on the growth in the number of benefits, in line with the scores on the theoretical index:[4]

(2A) In the hybrid Dutch social security regime, the number of benefits grows more strongly than in countries with a corporatist regime;
(2B) In countries with a corporatist social security regime, the number of benefits grows more strongly than in countries with a social-democratic regime;
(2C) In countries with a social-democratic social security regime, the number of benefits grows more strongly than in countries with a liberal regime.

In abbreviated form the *benefit dependency growth rate hypothesis* can then be represented as follows:

$$\Delta_{HYB} > \Delta_{CRP} > \Delta_{SD} > \Delta_{LIB}$$

where Δ = percentage change in the number of benefit years (compared with the previous calendar year)
HYB = hybrid social security regime (NL)
CRP = representatives of the corporatist social security regime type (BE, DE, FR)
SD = representatives of the social-democratic social security regime type (SE, DK, NO)
LIB = representatives of the liberal social security regime type (US, AU, CA, GB)

Here again it is possible to examine whether there is a within-cluster ranking, which would be expected for the regime types on the basis of figure 5.1 (see the above secondary hypotheses).

(3) Volume composition

Based on the constituent scores which underlie the benefit dependency boost index, a number of hypotheses can also be formulated concerning the composition of the benefit volume. These apply to schemes for people below the standard pensionable age, where according to the constituent indices one type of social security regime theoretically brings about more benefits than others. Expectations are that:

(3A) The relative volume of early exit schemes (early retirement pension, long-term unemployment benefit for older persons, disability benefit for former employees) is highest in countries with a corporatist social security regime;
(3B) The relative volume of unemployment insurance benefit is highest in countries with a corporatist social security regime;
(3C) The relative volume of survivor's benefits is highest in countries with a corporatist social security regime;
(3D) The relative volume of employee benefits (sickness benefit, leave arrangements) is highest in countries with a social-democratic social security regime;
(3E) The relative volume of disability benefits for people not gainfully employed is highest in countries with a social-democratic social security regime;
(3F) The relative volume of social assistance benefits is highest in countries with a liberal social security regime;
(3G) The relative volume for all types of benefit is above average in the hybrid Dutch social security regime.

In brief, the *volume composition hypothesis* can also be formulated as follows:

$$V^{(A,B,C)}_{CRP} > V^{(A,B,C)}_{LIB, SD, HYB}$$

$$V^{(D,E)}_{SD} > V^{(D,E)}_{LIB, CRP, HYB}$$

$$V^{(F)}_{LIB} > V^{(F)}_{SD, CRP, HYB}$$

$$V^{(A-F)}_{HYB} > \overline{V}^{(A-F)}_{CRP, LIB, SD, HYB}$$

where
V^A = benefit years early exit schemes (as % of the relevant reference group)
V^B = benefit years unemployment insurance (ditto)
V^C = benefit years survivor's benefits (ditto)
V^D = benefit years employee dependency (ditto)
V^E = benefit years disability insurance for non-employees (ditto)
V^F = benefit years social assistance (ditto)
$\overline{V}^{(A-F)}_{CRP, LIB, SD, HYB}$ = average relative volume in the individual arrangements
CRP = representatives of the corporatist social security regime type (BE, DE, FR)
LIB = representatives of the liberal social security regime type (US, AU, CA, GB)
SD = representatives of the social-democratic social security regime type (SE, DK, NO)
HYB = hybrid social security regime (NL)

These expectations with regard to the volume composition in different regime types do not derive purely from the scores on the benefit dependency boost index, but can also be substantiated on other grounds. For example, hypothesis 3A is in line with Esping-Andersen's assertion that corporatist countries deliberately use early retirement schemes to regulate labour supply and unemployment.

That the volume of unemployment insurance benefits is expected to be highest in the corporatist regime type (hypothesis 3B) is a result from the typical combination of high benefits, long potential duration, and a fairly passive labour market policy. The latter aspect marks a key difference compared with the social-democratic regime, where the favourable benefit conditions are linked to an intensive policy of activation. The liberal group can be expected to have lower volumes because unemployment insurance has limited cover, benefits are far below previously earned salary, and benefit duration is limited, as the entitlements are intended to tide people over periods of temporary unemployment.

The high volume of survivor's benefits in the corporatist regime type (hypothesis 3C) can be argued from the basis of the breadwinner model prevailing in these countries. Sustaining that model means that the non-working female partner and children have to be well protected in the event of the loss of the man from the family. The arrangements are generous, long-lasting and do not require widowed women to go out to work. By contrast, in the social-democratic regime type the assumption is that the partner left behind already has a job or will go out to work; and in the liberal regime the collective provisions for surviving dependants have limited coverage, and are often wholly or partly means-tested. This explains why these two types theoretically have a lower benefit volume than the corporatist regimes.

In line with Esping-Andersen's observation on the large-scale take-up of benefits among the gainfully employed (the other side of the high labour participation rate), the social-democratic regime is expected to have the highest volume of employee benefits, especially for sick leave and care leave (hypothesis 3D). In the corporatist regimes coverage and duration are more limited (and the benefit volume is constrained by the low labour participation rate of women), while in the liberal cluster these provisions are low across the board.

The expectation that the social-democratic regime will generate the highest volume of non-employee disability benefits (hypothesis 3E) is based on the fact that groups such as the early disabled, the self-employed, housewives and students are covered by this collective arrangement. Elsewhere they are forced to rely on private insurance or social assistance. The picture here may be complicated somewhat by the substantial number of disability benefits paid to military veterans in some countries.

The reason for the high expected volume of social assistance benefits in the liberal regime type (hypothesis 3F) lies mainly in the limited role of the arrangements earlier in the 'benefit chain' (in particular employee insurance benefits), so that more people are forced to rely on the social safety net. The United States may be a special case here, because its social assistance benefit is fairly ungenerous, in terms of the net replacement rates, duration, and the indexing of benefits. The USA is far below the average on the social assistance score that forms part of the benefit dependency boost index, while the other representatives of the liberal regime type score significantly higher.

As stated above, the hybrid Dutch regime theoretically combines the 'worst of three worlds'. In practice, however, the volumes may not be extreme across the board, because of the substitutability of some benefits mentioned above. This is reflected in the terminology chosen in hypothesis 3G: a large number of benefits is expected for all of these arrangements in the Netherlands, to be understood as a relative volume which is higher than the average.

The remainder of this chapter examines whether the available empirical data support the assumptions. The possibilities for statistical testing of the hypotheses are limited, because we are dealing here with macro-data with a small number of observations. This, however, is only one of the complications in the comparative empirical analysis of these issues. It will therefore be useful first to look more deeply at the problems that can arise when measuring benefit dependency, and to explain the data used.

5.2 Measuring benefit dependency

Although the concept of benefit dependency is fairly straightforward, this does not imply that the phenomenon can be measured easily. At the collective level, the term simply refers to the number of people in receipt of social security benefits; or, following the logical fundamental structure of social security institutions discussed in chapter 3, to the size of the subset of group A (entitled actors) that actually takes up benefits, plus the group of non-entitled recipients. The rights R are related to the occurrence of certain risks (old age, unemployment, etc.) and are granted in a process of application of social security rules that includes monitoring and sanctioning (see the theoretical interaction models in the previous chapter). In the case of benefit dependency, R typically refers to transfers which target a lack or loss of income on the part of the recipients. Although the rules may allow for preventive and restorative interventions, these are not relevant for the calculation of benefit dependency.

Conceptually this is fairly clear; yet measuring benefit dependency at national level is not simple, and in cross-comparative research issues of data reliability and validity tend to multiply. A first measurement topic that arises is what kinds of social security one should study. Theoretically it is desirable to include all theoretical risks, no matter how they are covered. This implies that one should take into account the volume of regulations which target both the classic and new risks mentioned in chapter 3: not only pensions, early retirement benefits, unemployment benefits, sickness benefits, disability benefits, survivor's benefits, social assistance benefits, family benefits and health costs insurance, but also arrangements covering the costs of parental leave and divorce, income fluctuations as a result of freelance labour, the costs of social participation, etc. These should preferably include both formal and informal social security schemes; i.e. social security provided or enforced by central and local government, occupational schemes, and communal and familial arrangements. In practice, however, an analysis of benefit dependency in such a wide institutional sense tends to be impossible because a complete set of data on all these different types of arrangements cannot be obtained.

Even where data on benefit volumes are available, they may be measured inadequately. Due to low response rates by benefit recipients, and under-reporting of benefit receipt by respondents, surveys are generally not a reliable source for assessing the total benefit volume. Figures on benefit dependency therefore usually need to be compiled from several different administrative databases and national statistics, often designed for the specific regulations they cover. These sources may not be accurate or up to date, and even if they are, they may not be very 'rich': in practice they often contain only the basic information that is essential in terms of the specific regulation and the current administrative procedure (e.g. little data on the accumulation of benefits, employment history, level of education, distribution by age and gender). It is also quite common for each database to have its own design, with particular variables and specific definitions. Trend-breaks may occur due to changes in the statutory regulations, in the structure and administrative processes of the social security organisation, or in the data-gathering procedure. This makes it difficult to integrate volume figures from different benefit schemes, even at the national level. If the aim is to compare benefit dependency internationally, such integration becomes more problematic as the number of countries increases.

The unit of benefit payment is also a matter of interest. Some types of benefit may be provided to individuals, while others may be paid to households. An integrated national database needs to apply some kind of conversion formula, preferably to the level of individuals (because a member of a household is covered, even if he or she does not receive the benefit in person). In comparing national benefit volumes, an additional complication may arise, in that the same kind of benefit may in some countries be paid to individuals, in others to households. This difference is especially prominent in national pension schemes and social assistance arrangements.

Another complication is the treatment of benefits of different duration. Person A may receive an unemployment benefit for just a few weeks, while person B's benefit dependency could last for years. Of course, it is not sound arithmetic to count these as two equivalent benefits. The obvious solution is not to look at the number of people receiving a benefit, but to convert volume figures to a standardised unit of time, for instance benefit years. However, this requires detailed data on benefit duration, which are not always available.

It is also possible that the same person may receive several benefits within a certain period of time. This can happen sequentially, for instance if the unemployment benefit of person C expires, and he or she applies for social assistance. But it may also be a conjuncture: if person D has lost his job, but is partially disabled, he or she may receive both unemployment and disability benefit. If these do not add up to the national minimum income standard, a partial social assistance benefit may even be granted on top of this. Of course, theoretically this can also be accommodated by a correction to full-time benefit years, provided the administrative databases are linked. In cross-national studies, both the number of coinciding benefits and the possibilities for applying corrections may vary. This of course may lead to different degrees of reliability.

A final issue is how to deal with partial benefits. Take person E, who used to work part-time. If he applies for unemployment benefit, it is commonly awarded in proportion to the level the applicant would have received if he had worked full-time. In terms of duration, however, there is often no difference between unemployed part-timers and full-timers. Should one then count the part-timer's benefit as, say, half a benefit year? Once again, in comparative research the complications that arise are even greater. Countries may differ in the prevalence of part-time work, in the rules for granting partial benefits, and in the possibilities for detecting and correcting them in the available databases.

Precisely because of measurement problems such as these, official international statistics have to date contained few data on the number of people in receipt of benefit, though the situation has improved somewhat in recent years (see e.g. Eurostat, 2004a). The best available database contains time series for a number of countries based on national statistical data for the period 1980-1999, with consistent definitions being used where possible. These data were originally gathered by Ecorys/NEI at the request of the Dutch Ministry of Social Affairs and Employment (cf. Arents et al., 2000; Moor et al., 2002). The OECD subjected the data to secondary analysis and added a number of countries (OECD, 2003a: 171-235; see also Carcillo & Grubb, 2006: 55-60; Grubb et al., 2009: 21, 70). The latter dataset has been adapted here and used to test the hypotheses formulated earlier as adequately as possible.[5] Even so, in order to obtain a comprehensive picture of all the different regulations in the various countries, it was unavoidably necessary to introduce assumptions and estimates in some parts of the data; and in order to obtain complete time series, interpolations were sometimes necessary.

In the analysis, social security has been limited to formal institutions only; the data relate to regulations founded in national law, whether these are administered by a government agency or otherwise. As a result, occupational social security arrangements are included as long as they have a statutory basis;[6] e.g. Dutch sick leave figures have been incorporated even after the privatisation of 1996, because the legislator obliged employers to continue payment of salary for a certain period in the event of sickness. A further selection has been made by confining the dataset to the major income replacement programmes: statutory old age and survivor's pensions, early retirement schemes, sick leave, disability benefits, unemployment insurance, maternity and care leave, and periodic social assistance payments. Child benefit, childcare facilities, incidental benefits (such as one-off social assistance payments), benefits for earmarked costs (e.g. housing benefit) and benefits in kind, such as medical care, are left out of consideration.

The measurement issues discussed above have been tackled by adopting the following strategies (see also Arents et al., 2000: 8-12):
- All benefits, including partial benefits and benefits which were not paid for a full year, are in principle converted to complete benefit years of persons. Supplementary benefits were counted only if they do not coincide with other benefits.[7]
- The problem that certain benefits are paid to households applies particularly for retirement pensions and social assistance. The number of retirement benefit years for people aged over 65 has been maximised to the size of the population in that age group in each calendar year. In virtually all countries studied, social assistance benefits are paid to households and usually cannot be converted to individualised benefit years. As a result, the social assistance volume tends to be underestimated for couples, possibly in differing degrees across countries.[8]
- A correction for conjuncture of benefits was applied by using the available national information. Where there is a clear risk of duplicate benefits (e.g. early retirees who also receive unemployment benefit) the volume of an entire regulation has sometimes been discarded for certain groups (for example on the basis of the age distributions of benefit recipients).

A complication is that the data were only available at the aggregate level of countries, not for individual benefit recipients. This rules out the use of certain statistical methods, such as multi-level analysis (cf. chapter 6). Furthermore, the effects of the regime types on benefit volume cannot be studied for all countries included in the previous chapter, because Norway is missing from the data set. The volume trend between 1980 and 1999 is therefore analysed here for two social-democratic social security regimes (Sweden and Denmark), three corporatist regimes (Belgium, Germany and France), four liberal regimes (Australia, Canada, Great Britain and the United States), and the hybrid Netherlands.[9] These ten countries offer sufficient institutional variety to enable us to study whether social security regimes differ in the volume and type of benefits they generate; but of course the number of observations at the collective level remains rather small, especially considering the fact that the underlying data on individual recipients are not available.

The limitations noted above call for a degree of caution, but the data used here probably still give a fairly accurate indication of the volume and composition of benefit dependency in the countries studied. Undoubtedly, however, the information provision on this point leaves room for future improvement (see also OECD, 2003a: 221-222).

5.3 The development of benefit dependency

This section investigates whether the data on the development of benefit volume support the theoretical expectations formulated above. The relative volume hypothesis is first examined (§5.3.1), followed by the benefit dependency growth hypothesis (§5.3.2) and the volume composition hypothesis (§5.3.3). The analyses in this section are bivariate: the aim is to ascertain whether there is a direct relationship between the regime type and the three volume aspects. This not only provides a detailed picture of the actual trends in benefit volume in the various countries, but also enables the adequacy of the simplest explanation (there is a monocausal relationship between regime type and benefit volume) to be tested. Bearing in mind *Ockham's Razor* and Popper's ideas on methodological simplicity[10] a more complex, multivariate approach should only be preferred if the bivariate hypothesis proves untenable. A priori the latter seems rather likely, because the countries studied here differ not only in terms of their social security regime, but also in their demographic structure and wider socio-economic context. Aspects such as these, however, will be explored in the next section; first, the explanatory power of the simplest approach will be assessed.

5.3.1 Relative volume

The expectation was expressed earlier that the relative benefit volume in the hybrid Dutch regime would be higher than in countries with a corporatist social security regime (hypothesis 1A); the latter would score higher than the social-democratic cluster (1B), which would in their turn generate comparatively more benefits than the liberal group (1C). Figure 5.2 shows the ranking of the ten countries studied as regards relative volume in three reference years: 1980, 1990 and 1999. The relative volume is defined here as the total number of benefit years divided by the population aged 15 years and older.[11]

In none of these years the picture corresponds entirely with the theoretical expectations. In 1980 the Netherlands is not at the top of the ranking: the benefit dependency of the hybrid regime is comparable with the medium score of the United States. The relative benefit volume is highest in Denmark and Sweden, where one third of the population are in receipt of benefit. These countries thus come higher than the corporatist countries: Belgium follows the social-democratic countries fairly closely, but Germany and France rank much lower than hypothesised. In the liberal social security regimes, only Canada and Australia occupy the expected positions at the bottom, with relative benefit volumes that are much lower than in all other countries, no less than 10 percentage points behind Denmark and Sweden. Great Britain and the USA, however, do not record extreme low scores; in 1980, Great Britain comes slightly higher than the corporatist France in the benefit dependency rankings, and the USA slightly lower. In the first measurement year, therefore, support is only found for hypothesis 1C: the relative volume is indeed higher in the countries with a social-democratic regime than in all countries in the liberal cluster. According to the bivariate analysis, the other hypotheses must be rejected.

Between 1980 and 1990 the benefit volume swells in most countries. The biggest increase is in Canada, but Belgium, France and the Netherlands also show strong growth. Two liberal countries are exceptions to the rule: the number of benefits in the USA keeps pace almost precisely with population growth during this period, while in Australia the relative volume actually falls.[12]

These developments lead to a somewhat changed ranking of countries in 1990, but the picture still does not correspond with the hypotheses formulated earlier. In line with the expectations, a corporate country, Belgium, does now top the ranking (with over 38%). The bottom three positions are now also occupied by the liberal regimes (Canada, USA and Australia), and the Netherlands has climbed up the rankings – though is still far from the postulated top position. Even so, benefit dependency in the two countries in the social-democratic cluster is still higher than in France and Germany, while one liberal regime, Great Britain has a rather large share of benefit recipients. To sum up: for 1990, too, based on the bivariate analysis only hypothesis 1C ($v_{SD} > v_{LIB}$) is not rejected.

In the 1990s there was wide divergence between the developments in different countries. Australia, France and Germany saw a sharp increase in the relative benefit volume; reunification had an impact on the figures for the latter country – the new *Bundesländer* were incorporated in the volume figures from 1992. Belgium, Great Britain and Sweden[13] showed a modest increase between 1990 and 1999. The third group consists of Denmark, the Netherlands, Canada and the United States, where the relative volume reduced in this period.

The result of the changes in this decade is that the outcomes in 1999 correspond most closely with the postulated hypotheses. Corporatist Belgium and France are at the top of the ranking, followed by the two countries with a social-democratic regime. Germany has overtaken Great Britain, but ranks below Sweden and Denmark. There is a fairly homogenous grouping of countries in the liberal cluster at the bottom of the ranking. The hybrid Netherlands remains the odd one out, however: as in 1980, the benefit dependency is lower than in the corporatist and social-democratic countries. Thus, hypothesis 1A is still rejected in the final measurement year: the relative volume in the Netherlands is lower than in all corporatist countries. It is less easy to discard hypothesis 1B in 1999, since two of the three representatives of the corporatist regime now rank higher than Sweden and Denmark, and the group averages differ as expected. The relative volume in Germany, however, still lags behind that of the social-democratic cluster. Sweden and Denmark rank higher than the countries in the liberal group, which means that hypothesis 1C can also not be rejected in 1999.

The fact that the relative volume in the USA is significantly lower than in Canada in 1999, which in turn lags behind Great Britain, is in line with the country scores on the benefit dependency boost index. However, Australia comes out lowest in the liberal group, and that was not expected. The slightly higher score for Sweden compared with Denmark does in turn correspond with the secondary hypothesis concerning the within-cluster ranking, though the difference is small. This does not apply in the corporatist group, within which Belgium, instead of having the lowest volume, in fact has the highest.

All in all, hypothesis 1 is supported to a limited extent by these empirical data. The theoretically expected ranking of countries is reproduced most clearly in 1999, especially if one considers the group averages. This is somewhat remarkable, because the benefit dependency boost index reflects the situation in around 1990 (though the typology as such is empirically valid over the entire period; cf. §4.3).

Relative volume among the population of working age

One possible explanation for the weak support for the relative volume hypothesis is that figure 5.2 may not be based on the optimum indicator for differences in the relative number of benefits between the regime types. A large share of the total benefit volume in all countries (roughly half) is made up of old age pensions. Since the coverage of the benefits for the over-65 population is generally high, the total volume encompasses a large demographic component. As a result, the volume data in figure 5.2 will be relatively low for countries with a comparatively young population and higher in countries where population ageing has proceeded further. With this in mind, it is perhaps better to test hypothesis 1 by considering benefit dependency below the age of 65 years.

Figure 5.3 portrays this. Here, for the same measurement years the total number of benefits paid to people younger than 65 years is divided by the size of the potential labour force (the population aged 15-64 years). Compared with figure 5.2, the relative benefit volume in all countries is significantly lower (13-24% instead of 23-39%). This is logical, because benefit dependency in the group left out of figure 5.3, namely the over-65s, is much higher than among the potential labour force. Moreover, the dispersion at each

Figure 5.2
Relative benefit volume in 10 countries, 1980, 1990 and 1999

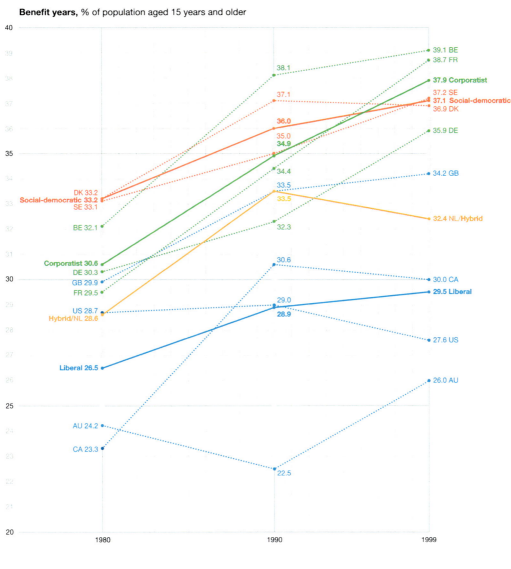

Sources: Arents et al. (2000); Moor et al. (2002); OECD (2003a: 171-235); adapted

measurement point is smaller in figure 5.3: below the age of 65 the relative benefit volume in the various countries differs less than for the population as a whole.

However, the relative volume compared with figure 5.2 does not decrease to the same extent in all countries. This is due to differences in the share of older people in the total population in 1980, diverging population ageing rates in the subsequent two decades, and small variations in the coverage of old age pensions. The alteration due to leaving out the over-65s is smallest in two countries with a relatively young 15+ population (Canada and Australia). This pushes these two countries up the rankings. The same applies, albeit to a slightly lesser extent, for the Netherlands and the United States. Sweden, by contrast, falls rather sharply through the rankings, because the proportion of people aged 65 years and older is the highest in all measurement years. Denmark and Great Britain come out somewhat higher due to the incomplete pensions coverage for the elderly (which implies relatively fewer benefits have been discarded in figure 5.3).

The rankings presented in figure 5.3 do not correspond fully with the expectation expressed in hypothesis 1 either. In 1980, the top position is not occupied by the Netherlands, but by the social-democratic Denmark (20%), followed at some distance by a very mixed cluster consisting of a corporatist, a liberal, a hybrid and a social-democratic country (Belgium, USA, Netherlands and Sweden: 16-17%). Great Britain and Australia lag slightly behind (15%) and at the bottom we find two representatives of the corporatist regime and only one from the liberal cluster (Germany, France and Canada: 13-14%). The relative positions of Denmark, the USA, Great Britain and Australia are much higher than expected, while those of Germany, France and the Netherlands are substantially lower. Hypotheses 1B must certainly be rejected for this year; but according to the group averages, hypothesis 1A and 1C are sustained. In spite of its moderate score, the hybrid Netherlands exceeds the average of the corporatist group. And although the USA attains a higher relative volume than Sweden, the liberal group average is clearly below the social-democratic one.

Between 1980 and 1990 Belgium, France and Canada rise strongly through the rankings, with an increase in the relative benefit volume of around 7 percentage points. In Denmark, the Netherlands, Great Britain and Germany the growth is less marked (between +3 and +5 percentage points), while in Sweden it is modest (+0.9 percentage points). The relative volume in Australia remains constant in this period, while in the USA it falls slightly (-0.9 percentage points).

This of course changes the ranking. Although the Netherlands moves up, it remains more than 3 percentage points behind the leader, Belgium. However, because Germany and France achieve only middling positions in 1990, the relative volume in the hybrid regime is higher than the corporatist group average; and in that sense hypothesis 1A is corroborated. Similarly, on average the relative volume of the corporatist countries exceeds that of the social-democratic group, even though Denmark attains a much higher level than Germany and France. The ranking of the social-democratic and liberal group averages is consistent as well, in spite of the fact that the relative volume in Sweden is lower than in Canada and Great Britain. Within the liberal cluster, it is notable

Figure 5.3
Relative benefit volume among the population of working age
in 10 countries, 1980, 1990 and 1999

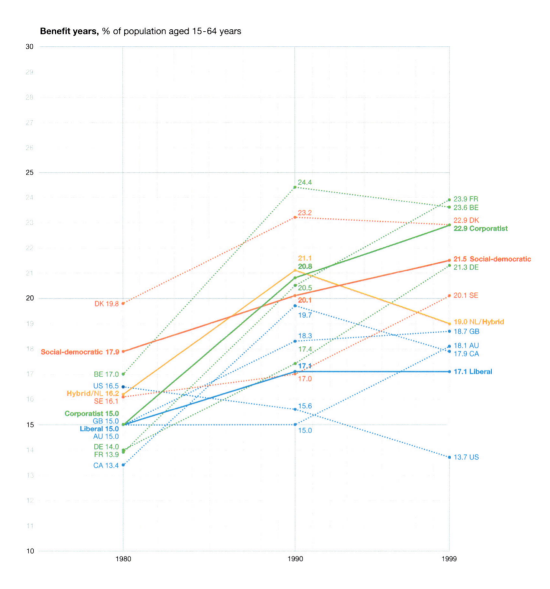

Sources: Arents et al. (2000); Moor et al. (2002); OECD (2003a: 171-235); adapted

that the USA and Australia are in the postulated position at the bottom of the rankings, as expected. On balance, according to the group averages hypotheses 1A-1C cannot be rejected for 1990; but there is a rather wide dispersion within each country group, and therefore no clear clustering of countries by regime type.

In the period 1990-1999, the benefit volume in four countries rises sharply (Australia, Sweden, France, Germany: +3 to +4 percentage points). Great Britain records a small increase (+0.4 percentage points) while Denmark and Belgium show a slight reduction of between 0.2 and 0.8 percentage points. In the remaining three countries, the relative benefit volume falls fairly sharply between the measurement points in the 1990s (Canada, the USA and the Netherlands: approximately -2 percentage points).

Due to these changes, the ranking in 1999 corresponds somewhat more closely with the theoretical expectations.[14] The biggest exception remains the Netherlands, which has sunk to a position in the middle – far from the anticipated position at the top of the ranking. The corporatist Belgium and France, however, move above the two social-democratic regimes, as predicted. Germany has overtaken Sweden, though still has relatively fewer benefits than Denmark. The corporatist group average clearly lies above the social-democratic one in this year. The four countries in the liberal cluster are at the bottom of the ranking as expected. Taking all this information together, hypothesis 1A must be rejected; in 1999 the Netherlands has by no means the highest benefit volume among 15-64 year-olds and is well below the corporatist group average. It is less evident that hypothesis 1B has to be discarded; although the position of Germany relative to Denmark is not as expected, on average the volume in the corporatist group is higher than in the social-democratic cluster. Hypothesis 1C cannot be rejected, as there is a large difference in the anticipated direction between the countries representing the social-democratic and liberal regime types, and the latter form a distinct cluster in the ranking.

The secondary hypotheses on the within-cluster ranking are not supported in 1999. In the corporatist group the score of Belgium is too high, while in the social-democratic cluster Sweden turns out lower than Denmark, and in the liberal cluster the relative volume in Australia is on the high side. On the other hand, the USA is firmly in bottom place, as expected.

Yet the results provide a rather narrow basis for concluding that hypothesis 1 holds entirely. In 1980 the regime typology is hard to recognise in the rankings, with the high score in Denmark and the low to moderate benefit dependency in France, Germany and the Netherlands going against expectations. This is incidentally not accompanied by a comparatively high number of employment years in the latter group: viewed over the whole period, the participation rate in the corporatist countries and the Netherlands is significantly lower than in the representatives of the liberal and social-democratic regime types. The difference lies mainly in the large residual category of housewives, students, etc.[15]

For the moment, therefore, the relative volume hypothesis receives limited support from the empirical data. It is by no means the case that the Netherlands is consistently at the top of the ranking, that the benefit volume in all corporatist countries is structurally higher than in all the social-democratic regimes, or that the members of the latter group come out higher in all years than all the liberal countries. Often there is a wide dispersion within the country groups, implying a considerable overlap of the regime types (no clear clusters). Nevertheless, some outcomes are very much in line with the theoretical expectations. At all measurement points, the average relative volume in the social-democratic group is clearly higher than in the liberal cluster, both in the total population and in the population of working age. According to that criterion it is a robust conclusion that hypothesis 1C cannot be rejected. The contrast between the corporatist and social-democratic type seems to become sharper over time. In the population at large, hypothesis 1B only holds for 1999; but in the category below the age of 65 years, the average relative volume of the corporatist countries was already higher than that of the social-democratic group in 1990, and became increasingly so in 1999. In the total population, the relative volume of the Netherlands is below the corporatist group average at all points of measurement, which was not expected. Yet among the population of working age some support was found for hypothesis 1A in 1980 and 1990; while the Netherlands did not reach a top position in those years, its relative volume was somewhat higher than the average of the corporatist countries. This difference was reversed during the 1990s, though.

5.3.2 Growth rates

The hypotheses formulated earlier on growth rates were in similar vein. The expectation was that the percentage growth in the number of benefits would be greater in the Netherlands (hybrid regime) than in the countries with a corporatist social security regime (hypothesis 2A). The latter would score higher than the countries in the social-democratic cluster (hypothesis 2B), which were supposed to show stronger volume growth than the representatives of the liberal social security regime (hypothesis 2C).

Figures 5.4a-5.4c show the growth rates as compared in the various hypotheses. There is little surprise that the volumes in all countries go against the economic tide to some degree, with large increases in periods of stagnating economic growth, as in the first half of the 1980s and 90s. This anticyclical pattern is related to the fact that in times of recession unemployment rises, and this translates into a growing number of unemployment and social assistance benefits. Sometimes the economic trend has a similar impact on the take-up of other schemes with a hidden unemployment component (such as disability or early retirement benefit). The pattern is broken somewhat by the fact that the growth in the number of benefits paid to people in employment (sickness benefit, leave arrangements) generally runs in line with the cycle: if the economy stagnates, there are fewer working people and the take-up of such arrangements tends to decline.

There are some phase differences in the economic cycles in the countries studied here: periods of economic recovery and downturn often manifest themselves earlier in the usa and Great Britain than elsewhere, something which was particularly apparent in the volume growth figures in the early 1990s.

One pronounced outlier has been excluded from figure 5.4a: following reunification, the number of benefits in Germany rises very strongly in 1992 (+31%), as a result of the inclusion of the new *Bundesländer* in the statistical data.

Hypothesis 2A would be empirically supported in the strongest sense if the percentages in figure 5.4 at all measurement points were higher in the Netherlands than in the corporatist countries. This is anything but the case, however. Although the hybrid regime comes on top in the period 1981-1984, this is countered by seven observations in the 1990s where the growth rate in the Netherlands is lower than that in Belgium, France and Germany. If we look at a weaker criterion – the average growth rates over the period 1981-1999 – the expectation is still not borne out. France has far and away the highest average growth (2.2% per annum), while the Netherlands, with 1.5%, ranks only slightly above Germany and Belgium (the German outlier in 1992 is left out of consideration here) and lags behind the average of the corporatist countries. In the 1980s, however, the Dutch per annum volume growth is clearly higher than the corporatist group average; but in the 1990s the reverse happens. If the analysis is limited to the population aged 15-64 years, the data contradict the hypothesis even more: the average growth rate in the Netherlands is much lower than in France, Germany and Belgium (1.7% versus 2.1-3.6%), and a full percentage point below the per annum average of the corporatist group. Based on this bivariate analysis, hypothesis 2A must therefore be rejected, possibly with the exception of the 1980s.

Hypothesis 2B is not contradicted by the figures in every respect (see figure 5.4b). Denmark and Sweden do not record a lower score than Belgium, Germany and France in each year; in 1981, 1988 and 1992-1993 the mean growth is higher in the social-democratic group. However, if we consider the entire twenty-year period, the growth rates of the two Nordic countries are much lower (0.9-1.0% per annum) than in Belgium, Germany and France. Among the population aged 15-64 years, the differences between the social-democratic and corporatist regimes run in the expected direction as well, and are even more marked.

Comparison of the growth rate in the liberal and social-democratic regimes (figure 5.4c) shows that the US, Australia, Great Britain and Canada do not come lower in all years than Sweden and Denmark. In 10 years (1982-1984, 1986, 1990-1992 and 1996-1998) the group average of the liberal countries is distinctly higher as well. This can be partly explained by the high volatility of Canada and Australia: these countries attain comparatively high peaks and deep troughs in their growth figures.[16] Over the entire period, the average growth rates of Great Britain, Australia and Canada lie above the Swedish and Danish figures; and the mean of the liberal group is clearly higher than the social-democratic one as well. This applies both for the total volume and for the benefit dependency among the population of working age. It is only in the USA that the average 1981-1999 growth rates are lower than in Sweden and Denmark – most prominently among the population aged under 65 years, where the growth in the American liberal regime is nil taken over all years together. However, this provides insufficient support for the hypothesis, and on the basis of this analysis hypothesis 2C must also be rejected.

Figure 5.4a
Growth rates: corporatist and hybrid regimes, 1981-1999

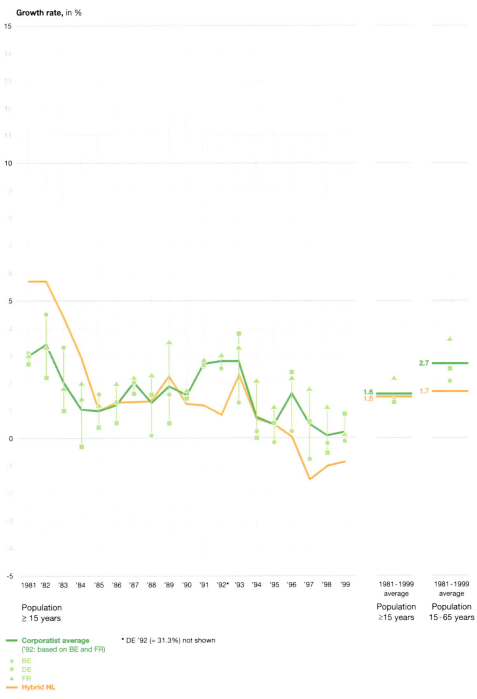

Sources: Arents et al. (2000); Moor et al. (2002); OECD (2003a: 171-235); adapted

BENEFIT DEPENDENCY

Figure 5.4b
Growth rates: social-democratic and corporatist regimes, 1981-1999

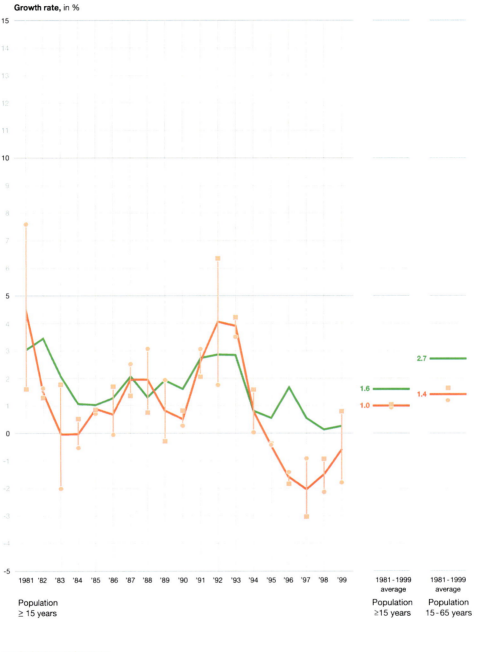

Figure 5.4c
Growth rates: liberal and social-democratic regimes, 1981-1999

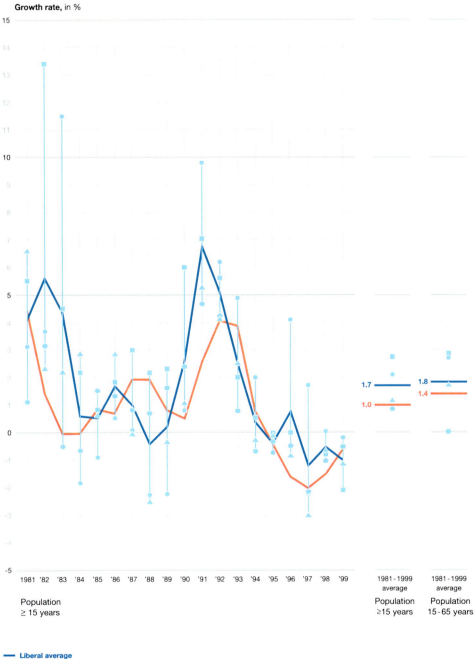

BENEFIT DEPENDENCY

This leads to the conclusion that hypotheses 2A, 2B and 2C to a large extent are not backed by the empirical data. Neither the annual growth rates of the individual countries nor the annual mean scores of the regime types show a consistent ranking as predicted. If the weaker criterion of the average growth rates over the entire twenty-year period is applied, hypotheses 2A and 2C must also be rejected. Hypothesis 2B is corroborated, however: in 1981-1999, the average per annum growth rate of the corporatist group is clearly higher than the social-democratic one (both in terms of the individual countries and the regime type means.) Even so, the empirical support for the benefit dependency growth rate hypothesis is rather limited.

These conclusions are underscored by the relatively arbitrary ranking that is obtained when viewing the average twenty-year growth figures across all countries together. For the population as a whole, benefit volume growth is strongest in the liberal Canada (2.8% per annum), followed at some distance by another liberal country, Australia, and the corporatist French regime type (2.1-2.2%). The Netherlands (hybrid) and Belgium (corporatist) occupy a middle position (1.4-1.5%), followed by Germany (also corporatist) with 1.3% and Great Britain (liberal: 1.2%). The two social-democratic countries and the liberal USA have the lowest average volume growth (0.9-1.0%). The strong growth in Australia and Canada, the rather high growth in France, the moderate growth in the Netherlands and the comparatively low growth in the two social-democratic countries, in particular, are not as postulated.

The ranking of the countries is also ambiguous when it comes to the average twenty-year growth in the benefit volume among the population of working age. The corporatist France heads the ranking (3.6% per annum), followed by a liberal/corporatist cluster comprising Canada, Australia and Germany (2.5-2.9%). Belgium follows at some distance (2.8%), while Great Britain, the Netherlands and Sweden constitute a group of mixed regime types with average growth of between 1.6% and 1.7%. Denmark scores notably lower (1.1%) and the USA has the lowest average growth (0.0%). It is above all the moderate growth in the Netherlands, the very high growth rate in France, the high growth figures in Canada and Australia and the relatively limited growth in the social-democratic countries (especially Denmark) which run counter to expectations.

One explanation for the limited support of the hypothesis may be that the growth rates are not determined just by the regime type, but also by other factors, such as demographic changes, country-specific economic developments, expansion and curbing of social security schemes, and so on. This is discussed later in this chapter. First, however, the next subsection explores whether the representatives of the regime types differ in terms of benefit dependency in specific social security arrangements.

5.3.3 Volume composition

Expectations were articulated earlier regarding the extent to which certain forms of benefit dependency would occur in the population aged under 65 years in the different regime types. Hypotheses 3A to 3F posit which social security regime theoretically generates the highest relative benefit volume in exit routes, unemployment insurance, survivor's benefits, benefits among the gainfully employed, non-employee disability insurance and social assistance, respectively. Hypothesis 3G postulates that the hybrid Dutch regime will score above the average on all social security schemes (the 'worst of three worlds' hypothesis).

A theoretical profile of the volume composition for the population aged below 65 years can be derived for each regime type from these hypotheses. This information can be presented succinctly in the form of a wind rose graphic, which is used in meteorology to portray the prevailing wind directions and speeds. Such graphs are also informative for detecting patterns in other multivariate data. Figure 5.5 plots the theoretical relative benefit dependency in each of the six schemes for the regime types in this way. For each social security arrangement the expected volume is plotted on a separate axis (a 'wind direction'). If a regime theoretically has the highest volume for a certain scheme, a maximum value of 10 has been assigned, while arrangements which are a-typical for that regime are given a score of 1. A value of 6.5 has been assigned in the graph for volumes that are predicted to be above the average. The higher the expected relative volume in a given arrangement, the stronger the 'wind' from that direction becomes (a longer and broader line towards the centre of the wind rose). In combination, the six dimensions represent the profiles of the expected composition of the benefit volume in typical corporatist, social-democratic and liberal regimes and in the hybrid Netherlands.

A corporatist regime will theoretically score highly on three of the six dimensions: exit routes, survivor's benefits and earnings-related unemployment insurance. This is visualised in figure 5.5 as lots of 'wind' from the easterly and southerly directions. The social-democratic regime type is predicted to score highly on employee dependency and disability insurance for non-employees, which is represented in the figure as northerly winds. A liberal regime is expected to score highly only on social assistance, depicted as a westerly wind. In the hybrid Netherlands the wind blows from all directions; for each arrangement the expected volume is lower than in the pure regime types, but is well above the average.

To test whether these patterns occur in practice, the volume figures for the population below the age of 65 years were broken down by type of scheme.[17] *Social assistance* as defined here relates to means-tested benefits that are not linked to past earnings, which are funded out of the general revenue.[18] *Unemployment insurance* relates to earnings-related income replacement schemes for the unemployed, without means testing and funded from contributions. *Exit routes* include both pre-pension benefits and social assistance benefits paid to older persons who no longer have a statutory duty to apply for work. The take-up of disability benefits by former employees has also been included here.[19] *Disability insurance for non-employees* refers to benefits paid to the former self-employed, early disabled people, housewives, veterans, etc. The classification used by the OECD (2003a) is followed for *survivor's benefits*. The *employees' dependency* consists of maternity, paternity and care leave benefits, in so far as they relate to current or former employees (i.e. excluding the self-employed and people without an employment history).

Figure 5.5
Theoretical composition of benefit volume (< age 65) in different social security regimes

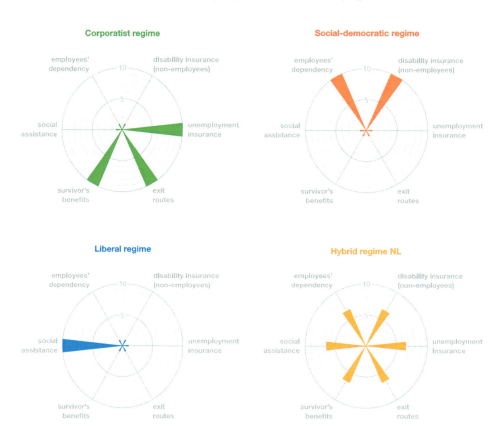

The relative volume in the years 1980, 1990 and 1999 is taken as a basis for each type of scheme. This produces 30 observations per arrangement: ten countries with three measurement points for each. Per type of scheme, these observations have been placed on a scale ranging from 1 to 10. The value 1 was assigned to the observation that produced the lowest relative volume over all countries and all three measurement years, while a score of 10 was assigned to the observation with the highest relative volume. The remaining observations have been ranked in between proportionally (based on the ratio of their relative volume vis-à-vis the minimum and maximum values).

Figure 5.6 shows the scores per arrangement for each country at the three measurement points, combined in a wind rose graphic. This makes it possible to compare the actual country profiles with the theoretical expectations in figure 5.5 at any given point in time. A number of trends appear to occur in virtually all countries between 1980 and 1999: the relative volume in exit routes and social assistance increases over time, while dependency on survivor's benefits generally falls.[20]

The corporatist profile in *Belgium* is very clear: the scores from the easterly and southerly directions are high, as expected. In 1990, Belgium even achieves the maximum scores on exit routes and unemployment insurance, and the relative volume in the survivor's benefits is also high, though does fall somewhat over time. A part of the high Belgian take-up of unemployment insurance can be attributed to a benefit arrangement for people who are involuntarily working part-time. The volume in employees' dependency, disability insurance for non-employees and social assistance benefit[21] is limited, as predicted.

Germany does not show a pronounced corporatist pattern in 1980. The score on survivor's benefits is very high, as expected, but the volume of unemployment benefits and exit routes is moderate. The low take-up of social assistance and disability benefits for non-employees is in line with expectations, but the employees' dependency (especially sickness benefit) is higher than would be expected for a corporatist regime. The score on the unemployment dimension rose slightly in 1990, but the score for exit routes hardly changed. This is surprising, since on the basis of Esping-Andersen's analysis it would be expected that there was a large influx of workers into exit routes in Germany in the 1980s, as a prime example of the corporatist strategy for dealing with unemployment. In practice, the volume in the German exit routes in the period 1980-1990 did grow, but only slightly more than the number of potential recipients. Two explanations can be offered for this. The first is that the growth in this type of benefit dependency was partly offset by the reduction in the number of disability recipients in the 1980s. The second explanation is that the effect of the temporary arrangement for early retirement (1984-1988) – which very much shaped the image of the German early retirement policy – is reflected to only a limited extent in the figures for 1990.[22] By contrast, at the final measurement point the distortion in the southern and easterly direction is clearly visible in Germany. The volume of unemployment insurance and exit routes in the 1990s increased relatively strongly, while the volume of survivor's benefits remained high, though did fall somewhat. This corporatist pattern is however found only in 1999, and it is questionable whether this would have been so manifest without the effects of German reunification.

France exhibits no clear profile in 1980: the volume is limited in all six arrangements, suggesting a welfare state in a nascent stage rather than a fully developed corporatist social security regime. In the later measurement years, it is the score on early exits and social assistance which increases particularly strongly. The first rise is in line with expectations, but the second is not. Following the introduction of the *Revenu minimum d'insertion* in 1988, France saw strong growth in the take-up of social assistance, which of course does not fit the theory for a corporatist regime. In 1999 only three countries in the liberal cluster (Australia, Canada and Great Britain) achieved a higher relative volume. The number of recipients of survivor's benefits in France, by contrast, is much lower than expected in the corporatist type. Although there is an extensive system of survivor's insurance,[23] the number of recipients aged under 65 years is rather low because of the fairly stringent entry conditions (related to employment history, care for young children, insufficient means of subsistence) and the sometimes limited duration (the *Allocation de veuvage* ends after three years). In addition, the take-up of unemployment insurance in France is not especially high, though does increase over time, while the employee dependency volume is certainly not low in 1999 (partly because of the strong growth in the take-up of the *Allocation parentale d'éducation* after 1995). The consistently low score for disability insurance for non-employees is in line with expectations.

The composition of the benefit volume in France thus cannot be described as distinctly corporatist. In 1980 the volume is low in all respects. In the two later measurement years, France achieves higher scores on exit routes and employment insurance, so that some of the expected pattern becomes visible. In most other domains, however, the picture does not correspond with the theoretical predictions. The number of social assistance benefit recipients and the employee dependency are higher than postulated in 1990 and 1999, while the volume in survivor's benefits is lower than expected. The corporatist profile is approximated most closely at the last measurement year.

Sweden shows the expected Nordic bias in all three years in figure 5.6, though there is some variation between the points of measurement. The score on employees' dependency is already fairly high in 1980 and rises over time, reaching the maximum of 10 in 1999. The reverse trend occurs with disability benefits for non-employees: the volume at the start of the series is high (partly because of a benefit housewives were entitled to) but is much less pronounced in 1999.

The profile in the first measurement year is also less clear, because Sweden at that time had an unexpectedly high volume of survivor's benefits. However, this volume fell sharply over time, especially in the 1990s, when the arrangement was gradually phased out. The substantial increase in the number of unemployment insurance benefits during the 1990s means that Sweden also scores fairly highly in 1999 for this theoretically non-characteristic dimension. In all years, the low volume of social assistance benefits and exit route arrangements is in line with expectations, though the latter rises over time. All in all, Sweden fits the postulated social-democratic pattern reasonably well, especially in terms of the high employees' dependency.

The composition of the volume in *Denmark* is also in line with expectations. Although the relative number of benefits due to employees' dependency is lower than in Sweden in all years, it is higher than that in all other countries. The benefit volume in disability insurance for non-employees is also considerable and more consistently so than in Sweden. Between 1980 and 1999 the relative take-up of these schemes rises, overtaking the Swedish rate, and in the final measurement year this type of benefit dependency is highest in Denmark of all countries studied.

Yet the relative number of unemployment benefits in Denmark is higher than would be expected for a social-democratic regime, especially in 1990. The score on exit routes increases over time and is above the average in 1999, though Denmark is still below the three corporatist welfare states. The take-up of social assistance benefit is not high, though there are comparatively more benefits than in Belgium, Germany and Sweden. This makes Denmark a somewhat less pure representative of the social-democratic regime type than Sweden as regards the composition of the benefit volume. The characteristic bias is however still visible.

Among the liberal social security regimes, the postulated pattern emerges clearly in *Australia*, with a predominantly westerly wind in 1999 in particular. The social assistance benefit volume reaches the maximum score in that year, while the take-up of other schemes is low. The employees' dependency remains limited to a fairly modest level of sickness absenteeism,[24] and the number of surviving dependants and former employees in early exit schemes is rather small (though the latter group grows in the 1990s). Australia has no social insurance for unemployment, and therefore achieves the lowest possible score on this dimension in all years. This helps to explain the high social assistance distortion: Australian unemployment benefits are to be regarded as a form of social assistance.[25]

In the earlier years the liberal pattern in Australia is less clear. The relative social assistance volume is lower in 1980 and 1990, though even then Australia comes in third place. By contrast, the take-up of survivor's benefits is higher, as is the take-up of disability insurance for non-employees (especially service pensions for military veterans). Despite this, the composition of the benefit volume in Australia corresponds fairly well with the hypothetical pattern in all years.

Canada has relatively fewer social assistance benefits than Australia, but the volume is still high: in all years Canada comes in second place in the rankings. The volume in exit routes, employees' dependency and disability insurance for non-employees is limited, as expected; in fact the exit of employees via collective retirement schemes in 1980 is the lowest of all observations (score 1). The liberal pattern is less clearly evident than in Australia, not only due to the lower score on social assistance, but also because Canada achieves a fairly high ranking on two typically corporatist arrangements: the volume of survivor's benefits is among the highest of all countries – and actually increases over time – while unemployment insurance also has a fairly high take-up, especially in 1990.

The composition of the benefit volume has become more and more liberal over time in *Great Britain*. Initially the score on virtually all dimensions, including social assistance benefit, is fairly low; only the volume in survivor's benefits is on the high side in 1980, but this reduces in the two later measurement years, as does the volume of unemployment insurance benefits. The number of people on social assistance benefits, by contrast, rises sharply in 1990 and 1999. These shifts are in line with the observation by Eardley et al. (1996: 388), that the system reforms in Great Britain in the 1980s implied a break with Beveridgean principles, with "social assistance becoming a mass scheme instead of a residual safety net". As a result, the liberal profile is clearly visible in the final measurement year, though the take-up of social assistance benefits in 1999 is still relatively lower than in Australia and Canada. In addition, the British volume in exit routes, disability insurance for non-employees and survivor's benefits is greater than would be theoretically expected.

Figure 5.6
Empirical composition of benefit volume in 10 countries; 1980, 1990 and 1999 (< age 65, ranking scores)

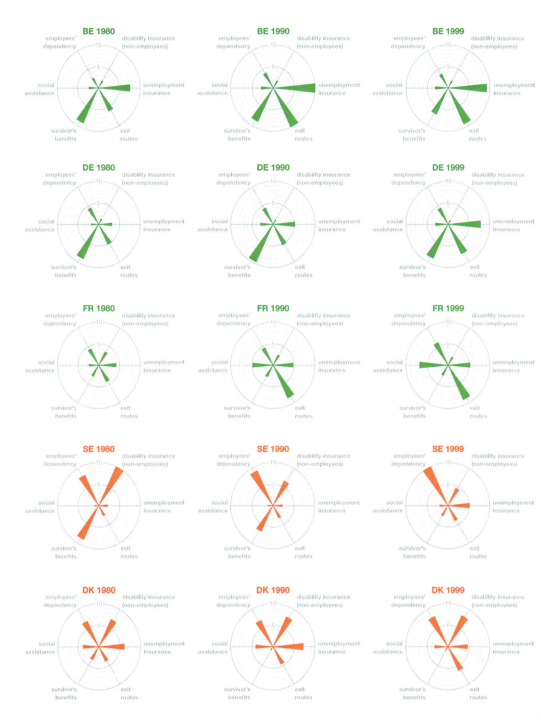

Sources: Arents et al. (2000); Moor et al. (2002); OECD (2003a: 171-235); adapted

The assumed liberal distortion is the least clear in the *United States*. In 1980 the number of social assistance benefits is not extremely high in the US, being relatively lower than in Australia and Canada. Contrary to the theoretical expectation, in that year there is a fairly high take-up of survivor's benefits and disability insurance for non-employees (mainly war veterans). In 1990 the latter distortions have disappeared, while the number of social assistance beneficiaries has risen in relative terms. The postulated liberal profile is approached most closely in that year, with the caveat that the social assistance volume is still not very high: at the second measurement point the three other liberal regimes achieve higher scores.

The last measurement year shows a reduction in the relative social assistance volume to a level far below that in the other three liberal countries and France. In the 1990s there is also a slight fall in most of the other arrangements, where the relative volume was already modest; only the take-up of early exit arrangements remains virtually constant in relative terms. As a result, the USA scores fairly low in 1999 on *all* dimensions and shows no characteristic bias at all. The conclusion that can be drawn from this is that the composition of the benefit volume in the USA does not correspond with the expected picture, and that the composition hypothesis for the final year therefore has to be rejected. Substantively, this could be interpreted to imply that during the course of these two decades the USA intervened so radically in its benefit schemes that in 1999 it was no longer a true liberal social security regime, but more of a welfare state in decline. The fact that the profile of the USA at the last measurement point in figure 5.6 corresponds so closely with that of the French system in its build-up phase (1980) supports this interpretation.

Given the rather pure liberal character of the American social security regime which emerged from the theoretical analyses, however, it may not be entirely correct to reject the composition hypothesis. Another possible interpretation is that the residuality principle which is central in the liberal regime (see chapter 4) is strictly applied in the United States in the social assistance arrangements as well – a view that is supported by the fairly low score for social assistance on the theoretical benefit dependency boost index around 1990. The radical changes made to the American social assistance arrangements in the 1990s[26] can be regarded as the ultimate consequence of this principle. Seen from this perspective, the absence of any social assistance bias in the last measurement year does not disqualify the USA as a liberal regime, but rather means that the regime is *plus libéral que les libéraux*: the take-up of all arrangements is reduced as far as possible, including the last resort that is social assistance. The limited duration of the *Temporary Aid to Needy Families* (TANF) is a clear example of this.

The hybrid regime in *the Netherlands* would be expected to score highly for all arrangements, but without reaching the level that characterises the purer types. In 1980 this is found to be only partially the case: the Dutch volume of social assistance, unemployment insurance and non-employee disability insurance benefits was relatively limited in that year. On the other hand, the volume in employees' dependency was substantial (as expected, mainly sick leave and little parental and other leave), as was the take-up volume for exit routes (especially disability benefits for former employees). The number of people in receipt of survivor's benefits is so great that it would fit in with a pure corporatist regime.

In 1990 the 'worst of three worlds' pattern is clearest. The number of survivor's benefits remains high and there is a substantial increase in early exits (more disability benefit recipients, but also a growing take-up of early retirement schemes and unemployment arrangements for the elderly), to slightly below the volume of Belgium and France. The relative volume in the four arrangements where the Netherlands achieved a low score ten years earlier, has risen in 1990 to a score of between 5 and 6. This approaches the postulated value, though the volume in unemployment insurance is lower.[27]

In the final measurement year, however, the expected pattern is again less clear. In the 1990s the relative volume of exit arrangements, social assistance, unemployment insurance and employees' dependency fell in the Netherlands. To some extent this has to do with system changes, but the economic climate and rising labour participation of women also had an influence.[28] Changes in the legislation on survivor's benefits, culminating in the introduction of the *Algemene Nabestaandenwet*, reduced take-up, but because this also happened in most other countries the Netherlands still scores highly in 1999 in relative terms; only Germany and Canada rank higher in that year. It is only for disability insurance for non-employees that the Dutch relative volume rises in the period 1990-1999.

If countries are compared with each other, the assumed corporatist pattern emerges most clearly in Belgium. In Germany it is only observable in 1999; in the other measurement years the relative volume in the exit routes and unemployment insurance is lower than postulated. France had a limited take-up of all benefit schemes in 1980, and was at that time more a welfare state in formation than an example of the corporatist type. At the later measurement points the volume of exit routes rises strongly, and the number of recipients of unemployment insurance benefits also increases; but for a corporatist regime, the score on survivor's benefits is too low, that for social assistance and employees' dependency too high (especially in 1999). The corporatist pattern is approached most closely in France in 1990.

Due to the high employees' dependency, Sweden is the prime example of the social-democratic regime type. The score on the other characteristic Nordic scheme, disability insurance for non-employees, however, decreases over time; and in the 1990s the take-up of unemployment insurance benefit and early exit schemes is somewhat higher than expected. Denmark also fits the theoretical type fairly well. It has a less marked profile than Sweden in terms of employees' dependency, but a more consistently high score on disability benefits for non-employees. In the 1990s, the volume of unemployment benefits and exit route schemes became larger than was expected.

In the liberal cluster, the postulated profile is most evident in Australia, especially in 1999. The pattern is also rather clear in Canada, though this country also has a number of corporatist traits: large numbers of survivor's benefits and (in 1980 and 1990) unemployment insurance benefits. Great Britain does not have a liberal pattern in 1980, but develops this increasingly during the period studied due to the strong rise in the number of social assistance benefit recipients. Even so, in 1999 there is still a fairly high take-up of exit route schemes, survivor's benefits and disability insurance for non-employees. The postulated pattern is least evident in the United States. There is a substantial social assistance volume in 1980, but also a rather high take-up of the (corporatist) survivor's insurance benefit and the (social-democratic) disability insurance benefit for non-employees (due to war veterans). In the later years the social assistance bias has disappeared, and the volume in all other arrangements is also relatively low. As stated earlier, however, this need not necessarily be in conflict with a liberal social security regime.

The following conclusions can be drawn regarding the hypotheses formulated above:
- *Hypothesis 3A* cannot be rejected. At all three measurement points, the relative number of recipients of early exit benefits is highest in the countries with a corporatist social security regime (in 1980 the differences are rather limited, though). Belgium comes in first place in all years, and the average score of the corporatist group is 2 to 4 points above that of the liberal and social-democratic clusters. However, in the earlier years the hybrid Netherlands also achieves a 'corporatist' score (2nd place in 1980, 3rd in 1990).
- *Hypothesis 3B* cannot be rejected either, though the pattern here is somewhat less convincing. In all years the number of recipients of unemployment insurance benefits is highest in the corporatist Belgium, and the group average is highest in the corporatist cluster. In 1999 the two other representatives of this regime type occupy second and third place, as expected. In the earlier measurement years, however, this is not the case; in 1980 Germany scores fairly low (8th place), while France achieves a low score in 1990 (6th). In those years the social-democratic Denmark (2nd place) and the liberal Canada (3rd) take the other two places in the top three;
- *Hypothesis 3C* receives limited support. The number of recipients of survivor's benefits in Belgium and Germany is relatively high in all three years, as expected; but in 1980 and 1990 the top position is taken by the hybrid Dutch regime, and in 1999 by Canada (where the relative volume hardly falls at all over time, in contrast to most other countries). The difference between Belgium and Germany compared with some other non-corporatist countries (in particular Great Britain and Sweden in 1980) is moreover not particularly large.
In the corporatist France the relative survivor's benefit volume is low, entirely at odds with the expectation: 10th place in 1980, 9th in 1990, 7th in 1999. In the 1990s, however, the average of the corporatist cluster is higher than that of the liberal countries, and it exceeds the mean of the social-democratic group by a considerable margin.
- *Hypothesis 3D* cannot be rejected. In all three measurement years the number of recipients of employee benefits (sickness benefit, leave arrangements) is highest in Sweden and Denmark, and over time the differences with the other regime types increase. In 1980 the average of the social-democratic group on the scale was 3 to 5 points higher than that of the corporatist and liberal clusters; by 1999 the difference had risen to 4 to 7 points.
- *Hypothesis 3E* is supported by the data as well. The number of recipients of disability insurance benefits for people who were not gainfully employed is comparatively

highest in Denmark and Sweden in 1980 and 1990. The social-democratic Danish regime again comes top in 1999, but Sweden has been overtaken by the Netherlands and Great Britain. Over time the average score declines in all regime types (with the exception of the Netherlands), with the steepest drop occurring in the social-democratic group. Although the differences have become smaller, therefore, in 1999 the social-democratic mean is still 3 to 5 points higher than that of the liberal and corporatist countries.

- *Hypothesis 3F* also finds support. In all measurement years the first three places on the relative volume of social assistance benefits are occupied by representatives of the liberal regime type. In Australia, Great Britain and Canada the social assistance bias increases over time. The United States distorts the pattern somewhat: the relative volume falls steadily here, causing the USA to drop from third place in 1980 to a middle position (5th) in 1990 and 1999. In terms of group averages, the difference between the liberal and corporatist clusters remains fairly constant over the years (3 points), while the gap between liberal and social-democratic countries becomes wider (3 points in 1980, 5 points in 1999).

- *Hypothesis 3G* cannot be rejected for 1990. In that year the hybrid Dutch social security regime has an above-average number of recipients of all the above arrangements, though the threshold value of the theoretical profile is not always achieved. However, the position in the ranking is largely as expected. In 1990 the Netherlands has fewer social assistance benefits than the liberal countries, but much more than the social-democratic and corporatist regimes. The employee dependency and disability insurance for non-employees are lower than in Sweden and Denmark in that year, but higher than in all other countries. In the exit routes, only Belgium and France come higher. The hybrid regime also scores below the corporatist group average on unemployment insurance benefits, but that is mainly a result of the very high level of Belgium; in the Netherlands, the take-up of this scheme is comparable with France and Germany. Finally, the Netherlands comes on top for survivor's benefits, and thus overtakes the corporatist countries. To a large extent, the 'worst of three worlds' hypothesis is corroborated in 1990. The picture in 1980 and 1999 is less convincing, largely due to the fairly low volume of social assistance and unemployment insurance benefits. As a result of the absence of a social assistance bias, the situation in the Netherlands in these years can at most be described as 'the worst of two worlds'. A fairly high volume in employees' dependency and disability insurance benefits for non-employees (characteristic for the social-democratic regime) is combined with a rather large number of exits and survivor's benefits, as would be expected in a corporatist system. The composition of the benefit volume is therefore still hybrid in these years, but in a different way from that postulated.

5.3.4 Summary of the bivariate analyses

Reviewing the results in this section, hypothesis 1, concerning the relative volume in the three regime types and the Netherlands, is confirmed to some degree. While there is no consistent ranking of countries in distinct clusters in the three years considered here (1980, 1990, and 1999), the expected pattern emerges to some extent from the group averages. Both in the total population and among the population of working age, the average relative volume generated by the social-democratic group is clearly higher than that of the liberal regime; in that sense hypothesis 1C cannot be rejected. In addition, as time goes by the distinction between the corporatist and social-democratic types shows more prominently in the average scores. In the population at large, it is only in 1999 that the relative volume was higher in the corporatist group than in the social-democratic cluster, as presumed in hypothesis 1B. Among the population of working age this already occurred in 1990, and more convincingly so in 1999. The expected difference between the hybrid Dutch type and the corporatist group average only showed in 1980 and 1990, in the category below the age of 65 years.

The empirical results on growth rates are not entirely as expected. In the early 1980s, the percentage change in the number of benefits is higher in the Netherlands than in the corporatist regime, but it lags far behind in the 1990s. The growth in France, Belgium and Germany is not higher than in the social-democratic countries in every year, and they in turn are not structurally higher in the rankings than the liberal regimes. When the average growth rates over the period 1981-1990 are considered, the support for the benefit dependency growth rate hypothesis is rather limited as well. Both in the total population and in the population of working age, only the assumption that the growth in the corporatist countries would be greater than in the social-democratic regimes (2B) cannot be rejected. The high average growth rate in France, Australia and Canada, the moderate rate in the Netherlands and the relatively limited growth in Sweden and Denmark are all contrary to the expectations.

On the other hand, the assumptions on the composition of the benefit recipient population below retirement age are largely supported by the empirical data; none of the hypotheses can be completely rejected. In the population of working age, corporatist countries have a large number of early exits, recipients of unemployment benefits and – with the exception of France – survivor's pensions. Representatives of the social-democratic regime type have comparatively large numbers of employees' dependency and disability insurance benefits for non-employees, while the liberal cluster (with the exception of the US) has a large social assistance volume.

The volume composition in Belgium meets the postulated corporatist profile best. In the liberal group this applies for Australia. In the terms of Arts and Gelissen (2002), these 'real' types most closely approach the theoretically expected volume composition of their regime. Denmark and Sweden both score highly on the expected dimensions, but also have a number of atypical deviations (large numbers of survivor's benefits in the earlier measurement years in Sweden, considerable unemployment insurance and early exit volumes in Denmark).

The Netherlands scores fairly highly on all arrangements in 1990, and thus combines 'the worst of three worlds', as predicted. Yet the composition pattern in 1980 and 1999 tends towards a more partial hybrid, with a high benefit volume in schemes that theoretically are characteristic of the social-democratic and corporatist regime types.

One possible explanation for the limited support for the relative volume and growth hypotheses is that the development of benefit dependency has been analysed in this section only in relation to the type of social security regime. As pointed out in chapter 3, however, the benefit volume theoretically also depends on other factors. If these were taken into account the differences between the regime types might emerge more clearly. This requires a model-based approach, which is the topic of the remaining sections of this chapter.

5.4 A causal model for benefit dependency growth

It can be deduced from chapters 2 and 3 that there are many factors which theoretically affect the benefit volume. The formal social security institutions of modern welfare states lay down rights, duties, conditions and potential sanctions (see figure 2.1 and §3.5). These determine the conditions under which people may receive benefits for unemployment, old age, disability, etc. The number of benefit recipients thus depends in the first place on the statutory or government-enforced social security rules: the retirement age, the entry and duration conditions for unemployment benefits, the existence of arrangements for early or flexible retirement, the definition of incapacity for work, etc. Regime types are sparse models of the wide variety of possible formal institutions.

The impact of formal institutions on benefit volumes is not fixed in stone. Rules govern behaviour at a certain point in a historical process, something that was described earlier as the 'context of rule application'. This means that the number of benefits, with unchanged formal rules, can vary according to the economic, demographic, social, technological and ideological developments. The interplay of institutions and historical circumstances in the evolution of the number of benefit recipients can be illustrated using a simple example. Suppose two countries have the same number of inhabitants, but that in country A the effective retirement age is 65 years and in country B 63 years. If all historical circumstances are identical, this will mean that the number of retirement pensions is higher in country B. But if, for example, the demographic profile of the two countries differs, this need not be the case. This can happen if country A has experienced a baby boom at some point in the past and this generation is now reaching retirement age, while country B did not go through a comparable demographic peak. Similarly, if certain pension cohorts are small in country B, the total number of retirement pensions in country A can turn out higher as well, even though the prevailing social security rules imply that country B has two extra year-cohorts that are eligible for pensions. Such a historical situation may occur, for example, as the result of the victims of a war which country B went through around 40 years ago, or due to a low birth rate around 65 years earlier, when a high proportion of the country's young men were fighting on the Front. Long-term historical processes like these may influence the benefit take-up just as much as the internal rules of the social security system. Theoretically this applies for the entire context of rule application: if the population ages, the economy falls into recession, the divorce rate increases, people wish to retire earlier, the social definition of disability broadens, etc., this can have a substantial effect on the number of benefit recipients.

However, this is not an automatic process: the motivations of individual and collective actors, and their mutual relationships, theoretically 'filter' the prevailing set of formal institutions and the historical context of rule application. In addition, the benefit volume is also determined by the actual course of the rule-driven social security interactions. The application behaviour of potential recipients; fraud and non-take-up; the actions of social security organisations; the approach to the principal-agent problem within these corporate actors; the hiring and firing behaviour of employers; the actions of supervisory board and the social security court: in principle these all have their own influence on the number of benefits for a given set of rules and historical circumstances. The models of rule-driven social security interactions discussed at length earlier (see §3.5) indicate that there may be wide variety in this intermediary process.

In formal systems, informal rules can partly determine the course of such interactions, and thereby also influence the benefit volume. Examples include the impact of public opinion on how 'deserving' different categories of social security recipients are. In addition, defective cultures can occur among benefit recipients, which may imply that residents of certain neighbourhoods have a low work ethic or consider social security fraud acceptable. The officials of the social security organisation can also base their behaviour on diverging informal rules, because they themselves gain from such a course of action (e.g. because their own caseload is reduced), because they regard this as efficient for the organisation, or because this is in line with their professional ethic (e.g. medical assessors who for health reasons award or continue a disability benefit *contra legem*). Chapter 3 also looked at these aspects in more detail.

Finally, the number of benefit recipients may also change because the formal institutions themselves are transformed, via a sometimes complex process of rule generation (cf. §2.9 and §3.7). Such institutional change can take many forms: a new scheme is introduced or an old one abolished, the statutory definition of 'unemployment' or 'incapacity for work' is tightened up or relaxed, the group of entitled beneficiaries is restricted or enlarged by setting different conditions in terms of employment history, supplementary income, household status, job search behaviour, etc. Where these and similar system changes are radical, do not lead to a substitution of recipients from one benefit scheme to another, and are introduced suddenly (without a lengthy transitional period for current beneficiaries), they can lead to major increases or reductions in the benefit volume.

As the benefit volume is theoretically not determined solely by the formal configuration of the social security system, it is plausible that the weak contrasts found in the previous section between the different regime types are connected to the divergent impact of non-institutional factors and system changes. In order to test this, an aggregate model is developed in this section. The model explores the influence of a number of characteristics on the benefit volume at the country level. For two reasons, however, the results of the model have to be interpreted with caution. In the first place, as is often the case in international comparative studies, the number of theoretical determinants is large, whereas there are only a few observations. This 'small-N problem' makes it necessary to restrict the number of explanatory variables in the model, and implies that the impact of causal factors cannot be estimated simultaneously. As Goldthorpe (2000: 49) remarks, this means that it is difficult to make a decisive evaluation of the various determinants of the benefit volume on the basis of the model developed here.[29] Because the volume data used here are available only at the macro-level of countries, the small-N problem cannot be circumvented by performing a multi-level analysis on micro-data (with individual recipients as the basic unit and various country traits as second-level determinants; cf. Snijders & Bosker, 1999). The restriction in terms of the number of variables which can be included in the model implies that estimates are somewhat uncertain; given the small set of countries, it is not possible to include all theoretically important factors in the model simultaneously for each nation.

But even if more country observations were available, the model would still be partial, because for some theoretical determinants there are simply no internationally comparable, reliable quantitative time series on hand covering the period studied here. This is notably the case for the informal social security rules analysed in §4.3. Data on the preferred distribution of rights and duties (government responsibility for the standard of living, the provision of jobs etc.; income differentials; post-materialism; the labour participation of women; the position of civil servants, and the like; cf. figure 4.3) are not available on an annual basis for all countries considered here. This makes it difficult to relate the development of the national benefit volumes to country-specific changes in such informal rules. The data problems are even greater when it comes to differences in the administrative processes of the social security organisation in the various countries. Here, only fairly rough national budget figures and performance indicators are available, for which it is often unclear how they impact on the number of benefits. For example, if the per capita administrative costs of the social security organisation are on the rise in a given country, this could indicate that more efforts are being made to help benefit recipients find work, possibly leading to a reduction in the national benefit volume. However, rising per capita outlays may also be the result of more inefficient case management, growing expenditure on office rent or ICT facilities, or may reflect the growing weight of fixed costs if the number of unemployed or disabled benefit recipients falls (implying a reverse causal relationship).

Figure 5.7 describes a rather simple theoretical model that was developed for the causal analysis. The dependent variable is the benefit dependency growth rate among the population aged 15 years and older in the last two decades of the 20th century, as discussed earlier in §5.3.2 (cf. figures 5.4a-5.4c). The basic analytical unit consists of the countries (representing various regime types) analysed in the previous section, in as far as adequate data were available. For each country included in the analysis, the data consist of time series of the annual percentage mutations in the dependent and explanatory variables in the period 1981-1999; this amounts to a maximum of 19 observations per variable in each country (evidently there is no mutation for 1980, the starting year of the benefit dependency data).

It was decided to use annual percentage mutations[30] because this offers a number of practical advantages. The scale differences between the absolute changes in the various countries disappear, while time series for the determinant variables in the model are also largely available as annual changes in percentages or percentage points. This has the technical advantage that the model is less sensitive to autocorrelation.[31] Substantively, the variable definition chosen implies that unstandardised regression coefficients can be interpreted as elasticities: the estimated values indicate the percentage change in the benefit volume if the independent variable increases by one percentage point.[32]

There are three types of determinant in the model: demographic developments (D), changes in the economy and on the labour market (E), and institutional changes (I). Other things being equal, the total benefit volume may be expected to increase if:
- the elderly population grows (D);
- the population of working age grows (D);
- the population of working age becomes older (D);
- the number of lone parents increases (D);
- the number of unemployed within the labour force rises (E);
- the labour participation rate of elderly men falls (E);
- the labour participation rate of non-elderly women rises (E);
- the coverage of pension schemes increases (I);
- major expansions of the social security system occur; if benefit schemes are curtailed the total benefit volume may be expected to decline (I).

These nine variables are assumed to have a direct impact on the benefit volume, which in some cases is reinforced or mitigated by indirect effects via the number of unemployed. In addition, four variables influence the number of benefits only through their effects on other determinants. *Ceteris paribus* the benefit volume is expected to rise indirectly if:
- the gross domestic product falls in real terms (E);
- real labour costs increase (E);
- the share of the services sector in total employment grows (E);
- the level of unemployment benefits rises (I).

Obviously, the model covers the process which theoretically may bring about benefit dependency only partially. Due to its aggregate nature, it is confined to the relationship between the historical process at country level and the collective outcomes. What happens in between – the translation of the context of rule application into actors' perceptions and motivations, the individual outcomes of social security interactions in the various nations, the impact of informal rules – remains hidden in a black box. This implies that it cannot be ascertained to what extent similar historical circumstances and institutions produce diverging results (or varying contexts lead to comparable outcomes) due to different processing at the micro-level. Furthermore, the historical process has been reduced to a limited number of demographic, economic, and labour market developments. And although it includes some institutional factors, the actual interaction

Figure 5.7
Causal model for benefit dependency growth: theoretical relations

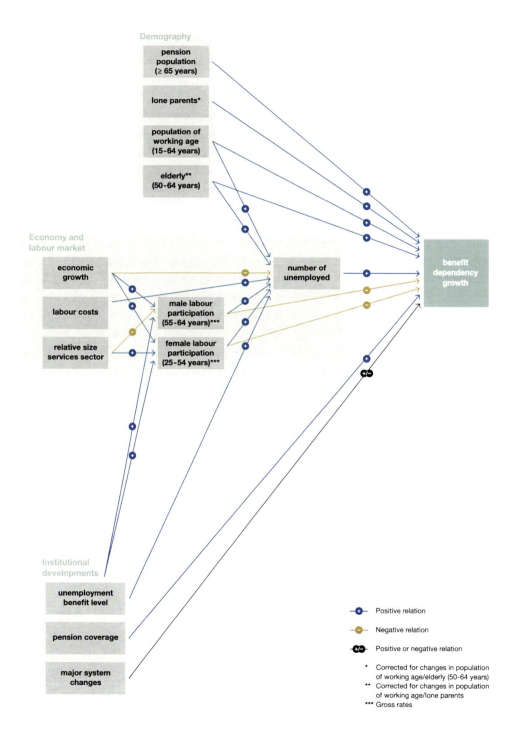

of the causal variables with social security regimes is not observed empirically in the model (cf. below).

Finally, the model does not allow for any feedback mechanisms. These occur if, for instance, an increase in benefit dependency results in less economic growth, higher labour costs, fewer work incentives, a reduction in the unemployment benefit level, or the implementation of major system changes. Theoretically some of these processes may apply, but, given the small number of observations available in each country, their impact could not be tested here. Following the analysis in §3.6.3, it could be added that some of these inverse effects are likely to be less influential than the causal mechanisms postulated in the model. Thus, the impact of economic growth on the level of unemployment and on the benefit volume is theoretically rather straightforward and substantial; whereas the number of benefits, and the ensuing social security expenditure, is only one of the factors determining GDP growth (in addition to a country's natural resources, human capital, infrastructure, technology, etc). Similarly, major system changes may be implemented as a result of the evolvement of benefit dependency, but other factors can also be quite important in bringing them about. This is demonstrated by the two biggest system overhauls in the current dataset. The revision of US social assistance in the 1990s occurred while the relative benefit volume was low by international standards (it even fell in the previous decade; cf. figures 5.3 and 5.6), and was partly inspired by ideological motives; and obviously the *Revenu minimum d'insertion* has not been introduced because benefit dependency in France was comparatively limited or decreasing during the 1980s, but as a result of the political commitment to fight poverty and social exclusion.

Simple as it may be, the model allows us to grasp some of the main forces driving benefit dependency; and by cancelling out the impact of other factors, it may be possible to obtain a more accurate picture of the impact of regimes than through the bivariate analyses of the previous section. Before discussing the empirical results, some of the causal relationships require further qualification, and a few comments need to be made on the data that have been used for the independent variables.

Pension population

The model assumes that if the number of people aged 65 or over increases, more benefits will be taken up. Because recipients of old age pensions are a subset of the total group of benefit recipients, this direct effect will be inelastic. Given the size of this age category and the generally high benefit take-up, it is likely that the benefit volume will be fairly sensitive to changes in this variable. Data for this factor are taken from the Ecorys/NEI database as adapted by the OECD (2003a), and consistent with the series on the benefit volume.

Population of working age

The direct effect of changes in the size of the population of working age refers to changes in the number of benefits awarded to the persons outside the labour force: if there are more people in the 15-64 years age bracket, there will be more recipients of early exit benefits, disability benefits, survivor's benefits and social assistance.

The indirect effect postulates that an increase in the number of 15-64 year-olds will lead to more unemployed persons (given constant participation and unemployment rates): any accrual to the labour force partly becomes unemployed or displaces existing workers. In the short run this growth in the number of unemployed will cause a higher take-up of unemployment benefit and social assistance.

The total effect of changes in the size of the potential labour force can be presumed to be inelastic, because these changes also affect only a part of the total benefit volume (not pensions, for example). The data source is the same as for the pension population.

Ageing of the potential labour force

The ageing of the potential labour force is important because elderly persons are more likely to retire early, to lose their spouse, and to become sick, unemployed or disabled; ageing therefore leads to higher benefit dependency. The variable has been defined as percentage changes in the number of 50-64 year-olds, corrected for the growth in the total potential labour force and the number of lone-parent families (two factors that are already in the model). The impact of ageing on the benefit volume is also broken down into a direct and an indirect effect, with the former reflecting the greater risk of early exits, incapacity for work and death of the partner, and the indirect effect representing their higher likelihood to lose their job. The effect on the benefit volume can be postulated as being inelastic, because the benefits to this group also make up only part of the total. The time series on this factor was constructed from several international databases (mainly Eurostat and ILO) and has been made consistent with the size of the potential labour force according to the OECD series.

Lone-parent families

The development in the number of lone-parent families is important because this group are relatively frequently dependent on social assistance and survivor's benefits; more single parents therefore implies more benefits. No indirect effect is specified in the model via the number of unemployed, because the growth in the number of lone-parent families theoretically impacts mainly on benefits for the population outside the labour force. Here again, the annual mutations have been adjusted for the portion that can be attributed to other model variables (the size and ageing of the potential labour force), and it may be assumed that the effect on the volume is inelastic.

No comparative time series are available for the number of lone-parent families covering the period 1980-1999. Use was therefore made of data from national statistical agencies, where necessary supplemented by estimates. Lone-parent families are in principle defined as households with one adult head and at least one child aged under 18 years living at home.[33]

Number of unemployed

The effect of this variable is considered positive: an increase in the number of unemployed will lead to higher benefit dependency. Although this may seem an evident assumption, the theoretical relation with the benefit volume is rather complex. More unemployed people of course translates into more unemployment benefits, but there is also an effect in the opposite direction. If the number of unemployed people grows, the number of people gainfully employed[34] reduces (assuming a constant labour force size and participation rates). This leads to a fall in employees' dependency: if there are fewer people working, the take-up of sickness benefits and leave arrangements will decrease. This is theoretically due not only to the fact that the working population has become smaller, but is also related to behavioural and selection effects: in a weak economy, employees will be less inclined to make use of such arrangements (they take less leave and fewer days off sick, out of fear of losing their job) and employers will dismiss people with a high absenteeism risk first.

The effect of the number of unemployed on the benefit volume reflects the net result of these opposing developments. The relationship is supposedly inelastic: a one percent change in the number of unemployed persons will lead to a proportionally smaller change in benefit dependency. This is mostly because unemployment benefit recipients form a subset of the total volume. In addition, the trade-off noted above, and the fact that not every unemployed person will be entitled to a full benefit (as a result of means testing, conditions on labour experience), imply that changes in the volume of unemployment typically do not translate fully in benefit mutations.[35]

The mutations in the number of unemployed are based on the standardised OECD series, with the unemployment definitions and population demarcations for the different countries being harmonised. In practice the figures are reasonably comparable, though there are a number of subtle differences, in particular between the USA and the European countries (see e.g. Sorrentino, 2000). Their influence is limited, however, and the OECD-based series is therefore preferable to the unemployment figures provided by the national statistical offices.

Labour participation of elderly men

In all countries studied, the labour participation rate of men aged 55-64 years declined between 1980 and 1999, and there was a general increase in the take-up of early exits (cf. figure 5.6). In line with the assumptions of Esping-Andersen, this growth was found to be fairly pronounced in the corporatist welfare states (Belgium and France), but was also occasionally substantial elsewhere (the Netherlands, Denmark, Great Britain). In the model, the effect of changes in the gross participation rate of elderly men on the benefit volume is intended to quantify the influence of this process. The gross participation rate equals the number of working people and unemployed divided by the size of the population in the relevant age category. The participation effect among elderly men does not refer to the impact of changes in the size of this age group, which has already been taken into account via the volume and ageing of the potential labour force.

Here again there is both a direct and an indirect relationship. The direct negative effect indicates that the take-up of early exit arrangements rises when the participation rate of older men declines. The indirect effect operates via unemployment, and theoretically runs in the opposite direction: if the labour participation of elderly men falls, the actual labour force becomes smaller and the number of unemployment benefits and employees' dependency (sick pay, leave arrangements) will shrink. It is assumed that on balance the direct correlation dominates, so that the total effect with respect to the benefit volume will be negative; due to size of the group in relation to the total number of benefits, it will probably also be inelastic.

The data series on the gross participation of the older section of the male labour force are taken from the *Labour Force Statistics* (OECD, 2000, 2003b). In some countries corrections were applied to compensate for trend breaks in these series.[36]

Labour participation of women

Many countries saw an increase in the participation rate of women in the period studied here, though it was not equally strong everywhere: in Sweden and Denmark, for example, the labour participation of women was already high in 1980 and could not rise as much as in countries with a lower base rate. Both a direct and an indirect effect are assumed for the variable 'labour participation of women aged 25-64', too.[37] The negative direct effect mainly indicates that a higher female participation rate will be reflected in fewer widow pensions and social assistance benefits. The positive indirect effect again operates via the unemployment variable: more working women theoretically leads to more unemployment benefits and higher take-up of sickness benefit and leave arrangements. Here, it is assumed that the overall effect is positive. This means that the indirect effect is the stronger, something that can be substantiated by the fairly limited share of widows and lone-parent families in the non-working population. Data are from the same source as the series on elderly male participation.

Pension coverage

In the event of incomplete pension coverage, the number of pension beneficiaries aged 65 years and older is smaller than the population in this age group. This may occur in countries where deferred retirement is possible or where the formal retirement age is above 65 years. Where this is the case, the development of the pension volume not only depends on changes in the size of the population aged 65 years and older, but also on mutations in the pension coverage. In so far as this is driven by changes in the formal entitlements structure (such as increased opportunities for flexible retirement), this variable can be regarded as an institutional determinant of the total benefit volume. During the two decades studied here, pension coverage of the over-65s is incomplete in Denmark and Great Britain. In the other countries this is a constant to which a value of 0 has been assigned.[38]

Major system changes

It was stressed earlier that formal institutions need not be unchangeable; and revisions of the social security system can influence the benefit volume substantially. Examples might include the introduction of entirely new arrangements, or extensions of the scope of existing arrangements, but also volume restrictions through the application of stricter entry or duration conditions, or through the complete abolition of certain schemes. Such system changes are of importance for the estimation of the benefit dependency growth mainly where they create major effects in the short term, and are not accompanied by substitution of benefit recipients from one benefit scheme to another.[39] If there are genuine system expansions or restrictions, it can be desirable to incorporate these in the model in the form of dummy variables. The system changes that have been included will be discussed at length in the country-specific analyses.

Economic growth
Economic growth has no direct impact on the benefit volume; it operates mainly via a negative relation with unemployment. A real increase in gross domestic product boosts the number of people needed to achieve the higher production. Assuming a constant potential labour force, stable participation rates and unchanged labour costs, unemployment will fall as production increases, and this in turn leads to a decrease of the total benefit volume.

However, there are also theoretical effects via the participation rate: in a growing economy, women and older men will less readily withdraw from the labour market, while a recession can lead to discouraged workers. The effect of economic growth on the two participation variables is thus positive. Given the theoretical total effects discussed above, this will lead to a fall in the number of benefits via the labour participation of elderly men, and to an increase via the participation of women. It is assumed that the overall effect of economic growth operates mainly via unemployment, and is thus negative: real growth in GDP leads to a fall in the number of benefits.

For this variable the series of annual percentage changes in gross domestic product (GDP) from the OECD *Economic Outlook* database was used. This indicator refers to the real changes in the total added value of the goods and services produced within a country in one year, valued at market prices.[40]

Labour costs
The central assumption here is that wage moderation makes it more attractive to employ personnel. If labour costs rise less than productivity, unemployment will fall, leading to a reduction in the benefit volume. This need not happen at once: wage mutations in preceding years may determine the amount of labour that employers wish to hire. Wage moderation therefore leads theoretically to a fall in the benefit volume after a certain period has elapsed; a wage explosion, on the other hand, eventually will cause the number of benefits to rise.

The development of labour costs was derived from the deflated OECD-series 'Unit labour costs in the total economy'. This variable is expressed in the form of deviations from the economic growth rate, and therefore indicates the degree to which labour costs keep pace with changes in productivity. It can therefore be interpreted as an indicator for (a lack of) wage moderation. Based on a sensitivity analysis, a lag of one year has been applied for all countries. Since the labour cost variable is exogenous, building in a lag does not introduce autocorrelation into the model (cf. Ostrom, 1990: 58-74).

Relative size of the services sector
Two indirect causal paths are specified here, both deriving from Esping-Andersen's analysis. First, a negative effect is assumed on the labour participation rate of elderly men. This

is based on the notion that in the period studied here a considerable part of this group did not have the skills to enable them to switch from jobs in the shrinking primary and secondary sectors to positions in the growing private or public services sector. As a result they ended up outside the labour force and went on to benefit; the saving in terms of a lower number of unemployed is not sufficient to offset this effect.

The impact of a growing services sector on the gross participation rate of women aged 25-54 years is considered positive. It is assumed that more women go to work as the share of the services sector increases. This corresponds with Esping-Andersen's expectation that it was mainly women who benefited in the period studied from growing post-industrial employment. Following the assumption on the total effect of female labour participation made earlier, this will lead to an increase in the benefit volume. A growing services sector implies that more women go out to work; this will lead to an increase in the number of unemployment benefits and the take-up of leave arrangements, a development only partly offset by the reduction in the number of recipients of social assistance and survivor's benefits.

On balance, the different causal paths on benefit dependency growth are expected to show a positive overall effect. A growth of the services sector has a negative impact on the participation rate of elderly men; and because the total effect of the latter variable on the benefit volume was assumed to be negative as well (cf. above), the effect of this path is positive. Changes in the relative size of the services sector have a positive impact on the participation rate of women, which in its turn is assumed to have a positive total effect on the benefit volume. Through this path, a relative growth of the services sector is therefore also expected to have a positive impact on the number of benefit recipients.

Data for this independent variable have been taken from the OECD *Labour Force Statistics*.

Unemployment benefit level

The effect of this institutional variable operates entirely indirectly, via the number of unemployed and the participation variables. The influence of benefit levels on unemployment was considered at length in §3.6.3. The main effect in the model is a standard assumption in the neo-classical economy: if the replacement rate increases, unemployed people will seek work less intensively and workers will be more inclined to fall back on unemployment benefit. Assuming an unchanged labour supply, an increase in the benefit level will therefore lead to a higher unemployment rate, which translates into a growing take-up of unemployment benefits.

The model also incorporates indirect supply effects via the two participation variables. If benefits increase, the labour participation rate of elderly men is expected to rise; and given the assumed negative total elasticity of this participation factor with the dependent variable, a net fall in the number of benefits will ensue. If unemployment benefits increase, the participation rate of women also increases. Because this latter factor is assumed to drive up the benefit volume, the total impact of this path will be positive.

The overall effect of all paths emanating from changes in the unemployment benefit level on benefit dependency growth is assumed to be positive. If unemployment benefits increase, this leads in theory to more unemployment in the labour force and a greater labour supply of women, and both paths are supposed to increase the benefit volume. This effect will only partially be mitigated by the positive impact of the benefit level on the participation rate of elderly men, which on balance reduces the number of benefits.

For this variable, the benefit entitlement index as constructed by the OECD was used. This index is an average of the gross replacement rates – the percentage of a person's salary that they receive back in the form of benefit when they lose their job – for various income levels, types of household and unemployment durations (OECD, 1994: 171-181; OECD, 1997a: 17-20; OECD, 2002; and supplementary data provided by the OECD).[41] It therefore provides some insight into the financial appeal of unemployment regulations, but the measure is a fairly crude one. Gross figures may offer an inadequate view of the financial incentives to work or remain dependent on benefit, because people are more likely to respond to the (perceived) net differences between earnings and benefits. A further limitation is that the index is calculated by the OECD only for uneven years; the even years have been interpolated here.

Theoretically, it could be assumed that changes in benefit levels will work through with some delay into the unemployment and gross participation rates. Following a sensitivity analysis, however, it was decided not to apply a lag to this variable.

Test of the causal structure across countries

As a preliminary step, consideration was given to whether the structure outlined in figure 5.7 matches the empirical data. A set of regression equations was estimated using the *Amos* program (Analysis of Moment Structures; see Arbuckle, 2006). Because the number of observations per country is limited, a simultaneous analysis across countries was first performed, with Canada and Australia being excluded due to limitations in the available data.[42] Based on 19 years and showing the mutations for eight countries, the number of observations then turns out at 152. Since outliers can easily occur in such a small dataset, a sensitivity analysis was performed in order to detect any influential observations.[43] This proved to be the case in years when unemployment rose very steeply in some countries, and in Germany in 1992, the year that reunification was incorporated in the figures.[44] These measurement points were removed from the analysis; ultimately, the model was tested on the basis of 120 observations.

The structure of the across-country model is as depicted in figure 5.7, with the exception of the variable 'system changes'. Modifications of social security schemes which are important in the country-specific analyses (cf. below) – such as the introduction of *Revenu minimum d'insertion* in France at the end of the 1980s – were not influential enough to warrant the incorporation of dummy variables in the across-country model. In addition, a number of covariates between the exogenous variables were introduced; e.g. the ageing process occurring in most countries is reflected in a negative relationship between the percentage changes in the pension population and the number of 50-64 year-olds in the labour force. Of course it would have been possible to include dummy variables for the regime type in the model as well, so as to obtain estimates which could be used to test the hypotheses directly. However, because it is quite likely that some of the effects of the independent variables will diverge between nations – whereas they have been assumed

Table 5.1
Standardised effects and goodness-of-fit-indicators of the eight-country model

	Direct effects[a] on:				Total effects on:	
	benefit dependency growth	number of unemployed	male labour participation (55-64 years)	female labour participation (25-54 years)	benefit dependency growth	number of unemployed
pension population (age ≥ 65 years)	0.17***				0.17	
lone parents	0.18***				0.18	
population of working age (15-64 years)	0.02	0.19***			0.13	0.19
elderly (50-64 years)	-0.22***	-0.08			-0.27	-0.08
number of unemployed	0.60***				0.60	
economic growth		-0.64***	0.09***	0.13	-0.39	-0.63
labour costs		0.24***			0.14	0.24
male labour participation (55-64 years)	*-0.17****	-0.01			-0.17	-0.01
female labour participation (25-54 years)	*-0.02*	0.08			0.02	0.08
relative size of services sector			*-0.15**	-0.03	0.03	0.00
unemployment benefit level		0.08	0.05	0.03	0.04	0.08
pension coverage	0.12**				0.12	
r²	0.60	0.64	0.04	0.02		

Goodness-of-fit indicators	Threshold value for good fit[b]	Model value
χ^2 (df, p)	p > .05	50.0 (df=42, p=.19)
χ^2/df	< 3.00	1.19
Goodness-of-Fit Index (GFI)	> 0.90	0.94
Adjusted GFI (AGFI)	> 0.85	0.87
Incremental Fit Index (IFI)	> 0.90	0.98
Tucker-Lewis Fit Index (TLI)	> 0.90	0.96
Comparative Fit Index (CFI)	> 0.90	0.98
Root mean square error of approximation (RMSEA)	≤ 0.05	0.04
(p) RMSEA=.05 (PCLOSE)	p > .05	p=.63

a. Coefficients printed in italics: postulated negative direct effects.
b. Cf. Arbuckle (2006); Kline (1998); Verschuren (1991).
Statistically significant at: ***p < .01 **p <.05 *p< .10.

to be constant across countries in the current model – this would probably not be very informative. Regime impact will be discussed separately in the next section, after various country-specific models have been developed.

Table 5.1 shows that of the 21 direct effects in the model, 17 operate in the postulated direction, and 10 of them are statistically significant (two others are borderline cases).[45] Of the four unexpected results, only one cannot be attributed to chance factors: a substantial negative direct effect (-0.22) of the number of 50-64 year-olds on the benefit volume. On closer inspection, however, this anomaly is easy to explain.[46]

Among the expected relationships, the standardised total effect on the benefit volume is strongest for the number of unemployed (0.60), followed by economic growth (0.39;

indirect effect only). In addition, changes in the number of pensioners and lone-parent families, and in the employment rate of elderly men, are fairly influential factors, with coefficients of 0.15 or more. Mutations in the size of the potential labour force largely impact via the number of unemployed. From the unstandardised coefficients (not included in the table) it is apparent that all direct effects on the benefit volume are inelastic, as predicted. The elasticities are highest for the relationship of benefit dependency growth with changes in the size of the pension population. The model factors explain a good deal of the variance in the benefit volume (r^2=.60) and in the number of unemployed (r^2=.64). The two endogenous participation variables, however, have low explained variances.

A common method to assess the goodness of fit of the entire model is the chi-square test. χ^2 indicates to what extent the relationships specified in the model reproduce the original variance/covariance matrix. A χ^2 value of zero means there is no difference between the estimated and the actual (co)variances, thus indicating a perfect fit. For higher values, the significance of χ^2 can be assessed using a standard statistical test. However, since the level of χ^2 is sensitive to the number of degrees of freedom[47] it is standard practice to correct for this (χ^2/df). Even then, this goodness of fit indicator has a number of disadvantages, including sensitivity to the sample size.[48] For this reason, many alternative fit indicators have been developed; a number of these (various fit indices, the root mean square error of approximation) have been included in table 5.1. According to all criteria, the specified model is in line with the empirical observations: the fit exceeds the applicable threshold values.

Both the direction of the standardised effects and the fit indicators therefore suggest that the specified model reflects the actual causal structure across countries fairly well.

5.5 Country-specific models

In principle, each coefficient in the model can differ for each country. To investigate the extent to which this is the case, it is theoretically most appropriate to specify what is known as a multi-group model. In such a model the specific coefficients for each country are estimated simultaneously, and it is possible to test whether the differences found between the countries are statistically significant (Arbuckle, 2006: 381-388). However, the 'small-N problem' highlighted earlier (a maximum of 19 observations are available per country) means that the estimates obtained by such an approach will not be robust and there is a considerable risk of multicollinearity. In a test of the multi-group model in which all coefficients were left free, the fit was found to be too low. This was the case both for an analysis of the individual countries and for an analysis in which nations were grouped by regime type. It was therefore decided to perform a separate modelling for each country, in which an attempt was first made to minimise the number of parameters that had to be estimated. Subsequently, for each country the remaining coefficients were modelled through a stepwise procedure.

The coefficient is fairly easy to establish for some of the causal relations in the model. For example, the influence of the growth in the pension population on the benefit volume does not have to be estimated using a regression analysis, but – assuming constant pension coverage – can be determined exactly. If it is known how many over-65s have been added to the population, and what proportion of them are in receipt of benefit, the unique effects of changes in the size of the pension population and in the pension coverage on the benefit growth rates (the elasticities) can be calculated directly.[49]

The direct effect of the size of the population of working age on the benefit growth seeks to map the extent to which changes in the size of this group work through into the number of benefits assigned to the population outside the labour force (early exits, survivor's benefits, social assistance and disability benefits). The elasticity has been calculated on the basis of the country-specific benefit fractions that applied in 1980, given a constant gross participation rate. The same approach was followed in estimating the direct effects of the two other demographic variables: the number of 50-64 year-olds and the number of lone-parent families.[50]

The indirect effect via unemployment of changes in the size of the population of working age and its ageing was determined in a similar fashion. It was assumed that both the gross and net participation rates do not change: thus, the labour force is a constant proportion of all 15-64 year-olds, and the unemployment rate remains constant from 1980. Given these assumptions, the elasticity of the potential labour force with the unemployment volume is by definition equal to 1 (if the number of 15-64 year-olds changes by 1%, the number of unemployed rises by the same percentage). The effect of the ageing of the labour force is smaller (and therefore inelastic), since the 50-64 years-old account for only a fraction of the potential labour force.

The impact on the unemployment volume of changes in the participation rate of older men and of women aged 25-54 years was determined in a comparable way. It was assumed that the size of these groups had remained constant since 1980, and that the unemployment rate in these two groups also remained unchanged. Based on these assumptions, it is possible to calculate directly how much the number of unemployed people has changed due to changes in the participation rates, and an elasticity can be determined. By contrast, the direct effect of these two participation variables on the benefit growth rate had to be estimated.[51]

Using this method, nine parameters were fixed in advance. The other 12 causal effects in the model and any influence of system breaks were then estimated using a stepwise hierarchical procedure. First, the impact described above of the demographic variables and the pension coverage on the benefit volume and unemployment were incorporated. Stepwise regression analyses were then performed on the residual variance in the endogenous variables. The variable which according to the analysis offered the most explanatory power as a determinant for all eight countries was included first. On the residual variance that remained, the next strongest explanatory factor was regressed, and so on until the entire hierarchy of determinants had been analysed. A detailed inspection of influential outliers was carried out in each regression analysis, in the same way as indicated earlier for the across-country model.[52] For a number of weak relationships, however, these outliers proved to be too dominant, and in these cases it was decided to constrain the coefficient for all countries to be equal.[53]

Some allowance was made in the country-specific models for the potential influence on the benefit volume of changes in the formal social security schemes (system expansions or curtailments), of which each country went through many in the decades studied here. Provided the following criteria were met, an estimate was made of the volume effect of such system breaks:
- There must be a documented change in the national legislation in specific years;
- This is combined in these years with a high residual in the benefit volume in the model without any system breaks. This implies that the rule change has not already been incorporated in the model through the impact of one of the independent variables;[54] and that the system break impacts suddenly on the benefit volume, with little substitution to other benefit schemes (as there would be no high residuals in these cases);
- It must also be possible to trace the system break at detailed level in the original data, i.e. in one of the time series underlying the mutations of the total benefit volume. There must for example have been a sudden marked decrease in the number of recipients of survivor's benefits.

5.5.1 Impact of model variables

The country-specific models are reproduced in detail in Annex 2. In all countries, the unstandardised coefficients (elasticities) have the sign that was assumed in figure 5.7, in other words all relations operate in the theoretically expected direction. As expected, among the demographic factors the *pension population* has the highest elasticity with the benefit growth rate. If the size of this group increases by 1%, the number of benefits grows by 0.5-0.6%. This reflects the large share taken by pensions in the total number of benefits: a substantial proportion of the population are of pensionable age, and the take-up is generally very high.

Changes in the size of the *population of working age* also weigh fairly heavily, with a total unstandardised effect that is usually[55] around 0.40. The direct effect among the population outside the labour force (the take-up of early exit arrangements, survivor's pensions, disability benefits and non-unemployment related social assistance) is generally stronger than the indirect effect via the *unemployment* variable. As noted, the latter relationship reflects the net take-up of unemployment, sickness and leave benefits in the labour force. This indirect effect is around 0.15 in most countries, but is lower in Sweden, Germany and the Netherlands (0.08-0.10), as a consequence of the wide dispersion of the unemployment variable in these countries.[56]

The *ageing of the potential labour force* has a substantial impact as well: in most countries, a mutation of 1% leads to an increase in the benefit volume of around 0.2%, chiefly due to the direct effect. The coefficient of the number of *lone-parent families* is lower (0.02-0.09), because this group is relatively small in all countries compared to the total number of benefit recipients (though in the period studied here it did grow strongly in some countries).

The dominant causal path of the two participation variables differs. The *participation rate of elderly men* has a considerable direct effect on the number of benefits (-0.20 to -0.40), which is only slightly mitigated by a weaker indirect effect via unemployment.

Substantively, this suggests that a declining participation rate leads to a net increase in the number of benefits: the rising take-up of early exit arrangements is offset to only a small degree by the fact that those who leave the labour market completely can no longer become unemployed and no longer have an entitlement to sickness benefit and occupational leave arrangements. The *participation of women aged 25-54 years*, by contrast, has a weak negative direct effect and a somewhat stronger positive indirect effect via unemployment. On balance, the increased participation rate of women appears to have driven up the benefit volume slightly: more women receive an employment-related benefit, and the reduction in the number of social assistance and survivor's benefits does not compensate for this. The total unstandardised effect on the benefit volume is however limited in all countries (0.02 to 0.06).

Economic growth has a strong effect on the unemployment volume,[57] with an elastic, negative coefficient: a growth mutation of one percent reduces the number of unemployed by between 4.3% and 8.7%. Compared with the effect of the number of unemployed on the benefit volume, the ranking of the countries is reversed. The peaks which occur in certain years in the changes in unemployment in Sweden, Germany and the Netherlands ensure that these countries have the highest coefficients in the regression of unemployment on economic growth. Since the country differences in the two effects are more or less compensatory this way, the total unstandardised effect of economic growth on the benefit volume is around 0.70 in all countries.

System changes have a considerable impact on benefit dependency in some countries, and will be discussed further below. The total effect of the remaining model variables, however, is limited. Worthy of note are the rather more substantial effects of *labour costs* on the number of unemployed (0.48 in Sweden, around 0.40 elsewhere), and the effect of the *size of the services sector* on the labour participation rate of elderly men (between -0.32 and -0.43).

The predictive power of the model for the final dependent variable, the benefit volume, is fairly high. Table 5.2 shows that the discrepancy between the actual and predicted change in the benefit volume over the entire period 1980-1999 amounts to less than one percentage point in all countries. The proportion of explained variance in benefit dependency is high in all cases as well: 0.51-0.52 in Belgium and Denmark, 0.70 in Sweden and 0.80-0.84 in the other countries.

A second dependent variable, the trend in the number of unemployed, also has a high explained variance, generally between 0.55 and 0.65. The USA comes out higher (0.81), Belgium somewhat lower (0.45). The two participation variables are less well predicted by the model, however. The explained variance is generally less than 0.06; it is only higher in Denmark for the labour participation of elderly men[58] (0.17).

Table 5.3 indicates the extent to which each model variable changed in the period 1980-1999, and how this influenced the number of benefits at the end point.[59] The table shows clearly that the number of benefits in all countries is influenced to a substantial extent by demographic changes. In four countries the number of benefits grows as a result by 12-16%; the growth in Denmark is lower (+8%), and is substantially higher in France, the

Table 5.2
Predictive power of the country-specific models

model	Benefit dependency 1999 (Index value, 1980=100) actual	model estimate	difference	r² benefit dependency	number of unemployed	male labour participation (55-64 years)	female labour participation (25-54 years)
US	117.8	118.1	0.3	0.816	0.812	0.056	0.014
GB	123.6	123.1	-0.5	0.844	0.565	0.022	0.031
DK	118.4	117.8	-0.6	0.515	0.621	0.170	0.024
SE	121.3	121.6	0.3	0.702	0.647	0.036	0.007
BE	130.0	129.9	-0.1	0.513	0.449	0.005	0.005
DE	125.0	125.3	0.4	0.838	0.548	0.022	0.033
FR	150.4	149.6	-0.8	0.810	0.653	0.005	0.011
NL	133.5	133.6	0.2	0.801	0.558	0.011	0.008

Netherlands and the USA (+22 to +33%). These differences arise in the first place due to the growth in the *pension population*. This group saw the strongest growth in the latter countries between 1980 and 1999. In the USA the rising number of people aged over 65 led to an 18% increase in the benefit volume; the increase in the Netherlands was 17%, in France 14%.

The growth in the size of the *population of working age* reinforces these differences. The potential labour force increased by 20% in the USA, driving up the number of benefits by an estimated 10%. Here again, France and the Netherlands also saw strong growth, so that the number of benefits increased more (+5% to +6%) than in the other European nations (+2% to +4%).

The *ageing of the potential labour force* had virtually no impact on the number of benefits in most countries. There was a slight rejuvenation of the labour force in the USA and Great Britain, which translates in a very modest decrease of benefit dependency. In Belgium, Sweden and France the potential labour force aged very little in the period considered here, resulting in a rise of less than 1% in benefit dependency. The Netherlands, Denmark and Germany are the exceptions here; in the first two countries the benefit volume rose by an estimated 2% due to this factor. This was because in the 1980s the labour force was rejuvenated to a lesser degree than elsewhere, while it aged markedly in the 1990s. The effect in Germany is somewhat stronger (+3%); it occurs mainly in the 1980s, and is fairly complex.[60]

The impact of the growth in the number of *lone-parent families* on benefit dependency varies: in four countries it is significant (approx. +3%), while in another four it is slight (less than 1%). The influence of this variable depends on three factors: the number of lone-parent families in 1980 (the base rate), the proportion of these families who were in receipt of benefit, and the growth in the size of this group between 1980 and 1999. The

Table 5.3
Impact of changes in model variables on benefit dependency, 1980-1999

	US	GB	DK	SE	BE	DE	FR	NL
Demography								
Pension population (age ≥ 65 years)								
- changes in X[a]	135	111	108	114	118	108	123	132
- impact on benefit dependency[b]	17.9	6.7	3.9	8.5	10.4	5.0	14.3	16.5
Population of working age (15-64 years)								
- changes in X[a]	120	107	106	106	104	111	113	115
- impact on benefit dependency[b]	9.9	2.9	2.3	1.8	1.7	3.6	4.8	6.1
Elderly (50-64 years)								
- changes in X[a]	99	97	111	104	102	116	105	115
- impact on benefit dependency[b]	-0.2	-0.5	1.7	0.8	0.4	3.3	0.9	2.2
Lone parents								
- changes in X[a]	138	192	113	130	227	142	170	198
- impact on benefit dependency[b]	3.1	3.5	0.3	0.5	2.7	0.6	0.8	2.6
Economy and labour market								
Number of unemployed								
- changes in X[a]	77	100	108	219	142	199	202	108
- impact on benefit dependency[b]	-2.2	2.2	3.0	10.6	6.5	8.3	12.1	3.1
Economic growth								
- changes in X[a]	184	158	143	145	146	144	146	161
- impact on benefit dependency[b]	-2.1	2.3	2.9	10.8	6.7	8.2	12.1	3.1
Labour costs								
- changes in X[a]	56	60	67	63	59	64	65	53
- impact on benefit dependency[b]	-3.1	-2.9	-2.0	-1.7	-2.9	-1.8	-2.2	-2.4
Male labour participation (55-64 years)								
- changes in X[c]	-4	-17	-11	-6	-22	-9	-23	-16
- impact on benefit dependency[b]	0.6	4.0	4.4	1.1	6.1	3.5	7.2	3.8
Female labour participation (25-54 years)								
- changes in X[c]	14	10	6	3	23	14	16	32
- impact on benefit dependency[b]	0.3	0.3	0.1	0.0	1.3	0.4	0.6	0.2
Relative size of services sector								
- changes in X[c]	9	17	8	11	11	16	17	12
- impact on benefit dependency[b]	0.4	1.3	0.9	0.6	1.1	2.3	1.7	1.0
Institutional developments								
Unemployment benefit level								
- changes in X[c]	0	-7	9	-1	-6	-2	10	-7
- impact on benefit dependency[b]	0.0	-0.2	0.2	0.0	-0.1	0.0	0.2	-0.1
Pension coverage								
- changes in X[c]	-	5	6	-	-	-	-	-
- impact on benefit dependency[b]	-	3.2	3.3	-	-	-	-	-
Major system changes								
- impact on benefit dependency[d]	-7.5	0.5	-1.2	-2.5	-	-	4.2	-2.0
All variables								
- impact on benefit dependency[b]	18.1	23.1	17.8	21.6	29.9	25.3	49.6	33.6

a. Index value 1999; 1980=100.
b. Estimated change in benefit years 1980-1999, in % (expected value).
c. In percentage points, 1980-1999.
d. Estimated change in benefit years 1980-1999, in % (net result of all system changes).

increase in the number of benefits is strongest in Great Britain (+3.5%); this country combines a fairly high starting level and a high benefit fraction with a sharp increase in the number of lone-parent families (+92%). The USA scores highs as well (+3.1%). Here, both the number of lone-parent families and the benefit fraction were already high in 1980. As a consequence, the more modest growth in the size of this group (+37%) still leads to a substantial growth of benefit dependency.

The Netherlands and Belgium combined a high initial benefit fraction with a fairly low number of lone-parent families in 1980 and the strongest increase in the size of this group. On balance, the number of benefits grows fairly strongly in the Low Countries (+2.6-2.7%).

The Scandinavian nations score lowest, with a volume increase of between +0.3 and +0.5%. Although Denmark and Sweden already had a large number of lone-parent families in 1980, these did not often receive benefit. The modest increase in the size of the group accordingly has virtually no effect. The volume increase in France was slightly higher (+0.8%), due to a combination of a low starting level and low benefit dependency in 1980 with fairly strong growth in the number of lone-parent families. Germany achieves a comparable score (+0.6%). Here, the base rate was similar as in France, and the initial benefit fraction was slightly higher; but the increase in the number of lone-parent families was comparatively smaller.

The table then shows the impact of the variables relating to the economy and the labour market. The development in the *number of unemployed* leads to a modest fall in the benefit volume in the USA (-2%) and to a slight increase in Great Britain, the Netherlands and Denmark (+2 to +3%). The influence of the unemployment variable on the benefit volume is more marked in Belgium and Germany (+7 to +8%), and is greatest in Sweden and France (+11 to +12%). In the three latter countries the number of unemployed was almost twice as high in 1999 as in 1980; in Sweden and Germany the impact on the benefit volume is somewhat mitigated by the low elasticity (cf. Annex 2).

Economic growth was highest in the USA between 1980 and 1999 (+84%), followed at some distance by the Netherlands and Great Britain, where GDP rose by around 60%. The economies of the other countries grew by around 45% over the period as a whole. Because the influence of economic growth operates mainly via the strong effect on the unemployment variable, the estimated impact on the benefit volume is in all cases virtually equal to that of the number of unemployed.

Labour costs in all countries lag a fairly long way behind economic growth between 1980 and 1999 (the index stood at between 53% and 67% of the initial value). After allowing for the lag of one year referred to earlier, this leads to a fall in the number of benefits of between 2% and 3% everywhere. The (small) differences between the countries are mainly caused by the divergent effects of unemployment on benefit volume. Wage moderation was most marked in the Netherlands in this period, but because here the unemployment effect is somewhat weaker than in the USA, Great Britain and Belgium, the impact on the number of benefits is less marked than in those three countries.

Although the downward trend came to an end in the second half of the 1990s, the *labour participation of elderly men* in 1999 was lower everywhere than in 1980. The development in the Netherlands is most remarkable, where the participation of this group rose by 5 percentage points from 1994 onwards. The influence on the benefit volume is cumulatively the highest in Belgium and France (+6% to +7 %), followed at some distance by Germany, the Netherlands, Great Britain and Denmark (approx. +4%). The USA and Sweden score much lower (+0.6% to +1.1%)

The *labour participation of women* rose very strongly in Belgium and the Netherlands (+23 to +32 percentage points), and also moved ahead considerably in the other non-Scandinavian countries. Yet this had virtually no influence on the number of benefit recipients, because of the low elasticity already mentioned: the weak direct negative effect of higher female participation (fewer recipients of social assistance and survivor's pensions) is offset by a slightly stronger indirect positive effect (more women who become unemployed and make use of sickness benefits and leave arrangements). Only in Belgium, where the indirect effect is greatest, does benefit dependency increase by more than 1% because of this factor.

The *relative size of the services sector* also had a modest influence on the number of benefits. In most countries the estimated impact over the entire period was no more than 1.1%. The three countries where the services sector grew most strongly – Great Britain, France and Germany – score slightly higher, with between 1.3% and 2.3%. The influence operates almost exclusively via the labour participation of elderly men. The growth of the services sector was accompanied by a reduction in the participation of this group, something which resulted in a rising take-up of early exit arrangements (early retirement, incapacity for work, long-term unemployment) and a small fall in the number of recipients of unemployment, sickness and leave benefits.

A further block consists of institutional developments. In all countries, the *unemployment benefit level* as measured by the OECD index does not change particularly strongly in the period considered here (between -7 and +10 percentage points). Combined with the low total elasticity (a maximum of 0.024), this leads to a limited cumulative impact on the number of benefits (between -0.1% and +0.2%). Given the somewhat problematic nature of this variable (see §5.4), this result may not be surprising. It could be that the postulated effect would show more clearly if benefit entitlements were assessed more adequately (use of the net rather than growth replacement rates, and of annual rather than biennial mutations; including non-unemployment entitlements in the index; weighing the coverage of the schemes). For the time being, however, it must be observed that this factor appears to have less of an influence on the growth in the total benefit volume than is generally assumed in neo-classical economic theory. In the current analysis, demographic changes and general developments in the economy and on the labour market emerge as more important driving factors.[61]

A second institutional variable, *the pension coverage*, is relevant only in Denmark and Great Britain, where it causes the number of benefit years to rise by more than 3%. This partly compensates for the fairly modest impact of the growth in the population aged 65 years or more in these countries.

Finally, *system changes* which met the criteria listed at the start of this section occurred in many countries. France underwent relatively large system expansions. The introduction of the *Allocation parentale d'éducation* (1985), and more especially the general social assistance legislation (*Revenu minimum d'insertion*, 1989), drove up the benefit volume by an estimated 4%.[62] In Great Britain, too, a system extension took place in the 1980s; the *Invalid Care Allowance* pushed up the British benefit volume by approximately half a percent.[63]

The benefit volume fell due to system changes in four countries. Denmark introduced a restriction in the sickness benefit scheme in 1983 (introduction of a maximum benefit duration), leading to an estimated fall in the total number of benefits of more than 1%.[64] In the Netherlands, changes in the sickness benefits and surviving dependants' arrangements[65] resulted in an estimated reduction in the benefit volume of 2%. Sweden imposed limits in 1995 on the arrangements for parental leave, contact days, caring for sick children, etc. Moreover, survivor benefits were gradually phased out, which was reflected from 1997 in a sharp fall in the volume. These changes led to a reduction of 2.5% in the total number of benefits.

The biggest system contraction took place in the USA (-7.5%). The most important change was the amendment of the social assistance scheme in 1996/97, with the abolition of the *Aid to Families with Dependent Children* (AFDC) and the introduction of *Temporary Aid to Needy Families* (TANF). The number of social assistance benefits in the USA fell from 6.7 million in 1995 to 3.2 million in 1999. This can be explained only partially by the falling unemployment rate in this period (an effect which is moreover mitigated by the rising number of lone-parent families); a considerable share of the reduction in benefit dependency is a result of this system change (an estimated -5.5% of the total volume in 1999). In addition, a number of modifications introduced in the early 1980s also helped push down benefit dependency in the USA.[66]

All in all, the benefit volume in the majority of countries is driven up mainly by demographic trends, in particular growth in the number of pensioners, the size of the potential labour force and – in four countries – the number of lone-parent families. Unemployment (and the underlying economic growth) also led to a substantial increase in the number of benefits in some countries in 1999 compared with 1980; this applies in particular for France, Sweden, Germany and Belgium. The falling labour participation of elderly men also had a clear upward impact on the number of benefits in all countries; Sweden and the USA are the only countries where this effect was more limited. The trend in labour costs reduced the benefit volume everywhere, with little variation between the countries. System breaks had a major influence mainly in the USA and France.

In most countries, the number of benefits grew by 21-30% in the period considered here (cf. table 5.2). The somewhat lower growth in the United States is found to be primarily the result of the stable number of benefits among the population of working age: the total increase of almost 18% is accounted for entirely by the growth in the number of pension recipients. Below the age of 65, the growth of the potential labour force and in the number of lone-parent families leads to a fairly sharp increase in the benefit volume (+13%), but this is cancelled out by the strong influence of the system changes in the USA and the fall in the number of unemployed.

Denmark also saw a relatively modest increase in benefit volume (just over 18%). This is due chiefly to the low growth of the labour force and the pension population, even allowing for the rising coverage. The limited increase in the number of lone-parent families and unemployed people also plays a role here.

The Netherlands scores higher than most countries (+34%). This is due mainly to population growth, which was the second-highest after the United States in both the population below and above the age of 65 years. This effect is reinforced by the growth in the number of lone-parent families, the ageing of the labour force and the decreased labour participation of elderly men (although the latter improved considerably since 1994).

France records far and away the highest volume increase (+50%). The influence of the growth in the pension population and in the population of working age is also fairly strong (in third place after the Netherlands). The benefit volume is driven up even further by the higher number of unemployed and the falling labour participation of elderly men, two variables whose influence is highest in France. In combination with the fact that France is the only country where system changes had a considerable positive impact, these developments led to the benefit volume in 1999 being one and a half times as high as at the start of the 1980s.

5.5.2 Regime impact

The above results say little about the impact of the different types of social security regime. To determine that influence one could try to argue for every relationship in the model whether there is a theoretical interaction with the type of social security regime. Sometimes, assumptions of this type can be deduced from Esping-Andersen's theoretical argument. The most interesting[67] is his thesis that corporatist regimes pursued a mass exit strategy from the 1980s onwards, leading to a strong increase in the benefit volume in countries with this institutional structure. This assumption is supported to some degree by the model outcomes. The labour participation of elderly men did indeed decrease most strongly between 1980 and 1999 in the corporatist Belgium and France (by between 22 and 23 percentage points), leading to the biggest increase in the number of benefits in these countries (+6-7%). Germany scores slightly lower (partly because one observation year was left out of the model), but still records a substantial increase in benefit volume (+3.5%) due to the falling labour participation of elderly men. However, the effect also occurs in some non-corporatist countries. The fairly strong volume growth that can be attributed to this factor in the Netherlands (+4%, comparable with Germany) may perhaps still be reconciled with Esping-Andersen's assumption, in the sense that the hybrid system shares this characteristic with the corporatist type. This does not however apply for the considerable increases in benefit volume attributable to the falling elderly male labour participation which occurred in the liberal Great Britain and the social-democratic Denmark (again approximately +4%). This confirms the picture that emerged earlier in the decomposition of the benefit volume (see figure 5.5). The growth in the number of early exits is a broad phenomenon which drove up the number of benefits in many nations. In the group of countries studied here, only Sweden and the United States were able to avoid this to any extent. At most the phenomenon occurs to a slightly greater extent in some corporatist countries than elsewhere; it is however by no means reserved exclusively for this regime type.

In many cases, however, the theoretical interaction effect of the regime type with the causal relationships specified in the model is less clear. To test the plausibility of the hypotheses formulated earlier, it may be useful to try and answer a more general question: how did the benefit volume develop after equalising the countries in terms of model characteristics which are *not* likely to be related to social security regimes? Both the relative volume (hypothesis 1A-1C) and the growth rates (hypothesis 2A-2C) may be examined in this respect. The volume composition (hypothesis 3A-3G), however, is left out of consideration here, since no statements can be made about this on the basis of the dependent variable in the model. This would require that the volume be broken down into the six types of benefit shown in the earlier wind rose graphics, with all direct effects in need of re-estimation.

The equalisation of countries was achieved in three ways. First, demographic factors were cancelled out by imposing the initial situation and subsequent developments of the United States on all countries.[68] In this *us demography simulation*, the population size for each country remains unchanged in 1980, but the composition in terms of the pension population, the potential labour force, the number of 50-64 year-olds and the number of lone-parent families is made the same as in the USA. The countries also undergo the same percentage change in these four variables as in the USA in later years. In this simulation the elasticities with the benefit volume were recalculated, based on the assumption that the country-specific benefit dependency risks of the different demographic groups do not change. As a corollary to this, a number of other effects in the model were also reassessed, because they are sensitive to changes in the population composition[69] (cf. Annex 2). This simulation results in an estimate of the benefit volume produced by the representatives of the various social security regimes under the same demographic conditions.

A second means of equalising the countries relates to the influence of *system revisions*. As we saw earlier, these changes can have a considerable impact on the benefit volume in different countries, and in divergent directions. It is therefore better to investigate how the number of benefits would have developed if the countries had not undergone these major changes. The qualifying comment can be made here that system revisions can theoretically be path-dependent (see e.g. Soede et al., 2004). In that case, to obtain a pure comparison between the countries it would perhaps be better *not* to leave them out of consideration. And indeed, some of the alterations to the various social security schemes do seem to be in line with basic regime principles; especially the further targeting of American social assistance at the most needy (thus making it even more liberal)[70] and the abolition of surviving dependent's benefits in Sweden (thus eliminating the corporatist regime's favourable treatment of breadwinners) could be considered exemplary in this respect. In practice, however, the majority of the system changes incorporated in the model do not appear to be particularly consistent with any institutional path. The introduction of a large-scale social assistance scheme would by no means be regarded as typical for the corporatist French system, any more than the introduction of a care allowance for invalid persons in Great Britain is a textbook example of the principles of the liberal regime; and most system curtailments in the model reflect austerity measures rather than path-dependent redesigns. For that reason, all schemes have been analysed frozen in time; i.e. in this simulation the basic assumption is that no major system changes meeting the criteria listed earlier occur after 1980. As a corollary to this, the comparison between countries becomes more accurate if the rising *take-up of pensions* in Denmark and Great Britain is discarded. These increases are probably not characteristic of the regime types to which these countries belong.

The third means of correcting for non-institutional differences between the countries is to eliminate the influence of the economic cycle. As became clear from figures 5.4a-5.4c, volume growth rates tend to show an anticyclical pattern, with more (hidden) unemployment benefits as economic growth decreases (partly mitigated by a reduction in employee dependency). Since the level and phasing of economic booms and recessions may vary across countries, the comparison of benefit dependency can easily become biased. The obvious way of correcting for this is to take the development in *structural unemployment* as the reference point in all countries and to determine how this has impacted on the number of benefits. Here this was achieved by imposing the 'non-accelerating inflation rate of unemployment' (NAIRU) in the model: the unemployment rate above which inflation is expected to fall, and below which inflation is expected to rise. The NAIRU is more or less synonymous to the 'natural unemployment rate'; it is not a constant, but may change as a result of technological developments, the availability of natural resources, the skill level of the population etc. Use was made of the historical NAIRU series provided by the OECD (Turner et al., 2001).

Simulations of benefit dependency growth

Since the simulations carried out with the help of the model relate to the percentage changes in the volume, it is logical to look first at the assumptions on the benefit dependency growth (hypotheses 2A-2C). The first ranking in figure 5.8 shows the development in the actual volume figures as already discussed, as well as the minor deviations from those figures in the estimates based on the country-specific models. As established earlier, it is only in the 1980s that hypothesis 2A cannot be rejected. In that period, the volume grew more strongly in the Netherlands than in the three corporatist countries and the hybrid regime occupied the expected top position, as the solid bars in the graph show. Viewed over the entire period (including the shaded bars), however, the increase in France is by far the strongest, and the average growth of the corporatist countries exceeds the Dutch score.[71] By contrast, the expectations in hypothesis 2B held: the growth in the benefit volume is indeed substantially greater in the corporatist group than in the social-democratic one, both on average and in the individual countries (although Denmark recorded stronger growth in the 1980s than Belgium). Hypothesis 2C had to be rejected, because there are virtually no differences between the representatives of the social-democratic and liberal regimes. The benefit volume in Denmark grew just as little as in the US, while

Sweden came out slightly lower than Great Britain. If Canada and Australia would have been included in the model-based analysis, the hypothesis probably still would have to be rejected, as these two liberal countries showed a theoretically unexpected strong volume growth (cf. figure 5.4c).[72]

The second ranking in the figure shows the result after the imposition of *us demography*. The models depicted in Annex 2 also contain the elasticities that apply for this variant.[73] In most countries the demographic equating with the USA means that in 1980 there are fewer over-65s, but that this group grows more strongly in the subsequent years than in the original figures. If the American population data are used, the group younger than 65 years is greater in 1980, and this category also expands more quickly in the period 1981-1999 than on the basis of the countries' own demography. On balance, the growth in the number of benefits based on these factors is greater in most countries after the US demography simulation. The smaller number of pensioners in 1980, in particular, does however mean that this growth usually starts from a lower base rate.[74] The exception to this general picture is the Netherlands. Here, the ratio of the over-65s to younger people in 1980, and the subsequent development in the pension population, do not differ markedly from those in the United States. As a result, the simulation leads to less changes in the Netherlands than elsewhere. The volume increase is slightly greater than previously, because the population aged under 65 years grows more strongly after imposing US demography.

In addition, after this simulation the potential labour force is younger in almost all countries: the share of 50-64 year-olds in the initial year shrinks, and increases to a lesser extent between 1980 and 1999. This reduces the growth in the benefit volume, most notably in Denmark, Germany and the Netherlands. Great Britain is the exception here; the original figures already implied a slight rejuvenation of the potential labour force, and this is less clearly so in the US demography variant. This means that the volume decrease attributable to changes in the size of the 50-64 year-age group is less after the simulation than before it.

The share of lone-parent families assumes a higher starting point in most countries after the imposition of the US demography, but the growth between 1980 and 1999 is generally less strong. This does not however apply for Sweden and Denmark, which already had a large number of lone-parent families in 1980 and subsequently experienced rather lower growth than in the US. The impact of this variable on the benefit volume is rendered slightly smaller by the simulation in Belgium and Great Britain, while it increases somewhat in the remaining countries.

The relative position of the Netherlands and the United States has changed markedly after imposing the US demography in all countries. In these two nations, the percentage mutation in the benefit volume over the entire period remained (virtually) the same, while elsewhere the simulation gave rise to a much stronger volume growth (+16-20 percentage points in most countries). In France, the estimated additional increase in the benefit volume is somewhat less (+10 percentage points); here, total benefit dependency rises by almost 60% between 1980 and 1999 after applying the American population figures, more than three times as much as in the USA.

Hypothesis 2A is rejected even more empathically in this variant. After imposition of the American demography, the Netherlands still experiences less benefit growth than the average of the corporatist group, but the difference in the 'wrong' direction has increased (-15 percentage points, against -1 percentage point with the countries' original demography);[75] and over the entire period Belgium, Germany and France each show more growth than the hybrid regime. Only in the 1980s the Dutch volume growth was high, though the Netherlands no longer occupies the top position (France comes higher) and the difference with the corporatist group average has become much smaller.

The theoretical expectations in hypothesis 2B still hold. After imposing the American demography, the growth in the corporatist group is substantially higher (+11 percentage points) than in Sweden and Denmark. Hypothesis 2C is partially confirmed in this variant: as expected, the group average in the social-democratic group is decidedly higher than in the liberal one (+9 percentage points). However, this is due to the very low score of the USA: the benefit volume in Great Britain has in fact grown slightly more strongly than in Denmark and Sweden.

Although the division in three regime types is clearly manifest in the US demography variant, this does not apply to the low growth in the hybrid regime in the 1990s: with the exception of the US, the Netherlands produces the fewest benefits over the whole period, leaving it far removed from the postulated top position. In Great Britain the number of benefits increases fairly sharply for a liberal social security regime, to a level just above the social-democratic group.

However, the picture is influenced by the *system changes* which took place in many countries. In Denmark and Great Britain, the growth was also determined by the rising pension take-up in the 65+ age group (elsewhere this was already incorporated almost fully in the volume figures for 1980). In the third ranking in the figure, the impact of these factors is left out of consideration, once again after application of the American demographic trends. In this simulation volume growth in the USA increases considerable, especially in the 1990s, because the *Aid to Families with Dependent Children* would not have been replaced by the *Temporary Aid to Needy Families*. The growth in France is substantially lower, mainly in the first decade, because the *Allocation parentale d'éducation* and the *Revenu minimum d'insertion* would not have been introduced in the 1980s. Great Britain also comes out significantly lower down the rankings: the scope of *Invalid Care Allowance* would not have been extended and the pension take-up would not have increased. In Denmark the latter factor also reduces the volume growth, but this is partially cancelled out by the assumption that a number of system restrictions would not have occurred; in comparison with the previous variant, a slight fall remains. Sweden and the Netherlands do see a small increase in benefit dependency growth due to the elimination of the effect of volume-reducing measures (among other things in the surviving dependants' legislation).

The difference between the countries with the highest and lowest growth figures shrinks in this variant: the volume increase in France is now less than twice as high as in the USA. Little support is still found for hypothesis 2A, though the difference between the hybrid regime and the average of the corporatist group in the unexpected direction

Figure 5.8
Benefit dependency growth in eight countries, 1980-1999 (actual and estimated)[a]

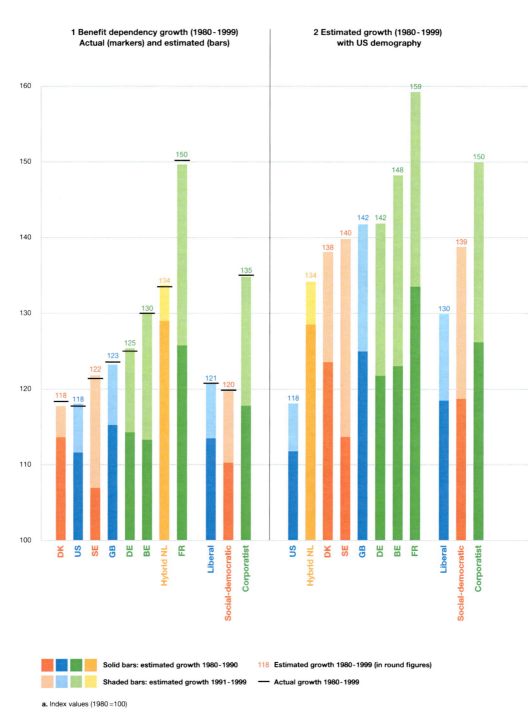

a. Index values (1980 = 100)

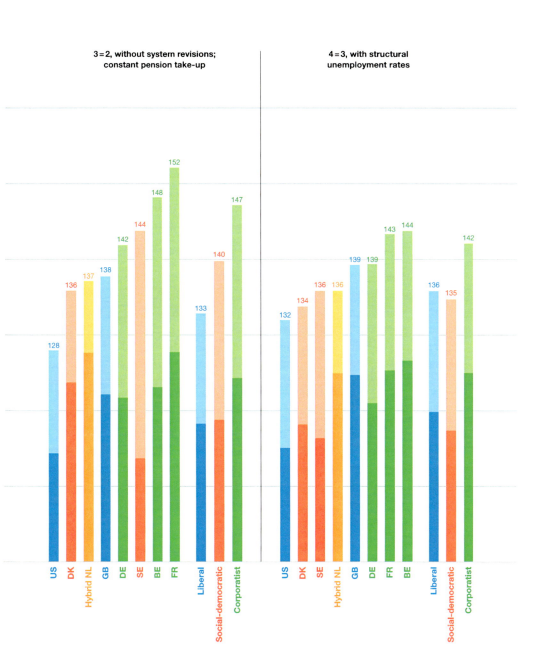

(-10 percentage points) over the entire period has become smaller. However, the Netherlands does top the ranking as expected in 1990: in the 1980s the volume growth here was the highest. Hypothesis 2B seems tenable at the level of group averages: benefit dependency in the corporatist regime grows stronger than in the social-democratic one, although the gap (+8 percentage points) is less wide than in the previous simulation. However, in the individual ranking Sweden occupies a midway position between that of Germany and Belgium, so the contrast between the groups is mainly based on the low Danish growth. Regarding hypothesis 2C the expectations are met more closely: the difference in the averages of the liberal and social-democratic group remains roughly the same (8 percentage points), but Sweden and Great Britain swap places in the country ranking. As a result, Sweden leaves both liberal countries behind, as expected; the Swedish score even appears to be on the high side for a social-democratic regime. Moreover, Great Britain now ranks considerably lower than the corporatist countries; yet the British volume growth is still greater than in Denmark. The gap of the latter country with the USA has closed somewhat.

If the *structural unemployment rates* are taken as a basis, the differences between the countries are much smaller. Belgium shows the biggest increase in the number of benefits in this final simulation: +44%, more than one third higher than in the USA (+32%). Compared with the previous variant, the benefit volume in Great Britain and the USA is between 2 and 4 percentage points higher, while in the other countries it declines. The fall is fairly modest (-1 to -2 percentage points) in the Netherlands, Denmark and Germany, and rather more substantial in Belgium (-5 percentage points). The steepest drop occurs in Sweden and France (-8 to -9 percentage points).[76]

In this final variant, too, hypothesis 2A has to be rejected. After imposing the structural unemployment levels, the benefit volume in the Netherlands still grows less between 1980 and 1999 than in the three corporatist countries, though the difference has become smaller (+36% versus +42% on average). In the 1980s, the benefit volume increases to roughly the same extent as in Belgium, France and Great Britain, giving the Netherlands one of the highest growth figures – though not a clear top position, just above the corporatist group average. In the following decade, however, according to this variant the Dutch benefit volume grows the least of all countries.

Hypothesis 2B is corroborated more clearly than in the previous simulation model. Not only is the average of the social-democratic group clearly below the corporatist level (+34% versus +42%), but due to the considerable decrease in Sweden the expected divergence also shows in all individual countries.

Hypothesis 2C, on the other hand, can no longer be maintained. There is hardly any difference between the group averages; in fact, the social-democratic average lags behind the liberal one (-1.0 percentage points). While, as expected, Sweden and Denmark come out higher than the USA (which holds the bottom position), in terms of volume growth these countries are surpassed by Great Britain. It was noted earlier that the British system could be regarded as an example of regime shift, where a fairly social-democratic system (designed on the basis of Beveridgean principles) was largely liberalised in the Thatcher years. The result may be characterised as an example of 'stalled social democratization' (Esping-Andersen, 1999:87) or, bearing in mind figure 4.2, perhaps more accurately as a liberal system with social-democratic residues. In terms of volume growth, however, the British system appears to perform less well than the purer representatives of the regime types with which it shares characteristics.

The secondary hypotheses relating to the within-cluster ranking cannot be rejected for the liberal and social-democratic regimes. As expected, the volume growth in the USA is lower than in Great Britain, and in Denmark it is lower than in Sweden. In the corporatist cluster the ranking is not as postulated: while the number of benefits in Germany grows less than in France, in line with expectations, Belgium ranks at the top and therefore has the highest rather than the lowest growth within its cluster.

Taking everything together, the final variant indicates that the benefit dependency growth hypothesis is supported to a limited extent. In the period analysed here, the representatives of the corporatist social security regime did indeed undergo stronger growth in the benefit volume than the representatives of the social-democratic type; these in turn, as expected, surpassed the liberal regime of the USA (but not Great Britain, a less pure representative of the type). The Dutch hybrid regime exceeds the corporatist group (but not France) in the 1980s, but had the lowest estimated growth rate in the 1990s.

This conclusion needs to be further qualified with the comment that the differences between the regime types are fairly limited after correcting for the influence of non-institutional factors (demographic differences, major system changes, the influence of pension take-up in Great Britain and Denmark, and the impact of the economic cycle on unemployment). On an annual basis, the number of benefits in the corporatist regime grows by an average of 0.4 percentage points more than in the social-democratic cluster, which in turn exceeds the growth in the liberal regime of the USA by slightly more than 0.1 percentage points per year. If Denmark, the country with the fewest inhabitants in this comparison, would have had a corporatist system, the volume of benefits in 1999 would have increased by around 6,000, while under an American system the decrease would have been approximately 2,000 benefits. If the USA, the most populated country, would have had a social-democratic regime, the 1999 benefit volume would be higher by almost 90,000; and a corporatist regime would add another 260,000 benefits – a fairly limited change, given the fact that actual US benefit dependency amounted to more than 59 million that year.

A point that must be considered is whether it is plausible that these fairly limited differences are actually 'produced' by the regime types. It is after all possible that the variation in benefit production between the country groups is a chance outcome; or that it is not brought about by diverging formal social security institutions, but reflects discrepancies in other factors that were not included in the model (such as the education level of the labour force, the prevailing informal rules, and the interaction processes occurring at the micro level).

Looking at the contributions of the individual direct determinants to the development of the benefit volume, rather more specific conclusions can be drawn. In the first place, a substantial part of the volume growth in all countries can be attributed to general population developments. According to the final simulation model, the benefit volume in most countries increases between 1980 and 1999 by 17-18% due to the growth in the population aged 65 years and older,[77] and by 5-7% due to changes in the size of the group below this age. Thus, these basic demographic trends together account for a growth in the number of benefits of around a quarter everywhere, all other things being equal. These two variables are therefore the most important factors driving up the benefit volume. At the same time, however, the country variation in their combined impact is limited; in equalised circumstances, a large share of benefit dependency growth is not related to the regime typology.

With regard to the differences between the hybrid and corporatist regime types (hypothesis 2A) the question may be raised of whether the fairly strong growth in benefit dependency which occurred in the Netherlands during the 1980s does indicate some support for the 'worst of three worlds' thesis. On the basis of the benefit dependency boost index it was expected that the Netherlands would have high volume growth due to widespread early exits and survivor's benefits, like the corporatist countries; due to a high take-up of disability insurance and employee dependency, like the social-democratic group; and due to considerable social assistance dependency, like the liberal countries. It was therefore postulated that the hybrid regime would generate the highest volume growth overall, exceeding the corporatist group. And indeed, between 1980 and 1990 the actual growth in the number of benefits was higher in the Netherlands than in the three corporatist countries; and over the entire period the Netherlands comes in second place in this set of eight countries[78] (see the first series in figure 5.8). Yet the results of the simulations suggest a different picture. The difference in the volume growth of the Netherlands and the corporatist group average in the period 1980-1990 dwindles from +10 to only +2 percentage points after the application of US demography; and this is reduced even further, to an estimated +0.7 percentage points, after correcting for system breaks and using structural unemployment rates. This indicates that the Netherlands was to a large extent a victim of its demography, not so much of its institutions. The strong increase in the number of benefits in the 1980s largely ensued from the growth in the labour force and the pension population, which was much larger than in the other European countries. The conclusion is that hypothesis 2A must ultimately be rejected, even for the 1980s: by the end of that decade the Netherlands may appear to have combined the worst of three worlds, but in fact it is far more likely that the high Dutch volume growth in this period reflects a general rise in benefit take-up due to specific demographic circumstances.

In the 1990s the actual volume growth contradicted the theoretical expectations: in the hybrid regime, the number of benefits increased far less than in the corporatist group. According to the final simulation variant, this was mainly achieved by a falling structural unemployment rate and the rising labour participation rate of older persons in the Netherlands, something that did not happen in the corporatist cluster, or only to a very limited extent. Somewhat speculatively, the suspicion could be voiced that the Dutch reform policy in the 1990s pushed some corporatist elements of the hybrid system to the background, but that this did not lead to a further liberalisation (i.e., greater take-up of social assistance benefits). The discouragement of the labour participation of older workers became a much less central feature of social policy, and the many changes in the Dutch unemployment benefits and social assistance schemes may have helped to reduce structural unemployment.

According to the final simulation, the fact that the corporatist countries are found to produce more benefits than the social-democratic cluster (in line with hypothesis 2B) is partly due to the regulation of the exit process. The benefit volume growth owing to the dwindling labour participation of older men is much stronger in Belgium, France and Germany than in Sweden (+4 to +7% versus +1%, respectively). This is consistent with the high score for the corporatist group and the low score achieved by Sweden on early exits in the theoretical benefit dependency boost index. The Danish case is more complex; here, the falling labour participation of men aged 55-64 years leads to a fairly sharp increase in the number of benefits, and the gap with respect to the corporatist group average (-1%) is much smaller than Sweden's (-5%). This difference, however, is enlarged by the fact that the benefit volume among the over-65s in Denmark grew less strongly than in the corporatist countries (-2%) owing to the higher statutory retirement age. The Danish strategy was to make early exits possible, but to curb the total benefit volume by a full retirement age which was high by international standards. This also showed in the theoretical benefit dependency boost index, where Denmark scored fairly high on early exits but was lowest on pension arrangements.[79] The Danish volume growth was furthermore mitigated by the development of structural unemployment, which over time increased more moderately than in the corporatist countries and Sweden.
    Finally, the corporatist countries come out higher than the social-democratic group because lone-parent families are more likely to be on benefit in Germany, France and Belgium than in Sweden and Denmark. The impact of this factor is limited, however (a difference of 0.4 percentage points in the benefit volume in the final simulation).

The outcome that the volume of benefits increases more in the social-democratic countries than in the liberal USA (in line with hypothesis 2C) is attributable to the trends in structural unemployment and in the labour participation of elderly men. Over the entire period, the mutations in structural unemployment lead to a volume change in the USA of less than 1 percentage point, the lowest of all countries. This is due both to the fact that this form of unemployment increased to the smallest extent in the USA between 1980 and 1999 (though as stated, starting from a fairly high initial level), and also to the lower elasticity: a change in the number of unemployed has less of an impact on the benefit volume in the USA than it does elsewhere. This latter aspect can be regarded as characteristic of a liberal regime. The changes in the labour participation of men aged 50-64 years also leads to the lowest volume increase in the USA, slightly below the Swedish level and well below the Danish level. The USA would have seen an even smaller increase in the number of benefits if the potential labour force and the number of lone-parent families had not led to somewhat stronger growth than elsewhere.[80] The lower volume growth in the USA compared with the social-democratic countries seems partly a result of the institutional setup: the lower probabilities of unemployed people to be on benefit and the extent to which early exits are promoted. This is in line with the theoretical index, where the USA achieved a low to very low score on boosting the benefit volume via unemployment benefits and early exits.

Because Great Britain was a less pure example of the liberal regime than the USA, theoretically the more substantial increase in benefit volume according to the final simulation does not come wholly unexpected; yet it is striking that Great Britain comes out higher than Denmark and Sweden. This can be traced to two factors. The labour participation of older men pushes up the volume of benefits in Great Britain far more than in the social-democratic countries (taking into account the Danish volume curtailment due to the higher retirement age). Secondly, the growth in the number of lone-parent families in Great Britain leads to far more benefit dependency than in the Scandinavian countries: the likelihood of becoming dependent on welfare is much higher. According to the constituent scores on the benefit dependency boost index, Great Britain was presumed to generate a fairly large benefit volume via early exits and social assistance, so both developments are in line with the theoretical expectations. However, compared with Sweden and Denmark the volume was supposed to be pegged back by the flat-rate nature of the disability benefits and the less attractive sickness and unemployment insurance benefits. In practice, especially the presumed dampening effect of the disability arrangements appears to be absent in Great Britain. This ought to be reflected in a relatively low direct impact of the size of the potential labour force on the benefit volume, but this is not found to be the case. In practice, the British disability benefit volume in 1980 was significantly lower than in the two social-democratic countries, but the growth in the two decades thereafter was much stronger. Expressed as a percentage of the population of 15-64 year-olds, the disability benefit volume[81] in Great Britain rose from just over 4% in 1980 to almost 10% in 1999. The latter is comparable with the relative number of benefits in Sweden and Denmark in the same year, but those countries started from a much higher level (7.5% and 9%, respectively, in 1980).

The general conclusion must be that hypothesis 2A has to be rejected, while hypothesis 2B is supported. Hypothesis 2C only holds if one compares the social-democratic regimes with the USA, as a purer specimen of the liberal type than Great Britain. The difference between the regime types is caused primarily by the influence on the benefit volume of the exit of older men from the labour market and of lone-parent families. The opportunity for early exits is greater in the corporatist than the social-democratic countries, while in the latter group (Denmark in particular) they are in turn more generous than in the USA. All other things being equal, this translates into concomitant differences in the growth in the benefit volume. The same applies for the operation of the factor 'lone-parent families': in demographically comparable circumstances the corporatist countries entitle lone-parent households more often to benefits than the social-democratic countries. The impact of this variable on benefit volumes in the USA is however much greater than in the corporatist group – something that may be related to the large number of young single mothers, and to the fact that in the USA divorce is more concentrated in the lower social strata than in most European countries (Härkönen & Dronkers, 2006).

To the extent that differences between the regime types derived from the trend in structural unemployment, it is less clear-cut that this purely reflects the influence of the different labour market and social security institutions. It is only in the USA that the elasticity of the changes in the number of unemployed with the benefit volume is clearly lower than elsewhere, but the differences between the other countries are small. Except where the USA is compared with the rest, therefore, the differences between the countries are primarily the result of the divergent development of structural unemployment, not of differential benefit probabilities among the unemployed. It is conceivable that the development in the level of structural unemployment is linked to the regime types; it could for example be assumed that the monies that are locked up in a corporatist regime in costly exit arrangements for older workers drive up structural unemployment, since they cannot be used to fund investments by businesses or to increase the production capacity via education. In practice, however, this is a complex relationship (cf. §3.7), and the development of structural unemployment also depends on non-institutional factors which are left out of consideration here: changes in the availability and price of natural resources, the skills level of the population, the degree to which countries implement technological innovations (such as ICT), migration flows, etc. Therefore the differences in the benefit production due to the evolution of structural unemployment can probably be ascribed only partially to the institutional structure embodied in the regime types.

Ultimately, this implies that the ranking of the purer representatives of the regime types (excluding the Netherlands and Great Britain) can to a certain degree be linked to their institutional differences: the regulation of labour market exits, the benefit probabilities of lone-parent families, and to some extent the level of structural unemployment. The theoretical expectation that the three social security regimes will differ in their benefit production under comparable circumstances thus finds some empirical support as far as benefit volume growth is concerned.

Simulation of relative volume

Figure 5.9 shows the benefit volume as a percentage of the population aged 15 years and older for three measurement years, after the final simulation (imposition of US demography and structural employment rates, no major system changes). This sheds light on the expectations regarding the relative volume (hypotheses 1A-1C) in equalised circumstances. Compared with the similar figure 5.2, the dispersion has reduced at all three measurement points – and this is not due solely to the fact that Canada and Australia have been left out of consideration in the simulation model.

In 1980, the relative volume after the simulation is lower in most countries than it is according to the original data (26-30% instead of 28-33%). This fall is due mainly to the fact that the imposition of the American demographic model leads to a reduction in the number of pension benefits. The Netherlands is the only country where the relative volume in the starting year has increased. The correction due to the imposition of the

American demography is relatively small here, and because structural unemployment in the Netherlands was higher in 1980 than cyclical unemployment, the relative volume turns out higher on balance. This means that hypothesis 1A cannot be rejected for the first measurement year: in 1980 the relative volume in the Netherlands was higher than in the three corporatist countries. Hypothesis 1B does not hold for that year, however. Denmark has the highest relative number of benefit recipients of all countries, and comes well above the representatives of the corporatist regime type. The relative volume in Sweden in 1980 is lower than that in Belgium, but comparable with Germany, and slightly higher than in France. As a result, the average of the social-democratic regime is clearly higher than that of the corporatist cluster. Hypothesis 1C is corroborated: the average of the social-democratic countries exceeds that of the liberal group. Yet the ranking in the latter group is contrary to what was assumed in advance, with the USA having a relative volume comparable with that in Germany and Sweden, and Great Britain attaining the lowest score of all countries.

Ten years later the dispersion among the countries is again smaller than in the original data (29-35% versus 29-38% according to figure 5.2). This not only reflects the imposition of the American demographic trend and the changes in the level of structural unemployment; the effect of system changes in the 1980s has also been eliminated here, and this pushes up the volume growth in some countries while holding it back in others (mainly France). According to the group averages all hypotheses hold in 1990, but there is little homogeneity within the regime types. The Netherlands has been overtaken by Belgium, but still has a higher relative volume than the average of the corporatist group; and in that sense hypothesis 1A is tenable. Sweden comes in below all corporatist countries now, as expected; the relative volume in Denmark is still high, but lower than in Belgium. Consequently, the social-democratic group average is well below that of the corporatist cluster, and hypothesis 1B cannot be rejected for 1990. The USA has dropped to the expected bottom position; and although Great Britain has overtaken Sweden (and two corporatist countries), the average of the liberal group is still below that of the social-democratic cluster, and hypothesis 1C is therefore also upheld.

In the final measurement year there is a threefold clustering. The USA has far and away the lowest relative volume (30%), while Belgium and Denmark clearly come out highest (39%). The other countries are clustered fairly close together, with a maximum difference between them of one percentage point: just over 34% in the Netherlands and France, slightly more than 35% in Germany, Sweden and Great Britain. Hypothesis 1A has to be rejected in 1999: the relative volume of the Netherlands is below the corporatist group average (due to the high score of Belgium). Hypothesis 1B is not supported either. In the corporate group a single high score (Belgium) is combined with two medium scores (Germany and France), while the social-democratic group has a single high (Denmark) and a single medium score (Sweden). Obviously, this results in a higher average in the latter cluster, something which was not predicted. Only hypothesis 1C cannot be rejected: due to very high relative volume in Denmark, and the low level in the USA, the group averages diverge considerably, and in the expected direction. Sweden and Great Britain do however achieve very similar scores.

Figure 5.9
Relative benefit volume in eight countries, 1980, 1990 and 1999 (estimated results)[a]

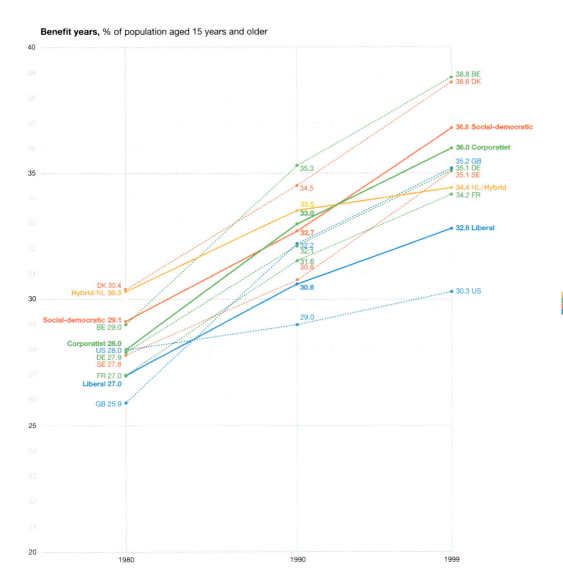

a. Estimated with US demography, structural unemployment rates, constant pension take-up and without system revisions

Sources: Arents et al. (2000); Moor et al. (2002); OECD (2003a: 171-235); adapted

In sum, support for the hypotheses concerning the relative volume increases following the simulation with the American demography, removal of the impact of system changes and pension take-up, and the use of the structural unemployment rates. In 1990 all hypotheses were sustained, and hypothesis 1C (the social-democratic versus the liberal regime) remained intact in all years. Hypothesis 1A (the hybrid versus the corporatist regime) was corroborated for both 1980 and 1990. This makes the contrast between the corporatist and the social-democratic types the least convincing, as hypothesis 1B had to be rejected in 1980 and 1999.

5.6 Conclusions

At the outset of this chapter it was stated that the number of benefit recipients is the most direct indicator for the output of the social security system. It was also commented that the size and development of this benefit volume theoretically depends on the formal institutions: the allocation of rights, or entitlements, to the potential beneficiaries. A priori it seems feasible that the rule-driven benefit production diverges between social security regimes; but there is no evident premise, either based on Esping-Andersen's theory or on the scaling of the formal institutions of the countries in the previous chapter, indicating the degree to which the regime types theoretically differ in this regard.

Theoretical expectations

For this reason, a benefit dependency boost index was developed in §5.1 (see also Annex 1). This was an attempt to map the extent to which the benefit volume in each country is theoretically driven up by 60 formal institutions. Constituent indices were calculated for different aspects of the social security system and the labour market (old age pensions, early exit regulations, unemployment insurance, disability benefits, social assistance, survivor's pensions, sickness benefit, leave arrangements and labour market measures). These were then weighted and added together, taking into account the maximum potential impact of the various regulations on the total number of benefits in the population aged 15 years and older. The total index reflects the situation in around 1990.

Based on this benefit dependency boost index, a number of hypotheses were then formulated which run as a common thread through this chapter. It was postulated in advance that the hybrid Dutch regime would come out higher than the three representatives of the corporatist regime (Belgium, France and Germany) both for the relative volume (the number of benefit years as a percentage of the population in the relevant age group) and for the growth rates (the annual percentage change in the number of benefit years). The corporatist countries, it was hypothesised, would in turn score higher than the social-democratic countries (Sweden and Denmark), while the latter were expected to come above the liberal group (USA, Canada, Australia and the United Kingdom). A number of expectations were also formulated regarding the composition of the benefit volume among the population of working age. In the corporatist social security regimes it was expected that a relatively high proportion of the benefits would relate to exit routes, unemployment insurance and survivor's benefits. The social-democratic regimes were expected to score relatively highly on employees' dependency (sick leave and care leave) and on disability insurance for non-employees. The liberal welfare states were postulated to have a relatively high number of social assistance benefits owing to their residual design. In the hybrid Dutch system, a 'worst of three worlds' hypothesis was formulated for the volume composition: an above-average volume on all six arrangements, without reaching the levels that characterise the pure representatives of a regime.

Data

The plausibility of these hypotheses was tested in ten countries for the period 1980-1999, on the basis of adapted time series of the annual benefit volume at the national level. These were originally published by the OECD (2003a), and derive partly from data gathered by NEI/Ecorys for the Dutch Ministry of Social Affairs and Employment (Arents et al., 2000; Moor et al., 2002). There are some limitations to the time series, and for Norway (one of the social-democratic regimes in the previous chapter) no commensurable information was available; but they probably still provide a fairly accurate picture of the historical development of benefit dependency (cf. §5.2).

Bivariate approach: volume indicators by regime type

A direct comparison revealed that the relative volume (the number of benefit years as a percentage of the eligible population) varies between the countries, but is linked rather weakly to the regime typology (cf. figures 5.2 and 5.3). The Netherlands is not consistently at the top of the ranking, nor do all corporatist countries structurally surpass Sweden and Denmark; and the latter two countries do not come out higher than all the liberal countries in each year considered here. While there are no consistent clusters (the scores of members of different regimes partially overlap at all measurement points), the group averages indicate that the regime typology does have some predictive value. Hypothesis 1C could not be rejected: on average, the relative volume in the social-democratic group clearly exceeded the liberal score at all measurement points, and both in the total population and among the population of working age. Hypothesis 1B had to be rejected in 1980. Yet in the category below the age of 65 years, in 1990 the average relative volume of the corporatist countries was higher than that of the social-democratic group, as expected; and the difference became even more marked during the 1990s. The postulated difference between the hybrid Dutch regime and the corporatist group average only emerged in 1980 and 1990, among the population of working age. The Netherlands did not reach the expected top position in those years, however, indicating little support for hypothesis 1A.

The growth rates (the percentage changes in the number of benefits) also failed to provide support for the theoretical expectations (see figure 5.4). The annual changes do not reveal consistent differences between the countries in the different regime types. Based on the average annual volume growth, only hypothesis 2B could not be rejected: for both the total population and the population of working age, the benefit volume grows over the period as a whole less strongly in Sweden and Denmark than in the three corporatist countries. Unexpected findings, however, include the high average growth rate in France, Australia and Canada and the modest growth rate in the Netherlands.

The assumptions concerning the composition of the benefit recipient population below retirement age, as shown in the theoretical profiles in figure 5.5, received more empirical support. The actual composition in many countries completely or largely matches the profile of their regime type (cf. figure 5.6). A characteristic feature of the corporatist countries is indeed a high share of early exits among the population of working age, as was theoretically posited in §5.1 (hypothesis 3A). This mainly occurred in the 1990s, however. Similarly Belgium, France and Germany score highly on unemployment insurance; this is in line with hypothesis 3B, with the caveat that the corporatist countries occupy the first three places only in 1999. When it comes to survivor's benefits, however, the reality matches the expectation formulated in hypothesis 3C less closely. Belgium and Germany do score highly here, but are not always in the top position (the Netherlands comes out higher in 1980, Canada in 1999). Contrary to expectations, for the population aged under 65 years France has a relatively low benefit volume in survivor's arrangements. Overall, Belgium has the most characteristic corporatist profile.

In the social-democratic group of countries, the expected bias towards employees' dependency and disability insurance for non-employees is indeed found. In all three measurement years considered here, the take-up of sickness benefits and leave arrangements is the highest in Sweden and Denmark, so that hypothesis 3D cannot be rejected. The benefit volume in disability insurance for people without an employment history is also very high in the social-democratic countries (hypothesis 3E), although Sweden is overtaken in 1999 by the Netherlands and Great Britain. Sweden most closely approaches the theoretical social-democratic profile of the benefit volume. However, both countries also exhibit a number of discrepancies: in the first decade of the time series Sweden has a large number of survivor's benefits, while in Denmark the benefit volume in unemployment insurance and early exits is not much lower than in the corporatist group.

As expected, the liberal countries – with the sole exception of the United States – have a high volume of social assistance benefits, as posited in hypothesis 3F: in all measurement years the first three places are occupied by representatives of this regime type. The USA falls steadily through the rankings over time, reaching a middle position by 1999. This difference was predicted theoretically; on the benefit dependency boost index, the USA achieved a low constituent score for social assistance, whereas the other liberal countries came out well above the average. This was a consequence of the low net replacement rates, the method of indexation and the strictness of the fraud policy prevailing in the USA at the time; and it has probably been reinforced by the transition from *Aid to Families with Dependent Children* to *Temporary Aid to Needy Families* in the 1990s.

The hybrid Dutch social security regime achieves a fairly high score in 1990 on all arrangements studied, in line with expectations. There are many social assistance benefits (though not as many as in the liberal group), and also a high take-up of sickness benefit and leave arrangements and disability insurance for non-employees (but lower than in the social-democratic countries). The Netherlands also scored highly in that year on the 'corporatist' schemes: a large number of early exits, just as many unemployment insurance benefits as in France and Germany, and the highest score for survivor's benefits. The 'worst of three worlds' assumption encapsulated in hypothesis 3G is thus not refuted in 1990. In the other two measurement years, however, the composition of the Dutch benefit volume points more in the direction of a hybrid regime which combines the worst of two worlds, since the volume of social assistance benefits is less high in 1980 and 1999.

Modelling

A multivariate approach was then adopted for eight countries; Canada and Australia were left out of consideration because of data limitations. The analysis in chapters 2 and 3 had already made clear that it was not only the formal institutions, of which the regime types are a condensed manifestation, which theoretically determine the production of benefit dependency. Even if the statutory or government-ratified 'rules of relief' are constant, the number of benefits still may vary depending on the context of rule application; economic, demographic, social, technological and ideological variations all may exert their influence, and lead to diverging outcomes. Different informal institutions among the actors concerned – the values, norms and conventions of benefit recipients, workers, employers, individual agents of the social security organisation, etc. – can also have an impact on the benefit production. Such influences can explain why the bare figures may not reveal a very strong relationship between social security regime types and the evolution of benefit dependency.

For this reason, an attempt was made to link the growth in the number of benefits in the eight countries cited above to the main underlying factors. A causal model was developed (see figure 5.7) in which the growth in the benefit volume is related to demographic trends, economic and labour market developments and a number of institutional changes, including major system revisions in the countries concerned. The model has some limitations, the most important of which is that the influence of informal institutions and administrative processes cannot be quantified due to a lack of suitable internationally comparable time series. The most evident structural factors were however incorporated in the model. The causal model proved to fit the data used well; an exploratory analysis covering all countries revealed a satisfactory goodness of fit, and virtually all relationships operated in the expected direction.

Model outcomes per country

It emerged from the country-specific analysis that in most nations the benefit volume rose during the period studied due to the growth in the number of pensioners and the swelling of the potential labour force. In four countries the number of lone-parent families also pushed up the level of benefit dependency quite strongly. The evolution of cyclical unemployment meant that the number of benefits in France, Sweden, Germany and Belgium was substantially higher in 1999 than in 1980. In the model, the number of unemployed is largely determined by economic growth, which consequently has a large indirect impact on the benefit volume. The development of labour costs also exerts its influence on the number of benefits through unemployment, but the indirect impact of this variable on the volume does not differ widely between the countries.

The reduction in the labour participation of elderly men was also found to be a factor which drove up benefit volumes substantially, with the exception of Sweden and the United States. System breaks were of major importance in the USA (fewer benefits due to cuts in social assistance in the 1990s) and France (more benefits due to the introduction of the social assistance laws at the end of the 1980s). The influence of the growth of the services sector, the rising labour participation of women and the level of unemployment benefits was found to be limited.

The number of benefits rose most strongly in France, growing more than one and a half times between 1980 and 1999. The model indicates that this was due to a combination of factors. In the period studied here, France saw fairly strong growth in the pension population and the potential labour force, and experienced the greatest impact of all countries of the rise in the number of unemployed and the falling labour participation of elderly men. All this was reinforced by the fact that France was the only country which saw a major system expansion, due to the introduction of the new social assistance legislation.

The Netherlands, where the number of benefits rose by a third, occupies second place. This country was largely the victim of its demographic development, which differs from that in the majority of Western European countries; both above and below the age of 65 years the Netherlands experienced the biggest relative population increase between 1980 and 1999, beaten only by the United States in this set of eight countries. The number of lone-parent families, the reduced labour participation of elderly men and the ageing of the labour force all helped to boost the Dutch benefit volume.

The USA and Denmark saw by far the smallest increase in the number of benefits (+18%). In the USA this was due to the fact that the number of benefits paid to the population aged below 65 years remained virtually stable between 1980 and 1999 because of the system changes and the favourable development of the unemployment rate. Without these two factors, this country would have realised a much bigger increase in the number of benefits, due to the growth of the pension population, the potential labour force and the number of lone-parent families. The limited volume growth in Denmark is the result of the modest increase in the size of the labour force, the pension population and, to a lesser extent, the number of lone-parent families and unemployed.

Impact of regime type in equalised circumstances

In order to establish the influence of the social security regimes on the benefit volume more precisely, the model was used to investigate how the benefit volume would have developed if all countries had started from the American demographic situation in 1980, and had undergone the same development up to and including 1999 as regards the number of pensioners, the potential labour force, the 50-64 year-old population and the number of lone-parent families. In this 'US demography' simulation the regime typology emerges more clearly than in the original growth figures (figure 5.8). This applies even more in a further simulation variant, in which the effects of system changes and the rising pension take-up in some nations have been discarded, and structural unemployment figures have been imposed for all countries, based on the OECD time series estimates of the non-accelerating inflation rate of unemployment (NAIRU).

According to this latter simulation, the percentage growth in the number of benefits between 1980 and 1999 was lowest in the liberal USA, slightly higher in Denmark and Sweden and highest of all in the three corporatist countries. This is in line with the expectations expressed in the benefit dependency growth rate hypothesis, in particular the sub-hypotheses 2B and 2C formulated in §5.1. The Dutch hybrid regime exceeded the corporatist group only slightly in the 1980s (by less than one percentage point); much of the previous difference was attributable to the specific demographic circumstances in the Netherlands. Hypothesis 2A therefore had to be rejected. However, the main thrust of the hypotheses cannot be discarded as long as the analysis is confined to the purer representatives of the regime types in this eight-country comparison (i.e., if the estimated growth rates of the hybrid Netherlands and Great Britain are ignored). Even so, the differences between the regime types are not very marked; under equalised circumstances the annual growth rate in the social-democratic countries is an average of 0.1 percentage points higher than in the USA, and 0.4 percentage points lower than in the corporatist cluster.

As regards the relative volume, hypothesis 1C holds at all measurement points (1980, 1990 and 1999) in the final simulation model. Under equalised circumstances, the number of benefits as a percentage of the population was higher on average in the social-democratic countries than in the liberal group. The difference between the average relative volume in the corporatist and social-democratic groups was in line with the expectations only in 1990; for the starting point and end point of the time series, hypothesis 1B had to be rejected. Hypothesis 1A was corroborated in 1980 and 1990, but not in 1999.

Thus, in 1990 none of these hypotheses can be discarded. At the end of the 1990s, only the average scores of the liberal and social-democratic regime types differ as expected in hypothesis 1C. According to the simulation many countries are grouped close together (34-35%) in 1999. The USA has the lowest relative volume in that year (30%), while Belgium and Denmark score highest (39%).

It should be added here that, based on the simulation model, no statements are possible on the composition hypothesis (3A-3G in §5.1); other dependent variables would need to be analysed for this.

An important question when considering the observed differences in the growth figures is whether it is plausible that the small differences can really be attributed to the differing formal institutions that characterise the regime types. Further analysis showed that in all countries the number of benefits increases mainly because of general demographic trends. The growth in the pension population and the potential labour force are the main factors driving up the benefit volume. The differences between the countries in this regard are small, however: under comparable conditions the resultant volume increase is approximately 25%, with no systematic variations between the regime types. Demographic factors therefore do explain a substantial part of the benefit volume growth, but in equalised circumstances are not linked to the regime type, so that they offer no explanation for the regime-specific differences.

Despite this, it would seem that the finding that the growth in the benefit volume is lower in the USA than in the social-democratic countries can be attributed largely to the formal institutionalisation. The difference is due mainly to the fact that there are fewer early exits in the USA than in the social-democratic countries (especially Denmark), and that the unemployed have a lower probability of receiving benefit. This is in line with the theoretical expectation, given the low score of the USA on the aspects 'early exits' and 'unemployment benefits' of the benefit dependency boost index.

The stronger growth in the corporatist countries compared with the social-democratic countries can also be linked to specific system characteristics. The regulation of the exit process is the most important. Under equalised conditions, Belgium, France and Germany undergo stronger volume growth than Sweden owing to the decreasing labour participation of elderly men. Denmark experiences a rise in early exits which is not much smaller than in the corporatist group, but the increase in the total benefit volume is held back by the higher retirement age in the period studied here (though this strategy became less successful over time due to the rising pension take-up). These differences in volume growth due to the exit process are consistent with the index scores on the aspects 'early exit regulations' and 'old age pensions'. In addition, there is a greater chance of benefit dependency among lone-parent families in the corporatist countries, where the rising structural unemployment also led to stronger volume growth than in Denmark.

One unexpected finding was that the less pure liberal regime in Great Britain underwent stronger volume growth than the two social-democratic countries under the simulation to make circumstances comparable. It seems that this can be ascribed to a strong increase in the take-up of disability benefits in Britain, something which was not predicted by the benefit dependency boost index. The Netherlands also did not occupy the expected top position over the whole period, so that hypothesis 2A proved not to be tenable. At the end of the time series the Netherlands, under equalised circumstances, occupies a middle position, with stronger volume growth than the USA and the countries in the social-democratic regime, but lower than Great Britain and the corporatist group.

In sum, the postulated unique position of the hybrid Dutch regime was not supported by the empirical analysis. After the equalisation procedure the relative volume (hypothesis 1A) and the volume growth (2A) were not clearly higher than in the corporatist group; and the 'worst of three worlds' hypothesis (3G) for the Netherlands holds only for 1990.

The corporatist countries do not exceed the social-democratic group in terms of relative volume (hypothesis 1B); but under comparable circumstances the average growth rates in the corporatist countries are indeed higher than in the social-democratic cluster, as postulated in hypothesis 2B. The differences between the social-democratic and liberal countries are largely as expected: in equalised circumstances the relative volume (1C) of Sweden and Denmark exceeds the average level of the liberal group, and with the growth rates (2C) the expected contrast was also found (though only if one compares the social-democratic regimes to the USA). It is plausible that the disparities in the growth figures are largely attributable to the differing design of the regimes.

Hypotheses 3A-3F, on the differences between the main regime types as regards the composition of the benefit volume in the population of working age, are also largely supported by the bivariate empirical analysis. The 'corporatist' distortion in survivor's benefits (hypothesis 3C) is however not very pronounced.

Some caution is needed with these conclusions. The limited number of observations meant there was little point in investigating the statistical significance of the differences between the countries and regimes using a multi-group model, which implies that the hypotheses could only be tested here at face value. In addition, the model developed here could not be used to verify the composition hypothesis, because it concerns the trend in the total benefit volume, not in individual social security arrangements. It is therefore not clear whether the same findings would emerge for hypotheses 3A-3G if the demographic development of the countries were equalised, if the influence of major system changes was eliminated, and if the evolution of structural unemployment were taken as the starting point.

The analysis performed here does however confirm to a certain extent that there is a relationship between the type of social security regime and the 'production of benefit dependency'. Of theoretical importance is the fact that fairly abstract and coherent variations in the formal institutions of countries lead to differences in the growth in the benefit volume which correspond with predictions. The ranking found here in terms of benefit production is also two-dimensional, in line with the typology of formal institutions in chapter 4. The most extensive welfare states do not automatically generate the largest benefit volume, because if that were the case Sweden and Denmark would have come out much higher in the figures. That the regime types are not meaningless concoctions of social scientists is also evident from the fact that they are found in practice to produce very different *kinds* of benefit dependency.

Policy implications

From a policy perspective, the findings imply that a country wishing to curb the growth in the number of benefits would probably do best not to opt for a corporatist path of development. Under comparable circumstances, a liberal or social-democratic regime performs better in this respect, though a number of caveats need to be mentioned here. In the first place, the differences between the regimes are not very great if a correction is applied for the impact of non-institutional differences, system changes and cyclical unemployment. In addition, the conclusion about the fairly good performance of the social-democratic regime as regards the growth in the benefit volume is based on results for only two countries, Sweden and Denmark, which moreover achieve that performance in partially different ways. Similarly, the favourable results of the liberal system emerge from the analyses chiefly as an 'American' achievement; in the British case, this regime type showed a growth in benefit volume which in equalised circumstances approaches the corporatist level (and in the raw data Australia and Canada ended up even higher). This may perhaps be expected with a less pure exponent of this regime type such as Great Britain. However, it is also possible that the liberal regime scores well mainly with US institutions in an American context of rule application: a politically powerful country with a great deal of economic capital and natural resources, which leads the way in technological innovations; a strong focus on competition and entrepreneurship; a stringent selection of migrants at the national borders based on economic motives, etc.

Finally, it is important to note that any policy choice for a specific path of institutional development must be made not only on the grounds of the expected impact on the benefit volume. Consideration must also be given to its significance for the fulfilment of the primary objectives of social security schemes: ensuring what is collectively deemed to be an optimum standard of protection in terms of income, employment, health and social participation. In addition, the expected external consequences of a given development path should play a role in the decision: the impact on economic growth and the financial sustainability of benefit schemes, the public support for the arrangements, the labour market participation rates, the redistribution of income, etc. It will therefore be interesting at this point to turn to the question of whether the effects of the different social security regimes go beyond the benefit volume.

Annex 1
Construction of the benefit dependency boost index

The benefit dependency boost index is the weighted sum of scores calculated for the main income-replacement social security arrangements and a number of labour market characteristics. It covers retirement pensions, early exit arrangements, survivor's pensions, disability insurance, unemployment insurance, sickness benefit, social assistance, leave arrangements for employees and labour market institutions. The constituent scores on these aspects are based on a total of 60 characteristics per country. These were calculated by first performing a categorical principal component analysis (CatPCA; see chapter 4) across the countries for each aspect. The degree of correlation between the individual characteristics was investigated, and also whether the scaling on the first dimension is consistent from the point of view of driving up the benefit volume. Items which did not scale, or which operated in the 'wrong' direction from the theoretical perspective, were removed from the CatPCA. This was the case, for example, if a short duration of benefits (which theoretically has less impact on the benefit volume than a long duration) empirically correlates mainly with benefits of a high level, with a low entry threshold, etc. (which theoretically push up the benefit volume). Such characteristics were added to the score on the first principal component in standardised form as separate items, in the theoretically correct direction. These were assigned a weight that was in proportion to the number of items remaining in the CatPCA. Such an added separate variable would thus for example have a weight of 0.167 if the scale of the other variables were based on six items.

A weighting was applied when adding the individual scores to the total index in proportion to the potential volume impact among the population aged 15 years and older. In theory, this depends on the size of the target group which may be affected by the risk or the arrangement, as well as the duration of take-up. For retirement pensions full year cohorts are eligible for benefits over a long period, while maternity leave, for example, is taken up by a part of the female labour force that is affected, and for a fairly limited period. The first score accordingly theoretically should weigh more heavily than the second in the benefit dependency boost index. To prevent tautologies, the potential volume impact was determined as far as possible on the basis of exogenous criteria, i.e. separately from the actual take-up of benefits. The weight of each arrangement in the total index was determined on the basis of the 1980-1999 average of the theoretical impact factors of the various countries.

The sources for the variables used in the construction of the index are largely the same as those reported in figure 4.1. Additional variables and data used for determining the weight of the constituent indices were drawn from several publications by the OECD (1993; 2001: 153-154; 2004), and the OECD Labour Force Survey database. Use was also made of demographic data from Eurostat and the United Nations, the European Foundation's EIRO system, and of Eardley (1996), Beaujot & Liu (2002) and Scherer (2002). The variables used to determine the theoretical impact factors and the weights are discussed in more detail below, in order of the contribution of the schemes to the benefit dependency boost index.

Old age pension (6 variables)
Variables: the statutory retirement age for men; the number of years by which the statutory retirement age is lowered for women; the number of years by which retirement may be deferred beyond the statutory age limit; means-testing of retirement pensions; the coverage of the collective retirement pensions; and the entitlement conditions in terms of domicile in the country, nationality or residence permits.

Impact factors and weight: for the statutory retirement the impact factor has been assessed as the average share of seven cohorts (aged 60-66, being the difference between the countries with the lowest and the highest statutory retirement age) in the population aged 15 years and older. The other characteristics weigh less heavily, because they are theoretically less important. This results in a weight of just over 39% for old age arrangements in the benefit dependency boost index.

Unemployment and financing (13 variables)
Variables: the maximum benefit duration; the minimum period needed to qualify for benefit (years in paid employment, payment of contributions); the statutory benefit level as a percentage of previous earnings; the net replacement rates at the onset of unemployment for a couple with children at two different income levels (that of the average production worker and two-thirds of this); the marginal tax rate for a double earner with two children and an above-average income; the average contribution for employers; the presence of means-testing; and the spending on activating labour market policy aimed specifically at the unemployed.

Impact factors and weight: the standardised unemployed figure according to the OECD definition was taken as a basis, corrected for the average benefit duration according to the Labour Force Surveys. Once again, this has been related to the 15+ population. It should be noted that this definition of unemployment does not look at receipt of benefit, so that housewives in search for a job, for example, are also included. This type of arrangement has a weight of 14% in the index.

Early exit regulations (6 variables)
Variables: the minimum age for early retirement in collective arrangements; the number of years that this lies below the statutory retirement age for a full regular pension; the possibility of exiting via unemployment or disability arrangements; the effective median early retirement age for men (1987-1992); the expected replacement rates for the coming five years in the event of early retirement at age 60.

Impact factors and weight: determined on the basis of the number of 55-64 year-olds who have stopped working (based on the participation figures and the average exit ages in the period 1987-1992), as a proportion of the population aged 15 years and older. This results in a weight of 11% in the index.

Disability (6 variables)
Variables: coverage of employment-related disability; minimum disability threshold in case of employment-related disability; benefit level in case of employment-related disability; coverage (*risque social*); minimum disability threshold (*risque social*); benefit level (*risque social*).

Impact factors and weight: first, the proportion of 15-64 year-olds reporting that they suffer from a 'chronic physical or mental health problem, illness, or disability', are consequently 'severely hampered in their daily activities' and regard their own health as 'bad or very bad' was determined for each country on the basis of the European Community Household Panel Survey (ECHP). This percentage was then standardised by age and gender, averaged out across the countries, and converted into absolute numbers of 15-64 year-olds according to the population statistics. The latter was then related to the population aged 15 years and older. This offers an approximation of the potential target group of the disability arrangements, regardless of whether people are currently receiving benefit. The weight in the total index was determined in this way at 10%.

Social assistance (13 variables)
Variables: strictness of means testing (four indicators: income test; capital test; housing test; work test); conditions regarding nationality or legal residence; minimum qualifying age for benefits; net replacement rates on social assistance after five years of unemployment (three household types: single person, lone-parent family with 2 children, couple with 2 children); indexation of social assistance benefits; limits on benefit duration; intensity of benefit fraud monitoring; take-up of preceding benefits.

Impact factors and weight: first an estimate was made for each country of the size of the main target group for social assistance, namely lone-parent families with a female head without work. No solid data are available on the number of potential users of social assistance who do not fit into this category (e.g. single men with social or medical problems, addicts, etc.). A somewhat arbitrary choice was therefore made for a multiplier, which is derived for each country from the proportion of lone-parent families versus other recipients of social assistance benefit. The number of non-working lone-parent families multiplied by this factor was then related to the size of the population aged 15 years and older. This results in a weight for social assistance benefit of 8% in the benefit dependency boost index.

Sickness benefit (5 variables)
Variables: coverage of sickness pay; conditionality of benefit on insurance period or payment of contributions; level of sickness pay; maximum benefit duration; number of waiting days.

Impact factors and weight: information is available in the OECD statistics for a limited number of countries on self-reported absence from work due to illness, regardless of whether the employee's salary continues to be paid by the employer or is met from a sickness benefit scheme. The average number of days' absence was divided by the average number of working days in a standard employment contract (less leave entitlements and public holidays). This percentage was multiplied per country and per calendar year by the number of employment years, producing an estimate of the absolute extent of sickness absenteeism. The potential impact on the total benefit volume was obtained by relating this figure to the size of the population aged 15 years and older. After averaging across all countries and years, sickness benefit contributes 8% to the total index.

Survivor's benefits (4 variables)
Variables: coverage of widow's pension; level of widow's pension; means testing; separate orphan's pension.

Impact factors and weight: the number of widows aged 15-64 years as reported by Eurostat for the 1990s was taken as a basis. This was adjusted for widows who are not eligible for benefit because they are working or have remarried. Widowers were left out of consideration. Their higher labour participation rate means they less often apply for this benefit (although their number is growing in most countries); moreover, widowers were not legally insured for this benefit in many countries during the first half of the period studied here (the 1980s). The number of potentially entitled widows younger than 65 years was related to the population aged 15 years and older in the countries. Calculated in this way, survivor's benefits contribute 4% to the benefit dependency boost index.

Labour market institutions (3 variables)
Variables: public expenditure on active labour market policy (as % of GDP); coverage of collective labour agreements; existence and level of statutory minimum wage.

Impact factors and weight: because the empirical material is limited, somewhat arbitrary assumptions were made concerning the proportion of people in receipt of sickness benefit, disability benefit, unemployment benefit and social assistance that are confronted with reintegration measures, and for what proportion of this group this leads to successful entry to the labour market. Here again, the shares were translated into absolute volumes. A multiplier was then applied to reflect the prevention of benefit dependency among workers through labour market policy. The numbers thus obtained were again related to the population aged 15 years and over to produce a weight in the total index (4%).

Leave arrangements for working parents (4 variables)
Variables: level of maternity benefit; coverage of maternity leave; total duration of maternity and parental leave; duration of paid and earnings-related maternity and parental leave.

Impact factors and weight: for maternity leave, an estimate was made for each country of the number of employed women giving birth on an annual basis, based on labour participation and fertility figures. This was related to the population aged 15 years and older, with a correction being applied for the generally limited duration of this type of leave. A multiplier was then applied to allow for other care tasks; it was assumed that this leave is generally shorter than maternity leave, but that the reasons for taking it (e.g. sickness of dependent children) will occur more regularly. The weight of these provisions in the benefit dependency boost index was determined in this way at 3%.

Annex 2
Country-specific causal models

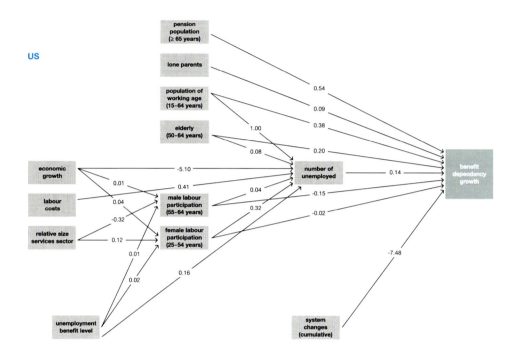

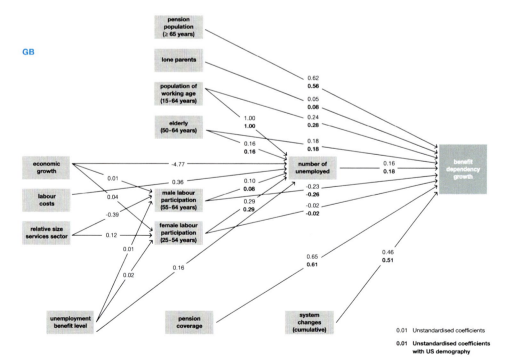

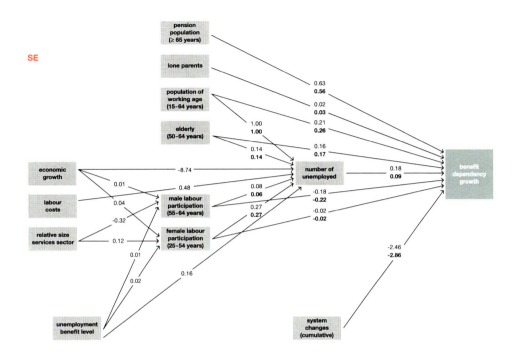
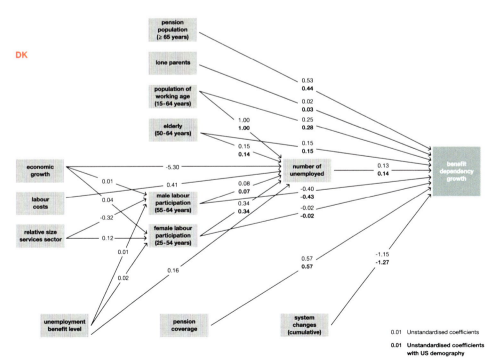

BENEFIT DEPENDENCY

(Annex 2)

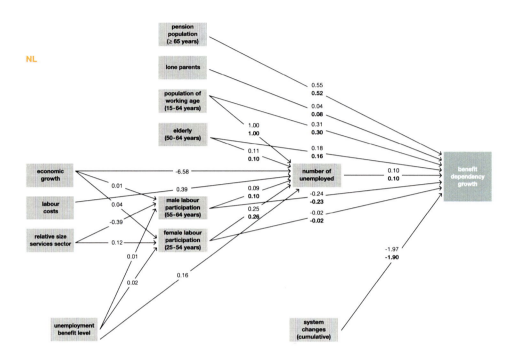

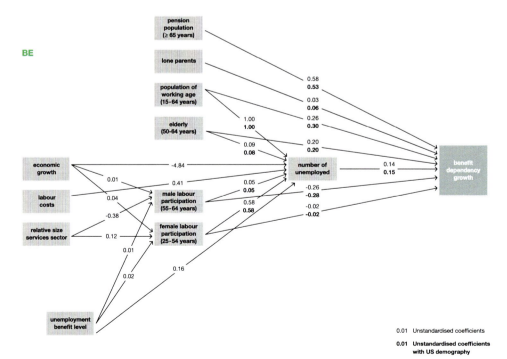

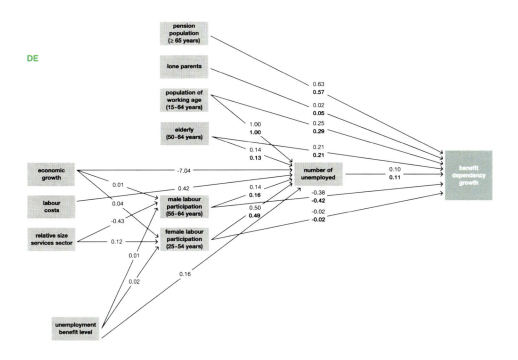

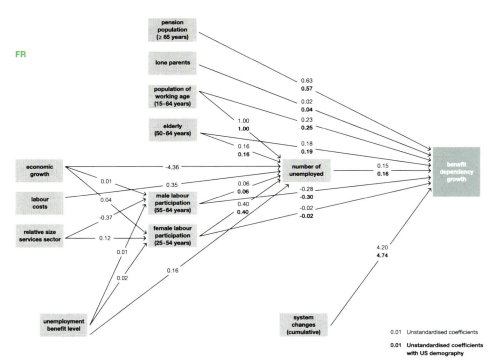

BENEFIT DEPENDENCY

6 Poverty

Historically, one of the main objectives of social security is to provide income protection; and in its early forms, this was reflected mainly in regulations that attempted to combat poverty. The first institutions, which were rooted in the family, the guilds and the local community, were concerned mainly with offering material and financial support to people facing acute want. In the process of the 'collectivisation of care' (see chapter 1), the fight against indigence gradually became the task of the government. In England, the *Elizabethan Poor Law* came into effect as early as 1601 and remained in force for more than two centuries, until the radical amendments[1] of 1834. Elsewhere, the first social legislation was also often concerned with combating poverty. In Germany, for example, government provisions had been in force long before Bismarck's social insurances (e.g. the Prussian *Armenpflegegesetz*[2] from 1842), and the Netherlands passed its *Armenwet* in 1854.

Other objectives of social security only later found their way into the formal rules. As the welfare state expanded, guarantees for the income continuity of workers were established, statutory regulation of the labour market and working conditions was imposed, and minimum standards of health care and social participation evolved. These developments can be regarded as later 'skins' around what is still the core of every social security system: provisions that bring down poverty to a level which the community considers acceptable. That level has risen over time. The old Poor Laws were replaced in many countries by a collective social assistance scheme, which covered more than just the bare minimum required for physical subsistence.

The social security regime types discussed in the previous chapters are all concerned with combating poverty, though each adopts a different strategy for doing so. From a social-democratic perspective, it is important that the entire population has access to a fairly high basic standard of living, regardless of how active (or inactive) they are on the labour market – although the system does aim to maximise the labour market participation rate. The purpose of this approach is to minimise the risk of poverty for all inhabitants.

In the liberal regime type, the key notion is self-reliance. The system aims to maximise the incentives for people to meet their own basic needs and secure their incomes (including their future pensions) through work. Those who fail to achieve this can fall back on a spartan subsistence provision which is subject to strict admission conditions and – as in the USA – may be of limited duration. This system type seeks to maximise collective wealth, partly by keeping social security spending to a minimum. The underlying idea is that even those with few resources will ultimately benefit from the resultant jobs growth and rising prosperity. This in turn will ultimately lead to a reduction in poverty, without the government having to redistribute money that could be used productively from the wealthier to the poorer members of society.

The corporatist regime type focuses mainly on the 'insiders'; people with a long employment history are assured of a high degree of income continuity, and this is especially profitable for persons whose occupational status is high. Theoretically there is little risk of poverty for these groups. This applies to a much lesser extent for the 'outsiders': people who have never worked, people in low-paid jobs or people with a short or interrupted employment history, including their dependent relatives. However, if such groups are not too large, this strategy can also keep poverty within bounds.

Against this background, it is useful to examine whether the regimes differ not just in the number of benefit claimants they generate, but also in their 'poverty production'. That is the central question addressed in this chapter. Before it can be answered, it is important to consider what can be defined as poverty, since the concept is theoretically much more complex than the benefit volume. Part of this chapter will therefore consist of an analysis of the meaning of poverty in prosperous societies, and of how the extent to which the phenomenon occurs can be investigated empirically. §6.1 outlines some of the main contours of the theoretical poverty debate in political philosophy. Taking this as a starting point, §6.2 discusses a number of basic principles and presents a theoretical definition of poverty. This section also analyses how this theoretical concept differs from two related notions in the scientific literature, namely inequality and social exclusion. In §6.3 a normative issue is raised: is it possible, from a sociological point of view, to make general statements about the rights that ought to be granted to the poor?

The operational poverty lines that have been used in empirical research to date are examined in §6.4. A central question here is whether practical measures of poverty such as these can be regarded as valid: do they adequately cover the theoretical content of the concept, as established in the basic principles and the definition? The operational lines are also assessed in terms of their reliability (do they make it possible to measure poverty accurately?); their ease of application; and their social and policy relevance.

Since none of the existing measures is satisfactory in all respects, §6.5 discusses an alternative operational criterion. This poverty line is based on a 'generalised budget approach', and will be used here to investigate whether there is an empirical relationship between social security regime types and poverty.

To this end, the theoretical relationship is first explored in more detail in §6.6. A theoretical 'institutional poverty risk index' is constructed and used as a basis to formulate a number of hypotheses concerning the degree to which the various regime types generate poverty. Whether or not these hypotheses correspond with the empirical data is assessed in §6.7, through a comparative analysis of 11 countries. The concluding section presents a summary of the main findings.

6.1 The theoretical poverty debate in political philosophy: some key elements

If we wish to study poverty, it is important to stipulate what we understand the concept to mean, in other words: what does the theoretical construct 'poverty' signify? Only when this is clear is it possible to specify an observable criterion for measuring poverty, which can then be used to test hypotheses empirically.

Based on the assumption that poor people lack something essential, it is first and foremost important to state what that deficit entails. It is then desirable to consider whether this concerns an absolute or relative shortage, and how much people have to do without in order to be classified as poor. Once this is clear, the next question to arise is whether there is a need to compensate the poor's deficits; and if so, who is to be responsible for that remuneration, and should it be tied to conditions? An extensive political and philosophical debate has been conducted on all these issues, of which only a few main points will be outlined here (see also e.g. Hayek, 1993 [1960]; Nozick, 1974; Harsanyi, 1976; Ackerman, 1980; Roemer, 1996; Scanlon, 1998).

6.1.1 Nature of the deficits: equality of what?

The question as to the aspects of life poverty relates to lies at the heart of the 'Equality of what?' debate in political philosophy (see e.g. Rawls, 1999 [1971]; Sen, 1980, 1992; Dworkin, 2000). There are three main trains of thought here: *welfarism*, the *capabilities approach* and *resourcism* (see White, 2004). The first perspective fits within the utilitarian philosophical tradition, and posits that welfare equates to happiness, generally defined as the net balance of pleasure and pain experienced by the individual. In the modern economic variant, this is equivalent to the satisfying of desires, preferences or needs. According to welfarism, a person is better off when they are happier or as they are able to fulfil more of their desires, preferences or needs. A poor person fails to achieve such a state to an adequate degree.

One frequently cited objection to this approach relates to adaptivity: people may get used to living under very unfavourable circumstances. It is questionable whether someone who has become accustomed to a very spartan way of life should be described as having an acceptable level of welfare if they – as in the 'poor but happy' stereotype – claim that they are content; or if they have resigned themselves to their fate, and their desires, preferences and needs go no further than short-term physical survival. A second point of criticism is that the 'core of existence' in the welfarism approach tends to be interpreted in too narrow a way: it may be that more is needed for an acceptable life than simply the achievement of utilities.

These criticisms are central to the approach advocated by Sen (1980, 1992, 1993, 1999), in which capabilities are the most important aspects. This concept refers to a person's ability to achieve certain functionings (valuable acts or states of being). It is more about possibilities than actual realisations[3] (Sen, 1999: 75):

> A person's 'capability' refers to the alternative combinations of functionings that are feasible for her to achieve. Capability is thus a kind of freedom: the substantive freedom to achieve alternative functioning combinations (or, less formally put, the freedom to achieve various lifestyles). For example, an affluent person who fasts may have the same functioning achievement in terms of eating or nourishment as a destitute person who is forced to starve, but the first does have a different 'capability set' than the second (the first *can* choose to eat well and be well nourished in a way the second cannot).

Another important difference compared with the previous approach is that capabilities embrace more than just welfare. As an example of capabilities, Sen cites in addition to the ability to be happy and to satisfy elementary desires or needs (food, health), aspects such as self-respect and possibilities to participate in social life. According to Sen it may be useful to acknowledge a 'capability for welfare'; theoretically, however, there are more capabilities than this. Following this approach, a poor person is not able to achieve the essential 'beings and doings' of the community in which they live at a minimal level. Poverty is about "the failure of basic capabilities to reach certain minimally acceptable standards"[4] (Sen, 1992: 109).

A criticism that can be levelled at the capability approach is that it easily becomes bogged down in abstractions. Although Sen mentions a number of examples of capabilities, he does not state clearly whether this is an exhaustive list, nor does he say anything about their relative weights.[5] Others have attempted to make the approach more specific (see e.g. Nussbaum,[6] 2000; UNDP, 1995: 11-23; UNDP, 2007: 229-354). However, they are often accused of 'sectarism': if a list of capabilities is drawn up, it is often difficult to make a neutral choice regarding the functionings to be included in the list; the preferences of the theoreticians concerned often play a decisive role. In addition, it is difficult to determine the relative importance of various capabilities on theoretical grounds.

In the resourcism approach, as propounded among others by Rawls and Dworkin, an attempt is made to avoid such sectarism.[7] It is assumed that certain resources are of universal importance for people, regardless of their actual circumstances or the lifestyle they prefer. These resources are often equated to income, financial assets and the attainment of a certain education level. Rawls (1999 [1971]) also sees 'basic liberties', 'equal opportunities' and 'the social basis of self-worth' as examples of the primary goods to which he believes people must have access.[8]

In a more sophisticated version of this perspective, a weighting is often included to take into account personal circumstances. According to Dworkin (2000: 79-81), for example, someone with a physical or mental disability in principle has a resource deficit. He or she will need a higher income or more support in order to achieve the same initial position as someone without such a deficit. The issue is then to determine which resources are the most important, how many of those resources people in a given society generally need, and how any resource deficits can be compensated. In this approach, a person can be described as poor if the resources to which they have access, allowing for any resource deficits, are insufficient for a minimally acceptable existence.

The resources approach is also not uncontroversial. The definition of resource deficits can readily become contaminated with value judgments about disabilities; which deficits prevent somebody from achieving a life that is good enough? Being blind or deaf probably do; but what about not having access to the latest textbooks or the most modern means of communication? And how are the deficits to be weighed against each other and translated into a total deficit in key resources? The more sophisticated form of resourcism often makes implicit choices on these issues, so that the danger of sectarism looms here, too, and the difference compared with the two earlier approaches becomes smaller than it initially appears. Its simpler manifestation, in which personal circumstances are not taken into account, is by contrast potentially 'fetishistic': the theoreticians concentrate on the presence or absence of resources, without asking themselves what kind of standard of living people are actually able to achieve with these.

6.1.2 Absolute or relative deficits

Given a particular selection of the aspects of life, a second question arises when conceptualising poverty: how can it be determined whether someone has too little in the way of welfare, capabilities or resources? A key point here is whether this should be determined in absolute or relative terms. Traditionally, the concept of poverty elicits mainly absolute connotations: people are poor if they suffer from hunger, become ill due to poor housing or are unable to afford medical care, have no shelter, and so on.

One result of the genesis of modern social security systems is that absolute poverty in such guises has become rather rare, though has by no means been eradicated entirely in prosperous societies (think of the homeless, illegal immigrants, etc.). If we were to limit ourselves exclusively to these phenomena, we would find relatively little poverty in the countries studied here. Yet it is questionable whether this is correct: in prosperous communities, attaining an acceptable standard of living generally requires more than simply being able to meet the most basic needs or being free of immediate threats to physical survival.

An alternative is to treat poverty as a completely relative matter. Individuals or households are then poor if they are considerably worse off than a reference group.[9] This approach has become the norm in recent decades in international comparative empirical research on poverty in developed societies. An example is the poverty line employed by the European Union (60% of median disposable income), which is intended to map out the 'at-risk-of-poverty' rate in the member states. This threshold not only raises all kinds of practical objections (these are dealt with in more detail in §6.4), but also objections of principle. In an entirely relative approach to poverty, the link is lost with what needs people have to meet in their society. Adam Smith (1909 [1776]: 541) long ago noted that the demarcation of this is not fixed, but depends on what is common practice in a society:[10]

> By necessaries I understand, not only the commodities which are indispensably necessary for the support of life, but whatever the custom of the country renders it indecent for creditable people, even of the lowest order, to be without.

This was an attempt by Smith to highlight the contextual nature of poverty. If people do not have the things that are necessary in their own community in order to survive not just physically but also socially, they are poor – even if they would not be poor according to the poverty standards used in the past or in distant countries.

Since a relative approach ignores the physical and social necessities it can give a distorted picture of poverty. An example is the case of an oil state with large income differentials, which however gives the least well off a high guaranteed income, good housing, free education, etc. In these circumstances relative 'poverty' will be substantial because inequality is high, but it is doubtful whether one would wish to describe those on the lowest incomes as poor: their necessities have after all been met. Conversely, in a country with a low level of prosperity and little inequality, people with an average income may have to do without the most basic goods and provisions. For example, in a communist society where incomes are virtually equalised around the median no one will fall below the relative poverty threshold. However, if that median income is not enough to buy food and clothing, one would still be inclined to describe the situation as one of mass poverty.

This problem also has a temporal aspect: in a relative perspective, people can become poor if the income of others increases to a greater degree than their own – even where in a material sense they lack nothing, and have experienced a considerable improvement in prosperity.

These limitations to an interpretation of poverty in terms of relative deficits do not however mean that it is better to measure poverty against an absolute criterion which applies everywhere and which fixes everything once and for all. The fact that 73% of the inhabitants of Eritrea were chronically undernourished in around 2002, or that many Europeans were confronted with housing shortages in the period after the Second World War, is not necessarily relevant for an assessment of current poverty levels in prosperous societies. As a society becomes richer and every one of its members benefits from this to some degree, a fixed and absolute criterion will in the long run imply that there are no poor people left. However, it is plausible that the higher level of prosperity also leads to a raising of the social standard of minimum necessities. A fixed, absolute approach does not reflect this evolution.

Sen (1983, 1985) chooses an elegant approach to this absolute/relative dilemma. He argues that the minimal necessary capabilities are invariant between communities and over time, and are absolute in that sense. However, the means needed to achieve them can diverge socially and historically. He elaborates on this as follows (Sen, 1985: 669-670):

> Poverty is not just a matter of being relatively poorer than others in the society, but of not having some basic opportunities of material well-being – the failure to have certain minimum 'capabilities'. The criteria of minimum capabilities are 'absolute' not in the sense that they must not vary from society to society […] or over time. […] People's deprivations are [to be] judged absolutely, and not simply in comparison with the deprivations of others in that society. If a person is seen as poor because he is unable to satisfy his hunger, then that diagnosis cannot be altered merely by the fact that others too may also be hungry (so that this person may not be, relatively speaking, any worse off than most others). The same applies to capability failures of other kinds, e.g., the more 'social' ones, such as being ashamed to appear in public because of the poverty of one's clothing. […] In the context of poverty analysis, it is a question of setting certain absolute standards of minimum material capabilities relevant for that society. Anyone failing this absolute level would then be classified as poor, no matter what his relative position is vis-à-vis others.

In Sen's view, therefore, poverty is ultimately absolute in nature: it is about whether people are able to achieve the minimum standards in respect of material things that are relevant in their society. Everyone who fails to achieve that absolute level should be regarded as poor, irrespective of their relative position compared with others. This does not mean that the content of those minimum standards is fixed; they can vary from time to time and from place to place, and in that sense can be regarded as 'relative'. The social and historical variation is related to what is regarded as socially necessary at a particular time and place, the statutory rules, the level of and trend in prices and prosperity, the availability of goods and services, and so on. However, this form of 'relativity' is not the same as equating poverty to not attaining a certain reference level of income or consumption. A person's relative position in such distributions in itself says little about whether or not they are poor, since such a ranking provides no direct measurement of their distance from the minimum standards which prevail in their society.[11]

6.1.3 Establishing thresholds

If one wishes to argue theoretically what poverty consists of, the next question that arises is where precisely the line demarcating the minimum standard should be drawn. This problem of establishing poverty thresholds occurs always. Whether the focus is on welfare, capabilities or resources, and whether an absolute or relative approach is chosen, a threshold value has to be declared, below which the deficits are so great that those concerned can be regarded as poor. In an absolute, welfare-based approach, for example, the problem of setting thresholds relates to the minimally required amount and quality of nutrition, housing, etc. In a relative approach based around resources, it is essential to establish how much income people should have vis-à-vis the reference group in order not to be classed as poor.

Several attempts have been made to resolve this issue theoretically. Dworkin (2000: 65-71), for example, has suggested the following thought experiment. Suppose a group of people have just arrived on an uninhabited island and have to distribute the available resources (land, water, timber, fruit trees, etc.) in an initial auction. Everyone receives an equal amount of 'money' (clamshells) and can bid in the auction. Initially, therefore, the external resources are equally divided. If the talents and disabilities of the people concerned were also equally distributed, the result of the auction would reflect the preferences of those involved, and would in that sense be fair. In practice, however, people's talents and disabilities differ, and in principle it is necessary to compensate for these resource deficits. According to Dworkin this can be resolved using the notion of a hypothetical insurance market. In this second part of his thought experiment it is assumed that the newly arrived islanders are not aware of their personal capabilities and limitations, but do know the distribution of limitations and talents across the group as a whole. It is then possible to determine what rationally acting persons would want to insure themselves against, and from this a theoretical threshold value for the necessary collective protection can be derived.

Dworkin (2000: 307-319) clarifies the problem using the example of health care. Every individual has an interest in ensuring their health. A community to some extent may regard this as a collective risk, and try to realise minimum health standards by funding medical provisions directly, or via a compulsory health insurance system, or by allowing people to deduct medical expenses when they make their income tax declaration, etc. However, not everything can be included in the collectively guaranteed minimum package; the ever burgeoning and often expensive medical technology and care tends to swallow up an increasing share of the communities' resources. At some point the rising medical expenditure will come into conflict with other things that people probably also regard as collectively desirable, such as the funding of infrastructure and good education, a fair remuneration of productive labour and encouraging business investments. Yet if limits are imposed on the package of communal health provisions, individual stakeholders are likely to oppose this. Such curtailments may seriously affect their quality of life, and in the most extreme cases can even be life-threatening. Where exactly should the limits of the collective guarantee be set in such a case?

In order to address the threshold-setting problem in relation to health risks, Dworkin proposes a fictitious rational young person operating on a hypothetical insurance market. He argues that such a person would not choose an insurance package which meant that in old age his life could be extended by a few months through expensive medical treatments, if he has to pay much higher contributions over the course of his life. Rather, he would probably prefer to invest the amount in things that produce greater returns on a lifetime basis (education, investments in shares) or to spend it on covering other risks which he considers more important (e.g. incapacity for work at an earlier age). Based on this argumentation, Dworkin states that it is possible in principle to decide whether specific provisions or treatments should or should not be included in the collectively guaranteed minimum package.

Rawls (1999 [1971]: 102-168) follows a somewhat comparable approach. In his thought experiment, people are placed behind a 'veil of ignorance'. They do not know what their natural resources are, how these can be exploited productively in their community, or what relative advantages and disadvantages ensue from their social, economic and cultural background. Rawls argues that a rational actor in this 'original position' will opt for the 'liberty principle' (secure all their basic political freedoms) and the 'difference principle'.[12] The latter means that differences in income and wealth are only to be regarded as fair if the worst-off group does better than they would have done without this inequality; and where such differences are linked to positions and offices which are attainable by everyone.

In order to resolve the threshold-setting problem, Rawls suggests starting from the assumption that people regard themselves as bound to the allocation principle which was chosen in the original position ('the strains of commitment'). Behind the veil of ignorance a rational actor must therefore also ask themselves whether, if the chosen allocation would imply that that actor turns out to be one of the least well off, he would actually be able to live under those circumstances. If he feels this would be unendurable for him, a rational actor would not wish to impose such a way of life on others. He therefore should opt for an allocation which makes the living conditions of the worst-off as good as possible, or in other words, a set of rules which maximises the minimum (*maximin*).

It is anything but certain whether the approaches put forward by Dworkin and Rawls can resolve the threshold-setting problem adequately. The elaboration of both the options of the rational young actor on the hypothetical insurance market and that of the maximin principle easily becomes bogged down in the detail. In many cases it will not be clear in advance what Dworkin's rational young actor will choose. What if a very expensive medical treatment extends the life of older people by three good or five ailing years? How to deal with costly interventions from which young people personally gain but which do not serve a clear collective purpose, such as breast enlargement for aesthetic reasons? Similarly, Rawls' maximin principle involving people operating behind a veil of ignorance can only be applied in fairly general terms. When seeking to utilise it in practice, the rational actor who tries to cast aside his own preferences and interests will need more information about the prevailing social conditions. The way of life that such a person considers the 'acceptable minimum' for themselves is difficult to ascertain in isolation from the customs and the prosperity of their community.

6.1.4 The need for compensation

Suppose that theoretically unambiguous answers were available to the above questions, so that one has arrived at a philosophical demarcation of what constitutes poverty: the aspects of life involved in poverty are given, the absolute/relative dilemma has been resolved satisfactorily, and the line which separates rich from poor is clear. In such a case, it is possible to identify the poor in a specific community; the question which then arises is whether there is a need to compensate the deficits of the poor, and if so, who should be responsible for doing so.

The contributors to the 'Equality of what' debate mentioned above tend to answer the question concerning the need for compensation in the affirmative. In their view, a certain minimum level of welfare, capability or resources has to be collectively guaranteed for three reasons: because it is useful for the community, because it serves freedom in society, or because it is fair. The welfarism approach generally attaches greatest importance to the first point, that of the net collective gains. If income has a declining marginal utility, and the utility of every citizen carries equal weight, the introduction of a guaranteed minimum will increase collective prosperity. Under those conditions poor people gain more utility through the extra means they obtain than wealthier people lose through the additional contributions they have to pay.

In the capabilities approach the freedom argument is stressed. If a certain minimum level is collectively assured, this increases the freedom of actors to realise 'valuable acts or states of being'.[13] In resourcism, fairness is often given the heaviest emphasis. In Rawls' view, for example, a self-interested rational actor operating behind the veil of ignorance would inevitably opt for fair principles which uphold a certain minimum standard (maximin and equality of opportunity). All three approaches accord a central role to government in compensating for the deficits, based on the idea that the government stands above the parties and is tasked with promoting general interests. The government is moreover in the ideal position to enforce the required redistribution via legislation.

However, from a theoretical standpoint it is not self-evident that the deficits experienced by the poor have to be compensated, nor that the government should bear a special responsibility for this. In neoclassical economic theory and libertarian political philosophy, both points are disputed. The argument that it is collectively *useful* to alleviate the indigence of the poor can be countered with the argument that the net result of income transfers may not positive at the level of the economy as a whole. Chapter 3 looked at this in some detail in the discussion of the economic repercussions of social security institutions. In addition to the potential benefits (promotion of public gains, prevention of public bad), it was pointed out that there are a number of potential negative effects of income transfers, and in particular the perverse incentives they can provide for economic actors: a reduced propensity to save, higher labour costs, more unemployment, and competition between income transfers and other government investments which could generate greater returns for the community. This puts into perspective the collective utility argument put forward by proponents of welfarism to underpin the need to compensate for deficits – though it is by no means firmly established that the negative effects will always dominate. Whether or not the collective benefits of a social minimum outweigh the drawbacks is ultimately an empirical rather than a theoretical question. In a certain socio-historical context, specific institutional arrangements guaranteeing a minimum standard of living may increase collective wealth; but it cannot be taken for granted that this would also be the case at a different time or place (cf. §3.6.3).

The logic of the *freedom* argument can also be contested from a theoretical standpoint (see e.g. White, 2004). Compensation for deficits by the government may well increase the freedom of the disadvantaged, but it also constrains the behavioural freedom of other actors (the wealthier, businesses), since they are no longer able to spend the levies they have to pay at their own discretion. A more subtle variant of this argumentation centres on the right to self-ownership. Through its taxation of productive labour, the government compels working people to support others. In this way the tax system uses their efforts, and such 'effort-harnessing' undermines individual freedom. The right to self-ownership is fundamentally attacked, because talented and productive persons are put in a position of being slaves: they have no choice other than to work for the untalented and the unproductive.

An argument against such 'freedom objections' is that at a collective level deficit compensation by the government does not by definition lead to less freedom, but rather to a different distribution of that freedom. One may also argue that the effort-harnessing by modern welfare states still leaves many freedoms unaffected, so that it is absurd to compare taxation with slavery. People who are obliged to pay taxes can still choose whether they wish to work and how much, and also what kind of work they do, and what remuneration they consider adequate – freedoms which a slave does not have. In this line of argumentation, some effort-harnessing is defensible as long as central freedoms continue to be guaranteed.[14] Finally, it is possible to take the stance that, while effort-harnessing is in principle undesirable, the right of some people to be spared any taxation has to be weighed against the right of all citizens to a minimal acceptable standard of living – and that the latter should weigh more heavily in the balance.

Although such refutations of the freedom objection to deficit compensation may be attractive to some, there is no theoretical need to regard them as decisive. Such arguments will not convince a consistent libertarian, who puts the right to self-ownership above all else.

The need to compensate the deficits of the poor can also be contested from the perspective of *fairness*. Suppose someone does not share the freedom objection, and thus in principle considers it acceptable that productive people should be forced to support those who are less productive. In that case, he may still feel that income transfers from the wealthier to the poor are not always fair, for example if hard workers are forced to maintain those who are too lazy to accept a job, or if those who are prudent and save are taxed to the benefit of spendthrifts. This is the 'fairness objection'; and the standard response to it is that such undesirable transfers can be avoided by conditioning the rights of the poor, for example by requiring that they actively look for work, follow a certain training course or be placed under tutelage. However, from a theoretical point of view there may also be drawbacks to such conditioning, which demand brief consideration here.

6.1.5 Conditions for compensation

If one thinks that deficits should in principle be compensated and that the government should be responsible for doing so, does this then apply for everyone and under all circumstances? Or should this compensation be subject to conditions? Such conditions may relate to certain qualifying properties; for example: the government only compensates for deficits if other actors (family, the Church, the employer) are unable to do so. The conditions may also refer to specific forms of conduct: moral requirements (behaving in a virtuous fashion, not having a criminal record), or obligations to do something in return (e.g. participating in sheltered employment). Rights are often also conditioned in the sense that certain eventualities (indigence, disability) must have occurred (cf. §3.2); and an important clause may be that compensation is withheld entirely or partially if the eventualities have been induced by the actions of the person concerned, i.e. when the deficits are self-inflicted.

Conditions of the latter type are regularly encountered in the political and philosophical debate, because they touch on a matter of principle:[15] it is perhaps not fair to compensate people who have become poor due to their own doings, at the expense of taxpayers and other contributors. Take a person who has the talents and qualifications to earn an adequate income through employment, and who has no impediments which prevent him from doing so. If jobs are available but the person concerned is lazy and chooses not to work, and as a result eventually ends up in financial difficulties, is it then fair that the government should compensate them for these deficits? Or, to give another example: what happens if someone is unable to generate sufficient income due to a physical disability which is the result of an accident during a risky leisure activity, such as mountaineering or parasailing? From a fairness perspective, it can be argued that compensation should only be granted on condition that the poor person did not cause their income deficit themselves.

Deficits that arise due to high expenditure which could in principle have been avoided can also be regarded as self-inflicted, leading to the argument that compensation should perhaps be ruled out via conditioning. Dworkin (2000: 48-59) describes this situation clearly in the examples he cites of cultivated expensive tastes, such as laying down an expensive wine collection, eating plover's eggs and visiting the opera frequently. If this causes someone to become poor, it is perhaps not logical that these deficits should be compensated.

If one wishes to exclude self-caused deficits from compensation, it must be possible to define them unambiguously. One way of doing this is to allow deficits to be eligible for compensation only if they do not ensue from the preferences of the person concerned. If the latter is the case, the deficit could have been avoided. Rawls (1999 [1971]) argues that people should always be held responsible for their preferences, regardless of how they arose. From that premise, it is logical to regard preference-related deficits as self-caused and therefore to exclude them from compensation.

Other political philosophers consider this unfair and argue that only preferences where people have a choice, and which they themselves would in reality not wish to have, should lead to a deficit being regarded as self-inflicted. Daniels (1990) illustrates this view using the following example. Suppose a family is poor because the wife prefers to stay at home to look after the children, while her husband would prefer it if she "brings the bacon in rather than cooking it". If this is her own will and free choice, the deficit should not be eligible for compensation. However, the situation is different if the woman in question would like to work but is unable to do so because her parents have brought her up in a traditional view of her role, and because her circle of friends hold very negative views on working women. In that case, the deficit should be compensated: although it is based on preferences, those preferences are unchosen and unwanted. A complicating factor in this approach is that it is necessary to investigate in detail which motives underlie the preferences, and that it may conflict with another notion of fairness, namely that people in equal circumstances and with identical preferences (not wanting to work in order to look after the children) are treated unequally if their preferences are based on different grounds.

Dworkin (2000) attempts to circumvent such problems by placing the emphasis on 'handicaps', which, as stated, he interprets as resource deficits that should in principle be eligible for collective compensation. As regards preferences, it makes no difference in his view whether they are wanted or freely chosen. The only thing that is important is the extent to which these impose certain mental or emotional constraints on people which cause them to become disadvantaged. He refers in this connection to 'handicapping tastes' (Dworkin, 2000: 82):

> Suppose someone finds he has a craving (or obsession or lust or, in the words of an earlier psychology, a 'drive') that he wishes he did not have, because it interferes with what he wants to

do with his life and offers him frustration or even pain if it is not satisfied. This might indeed be some feature of his physical needs that other people would not consider a handicap at all: for example, a generous appetite for sex. But it is a 'preference' (if that is the right word) that he does not want, and it makes perfect sense that he would be better off without it. For some people these unwanted tastes includes tastes they have (perhaps unwittingly) themselves cultivated, such as a taste for a particular sport or for music of a sort difficult to obtain. They regret that they have these tastes, and believe they would be better off without them, but nevertheless find it painful to ignore them. These tastes are handicaps; though for other people they are rather an essential part of what gives value to their lives.

Dworkin argues that in such circumstances preferences are the same as normal handicaps, and like other resource deficits should be eligible for compensation. Someone who is too lazy to work and becomes poor as a result has a right to compensation if that laziness is a personality trait which dictates his behaviour, no matter whether he wants it to or not; thus, if Ivan Goncharov's novel character *Oblomov* had been poor, he could have appealed to his 'handicapping taste'. And if excessive spending drags someone into poverty, but is the result of a physical dependency on alcohol or other drugs, compulsive gambling or addictive bargain hunting, he or she has a right to compensation for the resultant deficits – despite the fact that those deficits are self-inflicted. Deficits which result from tastes that are not handicapping, by contrast, need not be compensated from the collective purse.

Yet it is doubtful whether, in presenting this argument, Dworkin has produced the golden rule for conditioning the compensation of deficits. A first problem lies in establishing once and for all when a certain taste should be regarded as handicapping; it always depends on the traits of a specific person, their circumstances, and the one who is judging those. This implies that application of the principle may lead to arbitrary or unstable outcomes.

It is also difficult to determine whether deficits should be compensated if other factors are involved. For example, if someone does not work because they are fairly indolent by nature (a handicapping taste), and also because they do not find the work that they can find attractive enough (an 'ordinary' preference), should their deficit then be compensated fully, only in part, or not at all?

A final point is that it may also be considered unfair not to compensate for deficits when there are no handicapping tastes involved. An example is the familiar observation that poor people sometimes spend a lot of money on smoking, pets or lotteries, without being really addicted. This means that they could cease these activities, but prefer not to do so. This choice prolongs their poverty: they would be materially better off if they did not incur these expenses. Often, however, they justify their deeds with the argument that the easing of their material indigence that would result from abandoning such 'luxuries' is outweighed by the welfare gains that their unwise behaviour delivers: smoking and pets provide consolation, and the possibility of winning a top prize keeps alive the hope that they will be able to leave poverty behind them for good. Is it fair not to compensate people for their deficit if that deficit is not the result of a handicapping taste but of a subjectively understandable choice? Or, to put it in sharper terms, should poor unemployed dog owners, *ceteris paribus*, receive less social assistance than poor unemployed alcoholics who spend the same amount not on pets, but on hard liquor? When reviewing this debate, it is difficult to settle once and for all the issue of the forms of conditioning that are required from a theoretical point of view.[16]

6.2 The meaning of poverty

As stated earlier, the theoretical poverty debate in political philosophy breaks down into two core questions: what does poverty mean, and which rights should in principle be granted to poor people? The first is a 'What is?' question, on which a position will be developed here. The second is a 'What ought?' problem, which will be discussed in the next section.

The answer to the question as to the phenomena to which the notion of poverty refers depends among other things on the way the construct is embedded in theory, of which the debate outlined above provides various examples. The first issue to be addressed here relates to the theoretical meaning that one wishes to assign to the concept – the 'poverty concept by postulation', which cannot be observed directly (cf. Northrop, 1947). It is useful to say something about this, because in empirical research many divergent operational criteria are used. An ex ante theoretical conceptualisation may provide a touchstone for assessing the suitability of the empirical poverty lines that will be discussed in §6.4. The aim here is to formulate a limited number of basic principles of poverty. These should have heuristic value, in the sense that poverty and non-poverty are separated from each other theoretically in an unambiguous, straightforward and non-trivial way. After these principles have been elucidated a theoretical definition of the concept will be given, and the differences between poverty and a number of other theoretical constructs will be discussed.

6.2.1 Basic principles

As a corollary to the discussion sketched above – and in line with some of the ideas put forward in chapters 2 and 3 – four basic principles on the theoretical meaning of poverty may be posited.

1. Poverty relates to the aspects of life that are minimally necessary within a community.
This means that the question as to the aspects of life which are important in relation to poverty cannot be answered definitively; what is necessary at the minimum level cannot be seen in isolation from the society in which one wishes to debate or investigate poverty. It may thus relate to the most basic welfare (e.g. the need for sufficient food), but can also refer to higher capabilities, such as the opportunities to participate in social life. One point worth noting here is that it seems wise not to interpret the concept of poverty so broadly that we lose sight of the fact that we are talking here about a social *minimum*. In most communities it would probably be going too far to include people among the ranks

of the poor if they are unable to attain Sen's 'capability for self-respect' or Nussbaum's lofty ideal of the 'capability for connection with other species'.[17] Sen did not in fact mean this: as noted earlier, he sees poverty as "the failure of *basic* capabilities to reach certain *minimally* acceptable standards".

The premise is that an aspect of life is a minimum necessity if it is virtually indispensable for the members of a community to have access to it, because its absence would seriously affect their functioning within that community. This means in the first place that people must be able to obtain – in a socially acceptable manner – the things which are required for their physical survival: adequate food in terms of both quantity and quality, suitable clothing, satisfactory housing (including heating, water and energy) and sufficient medical care. What is considered the minimal acceptable level of these biologically rooted 'functionings' can vary according to time and place. Mindful of Adam Smith, for clothing this might be limited to a utilitarian minimum (enough to provide adequate protection against local weather conditions); but it could also include elementary social desiderata (clean clothing every day, which is not visibly worn out).

In addition, in order not to be poor a person must be able to meet the material obligations ensuing from the formal institutions of the community in which they live. In terms of the figural model from chapter 2, this relates especially to the rules which regulate government production, and private contracts that have been ratified officially (third-party recognition). Put simply: if a government levies taxes and social security contributions in order to pay for certain provisions, or makes it mandatory for people to take up medical insurance with a private company, this generates financial obligations which are almost impossible to avoid. If a citizen evades them he or she infringes the formal rules, and risks formal penalties if this defection comes to light (fines, dismissal, imprisonment); and possibly, by extension, negative informal sanctions, such as reputation damage.

Finally, to avoid poverty people must also be able to meet the (quasi-)universal material obligations associated with the informal institutions of their community, the infringement of which may have serious repercussions. It may be that there is considerable latitude in the way people are expected to dress, and that even a large deviation from the convention attracts no greater sanction than a curled lip or raised eyebrow. In such a community, it is not necessary to wear specific and possibly expensive clothes. However, where strict dress codes apply, and even a slight deviation from the standard brings great disadvantage (positions that become unattainable, public ridicule, expulsion from the peer group), a certain way of dressing may be considered a minimally necessary aspect of life. This can happen, for example, with school uniforms. If these are a *de facto* condition for being admitted to a mainstream secondary school, parents who cannot afford to buy a uniform for their children are poor.

2. *Poverty implies that it is impossible to attain the minimum communal necessities with the available resources.*
Following the capability approach, it is theoretically useful to conceptualise poverty as a lack of freedom: the inability to achieve the minimum that is indispensable in a given

community. It is not a matter of whether someone actually possesses all minimum necessary goods and services, but rather whether they could in principle achieve the prevailing minimum standard given their means of support.

There is a connection here with theoretical resourcism. It was noted earlier that it is 'fetishistic' to assess poverty by the presence or absence of resources if no link is made with the living standard that can be achieved with a certain income, financial assets, or education level. Thus it theoretically makes little sense to regard resources as an element of minimal necessities. However, if the latter have been specified, the available resources do offer an indication for the ability to achieve them. If a substantial part of the population has too little to eat, this can only be described as poverty if it is due to a lack of income, low yields from subsistence farming or home production, or a shortfall in other resources. However, if hunger ensues from widespread anorexia nervosa, the mass following of diets or compliance with religious rules dictating fasting (whereas those concerned have the resources to feed themselves), one would not wish to regard this as an indication of poverty.

3. *Poverty entails deficits in relation to an absolute standard.*
As argued by Sen, poverty is not about relative disadvantage. A person who is unable to realise the minimally necessary aspects of life of the community in which they live is poor, regardless of their position relative to others. Of course it is fairly likely that the risk of 'absolute' poverty will in many cases be greatest for those with a relatively low position on the central stratification ladders in their community (people with a comparatively low income, level of education, job prestige). However, this is not a one-to-one relationship: it is theoretically perfectly possible that even those on the lowest incomes are not poor, because they are able to achieve the minimum necessities.

It is important to stress that the absolute standard is flexible; it relates to what is minimally necessary within a community at a certain point in time. What is required for adequate shelter today in the Netherlands, Sweden or the USA, must not be assessed against the yardstick of housing conditions in 1900 or of the slums of Calcutta.

The absolute standard can change due to modifications in the formal and informal institutions (e.g. taxes may go up, the norms for socially acceptable housing may rise), but also due to developments in supply and demand (higher rents due to housing shortages) or technological innovations (the rise of the Internet is making it increasingly necessary to be connected). A general change in the level of prosperity (e.g. a real increase or decrease in median disposable income) does not of itself however mean that the poverty line has to be adjusted.

4. *A threshold value for the absolute standard can be identified if the minimum communal necessities can be valorised in terms of the available resources.*
It was concluded earlier that theoretical solutions for the problem of establishing a poverty threshold, such as the decision a rational young person would take on a hypothetical insurance market, or application of the maximin principle by a rational actor behind the 'veil of ignorance', are not satisfactory in all respects. The universalistic pretension is

especially problematic: any adequate solution for the threshold-setting problem demands that a limit is chosen which reflects the situation of real actors in real communities.

Given the above principles, a threshold value may be determined if it is clear what the minimal necessities are within a community, and what resources are needed in order to obtain them. This valorisation can be carried out for example by assessing the price of a certain minimum basket of goods and services and translating this into the net income required for its purchase. However, theoretically it is not self-evident that such a valorisation will be possible. If the minimal necessities in a given community also include things which are inherently difficult or impossible to observe (e.g. the frequency with which a person's aura turns dark brown must be minimised),[18] it will be impossible to identify what resources this requires. Similarly, if the available resources are unclear – for example in a community which does not recognise individual property and which does not grant rights of access to collectively owned goods and services – the valorisation is problematic. In such cases no threshold value separating the poor from the wealthier people can be established, and the degree of poverty cannot be assessed.

6.2.2 A theoretical definition of poverty

Based on these principles, poverty can be defined as follows:
An individual actor is poor if he consistently lacks the means to obtain the minimum necessities of his community.

What the 'minimum necessities of one's community' are was elucidated in the discussion of the first principle. A few other elements in the definition may require some explanation, however. First and foremost, poverty is interpreted as a characteristic of individual actors. Collective actors as described in chapter 2 (companies, the government) can thus not be poor. In principle, poverty is also not a trait of sets of individual actors, i.e. groups or communities; the theoretical reasoning behind this is that these cannot perform acts and can therefore not experience behavioural constraints due to a lack of means.[19] If so desired, such social entities can be called 'poor' when a substantial part of the group or community is unable to obtain the minimum necessities. However, this is then an aggregation of the poverty of the individual members, rather than a trait of the group or community as such. Empirically, there may be a high probability that all members of a household, an extended family or a particular caste will be poor; yet theoretically this cannot be taken for granted. It is possible that the available resources within such an entity are unequally distributed (a parent who goes without a meal so that the children can eat; a family head or clan leader who claims a high share of the limited collective means), or that some household members have specific necessities (for example because a child suffers from an illness for which the family cannot afford the medicines).

In a similar vein, countries are not necessarily poor if their national income is considerably less than elsewhere, or distributed more unevenly. They may be called poor if the means at the collective level are in principle not sufficient to meet the minimum necessities of each and every citizen; or if these means would be sufficient to achieve this goal had they not been allocated in such a skewed fashion that many people cannot fulfil their basic requirements, while others prosper. In both cases, however, ultimately it is the situation of individual actors that is decisive; a country can only be considered poor if its aggregate number of persons living in poverty is high.

In a different way communities are important in arriving at a demarcation of poverty as carriers of informal rules. In the definition, their 'rule-setting capacity' is reflected in the linkage of poverty to the minimal necessities as perceived within the community.

As stated, 'lack' must be interpreted absolutely: a person who does not have sufficient means to obtain the minimum communal necessities is poor, regardless of whether he is the only one or is one of many. When establishing the existence of poverty it is desirable to make a statement about the required duration of the absolute deficit. Describing someone who is short of money for a day or week as poor carries little conviction; therefore the deficit should be consistent. This means a longer period has to be taken as a basis, for example a calendar year. Where the deficits stretch over multiple years one can speak of 'protracted poverty'; if people move in and out of poverty over the years, this can be described as 'shuttle poverty'.

When it comes to means, the focus is on those resources which can be converted into economic value at short notice. They comprise the total of income from wages, profits and social security transfers, assets and income from assets, subsidies received, benefits in kind and home production (such as self-cultivated fruit and vegetables, subsistence farming). Even where such resources are obtained informally or illegally, they should in principle be taken into account. A drug dealer who has a lot of money obtained on the black market is not poor from a theoretical standpoint, although given the obvious observation problems it will generally be difficult to establish this empirically. Individual actors can in practice pool their resources within a certain group (e.g. a household), but this is theoretically not necessary.

Not all resources to which actors have access are relevant for poverty. A high education level, an attractive appearance or extensive social networks are only important to the extent that they increase the resources that can be deployed economically. This may be the case, for example, where an actor is able to obtain a well-paid job because of their qualifications, or is able to find work as a photographer's model because of their beauty, or if donations and bartering occurs within a group of relatives.

In the definition, the term 'obtain' signifies that actors in principle have access to the necessities via their available resources, not that they actually possess or consume those necessities. This is an expression of the second principle. It aligns with the emphasis placed on freedom of choice by the capability approach, and with the premise of resourcism that poverty has to do with universal opportunities to lead a minimally acceptable life, irrespective of the lifestyle individual actors would in fact prefer or adopt.

The definition deliberately says nothing about the voluntary or involuntary nature of poverty. In the approach chosen here, if deficits are self-inflicted it does not imply that people are not to be regarded as poor. If a person is not willing to work and ends up with too few resources, they are in principle poor. It is plausible that in such cases the community will take the view that the deficits should not be compensated, or at least not fully, from collective means. This does not however alter the fact such people are not able to attain the minimal communal necessities; and in that sense they have to be classed as poor. Their poverty has a clear reason, and an attempt can be made to show this by drawing a distinction between 'guilty' and 'deserving' poor – though in many cases it will not be simple to establish clear criteria for this, or to assess the guiltiness of individual actors. Theoretically, however, such a distinction is of secondary importance.

6.2.3 Poverty, inequality and social exclusion

Following on from this definition, it is important to indicate how poverty relates theoretically to two other concepts, namely inequality and social exclusion.[20] In chapter 2 it was argued that social inequality refers to the allocation of social positions and to the distribution of scarce goods at a given moment. As such, it is the outcome of the differentiation and ranking of groups in terms of the prevailing principles of hierarchy in the community (the social structuring process) and the growth and distribution of wealth (the economic process).[21] Income inequality is a specific manifestation of this. Poverty is related to such forms of inequality, but cannot be equated to them theoretically; a distinctive difference is that poverty refers to absolute deficits in relation to the minimal necessities, whereas inequality is by definition concerned with relative differences. In practice, a certain correspondence is to be expected between those in poverty and those who are at the bottom of the social ladders, but this is not theoretically necessary: in an egalitarian community mass poverty may occur, while in a country with great inequality but a high level of prosperity poverty may be virtually non-existent.

Since the second half of the 1990s, combating social exclusion has become an important element of policy in the European Union.[22] It is one of the goals set out in the Lisbon Strategy that was introduced in 2000. This obliged member states to frame their policy efforts in National Action Plans against poverty and social exclusion (subsequently renamed 'NAP-inclusion'), and led to the adoption of a set of quantitative measures to monitor their progress (the 'Laeken Indicators').

Historically, the theoretical distinction between social exclusion and poverty runs parallel to developments in the French and Anglo-American scientific tradition. The French school builds on Durkheim's (1897) theories on social cohesion and solidarity, the importance of normative integration and the risk of social alienation (anomie). This perspective tends towards the concept of social exclusion, which, according to Paugam (1996: 13-14), became a key issue in the 1990s after the new social assistance law (RMI) was introduced in France (see chapter 5). Poverty is still the dominant issue in the Anglo-American literature, where it is a separate line of research in the economic analysis of income distribution (Atkinson & Bourguignon, 2000). It is also prominent in the British sociological tradition which builds on Runciman's (1966) theory of relative deprivation, and in American studies of the inner-city underclass (Wilson, 1987, 1997; Small & Newman, 2001).

In the literature several theoretical distinctions between poverty and social exclusion are mentioned (cf. Room, 1995a, 1995b; Berghman, 1995; Saraceno, 1997, 2001; Littlewood et al., 1999; Hills et al., 2002). An important difference is that the aspects of life to which poverty theoretically relates are rather limited (a consistent lack of the means required to obtain the minimum necessities of one's community), whereas social exclusion would refer to a broader set of deficits (such as social isolation, a low work ethic, non-recognition of the rights of citizenship, etc.). One might thus be socially excluded without being poor, and vice versa; and indeed, in empirical work, the correlation between a low of income and several features of social exclusion often is not particularly strong (Gallie & Paugam, 2000; Saraceno, 2001).[23]

Jehoel-Gijsbers (2004) and Jehoel-Gijsbers & Vrooman (2007) therefore propose a direct definition of social exclusion, which separates it from the poverty concept. In their view, social exclusion may be conceived of as a state which reflects the economic-structural and socio-cultural positions of individuals in a community.[24] This implies that social exclusion refers to an actual situation, rather than a possibility; and that it is an inherently relative concept, while poverty as defined here is absolute. The authors suggest four theoretical sub-dimensions of social exclusion:
- actual material deprivation and financial hardship, such as non-possession of consumer durables, problematic debts and payment arrears;
- inadequate access to social rights provided by government and semi-government provisions. This includes obstacles to health care, education, housing, legal aid, social services, debt assistance, employment services and social security, but also to commercial services such as banking and insurance (e.g. not being able to obtain a loan);
- insufficient social participation: limited social networks, inadequate social support and social isolation;
- cultural non-integration: a lack of compliance with norms and values associated with citizenship, such as a weak work ethic, a low willingness to become sufficiently educated, tolerance of social security abuse and tax evasion, delinquent behaviour, and deviating views on children's education and the rights and duties of men and women.

In an empirical study conducted in the Netherlands, Jehoel-Gijsbers (2004) found three reliable sub-dimensions, which could be added together to construct a general index for social exclusion.[25] A causal model showed social exclusion, thus measured, to be mainly determined by health, income, benefit recipiency and command of the native language. Similar results were obtained in cross-comparative analyses based on a more limited set of social exclusion indicators (Jehoel-Gijsbers & Vrooman, 2008a, 2008b). This suggests that a theoretical distinction between social exclusion and poverty makes sense empirically. The concepts relate to different phenomena, each with distinct underlying causal mechanisms, and for that reason should not be equated.

6.3 Granting rights to the poor

A further question concerns the rights that should in principle be granted to the poor; as stated, this is a 'What ought?' question. From a sociological point of view it is doubtful whether a satisfactory solution can be derived from the theoretical poverty debate in political philosophy with regard to the issues discussed earlier – the need to compensate for deficits, the government's responsibility in this regard and the best ways to condition deficit compensation. This will be illustrated here using the analysis put forward by Coleman (1990), as discussed in chapter 2. His central postulate is that there is in principle no 'right division of rights'.

6.3.1 Compensatory rights

If we follow Coleman's argumentation, the question of whether compensatory rights should be granted to poor people is always an endogenous question, which can only be answered from within a certain system of action. Rights and the associated obligations, conditions and sanctions are always social constructs that apply within a given historical community. How this institutionalisation takes place in practice, as was argued in the earlier theoretical analysis, depends on changes in relative prices, power relations, conflicts of interest and support for ideals within the community.

Rawls and Dworkin, by contrast, deliberately choose an exogenous theoretical standpoint in their thought experiments (the 'original position', the residents of an uninhabited island). They ask which rights and obligations an abstract individual would want to assign, regardless of membership of any historical community. In that situation there are no predetermined formal and informal rules which have to be taken into account, the power relations are equal, there are no ideals, and relative prices initially play no role. Interests are important in the allocation of rights and obligations, but only in a very generic way; they do not ensue from personal talents, experiences and handicaps on the part of real actors within a specific community, but are ascribed to an abstract rational actor who is completely unaware of the actual circumstances.

In Coleman's view, such attempts at 'objectification' are fairly meaningless in the practice of social systems. There is no reason whatsoever why the members of a particular community should accept the outcomes of the hypothetical insurance market or the judgments made behind the veil of ignorance as a moral higher ground. They *may* do this; but then these are philosophically motivated ideals, which are in principle not of a different order from, for example, the expected salvation that drives Christian charity. From the perspective of the theoretical institutional analysis, it is not self-evident that poverty should be regarded as a social problem which has to be combated by granting certain rights. If there is a consensus in the community that only the strongest should survive, within that system it may be considered legitimate to leave the poor to languish – just as in certain social contexts actors may regard the duty to commit suicide or the offering of human sacrifices as justified. Such a consensus may arise if the 'incentives to regulate' identified in chapter 2 foster this. This is the case, for example, if powerful groups believe they can profit from large-scale poverty (e.g. because of the cheap labour); if the poor are completely powerless (no suffrage, no possibility for migration); if the dominant ideals regard poverty as the natural state of certain groups (as in a fatalistic religion or caste-based society); or where the poor are not able to defend their interests (ban on trade unions, repression of social protest).

However, the same critical comments can be stated here as were levelled earlier at Coleman's ethical relativism. Individual actors cannot interpret what constitutes poverty as they see fit, or decide independently what is a fair way of dealing with poverty. They are tied to the view that prevails in their community, and often perceive this as natural. It is also possible that certain notions of poverty acquire more or less universal status, forcing governments to combat the phenomenon in a certain way. This has in fact happened to a certain extent in the European Union over the last ten years, via the formulation of targets and action plans aimed at combating poverty and social exclusion. Also worth noting is that in most Western societies empirical data show a good deal of support among the population for some form of deficit compensation by the community.[26]

6.3.2 The role of the government

If people wish to grant rights to the poor, it is also by no means self-evident that the government should play a central role in this. This is clear from the simple fact that poor relief and other forms of social security initially consisted mainly of family and communal arrangements, as discussed at length in chapter 3. The theoretical conditions for regulation by the government were however present in most Western countries from the end of the 19th century, so that in practice social security rights were increasingly formally institutionalised (see §3.7). Even so, a strong government role is not a natural law, but is the outcome of a lengthy rule-generation process in a specific historical context, with variations between nations in its course and the results it produces. A salient point here is that over the last decades in many countries the scope of government intervention was actually reduced in a number of respects: lower benefits of shorter duration, more attention for activation and integration of benefit recipients, targeting of social security rights at the most needy groups, growing importance of individual and occupational social security arrangements. This underlines the fact that the rights guaranteed by the government are fluid even in a prosperous society, although the conditions for some kind of government regulation are often present. Once again, empirical research does show that a considerable share of the population of prosperous societies consider some government responsibility for combating poverty as desirable, though this does vary from group to group: some social categories are more deserving than others.[27]

6.3.3 Conditioning

Coleman's statement that there is no 'right division of rights' can also be extrapolated to apply to the conditioning of the rights of the poor. Whether deficits are compensated only under certain conditions is something that is determined endogenously, and can therefore not be seen separately from the community that establishes the rules. Thus, the 19th-century 'Regulations governing the provision of care to the home-dwelling poor in the town of Den Bosch' discussed in chapter 1 attached conditions to poor relief that were not uncommon at the time, but which are rarely found in modern welfare states. For instance, the then poor were not eligible for assistance if they could obtain support from their town of birth if this was somewhere other than Den Bosch, and the officials could exclude them from poor relief for "any ground deemed valid". In modern formal social security schemes, too, the conditioning is found to vary according to time and place. For example, countries operate differing work and means tests in their social assistance regulations, and these need not remain constant over time; in recent decades such conditions have in many cases been tightened up. Self-inflicted deficits may wholly or partly be covered by collective compensation, but this is not inevitably so. Examples are cases of 'culpable unemployment' (where a person has quit their job themselves, or has been fired for misconduct), or people who have landed in precarious financial circumstances because they have taken on debt in what is regarded as an irresponsible manner. Although these people may be poor, the community may not wish to compensate them for this and can specify this in its conditioning of rights.[28]

It follows from this institutionalist view that there is little to be gained from trying to settle the problem of poverty once and for all through a granting of compensatory rights that is considered universally fair, a standard demarcation of the government interventions this requires and a specification of conditions that should apply in all circumstances. Rather, it is important to investigate how the goal of combating poverty has actually been institutionalised in diverse socio-historical contexts, and what effects this has on the actors concerned and on the community to which they belong. That is a sociological, not a philosophical issue.

6.4 Operational poverty lines

Obviously, a general conceptualisation is not enough if one wishes to study poverty empirically. The size and composition of the poor population is determined by the way in which the concept is operationalised in an observable variable. All manner of such operational poverty lines are used in empirical research, each of which will be analysed here on the basis of a typology. Four criteria are applied to assess their suitability:
- validity: does the operational poverty line adequately cover the theoretical content of the concept as laid down in the principles and the definition? In Northrop's (1947) terms: is it plausible that the observable 'poverty concept by intuition' shows sufficient correspondence with the theoretical 'poverty concept by postulation'?[29]
- reliability: does the operational poverty line allow accurate measurements to be made of the incidence of poverty?
- ease of application: is the operational poverty line simple to calculate for households in diverse circumstances and different countries? Can it be established using fairly general, regularly available data? Can it be easily adapted to changing social circumstances, such as growing or decreasing national prosperity?

– social and policy relevance: is the operational poverty line normatively credible for the community to which it relates and for those who are involved in policymaking?

The latter point may require some explanation. As poverty often is a key topic of discussion in the political arena, it is desirable that a poverty criterion should to some extent be normatively convincing for policymakers, the media and a notable group of citizens. An operational poverty line which is regarded as scientifically valid and reliable but which is far removed from everyday notions is unlikely to be able to give much direction to the social debate. It will also offer politicians, civil servants and social security organisations little help in formulating and implementing the policy on poverty.

In addition to normative persuasiveness, the more practical requirement can also be imposed that the outcomes generated by a poverty line must not flagrantly contradict the perceptions of the actors concerned. This occurs, for example, if in a prosperous society with a relatively even income distribution a particular poverty line characterises a large share of the population as poor; or where an ordinary citizen observes poverty on a large scale (e.g. many starving children on the streets), whereas the problem is negligible according to the official poverty criterion. Developments over time can also lack credibility for those concerned. This is the case, for example, if the observed poverty according to a particular threshold fluctuates widely, whereas there is little change in the socioeconomic circumstances; or where measured poverty rises sharply when all citizens experience a strong growth in real income.

It should be emphasised that the social and policy relevance is an additional criterion when assessing the quality of a poverty threshold. It is not desirable to operationalise poverty in a completely nominalistic way, in the sense that poverty is whatever policymakers or the *vox populi* take it to be. What is necessary is to seek to ensure that the operational demarcation of poverty corresponds sufficiently with the notions that prevail in the community, among policymakers and officials, though without seeking to insist that all citizens and stakeholders must concur with it.

6.4.1 Notions on poverty among the population

Something more can be said about the normative persuasiveness of different poverty lines on the basis of the scarce empirical research into what the populations of developed societies understand by poverty.[30] It emerged from a series of Australian surveys that most citizens interpret poverty in a fairly restrictive way, tending to associate it with basic necessities rather than higher needs, wide-ranging capabilities or resources; and that they predominantly think of absolute lacks rather than relative deficits.[31] Saunders (2004: 7-8) concludes that, in the eyes of Australians, poverty means

> [...] not having enough to buy basic items, rather than being unable to buy the items that the majority can afford: it reflects need, rather than envy.

The same picture emerges from a Dutch survey in which more than 700 people were asked the open question "What do you understand by poverty?" (Vrooman, 2006; Soede

& Vrooman, 2008b). The largest group (22%) saw poverty as the inability to buy common basic necessities. This 'basic needs' interpretation is reflected in responses such as, "poverty means not being able to buy what you need"; "not being able to do anything extra", or "only being able to afford the absolute necessities". There was also a sizeable group of people with a stricter interpretation. One in 10 respondents felt that poverty only occurred if there was a threat to physical existence in the short or longer term. This category of 'unsustainable subsistence' included people who conceive of poverty as "dying of hunger", or who associate the phenomenon with homelessness. Twice as many people (19%) did not relate poverty to extreme physical indigence, but to a permanent battle to acquire essential goods. According to these 'sustainable subsistence' notions, poverty means that people "have to fight to eat every day", or are dependent on the food bank or charity.

Subjective poverty notions which aim at a higher minimal living standard are rare. A small group (1%) believe that poverty can be said to exist when people are unable to meet higher needs, such as "not being able to go on holiday", or "not having money for nice things". Perceptions of poverty as aspects of social exclusion are also sporadic: 3% associate poverty with "not being able to do things with the people around you", "loneliness", and so on. Notions of poverty relating to capabilities are fairly uncommon as well; only 1% see poverty as "not being free in your choices", "not being able to do things that others can do due to lack of money", etc. Sen's broader capability approach thus appears fairly academic; among the Dutch population, at least, the number of people sharing this view of poverty is negligible.

As in the Australian surveys mentioned above, few people in the Netherlands see poverty in relative terms: only 2% of respondents regard poverty as "lagging behind the rest of the population", or "being well below the modal income". Perceptions in terms of unspecified resources are more common (9%); e.g., "poverty is having too little money and too few possessions". This interpretation is 'fetishistic': poverty occurs whenever people have limited means, but it remains unclear what living standard they are supposed to achieve with those. The remaining responses (33%) in this Dutch survey were fairly mixed.[32]

These outcomes suggest that most people associate poverty more with an absolute lack of necessities rather than with relative shortages. The poverty line is fairly low in the dominant view: whilst it is above the subsistence level, it leaves little room for the fulfilment of higher needs and a broad range of capabilities. In order to be socially credible, a poverty line therefore probably needs to be absolute and rather strict. Of course, it may be that this conclusion does not hold for all modern societies, though the evidence emerging from the Dutch and Australian cases is remarkably similar.

6.4.2 A typology of operational poverty lines

The many operational definitions of poverty encountered in the scientific literature can be classified on the basis of three characteristic differences:[33]

- is poverty determined absolutely or relatively?
- is poverty measured by the available resources or by actual consumption and possession?
- is poverty established objectively or subjectively?

The absolute/relative distinction has already been discussed in §6.1. With absolute poverty lines, people are poor if they are unable to obtain a certain minimum level of necessities, while in relative approaches it is the disadvantage compared with a reference group which is key.[34] As argued earlier, the latter approach is theoretically less desirable for measuring poverty.

Poverty lines based on actual consumption and possession are sometimes described as the 'direct method' (see Sen, 1981).[35] This method involves establishing whether people actually have the minimally required goods or services; if this is not the case, they are regarded as poor. Resources-based poverty lines focus on the issue of whether people have adequate economic means to procure the necessary goods and services, regardless of whether they actually achieve the minimum package. This latter approach most closely matches the theoretical principles outlined above; even so, operational poverty lines based on consumption and possession can sometimes provide useful additional information.[36]

Table 6.1
A typology of operational poverty lines[a]

		Objective	Subjective
Relative	Means based	[a] - lower percentiles of income distribution - *percentage of median or average income*	[b] - relative minimum on income ruler
	Based on consumption and possession	[c] - consumer durables and services - *relative deprivation index*	[d] - common consensual necessities index
Absolute	Means based	[e] - expert budget standards	[f] - *minimum income question (MIQ), subjective poverty line* - *income evaluation question (IEQ), Leyden poverty line* - income satisfaction question (ISQ) - consensual budget standards
	Based on consumption and possession	[g] - food ratios - share of fixed expenditure - total expenditure	[h] - minimum spending question (MSQ) - *consensual necessities index*

a. In italics: commonly used poverty lines.

The terms 'objective' and 'subjective' are commonly used in poverty research, but often cause confusion. In reality, the important thing is whether the norms used to measure poverty are derived from decisions taken by 'outsiders' (e.g. scientists, budget experts or politicians), or whether it is the opinions of stakeholders (citizens, experiential experts) that are decisive. In the first, 'objective' case, people or households are described as poor if they are unable to achieve a minimum level defined by others. In the second, 'subjective' approach, they are poor if they are unable to achieve the standard that they themselves, or the members of their community, regard as the minimum necessary.

Table 6.1 presents the eight types of operational poverty lines obtained when the three dichotomies are combined. This classification builds on the earlier typologies developed by Hagenaars and others (1985, 1987, 1988), De Vos (1991) and Vrooman & Snel (1999). The variants that are commonly used in empirical research are italicised in the table and will be the main focus of the discussion in this section.

6.4.3 Relative poverty lines

Relative operational poverty lines are generally defined by 'outsiders'. Subjective variants are fairly rare and will be treated below; here we will therefore restrict ourselves to discussing the objective relative criteria.

With relative means-based poverty lines (cell a in the table) a person is regarded as poor if they have a substantially lower income than others. According to *percentile definitions*, people who are in the bottom 10% or 20% of the income distribution, for example, are classed as poor. More common are the objective relative approaches in which the poverty line is set at a given percentage of the *average or median*[37] *income* in a particular country. In empirical research, a norm of 50% or 60% is often used.

It is also possible to consider whether a person's actual consumption and possessions deviate from those of the average citizen (cell c in table 6.1). An obvious method is to explore whether households have to do without certain *goods or services* which most people have.[38] Examples might include a washing machine, a car, a telephone, a colour TV, DVD player or personal computer. It may also be relevant to establish whether households are unable to afford certain social activities, such as holidays or membership of clubs or associations.

A more elaborate version of this approach is the *relative deprivation index*, which has become known mainly through the work of Townsend (1979). Here, poverty is interpreted as the relative deviation from a standard consumption pattern. This is established by submitting a list of consumer articles and activities to survey respondents and asking them to indicate whether they have them or are able to undertake them. Among other things, Townsend asked about possession of a refrigerator, having meat on the table at least four days a week, regularly being able to invite family or friends round for a meal, being able to organise a birthday party for the children, but also being able to afford a cooked breakfast. The relative deprivation index is obtained by adding up the number of items which people cannot afford. It is possible to see this as a direct indicator for poverty; however, Townsend himself preferred to measure poverty using a combination of relative deprivation and low income.[39]

Assessment of relative poverty lines

If the first assessment criterion – the validity of the poverty line relative to the theoretical definition of poverty – is applied strictly, these relative poverty lines have to be rejected straight away. In the theoretical demarcation used here, the starting point is that poverty should be measured in terms of an absolute deficit in terms of minimal communal necessities, regardless of the circumstances of others. The relative poverty lines based on consumption and possession are moreover in conflict with the second principle, that poverty refers to the living standard that a person is able to attain given their economic resources. This would quickly end the discussion: following the theoretical principles and definition of poverty argued earlier, relative poverty lines are simply not valid. Moreover, they are not in line with the notions of poverty that prevail among the public (cf. above), which means they generally carry little normative cogency for the actors concerned.

Since some relative poverty lines have proven to be influential in empirical research, however, it will be useful to look more closely at their merits. The *percentile approaches* have the advantage that they are very easy to apply. They can also be regarded as fairly reliable, with the proviso that the measured income is not necessarily a good proxy for the available economic resources – a qualification which also applies to other means-based measures. There is however one specific reliability issue: the poverty rate obtained in this way is a constant rather than a variable. The proportion of poor people remains the same by definition; at most, the composition of the poor population can change. This implies that this criterion lacks credibility and is unusable from a policy perspective: no matter how many measures are taken to combat poverty, according to this criterion they will never lead to a reduction of the problem as observed empirically. Percentile-based poverty lines can at most be used to broadly identify the nature of the poor group, for example if one wishes to map out the evolution in the composition of people at the bottom end of society.

In its 'Laeken indicators' the European Union takes 60% of median income as the central criterion for measuring poverty and social exclusion. The *relative income threshold* therefore is of major policy importance, being used as a touchstone for the success or failure of the social policy of the member states. This threshold is easy to calculate and, unlike the percentile approach, does not invariably produce the same outcomes. Advocates of this approach often see it as an advantage that there is an automatic correction for differences in prosperity between different countries; when measuring poverty through this criterion, some allowance is made for the fact that per capita GDP in the Scandinavian countries, for example, is higher than in the Mediterranean states.

However, from the perspective of the theoretical definition of poverty advocated here, the relative income threshold is invalid in two respects. Since it is the income differential relative to the average citizen that is decisive, the poverty issue is equated to an issue of distribution. As a result, this operational poverty line refers more to the concept of income inequality than to the notion of poverty theoretically postulated here; in other words, it is "inequality in disguise" (Van Praag & Ferrer-i-Carbonell, 2004: 295).[40] Moreover, the relative income criterion completely ignores the extent to which people with an income at the threshold level are able to obtain the minimal communal necessities. To use Sen's terms, therefore, this criterion is by definition 'fetishistic'.

The reliability of relative income thresholds is equally unconvincing. The proportion of poor people measured depends on the reference group selected (the average or median citizen) and the distance relative to that group (e.g. 60%), both of which are arbitrary choices. It would be just as defensible to choose a higher or lower income group as the yardstick, or to take different threshold amount (e.g. 40%, 50% and 70% of the median, as in the EU's 'secondary indicators'). If this leads to divergent trends or rankings of countries in terms of the incidence of poverty, there is no substantive argument on the grounds of which one outcome should be chosen above another.

Another objection is that the relative poverty line does not comply with Sen's (1976) 'focus on the poor' axiom. He argued that the degree of observed poverty should depend solely on the resources of the poor themselves, and must not be influenced by the income and wealth development of the non-poor. If the relative threshold is derived from the median,[41] the poverty rate will rise if there is a real increase in median incomes and lower incomes lag behind. This can lead to counter-intuitive findings, especially in times of major shifts in prosperity levels. If these increase sharply, as happened in Ireland in the 1990s,[42] median incomes often rise more in real terms than the lower incomes. Although the standard of living of those on lower incomes improves in this case, there will still be an increase in measured poverty.

A final reliability issue is the ceiling effect that may affect median-based relative poverty lines. If one uses median income as a point of reference, the level of relative poverty can by definition never rise above 50%,[43] and in practice the ceiling often lies at around 30%. Poverty that occurs on a very large scale can thus not be reliably established using this criterion.

The social and policy relevance of relative income thresholds is limited. The outcomes can sometimes lack credibility for those concerned. The Irish example in the 1990s has already been mentioned, but the enlargement of the EU to accommodate 12 new member states in the period 2004-2007 is also illustrative in this respect. Some new member states in Central Europe traditionally combine a flat income distribution with a low median income. As a result, the degree of relative poverty in the Czech Republic is comparable to that in Sweden and the Netherlands; Slovakia and Hungary end up close to Germany and France, while Lithuania has the same share of poor people as the United Kingdom. In some of the new member states, however, the material hardship which people report is much greater (Vrooman, 2007, 2008b), as would be expected given their lower per capita GDP.[44]

The criterion is also problematic from a policy perspective. As long as the bottom incomes are distributed sufficiently uneven, through the relative threshold poverty will be detected. This gives policymakers a rather perverse incentive: in order to combat poverty it is always best to take measures which transfer income from the median citizen to the poorer classes. However, in countries with a comparatively low level of prosperity, it may be a more effective strategy to tackle poverty by maximising economic growth and accepting a somewhat greater income inequality, as long as the poor benefit sufficiently from the increasing prosperity.

Figure 6.1 illustrates some of the limitations of the relative threshold. On the y-axis, the poverty rate based on the 60% threshold is plotted for 38 countries, where available at six moments in the period 1980-2003. The data are drawn from the Luxembourg Income Study (LIS) and the European Community Household Panel Survey (ECHP). In total there are 150 observations, 63 of which relate to the 11 countries that are the central focus of this study.[45]

The figure shows that relative poverty does indeed correlate strongly with the degree of inequality, which is plotted on the x-axis. The correlation coefficient between the Gini indicator of inequality and the relative poverty rate is 0.89. This is thus a strong relation, but not perfect. For example, the proportion of people below the relative threshold given a Gini coefficient of 0.28 is between 10% (Luxembourg 2000) and 19% (Canada 1981); and 15% relative poverty corresponds with Gini-scores of between 0.24 (Denmark 1994) and 0.32 (Hungary 1992).

The ceiling effect is also clearly visible in the graph. If income inequality reaches higher levels, the poverty rate no longer rises proportionally, and the relationship between the two ceases to be linear. The empirical ceiling lies far below the theoretical maximum (50%). In Russia, Mexico and Turkey relative poverty is between 25% and 28%, which is much lower than would be expected based on the linear relationship of poverty and inequality in the other countries.

The *relative deprivation indices* put forward by Townsend and his followers are less fetishistic than the relative income thresholds. These types of indices generally include indicators for the ability to meet basic needs such as food and shelter. This increases the validity of this criterion, which is also fairly simple to apply in research (though it does require a dedicated data collection). The reliability and social credibility are however more questionable.

First and foremost, the measurement of deprivation is fairly limited. Relative deprivation indices are generally constructed on the basis of surveys, and these do not provide sufficient scope to include a complete budget, with detailed items for clothing, housing, social participation, and so on. The researcher thus has to select from the different possible necessities, and that selection may not be representative, but may reflect the researcher's own cognitive frame and moral bias.

In addition, when constructing the index, equal weights are often assigned to each of the different necessities; yet theoretically it is not self-evident that the inability to pay

Figure 6.1
Relative poverty and income inequality in 38 countries, 1980-2003[a]

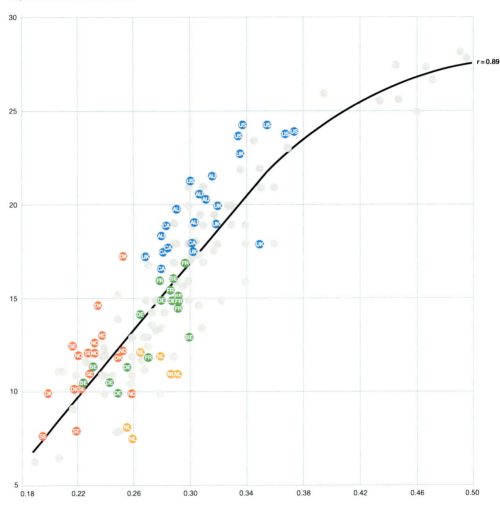

— Regression line
● Liberal: AU, CA, UK, US
● Corporatist: BE, DE, FR
● Social-democratic: DK, NO, SE
● Hybrid: NL

a. 5-year intervals: circa 1980, 1985, 1990, 1995, 2000, 2002/2003

Other countries: Austria (4 years included), Bulgaria (2), Croatia (1), Cyprus (2), Czech Republic (4), Estonia (2), Finland (5), Greece (3), Hungary (4), Ireland (4), Israel (5), Italy (4), Latvia (1), Lithuania (1), Luxembourg (5), Malta (1), Mexico (5), Poland (5), Portugal (2), Romania (3), Russia (3), Slovakia (4), Slovenia (2), Spain (5), Switzerland (4), Taiwan (5), Turkey (1)

Sources: Eurostat; Luxembourg Income Study

the electricity bill should weigh as heavily as having to cut back on going out. The index also takes no account of household-specific variations. A washing machine may be indispensable for a large family, whereas for a young single person looking for a partner being able to visit a bar may be regarded as crucial. There is also a problem with deviating preferences. If there are groups which do not want to have certain things, this influences the measured relative deprivation, whereas they may not see themselves as deprived. Examples include vegetarians who do not wish to eat meat, deaf people who have little use for a CD player, strict Protestants who do not want a TV, and older children who no longer want to have a birthday party.[46]

Once the individual items have been combined to form a single index, there is no convincing procedure for determining a threshold which separates the poor from the non-poor. In the original list compiled by Townsend (1979: 250-251), which contained 12 items, a score of 5 to 6 was regarded as "highly suggestive of deprivation". However, it is unclear why this should be the case; and this logically implies that the poverty rate is heavily dependent on the limit the researcher prefers.[47]

Finally, comparisons over time or between countries are often problematic using this measure. If certain consumer durables were once commonplace but have become out-of-date (e.g. a record player), non-ownership of those products initially may have been indicative of poverty, but has taken on a different meaning over time. Similarly, some items have divergent connotations in different countries. It may even be impossible to present them to foreign respondents in a meaningful way: Townsend's 'cooked breakfast' and 'a Sunday roast joint', for example, are eminently British concepts.

These shortcomings make objectively established relative deprivation indices vulnerable to criticism by other experts, policymakers and citizens. Depending on the decisions taken by the researcher, the percentage of deprived people may fluctuate widely, and sometimes rises to implausibly high levels. With a selection of six items, Townsend (1979: 252) found that 20% of British households were relatively deprived. For the Netherlands, Berghman et al. (1988: 33), using a comparable index, counted no fewer than 38% poor households in 1985. The socio-political credibility of such measures tends to be limited.

6.4.4 Subjective poverty lines

In the subjective approach the poverty line is not established by researchers or experts, but is determined (indirectly) by the respondents themselves. This often takes place via surveys. The oldest example of this methodology has been part of the American Gallup Poll since 1946, and seeks to ascertain what respondents consider to be the minimum cost of living for a standard family.[48] There are many variations of such *absolute, means-based* subjective poverty lines (cell f in table 6.1). The most usual formulation is the Minimum Income Question (MIQ): "We would like to know which net family income would, in your circumstances, be the absolute minimum for *you*. That is to say, that you would not be able to make ends meet if you earned less". Based on this question, there are several ways of arriving at a poverty line. The simplest is purely subjective, by simply comparing the actual income of a survey respondent with the minimum income they consider necessary (see e.g. Vrooman & Hoff, 2004: 27-28; Thijssen & Wildeboer Schut, 2005: 46-48). This is also known as the 'individual method'. An alternative is to take the average amounts given in response to the MIQ for different types of households. These amounts can then be regarded as the group-specific poverty lines, hence the term 'group method' that is sometimes used here.

The subjective poverty line (SPL) developed by Dutch researchers goes a step further. Here, the thresholds are estimated on the basis of a regression analysis, in which the amounts given in response to the MIQ are related to actual income and household composition. Including this latter characteristic means the model automatically delivers threshold amounts for different types of household[49] (see Goedhart et al., 1977; Kapteyn et al., 1985, 1988).

An alternative approach developed at Leyden University uses the Income Evaluation Question (IEQ) (Van Praag, 1971; Van Praag & Kapteyn, 1973; Goedhart et al., 1977). Here, respondents are asked to indicate which income levels they regard as 'very bad', 'bad' 'insufficient', 'sufficient', 'good' and 'very good'. It is then possible to calculate a welfare function of income (WFI) for each respondent, which shows the relationship between the verbal qualifications and the income amounts cited. Here again, the norm amounts for various household types can be derived through a regression analysis;[50] the resultant equivalence scale (see §6.7.2) is however usually much less steep than with the objective methods.

A third variant uses the Income Satisfaction Question (ISQ), in which respondents are asked to indicate how they assess their own current income.[51]

Another absolute means-based method does not use survey questions, but aims to develop *consensual budget standards* (Walker, 1987: 220-225; Middleton, 2000; Bradshaw et al., 2008). This involves the ascertainment of a detailed minimum standard budget for various household types. Unlike the objective expert method (see below), it is the opinions of citizens that are decisive (Walker, 1987: 222):

> What is suggested is a 'democratisation' of the budget standard approach ...; or, more accurately, a method for developing a budget standard through a process of public participation.

A citizen's panel first discusses what they consider to be a correct definition of poverty. Once consensus has been reached on this, the panel explores which life style various types of households should be able to obtain in order not to be classed as poor. If this has been agreed upon, the panel members discuss the specific goods and services different households should be able to afford at the minimum level. The individual items are then priced by the researchers, based on amounts charged in the shops and by the suppliers recommended by the panel. This produces a draft minimum budget standard. The panel members discuss this and are allowed to make changes. As a final test, they are asked to assume that the Chancellor of the Exchequer has examined the list and believes the nation cannot afford all these things. The panel are then asked to reconsider the budget once more; they may make further changes, but are not required to do so. The final budget they decide upon can serve as a poverty line.

The consensual budget method has to date been used to only a limited extent, in research on the island of Jersey, in New Zealand and in Canada. Fisher (2001, 2007) provides a discussion of the method. In these studies the approach produced fairly spartan budgets which could certainly not be described as 'wish lists', but which in the eyes of the panel members referred to a minimum without any luxuries:

> Parents felt that their lists represented an absolute basic minimum, and would have been devastated if this was all their own children had.

In the subjective approach to poverty, too, it is possible, rather than asking about the required means, to take the *minimum necessary consumption* (cell h in table 6.1) as a starting point. In American research a simple Minimum Spending Question (MSQ) sometimes is used for this purpose. If people's actual expenditure is below the level that is considered the minimum necessary, they are classed as poor.[52]

An alternative focuses on *consensual necessities*, a method developed by Mack & Lansley (1985: 42). They attempted

> [...] to identify a minimum acceptable way of life not by reference to the views of 'experts', nor by reference to observed patterns of expenditure or observed living standards, but by reference to *the views of society as a whole*.

The consensual standard of living was established by asking respondents in a survey how essential they considered about 30 goods and services. In Mack & Lansley's study, items such as having sufficient heating, an indoor toilet, a home that was free from damp and three meals per day for children were regarded as a necessity by more than 80% of respondents. Things such as having an evening out, having a car and being able to buy a pack of cigarettes every other day scored much lower. People were subsequently asked whether they themselves had the necessities, and if not whether they had to do without them for financial reasons. In the latter case, Mack & Lansley diagnosed an 'enforced lack of socially perceived necessities', their definition of poverty. Households which had to do without three or more of the necessities for financial reasons were regarded by these authors as poor – almost 14% of their British sample from 1983. The threshold value was underpinned by an empirical argument: in the higher income classes there were virtually no households which lacked three or more necessities, and Mack & Lansley concluded from this that such a level had to be involuntary. Unlike in Townsend's approach, this poverty line thus has pretensions of being absolute.

Relative subjective criteria are not commonly found in the literature.[53] There is thus no research tradition in which the poverty line is defined on the basis of preferred income differentials between social groups. Given the central place accorded in international comparative research to the poverty line based on 60% of median income, it is surprising that there is no subjective counterpart to this threshold. The *income ruler method* developed by Bunjes et al. (1977) and elaborated by Szirmai (1986) probably provides the best point of departure for such a poverty line.[54]

Relative approaches are also thin on the ground when it comes to subjective poverty lines based on consumption. An example is a variant of the Mack & Lansley's (1985) method discussed above. With the *common consensual necessities index* (cell d in table 6.1), poverty is established by counting the extent to which people for financial reasons do not possess or consume items that are regarded as essential in their community, and which a large majority of that community do have. Adding this latter requirement transforms the method into a relative consumption standard. In practice, however, such an approach often leads to virtually the same outcomes as the original method put forward by Mack & Lansley.[55]

Assessment of subjective poverty lines

If it is felt that "all 'objective' definitions lack credibility, because poverty is a *feeling*" (Van Praag & Ferrer-i-Carbonell, 2004: 316), then subjective poverty lines are the only way of measuring poverty in a valid manner. That is not the theoretical starting point here, however. Following the earlier definition, a person who consistently does not have the means to acquire the minimal communal necessities is poor, regardless of whether they consider themselves to be so. Even so, subjective perceptions could perhaps provide good approximations of such a state. Unlike the objective relative measures discussed earlier, therefore, not all subjective poverty lines are automatically invalid from a theoretical perspective. The two 'exotic' subjective criteria (the relative minimum on the income ruler and the common consensual necessities index) are however rejected because of their relative character. The Minimum Spending Question[56] and Mack & Lansley's consensual necessities index[57] are also regarded as invalid here on theoretical grounds; they are based on consumption and possessions, while it was argued earlier that such criteria are less suitable as primary poverty lines (though they can sometimes offer interesting supplementary information).

From a theoretical perspective, subjective poverty lines with an absolute, means-based character (cell f in table 6.1) are in principle the most appropriate. Of these, the consensual budget standard method is still rather experimental; only a preliminary evaluation can be made.[58] We will therefore restrict the evaluation here to the 'mainstream' subjective approaches: the Minimum Income Question/SPL, the Income Evaluation Question/LPL and the Income Satisfaction Question. In principle, these are all valid representations of the definition of poverty postulated here. Whether they can be adopted as operational poverty lines depends chiefly on their reliability, ease of application and relevance for the socio-political debate.

One advantage of these methods is that they are fairly simple to use, although the questions do have to be included in surveys – unlike the objective income assessments, they are not standard items in all manner of data sets. A further strong point is that in the advanced variants (SPL and LPL), the equivalence scales do not require arbitrary assumptions by the researcher, but can be derived directly from the answers given by respondents.

The reliability of the subjective income approaches is however limited, as the detailed overview study by Van den Bosch (2001) reveals. His opinion of the *income satisfaction method* is particularly negative. He notes that income satisfaction correlates much less strongly with actual income than would be expected: even the highest income brackets contain a substantial group of people who are dissatisfied. This suggests that satisfaction also depends on the consumption pattern to which people aspire, the financial self-reliance, and personal circumstances (fixed costs, debts, alimony allowances, etc.). Also striking is the asymmetry in the influence of income mutations. Any noticeable increase in income satisfaction requires a considerable improvement in real income; but even a slight income deterioration results in a sharp reduction in income satisfaction. In addition, the responses to the ISQ tend to be much less stable over time than the answers to the MIQ and the IEQ. Van den Bosch (2001: 376) concludes from this that this instrument is not an adequate criterion for measuring poverty:

> In the context of poverty measurement, the income satisfaction method is … clearly unsuitable for the determination of income thresholds.

The reliability of the other subjective income methods is equally unconvincing. With the *Minimum Income Question* and the *Income Evaluation Question* the assumption is that people mean the same thing when they say that a certain income is the 'absolute minimum', 'bad', 'sufficient', etc.; however, this assumption is probably not justified. Research in cognitive psychology has shown that people can attach very different meanings to verbal qualifications of income (Stinson, 1997, 1998; Garner et al., 1998). This is particularly relevant for the MIQ and the derived SPL. If people are asked at which level of income they would not be able to make ends meet, it makes a considerable difference whether respondents think of bare survival or the ability to continue their present lifestyle. In practice, some people are found to apply the first meaning, others the second. Several researchers argue that the IEQ and the LPL based on it are more precise than the MIQ/SPL, because these take into account more income levels. However, this method can also give rise to problems of reliability, as respondents may interpret the contrasting twin concepts in the question differently.[59]

A second measurement problem is that by no means all respondents are able to estimate the required income. Those who run the household finances often have a more realistic picture of income and expenditure than the other household members. This means that variable measurement errors can arise, depending on who completed the questionnaire.[60]

The results of these methods are moreover anything but stable. In the available time series, these subjective thresholds tend to fluctuate considerably from year to year, in a way which is not in line with the trend in economic growth, the average income and other socioeconomic indicators. As a result, poverty rates may also show large mutations over time, often in an apparently capricious way. The measurement problems associated with these methods only increase in international comparative research[61] (Van den Bosch, 2001: 98-110, 297).

It may be felt that the credibility of these subjective methods is high because the input is not provided by experts. However, this needs to be qualified with the comment that the threshold is ultimately still established by the researcher; unlike the consensual budget standard, there is no interaction between the respondents, in which the poverty lines are tested intersubjectively. Walker (1987) therefore argues that the best these methods have to offer is a 'consensus by coincidence'; but in truth there is no way of knowing whether the participants in the survey agree with the threshold amounts established by the researchers.

A more important credibility problem is that these methods can sometimes lead to very high poverty rates in fairly prosperous countries, as was the case with the relative deprivation index. The literature survey compiled by Van den Bosch (2001: 157-158) for the period 1975-1992 shows that poverty rates in countries such as France, Greece, Ireland and the United States according to these criteria[62] can rise above 40%. Strengmann-Kuhn (2004: 23) found that applying the SPL method to the 2001 wave of the ECHP generated poverty incidences of around 18% for the Netherlands and Belgium, 30% for France, 47% for Spain and 75% or more for Italy, Greece and Portugal. Not surprisingly, such high percentages are not regarded as credible by the public and policymakers in these countries.

6.4.5 Objective absolute poverty lines

Objective absolute thresholds have a long tradition. The first studies of poverty which were carried out in England in around 1900 took basic human needs as their starting point. These were generally limited to the purely physical necessities, such as food, clothing and shelter[63] (Seebohm Rowntree, 1901; Booth, 1902 [1889]). In this tradition, households are regarded as poor if their income is insufficient to cover the minimal necessary expenditure for those needs. In the case of food, for example, the cheapest possible food basket is put together which provides the required number of calories.

Theoretically, a broader definition of needs or necessities can be used (cf. Doyal & Gough, 1991).[64] Gradations are therefore sometimes used with these kinds of poverty line; see e.g. Sarlo (2001).[65] Modern empirical research often uses detailed *expert budget standards* (cell e in table 6.1), which have been developed for many countries over the last decades (cf. Fisher, 2007). The British study edited by Bradshaw (1993) has been a particular source of inspiration here. In this approach, the researcher first draws up a detailed list of the goods and services he regards as the minimum necessary.[66] This list includes what different types of households need to eat and to heat the home, and what level of rent they have to pay for an acceptable home, but also includes things like how many winter coats and how much underwear people need, what constitutes an acceptable inventory for the home (furniture, carpets and curtains, linen, kitchen equipment), how often people have to wash clothing, how many insurance premiums and local taxes people have to pay from their income, what they have to spend on memberships, subscriptions, transport and recreation, etc. A realistic price is then assigned to each of these items, and an estimate is made of the quantity a person needs in normal usage. If it is relevant, allowance is also made for the expected life of the item: if a winter coat normally lasts two years, half the purchase price is included each year. By adding up the annual monetary value of all items, standard budgets are constructed for different types of households. If the net disposable income is lower than this standard budget, the household is classed as poor. It makes no difference here whether households actually consume the different budget elements in this way: in the expert budget method, the measurement of poverty usually is means-based.

Less common are objective absolute thresholds which are based on consumption and possession (cell g in table 6.1). A first option is to look at the proportion of total household income which is spent on food. Such a *food ratio* poverty threshold starts from the observation that the higher the income, the smaller the share of food in total household expenditure ('Engel's Law'). If a high proportion of income is spent on food – 30-35% is a common norm – this therefore can be regarded as indicative for poverty. Another option is to look at the share of household income taken by *fixed costs*; these are regular expenses that cannot be avoided, because they ensue from contractual obligations (e.g. rent, water and energy) or government regulations (e.g. co-payments for care provisions, local taxes). A high proportion of fixed costs leaves little room for other expenditure (food, replacement of furniture), and reduces the ability to cope with financial setbacks. Finally, in the *total expenditure* approach, a person is considered poor if they spend more than they receive, or in other words if they have to get into debt or use up their savings in order to make ends meet.

Assessment of objective absolute poverty lines
Here again, poverty lines based on actual consumption and possession can be regarded as an invalid translation of the theoretical definition of poverty discussed earlier. The approaches based on food ratios, fixed costs and total expenditure moreover suffer from a number of reliability problems.[67]

The *expert budget standards* method does however adequately meet the theoretical definition of poverty. It makes explicit what the minimal communal necessities are and is therefore not fetishistic. This also makes it possible to apply gradations to the poverty criterion, for example a subsistence level for the homeless, a basic minimum amount that is needed in order to run an independent household, or a threshold which makes possible social participation and recreation on a wide scale. Moreover, taking the available resources as a basis implies the focus is on the spending possibilities, rather than the actual consumption and possession of goods and services. This largely circumvents the issue of preferences, which is often difficult to resolve with consumption-based poverty lines. Within the theoretical framework adopted here, therefore, this method is valid.
    The social and policy relevance of these types of threshold will also be fairly high. They are in line with the notions on poverty among the public as discussed earlier, and the detailed nature of the individual budget items lends them a high degree of credibility.

But is the method reliable? One objection that is often levelled at the expert budget standards approach is that the researcher by definition determines the standard. Scientific standards exist for only for a few of the budget components (mainly food and housing)

– e.g. minimum standards for a healthy diet – and even those often are debatable. As a result, this 'objective' method can still be normatively tainted: arbitrary perceptions and preferences of the experts involved may influence the number of poor people detected using this method.

This can happen because the researcher is highly educated and has a relatively high income (so may take their own needs as an implicit criterion), because of the researcher's possible ideological bias (wanting to help the poor or to fight injustice), or because of the researcher's own interests (scientific status, wanting to secure research funding). In practice, however, the detailed nature and transparency of the method constrain this discretionary scope somewhat. Unlike the relative deprivation index or the consensual necessities index, for example, this method involves a complete consumption basket, not a limited selection of goods and possessions the absence of which is considered by the researcher to be indicative of poverty. For each item, the researcher should argue why it has to be included in the budget standard in a specific way. If he is conscientious, he will use verifiable decision rules, information on the actual spending patterns of households and the opinions of other budget experts (fellow scientists, social services employees, debt counsellors). It is also possible to have the expert budgets tested by the public, via surveys or by the development of consensual budget standards. This can help keep the influence of researcher bias within bounds.

Adaptivity of the standard is a bigger risk. In practice, budget standards may tend to correlate with the applicable minimum benefits amounts. If benefit levels in a given country are greatly reduced or increased, people at the bottom of the distribution will adapt their spending pattern accordingly, and this can eventually work through into the standard. It is therefore possible that using this method ultimately produces low and fairly stable poverty rates. Sarlo (2001: 35), for example, discusses the results obtained by a 'basic needs' budget approach, and concludes that

> [Poverty in Canada] has not fallen for about the past 20 years. Despite a huge increase in social spending since the 1980s, the poverty rate [...] has apparently settled on a plateau.

It is however not certain that the adaptivity problem will by definition occur.

In terms of applicability, the expert budget method has a number of advantages. The poverty lines for different types of household (compare the discussion of equivalence scales in §6.7.2) are not determined on theoretical grounds, but emerge automatically from the ratios between the established budgets. The method is transparent and flexible: the items in the standard are clearly described, and product innovations, price and volume changes, and increases in national prosperity can in principle be easily incorporated. For example, if rents go up because of housing shortages, the threshold moves to a higher level and the proportion of rent in the budget increases. The same thing happens if quality improvements that are generally regarded as necessary (separate bedrooms for the children, a bath instead of a shower) push up the rent. If incomes do not keep pace with rent increases (after allowing for housing benefit), this will lead to higher poverty rates. In such cases, the underlying causes of the poverty trend can thus be easily identified.

Yet there are also major problems of applicability. Since the available goods and services, prices and spending patterns are constantly changing, the budget standards are never finished. This implies that the poverty line is continually moving, in a sometimes erratic way, which may complicate the analysis of time series; in addition, keeping the standards up to date requires a good deal of work. As a result of their labour-intensive nature, detailed budget standards are generally drawn up for only a limited number of household types, with little differentiation by age, income group, health impairments, region and ethnic origin. If a reference budget is not available for every household, it becomes difficult to establish generic poverty thresholds. Application of the method in international comparisons is even more complicated. Not all countries have developed detailed budget standards, and where they are available, methodological differences often imply that they cannot be used directly for comparative analyses.[68]

6.5 A generalised budget approach

No single poverty line emerges from the overview of operational poverty lines which can be regarded as suitable on the grounds of the criteria formulated earlier. Relative poverty lines are not valid within the theoretical framework employed here. Even if one were prepared to ignore this, there are serious complications with the two most commonly used methods, namely 60% of median income and the relative deprivation index, as regards their reliability and normative credibility. Subjective poverty lines may be valid, but also suffer from measurement problems and regularly generate implausibly high or unstable poverty rates. Although the subjective evaluation of income and spending capacity may generate interesting supplementary information (cf. Vrooman & Hoff, 2004), it provides too weak a foundation to serve as a primary poverty threshold.

Expert-budget standards fit in well with the theoretical definition of poverty proposed here. They are moreover recognisable for the public and policymakers and, if properly implemented, fairly reliable. They are however also very labour-intensive, often leading to a limited differentiation of household types. This makes this method less suitable for use in practical research, especially in cross-comparative analyses of poverty.

This creates a need to search for a poverty line which retains the theoretical and practical advantages of the expert budget method but which is easier to apply. The 'generalised budget approach' developed by The Netherlands Institute for Social Research | SCP (Vrooman & Snel, 1999; Vrooman, 2000; Soede, 2006; Soede & Vrooman, 2007, 2008b) is an example of such a criterion. Here, two detailed minimum budgets are first determined for a single reference household in a given starting year. Using an empirical equivalence scale, this is then generalised to an initial poverty line for all household types. A historical series of threshold amounts is subsequently obtained by applying a dedicated index to the initial norms.

6.5.1 Reference budgets for a single person

The initial level of the poverty line was determined by The Netherlands Institute for Social Research | SCP on the basis of the budgets drawn up by the Dutch National Institute for Family Finance Information (Nibud). Each year, Nibud publishes highly detailed budgets for a number of household types, in which minimum norm amounts are set for all kinds of expenditure items. These norms are based on the opinions of experts (e.g. on the required quantity and quality of food), the availability of goods and services, and actual consumption patterns at the bottom end of the income distribution. The method used by Nibud rests on years of experience and detailed knowledge of the actual expenses faced by households. The Nibud budgets are also used by municipal social services, lenders, debt support organisations, etc.

Based on the detailed budgetary data provided by Nibud, two reference budgets were compiled for a Dutch person living alone[69] (table 6.2). The first variant, the *basic needs* criterion, was based on the expenses that can be regarded as the minimum necessary in the Netherlands. These include costs that are difficult to avoid for things such as food, clothing, housing (including rent, insurance, energy, water, telephone, furnishings, home maintenance and local taxes) and a number of other expenses (transport, extra medical expenses, personal care, washing detergents, etc.). For food, the diets published by The Netherlands Nutrition Centre (*Voedingscentrum*) were used; for clothing purchases, the minimum norm was drawn from the National Textile Barometer (NTexB). The calculation of housing costs was based on the minimum costs for a rented two-bedroom flat. It was assumed that a household is privately insured for medical expenses through a shared contract (e.g. through one's employer), and that the premium has been deducted from disposable income. As a result, only out-of-pocket medical expenses not covered by the insurance were included in the budget. Fire and theft insurance and funeral insurance were deemed to be necessary, and the contributions due have therefore also been incorporated. The amount for transport costs is based on one national multi-journey bus and tram ticket (*strippenkaart*) per month, plus the maintenance and depreciation costs of a bicycle.

The total threshold amount obtained on the basis of these norms covers a minimal, but complete package of expenditure items. As long as no exceptional costs occur which are not reimbursed by the government or insurance companies, the budget is in principle sufficient to run an independent household without incurring debts or becoming dependent on charity (e.g. church social welfare, Food Banks). In order to attain this standard of living, a single person in 2000 needed a total of EUR 667 per month, as table 6.2 shows. If their disposable income is lower than this, they will very probably have too little money in the Dutch context to make ends meet. They can accordingly be described as poor.

The basic needs criterion includes the most necessary expenditure items, but no extras, such as the costs of social participation. The second variant does allow some scope for this. Modest amounts have been earmarked for recreation, membership of a library, sports or hobby club, subscription to a newspaper and magazine, and a pet. The selected items correspond almost exactly with one of the 'residual packages' used in the model

Table 6.2
Reference budgets and poverty lines by family type (monthly amounts in euros, 2000)

	Single	Single parent			Couple	Couple with children			
Number of adults	1	1	1	1	2	2	2	2	2
Number of children	0	1	2	3	0	1	2	3	4
Budget items									
Food and non-alcoholic beverages	142								
Clothing, shoes	32								
Rent	216								
Gas/fuel	30								
Electricity	22								
Water	7								
Local taxes	24								
Telephone	21								
Various insurances (excluding health care)	23								
Furniture, maintenance house	69								
Transport	9								
Uncovered medical expenses	11								
Other	61								
Total = basic needs reference budget	**667**								
Recreation	37								
Public library	2								
Newspaper and magazine	23								
Sport/hobby club	9								
Pet	20								
Total = modest but adequate reference budget	**758**								
Basic needs poverty line									
- with Dutch equivalence scale (Statistics Netherlands)	667	888	1008	1175	914	1115	1255	1375	1522
- with alternative equivalence scale[a]	667	934	1157	1354	1012	1225	1415	1590	1753
Modest but adequate poverty line									
- with Dutch equivalence scale (Statistics Netherlands)	758	1007	1144	1333	1038	1265	1424	1560	1727
- with alternative equivalence scale[a]	758	1060	1313	1536	1148	1390	1606	1805	1990

a. Cf. §6.7.2.

Sources: Soede (2006); Soede & Vrooman (2007, 2008b)

minimum budgets drawn up by Nibud (2006: 50). This *modest but adequate* reference budget includes expenses which strictly speaking exceed that which is unavoidable, but there is no question of luxury, such as a car or foreign holidays. For a single person, the total amount needed to maintain such a lifestyle in 2000 was EUR 758 per month.

6.5.2 Initial poverty lines

The initial poverty lines were subsequently determined by applying equivalence factors to non-single households; these indicate how much more on average, say, a couple with two children of a certain age spend than a single person. The additional expenditure items include extra food and housing costs, but also non-reimbursed school and study fees for children living at home, etc. The equivalence scale for various household types was established empirically by Statistics Netherlands (CBS) by applying the 'budget distribution method' to data from the Dutch Household Budget Survey. With this method, it is first determined what proportion of each expenditure item can be attributed to the individual family members. The additional costs of extra adults and children are then determined using regression analysis; and from this for each type of household ratios to a single person are derived which represent comparable levels of welfare (Siermann et al., 2004). Table 6.2 shows the norm amounts thus obtained for a number of typical household types. It also includes the amounts resulting from an alternative equivalence scale; this is somewhat steeper and will be discussed below.

6.5.3 The indexation method

For comparisons over time, it would be possible to use the updated norm amounts published by Nibud on an annual basis. However, this method can lead to complications if the expert judgment on what is minimally necessary changes markedly over the years, and if the norm amounts consequently have to be adapted. For example, if Nibud in a given year includes a mobile telephone or Internet connection in the minimum household budget, making the basic basket of goods and services more expensive in real terms, this may have saltatorial effects on measured poverty. In order to avoid this, it is preferable to determine the year-on-year evolution of the threshold amounts using a theoretically substantiated indexation of the initial levels. The precise content of the basket of goods and services can then be reviewed at greater time intervals (for example every five or ten years).

In order to be able to map out the development of poverty in the Netherlands over time, the norm amounts from 2000 were indexed using a method recommended by the National Academy of Sciences (NAS) in a report to the US government (Citro & Michael, 1995).[70] The Academy suggested that the poverty line be linked to changes in median expenditure on the basic items food and drink (excluding alcohol), clothing and housing. It was anticipated that this would cause the threshold amounts to rise faster than inflation, but more slowly than a completely relative threshold; the indexation was supposed to be 'quasi-relative'. This is because, with rising incomes and unchanged preferences, people generally spend a declining share of their income on food, clothing and housing. The threshold thus reflects growing prosperity, though not completely.

In line with the NAS recommendations, the indexation was based on the three-year moving average in median expenditure on the basic items. The mutation in the index for 2000 thus reflects the development of real median expenditure in the period 1998-2000. One advantage of this is that the threshold amounts are less sensitive to sample fluctuations and the economic cycle. In addition, the poverty line adapts with a certain time lag to changes in actual spending patterns – just as the social perception of the minimum necessary generally typically reacts with some delay to socioeconomic developments. The index was calculated on the basis of the median expenditure on housing, clothing and food (excluding alcohol) from the Dutch Household Budget Survey. In the period 1990-2000, that expenditure rose by 10% in constant prices, exactly equal to the real increase in the model minimum budgets published by Nibud for those years (cf. Soede, 2006: 53). The changes experts perceive in the budget standard are thus well replicated via the indexation mechanism.

This combination of:
- meaningful initial levels for the reference household in an initial year,
- the derivation of the norm amounts for other household types via equivalence factors,
- and a quasi-relative, delayed indexation based on actual expenditure trends on the basic items

could be described as a 'generalised budget approach'. This retains the conceptual advantages of the expert budget method. The poverty line is not fetishistic and reflects the absolute character of poverty; the current necessities have been specified in the reference budget, and whether or not people are poor does not depend directly on the circumstances of others. As with poverty lines based on the expert budget method, it focuses on people's consumption possibilities rather than their actual consumption. For these reasons, this method can be regarded as a valid operational translation of the theoretical poverty definition.

However, this method is much less labour-intensive than the traditional expert budget method, and can therefore be applied more easily in the practice of research. The norms are fairly simple to calculate for each year and each household type. The threshold amounts do not depend on the verbal qualifications assigned to income by respondents in a survey, so that the method does not suffer from the reliability problems of the subjective poverty lines.

The threshold is probably also normatively credible and transparent for policymakers and the general public. The two variants appear to fit in with the poverty notions of the Dutch population as outlined earlier. The 'basic needs' variant can be seen as a good elaboration of the most common subjective definition of poverty. The 'modest but adequate' variant turns out slightly higher. Together, the two criteria probably provide a plausible bandwidth for the degree to which the theoretical notion of poverty applies to the actual living conditions of the population.

6.5.4 Outcomes of the generalised budget approach in the Netherlands

Figure 6.2 provides some insight into the results obtained using this method. It shows the trend in the norm amounts and poverty rates over the period 1985-2005. The degree of poverty has been assessed via the Dutch Income Panel Study (IPO), a large database (approx. 245,000 individuals in 85,000 households) built from administrative data held by the Dutch tax authorities, the population register and various benefits agencies. For comparison, the trends based on the relative 60%-median criterion and the Dutch low-income threshold (cf. Vrooman & Hoff, 2004) are also shown. The latter is based on the minimum social assistance level for a single person in 1979, adjusted for price inflation;

norm amounts for the other households have been derived by applying CBS equivalence factors.

Because all poverty lines in the graph are in constant prices, and the low-income threshold is indexed to price inflation, the norm amount for this criterion remains constant and appears as a horizontal line. Median income in the Netherlands rose between 1985 and 2005 by roughly a third in real terms, and the relative income threshold level therefore shows the same increase. The norm for the two variants of the generalised budget approach rises in line with collective prosperity, but does not fully keep pace. Over the period as a whole, this amount rises by around a sixth (+17%) in real terms; a quasi-relative development, as expected.

According to the low-income threshold, the poverty rates trend downwards over the period; in 1985, one in five people were poor, while by 2005 this has reduced to 9%. This is mainly because his threshold is indexed only to price inflation, whereas the level of prosperity rose more strongly in the period concerned. Measured against the relative poverty line, the poverty incidence rises sharply between 1985 and 1990, from just over 4% to 9%. It then remains rather stable at 10%, with minor fluctuations. This is in line with the evolution of income inequality in the same period: the Gini coefficient rose in the Netherlands between 1985 and 1991, after which it remained fairly constant (Pommer et al., 2003: 48; Vrooman et al., 2007b: 129).

The poverty rate measured using the 'basic needs' and the 'modest but adequate' variant is lower in virtually all years than that measured using the other two poverty lines. In 1985 the gap compared with low incomes is very wide (14-17 percentage points), but this difference reduces steadily over time. Since the poverty line partially follows the welfare trend, the poverty rate does not show a structurally downward trend. Apart from this, the mutations often move in the same direction as with the low-income threshold, with peaks around the economically weak years 1994 and 2003/2004. The incidences according to the relative poverty line, on the other hand, are not sensitive to the fluctuations in the economic cycle.

Evidently, the poverty rates generated by the basic needs criterion are consistently lower than according to the modest but adequate variant. The trends are broadly similar, with the exception of the period 1995-2000, when the poverty rate based on the basic needs criterion was virtually stable, while according to the modest but adequate variant it fell.
This suggests that those on the very lowest incomes benefited less during that period from the economic upturn than those with a slightly higher income. In addition, it turns out that the composition of the poor population can be readily interpreted in all years, though it is striking that the weight of the working poor in the total increases over time (cf. Soede, 2006; Vrooman et al., 2007b).

All in all, the generalised budget approach seems to offer a plausible picture of the actual evolution of poverty in the Netherlands. In this way, a good insight is obtained into the size and composition of the group whose income is almost certainly inadequate according to current Dutch standards. The trend found is more plausible than the structurally

Figure 6.2
Poverty lines and poverty rates in the Netherlands, 1985 - 2005 [a]

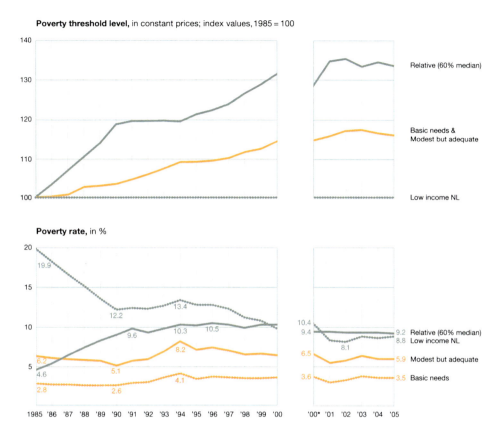

a. Poverty lines in constant prices; poverty rates based on equivalised disposable household income of persons
* In 2000 the Income Panel Study was revised, leading to a fall in median disposable income.

Sources: Dutch Income Panel Study; Dutch Household Budget Survey (Statistics Netherlands); Soede & Vrooman (2008b); adapted

falling poverty rates based on the low-income threshold, or the very even picture suggested by the relative approach. The levels are low, but this is not unexpected in a fairly prosperous country with a rather equal income distribution. It is however not the case that this method defines the poverty problem out of existence: according to the lowest variant, the basic needs criterion, 560,000 people were qualified as poor in 2005; that is one in 25 Dutch citizens, and more than 30 times as high as the client base of the Dutch food banks (approx. 8,000 households in February 2006). Based on the higher 'modest but adequate' variant, still one in 16 inhabitants of the Netherlands qualified as poor.

In the remaining part of this chapter, these two thresholds will be used to test a number of hypotheses concerning the impact of regime types on poverty rates. In principle, the method can also be applied in other countries and in international comparative research.

The royal road would be to determine the initial threshold amounts for the reference household in other countries, too, in accordance with the Nibud methodology; and then to apply suitable national equivalence scales and a similar country-specific indexation mechanism to these. A simple approximation of this can be obtained by translating the Dutch norm amounts to other countries using purchasing power parities, and by applying the same equivalence scale in all countries. For country comparisons over time, the indexation perhaps could be based on expenditure data from the National Accounts. A single-year example of such an approach will be given later in this chapter. First, however, it is important to specify the research questions for this empirical cross-comparative analysis.

6.6 The theoretical relationship between regime types and poverty

The introduction to this chapter gave a brief outline of the different strategies followed in the social-democratic, liberal and corporatist social security regimes to combat poverty. In the first regime type the emphasis is on de-commodification. According to the social-democratic approach, the best way of tackling poverty is to give all residents an entitlement to a guaranteed minimum living standard, regardless of their present or former position on the labour market. In order to finance this, it is desirable that as many people as possible should be active on the labour market: this increases the tax proceeds and the revenue from social insurance contributions, and reduces the costs of benefit dependency.

The liberal strategy is based on the idea of individual responsibility within a market setting. People are expected as far as possible to generate their own present income and their desired future income security (e.g. on retirement) via private arrangements. There is only a limited collective safety net, in the form of a sparse social assistance scheme which is subject to strict conditions and may be limited in duration. Since the government extracts less money from private households and businesses, more remains for consumption and investments. This is supposed to increase the national wealth and jobs growth; and such collective gains will ultimately trickle down to people at the bottom of the income distribution, thus reducing the level of poverty.

The corporatist regime type emphasises the income continuity of the traditional wage earner. Provided people have an adequate employment history, their loss of income in the event of unemployment, retirement or sickness is limited. When these eventualities occur, these insiders can claim high wage-related social insurance benefits. The poverty risk mainly affects outsiders: people who are not or insufficiently covered by the elaborate social insurance schemes. This concerns especially those who have never held a job, who perform low-paid work or who have a short or interrupted employment career (and their dependent relatives). As long as the number of outsiders remains limited, the strategy of the corporatist regime can theoretically also offer a successful means of combating poverty.

Based on these model strategies, it is not possible to say in advance which regime type will in theory generate the least poverty. The wide protection that is the aim of the social-democratic and corporatist strategies may at first sight offer the best recipe for combating poverty, but there is no logically compelling reason for this assumption. It is also conceivable that such comprehensive systems will lead to adverse and unintended economic effects, so that they ultimately produce more poverty (less collective prosperity, destruction of jobs, lower disposable incomes, poverty traps). This is the familiar essence of the neoclassical thesis of the negative impact of the welfare state on the economic process (see chapter 3.6.3). In fact, the strategy of each regime type can for various reasons lay a theoretical claim to the lowest 'poverty production'.

The actual institutional structure in the countries concerned may offer more clues for hypothesising about the relationship between regime type and poverty than the model strategies. On the basis of the scaling procedure it was concluded in chapter 4 that, based on the actual institutional differences, the three regime types can be interpreted in terms of two dimensions (figure 4.1): the scope of social security (residual/ extensive) and the degree of particularism or universalism. The liberal regime type is residual; the corporatist type is extensive and particularistic; and the social-democratic system is extensive and universalistic. In Hempel's (1966) terms, these dimensions can be regarded as an interpreted variant of the theoretical regime construct. The country scores on the two dimensions (figure 4.2) can then be understood as the observed manifestations of the theoretical regime concept, interpreted in terms of divergent formal institutions. Does this 'operational classification' of countries provide any leads about the empirical relationship of regime types and poverty that is to be expected?

In contrast to their postulated influence on benefit production (cf. §5.1), it may be assumed that the two underlying dimensions of the social security regimes theoretically reinforce each other in their impact on poverty. A wide scope on the first dimension means among other things relatively high benefits, of longer duration and with relatively little means-testing. On the second dimension, a universalistic regime implies wide coverage, entitlements that are not linked to the employment history, a social assistance scheme which serves as a fully fledged safety net, and many incentives to work, thus fostering the economic independence of all citizens. These factors may all be assumed to reduce the risk of poverty.

The risk of poverty is therefore likely to be lowest in the social-democratic regime type, as the countries in this cluster combine wide scope with a universalistic structure (see figure 4.2). The Netherlands would be expected to follow at a short distance, because this hybrid regime is slightly less extensive and universalistic. However, the positioning of the representatives of the corporatist and liberal regimes is less clear. The expected poverty risk associated with these regime types depends on the relative weight one assigns to the two dimensions. If they weigh equally heavily, the 'institutionally determined' poverty risk of the corporatist and liberal countries is more or less comparable. The representatives of the corporatist systems are then likely to generate less poverty because of their broader scope, but this is cancelled out by their less universal design. By contrast, if the first dimension weighs more heavily than the second, the poverty risk would in theory be smaller in the corporatist countries than the liberal states.[71] It is therefore not possible to derive an unambiguous theoretical expectation from the scores on the two dimensions concerning the ranking of the 'institutional' poverty risk in all countries studied here.

There are a number of other reasons why the country scores on the two dimensions are less suitable as a basis for deriving theoretical expectations about the extent of poverty in the different regime types. A first problem is that the individual regime characteristics in the earlier categorical principle component analysis (CatPCA) were not scaled by their theoretical significance for the extent of poverty, but purely on the grounds of empirical correlations. Theoretically, it may for example appear plausible that the risk of poverty for people who are not able to work reduces if their benefits are higher and the admission criteria for receiving benefit less stringent. Yet figure 4.1 makes clear that such poverty-reducing regime characteristics can in practice sometimes show a negative correlation. Thus, countries with generous benefits for occupational disability (*risque professionnel*) often put up high barriers for actual take-up, for instance in the form of a minimally required degree of incapacity. From the perspective of the institutional poverty risk as theoretically intended, the scores on the empirical dimensions are thus not by definition optimal.

Another issue is that the relative importance of social security arrangements for the risk of poverty was not made explicit in the earlier analysis. It is for example logical that differences in retirement pension are more important for the poverty risk generated by the different regime types than the various arrangements for parental leave for employees; the potential target group for retirement pensions is bigger, pension benefits are generally utilised for a longer period, and they account for a larger proportion of the total income of the households concerned. However, figure 4.1 shows that the level of maternity benefit, for example, weighs of more heavily on the first dimension of the CatPCA (it has a higher component loading) than the minimum level of collective retirement pensions for non-employees and the gross replacement rates for earnings-related occupational pensions. This does not appear to reflect the theoretical weight of these provisions for combating of poverty adequately.

A final point is more practical in nature. The regime typology in chapter 4 represents the situation in around 1990, whereas here poverty will be analysed for the same countries in around the year 2000. It is desirable to base the theoretical expectation on the relationship between regime types and poverty rates on more recent traits of the formal social security institutions in the 11 countries concerned.

For this reason, an 'institutional poverty risk index' (IPRI) was developed which seeks to accommodate these objections, by analogy with the 'benefit dependency boost index' from the previous chapter. The index is based on around 50 characteristics of social assistance, old age pensions and benefit schemes for the unemployed, disabled, surviving dependants and the costs of children. The underlying data relate to the same 11 countries as in chapter 4, but this time for the situation in around the year 2000. This is explicitly an *institutional* index: it seeks to give an indication of the theoretical poverty risks that may be expected on the basis of the formal social security institutions, assuming that the other circumstances (national prosperity,[72] demographic conditions, and so on) remain the same. The details of the construction of the IPRI are given in Annex 1. Figure 6.3 shows the index scores for the countries studied according to the regime type to which they belong. Generally speaking, these are negatively related to the scores on the benefit dependency boost index depicted in figure 5.1 (a high poverty risk tends to be associated with a limited boosting of benefit dependency, and vice versa), though the statistical correlation is not perfect (r = -0.81, excluding Norway).

The index values suggest that the poverty risk based on institutional characteristics is theoretically greatest in the liberal regimes, with an average score of 0.77. There is however some dispersion within this regime type. The institutional poverty risk index is far and away the highest in the USA; the social security arrangements in this country generate the highest poverty risks with respect to pensions, social assistance, disability benefits and family benefits. The USA comes in second place for unemployment benefits, and achieves a lower (and therefore more favourable) score only on survivor's benefits. In Australia the poverty risk is a bit less, mainly because collective pensions and family benefits are wider in scope than in the US, even though they are means-tested. The United Kingdom has a substantially lower index value. This country scores second for pensions and disability benefits, but this is offset by lower contributions to the poverty risk from social assistance, survivor's benefits and family benefits. Based on the formal institutions, Canada theoretically generates the lowest poverty risk of the liberal countries. It achieves a fairly reasonable score (from 6th to 9th place) for disability benefit, survivor's benefits and social assistance, but does worse (second and third places) on unemployment and family benefits.

The countries with a corporatist regime occupy a middle position; their average IPRI-score (-0.05) is slightly below the general average (zero). The differentiation within this regime type is low: theoretically the poverty risk in Belgium and Germany is slightly lower than in France. The latter country has the best pension provisions of the corporatist group; it attains the 8th place in the ranking. This is due to the fairly high replacement rates for the lower incomes in old age, wage indexation of first pillar pensions and a relatively short build-up period; these are mitigated by the absence of separate collective pension entitlements for people without an employment history. Nonetheless, France ends up higher on the IPRI then the other two corporatist countries because of the higher poverty risk generated by social assistance and survivor's benefits.

Belgium has the poorest pension provision within the corporatist group (the second highest poverty risk of all countries). This is mainly due to the poor provisions for people who never held a job, the limited indexation mechanism (price inflation only), and the long period required to build up a full standard pension (42 years). On the other hand, Belgium compensates for this with fairly good scores on unemployment benefits, social assistance, family benefits and survivor's benefits. In Germany the protection via pensions is moderate, mainly because of the low net replacement rates at minimum level and the lack of collective entitlements for people who never worked. The country also achieves a low score for disability benefit, due to the limited coverage of the *risque social*.

Figure 6.3
Theoretical institutional poverty risk index for 11 countries, by regime type (1999-2001)

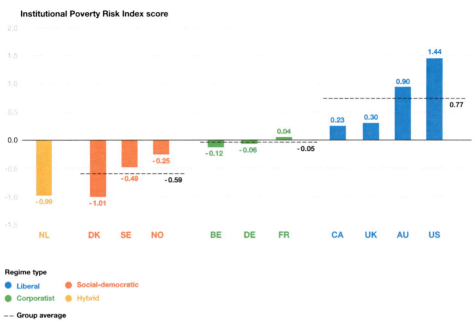

Sources: Soede et al. (2004); OECD (2002); EC (2002); SSA (2002); adapted

This is offset to some extent by reasonable scores for social assistance and by the fact that family benefits in Germany carry the lowest poverty risk of all countries studied.

The poverty risk theoretically generated by the formal rules is lowest in Denmark (-1.01) and the Netherlands (-0.99). Sweden and Norway score slightly higher on the index, but are still well below the general average. Across all social-democratic countries together the poverty risk score (-0.59) is considerably lower than in the corporatist group. Denmark achieves a low score on all constituent indices (ranging from 8th to 11th place), with the exception of survivor's benefits, for which the country has no separate scheme. Sweden also scores high on the latter aspect; it ends up above Denmark on the total index because of the moderate poverty risk generated by old age pensions, family benefits and social assistance. The theoretical poverty risk for unemployment and disability benefits is by contrast very low in Sweden (10th and 11th place, respectively). Norway offers good protection against poverty via pensions (10th place on the risk index) and also achieves a reasonable score for disability benefits (7th place), but generates a higher poverty risk on the other arrangements (3rd to 5th place).

The low poverty risk generated by the hybrid Dutch social security regime is due mainly to the low score on old age pensions (11th place), which weigh heaviest in the total index. Compared to Denmark, the Dutch pension schemes offers higher replacement rates, has slightly broader coverage for people without an employment history, and both first and second pillar pensions are indexed by the evolution of wages. Unlike Sweden and Denmark, the Netherlands moreover has an extensive collective survivor's insurance system by international standards. The other schemes also theoretically generate little poverty in the Netherlands (8th to 9th place), with the exception of family benefits (5th place), which are much lower than in the neighbouring corporatist countries.

Set against the typology presented in chapter 4, the ranking on the institutional poverty risk index (IPRI) corresponds quite closely with the ranking on the scope dimension. Apart from the difference in sign (a country with a wide scope generally has a low poverty risk and vice versa), however, there are also a number of salient differences:
– the corporatist regime type is a more average category according to the IPRI. Whereas these countries are fairly extensive on the scope dimension (and consequently tend towards the social-democratic group), on the index they fall almost precisely between the social-democratic and liberal groups, at around the origin. Furthermore, in the corporatist group, the differences on the IPRI (maximum 0.16) are much smaller than on the scope dimension (0.38). The ranking is also slightly different: Germany has the widest scope, but Belgium has the lowest institutionally determined poverty risk;
– within the social-democratic group the country with the broadest scope overall, Sweden, occupies a much more central position on the IPRI (third from bottom). Norway also moves to a more central position. Denmark achieves roughly the same score on both indicators and theoretically has the lowest institutional poverty risk, closely followed by the Netherlands, which occupies a much more peripheral position on the IPRI (second from bottom) than on the scope dimension;
– in the liberal group, the USA has a similar ranking overall, but it occupies a less peripheral position on the IPRI than on the scope dimension. As a result, the gap relative to Australia and Great Britain becomes smaller, but the distance compared with Canada increases. In terms of the poverty risk that its institutions theoretically generate, the latter country is far more central than on the scope dimension.

Based on the average scores on the IPRI, three simple hypotheses on the relationship between regime types and the extent of poverty can now be formulated:
(1) In countries with a liberal social security regime, poverty is higher than in countries with a regime of the corporatist type;
(2) In countries with a corporatist social security regime, poverty is higher than in countries with a regime of the social-democratic type;
(3) In countries with a social-democratic social security regime, poverty is higher than in the hybrid Dutch regime.

In formal terms, these poverty hypotheses can be expressed as follows:
All other things being equal, $P_{LIB} > P_{CRP} > P_{SD} > P_{HYB}$

where

P	=	degree of poverty
LIB	=	representatives of the liberal social security regime type (US, AU, CA, UK)
SD	=	representatives of the social-democratic social security regime type (SE, DK, NO)
CRP	=	representatives of the corporatist social security regime type (BE, DE, FR)
HYB	=	hybrid social security regime (NL)

The next section explores how far these hypotheses are supported by the empirical data. One qualifying comment needs to be made at this point, though. Arts & Gelissen (2002: 155) state that much research in this field

> ...has a bearing on the distributive effects of welfare regimes. Because they are often described in terms of their intended social stratification, a tautological element easily sneaks into the explanations.

As such, this observation is quite correct. However, it should be noted that in the current analysis the social security regimes have not been defined *a priori* in relation to the desired stratification effects. Rather, the actual institutional characteristics of the countries concerned are taken as a starting point here, regardless of the effects they are intended to bring about. Based on the poverty risk theoretically generated by the various sets of formal rules (viz., the average IPRI scores of country groups), hypotheses have been formulated with respect to the effects of different social security regime types on the extent of poverty. This is a postulated relationship which must be empirically investigated, rather than a tautological explanation.

6.7 Empirical results

The correlation between regime types and poverty has been the subject of earlier empirical studies. Korpi & Palme (1998), for example, drew up their own classification of four welfare state types, and subsequently analysed how these correlated with a number of distributive indicators. Their 'encompassing' type comprises the social-democratic countries (minus Denmark), while the 'corporatist' type consists of the continental countries of Western Europe, plus Italy and Japan. Korpi & Palme assign most of the countries that are regarded here as liberal to the 'basic security' category, but also include Denmark and the Netherlands in this group. These authors place Australia in a separate 'targeted' category. Their classification is contestable, because it is not based on an analysis of the connection between regime characteristics such as that carried out in chapter 4. This applies in particular for the separate targeted type: the institutional characteristics of Australia are not so unique that the country could not have been included in the liberal cluster; and if one wished to identify a separate 'Antipodean' cluster, New Zealand would probably also have to be included in it, but according to Korpi & Palme this country belongs to the basic security group. Placing Denmark and the Netherlands in the same cluster as the USA is also striking. While it is true that the social security systems of these two countries have some universalistic elements, as figure 4.2 showed, the level of social protection they offer is so much higher than the residual American system that it is difficult to justify placing them in the same group.

Notwithstanding these reservations, Korpi & Palme do find some correlation between their institutional types and a number of indicators for poverty and inequality (the 50% median threshold and the Gini coefficient). Using data from the Luxembourg Income Study in around 1985, they concluded that there is an opposition between systems with generous wage-related benefits for all inhabitants (the encompassing model) with little poverty or inequality, and those countries which offered only basic security or which were highly targeted (high levels of poverty and inequality). The corporatist countries fell between these two groups. Korpi & Palme (1998: 675) therefore concluded that institutional arrangements determine the income distribution and the concentrations at its lower end:

> These results give considerable support for our hypothesis about the overall role of welfare state institutions in the distributive processes of the Western countries.

The fit is however by no means perfect. The Netherlands, placed by these authors in the basic security group, has just as little poverty and inequality as the countries with an encompassing system, while the Australian type which they consider to be unique achieves the same levels of poverty and inequality as the USA, Canada and the United Kingdom.

Vogel (2003) also finds indications for a relationship between regime types and the distributive outcomes, based on data from the European Community Household Panel Survey from 1994. He draws attention to the contrasts between the Nordic countries (little poverty or inequality), a Central European cluster (an intermediate position) and a Mediterranean group (high rates of poverty and inequality). Analyses based on later waves of the ECHP, and using different versions of the relative poverty line (the 60%-threshold), lead to comparable conclusions (see e.g. Ras et al., 2002; CPB/SCP, 2003; Eurostat, 2004b). Wildeboer Schut et al. (2001) also included a number of non-European countries in their analysis and, like Korpi & Palme, found a dichotomy. In their case, however, the dividing line was not positioned between the 'encompassing' countries of Scandinavia and the rest, but between the liberal countries on the one hand (high relative poverty rates with the exception of Canada) and the corporatist and social-democratic regimes on the other (low poverty rates, with the exception of France). Wildeboer Schut et al. concluded that Esping-Andersen's 'three worlds of welfare' can be clearly separated from each other empirically in terms of the institutional arrangements, but that they are not entirely reflected in the distributive results.

The contours of the typology can also be clearly observed in figure 6.1, in which the poverty rate according to the 60%-threshold is included for various countries and two decades. Viewed over the whole period, the liberal countries generally attain the highest poverty rates. The social-democratic group and the Netherlands achieve the lowest rates, with the LIS observations for Denmark in the mid-1980s and early 1990s as outliers. Countries with a corporatist regime have lower poverty rates than liberal countries, but on average slightly higher rates than the social-democratic regime types.[73]

These results appear to confirm the hypotheses to some extent. Given this, is further research into the relationship between regime types and poverty necessary at all? The answer to this question is 'yes', and for a number of reasons. The most important are the limitations already highlighted of the poverty line used in these studies: the relative poverty threshold at the level of 50% or 60% of median income. This threshold was considered invalid earlier, and also failed to meet the requirements of reliability and socio-political credibility. The correlations found in the research carried out thus far chiefly reflect the fact that the regimes differ in the degree of inequality they produce. The latter is in line with Esping-Andersen's original theory; he posited that the 'three worlds of welfare' differ in their intended stratification (see chapter 4 and the qualification made in the previous section). In terms of poverty as theoretically demarcated here, however, these outcomes provide little information.

Another point of criticism that can be levelled against many of the earlier international comparative studies is that the relationship between regime type and poverty is often analysed as an isolated bivariate correlation. No allowance is generally made for the influence of other characteristics which can affect national poverty rates, such as the demographic profile. If retired people and young people are generally more often poor, for example, a country with a relatively elderly or very young population will – all other things being equal – produce more poverty than a country with a more balanced demographic composition. Allowing for this requires a multivariate analysis which establishes the effect of regime type on the poverty rate after controlling for the influence of alternative explanatory factors.

A third objection is more technical in nature. In most poverty research, and thus also in comparative studies focusing on the relationship between regime types and poverty, the emphasis tends to be on the headcount ratio or poverty incidence, i.e. the percentage of people living below a given poverty line. This is understandable: it is in principle an easily understood criterion, which leads to an unambiguous ranking of empirical observations. It is however questionable whether it provides an accurate reflection of the true level of poverty. With one and the same poverty rate, the depth of poverty (the average amount by which poor people fall short) and the poverty inequality (the distribution of shortfalls within the poor group) can be very different. These aspects really ought to be taken into account, but in research practice this does not happen very often, even though it is possible to capture them in composite poverty measures (see e.g. the overviews in Zheng, 1997 and Jäntti & Danziger, 2000; and for a practical international comparative application Ras et al., 2002).

All in all, therefore, there is sufficient reason to examine the relationship between regime types and poverty again. This is done here using data from the Luxembourg Income Study that are available for the 11 countries studied for around the year 2000. The LIS is a harmonised database containing detailed micro-income data from a large number of countries (see also figure 6.1). The equivalised disposable household income of persons in the database is used to establish whether people fall below the two variants of the poverty line according to the generalised budget approach.[74]

The LIS data used here ('wave 5') shows a number of improvements compared with earlier editions. The household definition is more consistent across the different countries – in earlier waves, for example, tax units, which could belong to the same household type, were taken as a basis in Sweden – and the quality of the income information has been improved in some countries (among other things by adding income data drawn from administrative sources). One drawback of the LIS data is that they are only available via remote access, which imposes constraints on the statistical analyses that can be performed. Another limitation is that only one measurement point is considered here; detailed time series with annual measurements as discussed in the previous chapter are not available via the LIS. Although data are available for several other years on most of the countries discussed here, in some cases comparability over time is not optimum (e.g. due to changes in survey design).

A final limitation is that poverty is established here on the basis of the adequacy of the available annual income. Whilst a year in poverty is by no means a short period, for some groups (e.g. the self-employed) it could perhaps be desirable to consider a longer time span, as their incomes can fluctuate widely from one year to the next. That said, empirical analyses of Dutch multiple-year income data have shown that there is no clear 'breaking point', whereby the problems associated with poverty rises sharply after a particular period. The financial assets of poor households, and the extent to which they are able to make ends meet, are substantially less after four years than after one year; but in the Netherlands at least this is a fairly gradual process (CBS/SCP, 1999: 24).

6.7.1 Country-specific norm amounts for a single person

It was concluded earlier that the poverty line developed by The Netherlands Institute for Social Research | SCP is a good operational criterion for covering the theoretical denotation of poverty. The two variants of this criterion will therefore be used here to test the hypotheses. For the cross-comparative analysis the Dutch amounts from the two variants of the SCP threshold for a single person in 2000 (see table 6.2) have been converted to local currency using purchasing power parities.[75] It would of course be desirable to assess the threshold amounts for the individual countries using the same method as that applied for the Netherlands and taking into account national differences in prices, taxation and consumption patterns. However, the reference budgets and the data that would be needed for this are not available.

Table 6.3 shows the norm amounts for a single person according to the 'basic needs' and 'modest but adequate' variants of the poverty threshold. In the empirical analyses all amounts are in national currencies, as derived by the application of purchasing power parities (the first two columns of amounts in the table). To gain an impression of the relative level of the poverty lines, they have also been converted into euros (based on the official conversion rates for Eurozone countries and exchange rates elsewhere).

In five countries, the deviations from the Dutch norm amounts are found to be limited: Australia comes out 4% lower, France, Canada, Belgium and Germany between 1%

Table 6.3
Poverty thresholds for a single person, 2000 (annual amounts)

		In national currencies[a]		In euros[b]	
		basic needs	modest but adequate	basic needs	modest but adequate
AU	AUD	12,017	13,637	7,562	8,581
NL	NLG	17,652	20,032	8,010	9,090
FR	FRF	53,306	60,494	8,127	9,222
CA	CAD	11,178	12,685	8,169	9,271
BE	BEF	334,118	379,167	8,283	9,399
DE	DEM	16,773	19,034	8,576	9,732
UK	GBP	5,602	6,357	9,200	10,440
SE	SEK	82,658	93,803	9,792	11,112
US	USD	9,227	10,471	10,015	11,365
DK	DKK	75,187	85,324	10,096	11,457
NO	NOK	84,066	95,401	10,367	11,764

a. SCP poverty thresholds for the Netherlands transformed to national currencies by applying OECD purchasing power parities for actual individual consumption.
b. Poverty thresholds in national currencies recalculated by means of exchange rates 2000 (official conversion rates for euro countries).

and 7% higher. The UK norm amounts for a single person are 15% higher; but Sweden, the United States, Denmark and Norway are the most expensive countries (between 22% and 29% higher than in the Netherlands).

On an annual basis the 'basic needs' criterion for a single person ranges from 7,600 to 10,400 euros, while the 'modest but adequate' criterion is between 8,600 and 11,800 euros. In most countries, both threshold amounts for a single person are below the relative poverty line (60% of median income) in 2000 as published by the OECD (Förster & Mira d'Ercole, 2005). In Australia, France and Germany, however, the amount for the 'modest but adequate' variant is 4-7% above the national relative poverty line.

The amounts in table 6.3 apply for disposable income; after compulsory government taxes, social insurance contributions, etc. have been deducted from the received salary, benefits, profits etc., the remainder must be adequate to cover the other unavoidable or highly desirable expenditure items.

6.7.2 Sensitivity analysis of equivalence scales

The norm amounts for a single person cannot be applied directly to other types of household. A family with four children will find it more difficult to make ends meet from 10,000 euros than a single person: there are more mouths to feed, more furniture and beds are needed, the energy costs will be higher, expenses will be incurred for school and childcare, insurance is more expensive, and so on. To allow for this, an equivalence scale is often used. This comprises a set of ratios which indicate how much extra income households need in order to derive the same utility or level of welfare as a reference household. The ratios (or equivalence factors) then express, for example, how many 'equivalent single adults' there are in households with a certain composition.

Equivalence scales usually take account in some way of economies of scale. As a result, they generally do not increase directly proportional to the size of the household. A couple with four children will need a larger house than a single person in order to achieve the same level of welfare, and will therefore incur greater housing costs; on the other hand, they do not need to occupy six homes that are suitable for a single person.

Whether or not households are poor can then be determined by examining whether the equivalised income (the nominal income divided by the equivalence factors) lies below the norm amount for the reference household. Logically, the same result will be obtained if this latter amount is multiplied by the equivalence factors and the resultant household-specific poverty lines are compared with the original (nominal) incomes.

Naturally, the question that arises here is which equivalence scale is the best to use. This is not a trivial issue, because the equivalence scale chosen can influence the poverty that is detected. For example, the more steeply the equivalence scale rises with the size of the household, the greater the number of large families that are classed as poor (given a constant threshold amount for the reference household). With steeper equivalence scales, the factor by which the nominal income is divided becomes higher, so that more large families end up below the threshold amount. This implies that both the number of poor and the share of large families in the poor group will increase.

As stated, the Dutch version of the SCP poverty line uses equivalence factors calculated by Statistics Netherlands (CBS) (Siermann et al., 2004). This equivalence scale is fairly well approximated if each adult is counted as 1 and each child as 0.8, and the square root of the sum of all individual weights is then extracted. It then resembles the scales proposed in the report mentioned earlier by the National Academy of Sciences for the United States. The latter are however steeper: the NAS proposes giving all adults a weight of 1 and each child a weight of 0.7; the sum of all weights is then raised to the power of 0.65 to 0.75 (Citro & Michael, 1995). It can however not be taken for granted that the equivalence scales suggested by Statistics Netherlands or the NAS are suitable for other countries, as empirically the situation may be different there (e.g. less housing costs in more sparsely populated countries, fewer energy costs in milder climates).

By convention three variants are often used in international comparative research:
- the *(old) OECD equivalence scale*, also known as the 'Oxford scale'. This scale assigns a value of 1 to the first adult household member, 0.7 to each additional adult and 0.5 for each child. The household income is then divided by the sum of the values of the household members in order to obtain equivalent incomes. The OECD (1982) introduced this scale for use in "countries which have not established their own equivalence scale".
- the *modified OECD equivalence scale*, proposed by Hagenaars et al. (1994). This rises less steeply as the number of household members increases. The first adult household member is given a weight of 1; each additional adult counts for 0.5, and each child for

0.3. The European Union uses this scale to determine the level of relative poverty in the member states (see e.g. EC, 2007).
- the *square root equivalence scale*. Here, household income is divided by the square root of the total number of persons in the household. A family of four is thus considered to need twice as much income as a single person in order to achieve the same level of welfare. This equivalence scale (and not the one which bears its name) has often been applied by the OECD in recent years in international comparisons (see e.g. Förster & Mira d'Ercole, 2005).

Their conventional nature is at once the main objection to these equivalence scales. There are no compelling reasons to assume that they adequately reflect the actual welfare differences between various types of household; and no grounds at all to suppose that the equivalences must be the same in all countries and periods. Furthermore, the conventional scales are based on relatively few household characteristics. They differentiate according to household size and partially to age (the square root scale does not distinguish between adults and children). It is rather plausible that finer age distinctions (e.g. young adults, over-65s), gender, health status and present income level are also important in determining the experienced level of welfare.

To get round this problem, *empirical equivalence scales* are often used, especially in national research into poverty and inequality; at first sight, these are less problematic. The best known are the scales based on consumer demand models (see e.g. Lewbel, 1997). These models use a system of regression equations to estimate how consumptive units (households) with divergent characteristics distribute their total income, given specific prices, across consumer goods and services. Equivalence factors can then be derived from the ratios of the estimated expenditure of different types of households relative to a reference household.

The estimation of equivalence factors based on consumer demand models is intended to provide a 'technical' solution to the arbitrariness of the conventional scales. In practice, however, normative elements still creep in (Cowell & Mercader-Prats, 1999: 410-412; for an overview see Jäntti & Danziger, 2000: 316-322). An equivalence scale can be regarded as the rate of exchange between nominal and equivalised incomes. For households with specific traits it gives the function by which nominal income is transformed in such a way that the welfare or utility level of the reference household is attained. The equivalence scale can thus also be interpreted as a 'cost of characteristics' index:

$$e_h = \frac{C(u_o, p, z_h)}{C(u_o, p, z_o)}$$

where
e_h = equivalence for household with characteristics z_h;
c = cost/expenditure function;
u_o = utility level of reference household;
p = vector of prices (assumed constant across households);
z_h = vector of characteristics of household;
z_o = vector of characteristics of reference household

The formula makes clear that the equivalence factor is determined not *only* by the differences in the characteristics of the household (such as size, composition, age), but also by prices and by the adopted points of reference. The price vector is not necessarily the same for all household types (farmers spend less on food and milk than town-dwellers), even though this is generally assumed to be the case; and if a different reference level of utility is chosen, the ratios on the cost of characteristics index can turn out differently. Equivalence scales based on consumer demand models tend to make normative choices here.

More fundamental is the assumption that the utility levels of households with different characteristics can be compared accurately[76] (see e.g. Pollak & Wales, 1979). This is not however self-evident. Suppose a person has a motor disability, so that they spend more on transport (e.g. a wheelchair, taxis) than a healthy person and less on other items. In principle, the 'pure' additional costs of the disability (controlling for age, household size and composition, etc.) can be established reasonably well using consumer demand models, and from this the conditional equivalence factor relative to the reference household can be derived. However, the extra transport costs for people with a motor disability do not by definition imply that they achieve the same level of welfare as people without disabilities. If someone becomes disabled, their needs may change; transport becomes more important to them, and in order to achieve the same utility as before they may have to spend more than their income allows; or the extra transport costs may force them to economise on other items, which is also tantamount to a loss of welfare.

When determining the level of poverty and income inequality the researcher is interested in unconditional equivalence factors: "index numbers which reflect the ratio of expenditures required to attain a particular indifference curve under alternative demographic profiles" (Pollak & Wales, 1979: 217). Since budget data generally contain no information enabling the estimation of indifference curves, Cowell & Mercader-Prats (1999: 409) conclude that

> [...] econometric equivalence scales cannot in general be identified from observed micro-data; in practice, they are identified by making assumptions that are not ethically neutral, and that may be criticized as arbitrary and controversial. [Thus] there can be no one 'correct' equivalence scale.

In empirical comparative research it has been found repeatedly that, while the equivalence scale chosen influences the poverty rate and the composition of the poor population, the ranking of countries and the trends observed are however often comparable (Burniaux et al., 1998; Jäntti & Danziger, 2000). For this reason, a pragmatic approach is followed here. It involves an assessment of the degree to which the measured poverty rate varies if a large number of equivalence scales are applied to the norm amounts for a single person outlined earlier. These equivalence scales are captured by the formula

$$e(1 + aN + bK)^c$$

where
e = equivalence scale;
N = number of additional adults;
K = number of children below 18 years of age;

a = multiplier for additional adults;
b = multiplier for children;
c = exponent of sum score

The conventional equivalence scales discussed earlier, the equivalence scale developed by Statistics Netherlands (CBS) and the scales proposed by the NAS all are variants of this formula. Comparing the poverty rates and ranking of countries using a range of different scales provides some evidence on the impact of the chosen equivalence scale on the empirical results. Two comments need to be made about this sensitivity analysis, however. First, the number of characteristics on which the equivalence scale is based is again limited in this analysis: household size and a fairly rough division by age of the family members (older/younger than 18 years[77]). In addition, the most extreme variants of the equivalence formula probably will not be perceived as reasonable by many people. At one extreme is the *nominal income*, where the welfare differences between households with a different composition are ignored. Here, the poverty line for the reference household serves as the norm for all households, and it is therefore assumed the larger families do not need to spend more in order to achieve the same level of welfare. The variant at the other extreme assumes that welfare differences show a linear increase with the number of family members. This approach in terms of the *per capita income* ignores economies of scale, which for instance implies that the family with four children mentioned above would indeed need six single-person dwellings in which to live. Although the extreme variants have little credibility, therefore, they do provide an indication of the maximum bandwidth in the poverty rate using different equivalence scales.

Table 6.4 shows results of this sensitivity analysis in the 11 countries in terms of the headcount ratios. In variant 1 (nominal income) the poverty rate in the 11 countries lies between 2% and 7%. Variant 18 (Y per capita) delivers much higher figures: between 27% and 54% of the population are characterised as poor based on this equivalence scale. Between these two extremes the poverty rate in all countries rises steadily[78] if higher parameter values are chosen, with large jumps in variants 17 and 18. The increase between variant 1 and variant 18 is smallest in Denmark and Norway (approx. +10 percentage points), and greatest in France and Australia (between +40 and +47 percentage points).

The ranking of countries is fairly stable for divergent parameter values.[79] Regardless of the equivalence factor used, Australia always comes in first place, with the highest poverty rate. Similarly, Norway and Denmark record the lowest relative number of poor people for each equivalence scale. Belgium, the UK and Canada also occupy fairly stable positions in the poverty ranking. In a few countries this is not the case, however. With higher parameter values, France climbs higher up the ranking of poor countries (comparatively more poverty), while Germany falls (comparatively less poverty). The Netherlands has the fewest poor people for the two least steep variants, and thereafter remains for a long time in third place. With the 'steepest' variants (17 and 18), the poverty rate in the Netherlands rises rather sharply, pushing the country into a middle position. The reverse applies for the USA: in most variants this country has one of the higher poverty rates. For the final

Table 6.4
Sensitivity analysis: poverty rates according to a class of equivalence scales (around 2000)

	Equivalence scale*		$e=(1 + aN + bK)^c$			% of population below **basic needs** poverty criterion									
No.	Name	a	b	c	NL	NO	DK	SE	DE	BE	FR	CA	US	UK	AU
1	Nominal income	0	0	0	1.9	1.4	1.7	4.2	4.0	2.8	2.5	2.7	3.7	3.6	5.5
2	-	0.5	0.5	0.1	1.9	1.5	1.8	4.2	4.2	2.9	2.6	2.9	4.0	3.8	5.8
3	-	0.5	0.5	0.25	2.2	1.6	1.8	4.4	4.5	3.5	3.1	3.4	4.5	4.3	6.5
4	-	1	0.5	0.25	2.4	1.6	1.8	4.5	4.7	3.9	3.6	3.7	4.8	4.6	6.9
5	-	1	0.5	0.35	2.8	1.7	2.0	4.7	5.4	4.6	4.4	4.2	5.6	5.3	7.7
6	-	1	0.5	0.5	3.7	1.8	2.2	5.3	6.5	5.9	6.5	5.6	7.2	7.1	11.4
7	-	1	0.7	0.5	3.9	1.9	2.3	5.8	6.9	6.4	7.3	6.2	7.9	8.1	12.8
8	Statistics Netherlands	1	0.8	0.5	4.3	2.0	2.3	6.0	7.1	6.7	7.9	6.5	8.2	8.8	13.5
9	Square root scale	1	1	0.5	4.7	2.1	2.4	6.4	7.4	7.0	8.8	7.2	8.9	10.3	15.1
10	OECD modified scale	0.5	0.3	1	5.3	2.2	2.7	7.0	7.9	8.9	11.2	8.5	10.3	11.9	17.0
11	Alternative scale: (SN+NAS)/2	1	0.75	0.6	5.5	2.2	2.7	7.1	8.1	9.5	10.9	8.4	10.1	12.4	17.5
12	US NAS (low)	1	0.7	0.65	6.4	2.4	3.0	7.9	8.6	10.1	12.6	9.4	11.2	13.8	19.1
13	-	1	0.5	0.75	7.0	2.6	4.0	8.6	9.8	12.1	14.4	10.5	12.3	15.3	21.3
14	US NAS (high)	1	0.7	0.75	8.6	3.1	4.8	10.2	11.2	12.9	17.5	12.5	14.1	18.5	24.6
15	Oxford (old OECD) scale	0.7	0.5	1	11.2	3.9	6.0	12.0	13.2	14.6	21.1	14.8	16.1	21.4	28.1
16	-	1	1	0.75	11.7	4.3	6.8	13.7	14.0	15.8	21.9	15.3	16.6	22.2	28.8
17	-	1	1	0.9	24.7	9.9	13.2	25.0	22.6	24.3	33.6	23.3	23.4	30.3	39.1
18	Per capita income	1	1	1	33.2	17.2	20.3	33.8	30.4	32.1	41.6	30.3	28.6	36.4	46.3

	Equivalence scale*		$e=(1 + aN + bK)^c$			% of population below **modest but adequate** poverty criterion									
No.	Name	a	b	c	NL	NO	DK	SE	DE	BE	FR	CA	US	UK	AU
1	Nominal income	0	0	0	2.4	3.0	3.2	6.7	5.6	4.8	3.8	3.8	4.8	5.1	6.9
2	-	0.5	0.5	0.1	2.6	3.1	3.2	6.8	5.9	5.0	4.2	4.2	5.2	5.4	7.3
3	-	0.5	0.5	0.25	3.2	3.1	3.3	7.0	6.4	5.8	5.1	4.8	5.9	6.2	8.3
4	-	1	0.5	0.25	3.3	3.2	3.4	7.3	6.8	6.3	5.7	5.2	6.3	6.8	9.5
5	-	1	0.5	0.35	4.0	3.3	3.6	7.7	7.7	8.0	7.1	6.1	7.4	8.1	12.1
6	-	1	0.5	0.5	5.3	3.6	4.3	9.1	9.1	10.3	10.5	8.1	9.7	11.7	17.1
7	-	1	0.7	0.5	6.0	3.8	4.5	9.7	9.5	10.9	11.9	9.1	10.6	13.7	18.9
8	Statistics Netherlands	1	0.8	0.5	6.4	3.9	4.6	10.1	9.8	11.3	12.6	9.5	11.1	14.7	19.5
9	Square root scale	1	1	0.5	7.3	4.1	4.8	10.9	10.2	12.3	13.8	10.5	12.0	16.3	20.4
10	OECD modified scale	0.5	0.3	1	8.5	4.3	5.9	11.9	11.6	14.2	17.0	12.2	13.9	18.3	24.1
11	Alternative scale: (SN+NAS)/2	1	0.75	0.6	8.6	4.5	6.0	12.2	11.6	13.9	16.8	12.2	13.7	18.7	23.9
12	US NAS (low)	1	0.7	0.65	9.6	4.8	6.9	13.2	12.9	14.8	19.1	13.5	14.8	20.4	26.0
13	-	1	0.5	0.75	11.5	5.3	8.1	14.7	14.8	17.1	21.9	15.3	16.0	22.2	28.3
14	US NAS (high)	1	0.7	0.75	13.8	6.2	9.7	17.4	17.1	19.5	25.4	17.6	18.2	25.3	31.7
15	Oxford (old OECD) scale	0.7	0.5	1	17.9	7.8	11.6	21.1	20.1	22.3	29.9	20.4	20.8	28.0	35.5
16	-	1	1	0.75	19.5	8.7	12.6	23.4	20.8	22.5	31.1	21.1	21.4	29.0	36.6
17	-	1	1	0.9	33.8	18.4	21.9	36.8	31.9	33.4	43.3	31.1	29.1	37.9	47.1
18	Per capita income	1	1	1	43.7	26.9	30.8	45.7	39.8	43.9	51.3	38.4	34.5	44.1	54.1

* In formula, with
e = equivalence scale
N = number of additional adults
K = number of children below 18 years of age
a = multiplier for additional adults
b = multiplier for children
c = exponent of sum score

Source: Luxembourg Income Study (1999-2001)

two variants, however, the poverty rate rises less than elsewhere, moving the country to the middle segment. Sweden initially falls down the ladder, but according to the last two to four variants the poverty rate rises comparatively strongly.

For most countries, it makes no difference for their position in the ranking whether the basic needs or the modest but adequate variant of the poverty line is used. According to the latter criterion, Belgium and Sweden are one place higher up the ranking than on the basis of the basic needs criterion; applying the higher threshold thus leads to a comparatively large increase in these countries. The USA comes in most cases almost two places lower when the modest but adequate criterion is used; the growth in poverty is comparatively small if the higher threshold amount is used.

If only the familiar equivalence scales are considered, the picture is even more stable. If the headcount ratios are compared according to the two variants which are furthest apart from each other in the table ('Statistics Netherlands' and 'Oxford'), the changes in the rankings are very limited. If the basic needs poverty line is taken as a basis, there are seven countries in exactly the same place in variants 8 and 15. The other four move up or down the ranking by at most two positions. Based on the modest but adequate criterion, five countries share an identical position according to both the 'Statistics Netherlands' and 'Oxford' scales; with the other seven, the difference is no more than one position.

What then constitutes a reasonable equivalence scale? If the conventional methods are examined more closely, the objection may be levelled at the square root scale that it does not distinguish between adults and children. If a married couple has the same household income as a single-parent with a newborn child, they are therefore assumed to attain the same level of welfare. The OECD-modified scale does draw a crude distinction by age. Here, however, one may question the linear increase in the equivalence scale: each additional adult or child carries the same weight as the previous one; there are no economies of scale. The same applies for the Oxford scale, which seems moreover fairly steep, resulting in rather high poverty rates (8-36%) for prosperous countries.

The strength of the equivalence scales put forward by Statistics Netherlands (CBS) and the US National Academy of Sciences (NAS) is that they distinguish between adults and children and allow for economies of scale. Compared with the two conventional scales most commonly used in international comparative research (Square root and OECD-modified), however, the Dutch scale is fairly flat (leading to low poverty rates), while the two American variants are actually steeper than usual (resulting in fairly high poverty rates).

For practical reasons, it was therefore decided to base the further analysis on a hybrid form: an equivalence scale which follows a middle path between the CBS equivalence scale and the average of the two scales propagated by the NAS. In the chosen equivalence scale (variant 11), each adult carries a weight of 1, each child 0.75, and with a rising number of household members the equivalence factor exhibits a slightly stronger non-linear increase than with the square root scale ($c=0.60$). In table 6.2 the norm amounts for this alternative equivalence scale in the Netherlands were already presented for a number of household types.

Given the earlier discussion of the merits of different equivalence scales, this is inevitably a normative choice. It does however seem reasonable in view of the highlighted limitations of the existing conventional scales and the somewhat extreme nature of the Dutch and American approaches. The poverty rates produced by the adopted equivalence scale are virtually the same as those based on the OECD-modified scale, with a maximum deviation of +0.6 percentage points (UK, basic needs variant). The difference compared with the square root scale is greater, rising to +3.5 percentage points for Australia using the modest but adequate criterion.

Applying this equivalence scale, the correlation between the poverty rates and income inequality is much smaller than when the 60% of median income criterion is taken as the poverty threshold (cf. figure 6.1). For the 11 countries studied here in around the year 2000, the correlation between the Gini coefficient and relative poverty is 0.95, i.e. almost perfect. The basic needs and modest but adequate criteria also correlate with this inequality measure, but less strongly (0.70 and 0.65, respectively).

6.7.3 The 'three I's of poverty' and the regime types

It was noted earlier that much international comparative research focuses exclusively on the poverty rate, ignoring two other potentially important aspects of poverty, namely the income deficits of the poor and the distribution of those deficits among the poor. This is sometimes described as the 'three I's of poverty': the *incidence, income deficit* and *inequality* of poverty (see e.g. Jenkins & Lambert, 1997). The incidence (also referred to as the poverty rate or headcount ratio) is an intuitively clear indicator: the proportion of the population with an income below the poverty line is an obvious key indicator both for policymakers and in the public debate. If the poverty line amount is regarded as a fundamental right, it also has legal significance: the incidence of poverty then indicates how many people's basic entitlements are being infringed. Yet the indicator also has some drawbacks. It implies that households are either poor or not poor, and this simple dichotomy may not fully reflect the actual situation as experienced by people. Is someone really not poor any more if he has an income that is one euro below the poverty line and receives an additional two euros? And does his condition improve just as much as in the case of someone who has a deficit of 1000 euros and receives an additional 1001 euros? Moreover, there is a possible objection from a policy perspective: based on this indicator measures aimed at those just below the poverty line will be found to be the most efficient, as these reduce the poverty rate at the lowest cost.

There is thus some justification for looking at the income deficit as well. Based on this indicator, there is also a reduction in poverty if the incidence remains constant but the average or median deficit of the poor reduces. The depth of poverty thus helps determine the judgment as to the severity of the problem: if 5% of the population are below the poverty line, it is less serious if they fall short by an average of 10 euros per year than if their income deficit is 1000 euros. The income deficit provides an indication of the difficulty and costs that will be involved in lifting this group out of poverty, and is therefore also relevant from a policy perspective. One comment that needs to be made here is that the indicator becomes less relevant if the poverty line is set at a very spartan level or has little discretionary scope. In that case, poor people cannot keep their heads above water anyway, and just like drowning people who cannot swim, it makes no difference how far below the water surface they are – they will still drown.

As regards the third aspect, the income inequality within the poor population, the assumption is that there is more poverty if the dispersion of the deficits is greater. Income redistribution among the poor will therefore also alter the degree of poverty: if money is transferred from a 'wealthy' poor person (just below the poverty line) to a poorer person (a long way below the threshold) poverty will reduce, even if the incidence and median income deficit do not change. From a policy perspective, the inequality criterion quickly leads to the conclusion that it is efficient to redistribute income in order to decrease the deficit of the poorest. This can be justified if one supposes that the marginal utility of income decreases. For the very poorest people, the extra amount can mean that they will not die of hunger, while for the 'wealthier' poor the loss of income may merely imply that they can no longer pay their telephone bill. The former could be allowed to weigh more heavily than the latter. At first sight this is a defensible standpoint, but here again another line of reasoning can be followed. To use the analogy of the drowning person once more: if a few people are swimming slightly below the water surface, they may have a chance of escaping; that may be preferable to a situation where all swim at greater depth but drown.

Since these are all relevant aspects of income poverty, however, it is still useful – despite the objections that can be levelled at each – to analyse all three indicators here, and to explore to what extent empirical results are in line with theoretical expectations. Table 6.5 shows the poverty rates, the median percentage income deficits and the inequality of the deficits (measured using the Gini coefficient) for both variants of the poverty line and the equivalence scale selected earlier.

Three composite measures are also reported; these summarise the differences on some of these aspects simultaneously. The intensity index is simply the product of the incidence and the median income deficit. The Sen index and the Shorrocks index also take the inequality among the poor into account. If a few familiar axioms are accepted, the Shorrocks measure is the most attractive from a theoretical point of view.[80]

With both poverty lines, the differences between the countries are greatest with regard to the incidence. In the country with the most poor people, the incidence with the basic needs poverty criterion is eight times as high as in the country with the fewest poor; based on the modest but adequate poverty threshold, the figure is five times as high.

The spread in the income deficits is less marked (the maximum is roughly twice as high as the minimum), and the inequality among the poor varies even less (a ratio of between 1.2 and 1.4). This implies that for the composite measures the differences will be mainly due to the divergent poverty rates, and to a lesser extent to the median income deficits and the inequality in them. It may thus be expected that the three indices will lead to roughly the same conclusions as the incidence.

Basic needs criterion

According to the basic needs poverty criterion, the incidence is lowest in Norway and Denmark (2-3%). The Netherlands follows at some distance (just over 5% poverty) and Sweden comes in fourth place (7%). The three corporatist countries all score higher (8-11%), as do the four liberal countries (8-17%). Hypothesis 1 ($P_{LIB} > P_{CRP}$) is thus supported by the data: the poverty rate is higher on average in the liberal group than in the corporatist cluster (+2.6 percentage points). This is however attributable largely to the high incidence of poverty in Australia; if this country is left out of consideration, the differences are less obvious, with only the United Kingdom scoring clearly higher than the corporatist countries.

The picture is even clearer when it comes to hypothesis 2 ($P_{CRP} > P_{SD}$). All corporatist countries have higher poverty rates than the social-democratic countries, and as a result the averages in these regime types diverge in the expected direction (+5.5 percentage points).

Hypothesis 3 ($P_{SD} > P_{HYB}$) is however not supported as regards the incidence of poverty. Norway and Denmark have significantly fewer poor people than the hybrid Netherlands; only Sweden scores somewhat higher. The average poverty rate in the three social-democratic countries is lower than in the Netherlands, contrary to expectations (-1.5 percentage point). The hybrid regime type does however score below the average rates in the corporatist and liberal regime types.

Linking the income deficits to the regime types is a less straightforward matter. The deficits are greatest in the Netherlands, Norway and the USA (a median value of around 25%), followed by Germany and Canada (approx. 20%) and the other countries (approx. 15%). Due to the scores of the USA and Canada, the liberal countries on average have a higher median income deficit than the corporatist group. This is in line with hypothesis 1, but the difference is not great. The social-democratic countries come out roughly on a par with the corporatist group, so that hypothesis 2 is not supported. The score of the Netherlands is actually completely opposite to the theoretical assumption in hypothesis 3: the country does not have the smallest median income deficit, but the largest.

The differences between countries in terms of inequality of deficits also run contrary to expectations. The limited differences reveal a divide between the social-democratic countries plus the Netherlands on the one hand (slightly higher Gini coefficient of income deficits than elsewhere, with the exception of Denmark) and the corporatist and liberal countries on the other (lower Gini coefficients, except in the USA).

The three indices show the same pattern as the poverty incidence, but the differences are less marked because they are dampened by the other two I's. Denmark and Norway have the lowest scores, with the high income deficit of the Norwegian poor putting this country into second place. Sweden and the Netherlands come next; the hybrid regime ends up somewhat lower in the rankings due to the high median income deficit. The Netherlands

Table 6.5
Poverty indicators according to basic needs and modest but adequate criteria [a]

	Basic needs poverty criterion					
	Incidence (% poor)	Income deficit (median %)	Inequality of deficits (Gini)	Intensity index	Sen index	Shorrocks index
NL	5.5	25.2	0.256	1.4	2.5	2.8
SE	7.1	15.6	0.256	1.1	2.6	2.2
DK	2.7	13.1	0.231	0.4	0.9	0.7
NO	2.2	24.6	0.285	0.6	1.0	1.1
DE	8.1	20.7	0.234	1.7	3.2	3.3
BE	9.5	14.6	0.224	1.4	3.2	2.8
FR	10.9	16.3	0.216	1.8	3.8	3.6
UK	12.4	14.3	0.227	1.8	4.5	4.5
CA	8.4	21.8	0.239	1.8	3.1	3.0
AU	17.5	15.2	0.204	2.7	6.5	7.2
US	10.1	24.2	0.263	2.5	4.2	4.2
Regime type average						
Hybrid (NL)=ref.	1.00	1.00	1.00	1.00	1.00	1.00
Social-democratic	0.72	0.71	1.00	0.48	0.62	0.49
Corporatist	1.72	0.68	0.88	1.16	1.38	1.17
Liberal	2.19	0.88	0.91	1.56	1.88	1.71

a. Assessed against equivalised disposable household income of persons, around 2000

is below all the social-democratic countries on the intensity index and the Shorrocks index. On the Sen index, the Netherlands comes in roughly the same place as Sweden, even though the poverty rate is substantially lower.

The corporatist countries still form a homogenous middle group, and the liberal countries have the highest scores. Australia is again that the poorest country according to the three indices. Its distance from the other countries however, is less than in the case of the incidence because of the low median income deficit and inequality. The United States climbs up the rankings somewhat: the poverty rate is not exceptionally high, but the income deficit and inequality are.

    Based on these composite measures, the conclusion for the degree of poverty of the regime types is the same as for the incidence. Hypothesis 1 is sustained, with the difference between the liberal and corporatist group now being due not only to the high score of Australia, but also to that of the usa. In line with hypothesis 2, the corporatist countries score higher than the social-democratic cluster across the board on the composite measures. Once again, however, hypothesis 3 has to be rejected: the Netherlands does not attain lower, but higher scores than the social-democratic group on the composite poverty measures.

(Table 6.5)

Modest but adequate poverty criterion						
Incidence (% poor)	Income deficit (median %)	Inequality of deficits (Gini)	Intensity index	Sen index	Shorrocks index	
8.6	19.0	0.238	1.6	3.3	3.3	NL
12.2	15.2	0.246	1.9	4.4	3.8	SE
6.0	10.5	0.223	0.6	1.8	1.3	DK
4.5	12.4	0.252	0.6	1.5	1.1	NO
11.6	21.4	0.241	2.5	4.7	4.9	DE
13.9	16.5	0.213	2.3	4.8	4.6	BE
16.8	17.9	0.213	3.0	5.9	6.0	FR
18.7	17.6	0.219	3.3	6.7	6.6	UK
12.2	21.1	0.240	2.6	4.9	5.1	CA
23.9	20.9	0.211	5.0	9.0	9.7	AU
13.7	25.1	0.263	3.4	6.1	6.7	US
						Regime type average
1.00	1.00	1.00	1.00	1.00	1.00	Hybrid (NL)=ref.
0.88	0.67	1.01	0.62	0.79	0.63	Social-democratic
1.64	0.98	0.94	1.59	1.56	1.59	Corporatist
1.99	1.12	0.98	2.19	2.02	2.16	Liberal

Source: Luxembourg Income Study (1999-2001)

Modest but adequate criterion

Applying the more generous modest but adequate criterion leads to similar conclusions. The ranking for incidence is virtually identical, being lowest in Norway and Denmark (5-6%), followed by the Netherlands (9%). Germany overtakes Sweden in the rankings on this measure, but the difference is not great: when rounded off, both countries score 12%. Canada has the same poverty rate as Sweden; Belgium and the USA score slightly higher (just under 14%). As with the lower threshold amount, the incidence of poverty is highest in France (16%), the United Kingdom (17%) and Australia (24%).

The differences are somewhat larger when it comes to income deficits. These are no longer highest in Norway and the Netherlands, but in the United States. Australia undergoes a relatively sharp increase on this indicator. The country differences in the inequality of deficits are even smaller than with the basic needs criterion. On the three composite measures, Norway now scores lowest across the board, while the Netherlands consistently comes below Sweden. Australia again records by far the highest score on the three indices.

Hypothesis 1 receives most support with the three composite measures, with three of the four liberal countries (with Canada as the exception) coming consistently higher than

Germany, Belgium and France. The average incidence in the liberal group is also higher than in the corporatist regime types (+3.0 percentage points), but as with the basic needs criterion this is due mainly to the high scores of Australia and the United Kingdom. The income deficits and the inequality in them reveal no systematic difference between the liberal and corporatist regime types.

Hypothesis 2 also receives the most support based on the indices, with all social-democratic countries coming below all corporatist countries (though on the Sen index the difference between Sweden on the one hand and Germany and Belgium on the other is not very large). When it comes to the incidence, the differences between the groups are mostly in line with expectations as well (except for the positions of Sweden and Germany). On average the between cluster difference equals 6.5 percentage points. The median income deficits in the social-democratic countries are somewhat smaller than in the corporatist group, as expected; but this does not apply for the inequality of the deficits.

Hypothesis 3 is not supported on the basis of the incidence and the three composite measures: the Netherlands comes substantially higher than Norway and Denmark in all cases. On average, the incidence in the social-democratic group is 1 percentage point less than in the hybrid regime. The median income deficit in the Netherlands also runs contrary to expectations, being greater than in the three social-democratic countries. The differences in inequality of deficits are negligible.

In sum, regardless of the level of the poverty line chosen, support is found for hypotheses 1 and 2 based on the incidence and the three indices, and also partially on the grounds of income deficits. By contrast, hypothesis 3 is not supported by any indicator.

It is however questionable whether this straightforward, bivariate comparison of the poverty indicators is empirically sound; the countries studied here may differ from each other in more respects than the regime type. In order to obtain a clearer picture of the impact of the regime types on poverty, a model-based approach is required.

6.7.4 Explaining the poverty incidence: multi-level models

The regime types are theoretically not the only determinants of the differences in poverty; other macro-characteristics, such as differences in national prosperity, can have an influence as well. It is also possible that characteristics at lower scale levels explain part of the differences in the national poverty figures: characteristics of individuals and households at micro-level, labour relations and administrative processes at meso-level, and so on. Multi-level analysis is the most appropriate technique for establishing the influence of such hierarchically ordered causal factors (see e.g. Snijders & Bosker, 1999). This technique starts from the premise that the spread in the dependent variable stems from a number of nested sources: pupils in schools in neighbourhoods, employees in companies in countries, patients in hospitals in regions, and so on. The total variance in the dependent variable is decomposed across the different levels. At each level it is then possible to assess to what extent independent characteristics (age of the patient, size of the hospital, population density of the region, etc.) are able to predict the specific part of the variance. Unlike in the previous chapter, multi-level analysis can be applied here, because data on poverty and its potential determinants are available for persons living in households in the various countries. By contrast, the figures on benefit dependency were only available at aggregated country level.

In order to determine the pure influence of the regime types, a number of multi-level models were developed. In each case, being poor or not being poor (the incidence) is the dependent variable. The income deficits of the poor and the inequality therein are left out of consideration here. In many countries the number of observations for multi-level analyses with these variables as dependent is too small, due to the fact that the non-poor are by definition ignored with these criteria.[81] Moreover, as stated the between country variance is much more limited as regards the income deficits and the inequality than for the incidence of poverty.

When dealing with a dichotomous dependent variable (such as poor/not poor), multi-level logistical regression is the most appropriate technique to use. If an ordinary regression analysis were to be performed on such a variable, the probabilities predicted by the model may become smaller than 0 or greater than 1. In the logistical approach this is avoided by taking the logarithm of the odds ratios (in this case: the probability that someone is poor, divided by the probability that they are not) as a starting point. A predicted value of 0 in such a model indicates that the independent variable has no effect. In that case the probability that someone is poor is the same as the probability that they are not ($p=0.50$); the odds ratio is therefore equal to 1, and its logarithm is 0. In logistic regression models, a negative coefficient implies a low probability of the dependent trait to occur; a positive coefficient points to an increased risk (e.g. -4.6 corresponds with an estimated probability of being poor of 0.01, while +4.6 equals a probability of 0.99).

For technical reasons, only two levels are distinguished in the models: persons in countries. This is because the LIS data could only be analysed via remote access using standard software, and the available version of the Stata software package did not allow more than two levels of analysis.[82] Two problems arose here: the program is not good at dealing with weighted data, and a correction had to be applied for the fact that some people were members of the same household. This was resolved by drawing physical subsamples of equal size (approx. 1,225 persons in each country, making a total of over 13,000 observations), in proportion to the household weight and minimising the number of persons originating from the same household.[83]

At level 1 (persons), the models incorporate five explanatory characteristics. One of these is a pure person variable, namely age. Dummy variables were used here for three age categories, with 30-59 year-olds as the reference group. The other variables were household characteristics that are attributed to the person: number of earners, number of children, (not) living in a single-parent family, and (not) belonging to a poorly educated household. The latter is the case where the head and – if present – partner have completed an education no higher than level 2 of the UNESCO International Standard Classification of Education (ISCED 97), i.e. no higher than lower secondary education or initial vocational training.[84]

The number of explanatory characteristics at level 2 had to be restricted because the number of countries is fairly small. National prosperity was measured on the basis of GDP per head of the population (which in this analysis is not regarded as an endogenous characteristic of the regime types).[85] A number of variants for the regime classification were tested in separate models: the country scores on the two dimensions in figure 4.2 (scope and universalism), the scores on the institutional poverty risk index (IPRI), and dummy variables for the three regime types and the hybrid Dutch system. Based on the analysis in §6.6, it would be expected that the scores on the IPRI would provide the best explanation for the poverty incidences. The dummy variables make it possible to test the hypotheses formulated there, but would be expected to have less explanatory power than the IPRI.

Table 6.6 presents the outcomes of seven multi-level logistical regression models for the risk of poverty based on the modest but adequate criterion.[86] In the *unconditional hierarchical model* (model 1) no explanatory factors are incorporated; this 'empty' model serves as a reference point. It can be deduced from this that most of the unexplained variance[87] in the dependent variable is at the lowest level, that of the persons; only 7.5% of the variance is related to country level.

In *model 2* the person variables discussed earlier (level 1) and per capita GDP (level 2) are added. The proportion of explained variance is 0.38. Most of this is attributable to person variables:[88] but at level 2 the proportion of unexplained variance (0.029) is much lower than in the empty model. All coefficients are statistically significant, with the exception of the effect of gender (and the constant).

At level 2 the expected relationship is found: the more prosperous a country is, the lower the risk of poverty. At person level the effects also operate in the expected direction. The poverty risk rises as the number of earners reduces, the number of children increases, and if people belong to single-parent families or households whose head and partner (where present) have a low education level. Measured by age, the poverty incidence relative to 30-59 year-olds is high among children younger than 18 and young people aged 18-30 years. The latter group excludes students living outside the home; the effect thus mainly reflects the lower earnings of working young people and their higher risk of unemployment, often coupled with low benefits. The over-60s are poor significantly less often than 30-59 year-olds, mainly because of the correction for the number of earners, which is smaller on average in this group. After controlling for the effect of the characteristics cited, the influence of gender is negligible. Based on the z-values (not shown in table), the number of earners is the most important variable at level 1. The number of children, a low-educated household and the 18-30 years age group roughly exert the same influence on poverty and rank second. The pure effects of single-parent families and 0-17 year-olds are the least important, though unlike the effects of the gender variable they are statistically significant.

Table 6.6
Multi-level logistic regression models [a]

Model [b]	1 uncondi- tional hier- archical model	2 **level 1 + gdp/cap**	3 level 1 + gdp/cap **+ regime dimen- sions**	4 level 1 + gdp/cap **+ institutio- nal poverty risk index**	5 level 1 + gdp/cap **+ regime type (ref.=LIB)**	6 level 1 + gdp/cap **+ regime type (ref.=SD)**	7 level 1 **- gdp/cap** + regime type (ref. =SD)
Level 2 variables							
GDP per capita (* 1000 US $)		-0.05	-0.04	-0.05	-0.04	-0.04	
Scope (regime dimension 1)			-0.31				
Universalism (regime dimension 2)			*0.01*				
Institutional poverty risk index				0.52			
Hybrid regime type [c]					-1.02	-0.40	-0.14
Social-democratic regime type [c]					-0.63	ref.= 0.00	ref.= 0.00
Corporatist regime type [c]					-0.54	*0.09*	0.48
Liberal regime type [c]					ref.= 0.00	0.63	0.89
Level 1 variables							
Age < 18 years [c]		0.29	0.29	0.29	0.29	0.29	0.29
Age 18-30 years [c]		0.87	0.87	0.87	0.87	0.87	0.87
Age 30-59 years		ref.= 0.00	ref.= 0.00	ref.= 0.00	ref.= 0.00	ref.= 0.00	ref.= 0.00
Age > 60 years [c]		-0.59	-0.58	-0.59	-0.59	-0.59	-0.59
Number of earners		-1.57	-1.57	-1.57	-1.57	-1.57	-1.57
Number of children		0.53	0.53	0.53	0.53	0.53	0.53
Single parent		0.28	0.28	0.28	0.28	0.28	0.27
Gender		*0.03*	*0.03*	*0.03*	*0.03*	*0.03*	*0.03*
Low level of education		0.65	0.65	0.65	0.65	0.65	0.65
Constant	-2.00	*0.69*	*0.55*	*0.75*	*0.97*	*0.34*	-1.01
Fit indicators							
Prop. explained variance (level 1+2)	0.000	0.384	0.401	0.408	0.401	0.401	0.395
Prop. unexplained variance (level 1)	0.925	0.587	0.588	0.587	0.591	0.591	0.592
Prop. unexplained variance (level 2)	0.075	0.029	0.010	0.005	0.008	0.008	0.014
Residual intraclass correlation (rho)	0.075	0.047	0.018	0.009	0.014	0.014	0.023
Log Likelihood	-5038.4	-3994.5	-3989.5	-3986.5	-3988.4	-3988.4	-3990.7
Δ −2 Log Likelihood (Δ df); ref.=model 2	.	.	10.0 (2)	16.0 (1)	12.2 (3)	12.2 (3)	.
Probability	.	.	0.01	0.00	0.01	0.01	.
Wald χ^2	.	1431.9	1450.4	1468.7	1457.3	1457.3	1448.7
Probability	.	0.00	0.00	0.00	0.00	0.00	0.00
Δ Wald χ^2 (Δ df); ref.=model 2	.	.	18.5 (2)	36.9 (1)	25.4 (3)	25.4 (3)	.
Probability	.	.	0.00	0.00	0.00	0.00	.
number of persons (level 1 observations)	13483	13483	13483	13483	13483	13483	13483
number of countries (level 2 observations)	11	11	11	11	11	11	11
number of persons in countries (range)	1224-1232	1224-1232	1224-1232	1224-1232	1224-1232	1224-1232	1224-1232

a. Dependent variable: non-poor/poor according to modest but adequate poverty line.
b. Changes in comparison with previous model are printed in bold.
c. Dummy variable.
Coefficients printed in italics are not significant at p<.05

Source: Luxembourg Income Study (1999-2001)

In models 3, 4, 5 and 6 a number of variants of the regime typology were then introduced at the second level. Since the group of countries studied here does not exhibit very strong correlations between national wealth and regime type, these additions to the model do not lead to multicollinearity problems. The explained variance is higher in all cases than in the model incorporating only per capita GDP. The other indicators also suggest a better fit: the log likelihood is lower and the Wald χ^2 higher than in model 2, and the differences compared with that model are statistically significant[89] in all cases.

In *model 3* the country scores on the two separate regime dimensions in figure 4.2 – scope and universalism – are added as explanatory characteristics at the second level. The proportion of unexplained variance at level 2 now falls to 0.010. Only the first dimension is found to have a statistically significant effect: a more extensive system reduces the risk of poverty, even after controlling for the level of wealth. The degree of universality (the second dimension) has no influence, however: this effect is negligible and not statistically significant.

In *model 4* the score on the institutional poverty risk index is included as a determinant. Here again, the effect operates in the expected direction: the higher the score on the index, the greater the extent of poverty. However, the fit is better than in the previous model, as borne out by the lower proportion of unexplained variance at level 2 (0.005), the lower log likelihood and the higher Wald χ^2. As expected, therefore, the institutional poverty risk index explains the empirical differences in poverty incidence in the countries somewhat better than the scope and degree of universalism of the regime.

Models 5 and 6 contain separate dummy variables for the regime types at level 2, with the liberal and social-democratic type, respectively, as reference group. This enables the hypotheses formulated earlier to be tested in a targeted way. As predicted, these models fare slightly less well with the empirical data than model 4. The proportion of unexplained variance at the second level is 0.008, and the log likelihood and Wald χ^2 are between those of model 3 and 4. The model with the institutional poverty risk index thus has the greatest explanatory power, as predicted. What is however striking is that the fit of the models with dummy variables is slightly better than the model with the dimensions of the original regime typology. These dimensions thus do not have exceptional explanatory power; in section 6.5 it was argued that they are also theoretically less suitable for testing the relationship between regime type and poverty.

Based on *model 5*, hypothesis 1 cannot be rejected. As expected, after correction for per capita GDP, the poverty incidence in the corporatist regime type is significantly lower than in the liberal countries. Remarkably enough, the difference between the two country groups is greater after correction for national wealth than before. This can be deduced from the coefficients in *model 7*, in which per capita GDP is omitted. Here, the low poverty rates in Canada and the USA push down the average poverty rate in the liberal cluster, while the higher poverty rate in Australia pushes it up. The outcomes in model 5 suggest that this is partially due to differences in prosperity. The North American countries are richer than the corporatist countries, while Australia is poorer; and if this is taken into account, the average gap in poverty rates between the two regime types widens somewhat.

Model 5 also shows that poverty in the social-democratic cluster is lower than in the corporatist group, and that the hybrid Dutch regime type scores lowest. This ranking is in line with expectations, but it emerges from *model 6* that the differences vis-à-vis the social-democratic group are not statistically significant. For hypothesis 2, it is interesting to compare the outcomes with those of model 7, which does not contain per capita GDP. In that case the poverty incidence in the corporatist countries is significantly higher than in the social-democratic group, and hypothesis 2 can thus not be rejected. In model 6, however, the hypothesis received no support: after correction for differences in national wealth, the difference still operates in the expected direction, but is no longer statistically significant. Substantively, the multi-level analysis leads to the conclusion that the corporatist group does indeed have a higher poverty incidence than the social-democratic regime type, as expected, but that this is to some extent due to differences in prosperity. In Norway, in particular, but also in Denmark, per capita GDP was significantly higher than in Germany, France and Belgium. Although the pure difference between these regime types operates in the expected direction, it is modest and insignificant in statistical terms.

It is also useful to compare the outcomes of model 6 and model 7 with regard to hypothesis 3. If no allowance is made for variations in national wealth (model 7), the Netherlands has a slightly lower poverty rate than the social-democratic group of countries, but the effect is not significant. However, it turns out that this difference is mitigated because per capita GDP in the social-democratic group is higher on average than in the Netherlands. Correcting for this (model 6) produces a greater gap between the hybrid regime and the social-democratic cluster, though yet again this is not statistically significant.

Taking the analyses as a whole, it is apparent that there is little variance in the incidence of poverty at the level of the countries. The combination of regime characteristics and per capita GDP does however explain a large part of the limited level 2 variance (models 3-6) and leads to a better fit than the models in which the two macro-variables are incorporated separately (2 and 7).

Substantively, only hypothesis 1 is not rejected in these analyses: the liberal regime generates more poverty than the corporatist (and substantially more than the social-democratic and hybrid regimes). Hypotheses 2 and 3 receive insufficient support in the multi-level analyses and must therefore be rejected. The differences operate in the expected direction, but the pure regime effects are not statistically significant. It should be noted here that on the theoretical institutional poverty risk index the differences between the liberal and corporatist countries are greatest as well (there is a gap of 0.82 between the average scores on the index). The distances between the social-democratic and corporatist countries, and between the social-democratic cluster and the hybrid Dutch regime, are smaller on the index (respectively 0.54 and 0.40). The fact that it is precisely hypotheses 2 and 3 that have to be rejected is therefore somewhat understandable:

the institutional differences between the regime types are smaller according to the IPRI than in hypothesis 1, and this may explain why the differences in the poverty incidence are not large enough (after controlling for the divergent levels of national wealth) to be statistically significant.

6.8 Conclusions

This chapter explored whether the social security regime types identified in chapter 4 differ in the degree of poverty they produce. Since the definition of poverty in the theoretical and empirical literature has an ambiguous status, the chapter first explored what should be understood by the term theoretically.

The construct of poverty

Several choices arise in a theoretical construct of poverty. Should deficits be seen in terms of welfare, capabilities or resources? Are they relative or absolute, i.e. should the deficits be measured in relation to a certain reference group or not? And where should the line be drawn between the poor and the non-poor? A choice was made for a number of simple theoretical principles:

– Poverty is about the minimum necessities within a community. This may include both simple 'basic needs' (food, clothing, housing) and things which can be seen rather as capabilities (e.g. the possibility of taking part in social life) – with the qualifying comments that the definition of poverty must constantly refer to the prevailing sociohistorical minimum in the community, and that overly broad definitions are not credible. Three elements are included in the minimum necessities: things which are indispensable for the physical survival of the actor within the socio-historical community; the economic duties that are established in the formal institutions (e.g. taxation); and material obligations which ensue from the informal institutions within the community, if infringement attracts heavy sanctions (e.g. not being allowed into school because one cannot afford the uniform).
– Poverty makes it impossible for a person to achieve the minimal necessities with the available resources. The presence or absence of resources (income, financial assets, education level) should not form part of the definition of poverty; but such resources are important in assessing whether or not poverty exists, as they offer an indication of the ability to achieve the indispensable communal minimum.
– Poverty relates to absolute deficits. If someone is unable to achieve the minimum necessities within their community they are poor, regardless of what others have or do not have. The absolute standard is flexible, though. It refers to what is the minimum necessary within a certain community at a certain point in time, and this implies that the standard may change, for example due to technological developments (new products), different supply and demand (e.g. growing scarcity) or alterations in the formal and informal institutions (e.g. taxation, social norms).
– A threshold value for the absolute standard can be determined if the minimum necessities can be valorised in terms of the available resources. This can be done, for example, by converting the monetary value of a certain minimum basket of goods into

the required disposable income. If the necessities cannot be valorised, it is not possible to determine a threshold.

Based on these principles, a theoretical definition of poverty was suggested: *An individual actor is poor if he consistently lacks the means to obtain the minimum necessities of his community.* This implies among other things that collective actors (e.g. businesses, governments) cannot be poor, and that the lack of means has to relate to a minimum period of time (e.g., a calendar year).

With regard to three other elements from the theoretical poverty debate – should the deficits of the poor be compensated; is the government responsible for this; and which conditions should be attached to compensation? – it was observed that no satisfactory general statements can be made from a sociological perspective. Following Coleman (1990), there is no 'right division of rights'; rights, and the associated obligations, conditions and sanctions, are always constructed within a certain historical community. The course of this institutionalisation process theoretically depends on changes in relative prices, power relations, conflicts of interest and ideals within that community. From this institutional perspective, poverty cannot be seen in isolation from the community in question; it is an endogenous issue, which cannot be resolved by adopting an exogenous standpoint, such as the abstract rational actor operating behind Rawls' (1999 [1971]) 'veil of ignorance' or in Dworkin's (2000) 'hypothetical insurance market'. Rather than racking one's brains about the true nature of poverty and the universally fairest way of tackling the poverty problem, it is important to investigate how combating poverty is actually institutionalised in various contexts, and what effects this has.

Operational poverty lines

The chapter then investigated whether, given the theoretical demarcation, it was possible to find a suitable operational criterion for measuring poverty. The existing poverty lines used in empirical research were classified on the basis of three criteria: is the poverty line absolute or relative? Is it based on available resources or actual consumption and possession? And is poverty determined by 'outsiders' (objective: experts, policymakers) or by those involved (subjective: citizens, the poor)? Combining the dichotomies creates a typology of eight types of poverty line. The most commonly occurring were assessed on the basis of four criteria: validity, reliability, ease of application and socio-political relevance (or normative credibility). With regard to the latter, it is important to note that Australian and Dutch opinion research suggests that most people see poverty as an absolute shortage of necessities, not as a relative disadvantage compared with an average citizen. The absolute deficits are delineated rather strictly: for most people, poverty is about shortages at a fairly basic level, according to the standard that applies in their own society. Higher needs and capabilities are not rated as such, and therefore tend to be excluded from the public notion of poverty.

The analysis based on the above assessment criteria led among other things to the conclusion that relative poverty lines are not valid given the theoretical definition advocated here. The most commonly used variants of this type, namely the poverty line that equates to 60% of median income and the relative deprivation index, are moreover not satisfactory in terms of reliability and normative persuasiveness. Subjective income thresholds – particularly the methods which rely on the Minimum Income Question and the Income Evaluation Question – sometimes fit better with the theoretical conceptualisation; however, they suffer from major reliability problems which lead to unstable or unrealistically high poverty rates in empirical research. The objective expert budget method, finally, is valid, fairly reliable and credible. However, it is not simple to apply due to its labour-intensive nature; and the often limited differentiation of budget standards by household types makes it hard to derive poverty thresholds covering the entire population. Moreover, at present the approach is not suitable for comparative analyses of poverty, as international budget standards based on a common methodology are not yet available.

The generalised budget approach to poverty

An alternative poverty line was subsequently introduced; it can be described as a generalised budget approach, and was originally developed for the Netherlands (cf. Soede, 2006; Soede & Vrooman, 2007, 2008b). Based on the detailed budget inventories published by the Dutch National Institute for Family Finance Information, two reference budgets for a single person were first constructed. The 'basic needs' level incorporates costs that are virtually unavoidable for food, clothing, housing (e.g. rent, insurance, energy, water, telephone, furnishings, home maintenance and local taxes) and a few other expenditure items (such as transport, extra medical expenses, personal care and washing agents). This resulted in a sparse but complete budget which in principle makes it possible to run a household independently. The second reference budget, the 'modest but adequate' variant, allows scope for a few expenditure items which go beyond what is strictly unavoidable (recreation, memberships and subscriptions, a pet), but without any luxury (such as a car or foreign holiday).

The reference budgets were then generalised using equivalence factors to create two variants of the initial poverty line for the Netherlands. Following the recommendations of the US National Academy of Sciences, the threshold amounts over time have been determined by indexing the initial norms to the three-year moving average in median expenditure on the basic items food, drink (excluding alcohol), clothing and housing. This leads to an increase in the threshold amounts which exceeds price inflation, but lags behind the growth in national wealth and median income.

Like the expert budget method, this threshold reflects the absolute nature of poverty, and establishes a clear link with what is necessary at a given time and place. The threshold amounts refer to people's consumption possibilities, not to their actual consumption; and the limits have a meaningful interpretation, they are not 'fetishistic'. As a result, the threshold provides valid coverage of the theoretical definition of poverty applied here. This poverty line is probably also relevant for policymakers and citizens, since the two variants fit in well with the subjective perceptions of poverty among the population. In contrast to the traditional expert budget method, the new threshold is not especially labour-intensive, which means it lends itself well for use in practical research.

For the Netherlands, this approach led to a plausible and readily interpretable trend in poverty rates in the period 1985-2005. Subsequently, the threshold amounts in around 2000 were converted into similar norms for the ten other countries using purchasing power parities. Based on a sensitivity analysis, a slightly different equivalence scale was chosen for the comparative norms than in the original Dutch poverty line. The ranking of the countries in terms of poverty rates proved to be fairly stable when applying a variety of equivalence scales.

Postulated relationships between regime types and poverty

This translation of the Dutch threshold amounts to the other countries made it possible to test a number of hypotheses concerning the relationship between social security regime types and poverty according to the generalised budget approach. The hypotheses were constructed on the basis of the country scores on a theoretical institutional poverty risk index (IPRI; cf. figure 6.3); this index indicates to what extent the formal social security institutions of different countries are conducive to the risk of poverty, all other circumstances (wealth, demographic composition, etc.) being equal. The expectations were that

(1) In countries with a liberal social security regime (Australia, Canada, UK and USA), poverty is higher than in countries with a regime of the corporatist type (Belgium, France and Germany);
(2) In countries with a corporatist social security regime, poverty is higher than in countries with a regime of the social-democratic type (Denmark, Norway and Sweden);
(3) In countries with a social-democratic social security regime, poverty is higher than in the hybrid Dutch regime.

Empirical results

Based on adapted data from the Luxembourg Income Study, a bivariate analysis was first performed on the 'three I's of poverty': the incidence, income deficit and inequality of poverty. The scores on a number of composite measures, in which all three aspects of poverty are expressed, were also calculated. Hypotheses 1 and 2 received support on the basis of the poverty incidence and the indices, and to some extent were also sustained on the grounds of the income deficits. Hypothesis 3, by contrast, received no support in any of the bivariate analyses.

A multi-level logistical regression analysis was then performed, with the poverty incidence on the basis of the 'modest but adequate' criterion as the dependent variable. This enabled the pure effects of the regime types to be determined whilst controlling for other characteristics in which the countries differ, and also to test whether the differences between the regime types were statistically significant. It emerged from this that only a small proportion of the variance in the poverty incidence is related to differences at the country level (7.5%); the rest consists of differences between individual persons. The limited variance at the country level could however be largely explained by the model variables, whereby the differences between the countries in the scores on the institutional poverty risk index and national wealth (measured by per capita GDP) both made an independent contribution. After correcting for the impact of differences in national prosperity, the effects of the regime types on the poverty rate all operated in the theoretically postulated direction. The difference between the liberal and corporatist groups was found to be statistically significant, so that hypothesis 1 cannot be rejected. Hypotheses 2 and 3 received insufficient support in this analysis, however; although the differences found were in line with expectations, the pure regime effects were statistically too weak.

As in chapter 5, therefore, it appears that divergent sets of coherent formal institutions in similar circumstances generate different outcomes. The abstract classification of countries in terms of social security regime types has the postulated impact on the 'production of poverty'; however, the effects are modest and sometimes negligible in statistical terms. This calls for a reconsideration of the central theme of this study in the final chapter.

Annex 1
Construction of the institutional poverty risk index

The same procedure was used for the construction of the institutional poverty risk index (IPRI) as for the 'benefit dependency boost index' in the previous chapter. The criterion is related to some degree to the inverse of the de-commodification score calculated by Esping-Andersen (1990: 47-54). The underlying theoretical notions are however different. Corporatist systems are for example relatively highly 'commodified', because a person's position on the labour market and their employment history play an important role in the allocation of benefit rights. This does not however mean by definition that such systems will in theory generate more poverty. If elderly people and widows in a corporatist system are assured of a generous pension, their poverty risk can in principle be lower than in a 'de-commodified' system with a universal but low basic income for every citizen. In addition, there are a number of practical differences between the IPRI and Esping-Andersen's de-commodification score: the data used are more recent, they cover more aspects of social security, and the components of the index are added together in a different way.[90]

The analysis performed here incorporates 49 characteristics of collective old age pensions; statutory social insurance benefits and provisions for the unemployed, the disabled, and surviving dependants; social assistance; and family benefits (excluding childcare; see OECD, 2002: 13-17). For each of these arrangements, the extent to which rights are allocated that are theoretically important for the degree of poverty was assessed in the 11 countries concerned: the intended target group, the level of benefits (especially at the lower end of the scale), the method of indexation, any conditions attaching to the rights (job search requirements, means testing, residency, employment history) and the maximum duration of benefit. The formal institutions studied were as follows:

Old age pension (9 variables):
a) coverage: entitlement of persons with/without labour experience;
b) levels: net replacement rates at three lower income levels (50%-100% average production worker); mode of indexation of first, second pillar pension; target full mandatory pension for a single person;
c) conditions: number of labour years required for a full pension in the second tier public scheme.

Unemployment (7 variables):
a) coverage: covered unemployed persons (inhabitants, employees, certain employees only); percentage of unemployed receiving benefits;
b) levels: statutory benefit rate of unemployment insurance; net replacement rate for a single person in the first month of unemployment (two lower income levels);
c) conditions: minimum qualifying period (contributions, work history) for entitlement;
d) duration: maximum duration in months.

Social assistance (14 variables):
a) coverage: restrictions based on nationality, residency, or period of residence;
b) levels: net replacement rates after five years without gainful employment (three family types); maximum statutory benefit amounts (three family types); indexation of benefits (prices, wages, mix);
c) conditions: strictness of work test; income test; assets test; inclusion of private home in assets test; minimum age to qualify for a full benefit;
d) duration: maximum duration in months.

Disability (9 variables):
a) coverage: group eligible for sickness leave, work-related and social disability benefits;
b) levels: benefit level in case of work-related and social disability; indexation of work-related benefits;
c) conditions: minimum threshold work-related and social disability; minimum period of affiliation in case of social disability.

Survivor's benefits (7 variables):
a) coverage: scope of widow's pension; separate orphan's pension;
b) levels: benefit level of widows of residents, employees (long term benefits);
c) conditions: means testing; exclusion in case of remarriage/cohabitation with new partner;
d) duration: maximum benefit period for dependent spouse, below age 65.

Family benefits (3 variables):
a) coverage: benefits for dependent children of residents, employees, or none;
b) levels: benefit amount 1st child;
c) conditions: means testing.

Categorical principal component analysis (CatPCA, see chapter 4) was applied to each arrangement to examine whether the items correlated in such a way that they could be reduced to one or more underlying dimensions. Variables which produced scale scores on these dimensions that were not in line with their theoretical impact on poverty have been treated separately. For example, the indicators for social assistance were split up into a 'performance' scale (levels + duration, 8 items, Cronbach's alpha= 0.95), a scale with a number of conditions (3 items, Cronbach's alpha= 0.67) and three individual indicators (the coverage, the income test, and the minimum age to qualify for full benefit). A total score was calculated for each set of indicators, taking into account the number of characteristics included. The constituent indices thus obtained were then standardised and added together to produce a total score.

In calculating the total score, weighting factors were applied to reflect the average importance of the scheme types across all countries. These factors were determined on the grounds of:

a) the average take-up of each type of scheme in the period 1995-1999 among the population aged 15 years and older, as this emerged from the volume figures in the previous chapter and (for family benefits, assuming full take-up) the proportion of households with children;
b) the share of potential users of the arrangement among people at the bottom end of the income distribution (the lowest three deciles);
c) the share of the income source (pension, unemployment benefit, etc.) in the total income.

Pension arrangements carry the most weight in the total index (34%), followed by social assistance (29%). Unemployment benefits have roughly half the weight of pension arrangements (18%), disability benefits are about three times as low (11%). Family benefits (5%) and survivor's benefits (4%) are of relatively subordinate importance.[91]

The institutional poverty risk index probably gives a good picture of the theoretical likelihood of poverty in the regime types and the individual countries, because it includes the elements of the formal rules that are particularly relevant for poverty of all major social security schemes. Naturally, a different approach is also possible. It could for example be argued that fewer arrangements should be taken into account because the degree of protection against poverty in a given country is determined mainly by the provisions which establish the collective 'bottom line', such as old-age pensions for people who have never worked, social assistance benefit and family benefits. This is in line with the de-commodification interpretation of Esping-Andersen, who considered it important how well people are protected regardless of their relationship with the labour market. However, such an approach ignores the fact that in some countries the protection against poverty is achieved largely via social insurance arrangements for the unemployed, the disabled and survivors. If the social assistance benefits are rather spartan, this is then less problematic from the perspective of poverty, because not many people are dependent on this provision. In addition, it should be noted that in fact old-age pensions, social assistance and family benefits do weigh heavily in the total index (two-thirds of the total weight).

Alternatively, one could posit that more social security arrangements should have been included in the analysis, for example by adding employee benefits (leave arrangements, maternity/paternity leave, childcare facilities). It was decided not to do that here, however, because these arrangements are often temporary or supplementary in nature and are taken up mainly by a group with a low risk of poverty.

Consideration could also be given to including characteristics of the institutionalisation of the labour market, such as the degree of legal protection against dismissal. The theoretical impact of such arrangements on poverty is however difficult to indicate in advance. An extensive system of employment protection may guard working people against a severe loss of income, and can thus prevent poverty. At the same time, however, it could lead to an increasing poverty risk among the unemployed; employers may be less inclined to hire them permanently, out of fear of not being able to fire them when things go wrong. From a theoretical point of view, the net effect on the poverty rate is hard to determine in advance. Something similar applies for a labour market policy of active integration. If a country spends a good deal on such an activating policy, it is not certain that this will lead to a reduction in poverty; that will depend on the effectiveness of the measures and the income gains that are achieved. If, for example, an active labour market policy induces people systematically to perform subsidised work for a wage that is barely above the level of their previous benefit, they have become more active, and benefit dependency will fall; but this has no discernible influence on the poverty figures if many people merely experience a transition from being non-working poor to working poor.

It would on the other hand be desirable to add certain supplementary benefits to the index, such as housing benefits and one-off social assistance to cover special expenses, but it was decided not to do this for practical reasons (limited availability of comparative data). In any event, their supplementary nature would obviously imply that these arrangements would have had only a limited weight in the total index, so that the picture presented here would probably not change radically if they were to be included.

7 The collective significance of social security institutions

One of the central ideas of the 'new institutional economics' is that the rules created within a society matter for the outcomes brought about at the communal level. Although mechanisms of supply and demand are of great importance in transacting, markets are not self-regulating in the sense that they automatically lead to economically optimal outcomes. On the contrary, if the desired collective results are to be achieved, even the most liberal society is bound to impose some kind of regulation, in the form of legally enforceable contracts, a system of mutual trust between traders and customers, or other institutions. Stiglitz (2006: xiv, 189-190) phrases it like this:

> The eminent eighteenth-century economist Adam Smith has often been misunderstood. He argued that individuals, in pursuing their self-interest, would advance the broader interests of society: that incentives to outcompete rivals would lead to lower costs and to the production of goods consumers wanted, and that consumers, and society more generally, would benefit from both. [... Thus] markets and the pursuit of self-interest would lead, as if by an invisible hand, to economic efficiency. [...] However, even Smith realized that in an unfettered market economy private incentives are often not aligned with social costs and benefits – and when that happens, the pursuit of self-interest will not result in the well-being of society. [...] Research on the economics of information showed that whenever information is imperfect, in particular when there are information asymmetries – where some individuals know something that others do not (in other words, *always*) – the reason that the invisible hand seems invisible is that it is not there. [...] Market failures arise whenever there are externalities, consequences of an individual's or a firm's actions for which they do not pay the cost or receive the benefit. Markets, by themselves, lead to too little of some things, like research, and too much of others, like pollution. [...] Without appropriate government regulation and intervention, markets do not lead to economic efficiency.

The premise that 'institutions matter' has been fleshed out and investigated in this study for the 'rules of relief'; the principal *motif* is the collective significance of social security institutions. On the basis of a literature survey, the theoretical sections began by exploring the nature of institutions, and how they are embedded in society (chapter 2). An institutional demarcation of social security was then built from this (chapter 3). The empirical sections first ascertained whether the actual configurations of official social security rules in 11 countries diverge in such a way that there is justification for reducing them to a limited number of regimes (chapter 4). This was followed by an examination of whether the countries representing the various types of social security regime differ in the degree of benefit dependency and poverty they produce (chapters 5 and 6).

The outcomes of the theoretical and empirical analyses are presented here in broad outline.[1] Following on from this overview, an attempt is made to interpret in more detail the relationships found between regime types on the one hand, and benefit dependency and poverty on the other. The chapter concludes with a brief look at some of the implications of this study for further scientific research and for socioeconomic policy in developed countries.

7.1 Institutions and social security

This section elucidates the two concepts that lie at the heart of the theoretical analyses. It also indicates how the outcomes of the general examination of institutions can be applied to social security.

Institutions as social rules

Institutions are often equated with certain forms of social organisation, especially the more permanent ones which give direction to society (the Church, the family, education) or which serve higher social ends (voluntary associations, cultural organisations). That is not the meaning that is assigned to institutions in this study, however. In line with the view put forward by Durkheim (1901) – who regarded sociology as "the science of institutions" – the term here refers simply to the rules that a community applies in order to steer the behaviour of its members in a desired direction. This interpretation is also employed in the 'new institutionalism' in the social sciences, three variants of which can be distinguished: the sociological approach, the rational choice view and the historical perspective. Proponents of sociological institutionalism argue among other things that collective rules not only guide behaviour through the explicit prescriptions that are contained within them, but also because of the way in which they allow actors to see their world (via 'cognitive framing' and 'moral templates'); or, to put it differently, institutions not only indicate what people ought to do in certain circumstances, but also determine the behavioural alternatives they are able to imagine. This approach also stresses that the relationship between the rules of the community and its members is a dialectic one. On the one hand, social rules steer actors' behaviour; on the other hand, institutions are not a natural given, but are always a product of the rule-defining acts of people.

The rational choice perspective has been widely used in research into social dilemmas: situations where behaviour that is advantageous and sensible for individual actors generates major disadvantages at the level of the community as a whole, and can therefore not be described as optimal from that collective point of view (e.g. overgrazing, polluting the environment, tax evasion). According to this approach institutions make economic and social interactions predictable; they foster collectively desirable behaviour by indicating what is allowed and intolerable, making rule compliance profitable and punishing defection.

Historical institutionalism posits that although actors make the rules, they are not free in doing so: the development of institutions is characterised by a high degree of path dependence. The routines and the investments encapsulated in the rules imply that institutional change may involve high economic or social costs; as a result, they tend to be difficult to change, and often build on the existing structures. Proponents of this perspective also point out that the same institutions do not lead to similar results everywhere, but that those results depend on the historical context in which the rules are applied.

The economist North (1990, 1998) integrated some of these notions. In his view, institutions are "humanly devised constraints that shape human interaction". According to North, such 'rules of the game' must be separated from the 'players': the actors who make and apply the rules. He argues that institutions play an important role in economic transactions because they establish and protect property rights (for example via contracts, laws, etc.) and also contain stipulations on monitoring and enforcing compliance with the rules. In this way they coordinate economic exchange, and they may do this more or less efficiently, with higher or lower transaction costs. North draws a distinction between formal institutions (such as government laws) and informal institutions which apply between private actors (such as conventions in business). If the exchange takes place over a long period, between actors who know each other well and are dependent on each other (for example in tribal societies), unwritten informal rules may be efficient: the likelihood that actors will not meet their mutual agreements is small because the cost of this (disgrace, expulsion) is high. In modern societies, however, exchanges tend to be more impersonal and are repeated less often. In these cases there is a high chance of defection and it may be useful to have the government, as an independent third party, draw up formal rules. Although this is more expensive (because a police and judicial apparatus is needed to ensure compliance and to impose sanctions in case of defection), it may nonetheless be efficient for the economic interaction in society as a whole, as it increases the likelihood that actors will behave in a predictable and reliable way.

A number of these lines of thought come together in the figural model (see §2.3). Here, institutions are interpreted as socially constructed rules that delineate the rights and obligations of actors. They also indicate the conditions attaching to the granting of those entitlements and the imposition of those duties, and what positive and negative sanctions are possible.

The fact that institutions are social constructs implies among other things that they never simply appear of their own accord, or that they follow inevitably from certain religious, ethical or philosophical principles (the *Rule of St. Benedict*, Kantian ethics, utility maximisation, etc.). Sociologically, the rights, obligations, conditions and sanctions that apply in a community can only be described, and explanations can be sought for the existence of certain configurations. There are however no universal imperatives: institutions are always endogenous, their justification lies exclusively within the community in which they are applied. The rationale may be derived from higher principles, but that is not necessarily the case; from a sociological perspective, there is no "right division of rights" (Coleman, 1990).

A right means that someone is permitted to do something, to possess something or to acquire something; and that others may not hinder this. Rights generally imply that other actors have obligations towards those who are entitled: "rights are grounds of duty in others" (Raz, 1986). Entitlements and duties both reflect the interests of the actors concerned, the support for ideals, the power relations within their community, and the relative costs and benefits of different forms of regulation (including expenditure on vesting the rules, monitoring and sanctioning). Ultimately, both the rights and the obligations are based on a social consensus; if they are no longer supported by the actors in the community, the basis for assigning rights and imposing duties disappears.

Conditions may be attached to rights in the form of certain events (such as being needy), qualifying characteristics on the part of stakeholders (having a certain age, family composition, education level, etc.), or particular types of behaviour (e.g. showing a willingness to work).

Sanctions are rewards granted when the rules are observed and punishments imposed in the event of defection. They are not by definition 'heroic', in other words it is not necessary for there to be one actor who hands out non-recurring punishments and rewards; sanctions can also be imposed collectively and incrementally. Sanctions need not be applied by external agents either; individual actors may have internalised the rules of conduct, causing them to experience feelings of guilt, shame or superiority when they break or observe the rules, and thus to punish or reward themselves.

The traditional and institutional view of social security

Although the type of arrangements to which 'social security' refers has a long history (poor relief, Bismarck's social insurances), until the introduction of the American *New Deal* in the 1930s it was a term that was used only sporadically. In the us *Social Security Act* (1935) it related to all rights that fell within the scheme, and simply meant that society offered a degree of economic security to its citizens. The more recent scientific literature contains both narrow and broad demarcations of the concept. In the narrow approach, social security has the objective of offering a certain level of income protection. The instruments deployed to achieve this consist of statutory social insurance (e.g. old-age pensions for employees) and national provisions such as social assistance or a national health insurance scheme. Under those arrangements, benefits may be provided in money or in kind when a limited number of clearly defined risks occur. The contingencies as laid down in 1952 in a convention of the International Labour Organisation (ILO) are often taken as a basis here: old age; death of the breadwinner; the maintenance of children; unemployment; short-term sickness of employees; permanent incapacity for work; high medical expenses; a loss of earnings due to pregnancy and confinement; and the costs and losses ensuing from occupational illnesses and accidents. The disadvantage of this approach to social security is that it is equated to formal income schemes which target specific and traditional risks; for example, it does not include help given by relatives or measures to counter the financial and social consequences of divorce.

In the broad definition, which is propagated among others by a number of Flemish theoreticians (see e.g. Viaene et al., 1976, 1990), social security is not only about income protection, but also extends to job security, health and social participation. The instruments used to realise this are not restricted to statutory government schemes, or 'social welfare', but also include 'invisible' social security: tax reductions and allowances, employment-related provisions and insurance schemes, and household savings and insurances people arrange for themselves ('fiscal', 'occupational' and 'private welfare'; cf. Titmuss, 1958; Berghman, 1986). The interventions are concerned not only with partially recompensing a falling or excessively low income; in principle, prevention and restoration should be given priority. In the broad approach, moreover, social security focuses not just on the traditional risks from the ILO list, but on all forms of 'human damage', thus including things such as ecological harm or losses which manifest themselves only after many years. A strong point of this broad approach is that it is not restricted to the legal protection against the risks contained in a fossilised list. On the other hand, it also means that the social security concept is in danger of becoming all-embracing: the entire welfare state falls within its scope, plus all the arrangements that are not enforced by formal legislation. Another objection is that it is a fairly a-sociological approach; there is little attention for the socio-historical context of the prevailing rules (such as the goals and interests involved) and for the collective consequences of social security.

In the light of these considerations, in this study social security has been defined from an institutional perspective. The concept refers to the collectively defined rights, duties, conditions and potential sanctions which aim to generate positive social outcomes by protecting individual actors against economic deficits. Social security is thus a collection of rules that have been constructed within the community, i.e. institutions. These relate to deficits faced by individuals to which an economic value can be assigned (too little income, loss of employment, costs of medical provisions or social participation). The allocation of rights and duties is not only important for those concerned, but also serves a higher purpose, namely the expectation that the rules will generate net positive outcomes for the community: more collective wealth or a fairer distribution of prosperity, a healthier population, fewer social tensions, combating poverty. The way in which social security rights are allocated and the manner in which duties, conditions and sanctions are imposed always depend on the socio-historical context. Every community determines for itself where the optimum lies; this is based on a certain consensus – there is no universally applicable 'right division of social security rights'.

Theoretically, it is not essential for social security to focus on specific eventualities; for example, an unconditional basic income is not linked to any explicitly covered risk. The notion of risk is therefore not included in the definition used here. In practice, however, the allocation of rights will generally be connected with the reasons for the deficits; for example, a person who becomes fully incapacitated for work due to an occupational accident often will receive a higher and longer-lasting benefit than someone who is dismissed due to misconduct.

According to this institutional demarcation, social security encompasses more than the traditional social insurances and national provisions; yet it is not so comprehensive that it can no longer be analytically distinguished from the welfare state and its informal counterparts. Collective regulation of education, health care, the housing market, etc. is not regarded as social security, except for those elements concerned with the economic entitlements of people or households (e.g. student grants, health insurance, housing benefit).

Types of institution

In the figural model in §2.3 a distinction is drawn between formal and informal institutions. The former are promulgated or ratified by the government. Formal institutions can be divided into four hierarchically arranged types. First there are the *meta-rules* (such as the

Constitution, election laws), which describe the rights and duties applying for the establishment of formal rules. Then there are rules governing the production of goods and services by the government; examples include laws on the police force, national defence, state education, etc. These rules also establish the rights and obligations of other actors in connection with this *government production* (paying taxes, military service, compulsory education etc.). A third category is *recognition by the government*, as an independent third party, of the rights and obligations of private legal persons (citizens, companies). Provisions from the civil code (e.g. matrimonial law) or mercantile law (such as the statutory period within which companies must pay their bills) are examples of this. Finally, there are *formal contracts between private parties*: agreements that are embedded in legal stipulations, such as ownership and inheritance rights that are implicitly established when people marry, or the terms of delivery between suppliers and consumers which build on the general rules of the prevailing mercantile law.

Informal institutions are based entirely on social consensus in groups or communities, and can also be broken down into four categories. *Values* are collective guidelines for preferred behaviour, which do not indicate what people should or should not do in specific cases. By contrast, *social norms* are prescriptive; they are behavioural rules applying in specific circumstances and can often be regarded as an elaboration of the principles incorporated in values. Since it is possible to infringe against social norms (unlike values, towards which people may be more or less oriented), they also contain the possibility of imposing sanctions. *Conventions* resemble norms in many respects, but have no value component: they are arbitrary behavioural expectations which are fairly neutral in nature, and which are intended mainly to coordinate behaviour effectively and to affirm the membership of groups or communities (e.g. dress codes). Sometimes conventions may be codified, giving them a formal character (e.g. statutory traffic rules, the official spelling of a language). *Informal contracts* are promises and agreements on the rights and duties of actors which are not endorsed by the government, but are entirely based on what is customary within the community (e.g. an unofficial church marriage).

Every social security system contains informal elements: values such as solidarity and fairness, the norms which apply in a society for the minimum necessities of life, conventions that apply in the relationship between benefit recipients and help and support agencies (e.g. making benefits available on a specific day). Social security systems can also be entirely informal, for example taking the form of support from family members or the Church.

Modern social security systems, however, tend to be highly formalised. They are often enshrined in laws and government decrees as part of the rules concerning government production. In addition to this purely collective social security, the government may also endorse specific types of occupational social security, for example by legally ratifying an unemployment insurance scheme which is administered by companies or trade unions. Finally, there are private arrangements which are partly controlled by the government, such as commercial medical insurance contracts where the minimum cover and the maximum premium payable are established by law.

The social security 'regimes' discussed later can be regarded as qualitatively different, cohesive systems of formal institutions which are designed to achieve certain goals that are considered collectively desirable.

The relationship between institutional levels

While formal and informal institutions are often hierarchically arranged, it is not the case that the lower rules can be derived from the higher rules in only one way; there is no logically compelling entailment: the form in which high principles or meta-rules appear at a lower level is socio-historically determined. In social security, too, laws and regulations, and the informal rules that support or elaborate the formal rules, can theoretically be arranged in an infinite number of ways. In reality, however, there is often a hierarchy in terms of the level of abstraction. Thus the government, driven by supranational rules imposed by the European Union or the United Nations, may for example guarantee a constitutional right to support in the event of need. This may be elaborated in the form of a social assistance law, and fleshed out further in implementation decrees and the mutual informal behavioural expectations of the actors concerned. The links between these hierarchical levels invariably rest on consensual interpretations. The constitutional right to social assistance may remain unchanged for decades, while it may be interpreted more broadly or more strictly over time in the lower laws, depending on the changing perceptions and preferences of politicians, policy officials and citizens. In practice the rights and obligations at the bottom of the institutional ranking can play a bigger part in determining the behaviour of the actors concerned (applicants for and recipients of benefits, social security organisations, etc.) than the higher principles that are laid down in the Constitution.

The formal social security rules discussed earlier can exist alongside each other, in which case they are often referred to as the first, second and third pillars. The government is then for example responsible for providing social assistance to all citizens; employers are responsible for operating an unemployment insurance scheme for their own workers; and the individual is responsible for his or her own pension provision. The institutions can however also be built up in layers; for example, the government may guarantee a flat rate minimum retirement pension for everyone; employers or trade unions may then top this up for former employees to a certain percentage of their earlier wage; and in addition the individual may themselves take out a supplementary pension insurance or annuity.

Although this is not necessary, institutions may be strongly interrelated. This is often the case in closed communities (sects, monastic orders, a class-ridden society, etc.), where the values work through in an apparently inevitable way into precise behavioural prescripts, with heavy and well-known sanctions for defection. In the main, however, such 'thick institutions' are less typical of prosperous democratic societies.

For several reasons it is likely that formal and informal rules which relate to the same kind of behaviour will correspond with each other to some extent. Informal institutions may be an elaboration of the formal rules; the latter can never cover all circumstances that might occur in practice and therefore by definition leave some room for discretionary action. Conversely, formal rights and obligations can be a codification of informal institutions people were already subjected to within their community. Such a correspondence is not however necessarily present: the informal rules by which people live can also diverge considerably from what the law stipulates (for example in countries where tax evasion is the prevailing standard), or in specific communities may differ markedly from the official rules (Jews in the Diaspora, Christians living under communism). Whether informal rules dominate the formal rules, or vice versa, is ultimately an empirical, socio-historical question; that applies just as much for social security institutions as for other rules.

Individual and corporate actors

The figural model incorporates two processes: rule application and rule generation (cf. graph 2.1). Both come about via actors, which may be individual persons or corporate actors (organisations which form an independently acting legal persona, such as companies or foundations). Social security actors vary depending on the nature of the scheme. In addition to entitled persons and duty-bound contributors, they may include various parts of the social security organisation, employers, judges, etc.

The rule-driven and rule-generating behaviour of actors is not determined directly by the existing institutions. People are not slavish followers of the prevailing rules, but filter them and thus play an active role. They base their behaviour on their own interpretation of the institutions, and that is shaped by their earlier experiences, their resources and a number of motivations. In theory, those motivations relate to the goals, ideals and interests of actors; their assessment of the costs and benefits of perceived behavioural alternatives; the likelihood of achieving desired outcomes; and (for natural persons) the emotional aspects of their possible courses of action. In the case of corporate actors there is a complication in that the aims, ideological bias, interests and the motivations of the individuals who represent them may not correspond with those of the organisation itself: the principal-agent problem.

The origin of social rules

Institutions always arise and change through the behaviour of actors. The figural model indicates that this rule generation process is theoretically determined by changes in relative prices, power relations, conflicts of interest and support for ideals. If the socially weighted sum of these elements alters, actors may be prompted to establish new institutions or modify existing rules. The changes in these driving factors, and consequently in the actors' incentive to regulate, theoretically ensue from the interaction of the existing institutional structure with the historical process a community is experiencing.

Actors do not react automatically to such impulses, but weigh up for themselves whether they make new rules desirable for them. Path dependence acts as a brake on change: people cannot always imagine new rules, and stakeholders may feel that rule changes do not produce sufficient returns or will be accompanied by high social or economic costs. New actors – the coming young generation, counter-elites, new organisations – and individual 'normative entrepreneurs' often play a key role in the process of rule transformation. They less readily accept the existing situation as self-evident, and for them the benefits of changes are more likely to exceed the costs.

This does not imply that widely desired rule changes can be achieved without a struggle. In the case of formal institutions, the vesting or modifying of rules often requires complex forms of 'rule interaction': decisions on new legislation and regulations in parliamentary democracies are a characteristic example of this. However, informal institutions can generally not be created in such a more or less rational interchange of arguments on a platform of rule interaction. It is not possible simply to promulgate new values, norms or conventions, because such rules are based purely on social consensus and consequently arise and change in a process that takes place within the community. The evolution of social norms on extramarital sexual relationships may illustrate this. The introduction of the contraceptive pill (a technological innovation) lowers the material and social costs of extramarital sex, because the risk of unwanted pregnancy declines. As a result the incentive to regulate can change, and this may work through into actor perceptions: fewer people may accept the norm 'sex outside marriage is not permissible' as self-evident. Defection may increase and be sanctioned to a lesser degree (more extramarital sex that is left unpunished occurs). However, if the behaviour is still considered to have negative collective consequences (such as the spread of sexually transmitted diseases) a new norm is likely to emerge (e.g. 'sexual contact outside marriage is permissible as long as people practise safe sex'), provided it has the support of a critical mass within the community.

Generally speaking, with both formal and informal institutions it is easier to change the lower-level rules (e.g. implementation decrees, conventions) then higher guidelines (the Constitution, certain core values). This is largely because the costs of changing the more abstract institutions tend to be greater: if these are modified, that change often also affects the lower-level rules. Additionally, actors are more likely to have internalised the higher rules, and therefore may find it more difficult to envisage changing them.

The process of institutionalisation is clearly visible in the transition from informal to formal social security systems (predominantly statutory social insurance schemes) which took hold in many Western European countries between 1875 and 1930 (see also De Swaan, 1988). The low wages and greater risks which accompanied industrialisation (mass unemployment and indigence need on the part of workers, industrial accidents, etc.) implied a change in relative prices. The growing gulf between the economic classes led to sharper conflicts of interest. The power relations also changed, largely as a result of the emergence of a liberal bourgeoisie which partially took over the dominant position of the traditional, often aristocratic elite, and of the growth in a number of counter-elites (socialists, communists, anarchists, feminists, the petty bourgeoisie). The latter were inspired by different ideals, which attracted growing support among the population. The Enlightenment ideals of equality and emancipation took on a radical dimension in the reformist ideologies of the 19th century; and the traditional Christian ideals of charity, mutual care and striving for eternal salvation enjoyed a revival because they offered a means of countering the excesses that accompanied industrial production processes.

In this way socio-historical developments had an impact on all the driving factors, thus changing the incentive to regulate. This does not however mean that it was decided overnight to establish formal social security schemes. Ultimately, three changes in the perceptions of the relevant actors proved decisive. There was a growing consensus that unemployment, neediness, incapacity for work, and so on were not purely the result of individual moral failure, but of the way in which industrial production was organised and embedded in society; and macro-problems such as these demanded a collective solution. The idea also gained hold that the existing informal social security arrangements offered an inadequate response to the emerging modern risks. The extensive migration to the large towns and cities caused many local communities to shrink and become more unstable, so that the traditional family and community solutions, based on social norms, no longer worked. In the urban setting, large sections of the working population could be affected by unemployment and neediness, which went beyond the ability of the network of blood relatives, churches and local authorities to mitigate. Occupational provisions failed to materialise: the surfeit of available labour meant that companies saw no need for this, with the exception of a minority of socially aware entrepreneurs.

Finally, both the elite and the counter-elites increasingly felt that there was something to be gained from establishing statutory social security schemes. For the bourgeoisie it was a means of mitigating the disadvantages of industrial production. Expensive externalities (strikes and social unrest prompted by the mass poverty and poor working conditions, health risks that could affect all citizens) might be countered by social legislation, and it was believed that a healthy, rested and properly trained population would be more productive. The establishment of formal social security was also often seen as a means of generating loyalty on the part of the working classes to a strong nation-state, which would be able to compete economically and politically with other countries. For the counter-elites, formalisation of social security was above all a means of emancipating their followers and assuring them of a more decent standard of living.

The 'social question' was ultimately decided in many countries in a lengthy process of rule interaction, often in connection with the decision-making on other policy domains and political questions (such as compulsory education, public housing). Introduction of universal suffrage was of great importance here: it was often the changing alliances of the bourgeoisie with the counter-elites – which were now also represented in Parliament – that effected the transition from informal to formal social security systems.

The acquisition of rules by individual actors
Since institutions are social constructs, new members of a society (children, immigrants) have to be familiarised with the rights and obligations that apply in their community. This rule acquisition by new actors can be seen as a specific form of rule-driven interaction: the community has expectations regarding the kind of upbringing parents should give their children; teachers have to meet the standards of their profession and the statutory requirements regarding the curriculum, etc. In many theories it is assumed that this is an inevitable, one-sided process of imprinting the rules of the host community. For example, the functionalist school stresses that the steady "barbarian invasion of new-

born infants" (Parsons, 1951) poses a permanent threat to the social order, and argues that they must therefore be integrated via a process of socialisation. Initially, this takes place via the parents, who pass on to the 'newcomers' basic values, norms and skills. In complex societies, an extensive secondary socialisation process also takes place (mainly via education), which is based more on direct instruction and role models. In this way the new members of the community are prepared for the professional and social tasks they will fulfil in the future. Critical sociology broadly takes the same view of socialisation, but stresses that the process is often a differentiated one: girls and children from lower social classes or descending from ethnic minorities are taught different skills, rules of behaviour and cultural preferences than boys and children from the elite and the indigenous population. This differential socialisation reproduces the existing social inequality from generation to generation. In economic theories, too, socialisation has a mandatory nature; here, it is often stressed that all families have an interest in optimising the formal qualifications and the 'human capital' of their children. A rational parent will ensure that their child learns as many useful things as possible, since this increases the likelihood that their progeny will sustain and care for them in later life, and also prevents loss of reputation (in this case, being seen as a 'bad parent'). According to this view the children, for their part, are driven to obtain the right qualifications, social contacts, etc., because this increases their subsequent chances of securing a well-paid job, high status and an attractive partner.

More recent theories stress that the view in which socialisation is interpreted as a unilateral, inevitable transfer of rules to the new members of the community fails to do justice to the complexity of rule acquisition. New actors are not passive, but often play an independent role in the socialisation process, in particular when they are older and/or the rules more complex. The process is not always intentional, especially in its earliest phase: primary socialisation largely happens 'incidentally', in the everyday contact between parents and children. It is also not self-evident that socialisation will invariably be successful from a collective point of view; children may withdraw from the upbringing attempts of their fathers, mothers and teachers, and the socialisers do not necessarily act as agents of the community. Parents may not be aware of the dominant rules of the society, or may reject them, be unwilling to pass them on (for example because they expect little return from them) or be incapable of doing so due to a lack of resources (e.g. inability to pay school fees) or because of their limited parenting skills. The outcomes of the socialisation process, finally, are not uniform. This is because the socialisers differ in their interpretation of the rules to be imparted, and because the socialisees are not uniform in their potential for development and self-regulation. As a result, similar socialisation processes can be passed through differentially. This heterogeneity is reinforced by the fact that the content of the rules to be imparted can change over time, as can the dominant view on the most appropriate method of socialisation (the content of the school curriculum, teaching methods). The process in which new actors acquire rules also shows socio-historical variation as regards the phasing, the socialisers who are involved in it, and their relative strength.

It is plausible that the institutions of social security are somewhat 'undersocialised': on the one hand because, owing to their complexity and ambiguity, the rules are difficult to learn; and on the other because people do not normally need in-depth knowledge of social security in order to be able to function in their everyday lives. In informal systems, the family or community members have a certain interest in imparting an elementary awareness of mutual support rights and obligations to children; in formal systems this interest is lacking, and the rules are usually transferred to only a limited extent through the education system. Just a small group of professionals (for example people working for the social security organisation or as legal specialists in this field) learn the rules thoroughly; and sometimes people who claim a given benefit for a long period can also acquire a great deal of specific knowledge about 'their' benefit. However, generally speaking modern social security rules tend to be undersocialised; and this increases the likelihood of defection.

The application of rules

The process of rule application can take different forms: economic exchange between people and organisations, social contacts, political selection processes, etc. For social security this is reflected in six theoretical models of rule-driven interaction. Three of these models relate to informal social security; the remainder to formal regulations.

Family-based social security regulations (cf. figure 3.1) are normally aimed at combating acute indigence through the provision of material assistance among blood relatives. The interaction is limited to contributing and receiving support in money or in kind, and only a few categories of actors are involved (parents, children, possibly grandparents and other family members). It is driven by the informal expectations that exist within the family and which are normally embedded in the institutions of the community. The rules are often fairly vague and only weakly internalised. This gives the actors considerable latitude, so that rights and obligations are difficult to enforce and are not always observed. The risk of defection is particularly great if the mutual connectedness is low or if many family members are affected by the same risk simultaneously (e.g. widespread acute need in times of mass unemployment). *Communal* arrangements (figure 3.2) seek to alleviate indigence at the level of the local society, and are characterised by the existence of an intermediary social security organisation (such as a church charity council or a municipal poor house). In contrast to the family-based structure, a principal-agent problem readily arises in these schemes. The rules leave a great deal of freedom of interpretation for the board, the attendants and the collectors, which they sometimes abuse for their own gain; and the decisions they take about those in need may be considered arbitrary or unfair. *Informal occupational* social security (figure 3.3) is concerned with rights and obligations that are linked to an employment relationship, without being ratified by the government (for example benefits in the guild system, emergency funds for employees).

Of the formal interaction models, the *demographic* regulations (statutory or government-ratified old age and survivor's pensions, child benefit, etc.) are the simplest (cf. figure

3.4). In addition to the beneficiaries and contributors, there is often a large corporate actor: the social security organisation charged with awarding and paying benefits, collecting contributions, and monitoring and sanctioning. There is also a supervisory board which oversees the administrative process and a social security court which rules on legal complaints. The principal-agent problem is greater here than in the informal schemes. The impersonal and indirect nature of the interaction (which is usually a written one) increases the risk of abuse by the beneficiaries. On the other hand, the main benefit conditions (having a certain age, death of the breadwinner, presence of dependent children, etc.) can be verified relatively objectively and simply, thereby reducing the risk of non-compliance.

In the interaction structure that characterises formal *unemployment and social assistance* arrangements (figure 3.5), the likelihood of defection is greater. There is an additional category of actors involved (employers who hire and dismiss people), there are more – and more complex – benefit conditions, and clients can themselves to some extent bring about or extend the rights, for example by not actively seeking work; the 'moral hazard' is greater than in the informal and the demographic schemes.

The most intricate structure of interaction theoretically occurs in formal arrangements for *sickness leave and disability* (figure 3.6). Establishing the right to benefit is often complex and requires the judgement of medical experts (GP, specialist, medical examiners appointed by the social security organisation or an independent assessment agency). This increases the principal-agent problem: the professional code of the medical assessors may be at odds with the statutory provisions and the internal rules of the social security organisation.

The consequences of rule-driven interaction

Institutions are in principle established in order to achieve certain collective goals. In theory, the application of rules can influence various developments in the community: the degree of technological and scientific innovation, the economic process, the structuring of society, the formation of ideals and demographic trends. However, the relationship between institutions and social developments is a dialectic one; the prevailing institutions are not only important for the collective output – and thus help determine the historical process – but the trends at macro-level also serve as a 'context of rule application'. This means that rules can have differing effects depending on whether they are applied when the economy is booming or in recession, in a population that is ageing or relatively young, etc.

The interactions driven by social security rules have consequences for the individual actors, for whom receiving a pension, for example, enables them to maintain a certain living standard. Of more decisive importance, however, are the consequences for the community, since this is the *raison d'être* for the institutions. Theoretically, the effects of social security regulations on social structuring and the economic process are the most important. By implementing these schemes new social categories may be created (e.g. OAPs, single welfare mothers), and the position of various social groups on the prevailing ladders of stratification may change. Social security usually implies some redistribution from contributors to beneficiaries; the extent to which this reinforces or reduces the existing social hierarchy is not something that is fixed in advance, but is an empirical issue. Another structuring effect is the potential influence of social security issues and the votes of benefit recipients in political elections; views on the desirability of supporting weaker groups and the beneficiaries' vote may be decisive for the selection of the political elite.

The impact on the economic process mainly relates to the level, growth and distribution of collective prosperity. Theoretically, positive wealth effects may be expected to the extent that social security contributes to economic efficiency (because it combats social unrest and maintains productive capacity in times of recession) and to avoiding a collapse in demand. Examples of negative economic effects relate to the potential decline in the propensity to save or invest, and to the labour market disincentives social security may create (for example a low labour supply due to high benefits). Whether the economic functions or dysfunctions of social security dominate cannot be established on theoretical grounds, but is an empirical question whose outcome depends on the precise nature of the institutions, the context in which the rules are applied and the perceptions and preferences of the actors concerned. Thus, for instance, a pension system that initially contributed to sustaining consumer demand can become less efficient over time, for example if pronounced ageing of the population pushes up the costs and places a heavy burden on the shoulders of working contributors, or if it squeezes other collective investments that are deemed necessary (such as the budget available for education).

7.2 Regimes, benefit dependency and poverty

In the theoretical part of this study social security in general has been delineated from the institutional perspective. The empirical analyses focused on the collective effects of specific formal social security institutions. Since modern forms of social security are predominantly national in their structure, a country comparison is the obvious way to investigate their operation. It is in principle possible to map out the collective impact of individual arrangements (different types of social assistance, unemployment insurance, child benefit, etc.) in various countries, but it was decided not to make such a 'single scheme' comparison, among other things because it could present too limited a picture of the influence of social security rules. If a country has a spartan social assistance scheme, for example, this may lead to widespread indigence among the population. However, such a causal connection need not occur by definition: if a large proportion of the population are entitled to generous social insurance benefits, it is possible that most people will be guaranteed an acceptable standard of living through these. The limited scope of the social assistance scheme may then be less problematic in terms of the results obtained.

It was therefore decided to perform empirical analyses of the collective effects that certain *regimes* of social security bring about, building on the influential work of Esping-Andersen (1990). Eleven countries were selected which are supposed to represent different types of social security regimes, viz. the Netherlands, Belgium, Germany, France, Sweden, Denmark, Norway, the United States, Canada, Australia and the United Kingdom.

The study looked at whether countries belonging to the various regime types differ in the degree of benefit dependency and poverty they generate. At collective level these two phenomena are important in both the social structuring and the economic process. The degree of benefit dependency is theoretically linked to the differentiation in recognisable social groups and their position on stratification ladders, and to the growth and distribution of the collective prosperity. Combating poverty is a traditional objective of social security; social security systems seek to protect people from want, but application of the rules can also create new, weak social groups, who may find it difficult to escape from their dependency on the collective provisions. Combating poverty via social security also guarantees a minimum level of consumption and the retention of productive capacities for those with an entitlement. At the same time, however, it may be that such arrangements provide too little incentive for people to look for work or save for a rainy day.

Three types of social security regimes, and one hybrid system

The term 'regime' refers to different types of coherent formal institutions at the national level, which are designed to achieve distinct collective goals. These regimes encapsulate divergent formal rules relating to government production in an abstract, systemic way. Esping-Andersen (1990) uses the term 'welfare regimes', which in principle embraces more than social security arrangements alone. He describes a number of regime types, which he refers to as the 'three worlds of welfare capitalism'.

Theoretically, the collective, statutory social security regulations in the *liberal* regime type are limited (or 'residual') in scope. Benefits are low and of short duration, and are heavily targeted at the most needy; there are no collective provisions for meeting the costs of raising children, etc. Yet there is a well-developed system of private insurance aimed mainly at the middle classes. The 'de-commodification' (the degree to which people are able to achieve an acceptable standard of living regardless of their market position) is low in this system. It sharpens the social stratification, increasing the likelihood of a threefold division between benefit recipients and the working poor; the middle classes; and the privileged. According to Esping-Andersen, the social security systems of the United States, Canada, Australia and the United Kingdom belong to this category.

The *social-democratic* regime type is by contrast very extensive in its scope. Benefits are not reserved for the disadvantaged and deprived, but are available for all citizens. They are generous and last for as long as the covered risk is present. To limit the costs and promote social integration, however, attempts are made to help beneficiaries back into work as quickly as possible via an elaborate activation programme. The funding base is broadened by the high labour market participation rate of women, most of whom work in the non-commercial services sector (education, care). The large collective system means that taxes and social insurance contributions are high and private insurance is less important in this system. The social-democratic regime is characterised by a high degree of de-commodification and attempts to reduce the existing social differences. Sweden, Denmark and Norway provide examples of such a system.

The *corporatist* regime type is also theoretically extensive, but more selective. Rights are often linked to contributions paid and previous work experience. They are also not the same for all social groups; for example, civil servants enjoy very generous arrangements, matching their elevated status as agents of the highest authority in these societies. Rights are built up around the breadwinner model: there are good social insurance programmes for families with children, but the economic independence of both partners is not stimulated. The labour market participation rate of women is therefore low. The provisions for elderly and disabled workers are comprehensive, but these imply that these groups, too, tend to be excluded from employment. The degree of de-commodification is low, and corporatist regimes are largely designed to keep the existing hierarchy between different status groups intact. Belgium, Germany and France are regarded as specimens of this regime type.

According to Esping-Andersen (1990, 1999), the regime in the Netherlands is a *hybrid*: a "Janus-headed welfare regime" which displays both social-democratic and corporatist traits. There are other countries, too, which are not entirely pure representatives of their type. For example, the United Kingdom initially had a generous social security system, which expressed the ideas of its founder Beveridge. In the 1980s, however, many schemes were transformed into a more liberal direction; Esping-Andersen regards this as an example of "regime-shifting or, perhaps, of stalled social democratization".

In his analysis Esping-Andersen stresses that the regime types arose in a specific socio-historical context. They reflect broader trends in society (e.g. wealth, demography), the power of political actors and the alliances they concluded when the welfare state was being developed after the Second World War. The hybrid Dutch system, for example, is the product of the Catholic-socialist government coalitions of the 1950s. Once established, regimes are relatively stable because the existing institutional structure determines further development, in accordance with the notion of path dependence from historical institutionalism.

Esping-Andersen substantiated his classification by presenting empirical analyses, but these received a fair amount of criticism. One class of objection concerned issues such as the limited validity, reliability and accessibility of his data. Another objection related to Esping-Andersen's use of unnecessarily 'soft' or less adequate statistical techniques (mainly tabular and regression analysis). Later authors tried to test his typology more stringently by generating new data and applying more advanced and robust methods. These new datasets and analyses also have limitations, however. They often relate to only part of the social security system (for example social assistance), and are generally based on relatively few institutional characteristics. The latter are moreover often analysed as continuous, linearly correlated variables, using statistical techniques that are less suitable for measuring the qualitative differences on which the typology is based.

In order to accommodate such objections this study performed a categorical principal component analysis (CatPCA) on 54 aspects of formal social security, as these existed in the selected eleven countries in around 1990. Institutional characteristics of all important collective schemes were included in the analysis. The component loadings showed that the variables can be reduced to two underlying dimensions. The first indicates the *scope* of the social security rules (are they residual or extensive?); the second indicates the degree to which schemes have a *universalistic or particularistic* design (figure 4.1). According to their scores on these dimensions, the countries fall into the expected clusters (figure 4.2). The United States, Australia, Canada and the United Kingdom form a liberal group, which is represented most clearly by the first two countries. Denmark, Sweden and – slightly less clearly – Norway end up in a social-democratic cluster, while Belgium, Germany and France form a rather homogeneous corporatist group. The Netherlands is scaled between the exponents of the social-democratic and corporatist regimes and thus does indeed has a hybrid system. Cluster analyses of the country scores on the two dimensions result in the same classification.

A further CatPCA was carried out to investigate whether the countries also show systematic differences in their informal social security rules (such as public opinion on the preferred level of inequality and government interventions, the social status of civil servants, traditional gender roles, etc.; see figure 4.3). The same groups of countries emerged from this analysis, albeit with minor differences of emphasis. In Denmark and Australia the informal rules are less pure than the formal rules, while in Norway and Canada the reverse occurs (see figure 4.4). The correlation coefficient between the formal and informal institutions of countries is however high: 0.84 on the first dimension, 0.85 on the second. This correspondence came out less clearly in earlier research, probably because the indicators used did not always refer to informal rights and obligations, and because there was often a lack of informal counterparts for the second dimension of the regime classification (universalism/particularism). The latter may explain why much comparative research on 'welfare attitudes' only detected the scope dimension, i.e. an opposition between the liberal and non-liberal countries.

The analysis thus leads to the conclusion that Esping-Andersen's typology has a solid empirical basis as regards both the formal and informal social security institutions.

Benefit dependency and the regime types

Another comment on Esping-Andersen's work that is regularly found in the literature is that the typology relates only to the institutionalisation that is characteristic for a specific moment in time. Esping-Andersen (1999) himself acknowledged that his classification was a "snapshot of the worlds of welfare capitalism". In order to test the robustness of the typology over time, it was therefore decided in chapter 4 to look at a different sample year (1990) from that in Esping-Andersen's original work and its secondary analyses (1980). In addition, a project related to this study explored the situation in around 2000 (Soede et al., 2004). This led to the conclusion that the classification into the three types of regime plus the hybrid Netherlands is empirically fairly stable for the last two decades of the 20th century.

Chapter 5 went a step further by creating not a snapshot, but a film of the results associated with the 'three worlds'. The aim was to establish whether the regime types differed in their 'benefit production' in the period 1980-1999. First, the institutional characteristics of the national systems in around 1990 were analysed again from this perspective and scored on a benefit dependency boost index. This led to the hypothesis that the hybrid Dutch regime incorporated the 'worst of three worlds' and would therefore generate the most benefits, both in terms of the relative volume (the number of benefits as a share of the population aged 15 years and older) and as regards the percentage growth in the number of benefits. The corporatist group was expected to generate more benefit dependency than the social-democratic cluster, which was in turn predicted to exceed the liberal countries.

Hypotheses were also formulated relating to the composition of the benefit volume in the population of working age. In the corporatist group it was expected that there would be a comparatively high volume of benefits for early retirement, unemployment insurance and survivor's pensions; the social-democratic cluster was predicted to show a high volume in employee dependency (sickness benefits, leave arrangements, etc.) and disability insurance for non-employees (early disabled, self-employed, housewives, students). In the liberal group the expectation was that there would be high dependency on social assistance benefits, while the hybrid Netherlands was supposed to score above average on all these types of benefit.

Whether the theoretical expectations match the facts was investigated using data on the take-up of the main benefits over two decades in ten countries (Norway is missing in the dataset). The analyses were based on administrative data on full benefit years, which were processed in such a way that they could be regarded as reasonably comparable across countries. Since all the information was available only at aggregate national level, it was not possible to determine the effects of characteristics of individual beneficiaries (gender, age, etc.) on the volume.

The bivariate relationship between the regime types and the *relative volume* was found to be fairly weak (cf. figures 5.2 and 5.3). On average, the share of benefits in the population was higher in the social-democratic countries than in the liberal group, as expected, but the other differences are less pronounced. While it is true that the relative volume in the population of working age was higher in the corporatist group than in the social-democratic cluster from 1990 onwards, prior to this, and in the entire adult population (i.e. including old age pensioners), this assumed relation was absent. The Netherlands had a fairly high volume in the period 1980-1990, but fell down the rankings in the 1990s and did not occupy the expected top position in any of the years studied.

Similarly, the bivariate correspondence between the typology and the *volume growth* was fairly limited (figure 5.4). The corporatist countries did indeed undergo consistently higher volume growth between 1980 and 1999 than the social-democratic cluster, but the other hypotheses were not sustained. Unexpected were the high growth rates in France, Australia and Canada and the low percentage increases in the Netherlands.

The hypotheses concerning the *volume composition* did however find support in the data (compare figures 5.5 and 5.6). In all years considered here the corporatist countries, as expected, had a relatively high number of recipients of unemployment insurance and early exit benefits (though for the latter in 1980 the difference compared with the other countries was less pronounced). Their top position was less clear for survivor's pensions below the age of 65; this applies especially to France.

Generally speaking, the two Scandinavian countries do indeed score highest on sickness benefits, leave arrangements for employees and on disability benefits paid to non-employees. In other aspects, however, they deviate from the expected profile. For instance, Sweden had a high volume of survivor's pensions in the early 1980s, while in Denmark the relative number of unemployment insurance and early exit benefits approaches that of the corporatist group of countries.

The countries in the liberal cluster generate the most social assistance benefits, as predicted. However, in the United States this bias reduces steadily over time, partly due to the restriction of access to the American social assistance schemes in the 1990s. As a result, at the end of the period studied here, the composition of the recipient population in the USA is *plus libéral que les libéraux*: benefit volumes are low for all types of arrangement, even social assistance, a benefit which in other liberal countries often serves as a last refuge for people who are not entitled to employee insurance.

Since it is evident that the benefit volume is not solely determined by the structure of formal rules, a multivariate approach was then adopted. A causal model was developed (see figure 6.5) in which the growth in the benefit volume was linked to a number of aspects of the context of rule application: demographic trends, economic developments, and changes in the institutional structure. The model was tested for eight countries simultaneously (Canada and Australia were left out of consideration because of data limitations) and was found to fit the empirical data well. In general, according to the model the volume was boosted substantially between 1980 and 1999 by the growth in the population (both below and above 65 years). In some countries the increase in the number of single-parent families was also an important factor, as was the falling labour market participation of men aged 50-64 years. System changes had an influence particularly in France (especially the introduction of new social assistance legislation at the end of the 1980s) and the USA (the curtailment of social assistance entitlements in the middle of the 1990s).

The model was then used to establish the impact of the regimes more accurately, by equalising the countries in a number of respects. In a first simulation all countries were assumed to have the same demographic structure and trends as the USA, so that the volumes were corrected for the effects of differences in the population profile. In addition, the influence of system changes and of the rising take-up of pensions was left out of consideration. Finally, a simulation was carried out which included structural unemployment figures, so that the benefit volumes were no longer distorted by the business cycle.

These simulations greatly reduced the dispersion in the 'benefit production' of the countries. If the less pure regime representatives in the causal analysis (the Netherlands and Great Britain)[2] are left out of consideration, the expected differences between the regime types emerge, but these are not particularly large. Under equalised conditions the annual volume growth in the social-democratic countries is an average of 0.1 percentage point higher than in the USA and 0.4 percentage points lower than in the corporatist cluster. Over the whole period studied, this is equivalent to differences of 3 and 7 percentage points, respectively. These limited discrepancies can however be linked to differences in the formal institutions. The USA undergoes less marked growth than Sweden and Denmark mostly because unemployed people have less chance of receiving benefit (including social assistance) and because early retirement is less common. The social-democratic countries, for their part, score lower on average than Belgium, Germany and France because of the divergent arrangements for early exits[3] and the higher benefit dependency of lone parents in the corporatist group.

Actual benefit volumes in the hybrid Dutch regime grew strongly in the 1980s, but in the 1990s the increase was the lowest of all countries. Under equalised conditions, however, the growth in the first decade turned out to be virtually no higher than in the corporatist group. This suggests that in the 1980s the Netherlands was more a victim of its specific demographic context – a relatively young population which grew more strongly and aged more than elsewhere, a large number of single-parent families living on benefit – than of its 'worst of three worlds' institutions.

Poverty and the regime types

The first social security arrangements, such as England's *Elizabethan Poor Law* (1601), were intended to combat poverty. That aim is no different in modern social security regimes, though a diversity of strategies are pursued. In the social-democratic model, the emphasis is on guaranteeing a fairly high living standard for all citizens, regardless of their present or past position on the labour market. In order to keep this system affordable, it is essential that as many people as possible work; this broadens the funding base and keeps benefit dependency within bounds.

The corporatist system attaches great importance to income continuity of the male breadwinner. Through a system of compulsory social insurance, breadwinners largely maintain their standard of living when they are affected by unemployment, illness, etc., assuming they have an adequate employment history. The poverty risk mainly concerns outsiders: people who have not worked or who have had many career interruptions, and those who are dependent on them. If this group is not too large, poverty can be effectively combated by this system.

The liberal approach stresses individual responsibility and economic incentives. Collective social security is kept to a minimum through low benefits of short duration. This encourages people to take responsibility for their own income and to become productive; and because the statutory social security system is relatively cheap, there is more money left over for consumption and investment. On balance, this leads to an increase in the collective wealth and demand for labour, which ultimately will trickle down to those with the fewest resources, so that poverty remains limited.

It is not possible to say in advance which strategy is the most effective in combating poverty. It may be that the more generous social-democratic and corporatist systems offer the greatest social protection, but it is equally plausible that these systems generate negative external effects (less prosperity and fewer jobs), so that people are ultimately best off under a liberal regime. An attempt was therefore made to establish to what extent the concrete formal institutions in the eleven countries theoretically reduce the risk of poverty. The main regulations were scored on an institutional poverty risk index, which led to the prediction that countries with a liberal social security regime (USA, Australia, Canada and UK) would generate more poverty than the corporatist group (Belgium, France and Germany). It was also presumed that the latter would exceed the social-democratic countries (Denmark, Norway and Sweden), which in turn were expected to produce more poverty than the hybrid Dutch regime.

Poverty is a more complex theoretical concept than the degree of benefit dependency, and there are many possible ways of investigating the phenomenon empirically. For this reason, this study first explored what poverty means and how it can best be measured.

Based on a critical analysis of theoretical politico-philosophical literature, poverty was defined as follows: "an individual actor is poor if he consistently lacks the means to obtain the minimum necessities of his community". This implies that poverty ultimately always describes a situation affecting individuals: a collective actor, a group or a community cannot be poor, but at most may not have the resources to protect all individual members against indigence. That situation must also have a certain permanence: someone who cannot make ends meet for a single month is not poor. Poverty is an absolute phenomenon, in the sense that in determining whether someone is poor it makes no difference how many people experience the same situation; the mere fact that during a famine or a period of mass unemployment "this person may not be, relatively speaking, any worse off than most others" (Sen, 1985) does not imply he cannot be regarded as poor. In another respect, however, poverty is 'relative': the standard concerning the minimum necessities can vary according to time and place; it depends on the community the actor currently belongs to. Finally, the definition expresses that poverty relates to the ability to achieve the prevailing minimum standard, not to the actual possession or consumption of what is minimally required. Someone who lacks the minimum necessities because they spend more on items that are generally not regarded as indispensable (a large wine collection, weekly visits to the opera, etc.) is not poor.

A community can compensate poor people for their deficits by giving them a conditional right to a benefit or other forms of material support. In the literature calls are often found for a collective social minimum, arguing that this is beneficial for society, increases freedom or is fair. An example is the thought experiment that was proposed by Rawls (1999 [1971]). According to this author, a rational actor operating behind a 'veil of ignorance' (he does not know what resources he has and what they are worth in his circumstances) will inevitably reach the conclusion that differentials in income and wealth are only defensible if the highest positions are attainable by everyone, and if the poorest would have been worse off if those differentials did not exist. Since the hypothetical actor himself does not know whether he is one of the worst off, and as he should not wish upon others a life that he could not bear for himself, it is rational to maximise the minimum rights (*maximin*) and have these guaranteed by the government.

Sociologically, however, there is no need for communities to adopt such a philosophical line of reasoning. There is no "right division of rights", and therefore no universally just method of tackling the problem of poverty. The allocation of rights in the case of poverty cannot be seen in isolation from the socio-historical developments with which the community is confronted, and from the institutional path chosen earlier. These influence the way in which the actors concerned perceive the phenomenon of poverty and the merits assigned by them to the various solutions; and through this they impact on the course of the rule interaction, the outcome of which is not fixed in advance (cf. figure 2.1).

The operational poverty lines used in empirical research were then assessed on the basis of four criteria: their validity (does the measurement instrument correspond with the theoretical concept?), reliability (is an accurate measurement obtained of the degree of poverty?), ease of application (can the poverty line be determined simply and be applied in a straightforward manner in the available databases?) and socio-political relevance (is the criterion normatively credible for the community in question and for policymakers?).

This led to the conclusion that all existing instruments used to measure poverty have shortcomings. Relative poverty criteria, such as the EU threshold of 60% of median income and Townsend's relative deprivation index, are not valid in terms of the theoretical concept used here, because the poverty rate depends on the position of the reference group. They are moreover not reliable or normatively convincing in all respects; e.g., even substantial improvements or deteriorations in the position of the least well-off will not be detected if the dispersion of income or consumption remains the same. Subjective income thresholds, such as the 'Leyden poverty line', often fit the theoretical concept better, but frequently run into measurement problems (differing interpretations of survey questions by respondents), thus denting their credibility (for example by producing unstable and very high poverty rates). Objective expert budget methods are valid, fairly reliable and normatively credible, but are very cumbersome for use in research practice, especially in international comparisons.

For this reason, it was decided to use the 'generalised budget approach' as developed by the Netherlands Institute for Social Research | SCP for the Dutch situation (Vrooman & Snel, 1999; Soede, 2006; Soede & Vrooman, 2007, 2008b). First, two reference budgets for a single person in the Netherlands were constructed, based on detailed data from the Dutch National Institute for Family Finance Information. The 'basic needs' level is sufficient for running an independent household, but is meagre; it includes those expenses which are almost unavoidable, for food, clothing, housing in a broad sense (rent, insurance, energy, water, telephone, furnishings, home maintenance and local taxes) and a limited number of other items. The 'modest but adequate' variant adds a few other expenditure items which exceed that which is strictly necessary (recreation, memberships and subscriptions, a pet), but does not provide for any luxuries, such as a car or a holiday abroad.

Earlier Dutch studies obtained a historical series of norms by indexing the initial amounts using a three-year moving average in the actual median expenditure on food, non-alcoholic beverages, clothing and housing according to the national Household Budget Survey. This resulted in threshold amounts which over time rose more strongly than price inflation, but which lagged behind the increase in national wealth and median income. For the Netherlands, using this method the observed evolution in the poverty rates for the period 1985-2005 was plausible and readily interpretable. The 'generalised budget approach' is valid in terms of the definition used here, appears sufficiently reliable and is easy to apply. Public opinion research in the Netherlands and Australia suggests that such a poverty line is probably also credible for both citizens and policymakers.

Because the required detailed budget data were not available in the ten other countries, for those the 'basic needs' and 'modest but adequate' levels for a single person have been assessed by converting the Dutch norm amounts in around the year 2000 using purchasing power parities. National norm amounts for other types of households were determined by applying uniform equivalence factors that were chosen on the basis of a sensitivity analysis of different scales (cf. tables 6.2-6.4).

When imposing the two variants of the poverty threshold to the data on the eleven countries included in the 2000 wave of the *Luxembourg Income Study*, the bivariate results show some support for the hypotheses. This study looked at 'the three I's of poverty': the incidence of poverty, the median income deficits of the poor and the inequality in the distribution of those deficits. According to both the 'basic needs' criterion and the 'modest but adequate' threshold, the poverty rate in the liberal countries was greater on average than in the corporatist group (a difference of approximately +3 percentage points); this was caused mainly by the high incidence in Australia. As expected, the corporatist group in turn had a higher poverty rate than the social-democratic cluster (+6 percentage points). The Netherlands did not have the lowest incidence, however, but ended up amidst the three social-democratic countries, which scored slightly lower on average (-1 percentage point). The difference between the regime types was much less clear when it came to the income deficits and the inequality in their distribution.

A number of multi-level logistic regression models were then developed, with the poverty incidence based on the 'modest but adequate' criterion as the variable to be explained. A large part of the variance was found to lie not at the level of the countries, but had to be attributed to differences between individual respondents and households. The limited macro-variance was however largely explained by the country characteristics that were included as determinants in the model. A part of it could be ascribed to the wealth differentials between the countries (for example, the liberal group includes both the affluent USA and the poorer Australia). If allowance is made for this, all 'pure' differences among the regime types and the hybrid operate in the theoretically expected direction; but only the difference between the liberal and corporatist group turned out to be statistically significant.

7.3 The impact of social security regimes

Based on the empirical analyses, it may be asked why the differences between the three social security regimes are reflected to only a limited extent in the output indicators. In the area of benefit dependency, characteristic disparities were found in the composition of the take-up of different arrangements, but under equalised conditions the differences in the volume growth between 1980 and 1999 were fairly small. The growth in the corporatist group was not much stronger than in the social-democratic cluster, which in turn ended up only slightly higher than the liberal group, and even then only in comparison with the USA as the purer representative of the latter cluster. The multi-level analyses of the poverty incidence in around 2000 also revealed only a rather limited influence by the regime type. Ceteris paribus, the sign of the effect on the incidence was as expected in all cases, but only one hypothesis (the liberal/corporatist distinction) withstood statistical testing.

A number of possible explanations for the rather small differences in the output of the regimes are obvious. For example, measurement errors in the dependent variables and the empirical typology may have distorted the outcomes. The findings in relation to benefit dependency might perhaps have been different if adequate data had been available on individual recipients, enabling multi-level analyses to be performed here, too. Similarly, the outcomes in relation to poverty incidence could have been more robust if they had been based on a reliable time series covering several decades. And the empirical typology of the regimes might gain in predictive power if it was extended to include more countries, thus increasing the variance and enabling more macro-characteristics to be included in the multi-level models. It is also possible that the effects of the typology have been partly cancelled out by 'invisible' forms of social security, which are not reflected in the empirical classification of formal social security regimes. The residual nature of the liberal regime and the selectivity of the corporatist type may matter less if in practice such formal schemes are complemented by more extensive familial, occupational, or community-based social security arrangements than elsewhere.

A further possibility is that the ceteris paribus assumption has not been entirely met. Although major control factors (demography, national wealth, the business cycle) were included in the empirical analyses, it follows from chapter 3 that theoretically other characteristics may influence the benefit volume and poverty rate as well. Differences in the administration of the formal rules (e.g. variations in implementation decrees, bureaucratic routines, verification procedures, the actual imposition of sanctions, the supervision and internal structure of the social security organisation) and in the informal institutions at micro-level (the work ethic of benefit recipients, the 'culture' among social security officials) have been mentioned in this respect. Theoretically it is likely that such processes and informal rules reinforce the effects of the formal institutions, but that is not by definition the case; they may also suppress the impact of the regime types on the collective output indicators. This would occur, for example, if in equal circumstances exponents of the social-democratic regime type generate higher benefit volumes and poverty rates because their social security organisation is less efficient than elsewhere, the willingness to work among benefit recipients is lower, and so on. Intuitively this may seem unlikely, but it cannot be entirely ruled out on the basis of the analyses performed here either.

However, at present it is only possible to speculate about the relevance of such potential shortcomings. Clearer answers require more and better data, as well as further analyses if these data become available in the future. At this moment it is worthwhile to look briefly at another issue: do the social security schemes in the country groups studied here resemble their 'ideal' type sufficiently well to expect that they will produce wide differences in collective output?

Real systems and ideal-types

It was pointed out in chapter 4 that Esping-Andersen's classification portrays theoretical ideal-types; empirical systems of social security never precisely match the theoretical pattern, because they are historical constructs. As such, they reflect the circumstances under which they were established: the institutions that already existed, the prevailing conflicts of interest, power relations, relative prices and ideals, political alliances, the trade-offs during negotiations, etc. Arts & Gelissen (2002) commented in this connection that "a significant number of welfare states must be considered hybrid cases: no particular case can ever perfectly embody any particular ideal-type".

If the exponents of the regimes analysed here are a long way from their theoretical ideal-types, this may offer an explanation for the limited influence of the typology on benefit dependency and poverty rates. When the differences between the groups of real systems turn out to be much smaller than those between the theoretical ideal-types, we should perhaps not expect wide differences in collective outcomes. The actual spread in terms of the scope of the social security system and the degree of universalism/particularism then lags well behind the theoretical dispersion: on ideal-typical dimensions the country scores in figure 4.2 would implode, with all real models ending up close to the origin. In that case the variance in the independent institutional traits will be too small to explain much of the differences in the degree of benefit dependency and poverty between countries. An analogous line of reasoning can be followed with regard to the real and ideal-typical scores on the benefit dependency boost and institutional poverty risk indices.

In order to be able to say something about this, scores must be obtained for the ideal-typical regimes which can serve as a point of reference. This was achieved in a rather straightforward manner in figure 7.1, which shows the outcome of a categorical principal component analysis (CatPCA) of the same data as those on which figures 4.1 and 4.2 were based; they therefore relate to the early 1990s. However, in addition to the empirical institutions of the eleven countries, four hypothetical systems were included. The latter were constructed by theoretically appraising each variable in advance in terms of the two main dimensions of the typology (the scope of the social security system and its degree of universalism/ particularism). Subsequently three ideal-types were constructed by assigning them on each variable the scores that would be expected on theoretical grounds. The pure social-democratic regime, for example, has extremely high replacement rates (benefit levels as a percentage of previous earnings) and spends a large amount on active labour market policy, whereas the pure liberal regime achieves minimal scores on these aspects. Similarly, the ideal-typical corporatist regime has very favourable social security arrangements for civil servants and generous arrangements for early retirement by insiders on the labour market, a form of particularism which is theoretically completely absent from the social-democratic regime.

The analysis also included a 'generic hybrid', a theoretical system which achieves a score precisely in the middle for all variables.[4] This produces a second point of reference: the closer empirical systems approach the generic hybrid and the further removed they become from their ideal-type, the more they can be regarded as less pure cases.

In the process of coding the theoretical regimes, on each variable the constraint was applied that the scores for the ideal-types could never be higher or lower than the extreme values that actually occur in the countries studied here. For some variables this restriction is an obvious one: if the coverage or replacement rate of a certain scheme is already zero or 100% in any of the systems actually studied, the ideal-type can by definition not score lower or higher. Where there are natural dichotomies (a certain provision does or does not exist), the values for the ideal-types are also evident. For a number of other variables, however, higher or lower scores are conceivable. Even so, no categories were added for the ideal regime types which were more extreme than those occurring in reality. Such peripheral values may not be likely to occur in practice (e.g. an average income tax rate of 0% or 100%), and introducing them in the analysis performed here would by definition boost the distance between the ideal regime types and their empirical exponents.

The scaling in figure 7.1 is based on the scores assigned to the four theoretical types. The eleven empirical systems were treated passively in the CatPCA, which implies that they do not attribute to the underlying dimensions. As a result, the distances, unlike in figure 4.2, do not reflect the empirical similarities and differences of the countries, but rather the degree to which their social security system diverges from the three theoretically ideal systems and the generic hybrid. A 'passive' actual social security system having the same scores on all variables[5] as the corporatist ideal-type will coincide with the latter. Conversely, the fewer characteristics a real system shares with a theoretical type, the greater the distance between the two will be.

In this analysis, too, the dimensions can be described in terms of scope and universalism/particularism, and the observations belong to clearly distinct clusters in the presumed manner. The empirical types thus not only share many characteristics among themselves, but also correspond most closely with their own theoretical ideal-type. They are however not entirely pure exponents of that ideal-type: the countries come roughly halfway between their own theoretical regime type and the generic hybrid, with a few differences of emphasis.

On average, the empirical *social-democratic* systems most closely resemble their ideal-type and are furthest removed from the generic hybrid. The configuration is somewhat different from in figure 4.2: the three empirical systems are now much closer together. Denmark comes nearest to the social-democratic ideal-type, followed at a short distance by Sweden. Norway is still the least social-democratic country, but is much less peripheral than in the earlier analysis. This suggests that the difference found there was due partly to the fact that Denmark and Sweden share more characteristics with each other

Figure 7.1
Empirical social security systems and ideal regime types, early 1990s (CatPCA, object scores)

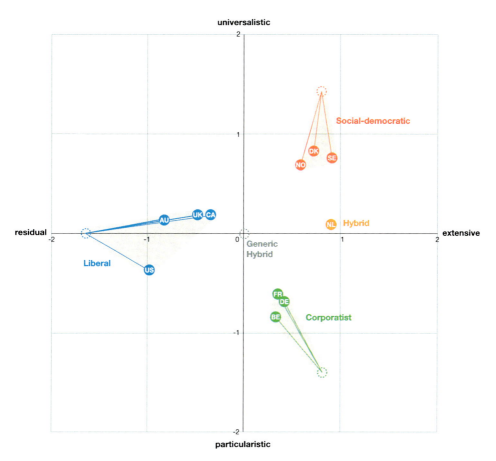

than with Norway. The three Scandinavian countries diverge from their theoretical ideal-type mainly because each of them sometimes fails to achieve the maximum characteristic score. This applies in particular for contribution levels and marginal tax rates, the gross replacement rates of social assistance benefit after five years of unemployment, care leave arrangements and the absence of a minimum wage. Sweden, Denmark and Norway also exhibit a number of corporatist traits. For example, the initial level of unemployment benefit is often high, and the earnings-related unemployment insurance benefit is often long-lasting. The separate orphan's benefits which are sometimes present and the child allowances in the income tax system are theoretically also more characteristic of the corporatist than the social-democratic regime type.

The empirical *corporatist* systems are somewhat further removed from their theoretical ideal-type on average. As in the earlier analysis, however, they do form a homogenous group. Belgium is positioned slightly closer to the fictitious ideal regime than Germany and France, and is thus the purest representative of the typical corporatist pattern. The differences compared with the theoretical ideal are mainly due to the fact that the three countries score lower than expected on marginal tax rates, replacement rates, financial provisions for children and the minimum wage protection. The provisions for the elderly are also often slightly less than those assumed in the theoretical ideal-type. The scope of leave arrangements and government spending on active labour market policy are somewhat greater in the empirical corporatist systems than in their theoretical counterpart, moving them in the direction of the social-democratic cluster.

On average, the empirical *liberal* systems differ most from their theoretical ideal, but as in figure 4.2 the spread is fairly wide. The USA and Australia are the purest exponents of their ideal-type; they are slightly further removed from their own theoretical reference point than Belgium. The United Kingdom and Canada have the most 'impure' empirical systems; these two come closest of all countries to the generic hybrid. In many respects the liberal countries are much more extensive than their theoretical ideal-type, and this applies in particular for the United Kingdom and Canada. Frequent anomalies include high tax breaks for breadwinners, the existence of a collective pension insurance for all residents, the high gross replacement rates for earnings-related pensions, the fairly good provisions for surviving dependants of employees, and the rather high social assistance benefit level after five years of unemployment (with the exception of the USA). Additionally, many liberal countries have arrangements for maternity leave and formal childcare. The means-testing of old age and surviving dependants pensions is often less strict than might be expected, and the thresholds for disability benefits are not as high as the theoretical ideal-type presumes.

The system in *the Netherlands* ends up between the social-democratic and corporatist ideal-types, with a slight distortion in the direction of the Nordic group. According to this analysis, too, therefore, the Dutch system is clearly a hybrid of two models of social security. It is generally extensive, as are the two ideal-types it reflects. In around 1990, the contribution rates, income provisions for the elderly and coverage of the *risque social* in the event of disability broadly correspond with the social-democratic model. The Dutch provisions for surviving dependants, civil servants and formal childcare tended towards the corporatist type at that time.

Although there are clear differences between the empirical institutions and the theoretical regimes, these are not so large that the real social security systems cannot be regarded as exponents of their ideal-type. When the scores in figure 7.1 are subjected to hierarchical cluster analyses, the expected grouping emerges once again. In a two-cluster solution, a contrast is found between the liberal ideal-type plus the four real liberal systems and the rest. The latter group becomes split if three clusters are specified in the model. The corporatist ideal-type and its representatives, plus the 'generic hybrid', then form a separate cluster, while the remainder consists of the social-democratic ideal-type and the actual systems of Denmark, Norway, Sweden and the Netherlands. If four clusters are specified in the analysis, the Netherlands ends up in its own separate category. Solutions which include more clusters lead to a more fragmented picture, but even then the ideal-types and their empirical representatives often coincide. For instance, in an analysis where the 15 cases are attributed to eight clusters, Germany and France still group together with the corporatist ideal-type, while Australia joins with the liberal ideal-type. Similar results emerge from a number of latent profile models.[6]

On balance these analyses, despite the sometimes subtantial distances (especially for the United Kingdom and Canada), give no reason to conclude that the empirical regime types reflect their theoretical ideal-types too weakly to be considered representative of them. Set against the ideal-typical dispersion in scope and universalism/particularism, the differences between the empirical types do not implode, and they are all placed in the same cluster as their theoretical ideal-type.

It would therefore seem that a low dispersion on the ideal-typical dimensions does not offer an adequate explanation for the limited effects of the real social security regimes on benefit dependency and poverty rates. Their impact could become somewhat greater if purer representatives of the theoretical ideal regime types were to be included in the empirical analyses – though it is not clear which countries these would be. However, even then the contribution of such institutional differences to these forms of collective production might not be very large. The nature of the regimes of formal institutions clearly matters; but the empirical differences between such abstract types are perhaps less decisive for the degree of benefit dependency and poverty than variations in the more specific benefit stipulations and in the socio-historical context in which the rules are applied.

7.4 Some implications

In conclusion, it may be interesting to look briefly at some of the scientific and policy implications of the analyses performed here. The study was set up first and foremost as an exploration of the significance of recent theory on institutions for the field of social security. The institutional perspective has a number of strong points:
1) It emphasises that rights and obligations are not self-evident, but are always constructed by rule-making actors, as are the associated conditions and potential sanc-

tions. They always reflect the circumstances and perceptions prevailing at the time of their establishment, and they often build on earlier rules.
2) Institutions are established in order to achieve a collective goal: the actors concerned have a reason for assuming that their community will benefit in some way from having certain rules (e.g. higher collective wealth, effects on social structuring).
3) Formal and informal institutions can be seen as functionally alternative forms of regulation. They can supplement and reinforce each other, but they can also exist alongside each other, or systems can be predominantly informal or formal. The establishing or changing of formal and higher rules generally involves higher costs than vesting or altering informal and lower institutions.
4) Actors do not follow established rules automatically, but make their own judgment, which means that defection is always a possibility. Corporate actors are often confronted with a principal-agent problem in this regard. If institutions are very thick, and are deeply embedded in the actors via the process of socialisation, they can however dictate behaviour to a great extent; but this is less usual in modern, open societies.
5) The result of established rules cannot be determined in advance, but depends on the context in which they are applied, their subjective filtering by actors, and the actual course of the interactions between the parties concerned.

Relevance of the institutional approach to social security

Not all these ideas are universally accepted in the current scientific approach to social security. Rights and obligations are sometimes apprehended from a one-sided legalistic perspective, with the emphasis on what has already been codified (the prevailing laws and regulations relating to a limited number of risks) or on what ought to be included in the official rules based on considerations of justice and fairness (such as ever better protection against human damage). The dominant economic approach tends to emphasise that social security arrangements can generate negative effects (less propensity to save, labour market distortions, the poverty trap, etc.). In the neoclassical paradigm, less social security is almost by definition better social security, thus losing sight of the potentially positive functions (combating poverty, providing income continuity, retention of productive capacity, sustaining demand) of collective social security: "the whole purpose of welfare state provision is missing from the theoretical model" (Atkinson, 1999). The institutional approach makes clear that what is ultimately important is to establish which effects different social security arrangements actually have at a certain point in time. It is also relevant to assess whether they serve the current goals of the community and whether, all things considered, they generate positive gains according to the prevailing consensus. The first of these is a scientific matter; the second is predominantly a policy issue.

The communal verdict on the existing rules may be negative, and may for example result in a wide consensus that it is best to constrain social security rights, increase obligations, make conditions more stringent, tighten up sanctions and punish defective behaviour more severely. In other cases, by contrast, the conclusion may be that more social security is useful or desirable. If the poverty rate in households with children is considered too high, for example, it may be deemed efficient to raise child benefits to a level which covers the minimum actual costs of rearing children, so that the material conditions for their development do not depend on the parental labour market position. On the other hand, it is also possible that other forms of social security are thought to fit the present society better. If the community agrees that it is useful for women to work more often and more hours, it may be considered a good idea to transform tax breaks for non-working partners and child benefit levels that are above the minimum into fiscal exemptions for those in work and better leave arrangements.

From the institutional perspective, it is however not automatically the case that the new rules will achieve the envisaged results; that will depend on the context in which those new institutions are applied (during a recession women may feel discouraged to work, or do not get the opportunity to extend their working hours, and tax changes may have little impact), and on the way in which actors respond to the newly established rules (if poor parents want to avoid means-testing or other conditions, they may not apply for the higher child benefit).

The idea that formal and informal institutions are functional alternatives does not fit with the paradigm that dominated in the 20th century for a long time in the scientific study of social security. Informal arrangements were something that belonged to the past: after the American *New Deal* and the British *Beveridge Report*, 'true' social security was a matter of rules laid down in national law or ratified by the government. It is no coincidence that in his inaugural lecture in 1986, Berghman described all forms of non-formal regulation as 'invisible social security'. Over the last two decades, in which governments have increasingly stepped back, there has been some reappraisal on this point. Nonetheless, in modern, prosperous societies social security still is a predominantly formal set of rules. The institutional perspective makes clear that this is not necessary: it is perfectly feasible to regulate some forms of social security outside the government sphere more than at present, for example by introducing greater individual responsibility for pension build-up and covering the risk of work disability. This does need to be qualified with the comment that, historically, the transition from informal to formal regulation has not been achieved without sound reasons. In some respects the incentive to regulate which applied in the past may no longer hold, for example because citizens today are more prosperous, better educated and healthier, and are better able to look after their own interests. On the other hand, people often value a collective protection against major economic risks. With regard to social security rights, some degree of paternalism from the government is appreciated by many citizens, at least in the Netherlands (see e.g. Hoff & Vrooman, 2002). That is probably because rights that are guaranteed by law are felt to be more secure than private insurance or individual savings, and because they may involve lower transaction costs than a system with a great deal of freedom of choice.

The institutional perspective has also revealed a major drawback of formal regulation: the high likelihood of non-compliance. This has to do with the 'thin', weakly socialised nature of formal social security rules; but specific characteristics of the institutions also theoretically increase the risk of defection. This applies in particular to benefit schemes where the rules are complex and difficult to verify, where there are regular mutations in the entitlements and many different actors (including a social security organisation with a principal-agent problem), and where the endorsement on behalf of the community is weak. Formal regulations on social assistance, unemployment, sick leave and disability benefits tend to be especially vulnerable in this regard. This can be combated to some extent through an intensive anti-fraud policy (for example based on electronic data exchange), the imposition of heavy sanctions on culprits, and promoting cooperative behaviour via the instilling of social norms. The institutional approach stresses that such attempts can result in high transaction costs, however, and that it is very difficult to banish defection altogether. Every regulation of rights and obligations leaves the actors some latitude, and some of them will attempt to turn this to their own advantage.

Regimes, science and social policy

This study also sought to establish the influence of the different types of regimes on collective output. Among other things, it can be concluded from this that the regime concept is not merely a notion invented by the "welfare modelling business" (Abrahamson, 1999) of political science, but refers to real differences between countries in the design of their formal social security system and the informal rules supplementing it. The concept is also found to have a demonstrable significance for collective output and is therefore a scientifically relevant predictor.

In practice, however, very wide differences should not be expected in the results produced by representatives of the different regime types. This is due to the abstract nature of the typology, the fact that all real systems imply a dilution of the ideal theoretical principles (precisely because they are socio-historically created systems), and the often strong influence of the context in which the rules are applied. From the perspective of policy, the question is whether it is worthwhile seeking to bring about some kind of regime shift: even where policymakers succeed in circumventing path dependence, the effects are likely to be limited, at least as regards the extent of benefit dependency and poverty, the outcome indicators that were the central focus here.

Benefit dependency: the potential for data improvements

The degree of benefit dependency is the most direct indicator of the collective effects of social security institutions, because it ensues directly from the prevailing attribution of rights and obligations. It is therefore all the more striking that this is relatively virgin territory in terms of scientific research. The analyses performed here offer a first insight, but it would be advisable to repeat them when better data become available, preferably at micro-level as well. Linking the records of the social security agencies, as in the Dutch Social Statistical Database (ssb), and enriching them with survey data, could enable considerable improvements to be achieved in this regard. It would also be desirable to include provisions that are not regulated by law. The harmonisation of such 'census data' in the field of social security between countries would require a great effort, but is likely to offer many possibilities for studying the effectiveness of policy interventions on the number of benefits.

An alternative poverty measure

By contrast, poverty is a fairly exhaustively explored terrain in scientific theory and empirical research. Yet the analyses performed here have produced several new insights. One of the most important is that it is useful to establish a relationship between theoretical notions and operational criteria. Here, this led among other things to the conclusion that the poverty lines that are frequently used in empirical research sometimes have a weak theoretical basis. This applies in particular for the widely adopted relative threshold of 60% of median income. In the theoretical definition of poverty chosen here that criterion is not valid, and moreover regularly produces outcomes that are not credible (e.g. Slovakia has around the same percentage relatively poor people as Germany, while Lithuania equals the UK level). This is all the more problematic because this poverty line has been agreed upon by policymakers, for example in the 'Laeken indicators' which are used as a touchstone for social policy in the European Union. The relative poverty line is unfit for measuring differences and trends in the poverty rate in the member states, and offers therefore no sound basis for policymaking.

The 'generalised budget approach' adopted in this study appears to be a suitable alternative: it is preferable on both theoretical and practical grounds to existing poverty lines. Here it was found that it not only leads to plausible outcomes in the historical series of Dutch poverty rates, but also in country comparisons. In order to be widely applicable in international comparative research, the instrument would however need some further refinement. For example, it would seem sensible to investigate whether the 'basic needs' and the 'modest but adequate' living standard of the reference household (a single person) is accurately approximated in different countries if the norm amounts for the Netherlands are translated directly using purchasing power parities. This demands a detailed and consistent analysis of the expenditure that would be unavoidable or highly desirable for meeting the minimum level in each country, using the same method as that applied by the Dutch National Institute for Family Finance Information, and taking into account national differences in consumption patterns, prices, and taxation. It would also be necessary to ascertain whether the equivalence scale selected here is adequate for all countries. Finally, it is important to investigate whether the 'Dutch' mechanism used to index the level of the poverty thresholds over time is suitable for use elsewhere and (given the differing structure of the various national Household Budget Surveys) can be applied consistently in time series analyses across countries. These aspects fell outside the scope of this study, but certainly warrant further research.

Rules of relief?

Reference was made in the theoretical analysis to the views of G.H. Mead (1934), who argued that institutions are not per se oppressive or conservative, but can also be "flexible and progressive, fostering individuality rather than discouraging it". Are the institutions of social security, based on the results of this study, 'rules of oppression' or 'rules of relief' for the actors concerned?

It is not possible to give a general answer to this question. In the Introduction a 19th-century regulation was discussed which established the conditions for the alleviation of poverty in the Dutch town of Den Bosch. Although such forms of social security at the time were described as 'poor *relief*', this should not be understood to mean that the arrangements increased the freedom of action of the recipients. On the contrary: in order to be eligible for material support which was just barely enough for survival, the needy had to meet strict conditions and carry out unpalatable tasks in return. They were also subject to the whims of the local officials, and were often disgraced in their own community. In many countries the rights to social security were formalised partly in order to bring an end to such distressful circumstances. Seen in this way, the modern formal arrangements thus represent a major step forward. People affected by misfortune nowadays can enforce their rights, and those rights guarantee a substantially higher standard of living than in the past. The officials of modern social security organisations are trained and are expected to deal with their clients in a professional manner. The statutory and relatively anonymous character of social security – with no direct contact between beneficiaries and contributors – means that people have less to fear in terms of loss of status and being shunned by their community.

Even though modern institutions offer much greater freedom than the old informal systems, however, they still contain mandatory elements in their terms and conditions. Strikingly, not all benefit recipients are confronted by these elements to the same degree. For someone who has taken early retirement in Western Europe, who no longer needs to work, who receives a benefit whose net value is barely lower than their previous earnings, and who is in good health, social security can indeed be described as a system that predominantly brings relief. This person's income hardly drops, and he gains a huge amount of free time. He is also released from the inconveniences that often accompany work, such as emotional and physical stress and the hazards of occupational diseases and injuries. Dutch research accordingly shows that these people often see their 'benefit dependency' as a positive experience: on average, such voluntary unemployed are in fact happier and more satisfied with life than employed persons (see §3.6.2). Their peers who are in receipt of social assistance benefit, by contrast, not only receive less money, but generally have to continue looking for work and are frequently confronted with means-testing and other infringements of their privacy (such as home visits to check that they are not cohabiting or out working and earning undeclared income). Such social security arrangements erode the freedom of action of the entitled persons and may be experienced by them as oppressive.

It has to be remembered, however, that social security schemes are not established in order to maximise the relief of individuals who are facing economic distress. Rules of this kind are always intended to achieve certain *collective* gains that the rule-makers perceive at a certain place and time, not to generate individual returns. The rights of the entitled persons (benefit recipients) must then always be weighed against the obligations imposed on the duty-bound (taxpayers and contributors), and against the transaction costs involved in implementing the social security rules.

Socio-historically, that weighing-up process can have different outcomes. In the corporatist early exit arrangements which came into being in the 1980s, the collective goal was a temporary curbing of labour supply, with a view to reducing unemployment and giving school-leavers a greater chance of employment (swapping 'old for young', avoiding the creation of a 'lost generation'). In practice, the arrangements were often structured as an offer elderly employees could not refuse. Precisely because of this attractiveness, early exits increasingly came to be seen by the population of many countries as an acquired right, even though the schemes soon became fairly expensive for the contributors and the original reason for their establishment largely disappeared in the 1990s.

Social assistance regulations were mostly vested in a different socio-historical context, and also served other collective goals. For example, when the Dutch National Assistance Act was introduced in the 1960s it was stressed that the arrangement should make possible a 'dignified existence'. The aim of the founders was to give expression to principles of fairness and solidarity for all, and to acknowledge that the risk of indigence was not an individual matter. Compared with the old Poor Law, the new legislation brought a considerable extension of rights, which could moreover be geared to the individual circumstances of the recipients. For example, it became easier for women to withdraw from the strains of a failed marriage, and to carry on their lives as single mothers on benefit; in this sense the arrangement did indeed bring more relief. However, the take-up of social assistance benefit increased over time, and some of that take-up was unintended or fraudulent. To prevent the collective costs from rising too high and to maintain sufficient social support for the scheme among taxpayers, the emphasis was shifted more and more towards uniform national norms, conditioning of rights, strict monitoring, heavier sanctions and more active guidance into paid work. This was partly legitimised by pointing out the importance of work as a vehicle for social integration and personal growth. As a result, the oppressive elements of the social assistance legislation and its implementation gradually came more to the fore.

Examples such as these underline the fact that it cannot be taken as read that modern social security is liberating and emancipating for the individual beneficiaries, or is becoming so to an increasing degree; sociologically, that depends on the goals that a community currently wishes to achieve with social security, the institutions that are established in order to achieve the collective purposes, and the way in which the rules are interpreted and applied by the actors concerned.

Acknowledgements

The first version of this thesis was conceived a long time ago and looked very different. My daughters Arlinde and Ellika, who are now approaching puberty, were still very young; and their growth since then has been both more rapid and more consistent than the genesis of this book. The project began under the guidance of my then supervisor at Utrecht University, Piet van Wijngaarden, who at that time was also a fellow member on the board of The Netherlands Social Security Society (NGSZ). He suggested me to systematise some of the ideas from my earlier – more policy-focused – research and to add a theoretical substantiation. Sadly, illness forced him to step down from his duties, and for want of a supervisor my study lay untouched for several years. However, thanks to Piet's enthusiastic encouragement, a solid foundation had been laid, for which I remain thankful to him to this day.

During an afternoon symposium that I was organising for the Dutch Sociological Association (NSV), Jaap Dronkers asked me in passing, "Isn't it about time you obtained your doctorate?". Those words were enough to breathe new life into the project, under the joint supervision of Jaap (who shortly afterwards left Amsterdam to take up a professorship at the European University Institute near Florence) and Wil Arts from Tilburg University, which eventually became the home for my thesis. Both supervisors gave me the freedom to carry out the study in the fairly ambitious – and protracted – way that I had in mind. Their suggestions and the close attention with which they read and commented on the draft versions of the manuscript improved the end product considerably. Wil was my main inspiration in the theoretical analyses and reflections on social security regimes, while Jaap impressed upon me the need for scientific rigour and stressed the importance of a multivariate perspective in the empirical parts of the study. I am grateful to both of them for all their support and patience.

The thesis was written alongside my responsibilities as Head of the Research Group on Labour, Income and Social Security at The Netherlands Institute for Social Research | SCP. This meant that these activities had to be carried out to some extent 'against the tide'; it was frequently inevitable to give priority to other matters, and so this project often became the residual item in my time budget. Even so, I greatly appreciate the fact that SCP allowed me the latitude to bring forth what is in reality a somewhat atypical product for the Institute. The exemplary research environment that SCP offers, the good access to empirical data and the professional support all benefited the study hugely.

In particular I should like to thank the colleagues who were members of the internal reading committee for the project: Gerda Jehoel-Gijsbers, Michiel Ras and (until her early retirement) Cora Maas-de Waal. They repeatedly provided in-depth comments on the draft texts, and made useful suggestions with regard to the methodology and structuring of the study.

Richard van den Brink, Ron Olij and the others involved in the SCP publishing department ensured that the manuscript was cast in an attractive form. Gerlinde Schuller and

Ralph Noordhoek turned my sketches into eye-catching graphics, and Julian Ross and I enjoyed a detailed and instructive exchange of ideas on the finer points of the English language. I express my gratitude to all of them for their contributions to this publication.

On receiving the *Times Literary Award* in 1949, Mr. Churchill said: "Writing a book is an adventure. To begin with it is a toy, an amusement; then it becomes a mistress, and then a master, and then a tyrant; and then the last phase is that [...] one kills the monster". There is a grain of truth in that statement, which also applies to the realisation of this thesis. Looking back, however, it is the pleasure and intellectual satisfaction of carrying out and writing up the study which were the most salient aspects for me. I hope the reader will obtain some sense of this.

Notes

Chapter 1

1. *Reglement op de verzorging der Huisarmen binnen de Stad 's Hertogenbosch, met overleg van Heeren Armverzorgers, door het Collegie van Regenten over de Armen, beraamd* (22 November 1817). The Regulations governed the general care for the poor in 's-Hertogenbosch (or Den Bosch), capital of the Province of Noord-Brabant in the south of the Netherlands, for more than 35 years, from 1817 to 1853. Wouters (1968: 244-245) presents a more in-depth discussion.
2. Given the standards of the time in which they were written, the rules set out in the *Reglement* were extremely detailed. Despite this, they covered only four folio sheets – a negligible volume when compared with the many thousands of pages of legislation and regulations governing modern social security systems, where an average administrative decree is longer than this.
3. As a corollary to this, De Swaan (1989: 12-13) therefore believes it to be fairly implausible that the process of the collectivisation of care will continue in the future to an even higher level of aggregation, such as the European Union: "An integration beyond the level of national states, for example in a European community, does not of itself lead to a social synthesis in which the provision of care is continued at continental level. [...] The states that sustain care in an international context stand in the way of an international social policy".
It is worth noting here that the number of member states of the European Union has increased greatly in the last two decades, and that they have also become much more interwoven with each other. The introduction of the euro brought monetary union to the countries which adopted it, and arrangements such as the Schengen Treaty have rendered the sharp delineation of national territories within the Union less important, while Europe's external borders have become all the more crucial. Reference can also be made to the allocation of social security rights to citizens from other member states, the growing influence of European social regulations and jurisprudence on national legislation, and the increased importance of the 'European social agenda' (objectives and national action plans in relation to labour market participation, poverty and social exclusion, pension and care systems). On the other hand, De Swaan is correct to the extent that the most important welfare arrangements are essentially still a matter of national responsibility: benefit levels, pensions policy, labour market regulation, etc. are mostly determined in the national parliaments and policy fora, not in Brussels (see also: Vrooman, 2008a).

Chapter 2

1   Zijderveld bases this on the work of Malinowski (1944).
2   Giddens (1984: 17, 24, 375) sees institutions as the rules, including the related resources, which determine the behaviour of many actors over a longer period. In his approach, not every social rule is an institution; this is only the case if the rule (or a complex of rules) is recognised by many actors, has a certain historical continuity, and is accompanied by a sizeable deployment of social resources (including collective organisation). Compare: "(Structure refers to) the structuring properties allowing the 'binding' of time-space in social systems, the properties which make it possible for discernibly similar social practices to exist across varying spans of time and space and which lend them a 'systemic' form. [...] The most deeply embedded structural properties, implicated in the reproduction of societal totalities, I call *structural principles*. Those practices which have the greatest time-space extension within such totalities can be referred to as *institutions*. [...] The most important aspects of structure are rules and resources recursively involved in institutions. Institutions by definition are the more enduring features of social life [...] (or) chronically reproduced rules and resources".

This view is therefore concerned exclusively with collectively important, permanent rules. Interpreting institutions in such a way, however, begs all manner of definition-related questions. How many rule-subjects, how much rule-continuity and how much deployment of resources are needed before rules can be regarded as central? Does an institution not exist if there is a deficit on one of the dimensions? And if the threshold values have been exceeded in one social system but not another, can one speak of an institution only in the former case? This underlines the fact that it may be more sensible to regard *all* socially constructed rules as institutions, regardless of the number of supporters, the historical 'expiry date', and the mobilisation of resources that actually occurs. It is however true that some institutions are more central than others, an issue which will be explored in §2.6.

3   A social dilemma can be interpreted as a prisoner's dilemma (PD) with more than two participants. Ross (2006) explains the classic prisoner's dilemma as follows: "Suppose that the police have arrested two people whom they know have committed an armed robbery together. Unfortunately, they lack enough admissible evidence to get a jury to convict. They *do*, however, have enough evidence to send each prisoner away for two years for theft of the getaway car. The chief inspector now makes the following offer to each prisoner: If you will confess to the robbery, implicating your partner, and she does not also confess, then you'll go free and she'll get ten years. If you both confess, you'll each get 5 years. If neither of you confess, then you'll each get two years for the auto theft".

The classic prisoner's dilemma dates from the 1940s and 1950s, when American scientists were studying the possible applications for game theory variants in the US nuclear strategy. Characteristic of the classic prisoner's dilemma is that the incentive structure causes a rational actor to adopt egoistical, non-cooperative behaviour. Mutual defection is the logical result – partly because it is a once-only choice that the two prisoners have to make simultaneously, and it is assumed that they each possess the same information and have the same costs, benefits and preferences, and are not able to confer. In later research many variants of the classic prisoner's dilemma were studied, where a modified incentive structure can lead to different results. If there are more than two actors, a volunteer's dilemma or social dilemma may arise. The former occurs when a certain activity requires a limited number of volunteers. Each actor is better off if someone else becomes a volunteer, but if the minimum number of volunteers is not achieved the collective will be worse off. A standard example relates to the bystander effect: if someone is assaulted, people witnessing the attack may think the police should be informed, but do not do so themselves because the personal gains do not outweigh the possible costs of getting involved in the dispute or a future legal procedure. In the case of the social dilemma there is a certain threshold value: if too many farmers graze their cattle on the common grounds, that land will be ruined. Theoretically there are two equilibrium states in a social dilemma: universal defection or minimal effective cooperation, where the number of co-operators approaches the limit value. Only the latter distribution is Pareto-optimal (each actor is at least as well off as with all other solutions, and some are better off). In order to approach this point, the defection must be limited; this entails tackling any 'free riders' (people who benefit from their defection without intentionally harming the interest of others) and 'foul dealers' (people who not only benefit through their non-cooperative behaviour, but also seek to put others at a disadvantage).

Other game theory variants stress the repetition of the interaction (PD's may be continuous or iterative), the transparency of the intentions of the players, and the evolution of certain strategies. Axelrod (1981, 1984) has pointed at the effectiveness of the 'tit-for-tat' (TFT) strategy in computer simulations. This strategy means that the actor in an iterative PD acts cooperatively in the first move, and thereafter follows the behaviour of their opponent: cooperation is rewarded with cooperation, defection with defection. According to Axelrod, the TFT strategy is successful on account of four characteristics: it is 'nice', because the actor is never the first to defect; it is 'retaliatory', which means it does not lead to exploitation if the incentive structure rewards defection; it is 'forgiving', as the actor remains capable of cooperation if the other player regularly defects; and it is 'clear' because of the predictability of the actor's behaviour.

Later variants of the strategy are slightly more efficient, as they take account of the possibility that the other actor will sometimes take a suboptimum decision due to an incorrect perception or by accident, and will therefore not always repay defectors in kind ('Generous TFT'). However, TFT is not necessarily optimal; for instance, in games of limited duration, the last players may choose to defect in the final round, thus making retaliation impossible.

4   In the first chapter of this novel McEwan (1997) describes six men, who do not know each other and who due to a "fatal lack of co-operation" do not manage to keep a stranded balloon with a child as passenger on the ground. If they were to undertake the same joint action (all holding onto the balloon together, lifting out the child who is paralysed with fear, deflating the balloon), they could have prevented a gust of wind carrying away the balloon and child. However, there is no history of co-operation, no shared morality, and no clear leader. One lets go of the balloon, causing the remaining weight of the others to reach a critical point. They see their own lives come under threat, and bring themselves out of danger. The most altruistic of them holds on until exhaustion forces him to let go, so that he falls to his death.

5   In a zero-sum game a person can only gain by putting another player at a disadvantage. A simple example is noughts-and-crosses (tic-tac-toe), in which a move that allows player A to win means that player B loses. In such finite zero-sum games, where both players have perfect information, the solution is equal to the Nash Equilibrium (NE) of their respective strategies. This is the case if neither player, given the strategy employed by the other, can increase his yield by changing his line of attack. If both players follow a rational strategy in this type of zero-sum game, in which they attempt to maximise their minimum gains (maximin) under the assumption that the other player will play as well as possible, this leads to a unique solution, which for this type of game is also the only Nash equilibrium. If played well, therefore, noughts-and-crosses always ends in a draw.

However, games as these are fairly atypical, and not very useful as models for social interaction. Non-zero-sum games are more instructive; these often have several Nash equilibria, so that the outcome is less clearly determined from the outset. In the classic prisoner's dilemma (see above), the solution that is optimal for both players is not achieved because the Nash equilibrium is not cooperation, but mutual defection (see Ross, 2006).

6   Liebowitz & Margolis (1990) have criticised David's 'Fable of the keys' in a number of ways. First of all they point out that the claims for the superiority of alternative keyboards –especially the Dvorak layout– are not convincing. The US Navy experiments comparing QWERTY and Dvorak in 1944 possibly were flawed; a more rigorous experiment conducted in 1956 suggests the gains in typing speed on the Dvorak keyboard are limited and do not outweigh the additional training costs (especially for trained typists). According to Liebowitz & Margolis this is corroborated by ergonomic studies, which state that optimal typing speed depends on three factors:
-   The loads on the right and left hands should be equalised;
-   The load on the middle row of the keyboard should be maximised;
-   The frequency of alternating hand sequences should be maximised, while the frequency of same-finger typing should be minimised.

The Dvorak keyboard outperforms QWERTY on the first two criteria. But Sholes's policy to put successively typed keys as far apart as possible favours the third criterion, and enables QWERTY-users to type rapidly (probably because during a keystroke the idle hand prepares for the next). "Thus Sholes's decision to solve a mechanical problem through careful keyboard arrangement may have inadvertently satisfied a fairly important requirement for efficient typing" (Liebowitz & Margolis, 1990: 17).

Apart from questioning the superiority of alternative keyboard designs, Liebowitz & Margolis (1990: 22) also point out that the market situation prevailing in the 1870s may have been less clear than David thinks: "Remington was not so well established that a keyboard offering significant advantages could not have gained a foothold". Finally, in their view David has not taken the true complexity of markets into account, by neglecting the role of entrepreneurs, guarantees, mergers, advertising, and other institutional factors: "[In] such a sterile model of competition, it is not surprising that accidents have considerable permanence, [and] embarking on some wrong path provides little chance to jump to an alternative path" (Liebowitz & Margolis, 1990: 22).

7   In Australia the *Terra Nullius* doctrine – at the time of the colonisation the continent was empty and belonged to no-one – has been used to substantiate the proposition that the government had a right to take the land for itself, and to lease land and concessions to farmers and mining companies. Others take the opposing standpoint that such a view repudiates the rights of the aboriginals already living in the continent at the time, and that these original inhabitants have a legitimate claim on some form of compensation.

Even in societies where land is less plentiful, it may be possible to appropriate no man's land. In Britain, for example, areas of land that belong to no-one may be appropriated provided a) these have not been declared to be common property pursuant to the *Commons Registration Act*, b) are permanently fenced, and c) are used without interruption for a number of years.

8   Weber's analysis is however more sophisticated in several respects. North regards the relationship between these informal institutions and the emergence of an efficient capitalist market system as a fairly direct one, whereas in Weber's approach it is an unintended consequence. The restless labour, thrift, sobriety and individual responsibility for performing one's work are, according to Weber, the result of the struggle by Calvinists to achieve their own salvation. Capitalism has evolved as the result of the co-incidence of this culture, changing market conditions, and the interests of the rising bourgeoisie.

9   The formula $P_D = \log_{10}(1+(1/D))$ describes *Benford's Law*, named after the physicist who pointed out the striking regularity that is found in all manner of non-uniformly distributed series of discrete numbers, such as tables in newspapers and magazines, population statistics, addresses, mathematical constants, certain sports results, etc. (Benford, 1938). Just over 30% of the observations in such number series begin with the figure 1, which is much higher than the 11.1% probability that would be expected if all starting figures were proportionally represented, as in a lottery. To give an actual example: of the more than 5,000 computer files created for this study, the size (in bytes) in 31.3% of cases is a number that begins with 1 – far more than would be expected in a uniform random distribution, and very close to the prediction according to Benford's Law. The other starting numbers in this series show the expected decreasing frequency.

An intuitive understanding of the mechanism at work here can be obtained by thinking of a stock market index which rises in equal steps. If the index starts at 100 and rises by 20% each year, it will be almost four years before the index reaches 200 and the starting figure changes. The jump from 200 to 300 takes significantly less time (just over two years); the change from 500 to 600 is even faster (precisely one year), while the change from 900 to 1,000 is the shortest (just over six months). The mechanism then begins over again: the change from 1,000 to 2,000 again takes almost four years, that from 2,000 to 3,000 just over two years, and so on. As a result, in such series the figure 1 dominates as a starting value, and the other figures occur with a decreasing degree of probability.

Hill (1996) provides a mathematical substantiation for this law, which has been used in actual practice for auditing purposes, e.g. to detect errors of calculation, computer bugs and tax fraud (Nigrini, 1996). Hill also demonstrates that the rule continues to apply when the figures are expressed in different units (e.g. hexadecimal notation). However, Benford's Law does not hold for all independent numerical series (e.g. telephone numbers in a certain town, which often begin with the same number). The logarithmic pattern emerges whenever "various distributions are being sampled in a presumably unbiased way", in other words in the case of random samples from random distributions (Hill, 1996: 361).

The content of a rule such as this is not institutional, because it is not socially constructed. However, its expression in the scientific discourse can be regarded as rule-driven, since it is related to accepted language conventions and the genesis of mathematical statistics.

10 This view on institutions resembles some of Wittgenstein's assertions in the *Philosophical Investigations* (1953). Wittgenstein presents an analysis on the nature of rules (PI 185 ff.), which he begins with the example of a student who makes a mistake in completing an arithmetical series. He links a large number of questions to this, such as: How do people learn rules? How do we follow them? Where do the standards come from by which we assess whether or not the rule has been followed? Is there a mental representation of the rule and the standards? Is this applied on the basis of intuition? Are rules socially learned and enforced? Rather than answering these questions directly, Wittgenstein questions the underlying dogmatic 'pictures' which give rise to them – his aim is to free philosophy from this straitjacket.

Winch (1958: 24-33) stresses that, in Wittgenstein's analysis, rules exist by the grace of the reaction of others who, because of a certain training, regard them as natural: "One has to take account not only of the actions of the person whose behaviour is in question as a candidate for the category of rule-following, but also the *reactions of other people* to what he does. More specifically, it is only in a situation in which it makes sense to suppose that somebody else could in principle discover the rule which I am following that I can intelligibly be said to follow a rule at all." (Winch, 1958: 30). Another feature of rules is that they are linked to a social recognition of compliance and defection: "The notion of following a rule is logically inseparable from the notion of *making a mistake*. [...] A mistake is a contravention of what is *established* as correct; as such, it must be *recognisable* as such a contravention." (Winch, 1958: 32). For there to be a rule, others must be able to check their compliance on the basis of a certain recognised standard. This social character of rules does not mean that private rules of conduct cannot exist. In Wittgenstein's analysis, however, these also contain social elements because:

(a) A rule cannot exist if others are in principle unable to understand it and assess whether or not it is being correctly observed;

(b) It is doubtful whether someone can develop personal behavioural standards if he has never had experience of "human society with its socially established rules" (Winch, 1958: 33).

Wittgenstein's view is also echoed in modern sociology of knowledge, in which it is stressed that scientific truths and the pre-eminence of a certain mathematical/philosophical logic are often based on peer consensus, which cannot be seen in isolation from the established interests and reputations. In this sense such paradigms can also be regarded as institutional.

11 The rational-ethical actor may be both a natural person and a collectivity, generally a society with a government and laws. An example of the first is Kantian moral philosophy. According to this scheme of thought, people should act in accordance with rules that correspond with the abstract principle that they would want them to become universal laws: "Act only according to that maxim by which you can at the same time will that it should become universal law". For example, a rational-ethical actor will believe that others must keep their promises, because he himself or society would suffer disadvantage if they do not. He then does not act proper if he does not apply a guideline to himself that he considers applicable for others. From this 'categorical imperative' it therefore follows that it should be a rule that people must keep their promises.

The theories on distributive fairness posited by Rawls and Nozick, for example, accord central importance to the collective ethic. Rawls (1999 [1971], 1993) adopts two principles of 'justice as fairness':

(1) The liberty principle:
"Each person has an equal claim to a fully adequate scheme of equal basic rights and liberties, which scheme is compatible with the same scheme for all; and in this scheme the equal political liberties, and only those liberties, are to be guaranteed their fair value."

(2) The difference principle:
"Social and economic inequalities are to satisfy two conditions:
a) They are to be attached to positions and offices open to all under conditions of fair equality of opportunity; and
b) They are to be to the greatest benefit of the least advantaged members of society".

Nozick (1974) takes a liberal-conservative view. A fair distribution need not have a particular form or pattern; the key thing is whether the individual actions that have led to the distribution were themselves just. He assumes among other things that it is permissible to claim the rights to a disproportionate part of the world if:
a) This will not worsen other people's circumstances;
b) The preceding actions that led to the acquirement and transfer of property rights comply with certain principles of justice; or
c) Past injustices are corrected via a procedure of rectification.

Coleman (1990: 53) rejects both the individualistic and the collective variants of normative ethics: "Moral philosophers searching for the right distribution of rights are searching for the pot of gold at the end of the rainbow".

12 In fact the rational conditions cited by Coleman were not met in the collective suicide at the People's Temple in Jonestown; see e.g. Johnson (1979) and Hall (1987).

13 Stirner (1971 [1845]) regards *Eigenheit* ('ownness', a specific form of egotism) as the highest goal for which a person can strive. This is in agreement with the *homo economicus* of rational choice theory, but someone who is guided purely by his material interests is not genuinely free according to Stirner. He regards *Eigenheit* as a natural state, which is suppressed in practice by external regulation. According to Stirner, *Eigenheit* is the only true moral, and in an ideal world it would take place of the existing social rules. In his view these are obstacles to this form of egoism and are therefore morally reprehensible; complying with them is regarded as a form of weakness of cowardice. In Stirner's ideal world, breaking the rules is defensible if it serves the cause of egoism, even if this involves the committing of serious offences such as murder. Although Stirner is often regarded as the inspiration for the later anarchism, he does not believe that the State should be overthrown. His ideal society is a 'Union of Egoists', consisting of individuals who associate voluntarily in order to increase their powers. The egoist, however, must free himself as far as possible from government authority, and where possible approach the State instrumentally: "Since the State is the 'lordship of law' ... the egoist, in all cases where *his* advantage runs against the State's, can satisfy himself only by crime." (Stirner, 1971 [1845]: 151).

14 In particular the *Genocide Convention* (1948), the *International Covenants on Civil and Political Rights* and on *Economic, Social and Cultural Rights* (1966), the *Convention on the Elimination of all Forms of Discrimination against Women* (1979), the *Torture Convention* (1984) and the *Convention on the Rights of the Child* (1989).

15 As noted, North (1990) considers institutions in terms of constraints, and not as rules that confer rights. His concept of rights is limited to property rights, which are central to his economic/historical analysis. He does not go into the relationship between such rights and institutions in any detail, but does regard them as being closely related: "Property rights are the rights individuals appropriate over their own labor and the goods and services they possess.

Appropriation is a function of legal rules, organizational forms, enforcement, and norms of behavior – that is, the institutional framework" (North, 1990: 33). Gaining rights as a function of rules does not differ much from the theoretical position adopted in this chapter, with one exception: in the model developed here rights are included in the exogenously given rules, which are then interpreted by actors.

16 Raz (1986: 166) defines this as follows: "An individual is capable of having rights if and only if either his well-being is of ultimate value or he is an 'artificial person' (e.g. a corporation)". 'Ultimate value' means that something is valuable irrespective of its instrumental value, in other words when its value cannot be reduced to the contribution it makes to something else (Raz, 1986: 177). Raz's definition of the potential holders of rights means that dogs, for example, are excluded: "Dogs can have no rights though we may have duties to protect or promote their well-being [...] Dogs have the same moral standing that many ascribe to works of art. Their existence is intrinsically valuable inasmuch as the appreciation of art is intrinsically valuable. But their value is derivative and not ultimate. It derives from their contribution to the well-being of persons" (Raz, 1986: 178). This view puts Raz in the middle ground as regards the definition of possible 'rights entities'. Rights philosophers who advocate the *Choice Theory of Rights* generally believe that not only animals, but also young children, people with mental disability, etc., can also not have rights. In this view the core of a right is that the holder of the right can exercise a degree of control over the duties of others. Owners of dogs or parents of young children have rights, but those without the legal capability of acting do not. Proponents of the *Interest Theory of Rights*, among whom Raz is also included, argue that interests are the only things that determine whether someone can have rights, not whether they are capable of action or are able to set in motion legal proceedings. A child has an interest and therefore has rights, something which is in fact acknowledged in many cases in practice. For example, in assessing the damages to be paid after physical injury has been caused to children (e.g. following a traffic accident), the loss to be suffered by the child in its later life is often taken as a yardstick, rather than the present suffering caused to the parents. In certain variants of this approach everything and everyone with interests in principle also has rights. Not only young children are then potential holders of rights, but also animals, landscapes, cultural heritage, the environment, etc. Raz limits the scope of rights to natural and artificial persons.

17 In the philosophy of rights literature this is often illustrated by citing the distinction between 'claim rights' and 'liberty rights'. According to Hohfeld (1919), a person has a claim right if he can demand that someone else does something for him; set against this right is the duty of the other party to act. In the case of a liberty right, a person may perform an act; set against this is the duty of the other person not to prevent the owner of the right from doing what they wish. Raz (1986) points out that rights and duties need not by definition be so directly linked.

The philosophy of rights literature also uses a number of related concepts, such as 'permissions' (A has legal permission to do X), statutory 'powers' (A can influence the statutory relationships of B) and 'immunities' (B cannot influence the statutory relationships of A); see e.g. Hohfeld (1919: 65). These topics are the subject of extensive debate. Raz (1986: 168), for example, regards 'powers' as aspects of rights, and "by extending the same reasoning rights can be shown to be grounds of immunities and liberties: they are reasons for not subjecting individuals to duties or powers of others".

18 Property rights are complete when an actor has the following rights vis-à-vis all others with regard to a good or service:
    - liberty of possession: the actor may exercise physical control and exclude others
    - liberty to use: the actor may utilise the good or service
    - liberty to abuse: the actor may damage or destroy the good or service
    - claim to income: any gains from the good or service accrues to the actor
    - liberty of alienation: the actor may give away, sell or refuse the aforementioned rights.

19 The will theory stresses that rights are created in order to give the holders control over the duties of others; i.e., an actor's right is an instrument for imposing his will on other actors. Each right therefore necessarily implies correlated duties; the right-holder is a "small-scale sovereign to whom the duty is owed" (cf. Hart, 1982: 183). The will theory has difficulty in explaining unwaivable rights (entitlements over which the bearer has no control, e.g. the right not to be enslaved) and the rights of actors that are not able to exercise sovereignty (infants, mentally insane or comatose persons, animals).

20 Raz, and other rights philosophers such as Hohfeld, see power as primarily a consequence of rights: the prerogatives to act that ensue from the right. And it is indeed possible that power is encapsulated in the rules, as in Weber's (1922) typology of authority (legitimised power). Sociologists and economists (e.g. Coleman, North), by contrast, assert that power is to some extent also a *cause* of a specific allocation of rights, which leads to a bias in the interests that are recognised in the rights structure.

21 In modern legal systems the laws on public decency are often rather liberal. It is a basic principle that the government has to apply its police and judicial powers with restraint, and should only infringe the freedom of actors in serious

cases. For example, a committee that issued recommendations on the modernisation of the Dutch public decency laws stated that, "(It) is not the task of the state to use the criminal laws to impose its views on what constitutes a morally good life". The freedom of private citizens has primacy, and the state may only interfere in that freedom if it leads to "unacceptable expressions and consequences vis-à-vis fellow citizens", and only if the infringements take place against the will of the victim (Melai Committee, 1980: 9-10). In such an approach the laws on public decency are often limited to the banning of behaviours that are broadly rejected and which involve violation of the interests of actors or public order. They then include things such as the prohibition of human trafficking, sexual contacts with young children, offensive behaviour in public, offering for sale or possessing certain types of pornography, etc. In some cases these have turned into 'complaint-led' offences: the government only acts as a third party when an interested party lodges a complaint.

22 As argued earlier, this relativist standpoint is an unavoidable theoretical consequence of the definition adopted here, in which institutions are ultimately social constructs. This also implies rejection of 'value platonism', of which the work of Nicolai Hartmann (1962 [1925]) is the best-known example. Hartmann regards values as the core of ethics. In his view they have an objective character, and only need to be historically discovered. He distinguishes four elementary values: *das Gute, das Edle, die Fülle und die Reinheit*. He places these at the top of the hierarchy of values, and they are a condition for the discovery of specific virtues (*spezielle sittliche Werte*). Historically this would first have taken place in ancient Greek times: the Platonic values of justice, wisdom, courage and control and the catalogue of virtues of the intellect and character in Aristotle's *Nicomachean Ethics*. According to Hartmann, Christianity 'discovered' virtues such as charity, reliability, faith, humility and "*Werte des äusseren Umgangs*". The modern age brought the individual personality, love for the distant other (*Fernstenliebe*) and between persons and, following on from Nietzsche's *Zarathustra*, the "*schenkende Tugend*" (spiritual giving not because there is a moral obligation or necessity, as with charity, but because of a "*Drang der Fülle*") (Hartmann, 1962 [1925]: 504).
However, the fact that Western religion and philosophy show a certain historical evolution of values does not necessarily mean that it is inevitable. That history could have developed in very different ways, and its reconstruction is debatable. Moreover, the articulation of certain values in religious and philosophical idea systems does not necessarily mean that they actually influence behaviour. Imposing any kind of universal hierarchy of values *a priori* and on theoretical grounds is most disputable.

23 Coleman (1990: 248) also acknowledges the special status of conventions: "In some cases the selection of the focal action is largely arbitrary ... It is arbitrary whether the action defined as correct is driving on the right or driving on the left. Once the convention has been established, however, all are better off if each follows the convention. The interests in a particular direction of action depend on whether the action is being carried out by others. If a convention has established the direction of a norm, I will call the norm a conventional norm". Here, preference is given to regarding conventions as a separate type of rule, not as a collective custom that translates into a special type of norms.

24 Spelling is conventional, but language also contains normative elements. It is the ultimate institution for imparting meaning. Language can create social distinctions (e.g. between 'high' and 'low' dialects, church and scientific Latin versus layman's language, etc.) and can also embody a shared value (a language as the cultural vehicle of a nation, or as a confirmation of the identity and solidarity of minority groups). Aspects such as these are central to sociolinguistics. Searle (1995) regards language as a kind of meta-institution, which makes possible all other rules.
It is worth noting that in language rules (word meanings, grammar, pronunciation rules), the duties are often more explicit than the rights. The latter do occur however, for example when the right to say holy prayers or pronounce words of absolution is reserved for priests. Language may also be a condition for the emergence of all manner of other rights: the right to enter a place may be regulated by codes (passwords); the right to belong to a group may require a command of the *argot* or professional *jargon*. The latter may be formalised, as in the case of immigrants where the government requires a basic command of the language before granting them the right to settle or work in a country.
De Swaan (2001) also refers to the central role of language when he argues that all relations between groups take place via verbal interactions, which are by definition embedded in a specific language. He also stresses the politico-sociological and politico-economic aspects of language. De Swaan points to the global, hierarchically arranged language system that has arisen in recent centuries. English is the hypercentral language, which is linked to a dozen supercentral languages, which in turn are surrounded by central and peripheral languages. According to De Swaan, language is a collective good which is used by actors strategically, for example when they have to decide whether or not to learn or use a foreign language. On a number of points, De Swaan's analysis touches on the institutional approach adopted in this study. For example, he regards language as collective cultural capital in which the users have invested, so that changes can entail high costs for professional users, such as writers, preachers, or politicians. This explains why precisely these actors often fight for the preservation of language and culture, and are only willing to tolerate path-dependent changes.

25 Searle (1995: 26, and more extensively in his 'hierarchical taxonomy of facts', 120-126), draws a distinction between 'brute facts', 'social facts' and 'institutional facts'. A social fact can be distinguished from a brute fact because it does not exist independently of human thought; more precisely, these are facts that are based on a collective intentionality. An institutional fact, according to Searle, is a social fact of a specific type, which is concerned with functions that can only be fulfilled "as a matter of collective acceptance or recognition". The statements 'this is a screwdriver' and 'this is money' both refer to social facts, but only the latter can be regarded as an institutional fact. The monetary system is based entirely on social recognition of the tender, whereas a screwdriver can still be used even if no one acknowledges it as such.

It might be expected that Searle would devote some attention in this context to Durkheim, whose views on social facts were discussed in the first section of this chapter. This author is however mentioned only in passing, and along with Weber and Simmel is immediately discarded, because they "… did not have the necessary tools. That is, through no fault of their own, they lacked an adequate theory of speech acts, of performatives, of intentionality, of collective intentionality, of rule-driven behavior, etc." (Searle, 1995: xii). Searle also states that he is not very familiar with the work of these classical sociologists.

26 McConnel (2002) discusses the (im)possibility of a hierarchical ranking of behavioural prescriptions in moral dilemmas, inter alia on the basis of two familiar examples. The first is taken from Plato's *Republic*: "In Book I [...] Cephalus defines 'justice' as speaking the truth and paying one's debts. Socrates quickly refutes this account by suggesting that it would be wrong to repay certain debts – for example, to return a borrowed weapon to a friend who is not in his right mind. Socrates' point is not that repaying debts is without moral import; rather, he wants to show that it is not always right to repay one's debts, at least not exactly when the one to whom the debt is owed demands repayment. What we have here is a conflict between two moral norms: repaying one's debts and protecting others from harm. And in this case, Socrates maintains that protecting others from harm is the norm that takes priority. [...] The Platonic case strikes many as too easy to be characterized as a genuine moral dilemma. For the agent's solution in that case is clear; it is more important to protect people from harm than to return a borrowed weapon. And in any case, the borrowed item can be returned later, when the owner no longer poses a threat to others. Thus in this case we can say that the requirement to protect others from serious harm overrides the requirement to repay one's debts by returning a borrowed item when its owner so demands. When one of the conflicting requirements overrides the other, we do not have a genuine moral dilemma. So [...] in order to have a genuine moral dilemma it must also be true that neither of the conflicting requirements is overridden".

The second example is from William Styron's novel *Sophie's choice*: "Sophie and her two children are at a Nazi concentration camp. A guard confronts Sophie and tells her that one of her children will be allowed to live and one will be killed. But it is Sophie who must decide which child will be killed. Sophie can prevent the death of either of her children, but only by condemning the other to be killed. The guard makes the situation even more excruciating by informing Sophie that if she chooses neither, then both will be killed. With this added factor, Sophie has a morally compelling reason to choose one of her children. But for each child, Sophie has an apparently equally strong reason to save him or her". This moral dilemma cannot be resolved by making one rule subordinate to the other, because the contradicting duties derive from the same rule. There is no solution to the dilemma, though some ethicists defend the standpoint that Sophie must always act in order to save one of her children; that is always better than not choosing and losing both of them – just as it is better to save one of two drowning men and not the other, rather than allowing both of them to drown. If Sophie cannot think of a justification for her choice, she would do well to take a random decision – this will prevent future remorse about the unused possibility of saving one of her two children. But this demands a rationality that is difficult to conjure up where there are strong emotional ties.

27 The costs of such a change in the formal traffic conventions are considerable: other rules, such as the right of way, also have to change, the signposting and routing of streets has to be modified, public transport has to be adapted (e.g. doors, platforms moved to the other side), car manufacturers must supply cars with the steering wheel on the other side, and there may initially be an increase in the number of traffic accidents because not all road users change their routines immediately. In practice, therefore, such a switch is often the result of a revolution or occupation by a foreign power. Driving on the right was introduced in France during the Revolution, and this convention expanded to the occupied states of Western Europe during the Napoleonic Wars. The growth of the British and French colonial empires meant that the colonised territories began driving on the left or right, respectively, while the German occupation during the Second World War led to the convention of driving on the right being imposed on many countries in Central and Eastern Europe (Lay, 1992: 197-201). Sweden is a special case, in that in 1967 it switched voluntarily to driving on the right. Here, however, there was the typical circumstance that the old convention of driving on the left also entailed considerable costs. Sweden was surrounded by countries which drove on the right, increasing the likelihood of accidents along the extensive borders; and there was also a fairly large automotive industry which produced mainly for countries that drove on the right. This limited the relative costs of switching to the convention of driving on the right.

28 An agreement that is not governed by rules at all is theoretically possible, but not probable. It may arise assuming there is no government or community, and actors are a-historical. Empirically this is rare, and actors usually are inclined to act in accordance with the procedures, values, norms and conventions they are used to.

29 All manner of further differentiations can be made within groups. For example, it is possible to distinguish primary groups (personal, emotional and direct relationships, as among family and friends; private life) from secondary ones (impersonal, non-emotional, indirect; public life). A distinction is sometimes also made between formal and informal groups. The former occupy clear positions based on an official or functional criterion, such as school classes or an orchestra; the second type is formed spontaneously, and may for example consist of people who come together during a course, or who spontaneously join singing during a music concert. In addition, groups of which a person forms part can be contrasted with groups to which he or she would like to belong (the functionalist 'reference group').

30 Coleman (1990: 197-240) provides an extensive summary of such forms of 'collective' action. He discusses the panic reactions exhibited by people during disasters and crises in the financial world and on stock markets, 'acquisitive crazes' (such as the Dutch speculative trade into tulip bulbs in the 17th century), contagious superstition (believing in flying saucers and magical cures), crowd behaviour, fashion rages, and so on. Apart from the fact that many people do the same things, Coleman points out that in situations such as these their behaviour can change rapidly, and that their actions are mutually interdependent. In his view this is an example of individuals partially and unilaterally transferring control of their behaviour to the collective so as to maximise their own utility. If a building has to be evacuated in an emergency, there is a need for coordination, and people gain by transferring control. According to Coleman, a rational actor will then set a good example (by listening to the person in charge of the evacuation), and will subsequently make his behaviour dependent on the actions of others (if everyone begins running, it is necessary to do the same in order to minimise the personal risk).

This is an interesting attempt to place seemingly irrational actions in a rational choice perspective, yet it has a number of weaknesses. Coleman assumes a process of weighing up the pros and cons for which people in such circumstances often have no time, and also ignores the emotional motivations of actors (their flight response, partly driven by biological processes). A single person who looks up to see a rock falling towards him and runs away in response is behaving in the same way as a crowd fleeing before a volcano eruption, without being capable of transferring his behaviour or convictions in a reasoned way to others. Collective phenomena such as these can be more easily understood in terms of equal reactions to equal stimuli, in which the actors reinforce each other's responses; it is thus an interaction process that leads to homogeneous outcomes, not collective, rational action.

31 Coleman (1990: 300) regards all manner of relational characteristics within social systems as forms of social capital; not only trust, but also relationships of authority and even norms. In his view, economic capital and human capital are not relational, but resources of individual actors.

32 *Herrschaft* is difficult to translate into English; it refers both to the legitimacy and the possibility of dominating through the use of coercive force. The revisers of the 1968 English edition of *Wirtschaft und Gesellschaft* state that "both 'domination' and 'authority' are 'correct', although each stresses a different component of *Herrschaft*" (p. 62), and translate the definition as "the probability that a command with a given specific content will be obeyed by a given group of persons".

33 In addition to the economic, sociological and psychological notions mentioned in the main text, Mead's (1934) theory on the social construction of the self is worth noting. He argues that actors place themselves in the roles of others, and in a socio-genetic process gradually develop a reflective consciousness ('mind') and an identity ('self'). The self is compartmentalised into the 'me' (the internalised collective expectations) and the 'I' (the individual component, which can respond to exogenous expectations and is therefore a source of freedom and innovation). If actors learn to take the standpoint of others towards themselves, Mead speaks of the 'generalised other'.

Later sociologists make similar distinctions. Thus Giddens (1984: 5-8), in line with the Freudian distinction of id, ego and superego distinguishes the unconscious motives and cognitions of actors, their practical consciousness and their reflective consciousness. He regards the practical consciousness as being particularly important in seeking to understand the behaviour of actors. This consists of "what actors know (believe) about social conditions, including especially the conditions of their own action, but cannot express discursively ... between discursive and practical consciousness there is no bar; there are only the differences between what can be said and what is characteristically simply done" (Giddens, 1984: 7, 375).

Bourdieu refers in this connection to a 'habitus' or a 'socialised subjectivity', a cognitive basic structure which gives direction to people's actions. The habitus is a stable, internalised thought pattern, on the basis of which behavioural alternatives are categorised and assessed unconsciously or semiconsciously. This is rooted in the experiences of individuals, groups and social classes. According to one of Bourdieu's definitions (1990: 91): "The habitus, which is the generative principle of responses more or less well adapted to the demands of a certain field, is the product of individual history, but also, through the formative experiences of earliest infancy, of the whole collective history of family and class".

Coleman (1990: 503-528) proposes a distinction between the 'object self' or 'receptor', and the 'agent self' or 'actuator'. He regards the former as "the storehouse of the person's values and experiences" and as having interests without being able to act. According to Coleman, the 'agent self' is comparable to Mead's 'I'. It can act but does not itself have any interests, serving those of the object self instead. In his view, the same principal-agent problems arise here as with corporate actors.

34 Cf. I Corinthians 3: 16, 17: "Know ye not that ye are the temple of God, and that the Spirit of God dwelleth in you? If any man defile the temple of God, him shall God destroy; for the temple of God is holy, which temple ye are."

35 For example in the Netherlands Criminal Code, where Sections 293 and 294 prohibit killing a person at their request or helping in their suicide, with a maximum sentence of twelve years imprisonment (the perpetrator is themselves not liable to prosecution, even if an attempt fails). Since the Euthanasia Act (*Wet toetsing levensbeëindiging op verzoek en hulp bij zelfdoding*) came into force in April 2001, doctors who help in the performance of euthanasia in the Netherlands are no longer subject to prosecution provided they meet a number of strict conditions. The doctor must be of the professional opinion that the patient is undergoing unbearable suffering with no prospect of improvement; the patient must be able to give informed consent (or, where this is no longer the case, must have issued a written declaration in advance), must submit a voluntary and a well-considered request, and must have been informed by the doctor of their situation and the prospects. Together, patient and doctor must have reached the conclusion that there was no other reasonable solution. The doctor must have consulted at least one other independent colleague, who has seen the patient and has issued a written opinion stating whether the conditions have been met. Finally, the ending of life and the provided assistance must have been carried out with all due medical care, and the doctor must report it to the local coroner.

36 As the historian Flavius Josephus says: "Let our wives die before they are abused, and our children before they have tasted of slavery; and after we have slain them, let us bestow that glorious benefit upon one another mutually, and preserve ourselves in freedom, as an excellent funeral monument for us. But first let us destroy our money and the fortress by fire; for I am well assured that this will be a great grief to the Romans, that they shall not be able to seize upon our bodies, and shall fall of our wealth also; and let us spare nothing but our provisions; for they will be a testimonial when we are dead that we were not subdued for want of necessaries, but that, according to our original resolution, we have preferred death before slavery." (The Wars of the Jews, or the History of the Destruction of Jerusalem; translated by W. Whiston). Also note that, in a strict sense, there was only one suicide in Masada, though even this is a taboo in the Jewish tradition. The other martyrs – according to historical records 959 – were killed by their spouses, fathers or comrades, and Josephus does not report whether they agreed with the argumentation of their leader Eleazar ben Yair. In addition, based on archaeological research, the historical evidence for the collective suicide does not appear strong in all respects (see e.g. Cohen, 1982).

37 For example, only 7% of those who committed suicide in the Netherlands in 2000 had physical disabilities as a motive, and could therefore possibly have been rational suicides. In the other suicide motives – including relationship problems, financial problems, work and study problems – this is less likely.

38 Frijda (2007: 4) gives a more formal definition of emotions: "states of action readiness, and feelings of readiness that bear on the aim of achieving or maintaining, or terminating or decreasing one's relationship to a particular object or event; and to have the characteristics of emerging involuntarily, of appearing to be set towards completing the aim in the face of delays and difficulties, and to seek precedence over ongoing behavior or interference from other sources". These states are induced by emotional events, and according to Frijda governed by several 'laws', e.g. the laws of 'situational meaning' (emotions are a reaction to the subjective interpretation of an event), of 'concern' (events are deemed important, because they refer to a motive, need, goal or value), of 'apparent reality' (the meanings attached to the events are perceived as real; and the higher this sense of realness, the more intense the emotions become) and of 'closure' (emotions are of prime importance, they are closed to considerations that its aims may be of relative and passing importance).

39 In fact the 'revolutionary suicide' of the *People's Temple* was legitimised by Jim Jones by references to Durkheim's altruistic type (Hall, 1989: 274-275).

40 In 1999 a controversial case of *sati* occurred in the federal state of Uttar Pradesh (*The Hindu*, 3 December 1999), and the article *The pull of the pyre* (The Indian Express, 9 January 2001) makes reference to five proven and successful widow-burnings between 1979 and 1987. Indian widows frequently did not climb onto the funeral pile willingly, but were forced to do so by their relatives. Economic motives also played a role here: widows were frequently not allowed to remarry, and their family members often did not wish to be saddled with the costs of maintaining them, or else had eyes for the inheritance. According to the latter source:

"Interestingly, every sati case is followed by nonsensical stories of the widow's eyes glazing with ecstasy as flames envelop her. This contradicts all sati literature which says that the self-immolations were never voluntary. The new widows were pressured into embracing death by in-laws who would crowd around her and tell her to join her dead husband. She would be made half-unconscious with narcotics. Invariably, she was tied to the husband's body and to heavy logs to prevent her from breaking free. And when the fire was lit, the spectators would set up a loud religious chant to drown out her cries. Yet in Devrala (Rajasthan, 1987), witnesses swear that nobody put a match to Roop Kanwar and that she was set ablaze by a divine force which approved of her fiery self-sacrifice. [...] Writers attribute the [historically high] prevalence of sati in Bengal to the worship of goddess Kali and the need to satisfy her bloodthirstiness. Ram Mohun Roy's explanation was more logical, however. He ascribed sati in Bengal to the Dayabhaga system of inheritance which gave the widow a right over her husband's property. Sati in Uttar Pradesh was rare because a Mitakshara law limited a widow's inheritance rights. So in-laws in UP had much less to gain from a widow's death."

41 Coleman (1990) clarifies the difference between individual and corporate actors by referring to the development of the legal doctrine on the legal position of the English king. From the 15th century onwards, the physical body of the king and his body politic were increasingly regarded as two separate personas. On the one hand the king was an individual actor or natural person; on the other he was a corporate actor or legal body (Crown). Having these two legal personalities enabled the king to perform acts which would not have been permitted as a natural person (such as selling land whilst still a minor). In addition, the continuity of the legal person no longer depended on the physical survival of the king: "The body politic had no birth or death, no age of minority or infirmity. [...] The distinction made it possible for Parliament to revolt in 1642 against Charles I as a physical person while continuing to uphold the Crown. This distinction, which did not exist in France, made it possible for a King to be beheaded while the monarchy continued" (Coleman, 1990: 540).

42 Acts are events of a specific type. They are constrained in time, but are not physically limited objects, although they can relate to them (physical manipulation of objects). This is not necessary, however; thinking can be a form of problem-solving behaviour.

43 Machines and tools are theoretically not actors, but objects which form part of the resources of actors. They are aids (extensions or substitutes) of the actor: an automobile or dishwasher takes over the task of transport or washing-up from individuals. This kind of automation can be very extensive, as in the case of robots and sophisticated user interfaces. However, machines and tools are not actors in the definition applied here, not because they are not 'organisms' – neither is a corporate actor – but because they cannot be carriers of rights and duties. Intentionality also plays a role. While it is true that the acts of individuals and legal persons are sometimes also involuntary, machines and tools by definition have no intentions with the actions they perform; in the final analysis an actor must desire the action (e.g. wanting the washing-up done) and must set it in motion (pressing the start button).

Animals are borderline cases; some people claim that they cannot perform acts. This follows, for example, from the standpoint of Raz (1986) discussed earlier, who believes that animals cannot carry rights and obligations. If animals are not actors, this implies that they can perform actions, but not acts. Against this it can be argued that the intentionality and motivations of the higher animal species (such as primates) differ from human behaviour only in degree, while the latter can also be involuntary. If the human knee reflex is an act, is the mutual de-fleaing of apes no more than an action, comparable with the cleaning function of a washing machine?

44 The view adopted here means among other things a rejection of the 'causal approach' to actions. In this line of thought, actions are movements whose cause lies in mental processes (desires, intentions, beliefs) which rationalise them. Without this causality, according to this view the events are not actions but 'happenings'. Frankfurt (1997 [1978]) counters this with the argument that, regarded in this way, actions and happenings can only be distinguished from each other by the preceding causal chain. The implication – the difference does not lie in the external appearance but in what has happened previously – is one that he criticises: "It is integral to the causal approach to regard actions and mere happenings as being differentiated by nothing that exists or is going on at the time those events occur, but by something quite extrinsic to them – a difference at an earlier time among another sets of events entirely" (Frankfurt, 1997 [1978]: 42-43).

45 In the philosophical debate the intentionality of an act is often assessed on the basis of trying, foresight and skill; that is, acts are intentional if the actor was aiming to bring about a specific outcome in a way he knew could be effective, and if he possessed the ability to perform the act adequately (see e.g. Mele, 2003). Someone who wants to win a rifle contest, who aims at the bulls-eye and who has proved able to hit such a target before, is acting intentionally. If he participates but is a poor shot who succeeds through sheer luck, some authors consider this a non-intentional act. Knobe (2008) has pointed out that in everyday life people intuitively tend to judge intentionality on moral grounds as well. Many regard the act of the unskilled rifleman who nevertheless wins the shooting contest as unintentional; but if he does not hit the bulls-eye, but his wealthy aunt in order to get hold of his inheritance, folk psychology often considers him blameworthy, because his act was intentional.

46 The concept 'interaction' can be defined more precisely. If, as argued earlier, acts are regarded as a special form of action, it is also logical to make a distinction between *interacts* and *interactions*. In that case the former relate only to

a series of acts by individual and corporate actors. Interactions are wider in scope: they also include the interactions between actors and machines and tools – the exchange of actions when typing or clicking on a PC – and the actions that take place between non-actors (two modems which send and receive bits of information using a specific protocol). Since all behaviour of actors is generally designated as interaction in sociology, this broader concept is also used to indicate the interacts that are the main focus here. However, this choice is based purely on the linguistic convention.

47 It is also possible to adopt the standpoint that the social act is the basic unit of all action, and that the behaviour of individual actors is a component of this. See for example the view of G.H. Mead (1938: VIII-IX), as summarised in the foreword to some of his posthumous essays: "The basic act is a social act, that is, an act that involves 'the co-operation of more than one individual, and whose object as defined by the act [...] is a social object. I mean by a social object one that answers to all parts of the complex act, though these parts are found in the conduct of different individuals'. The act of an individual organism is an abstracted fragment of such a social act".

48 Compare: "Because [the stranger] is not bound by roots to the particular constituents and partisan dispositions of the group, he confronts all of these with a distinctly 'objective' attitude, an attitude that does not signify mere detachment and nonparticipation, but is a distinct structure of remoteness and nearness, indifference and involvement [...] The stranger who moves on [...] often receives the most surprising revelations and confidences, at times reminiscent of a confessional, about matters which are kept carefully hidden from everybody with whom one is close" (Simmel, 1971a [1908]: 145).

49 Corporate actors are left out of consideration here. They acquire rules via their individual agents who act on their behalf. This means that the familiar principal-agent problem is also theoretically present in rule acquisition.

50 The differences in educational opportunity between different social milieus, genders and ethnic groups are in fact not stable over time. In the Netherlands, for example, the differences in the school achievements between people from different social backgrounds have reduced in recent decades. Furthermore girls, who initially lagged a long way behind boys in educational achievement, moved ahead of them slightly – although the sex-specific differences in the type of education followed remained stubborn (Vrooman & Dronkers, 1986; Dronkers & Ultee, 1995; SCP, 1998: 585-588). Based on research there is a tendency to attribute these changes more to general social processes (rising prosperity, women's emancipation, growing participation in education) than to the specific policy aimed at reducing social differentials through education (SCP, 1998: 584-585; Dekkers et al., 2000; Bosker, 2002). In as far as social reproduction through education still occurs it has at the very least altered in character.

51 Seen from a rational choice perspective, it is not self-evident that socialisation will take place: potential socialisers will embark on socialisation only if they expect to derive benefit from it. Coleman (1990: 292-297) outlines an interesting if rather narrow variant of the rational choice perspective on socialisation, focused on the internalisation of norms. In his view socialisation relates mainly to the establishing of an internal sanctioning system (conscience, superego), which ensures that the behaviour of actors corresponds with the interests of others. If this internalisation is successful, the socialisees will themselves ensure that they behave in accordance with the rules, or will punish defection by suffering from remorse. Coleman sees internalisation as an alternative to external policing, i.e. the direct imposition of positive and negative sanctions by the interested parties. The method chosen by an interested party depends in his view above all on the relative returns. Creating an internal sanctioning system involves costs for the potential socialiser (time, attention), whereas he will receive only a part of the future returns of the rule-compliant behaviour of the socialisee. Coleman therefore assumes that the willingness to socialise by parents reduces as children leave home earlier, the social status of the family is lower, the envisaged norm relates to fewer forms of conduct, and the behavioural rule is further removed from day-to-day family contacts. According to him, certain norms lend themselves better to socialisation than others. For example, parents can monitor characteristics such as 'cleanliness' in their children easily and it is simple for them to apply direct sanctions. 'Honesty', by contrast, is difficult to observe, increasing the chance that parents will try to socialise their child on this point.

According to this view, identification is the chief method of achieving internalisation of norms: "Socialization activities are attempts to create a new self so that the individual's actions will be dictated by the imagined will or purpose of the actor he has identified with: parents, nation-state, company, religious order, profession, or academic discipline. It is then this will which will generate the internal sanctions for future actions. [...] In attempting to internalize norms in another actor [a socialising actor] does not attempt to inculcate directly the belief that certain actions are right and others wrong. The strategy is to change the self and let the new self decide what is right and what is wrong" (Coleman, 1990: 295).

The strong point of this approach is that the transfer and internalisation of rules is not a premise. It is important to indicate the conditions under which actors will perform socialising acts. However, a number of comments can also be made about this rational choice perspective on the socialisation process. In the first place, socialisation involves more than simply the transfer of norms: it is also about the acquisition of knowledge as a personal resource in later life, and about values and meanings, such as learning the different aspects of language. Moreover, it is doubtful whether potential socialisers really make a conscious judgement, over such a long period, and involving all manner of possible socialisee behaviour in which they may have an interest now or in the future. The question can also be raised as to whether a socialisee must always meekly accept the interventions of his socialisers: can socialisation not better be described as more of an interaction, in which the responses of the new actor matter as well? Finally, it is unclear in Coleman's rational choice model under what conditions socialisation attempts will succeed and fail – a theme to which he devoted a good deal of attention in his influential early work (Coleman et al., 1966).

52 Erikson (1963), for example, argues in his epigenetic theory that every individual passes through eight 'ages': oral-sensory, muscular-anal, locomotor-genital, latency, puberty/adolescence, young adulthood, adulthood and maturity. Each phase builds on the ego-identity already developed to that point. A fundamental conflict has to be resolved in each phase, relating to the tensions between the individual's own drives and the requirements of their social setting. This results in the development of certain core aspects of their identity. In the first years of life in the family, the individual acquires a basic level of trust and autonomy; the early school period is concerned with the idea of initiative and producing things. In later youth the prime focus is on the development of the identity, while the three phases of adulthood are characterised by the development of a degree of intimacy, love, generativity, caring and wisdom. What is rather remarkable is that Erikson expects society to be correlated with these universal stages of personal development: "Society, in principle, tends to be so constituted as to meet and invite this succession of potentialities for interaction, and attempts to safeguard and to encourage the proper rate and the proper sequence of their enfolding" (Erikson, 1963: 270). Just as sociological theories sometimes tend to regard the socialisee as an epiphenomenon of his or her social setting, so such a psychological approach may reduce the macro-level of society to the demands placed on it by the ontogenetic process.

53 Simmel spoke in this connection of an unavoidable, tragic tension between 'individuality' and 'cultural forms' (social meanings and rules). The introduction to an English translation of his work summarises his view as follows: "To subordinate one's personal growth to the requirements of a boundless stretch of cultural materials is to betray one's individuality; in following that path, the self 'loses itself either in a dead end alley or in an emptiness of its innermost and most individual life'. Yet to abandon those requirements is an equally serious betrayal. One does injustice thereby not only to the claims of autonomous cultural forms but moreover, because self-cultivation entails mastery of the relevant objective culture, to the claims of individual self-development as well. 'The situation is tragic: even in its first moments of existence, culture carries something within itself which, as if by an intrinsic fate, is determined to block, to burden, to obscure and divide its innermost purpose, the transition of the soul from its incomplete to its complete state' "(Levine, 1971: xli).

54 Of course this does not rule out the possibility that people can acquire a good deal of knowledge about formal regulations with which they come into frequent contact: a good building contractor will have a more than rudimentary knowledge of local building regulations; a con man has to know how far he can go without committing a crime; a benefit recipient may become very knowledgeable about the rights and obligations that apply to him, etc.

55 This is not to say that such an autonomous decision on the prevailing rules always arises in a balanced way: one partner may for example be more powerful, more intelligent or more convincing than the other. And married life in particular (at least the visible part of it) is the subject of very strongly informal regulation in some societies and communities: the prevailing values, norms and conventions then leave the partners little scope in drafting their own informal arrangements.

56 As noted, on this point North (1990) diverges somewhat from the standard NIE train of thought. He posits that the changing preferences of actors are also important for institutional change, and that relative prices do not change solely as a result of exogenous developments, but rather as a consequence of an endogenous process, whereby entrepreneurs see their transaction costs reduce as their knowledge and experience increases. This would lead them to desire and aim for an increasing refining of the rules. North may be overestimating the significance of endogenous developments, however: in the economic sphere, too, new actors, who are not bound to existing knowledge and experience, can sometimes be the main drivers of rule change.

57 Compare the German edition: "Die wesentliche Bedingung für die Existenz und für die Herrschaft der Bourgeoisklasse ist die Anhäufung des Reichtums in den Händen von Privaten, die Bildung und Vermehrung des Kapitals; die Bedingung des Kapitals ist die Lohnarbeit", or: "The essential condition for the existence and for the sway of the bourgeois class is the accumulation of wealth in the hands of private individuals, the formation and augmentation of capital; the condition for capital is wage labour" (Marx & Engels, 1848).

58 Coleman (1990: 133) himself comments that this definition is somewhat circular. Frank (1991: 161) points out that this is not necessary, because in the definition of power the 'value of an event' does not lie solely in the interests of powerful actors: "an event in which many unpowerful people are interested can also have high value". The word 'powerful' could therefore be left out of the definition, so that it is no longer circular: the power of an individual actor

derives from his control over valuable events; the value of an event derives from the interests of all actors in that event.

59 In the English translation: "Power is the probability that one actor within a social relationship will be in a position to carry out his own will despite resistance, regardless of the basis on which this probability rests". The translators add that Weber frequently does not use *Chance* with a technical/mathematical meaning, so that in those cases it can also be understood as 'likelihood'.

60 Interests will not readily be *truly* general, in the sense that the well-being of all actors in a community can be secured to the same degree via the same rules. Issues that are often described as being in the 'general interest' – protecting the environment, world peace, emancipation of disadvantaged groups, repayment of the national debt – frequently turn out to be difficult to achieve in practice. Concrete rules which seek to secure the general interest often meet with resistance from actors who see their specific interests being harmed: owners and employees of environmentally harmful businesses, arms dealers, the privileged elite or middle classes, the present generation of taxpayers.

61 Compare for example Thoreau's famous exhortation against slavery in the US and the war with Mexico: "All men recognize the right of revolution; that is, the right to refuse allegiance to, and to resist, the government, when its tyranny or its inefficiency are great and unendurable. [...] When a sixth of the population of a nation which has undertaken to be the refuge of liberty are slaves, and a whole country is unjustly overrun and conquered by a foreign army, and subjected to military law, I think that it is not too soon for honest men to rebel and revolutionize. What makes this duty the more urgent is that fact that the country so overrun is not our own, but ours is the invading army." (Thoreau, 1849: 192)

62 Coleman asserts that revolutionary activities occur on a large scale if many people have an interest in overthrowing the *ancien régime* and believe that this can be achieved: "If revolutionary activity and support for the revolutionary activity of others are regarded as rational actions, it becomes evident that such activity will be more likely to occur as those who have an interest in seeing the authority system replaced come to have a belief that they will succeed. And support for revolutionary activity among those who are committed to neither side but hope to be on the side of the winners will increase as their estimation of the revolutionaries' chances of success increases. It is irrational to revolt and dangerous to support those who do if the revolution will almost certainly be suppressed. There is an expected gain only when two conditions exist: when the expected gain if the authorities are overthrown is positive and the expectation of overthrowing the authorities is high. This can be put more precisely (in particular, it depends also on the expected costs of failure so long as there is a nonzero probability of failure), but the point should be clear: the likelihood of revolution should increase if either of these two factors increases" (Coleman, 1990: 480).

Frustrations can come to light in a major way during revolutionary activity, but this does not mean that they are the cause of it, as some believe. Coleman (1990: 484) prefers to see them as a side-effect of a given *phase* in the revolutionary process: "If opponents of an authority system come to have a strong belief in their power to overthrow the regime, one consequence will be a sense of frustration that the regime remains in power. But this frustration will be only an epiphenomenon, an incidental consequence of the opponents' increased belief in their own capabilities. The frustration is without consequence, despite its occurrence preceding the revolt. It does serve as a measure for the potential of action, but the consequences are not due to frustration, but to the components that give rise to it: the existing dissatisfaction with the current authority system, and the newly acquired belief that there is some possibility of change".

63 Which does not imply that such pioneers will never be able to derive benefit from institutional change. Their social status may rise, they may acquire influential positions for themselves or their relatives, and their children may acquire better opportunities. Often, however, such potential gains are a priori uncertain; they will only be realised after a certain period of time and generally do not weigh against the high social and material costs that they may experience in the short term (being the subject of malicious gossip, social rejection, closed-off career paths, disinheritance, etc.).

64 North illustrates this by pointing out that a 17th-century pirate needed a completely different type of knowledge from a present-day chemical manufacturer. Such diverging needs may be reflected in a greater demand for, respectively, knowledge of maritime technology or theoretical and applied chemical research: "If the basic institutional framework makes income redistribution (piracy) the preferred (most profitable) economic opportunity, we can expect a very different development of knowledge and skills than a productivity-increasing (the 20th century chemical manufacturer) economic opportunity would entail" (North, 1990: 78).

65 Berting (1978: 477-479) distinguishes the following stratification forms:
   - Estates: strata consisting of families who regard each other as equals in terms of standing and honour, and who maintain mutual social relations in areas symbolising that equality (connubium, convivium). An 'estate society' is made up of a ranking of such strata.

- Castes: permanent social groups to which people belong by birth, with a strict hierarchy and without mobility, and which define each other in terms of pure and impure (prohibition of intermarriage, physical contact, certain food habits). The members of a caste often specialise in certain occupations.
- Economic classes: social groups that are defined in economic terms. More specifically this may relate to owners of the means of production versus the have-nots; or to stratification in terms of opportunities in economic life. The latter criterion leads to different distinctions from the former: the economic opportunities of highly educated technical specialists are better than those of unskilled factory workers, although in a Marxist sense they belong to the same class. A class society is a society in which the dividing lines are drawn on the basis of such economic differences.
- Social classes: statistical groups, which are often defined on the basis of empirical research, such as occupational prestige ladders.

The same author also refers to a number of common theoretical explanations for the occurrence of social rankings:
- Paretian: stratification is a result of the variation of individual talents in populations, and is generally not social in nature;
- Marxist: the power over the means of production enables those who possess it to claim a large part of society's wealth for themselves;
- Weberian: social hierarchies are a function of differences in economic power, social status, and the domination and authority that competing groups are able to acquire in the political arena;
- Functionalist: high social esteem, a high income and privileges motivate people to attain positions that are regarded as important;
- Exchange theoretical: stratification is the result of individual differences in the ability to procure scarce goods and services, so that others are able to meet their needs better and more quickly than if these goods and services are not offered. Subordination, demonstrating gratitude, honouring and granting senior positions are the things that are done in return.

66 There are many possible variants of political institutions which aim to select the ruling class. Strategic positions may be passed from father to son, the old leader may designate a new one, or the leader may be chosen on religious grounds (as with the Tibetan *dalai* and *panchen lama*, who are appointed on the basis of signs of the reincarnation of their predecessor in a newborn child). They may sometimes also be legitimately purchased, with the position going to the highest bidder. The sale to private persons of the government right to collect certain levies is an example of this.

Besides this, all manner of election are possible. In democratic societies the usual means of selecting members of the legislative assembly (parliament) is through direct elections based on the one man, one vote principle. The recruitment rules in the executive power and civil service are often less clear. In principle, general or indirect (for example from or by the current MPs) elections may be held for influential positions such as ministers, parliamentary speakers and committees, state governors and mayors, judges, and top executives. It is however also possible to appoint them in accordance with certain conventions or distribution codes. In that case, for example, the biggest political party may provide the chairman of the legislative assembly, the number of ministers in a coalition government must reflect the distribution of seats in parliament, etc. It may also be that the recruitment forms part of the ongoing negotiations between the political actors, which may mean for example that a representative of one party may occupy a certain key position in exchange for their support for a bill that is regarded as crucial.

Co-option from a group of equals occurs for example in the case of the conclave electing a new Roman Catholic Pope from their ranks, but also in large companies, where the members of the Supervisory Boards are recruited from a limited group of businessmen who are considered to be leading figures in their field. The obverse of this is a broadly accessible *concours*. Here, objectified criteria (e.g. expertise, experience, intellectual and social capacities) are used in the selection of candidates.

Mixed succession procedures are conceivable as well. The Roman succession system of adoptive emperors combined inheritance and designation. In modern democratic countries formal positions are generally no longer for sale, but the available campaign funds can nonetheless be decisive during parliamentary or presidential elections. Coleman (1990: 738) presents a model of this latter phenomenon. In his view political candidates receive votes from electors and money from interest groups in return for promises. The media buy entertainment from artists and supply it to the electors. The attention of the electorate can in turn be cashed in by the media from the political campaign funds, as candidates need media coverage in order to draw their political programme to the public's attention and be elected.

67 *Enarques* are graduates of the *École Nationale d'Administration*, the most important French *Grand École*. This was founded after the Second World War in order to train civil administrators. It is a small, stringently selected group: each year around 100 students are admitted after they have completed their university education, have followed one or two

years of preparatory study and have successfully completed the admission *concours*. Graduates can be recruited into promising positions in the civil service, with high marks giving access to the most prestigious official *Grands Corps*. The *Enarques* not only make up a large part of the senior figures in the French civil service, but are also overrepresented among the political and business leaders. Presidents Giscard d'Estaing and Chirac, and the Prime Ministers Fabius, Rocard, Juppé, Jospin and Villepin are all ENA alumni, for example (Presidents Mitterrand and Sarkozy are an exception to the rule). In its design, the ENA was meant to be meritocratic: the *concours* was intended to make the course accessible to a broad section of the population. Over time, however, the degree of self-recruitment has been shown to be large, and has probably even increased. Roughly two-thirds of the ENA students come from the upper echelons of society (parents who themselves work in the *Grands Corps*, the liberal professions or in senior positions in industry), so that in reality only a small section of the population supplies the new administrative elite. The Paris region (Île-de-France) is strongly overrepresented, and women are in the minority among the new students (cf. Gaillard, 1995: 218-219).

68 Middendorp (1978: 102-108; 1991: 60) defines an ideology as "a system of general ideas on man and society, centred around one or a few general and fundamental values, which has manifested itself historically as a doctrine adhered to by some major groups or categories, and which expressed the interest of some important category, or social class". Here, the preferred approach is not to link ideologies directly to their supporters, or to the interests they encapsulate. In addition, their forward-looking aspect is emphasised, not their historical form. A cohesive system of ideas for the future is an ideology, even if at a certain moment it has virtually no supporters or represents no clear interests.

69 North (1990: 32) puts it thus: "There is, in fact, an implicit contract between [master and slave]; to get maximum effort from the slave, the owner must devote resources to monitoring and metering a slaves output and critically applying rewards and punishments based on performance. Because there are increasing marginal costs to measuring and policing performance, the master will stop short of perfect policing and will engage instead in policing until the marginal costs equal the additional marginal benefits of such activity. The result is that slaves acquire certain property rights in their own labor. That is, owners are able to enhance the value of their property by granting slaves some rights in exchange for services the owners value more. Hence slaves became owners too. Indeed it is only this ownership that made it possible for slaves to purchase their own freedom, as was frequently done in classic times and even occasionally in the antebellum South".

70 Posner (2000) regards social norms as no more than empirical regularities in behaviour, which potential transaction partners deliberately observe or break in order to make clear their 'discount rate' to each other. By giving off signals such as these reliable, cooperative business contacts, friends, etc. can be distinguished from the 'bad types'; and through signalising people develop a certain reputation. According to Posner norms, in the sense of behavioural regularities, arise only if behaviour entails costs, is observable, and is arbitrary in nature. He does not however see them as a cause of behaviour: "Social norms describe the behavioural regularities that occur in equilibrium when people use signals to show that they belong to the good type. Social norms are thus endogenous: they do not cause behaviour, but are the labels that we attach to behaviour that results from other factors" (Posner, 2000:34). According to this view, norm change is primarily the task of competing norm entrepreneurs, who question the existing signals and propose new ones. They are motivated to do so by the anticipated individual gain (money, loyalty, fame) and certain personal characteristics: "People earn returns when they contribute to shifts in mass behavior [...], but norm entrepreneurship is risky precisely because one breaks a norm by challenging it. Few people take this risk, and those who do either have tastes or values that lie on the extremes of the distribution, or else have immense talent and charisma, so people cannot afford to shun them" (Posner, 2000: 32).

It is clearly the case that actors often try to signal something to each other, and this is also recognised in sociological theories. G.H. Mead (1934: 42-51), for example, building on the psycho-physiological theory of Wundt, sees 'gestures' as important expressive social actions. Gestures allow people to signal their emotions to each other in a socially acceptable way, and to construct meanings by exchanging significant symbols. The fact that people give out signals does not however mean that they always do so consciously, and it certainly does not imply that they do so only in order to make clear the mutual 'discount rate' in social contacts. Above all, it would seem conceptually inaccurate to equate such expressive gestures with the social rules which govern them. Wendel (2002), who discusses this and other rational choice approaches to social norms in more detail, accordingly criticises Posner by pointing out that his theory fails to do justice to the evaluative character of these informal rules: the "normativity of norms" is eliminated from the definition.

71 Other examples include Van Eeden's 'Walden' and Neill's 'Summerhill'. Inspired by the work of Thoreau and by socialist ideas, the Dutch writer Frederik van Eeden established the idealistic Walden colony in 1898 on the Cruysbergen estate near the town of Bussum. The colony focused mainly on horticulture and was based on shared land ownership. Its unbusinesslike management resulted in its bankruptcy in 1907, after the community had functioned for a while as a consumer cooperative. Alexander S. Neill founded the Summerhill School in 1921, and it continues to exist up to

present. It is characterised among other things by the democratic relationships between teachers and pupils, with the latter themselves determining the structure of their learning process and their attendance at lessons.

72 In the case of conventions, in particular, the externality is sometimes difficult to demonstrate. Coleman solves this by adopting a somewhat laboured reasoning, in which he asserts that in those cases the norm itself generates the externalities, in the form of confirmation of the group identity and the social distinction. Compare: "Dress codes illustrate a form of conventional norm for which externalities do not exist prior to and independent of the norm. They contrast with conventions such as driving on the right, for which negative externalities exist in the absence of the norm and the norm provides benefits by reducing them" (Coleman, 1990: 257-258).

73 Durkheim already stressed that institutions have a supra-individual character. This makes it difficult for individual actors to decree entirely new norms and conventions. If they nevertheless try to do so, for example because they believe they possess the necessary power, they run the risk that the new rules will not be accepted by the community. They can then attempt to force compliance by applying stringent sanctions or eliminating dissidents and people who fail to sanction deviations from the norm. Such classic dictatorial solutions, however, often do not lead to effective social norms, but at most create a situation where people pay lip-service to the new rules. It is equally not a simple matter to steer the consensus in the community using democratic means. An example of this is the government agencies that seek to enforce informal rules with a view to preventing the erosion of norms in public life. In 2002, for example, a Dutch municipality drew up a hierarchy of behavioural rules, based on the views of 3,800 inhabitants who responded voluntarily to a municipal survey. The list contained popularly formulated norms such as 'if you break something, you must pay for it yourself', 'do not use violence', 'hanging around on the streets in an intimidating way is antisocial', and 'speak Dutch, then we will understand each other'. The expectation encapsulated in the municipal policy memorandum was that formulating norms would contribute to compliance with them. In reality, however, the rules recognised the existing behavioural expectations of many residents, rather than breaking radically with the past. Attempts such as this often ignore two problems. The setting of norms reflects the views of the compliants, who were already behaving properly before the rule was promulgated by the local authority. It is doubtful whether the defectors, who probably responded in smaller numbers to the municipal questionnaire, will take much notice of the new rules. In addition, it is questionable that large-scale unfamiliarity is a problem with such norms. In all likelihood, a large part of the local population already know what is considered appropriate behaviour and what is not, but people are less willing than in the past to comply or sanction infringements. Such an attitude cannot be changed simply by putting down the rules in writing once more.

Chapter 3

1 Section 3.1 is partly new and partly a revision of elements from Geleijnse, Vrooman & Muffels (1993: 13-23) and Vrooman (1994, 1995).
2 Or: "The most perfect system of government is that which produces the most happiness, the most social security, and the most political stability."
3 In the USA, however, the concept is also used in its more restricted original sense, referring to the various elements of the Social Security Act.
4 The EU's official definition of social protection has been laid down in the manual of the *European System of integrated Social Protection Statistics*, or ESSPROS (Eurostat, 2008). It states that: "Social protection encompasses all interventions from public or private bodies intended to relieve households and individuals of the burden of a defined set of risks or needs, provided that there is neither a simultaneous reciprocal nor an individual arrangement involved. The list of risks or needs that may give rise to social protection is fixed by convention as follows: (1) Sickness/Health care; (2) Disability; (3) Old age; (4) Survivors; (5) Family/children; (6) Unemployment; (7) Housing; (8) Social exclusion not elsewhere classified."
5 Despite its universalistic principles, the Beveridge Report does not recommend that social security be entirely the responsibility of the government. The coverage provided by the government does not discharge the individual from his responsibilities. For example, the individual should take out voluntary insurance over and above the statutory minimum: "Social security must be achieved by co-operation between the State and the individual. The State should offer security for service and contribution. The State in organising security should not stifle incentive, opportunity, responsibility; in establishing a national minimum, it should leave room and encouragement for voluntary action by each individual to provide more than that minimum for himself and his family" (Beveridge, 1942: 6-7).
6 The causality triptych (see Veldkamp, 1984: 22) describes the following actuarial principles:
   - the contribution to be paid depends on the risk to which the person is exposed;
   - the level of the benefit or provision is a function of the contribution paid;
   - the level of benefit or provision is proportional to the loss actually suffered (the manifestation of the risk).
7 The full title of the Beveridge Report suggests that social insurance should be at the heart of the 'Plan for Social Security'. Social assistance is a secondary provision which should be used sparsely: "For the limited number of cases of need not covered by social insurance, national assistance subject to a uniform means test will be available" (Beveridge, 1942: 11). The report lists six principles of social insurance (Beveridge, 1942: 121-122):
   - flat rate of subsistence benefit
   - flat rate of contribution
   - unification of administrative responsibility
   - adequacy of benefit in amount and time
   - comprehensiveness, in respect both of the persons covered and their needs
   - classification, (or) adjustment of insurance to the differing circumstances of (insurance) classes.
   These deviate from the pure principles of social insurance (see table 3.1). Beveridge's notion of social insurance corresponds with them only in a semantic sense; he actually refers to a contribution-based national provision.
8 The European Code of Social Security (1964) contains a similar list of events. It was modeled on ILO Convention No. 102, but provides higher benefit levels.
9 Berghman's concept of social security as a 'state' refers to both the macro- and micro-level. On the one hand, quoting Van Kessel (1985), it concerns a "state of *society* in which every member is assured of help and provisions aimed at prevention, restoration and compensation of human damage". On the other hand, it is a state of *individuals*, or "social security as a subjectively experienced value" (cf. Berghman, 1986: 10-11). In terms of the figural model presented in the previous chapter, the macro state can be equated with the entire set of prevailing formal and informal social security institutions. The individual state corresponds to the subjective apprehensions of the rules and their consequences by actors, which form the basis of rule-driven social security interactions.
10 The term 'prevention' is used here in a narrow sense; it concerns interventions which aim to avoid the occurrence of social risks (unemployment, disability, indigence, etc.). In the literature this is sometimes referred to as 'primary prevention' or 'risk prevention'. In secondary prevention the risk has already manifested itself; this term refers to interventions directed towards restoration, but also to attempts to prevent long-term benefit dependency. Tertiary prevention relates to either 'curative' or 'ameliorating' interventions, or to interventions aimed at preventing permanent dependence on social security (Viaene et al., 1990: 34-35; Van den Heuvel & Vrooman, 1991: 12-13).
11 Searle (1995: 111-112) formulates a related elementary rule for the logic of institutions:
   "There is exactly one primitive logical operation by which institutional reality is created and constituted. It has the form: We collectively accept, acknowledge, recognize, go along with, etc., that (S has power (S does A))."

While this definition is very generic, a number of objections to it can be made. The formulation implies that rules always enjoy general support. However, actors are not always involved in the constitution of rules, and often have no choice but to regard the existing rules as a given: they have no power to change them, or only at prohibitive cost. Yet they may reject the rules or wish to modify it; but in Searle's logic of institutions, rule dissent is largely ignored.

In addition, in this definition rights are seen mainly as freedoms of action (legal 'power'), or: 'authorization, permission, enablement', with a conventional character (Searle, 1995: 96). This ignores the rights that actors award to others, such as those which are central to social security. Duties and sanctions, essential components in the definition of institutions because of their effect in regulating behaviour, are left out of consideration; and conditions are regarded as merely as an extension of the basic primitive logical operation (Searle, 1995: 111), while they may be crucial to the specification of rights.

12 The potential beneficiaries can be subdivided into *entitled actors*, or persons who meet the conditions: actual recipients (users) and those who do not exercise their rights (cases of non-take up); and *non-entitled recipients*: persons who do not meet the conditions, but nonetheless are granted rights (abusers). See Vrooman & Asselberghs (1994: 18-21) for a more detailed discussion.

13 The statement 'Peter is without a job' is an example of an actor state. Casati & Varzi (2002) point out that states are merely one sub-type of events (the occurrence of an eventuality). Others are activities ('Peter is writing one application letter a week') and performances, which can in turn be subdivided into accomplishments and achievements (the statement 'Peter has been invited for a job interview' refers to an intermediate step and is therefore an accomplishment; 'Peter has found a new job' refers to a final situation and is therefore an achievement). Events are not the same as properties because they are one-off or individual, whereas properties have a universal character: events occur, properties recur. Events are sometimes also interpreted as forms of time to which a qualification is linked: "temporal instants or intervals during which certain statements hold". In this terminology, the E and C conditions in the fundamental structure of social security institutions can be regarded as events (states, activities or performances) and the Q conditions as actor properties.

14 In the demarcation of group B, event conditions (E) and conduct conditions (C) generally do not apply. Of course, it may be that the duty-bound are required to perform certain actions in order to secure the rights of the beneficiaries; but that is part of their obligations, not a conduct condition which determines whether a person is to be included in group B.

15 Of course corporate actors do have an income: the rewards for entrepreneurship (profit) and capital (interest) to the providers of these factors (and, in the case of non-profit organisations, the budget that has been allotted); and they may experience difficulties hiring the labour force they need. However, it is generally not an objective of social security to tackle the lack of profit or interest, budgets that are too low, or staff shortages in firms and intermediary organisations.

16 In terms of the logical fundamental structure of social security institutions, in the classical basic income scheme the rights R are completely unconditional, apart from the general requirement of citizenship. There is no need for events E to occur in order to be entitled; the rules do not specify any risk which generates the rights. Similarly, people do not have to comply with Q-type conditions (e.g. having reached a certain age) other than citizenship, or with stipulations relating to their conduct (C), such as job search requirements. Even so, the fact that R is hardly conditioned does not mean that the classic basic income scheme does not carry any obligations (O) whatsoever. The duty-bound are still required to finance the scheme, by paying direct or indirect taxes or through alternative sources (e.g. levies on polluting behaviour or luxury goods). As there are no conditions attaching to the rights, the duty-bound are the only ones who may defect, and the possibility of imposing sanctions is limited to this group. This leads to the following reduced form of the classic basic income case:

(1) *Social consensus*   On the basis of prevailing relative prices, powers, interests and ideals there is a sufficient shared understanding that society gains if:
(2) *Conditioned rights* - A is entitled to R if (A=Q:citizen)
(3) *Conditioned duties* - B must fulfil O to secure R, or not interfere with A in exercising R, if (B=Q)
(4) *Potential sanctions* - S- is possible if (B ~fulfils O), or (B interferes with A)
   - S+ is possible if (B fulfils O), or (B ~interferes with A)

The full unconditional basic income is thus far a theoretical notion; such schemes have not been implemented yet anywhere. Partial basic incomes and categorical basic incomes do exist, but these are often of a low level or carry E-type conditions (having limited means, reaching a certain age). Examples are systems of earned income tax credits, guaranteed minimum state pensions for the elderly, and individual entitlements to a share of the revenues of the exploitation of natural resources, as in the *Alaska Permanent Fund Dividend*.

Proponents of a full basic income stress its egalitarian nature, its simplicity, the reduction of the transaction costs, control and alienation brought about by the massive social security administrations, and the abolition of the sometimes arbitrary nature of the conventional risk demarcation (for instance, it is not considered justifiable to treat long-term unemployed and disabled persons differently, as they often experience the same kind of problems). Standard objections to full unconditional basic income schemes include its presumed allocative inefficiency (people with a highly paid job may receive more than they need, while disabled persons with high costs for medical care may not be able to make ends meet), the possibility of unfair outcomes (uniform treatment of unequal cases), high costs which may prove prohibitive for individual contributors and society at large, and the labour market disincentives that may ensue from it (women with a partner, the disabled, the low-educated, and people with a strong preference for labour may not earn enough to make a full-time paid job worthwhile).

From a theoretical point of view, the classic basic income scheme has a limited objective, as it does not target deficits in terms of labour, health and social participation: it is restricted to the income dimension. Moreover, here the minimum income goal prevails; income continuity is not a primary objective, and may be difficult to attain for people with a higher income who lose their jobs.

17 By relating entitlements to risks it is possible to fine-tune the rights to the severity and the irreversibility of the income, labour, health or social participation deficits. Thus the rights of people who are considered permanently unfit for work (the elderly, the fully disabled) may be distinguished from those of temporarily unemployed young people. The former group could for instance be entitled to high, non-means-tested benefits, while the latter might be provided with a combination of means-tested workfare and additional training. From a collective point of view this may be considered more efficient than a uniform distribution of rights. If it comes to that, the most vulnerable groups would possibly not receive what they need or is deemed just, while the recipients with favourable labour market prospects might not be stimulated to obtain a paid job.

Risk diversification also increases the communal support for social security schemes. It allows for shared notions on justice, fairness and the deservingness of various groups to be taken into account, e.g. by placing migrants receiving social assistance on lower benefits and under stricter behavioural surveillance than disabled war veterans. This may increase the contributors' willingness to fulfil their obligations. Furthermore, actuarial principles are easier to maintain if the risks covered are set out clearly.

18 Not to be confused with the famous Beard Tax imposed by Tsar Peter I in Russia in 1705. This was part of Peter the Great's attempts to modernise and westernise the country. The traditional norms of the Russian Orthodox Church encouraged men to grow beards. The Tsar tried to discourage this by prohibiting the wearing of beards; only members of the clergy were exempted. People who in spite of this wanted to keep their beard had to pay a special tax, and received a token (*znak*) from the Tsar's officials to prove they had paid the dues.

This regulation did not relate to duty-bound contributors financing a provision, but was a specification of the right to wear a beard; the officials had to fulfil a duty in this case. As such, the Beard Tax was not part of a social security scheme but a condition for acquiring a privilege (a right which generally does not apply). A comparison of the following two sets of rules shows the distinction:

Shaving Fund
- Conditioned rights: A may (receive reimbursement of shaving bill) if (A visits barber) and (A is male 16+)
- Conditioned duties: B must (pay Shaving Fund contribution) if (B is gainfully employed)

Beard Tax
- Conditioned rights: A may (not wear a beard) if (A is not orthodox clergy) unless (A pays Beard Tax)
- Conditioned duties: B must (provide token) if (A pays Beard Tax) and (B is Tsar's official)

In both cases the social consensus and potential sanctions may be specified, following the logical fundamental structure of institutions sketched earlier.

19 There are a number of possible exceptions to this. Fire and theft insurance can (partly) be regarded as social security if a person works at home and loss of income due to loss of home contents is covered by the insurance; or if someone lives in a home belonging to their employer for less than cost (something that can be regarded as income in kind); or if the regulation stipulates that the government will assume all or part of the financial responsibility vis-à-vis households in the event of disasters with a collective nature (floods, war, terrorism).

20 The maintenance of children is not mentioned explicitly as a ground for poor relief in the Den Bosch *Regulations*, but was taken into account in the setting of the summer and winter relief amounts by the Council of Regents. The death of the male breadwinner is not included either, because the *Regulations* relate only to the poor living at home; at that time, surviving dependants generally resided in almshouses and orphanages.

21 These are the three binding legislative instruments in the European Union, which also apply to social security. EU regulations are immediately enforceable as law in all member states simultaneously. EU directives require member states to realise a particular result without dictating the means it should be achieved by; these usually need to be translated into national law. EU decisions only apply to their particular addressee, which may be a member state, company or individual. In addition, there are two non-binding instruments: recommendations (views and suggested

lines of action, often with the aim to provide an incentive for the preparation of national legislation) and opinions (specifications of the view of the EU on a certain issue, without any legal consequences).
22 According to the Dutch Survey on the Integration of Ethnic Minorities (SIM) conducted in 2005, 23% of the Moroccan households living in the Netherlands did sent money to their family in Morocco. The reported average annual amount was €700; the total of these remittances equalled about €17 million. Such transfers are not made purely out of charity, but also because the donors intend to return to Morocco one day and hope to have access to informal support then.
23 Some authors claim that the existence of an elaborate formal system of social security may even lead to a further decline of informal solutions based on authority, mutual trust, reciprocity and networks of civic engagement. The latter indicators of social capital would tend to erode in the case of a well-developed welfare state, as they are no longer needed for providing social protection (e.g. Etzioni, 1995; Putnam, 2000). However, the empirical evidence for this 'crowding out hypothesis' is rather limited; for instance, the extensive welfare states of the Nordic European countries and the Netherlands also show a high degree of trust in fellow citizens and political institutions, of active and passive participation, and of political engagement (cf. Van Oorschot & Arts, 2005: 15).
24 Excluding the rule driven interactions which aim at the acquisition of social security rules, the subject of the previous section.
25 Van Loo (1987: 26-27) points out that members of the poor relief boards were recruited from the well-to-do local citizenry. For instance, in the Reformed Church community in Rotterdam during the first half of the 19th century, roughly half the members were practitioners of one of the liberal professions or "major business figures". Often they were relatively young (below 30), though they also included persons of independent means. For the former group the office was often "a sort of training school for later positions in life, [...] a first step in a social career".
26 For instance, the regents of the board sometimes instigated drinking bouts during the meetings in which the poor relief was awarded, as illustrated for the Netherlands by Van Loo (1987: 27): "In Den Helder the members of the general poor relief board were doing very nicely in around 1850, judging from the amounts spent on wine, cigars and bread rolls during the meetings. The furnishing of the poor relief chamber must also have been very luxurious, judging from the prices paid." The church social welfare council in the town of Zutphen were even more lavish: "In those days [circa 1800-1840], heavy consumption and other excesses were by no means the exception. In one year, so we read, 6,000 bottles were drunk. The gatherings were not infrequently marred by coarse exuberance. Brother S., for example, threw his plate full of food through the window, which led Brother L. to remark: 'If that's how you're going to do things, I can pay for it just as well', and threw all manner of items to the floor, where drink and food, bottles and glasses were scattered in brotherly unison." Van Loo comments that these were unlikely to be bottles of wine: that would be equivalent to a consumption of more than eight litres per person in each weekly meeting.
27 For instance, an informal occupational system may also be the result of collective bargaining between trade unions and employers' organisations at different levels (companies, trade sectors, national agreements). In that case the number of actors and their mutual relationships (including consultations with the rank and file) is greater than in figure 3.3. The administration of the system need not be carried out by the firm itself, but may also be outsourced to external organisations such as administration offices, private insurance companies or sectoral funds. An interaction structure with such intermediate 'occupational social security organisations' evidently is more complex than one with self-administrators. Finally, the size of the firm and the nature of its activities theoretically also influence the structure and course of the interactions in the model. Large companies tend to have more complicated systems: the management is likely to be responsible for the content of the informal rules, which are implemented by the personnel and salary administration or is outsourced, with the whole process being overseen by an external auditor and a supervisory board. Companies where, e.g., hazardous work is performed (such as the construction industry) may have a greater interest in regulating working conditions than companies where this is not the case.
28 In addition this fraudster was also claiming four social assistance benefits (SCP, 2002: 360).
29 Verheul (1989: 70-71) summarised a number of specific forms of abuse of the demographic schemes. Examples in the old-age pension system include stating an incorrect date of birth registered in a foreign country, or failure to disclose the death of a claimant abroad, while the benefit is still claimed (on cases of death in the Netherlands the latter is difficult, because the population registry automatically notifies the benefits agency). In the surviving dependants' benefit system, the claimant may fail to report that they have remarried or that they are also in receipt of surviving dependants' benefit from another country. "Promoting widowhood by ending the life of a spouse or being complicit in such an act" may also occur. Child benefit can be wrongfully obtained by incorrectly stating the number of children or their date of birth (especially if they were born or live abroad), simulating situations which entitle them to higher benefits (children in education, living outside the home, disability of the carers), or failing to disclose information which would end the entitlements (the child having its own means, maintenance by third parties).

30 The moral hazard notion refers to situations where the likelihood of a risk to occur depends on the behaviour of the entitled party, and where it is increased by the fact that it is collectively covered.
31 Transference and compensatory efforts are two other possible behavioural reactions of contributors to the levies imposed. The former occurs when the contributor succeeds in transferring the costs to someone else, e.g. an employer who passes on a contribution increase to the consumer by raising the price of his goods. Employees may show a similar response by demanding higher wages if their social security contributions are raised. An example of compensatory efforts is the employee who begins working longer hours in order to keep their total income at the same level after a rise in contributions.
32 A special form of contributors' defection occurs when they claim conscientious objections to paying their dues, for instance on the ground that their religion forbids them from taking out any insurance against the risks that God visits on human beings. In the Netherlands this possibility is formally laid down in sections 64-67a of the Social Insurance Funding Act (*Wet Financiering Sociale Verzekeringen*). This does not generally lead to defection and a reduction in the total contribution revenue, because the employees and employers concerned are subject to an equivalent additional income tax levy.
33 The various tasks can of course be attributed to a more differentiated organisational structure, with separate agencies for prevention, job placement, reintegration, possibly with competing organisations for each type of intervention. They may also be privatised, with the board of the social security organisation acting as principal for outsourcing.
34 In a strict insurance model benefit recipients are not required to contribute, because the covered risk has already occurred.
35 Client organisations usually are not awarded a direct say in the administration of the system – e.g. through a seat on the board of the social security organisation – because it is likely they will slight the organisational goals in favour of their group interests. They may be expected to propose a generous interpretation of the legal rules, maximisation of entitlements, minimisation of duties and a lenient imposition of negative sanctions. As a consequence, client organisations often have no more than the right to be heard or to advise, without this imposing any obligation on the social security organisation. A number of factors make it difficult to fulfil even this limited role effectively. The variation within various groups of clients (unemployed school leavers, single-parent families, older workers) means that they may be internally divided. In addition, the number of unemployed people and social assistance benefit claimants with the administrative and strategic competence and the willingness to engage in a lengthy process are often limited. Moreover, there is generally little continuity in their ranks: capable client representatives have a good chance of finding a mainstream job.
36 These ideas are elaborated in the economic models of job competition, of which Thurow's (1975) labour queue theory is an example. According to this latter approach the available jobs are arranged by grade and salary in the labour demand queue, and individual job-seekers are ranked according to their qualifications in the labour supply queue. An employer who acts strategically will try to recruit the employees with the highest added value: those up front in the supply queue. Conversely, rational job-seekers will attempt to select a high-ranking employer in the demand queue. Neither possesses full information, so that they are guided by proxy criteria and subjective impressions. The likelihood of an unemployed person finding work is determined by their position in the queue of job-seekers, in combination with the length of the queue of available jobs. Both correlate with the state of the economy: if this deteriorates an unemployed person is likely to have more competitors in front of him in the supply queue, while the demand queue will become shorter.
37 For instance, the first national formal social security regulation in the Netherlands (after the Poor Law, 1854 and the Law on the Abolition of Child Labour, 1874) related to limiting the maximum of working hours and the introduction of a labour inspectorate (*Arbeidswet*, or Labour Law, 1889).
38 Or, in the classic formulation: "Into as many houses as I may enter, I will go for the benefit of the ill, while being far from all voluntary and destructive injustice... and I will use regimens for the benefit of the ill in accordance with my ability and my judgment, but from [what is] to their harm or injustice I will keep [them]" (*Hippocratic Oath*, translation in Von Staden, 1996: 406-408).
39 The peak of the ageing process, however, will in most countries not be reached when the baby-boomers start retiring, but around 2025-2040. This is because the development of the absolute number of pensioners depends not only on the number of new beneficiaries (and changes in the pensions coverage ratio), but also on changes in average life expectancy and the size of the 'dying' cohorts. Moreover, ageing is a relative concept: the percentage of older persons has to be set against the total population or the potential labour force. The degree of ageing therefore also depends on changes in the size of younger cohorts; and because of the arrival of the contraceptive pill in many countries the birth rate fell from the 1970s onwards. The issues of sustainability and adequacy of pensions as a result of ageing are even more complicated. This not only depends on the demographic situation, but also on trends in the national wealth (GDP, driven by technological and educational changes), the activity rates of males and females and their

implication for accrued pension rights, and changes in the pension formula and indexation mechanism (see e.g. EC, 2006; OECD, 2007; Soede et al., 2004; Vrooman, 2008b).

40 For example, analyses of developments in the Dutch labour market during the last two decades of the 20th century showed that jobs at the lower end of the labour market were not lost *en masse* as is often assumed, although a shift from industry to the service sector certainly occurred. However, the falling employment share of traditionally low-skilled jobs such as blast furnace labourers, timber and paper processing, clothing and shoemakers was largely offset by the growth in domestic and shop work, the hospitality industry and transport (De Grip & Dekker, 1993; De Grip & Van Loo, 2000; De Grip & Dijksman, 2004, 2008; De Beer, 2001: 31-33).

41 Van Praag et al. assume that an increase in social security contributions due to an external shock, such as a sudden sharp rise in unemployment, leads to a vicious circle which ultimately makes the system untenable. The rising contributions imply higher wage costs for employers, who will respond by setting higher productivity targets for their employees and/or raising his prices. The former will lead to the dismissal of employees who are not productive enough (low educated, low skilled, disabled, too old), the latter to a decline in the effective demand for the goods and services of the firms. Both strategies push up unemployment and benefit dependency even further, which in turn makes it necessary to raise the level of contributions once again. The cycle continues, and the social security system will in theory ultimately collapse entirely.

The authors themselves concede that this is not a very realistic scenario; a convergence towards a situation in which ultimately no-one works is not feasible, because rule amendments inevitably will be made. Van Praag et al. (1982: 1158-1159) also admit they ignore a number of factors. For instance, employers may be subjected to institutional constraints (they may not be able to simply dismiss employees as they see fit) and may take their hiring and firing decisions from a long-term perspective: employees are not laid off immediately as soon as their productivity is below a certain threshold value. More importantly, the higher social security costs need not be pushed solely on to employers; employees may also pay their share (via rising employee contributions) and not be able to realise compensating wage demands, and the government may provide some kind of tax relief. And of course, the model does not take into consideration the impact of the development of the capital stock and technological progress, which can generate a part of the required productivity increases.

42 Habermas in fact uses this term in a more precise sense. He refers to the growing dominance in modern societies of the politico-economic system, which he regards as a reality *sui generis*. This leads to the dismantling of the communicative infrastructure, the 'lifeworld'. The ever more complex system thus destroys a key condition for its own functioning, and is unable to repair or replace it. Compare: "In entfalteten modernen Gesellschaften [...] ist zu erwarten, daß die Konkurrenz zwischen Formen der System- und der Sozialintegration *sichtbarer* als bis dahin hervortritt. Am Ende verdrängen systemischen Mechanismen Formen der sozialen Integration auch in jenen Bereichen, wo die konsensabhängige Handlungskoordinierung nicht substituiert werden kann: also dort, wo die symbolische Reproduktion der Lebenswelt auf dem Spiel steht. Dann nimmt die *Mediatisierung* der Lebenswelt die Gestalt einer *Kolonialisierung* an" (Habermas, 1981: 292-293).

43 The theoretical limitations of the median voter hypothesis are also evident (cf. Milanovic, 2000). The model applies less well if the distribution of preferences is not unimodal, and if there are more than two competing political candidates or parties. Furthermore, and in line with the 'bounded rationality' perspective discussed in chapter 2, electors may not have all the information they need for a well-considered choice (e.g. they generally cannot estimate their long-term personal social security gains and contributions accurately) and may settle for 'satisficing', or cast their votes on non-rational grounds (ideals, collective interests, the personal qualities and image of the candidates). Media attention and the selective turnout of certain groups at elections can also play an important intervening role in voting behaviour.

44 Don & Verbruggen (2006) give an overview of the long tradition in the development of such models at The Netherlands Bureau for Economic Policy Analysis|CPB. Specific examples are the SAFFIER model, which is used for short-term and medium-term forecasting (Kranendonk & Verbruggen, 2007); and the applied general equilibrium MIMIC model, containing detailed modelling of labour market supply and social security institutions (Graafland et al., 2001).

45 More detailed accounts of the economic effects of social security are to be found in Aaron, 1982; Douben, 1986; Barr, 1992; Feldstein, 1998: 1-29; Aghion et al., 1999; and Atkinson, 1999.

46 Yet it should be mentioned that the use and non-take-up of social security provisions theoretically are not only driven by expected subjective utility. According to Kerr's (1983) 'threshold model' the likelihood of non-take-up increases when the potential client is not familiar with the social security scheme, does not need the benefit or provision or has not needed it for a sufficiently long time, does not expect to be entitled to it, expects little gains, and has subjective attitudes which hinder application. The latter may relate to the procedures (time, complexity, infringement of privacy, dislike of bureaucracy), but also to the anticipated social consequences (the stigma attaching to certain types of benefit) and the personal implications (not wishing to be dependent). Van Oorschot (1994) has moreover

pointed out that the interaction with the social security administration also is an important theoretical explanation of non-take-up. In empirical studies in the Netherlands, awareness of the schemes, expecting to be entitled, and subjective utility indicators (low needs, short expected duration, limited expected amounts) proved to be the strongest predictors at the micro-level (cf. Vrooman & Asselberghs, 1994; Wildeboer Schut & Hoff, 2007).

47 In the market sector, the added value consists of the difference between the market value of produced goods and the consumption of purchased raw materials, energy, semi-manufactured products and services by other parties. In the public sector this is difficult to establish; some government products have no clear price (administration, defence, etc.), while so-called 'merit goods' (education, cultural facilities) are deliberately provided below cost price. The total of the wages and salaries of government personnel is often used as a proxy for the added value of government provisions. Gross domestic product (GDP) is equal to the total added value realised within the national borders within one year. The gross national product (GNP) is obtained by adding the balance of the primary incomes from and to other countries. If one allows for the depreciation of the capital stock as a result of its use in the production process, this leaves the net domestic product (NDP) and the net national product (NNP), respectively. The added value after allowing for depreciation can be divided over the production factors: the labour of employees (wages) and businesses (profits), the making available of financial capital (interest) or land (lease, rent).

48 The maximum achievable output can be estimated via a production function, which indicates how the available means of production of the community are deployed. In a simple Cobb-Douglas variant, the theoretically attainable added value is determined by the available capital stock, the potential number of workers and the state of technology:

$Y = K^p \cdot L^{1-p} \cdot H$

where
Y = total output
K = capital stock
L = employment years
H = state of technology
p = share of profit in the value of output

Yet for several reasons this production function is too simple for modern societies. It describes a closed economy with a single sector of industry and with no government investments. There is no home production, no self-employed enterprise, and the labour market is not differentiated. All workers are identical and are fully employed at an equilibrium market wage. The capital stock is fully utilised at a given rate of interest. Furthermore, the 'new growth theory' argues that the three production factors need not develop independently of each other. An increase in the investments in capital (ΔK) can for example lead to an acceleration in the rate of technological innovation (ΔH).

The production capacity is not always fully deployed; the actual added value is equal to the maximum production capacity multiplied by the degree of capacity utilisation. A difference between theoretical and actual GDP (the 'output gap') suggests under-utilisation of the capital stock, unemployment, and non-participation by people who could work.

49 The theoretical significance of human capital for collective wealth is developed *inter alia* by G.S. Becker (1993 [1964]), Mincer (1993 [1984]) and Lucas (1988); see Engelbrecht (2003) for a country comparison.

50 However, this Keynesian perspective needs to be qualified in two ways. The influence of social security on consumer demand is selective because beneficiaries spend more on basic needs than on luxury consumer goods. Moreover, a large part of the take-up of formal social security arrangements (old age and survivor's pensions, disability schemes, child benefit, structural unemployment) is not tied to the economic cycle (see e.g. Douben, 1980: 71-73).

51 This is the total number of workers in the tax department, the agencies of the unemployment and disability benefit schemes, municipal social services, the Social Insurance Bank and the staff of sheltered employment support. It is of course possible that in the absence of these social security organisations their employees would perform other work, with which they would make a larger contribution to national prosperity.

52 Market clearing refers to the situation where the quantity supplied equals the quantity demanded; or to the price adjustment process that leads to such a state of affairs.

53 According to neo-classical theory a one-off fall in the output level will occur, but the growth rate will remain constant; cf. Atkinson (1999: 146) "if S/Y were to fall, then over time the capital output ratio falls, and in steady state the fall in (K/Y) fully offsets the fall in the savings ratio, leaving the growth rate unchanged". However, the wealth-reducing effect of savings depends on the chosen funding method. In fully funded schemes 'institutional' savings (i.e. enforced by the formal rules) largely may substitute private savings, and only the composition of the total amount changes. In pay-as-you-go schemes, however, total savings theoretically will decline.

54 Cf. the previous discussion of Van Praag et al.'s 'flywheel effect' of rising social security contributions.

55 On the one hand, an increase in social contributions makes it relatively more attractive to consume leisure time, as its shadow price falls. This theoretically leads to a decrease in labour supply and collective wealth. On the other hand, higher contributions increase the incentive to find work, since households will seek to offset their decline in income. If this greater labour supply can be deployed productively collective prosperity theoretically will increase.
It is not certain in advance whether the substitution effect or the income effect of higher contributions will dominate. Wildeboer Schut et al. (2001: 98-103) point out that this may vary across social groups. For working people (regardless of their income level) and benefit claimants, an increase in the contribution rate will lead to positive income effects and negative substitution effects, so that the overall effect is unpredictable. For non-working people without benefit the substitution effect dominates: it becomes less attractive for housewives in particular to start working.

56 Atkinson (1999: 9-11) argues in this respect that "there is a tendency for economists to analyze the impact of a hypothetical benefit that differs in essential features from real-world social security. [...] Unemployment benefit provides an illustration of the neglect of important institutional structure. Economic models regularly assume that the only relevant condition for the receipt of benefit is being unemployed. In fact, in the typical unemployment insurance program, benefit is subject to contribution conditions, is paid for a limited duration, and is monitored to check that the person is making genuine efforts to seek employment. Benefit may be refused where the person entered unemployment voluntarily or as a result of industrial misconduct, and a person may be disqualified for refusing job offers. The conditions for the receipt of unemployment insurance not only reduce its coverage but also affect the relationship between transfers and the working of the economy. The standard job research model, for example, assumes that workers can reject job offers that offer less than a specified wage. Such a reservation wage strategy may, however, lead to the person being disqualified from benefit."

57 These differences, however, partly reflect the impact of other factors. People on disability benefit and people who had taken early retirement displayed a stronger work ethic than working people, which can be ascribed to some extent to their comparatively high age (the work ethic of older people is generally higher). Unemployed benefit recipients had a lower work ethic than those in work, but generally were younger (De Beer, 2001: 168-170).

58 Social security also impacts on the sector income distribution, which is concerned with splitting the rewards over the various production factors: the share of the wage bill (salaries and social security charges), profits, interest and rents in total income.

59 The distribution of assets receives less attention in empirical research, mainly because of the scarcity of reliable data. This is regrettable, because the inclusion of this factor probably offers a better indication of the overall wealth position of actors than their current yearly income alone. Davies & Shorrocks (2000) point out that a person's wealth at a certain point in time (W_t) can be defined as the sum of previously gathered assets (W_{t-1}), the interest received on them ($r_t W_{t-1}$), current inheritances in a broad sense (I_t: gifts, legacies, prizes won) and current income (E_t), minus current consumption (C_t). In a more complete equation, human capital and future entitlements (annuities, social security pensions) should be added as well. The same authors tentatively conclude that:
    - Wealth generally is distributed less equally than labour income, total money income or consumption expenditure;
    - Financial assets tend to be less equally distributed than nonfinancial assets;
    - The distribution of inherited wealth is much more unequal than that of wealth in general;
    - In all age groups there is typically a group of individuals and families with very low net assets, and at all ages the majority have surprisingly low financial assets;
    - Wealth inequality has decreased during the twentieth century in most countries, with some reversals (e.g. the US since the mid 1970s).

60 Esping-Andersen (2003: 66) points out that in this "early formative epoch of model building" the dominant elites varied in the different countries: "In one large group of nations, the traditional authoritarian, anti-democratic conservative forces were already pretty much sidelined and emasculated by the time that the 'social question' arose. This was so in the Anglo-Saxon nations and, by and large, also the case in Scandinavia. In this same group, the political power of the Church – and especially of Catholicism – was marginal or almost nil. Hence, virtually from the very beginning of social policy, the axis of conflict was basically one-dimensional: workers' movements against a liberal-leaning bourgeoisie and petty bourgeoisie. In other countries, mainly concentrated on the European continent, the frontlines were messier because the neo-absolutist forces remained powerful and often decisive. The liberal impulse remained feeble and failed to assert itself in any hegemonic way in Germany, Austria, Italy or Spain. Within this political matrix, workers movements and conservatives could agree in terms of their shared antipathy to the naked cash nexus; and the liberals and socialists in terms of their shared preference for individual rights. On most other social welfare issues, the three clashed head on. More often than not, dictatorship helped silence the socialists."

Chapter 4

1 Parts of this chapter are based on the author's contributions to the SCP study *On worlds of welfare*. Section 4.1 has been edited and updated, while the analysis in section 4.2 is a variant of the one performed in the previous work (Wildeboer Schut et al., 2001: 5; 7-32).
2 This 'Mutual Information System on Social Protection in the EU countries and the EEA' (MISSOC) is available through http://europa.eu.int/comm/employment_social/missoc/index_en.html. A separate extension to incorporate Central and Eastern European countries (MISSCEEC) can be accessed through the same Internet address.
3 Esping-Andersen uses the expression 'liberal' in a classical European sense, referring to a regime which maximises individual freedom and limits state intervention. This, of course, is completely at odds with its standard meaning in current American English, as Murray (1997: xii) points out: "The correct word for my view of the world is *liberal* [and] the writers of the nineteenth century who expounded on this view were called liberals [...] But words mean what people think they mean, and in the United States the unmodified term *liberal* now refers to the politics of an expansive government and the welfare state". Murray proposes 'libertarian' as an alternative. That concept, however, may be rather confusing as well – at least from a European perspective, in which it usually is associated with individualistic variants of anarchism. Throughout this book the word 'liberal' is therefore adopted, in its classical meaning and in line with the Esping-Andersen nomenclature.
4 Viz. *Rerum Novarum* (1891) and *Quadrogesimo Anno* (1931).
5 Of course, the regime concept as defined here has nothing to do with the notion of 'regimentation', as discussed in chapter 2. The latter refers to rules which inevitably force actors to comply.
6 Goodman (1998) suggests that the historical roots of the Japanese social security system do not stretch as far as is often presumed, and that the notion of a traditional Japanese way of providing welfare was actually used to curtail the demand for a more extensive system in the post-WW II period: "The Japanese-style welfare state thesis is a classic example of what Hobsbawm and Ranger have called 'the invention of tradition'. It drew on idealised visions of a Japan where communities had always lived co-operatively and harmoniously, caring for each other, and especially for the aged and the sick. In doing so, it ignored compelling historical evidence of communal violence, rioting, the abandonment of the elderly and the culling of the sick or weak. Similarly the emphasis placed on Confucian values of filial piety, loyalty, obligation, respect for seniority and so on ignored the fact that until the Meiji period these values had very little to do with the lives of the common people of Japan, but were important only to the 6 per cent who constituted the samurai class. It was only the so-called 'samuraisation process' in the 1870s that led to these values being devolved, through state sponsorship and via the education system, to the rest of the population in a conscious attempt to construct a Japanese state. There is little doubt, however, that by drawing on the 'historical' precedent and Confucian 'tradition' – in particular the emphasis on care for the aged – the proponents of the Japanese-style welfare model were successful in deflating rising social expectations of state-provided welfare rights and citizenship" (Goodman, 1998: 150).
7 In Esping-Andersen's original typology the Netherlands belongs to the corporatist (or conservative) group on the basis of its 'de-commodification score', which is slightly higher than France's or Germany's, but does not reach the level of the Nordic countries. Belgium and Austria are on a par with the Netherlands. Esping-Andersen attributes this to the political power of the social-democratic labour movement in these three countries during the post-WW II period. In terms of pension benefit schemes, however, Esping-Andersen originally classified the Netherlands as a universalistic state-dominated system, rather comparable to Norway, Sweden and New Zealand (Esping-Andersen, 1990: 53-54, 85-87).
In his later work Esping-Andersen is more pronounced about "the Dutch enigma" and acknowledges the fundamentally hybrid character of the Dutch social security regime: "The original 'three worlds' typology focused rather one-sidedly on income maintenance. Herein lie perhaps the ambiguities of the Dutch case. When we study income maintenance, the Netherlands appears 'social democratic' in the sense of strong universalism, comprehensive coverage, and generous 'de-commodifying' benefits. But when we include social service delivery – and when, more generally, we examine the role of the family – the Netherlands becomes squarely a member of the 'conservative', Continental Europe fold" (Esping-Andersen, 1999: 88).
8 Shalev (2007: 300) argues that the multinomial logistic regression approach Esping-Andersen (1999) used in a later version of the typology "has the advantage of permitting explanatory weights to vary across different categories of the dependent variable. But in the context of cross-national research of this type, the category-specific coefficients must be estimated on a ludicrously small number of cases".
9 CatPCA was formerly known as Princals (Principal components analysis by alternating least squares). The procedure is available through the 'Categories' module of the SPSS software package. Gifi (1990) gives a more detailed description; see also the CatPCA algorithm document, available through the SPSS support site at http://support.spss.com/tech/default.asp).

10 To a large extent this is a replication of the analysis in Wildeboer Schut et al. (2001: 17-32). A description of the original variables and their coding scheme is listed in the appendix to chapter 2 of that publication. However, seven variables have been deleted from the dataset, because they resembled possible outcomes of institutions, rather than institutional characteristics. They are the labour market participation of women, elderly men (55-64 years), and males aged 65 or more; the share of the services sector in total employment; and the employment shares of specific segments of the services sector (social and community welfare; financial/business/real estate; and wholesale/retail employment). These have been replaced by three variables with a more 'institutional' content. The formal pension age for men (coded <65, 65, >65) may partly explain early exits of elderly men. The minimum annual statutory period of leave for employees (none; < 4 weeks; 4 weeks; >4 weeks) could influence labour market supply, especially of women . This also may hold for formal child care facilities available for children aged 0-3 years (<10% coverage; 10-30%; 30-45%; >45%). The *Employment Outlook* (OECD, 2003a: 135) suggests that "an extension of child-care support might increase women's labour force participation", although the direction of causality is not wholly clear.

A further deviation from the previous scaling procedure is that the CatPCA solution has been slightly rotated, in order to make the first dimension a clearer indicator of social security scope. In the analysis all variables were initially scaled on a single ordinal basis. This implies that the quantifications have been accredited in such a way that the original ranking of the categories was maintained; the distances between them, however, were free. For a number of variables this ordinality restriction resulted in a high loss of fit (more than 0.50 across two dimensions). In such cases a better fit may be achieved by making the measurement level less restrictive, through a multiple nominal quantification. This means that the original ranking of categories does not have to be maintained during the scaling procedure, and quantified categories do not need to be placed on one line in multidimensional space. For four variables such a quantification was applied in the final scaling, because it led to a meaningful interpretation in terms of regimes. They are the intensity of active labour market policy, the disability benefit threshold for the *risque social*, the presence of a collective surviving dependants' scheme for residents, and the statutory number of weeks leave per annum.

11 From a wider theoretical point of view the selection of institutional traits is somewhat limited, bearing in mind the social security definition and the interaction models of formal social security that have been outlined in the previous chapter. For instance, there are virtually no variables which refer to potential sanctioning, the structure and operation of the social security administration, differences in auditing actors and appeal procedures, etc. While it would be interesting to add such traits, it should be pointed out that these are not key elements of the typology which is tested here. In the next two chapters some of these attributes will be included in the construction of theoretical institutional indices which predict country differences in benefit dependency and poverty.

12 Together the two dimensions account for 61% of the total variance of the unrotated solution. A supplementary analysis was carried out over five dimensions. The eigenvalues of the three 'higher' dimensions were much lower, as was their contribution to the proportion of explained variance (0.14 for the third dimension, 0.11 for the fourth and 0.09 for the fifth). Moreover, this analysis did not produce any new substantive insights. On the first two dimensions the component loadings and country clusters were the same, while on the higher dimensions some less easily interpretable differences between separate countries were found (cf. Wildeboer Schut et al., 2001: 33-34).

As a final test, in an additional analysis *all* variables were scaled on a multiple nominal basis. This is not the obvious measurement level, because most original variables run from low to high (or vice versa), which suggests ordinal scaling is appropriate. However, such an analysis provides information on the impact of the ordinality restriction on the scaling results. In this multiple nominal CatPCA the same clusters of countries and regimes emerged, the main difference being that Norway was scaled closer to the Netherlands, and thus became more of a hybrid regime.

13 The low component loadings indicate that this is not a very consistent pattern, however. After optimal scaling, this variable shows a dichotomy between Australia and all other countries.

14 This means that several countries operating a 'liberal' regime type had high minimum wages, while these were absent in social-democratic regimes. One could argue that a statutory minimum wage is especially necessary where social security benefits are low, and there are no collective labour agreements between employers and trade unions. Some corporatist and social-democratic countries may not need statutory minimum wages, because the benefit levels and collective arrangements make the bottom rung of the pay ladder quite high, which in practice may have the same effects as a high statutory minimum wage.

15 There is no separate orphan's pension in Australia, Canada, France and Denmark. The component loading of this variable is lowest of all.

16 If one considers these variables over both dimensions, most also have nonzero component loadings on the first dimension. This is because corporatist countries often are rather extensive, but it is also a consequence of the score of the hybrid Dutch social security regime. If the Netherlands is excluded from the CatPCA-procedure, this group of variables falls apart. Most component loadings move closer to the origin of the x-axis, where one would theoretically

expect them. A few, however, become more outlying on the first dimension, because some social-democratic nations score consistent with countries representing the corporatist regime.

17 The collective pensions of surviving dependants of employees are in the highest category in the three corporatist regimes, but also in Canada and the USA. This explains why item no. 33 has a slight bias towards the 'residualist' side of the first dimension. Survivor's pensions for dependants of non-employees are included as a nominal variable, and therefore do not show up in the plot of component loadings, which are only available for ordinal or interval variables.

18 The component loading of the collective old age pension for all inhabitants (item no. 40) is lower on the first dimension, because this trait is not specific to social-democratic regimes, but shared with several countries belonging to the liberal type.

19 Full early retirement pensions are something of a borderline case in figure 4.1. After optimal scaling, there exists a dichotomy between countries who offered this opportunity (at the end of the 1980s) before 60 years of age and the other categories (no possibility of full early retirement, or only between ages 60 and 64). The first category consists of nations representing the corporatist and liberal regimes – but not all countries of either type, which explains the rather low component loadings. Full early retirement before age 60 was possible in Belgium, France, the UK and Australia, and in none of the social-democratic regimes.

20 This concerns the UK, Australia and Denmark.

21 In a hierarchical cluster analysis of the object scores on both dimensions, a two-cluster solution results in a contrast between the liberal countries and the rest. The three-cluster solution separates the liberal countries (Australia, Canada, UK, the USA) from the corporatist (Belgium, France, Germany) and social-democratic (Denmark, Norway, Sweden) clusters. The Netherlands is included in the latter group; but it emerges as a distinct case in a four-dimensional solution. With five clusters the USA split off from the liberal group, and in the six-cluster solution Denmark drops out of the social-democratic class. With a different measure for clustering (Euclidean or squared Euclidean distance instead of cosine) the two- and three-cluster solutions remain the same, but the higher solutions show a reversal: Denmark emerges as a single case in the analysis over four clusters, the Netherlands in the six-cluster solution.

Traditional cluster analysis does not allow the goodness of fit of the various solutions to be tested. This is however possible in latent profile modelling, which assesses whether the scores on a set of continuous indicators (in this case: the object scores) can be reduced to a single categorical latent variable; and cases are attributed to the classes of this latent variable with a certain probability (cf. Vermunt & Magidson, 2002). Latent profile modelling of the object scores with two and three clusters result in the same country classifications as the hierarchical cluster analyses mentioned above; that is, a distinction between liberal and non-liberal countries, or a separation of the representatives of the liberal, corporatist, and social-democratic (plus the Netherlands) regimes. The fit of the two-cluster model is not significantly better than the baseline model containing a single cluster; but the three-cluster model differs significantly from the baseline and two cluster models. Due to the small number of cases (n=11), latent profile models with four or more clusters are not identified (the three-cluster model was only barely so) and could not be tested.

22 Canada also shows considerable regional variation, as does the USA. Social assistance is partly funded at federal level, but provinces and local authorities have a wide degree of freedom in determining the eligibility criteria, the use of means tests, and the level of benefits. There is also a separate welfare scheme for 'native Canadians' living on the reservations. The norm amounts for child benefit vary widely as well: some provinces provide top-ups, or relate these benefits to the age and number of children. The system in Quebec, in particular, exhibits corporatist characteristics in this respect.

23 The post-war social security regime in the United Kingdom was initially universalistic. The system devised by Beveridge which was introduced after the Second World War, with a national social insurance scheme, contribution-based funding, flat-rate benefits and a limited social safety net, was developed even further in the following decades. In the 1960s and 1970s, benefits were increasingly related to earnings. Coverage was introduced for those who had not paid sufficient contributions, and entitlements to medical treatments were extended.

Under the influence of the economic crisis and the neo-liberal philosophy of the Conservative governments, however, earnings-related benefits were gradually phased out in the early 1980s, and the conditions for benefit eligibility were tightened up – among other things by stating that people had to be available for work. The changes culminated in the *Social Security Act* of 1986, in which the national earnings-related pension provision was abolished, the national assistance scheme was restructured, and incentives were built in to encourage a switch from public to private provisions. Eardley et al. (1996: 388-389) describe this development as a shift towards targeting and means-tested social assistance, which became the main scheme. This implied a weakening of the universalistic nature of the British social security system.

Esping-Andersen (1999: 87) considers Britain "mainly a problem because the typology does not take into account mutation. Had we made our comparisons in the immediate post-war decades, we would almost certainly have put

Britain and Scandinavia in the same cluster: both were built on universal, flat-rate benefit programmes, national health care, and a vocal political commitment to full employment". After the changes of the 1980s, however, "Britain appears increasingly liberal". This does not necessarily imply that Britain and the Nordic countries were social-democratic in the 1950s, since "the essence of social-democratic welfare regimes emerged in Scandinavia later".

24 The main difference is that in Shalev's results Germany loads lower on corporatism, and the UK comes out as less residual, which seems quite plausible for this pre-Thatcher period. However, Shalev's analysis is not wholly comparable to the one reported in section 4.2. He uses fewer variables but more nations; and some of his variables indicate the results of regimes, rather than the institutions they are made of (e.g. "full-employment performance"). Contrary to CatPCA, factor analysis assumes an interval measurement level.

25 In a CatPCA of 85 regime characteristics in 23 countries Soede et al. (2004) find five different clusters: the three presented here (with Norway at a larger distance from the other social-democratic countries), plus two separate groups, one consisting of the Mediterranean countries (with Greece and Spain as somewhat purer examples than Portugal or Italy), the other of the four recent larger EU member states of Eastern Europe (Poland, Hungary, the Czech Republic and Slovakia). The Netherlands is once again a hybrid.

While Soede et al.'s first dimension also indicates the scope of social security (residual-extensive), their second one refers to pension schemes rather than corporatism. Pensions are, relatively speaking, rather well-developed in Southern European countries, in contrast to their more residual arrangements for unemployment and social assistance. Since these countries do not form part of the analysis in this chapter, this influence does not show up. For the corporatist countries included here, it might be that particularistic traits have become less dominant during the 1990s. A more likely explanation, however, is that Soede et al. (2004) have less indicators for corporatism, while their total set of variables is larger (85 instead of 54), especially in terms of pension scheme characteristics. The latter seem to have 'taken over' the second dimension. This picture is corroborated by the analysis in Soede & Vrooman (2008a), where the existence of specific pension regimes in EU member states is explored further. It should however be noted that the three analyses do not provide any information on the stability of the between-cluster distances over time. In order to assess these, a simultaneous analysis of the same regime traits in different years would need to be performed. While the classification as such seems consistent over time, it may be that countries approximate their 'ideal-type' more closely in some years than in others (cf. §5.3.3 and §7.3).

26 This may apply to the structure of the education system but, following Blossfeld & Shavit (1993), the *results* in terms of educational opportunities and educational attainment of socio-economic strata do not vary systematically between the three regime types. Sweden and the Netherlands have accomplished a reduction in educational inequality over the years, while this remained fairly stable in eleven other countries. These authors also point out that the dual education system has expanded in several countries; not only in corporatist ones like Germany, but in Sweden as well. They conclude that this has facilitated the reproduction of the existing stratification: "The expansion of vocational, non-college education enabled these systems to incorporate growing proportions of children from lower strata who would complete secondary education but would not be considered for further academic education. This led to an opening up of secondary education without disturbing the basically exclusive character of higher education" (Blossfeld & Shavit, 1993: 20).

27 In practice, however, the French education system also tends to reproduce the social elite to a large extent through a process of self-recruitment (cf. the discussion of the *Enarques* in chapter 2).

28 Arts & Gelissen's (2001) item on equality refers to the elimination of large inequalities in income between citizens. The 'needs' question relates to guaranteeing that basic needs are met for all, in terms of food, housing, clothing, education, and health. 'Equity' is measured by the responses to the statement that a 'just' society should recognise people on their merits.

29 On preferred solidarity the level-2 modelled variance of the five regime types is 0.24, with only the social-democratic and Mediterranean types deviating significantly from the reference category, the liberal regime. On 'equality' the modelled variance of three regime types – the European Value Study does not contain data on the Antipodes and Eastern Asiatic countries – is even higher (0.49); but, as was noted earlier, with coefficients running in an unexpected direction. The modelled variance in 'need' and 'equity' that can be attributed to the regime types is much lower (0.08-0.09). The individual characteristics seem to have a limited influence as well, with a total level-1 modelled variance ranging from 0.02 to 0.09.

30 The analysis by Arts & Gelissen (2001) provides a few examples of this. Based on a review of the literature on welfare state classifications they make a distinction between six regime types: liberal countries (USA, Canada, Great Britain, Ireland), conservative ones (France and Germany), social-democratic nations (Sweden, Denmark, Norway, Austria, Belgium and the Netherlands), Mediterranean countries (Greece, Portugal, Spain and Italy), Antipodean types (Australia, New Zealand) and East-Asian communitarian regimes (Japan, the Philippines). Based on the scaling results of the previous section Arts & Gelissen's classification of Belgium may be questioned. Following Soede et al. (2004)

this also holds for Austria, which seems to belong to the corporatist/conservative cluster as well. Arts & Gelissen's straightforward inclusion of the Netherlands in the social-democratic group is also open to challenge.

Within these types, Arts & Gelissen consider some countries as less pure examples. This applies for Great Britain and Ireland in the liberal cluster; Austria, Belgium and the Netherlands in the social-democratic cluster; Italy in the Mediterranean group; and the Philippines in the East-Asian type. In their multi-level models they neglect these finer distinctions by using one dummy variable for each type, with the liberal regime as the reference category. Their motivation for this decision is not wholly convincing: "Some of these (countries) are close empirical representations of the ideal-type and others are hybrid cases, exhibiting traits of two or more regime-types. However, one has to keep in mind that, ultimately, even archetypes are not completely pure cases" (Arts & Gelissen 2001: 290). Part of Arts & Gelissen's unexpected results may be due to their specific *ex ante* definition of regime clusters.

31 Cf. the explanation that Gelissen (2002:[1] 214) offers in the Dutch summary to his thesis for some of the more singular results that were reported in Arts & Gelissen (2001): "Citizens [of the liberal and Mediterranean welfare regimes] may have more to gain from government intervention than those of social-democratic and conservative welfare states. In the former, people may be predominantly focussed on the benefits of increased state intervention whereas, in the latter, they may be more aware of the costs incurred".

32 This 'scope bias' is apparent, for instance, in Svallfors (1997), who studies preferred income differentials and attitudes to redistribution. The key dependent variables Arts & Gelissen (2001) analyse – solidarity, equality, needs and equity – mainly refer to Esping-Andersen's first dimension as well.

33 The *International Social Survey Programme* has been running since the mid-1980s. It consists of topical modules, which are harmonised across countries and added to existing national surveys. Currently 39 different countries are taking part. The sample size of the ten countries analysed here usually is between 900 and 1400 per wave. This adds up to a total of around 11.000-13.000 cases for each wave. More information can be obtained through www.issp.org.

The ISSP data refer to Great Britain, not to the United Kingdom (as in the previous section). For Germany the analysis was confined to the western part, because the majority of the inhabitants of the new *Bundesländer* do not share the corporatist legacy, and an explorative analysis showed them to have a different profile on the indicators used here. The 1999 data for Denmark and the Netherlands are not included in the regular ISSP-dataset. The Danish file is available upon request. The Dutch data were gathered through an access panel instead of a regular survey and are part of the 1999 edition of SCP's long-running series on *Cultural Changes in the Netherlands* (available through the Data Archiving and Networked Services (DANS) in The Hague, formerly Steinmetz Archives).

34 On the variables presented in figure 4.3 three countries still have missing values. Denmark and the Netherlands did not take part in ISSP 1996 (two variables), and Australia skipped 1997 (four variables). In the CatPCA-procedure these missing values were treated passively, in order to avoid extreme scalings. Most variables are expressed in discrete classes of response percentages (see the legend to figure 4.3). For instance, item 1 – "should it be the government's responsibility to provide a decent standard of living for the unemployed?" – is based on the share of respondents answering this should 'definitely' or 'probably' be so. Country percentages were divided into four classes: very low (9-13%: Australia and the USA), low (17-21%: Germany, France and Canada); moderate (28%: Great Britain) and relatively high (38-41%: Norway and Sweden). Two cases (Denmark and the Netherlands) are missing on this variable. It has to be borne in mind that the analysis charts the relative differences between countries over such categorised variables.

35 The CatPCA results of figures 4.3 and 4.4 have been rotated in order to enhance the interpretability of the dimensions in terms of the component loadings. The original solution accounts for 79% of the total variance.

36 Features 4 and 10 in figure 4.3 refer to preferred income differentials. The same underlying variables were analysed by Svallfors (1997) over a more limited set of countries from the ISSP-waves of 1987 and 1992. Respondents were asked about how much people in nine different occupations should earn (depending on the local custom earnings were measured before or after taxes, and weekly, monthly or yearly). For the present analysis, in each country the nine variables were concatenated in order to construct a distribution of preferred income differentials. This variable is not representative of the *entire* preferred income distribution, because the chosen occupations reflect earnings at the top and at the bottom, neglecting the middle segment of the labour market. Moreover, preferred income from pensions and social security is excluded. And of course most countries have more factory workers and shop assistants than lawyers, Supreme Court judges or cabinet ministers, while in the constructed variable the latter dominate (since it contains responses for six higher and three lower occupations). To take account of this two dispersion measures were calculated. The decomposable Theil-coefficient was used to assess the preferred earning differentials between lower and higher occupations; and the Gini-coefficient was taken as an indicator for the 'income inequality aversion' regarding the higher occupations (since this is less susceptible to extreme top incomes than the within Theil-coefficient).

37 Feature 8 is based on the ratio of the shares of female and male respondents who prefer working for the government or civil service. The ratio was used to correct for the *general* prestige of being a 'part of government' in a country, an indicator which was expected to load on the corporatist dimension (feature 13). It is about 2.0 in Sweden and Norway, against 1.1-1.3 elsewhere.
38 Theoretically several hypotheses may be put forward to explain a more lenient rule interpretation in corporatist regimes. First, the attitudes towards government may be different. While the state is the embodiment of public interest in social-democratic and liberal regimes (albeit with an entirely different scope), in corporatist ones it is a vehicle for group-based interests, controlled by a bureaucratic elite. In such a context, not paying taxes or benefit fraud may be more likely to be regarded as a way of 'beating the system', rather than as an offence against the common good. In line with this, solidarity in corporatist regimes is not universalistic, but limited to people in the same stratum. This may imply that defection is acceptable, as long as it does not affect the interests of the status group one belongs to. A third theoretical explanation is more down to earth. Liberal regimes may tend to enforce rules in order to keep the scope of their systems small, social-democratic ones so as to reduce costs and maximise contributions. Corporatist regimes, however, may be less inclined to enforce rules. The risk of being caught may thus be lower. Of course, factors that are not directly related to the regime types (e.g. varying degrees of secularisation between countries, a divergent impact of a predominantly Protestant or Catholic ethic) may be relevant as well.
39 A hierarchical cluster analysis with two clusters resulted in a contrast between the two corporatist countries plus the Netherlands, versus the representatives of the liberal and social-democratic regime. A three-cluster model is more or less in line with the theoretical expectations: (1) France, Germany, the Netherlands; (2) Denmark, Norway, Sweden; (3) Australia, Canada, Great Britain, USA. The latter group is split in the four cluster solution (Australia and Great Britain versus the North-American countries).

With (squared) Euclidean distances and four clusters a somewhat different classification emerges, consisting of the corporatist group (France, Germany), two clusters containing the more pure specimens of respectively the liberal (USA, Canada) and social-democratic (Norway, Sweden) groups, and a remaining cluster of less typical countries (the Netherlands, Great Britain, Australia, and Denmark).

It was not possible to perform a meaningful latent profile analysis, as in the additional analyses relating to the formal institutions (cf. note 21 to this chapter). Because data for Belgium are lacking, the number of cases (n=10) is too small for comparing the goodness of fit for models with three or more clusters.
40 As noted earlier, Australia has four missing values in the dataset. However, Australia's lower score on the first dimension cannot be attributed to this completely. Most variables loading high on the x-axis are valid in the Australian case; and if the USA values are imputed for the missing variables in Australia, its score on first dimension becomes more negative than the British one, but remains rather close.
41 The 'scope' dimension of social security regimes in figure 4.1 is similar to Larsen's 'generosity', and the 'universalistic/ particularistic' contrast resembles his 'selectivism'. Formal labour market institutions scaled on either of the two principal components. Larsen's 'job opportunities' therefore did not emerge as a separate dimension of social security regimes, even after extending the CatPCA to a solution with 3 to 5 dimensions.

Chapter 5

1 The standardised total scores on the index for Sweden, Norway and Denmark are then 0.17, 0.46 and 0.65, respectively.
2 The high score for Sweden for unemployment insurance is perhaps rather unexpected, because the 'Swedish model' has traditionally been associated with low unemployment rates. However, it has to be borne in mind that the benefit dependency boost index is concerned with the *theoretical* risk of a high volume based on the formal institutions with regard to unemployment arrangements (see Annex 1). The benefit percentages and the replacement rates at the onset of unemployment are high in Sweden. This also applies for the marginal tax rates and average contributions, and the duration of unemployment benefits can be long – all factors which theoretically increase the benefit volume. In the Swedish philosophy, a generous unemployment arrangement does not lead to high numbers of unemployment benefits because of a strict and effective activation policy and the promotion of full employment (among other things via the services sector). If the last two objectives cannot be realised, the risk of a substantial unemployment benefit volume is theoretically high. The index score reflects this; and the development of the Swedish unemployment volume in the first half of the 1990s suggests that this is not entirely without foundation.
3 The benefit dependency boost index was calculated as the weighted sum of the volume-boosting score on a number of formal institutions (see Annex 1). Theoretically, however, the volume of the various types of benefit is not completely independent, since substitutions occur. If a country has a financially and socially attractive early retirement scheme, for example, this is likely to reduce the number of disability and unemployment benefits (put differently, there is hidden disability and unemployment in the early exit arrangements). The same thing can happen between arrangements for disability and unemployment: depending on the entry conditions and the norms and conventions of the actors in the administrative process, there may be 'hidden unemployment' in the disability benefit system or 'hidden disability' in the unemployment benefit schemes. In the case of the Netherlands in the early 1990s it is plausible that the early exit arrangements depressed the disability and unemployment volume, and that the generous disability schemes led to less take-up of unemployment insurance. The high theoretical scores on unemployment and, to a lesser extent, disability, need not therefore by definition lead to high volumes in practice, because part of the theoretically expected high volume may be captured twice. However, as the same substitution mechanisms will also occur in other countries, it is difficult to determine in advance to what extent the relative position of the Netherlands on the benefit dependency boost index is influenced by this.
4 These hypotheses assume that there are no countries where the initial volume is very much lower or higher than elsewhere, leading to considerable base rate or ceiling effects. For the total benefit volume this assumption seems warranted, because in all countries analysed here the high take-up of old age pensions ensures that the initial number of benefit recipients consists of a substantial part of the population. Moreover, the dispersion is limited: while the 'growth potential' of Canada and Australia is higher than that of Belgium, Sweden, and Denmark, the difference is no more than about 10 percentage points (cf. the data on 1980 presented in figure 5.2).
The relationship between the two indicators can be demonstrated as follows:

$$G_t = \frac{N_t - N_{t-1}}{N_{t-1}} = \frac{R_t \cdot P_t - R_{t-1} \cdot P_{t-1}}{R_{t-1} \cdot P_{t-1}} = \frac{R_t \cdot P_t}{R_{t-1} \cdot P_{t-1}} - 1 = \frac{R_t}{R_{t-1}} \cdot \frac{P_t}{P_{t-1}} - 1$$

where
G = growth rate of absolute benefit volume (/100);
N = absolute benefit volume;
R = relative benefit volume;
P = population 15+

5 The most important changes compared with the original Ecorys/NEI data – partially incorporated in OECD (2003a) – are:
   - the benefit volume above 65 years has been re-estimated for all countries, correcting for recipients living abroad. Where this exceeds the number of residents aged over 65 years, the volume is equated to the population size above this age limit;
   - the volume of unemployment benefits is limited to those who are actually available for work. This means, for example, that Dutch unemployed people aged over 57.5 years (who previously were not required to search a job) were regarded as having taken early retirement;
   - in *Belgium*, the volume of survivor's benefits has been greatly reduced through the addition of a new series on the actual number of recipients younger than 65 years. The year in which the permitted early retirement age for women was raised from 60 to 61 years was also corrected (1997 instead of 1992, as assumed by Ecorys/NEI). The volume of maternity benefits in 1990 was modified relative to the OECD (2003a: 225);
   - the *German* figures for the number of disabled persons aged below 65 years originally included people above that

age limit. This has been corrected, leading to a substantial fall in the disability benefit volume. The volumes in the arrangements for widows and orphans in the period 1997-1999 have been adjusted downwards;
- in *France*, two arrangements have been added: the *Allocation de parent isolé* (API, a social assistance scheme for non-working lone-parent families) and the *Allocation parentale d'éducation* (APE, a benefit for parents interrupting their careers to look after young children). The time series for pensioners, surviving dependants and the unemployed were also re-estimated, among other things to correct for conjunctures;
- in *The Netherlands* the early retirement scheme (*vut*/pre-pension) has been added. Without this, the benefit dependency – and certainly the number of early exits – would be substantially underestimated. At the end of the 1990s approximately 130,000 benefit years were involved. NEI/Ecorys leaves these arrangements out of consideration for formal reasons: they are not established by law, but in the collective bargaining between employers and trade unions. In reality, however, the *vut* early retirement arrangement is at the very least partially ratified by the government, since the Minister of Social Affairs and Employment declares the Collective Labour Agreements in which it is laid down in most sectors to be 'generally binding'. Some benefit volumes at the end of the 1990s were also adjusted to take account of more recent Dutch figures. In the social assistance arrangements, the relative shares of unemployment assistance and other recipients have been estimated from 1996 on the basis of the trend in the number of lone-parent families receiving general social assistance;
- two arrangements were added to the *Danish* time series: the 'transitional allowance' (*Overgangsydelse*), which made it possible between 1992 and 1996 for older long-term unemployed to retire early, and the childcare leave arrangements that were introduced in 1994 (*Børnepasningsorlov*). For 1980-1983 the volumes of survivor's pensions (*Enkepension*) were added, which were abolished in 1984 and absorbed into the *Fortidspension*. The share of 66 and 67 year-old recipients of early exit benefits (*Efterløn*, *Overgangsydelse* and *Fortidspension*) was redetermined, leading to a reduction in the benefit dependency in the population younger than 65 years. Finally, a harmonised statistical series published by Statistics Denmark was used for social assistance benefit recipients, with a correction for a trend break in 1994. For 1980-1983, the mutations in social assistance benefit have been estimated. A correction was applied for duplications in the counting of social assistance benefit recipients who were already included in the unemployment figures as 'non-insured unemployment beneficiaries'. The Danish social assistance volume roughly halved compared with Ecorys/NEI, by taking full time equivalents as a basis and leaving a number of provisions out of consideration in the new series (including activation, educational grants, benefits to children aged under 18 years and housing benefits);
- the *Swedish* dataset is virtually unchanged;
- in *Great Britain* the OECD classified a large number of social assistance beneficiaries as recipients of unemployment or disability benefits, a method which is not followed in the decomposition of the benefit volume performed in this chapter. In 1999 a small change was made to the share in the population of residents below and above the age of 65. As a result, the working age benefit dependency rate in that year is slightly higher than in the OECD calculation;
- in the *USA* the time series for the volume of social assistance benefit was corrected, as a result of which it now comprises all recipients of *Aid to Families with Dependent Children* and *Temporary Assistance to Needy Families* (AFDC/TANF), the *Supplemental Security Income* (SSI) and the *Food Stamp Program*;
- *Australia* was not included in the original Ecorys/NEI dataset, but was added by the OECD. The Veterans Old Age Pensions have been included here, with an estimate being made of the share of beneficiaries younger and older than 65 years (taking into account cohort effects associated with the military conflicts in which the country was involved);
- *Canada* was also added by the OECD. Here, however, a different series was used for the allowances awarded to partners and surviving dependants aged 60-64 years within the context of *Old Age Security*. Moreover, for *Widowed Spouses Allowance*, only those receiving the maximum amount were included, in order to avoid conjunctures. Where lower amounts are paid this benefit is generally supplementary, being received alongside other benefits such as the *Canada/Quebec Pension Plan*.
6 However, to facilitate comparison between countries it was sometimes necessary to deviate from this principle. Ecorys/NEI and OECD did include the Danish unemployment benefits in the figures, even though this is a non-statutory and voluntary insurance operated under the responsibility of the trade unions.
7 For example, supplementary social assistance paid to recipients of retirement pensions are in principle left out of consideration, but where they are paid to workers they have been included.
8 Sweden is an exception, in that social assistance benefits here can be attributed to individuals. It should be noted that single persons and one-parent families are counted correctly in all countries, and that couples – who should be included twice in a person-based statistic – typically comprise only a minority of all social assistance beneficiaries (e.g., in the Netherlands around 2000 only 17% of the recipients lived with a partner).

NOTES

9   OECD (2003a) reports on 16 countries. For the sake of consistency with the country selection in chapters 4 and 6, the volume development in Austria, Ireland, Japan, New Zealand, Slovakia and Spain is left out of consideration here. Because Northern Ireland has different social security legislation for which not all data were available, the volume figures relate to Great Britain and not to the United Kingdom.

10 The maxim *Entia non sunt multiplicanda praeter necessitatem* is attributed to the 14th-century philosopher William of Ockham (though this does not in fact appear in this form in his writings). It has been variously translated as "entities should not be multiplied beyond necessity" or "Shave off [omit] unnecessary entities in explanations", or paraphrased as "Of two equivalent theories or explanations, all other things being equal, the simpler one is to be preferred". *Ockham's Razor*, also known as the *lex parsimoniae* (law of succinctness) or the "principle of simplicity", does not imply that the most parsimonious theory is always the best: if an apparently uncomplicated phenomenon is brought about by an intricate mechanism, simple explanations are simplistic. Ockham's heuristic principle merely recommends that the theory be selected which postulates the fewest entities and assumptions (cf. Spade, 2006).

In modern versions of the maxim, empirical validation is often added as a further condition, and the simplest theory is only considered best if it is in line with empirical observation; cf. "The supreme goal of all theory is to make the irreducible basic elements as simple and as few as possible without having to surrender the adequate representation of a single datum of experience" (Einstein 1934: 165).

Popper (1968 [1959]: 136-145) defines methodological simplicity in terms of the number of logical parameters in a theory. He defends the principle of parsimony not on aesthetic or pragmatic grounds, but by pointing out that theories with fewer parameters tend to be more informative and more general, and can be falsified more easily by observation: "[To explain] why simplicity is so highly desirable […] there is no need for us to assume a 'principle of economy of thought' or anything of the kind. Simple statements, if knowledge is our object, are to be prized more highly than less simple ones *because they tell us more; because their empirical content is greater; and because they are better testable*" (Popper, 1968 [1959]: 142; italics in the original).

11 The relative figures presented here differ from those in the report by Arents et al. (2000), which is mainly concerned with the ratio of the number of benefit recipients to the working population (the inactivity/activity or i/a ratio).

12 The fall which occurs in Australia between 1980 and 1990 is due mainly to the relatively modest growth in the number of pension beneficiaries aged 65 years and older, which lags behind the growth in the population in that age category (+5% and +34%, respectively; see also Eardley et al., 1996: 33).

13 Note that the very sharp increase in the Swedish benefit volume in the early 1990s is not visible because of the measurement years selected in the graph. Between 1990 and 1994, benefit dependency in Sweden rose from 35.0% to 39.7%, before falling back again to 37.2% in 1999.

14 The analysis by the OECD (2003a), which includes more countries, shows a similar ranking of the regime types in 1999 when it comes to benefit dependency among the population of working age. Of special interest are the positions of Austria, Ireland and New Zealand. The Austrian system can be regarded as corporatist (cf. Esping-Andersen, 1990; Soede et al., 2004), and in 1990 and 1999 the level of benefit dependency among the population of working age was lower than that in France and Belgium. Ireland and New Zealand theoretically belong to the liberal type. According to the OECD analysis in both countries the 1980 benefit volume was lower than in the other liberal regimes discussed in this chapter. Subsequently, the growth in Ireland and New Zealand was significantly stronger. As a result, in 1990 and 1999 Ireland has a higher share of benefit recipients than Great Britain, Canada, Australia and the USA. New Zealand, which started from a very low base rate in 1980, ends up slightly above the level of the USA in 1990 and 1999, but below the other liberal countries (OECD 2003a: 226). As mentioned before, the figures presented here are not wholly comparable with those in the 2003 OECD Employment Outlook.

15 In Germany, France, Belgium and the Netherlands the residual category (which is no part of the actual labour force) comprises an average of 25-32% of the population aged 15-64 years between 1980 and 1999, compared with 13-23% for the representatives of the liberal and social-democratic regimes studied here. This is in line with the corporatist philosophy of minimising labour supply.

16 The very high growth figure for Canada in 1982 (13.4%) is largely a result of the strong increase in the number of unemployment benefits, which rises by 44% from around 1 million to 1.5 million benefit years. This is consistent with the increase in the official Canadian unemployment rate, which rose in that year from 7.6% to 11.0%, a much bigger increase than in most other OECD countries. By way of comparison, the unemployment rate in the US also made the biggest leap in the whole of the 1980s in that year, but here it increased from 7.6% to 9.7% (OECD, 1996: A24). The peaks in Australia in 1983 and 1991 are also due to large increases in the number of unemployment benefits (approximately +260,000 benefit years, +60-70%).

17 The classification used here emphasises the *type of arrangement*, and therefore deviates partially from OECD (2003a), which focuses mainly on the composition by *risk*. This especially makes a difference for social assistance provisions to the unemployed and the disabled. The OECD classifies these under the risks 'unemployment' and 'disability', whereas

here they are placed under 'social assistance' (with the exception of early exits via social assistance). Both approaches are valid. The OECD classification is suitable for ascertaining which portion of the total volume is related to specific eventualities. However, when the emphasis is on the residuality and targeting of social security schemes, as here, a risk-based classification may make it difficult to assess the importance of social assistance schemes (the distortion in the 'liberal' direction).

18 Based on this definition, arrangements can often be unambiguously classified as being or not being social assistance benefits, but there are also a few borderline cases. An example is the German *Arbeitslosenhilfe*, characterised by Eardley et al. (1996: 161) as "a hybrid benefit, having some elements of both insurance and assistance". On the one hand it is insurance-like: the benefit is a percentage of previous earnings. On the other hand it has assistance elements: it is funded from general resources and is means-tested, although less strictly than the *Sozialhilfe*. The *Arbeitslosenhilfe* has been classified as an unemployment insurance here, as is customary in Germany, where it is generally regarded as an extension of the *Arbeitslosengeld*. The EU's MISSOC classification also places this benefit under 'Unemployment', though reference is made to the assistance-like elements. The implication is that a proportion of the volume of the German 'Unemployment Insurance' could also have been categorised as social assistance.

In Australia the classification problem is even greater, because virtually all benefits are means-tested and could therefore be classified as social assistance. However, this would not reflect the relatively high exemption threshold, especially in the pensions system. Eardley et al. (1996: 11) comment in this connection: "The means tests in much of the Australian system are primarily designed to exclude fairly well-off individuals, not to concentrate benefits on a residual group. The crucial fact about the Australian system is that there are no social insurance programmes at all. This means it is very hard to define what constitutes social assistance in the Australian (and New Zealand) context. At one extreme, it could be argued that virtually all payments are a form of social assistance, and at the other, that only the Special Benefit going to around one percent of all recipients is social assistance. Either extreme would be misleading, however, since benefits to the unemployed and short-term sick are virtually identical to Income Support in the United Kingdom… It is probably more accurate to see the Australian system either as effectively providing a form of negative income tax for the elderly and some other groups, or as an integrated system of social assistance and partial social insurance. The unemployed and the sick, however, receive payment under conditions similar to those applying under Income Support in the United Kingdom …". On this basis it was decided to equate the Australian social assistance volume with those receiving *Special Benefit* (for people "in severe financial need, for whom no other pension, allowance or other support is available"), the *Parenting Payment-Single* (for lone-parent families with "primary care of at least one child under 16 years of age") and the *Unemployment Benefit* (with the exception of the category 'incapacitated', which has been included under disability benefits). Recipients of the Australian *Sickness Benefit* have been classified under employees' dependency, because entitlement is linked to employment.

19 In a few cases supplementary estimates were made for the early exit arrangements. In Germany, unemployment arrangements are fairly widely used as an exit route. Part of the volume of *Arbeitslosengeld* and *Arbeitslosenhilfe* has therefore been transferred to the exit routes, based on estimates taken from Knuth & Kalina (2002) and Brixy et al. (2002). In Denmark, the *Fortidspension* is an important exit route until age 60, but not all recipients are former employees (widows and the needy are included as well). Estimates of the percentage with an employment history are taken from Bingley et al. (2002). The Swedish *Förtidspension* can also be partially classified under exit routes. Here it has been assumed that former employees consist of recipients who receive an earnings-related supplement (*Allmän Tillagspension*) under this arrangement (information obtained from *Statistika Centralbyrån*). The number of self-employed people was then deducted from this. Finally, it would have been more correct to include the disability volume for former employees and early exits only to the extent that they are aged over 50. However, since the information in the dataset is not broken down by age, this was not possible.

20 Exceptions to these general trends include the fact that the relative volume of exit routes in Australia decreased slightly between 1980 and 1990, as it did in Belgium and the Netherlands between 1990 and 1999. In the USA it remained virtually unchanged throughout the 1990s. In addition, the share of survivor's benefits in Germany and Canada increased between 1980 and 1990; in the latter country it showed virtually no fall in the 1990s. Finally, the relative social assistance volume in Denmark, the Netherlands and the United States was lower in 1999 than in 1990.

21 The comment should be made here that the Belgian social assistance volume may well have been overestimated, because it was not possible to apply a correction for the *Minimex* to take account of partial benefits.

22 Einerhand et al. (1995: 79-90) observe a "sharp and consistent fall" in the German disability volume in the period 1980-1990, which they ascribe to the tightening up of the entry conditions, in particular the introduction of the requirement that disabled persons must have worked for at least three of the last five years in order to be eligible for benefit.

Between May 1984 and December 1988 German employees were able to retire at the age of 58. Until they reached the age of 60, they were paid by their employer and the employment agency, after which they could move on to unemployment benefit. In 1990 only the latter elements can still be observed: people aged 60-64 years who were still on unemployment benefit in that year.

The volume effect of the special transitional arrangement for older unemployed persons in the former German Democratic Republic is also not visible in the data presented here. Benefits paid in the new *Bundesländer* were only included in the series for 1992, and this *Altersübergangsgeld* was abolished on 1 January 1995. As a result, the group of beneficiaries (a maximum 641,000 in 1993) had virtually disappeared by 1999 (553 cases).

23 France has a means-tested benefit for widows aged below 55 years (*Allocation de veuvage*); an earnings-related benefit, which depends on the number of years that the deceased person was insured, for widows aged over 55 years (*Pension de réversion*); and separate arrangements for widows of disabled persons, victims of occupational accidents and military personnel (*Pension d'invalidité de veuve/veuf; Rente de survivant de victime d'accident du travail; Pension militair d'invalidité reversée*). In 1999 an estimated 17% of all survivor's benefits were paid to people aged below 65 years.

24 Leave arrangements in Australia are generally voluntary, private-sector arrangements and are therefore not included here, in line with the methodological principles set out in § 5.2.

25 Compare note 18 in this chapter, which gives more detail on the classification of the Australian social security arrangements.

26 In the 1990s the USA replaced the *Aid to families with dependent children* (AFDC) with *Temporary Assistance to Needy Families* (TANF). The old scheme was operated by individual states; within federal guidelines, the states could determine for themselves who was eligible for the scheme and what level of benefits they would receive. TANF is a federal regulation which sets a time limit of 60 months, stresses work requirements, and gives states latitude in designing specific programmes. This 'system fissure' in US social assistance will be discussed more extensively in the causal analysis.

27 It should be borne in mind that the unemployment benefits paid to people aged 57.5 years and older in the Netherlands are not included under exit routes here because since 1984 this group have not been required to look for work actively (though since 1999 new cases do have to register with an employment agency and accept work offered). This pushes down the volume figure in the category 'employment insurance' considerably: it affected 20% of recipients of this benefit in 1990, and 28% in 1999.

28 The fall in the relative volume in Dutch exit routes between 1990 and 1999 comes about as follows. The absolute number of former employees receiving disability benefit declined, while the take-up of pre-pension and unemployment benefits by people aged 57.5 years and older (no duty to look for work) rose slightly. On balance, the absolute number of these benefits remained virtually constant. However, as the number of employees (part of the denominator) grew strongly at the same time, the relative volume reduced.

The reduction in the take-up of unemployment insurance not only reflects the favourable employment situation in 1999, but also the tightening up of the entry conditions and duration of the *Werkloosheidswet* (Unemployment Insurance Act). The fall in the social assistance volume occurs mainly among unemployment assistance beneficiaries aged below 57.5 years (formerly the target group of the Special Government Scheme for the Unemployed, RWW). An important aspect with regard to employee dependency is the phasing in of financial responsibility for employers for the first year of sickness during the 1990s. Since the number of employees rose at the same time, the relative volume of the sickness benefits decreased.

29 See also the more detailed discussion of the 'small-N problem' in chapter 4.

30 Five determinants in the model were analysed in terms of annual mutations in percentage points. This concerns the participation rates of women and elderly men, the share of the services sector in civil employment, the benefit entitlement index and the pension coverage. These five factors are expressed in their original form as percentages. If percentage changes were to be used for these variables, the annual mutations may be strongly influenced by the base rate (the value in the start year). For example, if the participation rate in a given year rises from 20% to 25%, the percentage change is 25% [((25-20)/20)*100]; but if the activity rate were to rise from 80% to 85%, the percentage change is only 6.25% [((85-80)/80)*100]. Using annual difference scores, the change in both cases is 5 percentage points.

31 This is the case when the values for the dependent variable correlate over time, for example where high defence spending in one year is offset by low spending in the next (negative autocorrelation), or where the prevailing budgetary rules effectively prohibit radical changes from one year to the next (positive autocorrelation). The residual values in such cases are not randomly scattered. In the case of a first-order auto-regressive process this does not affect the parameter estimates, but does render the standard significance tests unusable (Ostrom 1990: 9-14).

32 The price elasticities in demand models in the economic sciences are a familiar example. With a value of less than 1 the demand is described as inelastic: if the price goes down by 10% and demand rises by 5%, the price elasticity is 0.50 and the total revenue reduces (if the price of a good falls from 100 to 90 euros and the demand subsequently goes from 100 to 105 sold units, this implies a fall in revenue from 10,000 to 9,450 euros). With a value greater than 1 the demand is elastic: price falls lead to proportionately larger demand increases and therefore to rising total revenues.

33 The number of lone-parent families in the United States is available annually in a series published by the US Census Bureau, based on the Current Population Survey. The time series for Great Britain is derived from Haskey (1998, 2002), with a few interpolations in the 1980s. For Belgium, the figures on lone-parent families are taken from the *Nationaal Instituut voor de Statistiek*. Census material relates to 1981 and 1991, while register data are available for the end of the 1990s. The intervening years were interpolated. A correction was applied to restrict lone-parent families to the group with children aged under 18 years, based on the 'nuclear families' series (see NIS, 2001).
The German data for the years 1991, 1996 and 2001 are drawn from the series 'Allein Erziehende ohne Partner mit Kindern unter 18 Jahren' from the *Mikrozensus* (Statistisches Bundesamt, 2002). For earlier years, the mutations in a longer time series from the *Bundesinstitut für Bevölkerungsforschung* were used (BiB, 2003).
Algava (2002) reports the number of lone-parent families in France for 1975, 1982, 1990 and 1999. This is a fairly wide definition, however, which also includes households with children living at home aged between 18 and 25 years. A global correction was applied to produce the envisaged population with children younger than 18 years on the basis of the shares listed by Le Gall & Martin (1987) and the website of INSEE (1999 census). The intervening years were interpolated.
For Denmark, figures on the number of lone-parent families are available on an annual basis from *Statistikbanken*. The Swedish figures for 1980, 1985 and 1990 are taken from census data. After 1991, register data are available. The *Statistika Centralbyrån* supplied additional data for 1995, 1996 and 1999. Here again, the missing years were interpolated.
The official Dutch series on lone-parent families does not set an upper age limit for children living at home. For this reason, the time series from the large-scale Income Panel Survey carried out by Statistics Netherlands was used, in which only single adults with children below the age of 18 are counted as lone-parent families. These figures are available for 1977, 1981, 1985 and 1989-1999; the intervening years were interpolated.

34 Estimating the effect of changes in both the number of employed and unemployed persons on the benefit volume would make it possible to assess the impact of both factors separately (i.e., ascertain to what extent employee dependency falls and unemployment benefit dependency rises in times of recession). However, because changes in the volume of employment and unemployment have a strong negative correlation, this would introduce a high degree of multicollinearity in the model. For that reason only the unemployment mutations have been included.

35 Other complications are that the unemployment figures are generally expressed in persons and the volumes in years, which generally turn out lower; and that the official tally of the number of unemployment persons may be more prone to contamination than the registration of benefit volumes. Unemployed people generally have to register with an employment agency, but do not always notify the agency immediately that they have found a job; because the benefits administration has a duty of financial accountability, the receipt of benefits and their legitimacy is generally verified with more precision (though of course registration errors also occur here).

36 For the Netherlands, a correction was applied for trend breaks in the data gathering in 1987 and 1992. In Belgium and the United Kingdom there are no participation figures for the early 1980s. These were estimated on the basis of ILO figures and national sources. For Denmark, use was made of two series on participation rates from *Statistikbanken*.

37 The specification of the effect of developments in gross participation in the model is partial, because changes in the participation rates of young people, men aged 25-54 years and women aged 55-64 years are left out of consideration. In order to limit the number of variables it was decided to investigate the mutations in participation in the two groups with the largest theoretical impact on benefit volume, and for which Esping-Andersen assumes a relationship with the regime type: the exit strategy in the corporatist countries, and the maximisation of the participation rate of women in the social-democratic cluster. For young people aged 15-24 years, the changes in the participation rate between 1980 and 1999 are limited in many countries. According to the OECD *Labour Force Statistics*, they fell slightly in the United Kingdom, the USA, Germany and Denmark (by between 1 and 6 percentage points), and rather more sharply in Belgium, France and Sweden (by between 11 and 17 percentage points). This falling labour participation rate of young people is probably connected to increased duration of education. The labour participation rate of this age group rose strongly in the Netherlands, especially from the middle of the 1990s. This can be explained by reforms in the student grant system, which meant that students began taking up part-time jobs *en masse*. All in all, there is sufficient reason to assume that the changes in the gross participation figures of young people do not weigh very heavily in the development of the benefit volume: the mutations are often limited, and the relationship with the benefit volume is rather inelastic, as benefit dependency of young people tends to be low in all social security schemes, with the exception of unemployment benefits.
The changes in the labour participation rate of women aged 55 years and older are more complex than those for men or women aged 25-54 years, due to generation and period effects crossing each other in this group. Compared with elderly men, the early exit effect is generally more than offset by the fact that in every new cohort more women go to work; France is the only country where the participation rate of older women falls, elsewhere it increases. The increase in the participation rate is generally less marked than among women aged 25-54 years, however, as it is held

back by the growth in early exits. Such antagonistic mutations imply that the changes in the participation of older women have a less marked influence on the total benefit volume than changes in the two selected groups.

The participation rate of men aged 25-54 years is above 90% in all countries, and falls only slightly over time. This is largely attributable to the increase in the number of men living off their own wealth or receiving disability benefit. In so far as the latter volume increase can be traced back to changes in the participation rate (and not to the growth of the labour force), it is ignored in the model.

38 The Danish pension threshold in the period studied was set at 67 years, making it logical to assume that the pension coverage for the over-65s is not complete. In Great Britain it was possible to defer retirement by up to five years (for men until age 70), with an increase in benefit of 7.5% for each year that those concerned continued to work.

39 As an example, if a system constraint means that all people who under the old rules would have been entitled to disability benefit receive social assistance benefit in the new situation, the volume effect of the measure is nil. There may well however be a price effect: since social assistance benefits are generally lower and are dependent on other income and the assets of households, the benefit costs fall. In the short term, this has no impact on the benefit volume.

40 The definition used by the OECD is "the sum of gross value added of all resident producer units (institutional sectors or, alternatively, industries) plus that part (possibly the total) of taxes, less subsidies, on products which is not included in the valuation of output". This definition thus leaves unpaid work and 'green' production factors (unpriced natural and environmental goods) out of consideration.

It should be noted that data on Great Britain were not available for the variables relating to developments in the economy and on the labour market; in these cases UK figures have been used.

41 The benefit entitlement index is the average of the gross replacement rate (gross benefit level divided by previous gross earnings) for three types of household (living alone; with partner, not working; with partner, working) and two pay levels (average and two-thirds of the average) for three unemployment durations (one year; two to three years; four to five years). The benefits concerned are usually unemployment benefits and, where the duration is longer, social assistance for people with a duty to apply for work. Other limitations of the index are:
 - because gross figures are used, the index may suggest an improvement or deterioration in the benefit levels which does not correspond with the actual situation (e.g. if taxes are raised but the net amounts remain the same);
 - the benefit level is only one aspect of the attractiveness of unemployment benefits. The insured population and the eligibility conditions for unemployment benefits are equally important. There are wide differences here between the different countries, with a very large group of potential unemployed people entitled to benefit in Belgium and Denmark, for example, and much lower coverage in the United States and the United Kingdom;
 - when calculating long-term benefit entitlements, no allowance was made for renewed periods of unemployment for people who participate in a job creation programme. This occurs frequently in Scandinavian countries, and may distort the effective replacement rates over a longer period according to the index (where such cases are interpreted as new spells of unemployment; cf. OECD 1994: 175).

42 Not all required data on the independent model variables were available for Canada and Australia in the form of a detailed time series (e.g. data on lone-parent families). The dependent variable is more uncertain than elsewhere as well, because some smaller benefit schemes have not been included (e.g. orphan's benefits in Canada, war widows' pensions in Australia) and the times series relies on estimates to a greater extent (cases of conjuncture, e.g. Quebec Pension Plan with social assistance; several Australian schemes in the 1980s).

43 Single observations may be considered influential if they are distant from other cases in multivariate scatterplots and have high leverage (which typically occurs on the tails of the joint distributions): "the combination of high leverage with an outlier produces substantial influence on the regression coefficients" (Fox 1991: 21). Such influential points cannot be detected by simply inspecting the unexplained part of the dependent variables because "high leverage observations tend to have small residuals – a sensible result, because these observations can force the regression surface to be close to them" (Fox 1991: 25). Influential outliers can be detected by combining two indicators, the leverage or 'hat value', and the Studentised residuals. The indicator for the leverage lies between 0 (no influence on the model) and 1 (determines the model). Fox suggests that values with a leverage greater than $2(k+1)/n$ are suspect (where n is the number of cases and k is the number of independent variables). The Studentised residuals (SR) indicate the degree of discrepancy; these are obtained by leaving out observations of the estimation one at a time. Fox proposes that values outside the range $-2 < SR < 2$ should be regarded as questionable. In the sensitivity analysis performed here, the leverage and Studentised residuals have been plotted, and observations which are above the threshold values on both indicators are regarded as influential. This has been checked against the value on the Cook's Distance measure, which expresses leverage and discrepancy in a single figure; Fox (1991: 34) suggests a cut-off value of $4/(n - k - 1)$. Points which were influential according to both the plot and Cook's distance have been eliminated from the analysis.

44 The German trend break was synchronised for all model variables, so that the data from 1992 onwards relate to the total of the old and new *Bundesländer*.

45 The effects of economic growth on female labour participation, and of the benefit entitlement index on the number of unemployed, are statistically significant at p<0.15.
46 The unexpected negative effect (-0.22) of the number of 50-64 year-olds on the benefit volume arises due to two clusters of observations. In some countries in the early 1980s there was a combination of juvenescence of the potential labour force and a fairly marked increase in the benefit volume, mainly due to the rising number of unemployment and social assistance benefits. In the second half of the 1990s the reverse occurred in many countries. The potential labour force aged as the post-war baby boom generation reached their fifties, and the number of benefits paid to people below retirement age declined as the economy picked up in that period, sometimes reinforced by changes in the social security arrangements. These two clusters of observations lead to the observed negative direct effect. If they are removed the postulated positive relationship between ageing of the potential labour force and the benefit volume is found, though it is weak and not statistically significant.

The anomalous effect of the ageing variable on the number of unemployed is less strong (standardised coefficient -0.08) and not statistically significant. It reflects a combination of juvenescence of the potential labour force and rising unemployment in the early 1980s, and of ageing and falling unemployment in the second half of the 1990s. It was also found, contrary to expectations, that the change in the labour participation of elderly men had a small and insignificant negative effect on the number of unemployed (-0.01). The same applies to the impact of the growth of the services sector on the labour participation of women (-0.03).
47 The number of degrees of freedom (df) is equal to the number of variances and covariances in the observed variables, minus the number of model parameters to be estimated. The model parameters consist of the effects operating between the variables, the (co)variances of the exogenous variables (X) and the (co)variances of the error terms (disturbances) in the endogenous variables (ζ). The latter is the portion of the variance in Y that is not explained by the determinants and that has to be attributed to characteristics not included in the model, chance and measurement errors.

The number of degrees of freedom is important in determining whether the model is able to generate a unique solution. This is connected with the familiar condition that in order to solve an equation, the number of unknowns must be equal to or smaller than the number of equations. If df > 0, the model is over-identified, which implies that the parameters can be estimated and that the fit of the model to the data can be ascertained. If df = 0, the model is exactly identified; this is known as a saturated model, which by definition has a perfect fit. If df < 0, the model is not identified and no unique parameter estimates can be obtained, so that the goodness of fit can also logically not be determined.
48 The χ^2-test can be applied if the sample size is sufficient and variables are normally distributed. The sensitivity of the χ^2-test to sample size was already stressed for bivariate associations by Gulliksen & Tukey (1958: 95-96): "if the sample is small then the χ^2 test will show that the data are 'not significantly different from' quite a wide range of very different theories, while if the sample is large, the χ^2 test will show that the data are significantly different from those expected on a given theory, even though the difference may be so slight as to be negligible or unimportant on other criteria". With regard to the use of this test in determining the goodness of fit in structural modelling, Bentler & Bonnet (1980: 591) comment that: "in very large samples virtually all models that one might want to consider would have to be rejected as statistically untenable. [...] A non-significant chi-square value is desired, and one attempts to infer the validity of the hypothesis of no difference between model and data. [...] This procedure cannot generally be justified, since the chi-square variate v can be made small by simply reducing sample size".
49 The unique effects on the benefit growth rate of changes in the number of pension beneficiaries and in the pension coverage was calculated year-on-year for each country using the following decomposition rule (for a formal proof, compare: De Beer, 2001: 380):

If $C = A \cdot B$ then
$\Delta C = (B' \cdot \Delta A) + (A' \cdot \Delta B)$

where
$A' = (A_{t1} + A_{t2})/2$
$B' = (B_{t1} + B_{t2})/2$

If $\Delta A = 0$ then $A' = A_{t1}$
If $\Delta B = 0$ then $B' = B_{t1}$
50 For assessing the elasticity of changes in the size of the potential labour force with benefit dependency growth, the starting point was the total number of benefits paid in 1980 to the non-working population (retirement benefits paid to people younger than 65 years, social assistance benefits not related to unemployment, survivor's benefits and disability benefits). This was then related to the size of the population outside the labour force in order to obtain the initial benefit fraction. Taking this as a basis, the expected absolute changes in the total benefit volume were then

calculated for the period 1981-1999. The elasticity was determined by relating the percentage changes in this variable to the percentage changes in the size of the potential labour force.

For the impact of changes in the elderly part of the labour force and the number of lone-parent families, an estimate was made for the same four arrangements of the proportion accruing to these two groups in 1980. The absolute changes in the two target groups for the period 1981-1999 were then again multiplied by this benefit fraction, to arrive at an estimate of the absolute influence on the benefit volume. Here also, the elasticity was calculated by relating the estimated relative mutation in the dependent variable to the percentage changes in the independent variable. Note that the mutations in these two independent variables have already been 'cleaned' for the evolution of the total potential labour force, while the series for 50-64 year-olds has also been adjusted for the trend in the number of lone-parent families, and vice versa.

51 If the labour participation of elderly men reduces because they use early exits arrangements, the benefit volume increases, but this is mitigated by their reduced take-up of unemployment and sickness benefit. The same applies for the labour participation of women: if this rises, the take-up of survivor's benefits and social assistance benefits for lone-parent families will fall; against this, there are now more women who could become unemployed, or who could claim sickness and maternity benefits. The net impact of these mutations cannot be deduced in advance, but is an empirical matter.

52 The stepwise hierarchy for the regressions on the benefit growth (after elimination of the influence of the predetermined variables) was: number of unemployed, labour participation of elderly men, female labour participation, and system breaks. The trend in the number of unemployed was first decomposed into demand and supply parts. The effects of economic growth, labour costs and the benefit entitlement index were estimated on the demand side of unemployment; supply effects are assumed to show in the effects of the two participation variables. Regarding the latter, the effect of economic growth was estimated first, followed by the coefficient of the share in the services sector and finally that of the benefit entitlement index.

The method followed to discover influential points has already been described in note 43 of this chapter.

53 This concerns the effect of economic growth on the two participation variables; the effect of the benefit entitlement index on the number of unemployed and the two participation variables; the effect of the share in the services sector on the labour participation rate of women; and the effect of female labour participation on benefit dependency growth (see Annex 2).

54 If the introduction or expansion of, e.g., an early exit scheme means that the benefit volume increases considerably and at the same time the employment rate among older workers falls sharply, it may be that the latter variable already largely explains the effect. While the system change may have had a major impact on benefit growth, it is not problematic in terms of the model because the effect has already been captured.

55 In the us, however, the total effect of the population of working age on the volume is stronger (0.52). This is due in the first place to the low degree of ageing in the USA in the start year. As a result, benefits paid to the group under the age of 65 years weighed more heavily in the total volume, while those paid to the over-65s weighed less heavily than in most other countries – a phenomenon that is also visible in the coefficient for the Netherlands. This manifests itself mainly in the direct effects on the benefit volume. In addition, although the size of the population outside the labour force in the USA in 1980 was comparable with that in other countries (except for the Netherlands and Belgium, where this group accounted for a larger share of the population of working age), the benefit dependency in this group was higher. This was due to the high take-up of social assistance benefits in this group in 1980, while the number of disability benefit recipients was also fairly high, and the relative volume of survivor's pensions and early exits was not particularly low in the USA that year.

56 The variance in the unemployment variable is greater in Sweden, Germany and the Netherlands because in some recession years unemployment increased more strongly than elsewhere. For example, the number of unemployed in the Netherlands (after standardisation) increased by more than 45% in 1981 and 1982. In Germany the figure grew by over 60% in those years. The unemployment figure exploded in Sweden at the start of the 1990s, reaching a growth peak of almost 80% in 1992. Since the variation in the total benefit volume does not show such high peaks – unemployment benefits account for a limited part of the total volume – it is logical that a change of 1% in the number of unemployed in these countries has a comparatively smaller effect on the number of benefits.

57 With the caveat that unemployment only begins to fall once a certain level of economic growth is reached. In the data used here the turning point lies at a GDP growth rate of 2.2-3.1%. This phenomenon was taken into account in determining the estimated influence on the number of benefits by including an intercept in the prediction of the number of unemployed.

58 This is a consequence of the relatively strong impact of the size of the services sector on the labour participation of elderly men in Denmark. Because the services sector in Denmark increased less than elsewhere, the variance in this independent variable is smaller; as the decrease in elderly males' labour participation was fairly moderate, the unstandardised effect becomes rather high.

59 Provided the independent variables are not correlated, the expected values in table 5.3 are multiplicative (cf. Hays 1973: 874). Thus, in the USA the total expected value of changes in the size of the potential labour force, the population aged 50-64 years and the number of lone-parent families is equal to 1.099 * 0.998 * 1.031 = 1.131. This is a legitimate multiplication, because these variables were rendered independent of each other in the model (e.g. the mutations in the number of lone-parent families were corrected for changes in the size of the potential labour force and the share of 50-64 year-olds in it). However, it is not possible to multiply all expected values in this way, because the outcomes of the intervening variables (number of unemployed, labour participation of elderly men, female labour participation) are partly determined by exogenous characteristics, and these expected values therefore are not independent. Given their low explained variance in the model, this is not very problematic for the two participation variables; but the expected value for the number of unemployed on the benefit volume strongly depends on the preceding model variables (especially economic growth). If the expected values of economic growth and the number of unemployed were to be multiplied, the impact on the benefit volume would be seriously overestimated. The over-all prediction of benefit dependency on the bottom row of table 5.3 has therefore been calculated as the multiplication of the expected values resulting from the direct effects in the model. Given the decomposition rule cited earlier, the expected values following from changes in the pension population and pension coverage are additive; this was taken into account in the calculation of the combined impact of all variables.

60 In Germany the labour force aged markedly in the 1980s for two reasons. At the start of the decade, the small cohorts born during the First World War left the labour market as they reached retirement age. Because they were replaced in the 50+ group by the larger cohorts born in the early 1930s, the share of the elderly in the labour force grew. In addition, in the second half of the 1980s the fairly large cohorts born in the years before World War II (1935-1939) reached the age of 50. They replaced the smaller cohorts born after World War I (1920-1924), who were then attaining the age of 65. In the 1990s the share of 50-64 year-olds subsequently remained fairly constant (here again the influence of German reunification is left out of consideration), so that over the period as a whole there is a fairly sharp increase in the elderly population of working age: +16%, versus +5% in France, for example. This latter country underwent a partially different trend. As in Germany, the number of 50-64 year-olds grew strongly at the start of the 1980s as the small World War I cohorts exited from the labour market. However, in the second half of the 1980s there was a relative fall; the 1935-39 cohorts were much smaller in France. This decline continued until the second half of the 1990s, when the French labour force began to age again (cf. Burricand & Roth, 2000).

61 Admittedly, a part of the limited impact of the benefit entitlement index in the country-specific models is due to the fact that this variable was 'at the back of the queue' in the stepwise estimation procedure, after the effects of economic growth and other factors had been allowed for. Yet this cannot fully explain the limited impact of the variable. In the 'free' model across all countries – were no such stepwise procedure was applied –, the direct effects of the benefit entitlement index on the number of unemployed and on the two participation variables were statistically insignificant, and the total standardised effect on benefit dependency amounted to only 0.04 (cf. table 5.1).

62 The *Allocation parentale d'éducation* is a maternity benefit which continues until the youngest child reaches the age of three years. The *Revenu minimum d'insertion* was introduced in 1988 as a general safety net. In addition, France has a number of category-specific social assistance arrangements, often in the form of a supplement to social insurance benefits.

63 The *Invalid Care Allowance* can be paid to people below the retirement age who are responsible for caring for a severely disabled person for more than 35 hours per week. The carer may not be gainfully employed and may also not be in full-time education. The person receiving the care must be in receipt of disability benefit. Eardley et al. (1996: 389) also point out that in Great Britain "some improvements and extensions were made to some benefits over the 1980s (especially for carers)". In 1986 and 1987 the take-up of *Invalid Care Allowance* grew strongly, after which it increased more or less in line with the number of recipients of disability benefit (rather self-evident, as this is a criterion for entitlement). After allowing for this system break, only a small underestimate remains.

There was no need to model other larger system changes in Great Britain (such as the transition to *Income Support* in 1988, the introduction of the *Job Seeker's Allowance* in 1996), as these were not accompanied by abrupt mutations in the take-up of unemployment and social assistance benefits or by large residuals after the estimation procedure. In so far as these system changes had an effect, it is gradual and operates over the longer term; the reforms took place at a time of economic buoyancy, when the number of benefit recipients was already falling.

64 Denmark introduced many changes in the sickness benefits system in the 1980s (cf. Flora, 1986; Einerhand et al., 1995). However, the change in 1983 is the only one which was accompanied by a clear dip in the benefit volume, which cannot be explained by the other model variables. Before 1983 a much higher proportion of the labour force claimed sickness benefit than did so after that year. Part of this difference can perhaps be attributed to a registration effect: from 1983 onwards Denmark switched to an electronic system for the administration of sickness benefits.

The influence of other system changes in Denmark was also explored, such as the introduction of the *Børnepasningsorlov* in 1994 (a leave arrangement for looking after young children to which working people, students and unemployed people affiliated to an unemployment fund were entitled). This boosted the volume by around 35,000 benefits. However, this was largely offset by a substitution in social assistance benefit, which fell sharply in that year. The 'transitional allowance' (*Overgangsydelse*) which was introduced in the 1990s and offers long-term elderly unemployed the opportunity for early retirement also probably had a limited net influence on the total volume. It was introduced in 1992 for 55-59 year-olds; from 1994 onwards 50-54 year-olds could also claim this benefit. Entry to the scheme was ended in 1996, as a result of which only around 20,000 entitled persons remained in 1999.

65 From December 1988, widowers in the Netherlands gained an entitlement to survivor's benefit, leading to a rise in the total benefit volume of half a percent. The impact of this system expansion was largely cancelled out with the introduction of the Surviving Dependants' Act (*Algemene Nabestaandenwet*) in 1996. This limited the target group to older cohorts (born before 1950) and surviving dependants who were looking after a child or who had an incapacity for work of at least 45%. In 1998 an income test was also brought in, whereby higher incomes no longer had an entitlement to the benefit. This led to a volume reduction of 0.9%.

In the 1990s, the Sickness Benefits Act was reformed in two steps. In 1994 the first 2 to 6 weeks were made the responsibility of the employer; this was followed in 1996 by full 'privatisation' of the first year of sickness (with the exception of a safety net scheme for pregnant women, sick employees whose employer has gone bankrupt, etc.). Because the majority of sickness absenteeism is of short duration, the first step had the biggest impact on the benefit volume (-1% versus -0.6%).

The reforms of the disability laws in the 1990s did cause the disability benefit volume to reduce, but some of these recipients ended up on early retirement, social assistance or unemployment benefits. The remainder is largely captured in the model by the effect of the sharp rise in the gross labour participation of elderly men. Other system changes, such as the complicated *Stelselwijziging 1987*, various amendments to the Unemployment Act and the introduction of the new Social Assistance Act (1996) did not lead to sudden mutations in the benefit volume which were not predicted by the model (for a detailed overview see SCP 1998: 421-448).

66 The Social Security Disability Amendments of 1980 led to a fall in the number of disabled employees covered by *Old Age, Survivors and Disability Insurance* (OASDI), among other things because of the introduction of periodic individual reviews (see: SSA, 1986). The Omnibus Budget Reconciliation Act 1981 led to a fall in the number of survivor's benefits because the independent entitlement of 'children of deceased workers' who were no longer in high school or who were below the age of 19 was gradually phased out. This reform package also ended the OASDI disability benefit for partners of disabled workers who were looking after children if the child in question had reached the age of 16 (previously the threshold was 18 years) (cf. Kollmann, 2000). The combined effect of these measures on the total benefit volume in 1999 has been estimated at -2.1%.

67 A further point made by Esping-Andersen refers to the central place occupied by the services sector and female labour supply in the social-democratic regime. He argues that the extensive post-industrial employment, especially in the (semi-)public sector, is one of the conditions for a high labour participation rate of women (in addition to generous sickness benefits and leave facilities). Against this background the theoretical assumption might be that the development of the relative size of the services sector and the labour participation rate of women have a different influence on the 'production' of benefits in Sweden and Denmark than in the other countries. More specifically, it could be assumed that:
  a) an increase in the female labour participation rate of women leads to a higher volume in the social-democratic countries in particular, due to the greater weight of the employment-related benefits (unemployment benefit, sickness pay and leave arrangements).
  b) the growth of the service sector impacts more heavily on female labour participation in the social-democratic countries than elsewhere. This translates into a higher benefit volume.

The model estimates provide little support for these assumptions in the period studied here. In all countries the mutations in female labour participation had a negligible influence on the benefit volume. An increase in the percentage of women working leads to only slight growth in employment-related benefits: the positive relationship via the unemployment variable is not very strong, and is weakened even further by a limited negative direct effect (which indicates a reduction of social assistance and survivor's benefits). The total elasticity of the female labour participation rate with respect to the benefit volume is not highest in Sweden and Denmark (cf. Annex 2). Moreover, the participation of women in Sweden and Denmark increased only slightly between 1980 and 1999 – rather self-evident, given the high base rate. In combination with the low elasticity, this implies that the impact of the changes in female labour participation on the benefit volume is in fact the lowest in the social-democratic countries. The model shows no clear impact of the growth in the services sector via the labour participation of women either; to the extent that this factor is important, it operates via the falling labour participation of older men.

68 The decision to impose the demographic traits of the USA on the other countries is based on a number of considerations. Substantively, it is important that the United States is a relatively pure exponent of one of the regime types,

and is often used as a reference point in international comparisons. Technically, the decisive factor was that the time series for the four demographic variables on which the countries were equalised are of good quality in the USA (little missing data). Belgium, Germany, France and Sweden are less suitable because the time series for lone-parent families lacks detail (a limited number of measurement points). In Denmark these data are better, but not available for the beginning of the 1980s; an added complication is that in the Danish series a correction had to be applied for the 65 and 66 year-olds, which in the period analysed here formed part of the labour force. The demographic data in the Netherlands and Great Britain are of reasonable quality, but there are some missing years, and these two countries are less pure exponents of a particular regime type than the USA.

69 These are the elasticities with respect to the benefit volume of the number of unemployed, the labour participation of women and elderly men, the pension coverage and the system changes, as well as of the two participation variables in relation to unemployment. The values of the independent variables remain the same, except for the unemployment variable (where changes in the values of the predetermining factors lead to a correction of the annual mutations). The elasticities do generally change, however, because allowance has to be made for the changes in potential entitlements and total benefit dependency. An example may clarify this. Suppose that in the year that the *Revenu minimum d'insertion* was introduced in France the potential labour force and the number of lone-parent families have grown as a result of the imposition of US demography. All other things being equal, the system break will have a greater effect on the total French benefit volume: there are more potentially entitled people, and this shows in a higher elasticity. If moreover the total number of benefits in France has dropped as a result of the US demography simulation – e.g. because there are less aged people, leading to a lower take-up of pensions – the elasticity will increase even further: the claims for the new social assistance benefit weigh more heavily in the reduced total volume. It should be noted that the elasticity of the population of working age with the number of unemployed is always assumed to be equal to 1 in the country-specific models, and therefore does not change in the US demography simulation.

70 Yet there is room for discussion on the question of whether the introduction of the *Temporary Aid to Needy Families* in the USA fits in very well with the residual principles of the liberal regime, or whether it is indicative of a 'welfare state in decline' (see the earlier discussion on the composition hypothesis).

71 The relatively low score of Germany within the corporatist group is partly due to technical factors. In the extrapolation based on the original model, 1992 was left out of consideration because in that year the effect of reunification leads to a sharp rise in the absolute number of benefits. However, this also means that not all changes in the size and composition of the population, unemployment and the participation rates of the 'old' *Bundesländer* are reflected in the volume estimate. The effect on the benefit volume of this missing year, leaving aside the issue of reunification, is estimated at 1.7 percentage points at the end of the time series. If this is taken into account, the index for Germany in 1999 turns out to be 127, much closer to the score of Belgium.

72 It is plausible that the strong volume growth in Canada and Australia can partly be attributed to the population increase. The potential labour force in Canada grew by 25% between 1980 and 1999, and in Australia by 33%. In the other countries the increase was between 4% (Belgium) and 20% (USA). The differences are even greater in the population aged over 65. In the period studied, this group grew by 64% in Australia, and in Canada by 66%. The lowest growth among the countries included in the model analysis is 8% (Denmark), the highest (USA) 35%. The number of pensions, which weighs heavily on the total volume, therefore rises much more in Canada and Australia than elsewhere (also compare the difference between figures 5.2 and 5.3). If US demography were to be imposed upon these two countries, the benefit volume would probably grow less strongly.

73 Annex 2 shows that the elasticities with the benefit volume that are related to the over-65s (the effects of the pension population and the pension coverage) fall after the US demography simulation. This is because the weight of pension benefits in the total volume reduces. The elasticities that relate to the younger population are greater, by contrast: the weight of the benefits paid to this growing population group is increased by the simulation.

The elasticity of the number of unemployed relative to the benefit volume generally rises after the imposition of US demography, because:
- there are more unemployed people, since the potential labour force is larger after the simulation. This effect is usually mitigated somewhat by the fall in the share of 50-64 year-olds.
- the number of unemployed people weighs more heavily, because the total volume has generally decreased after imposition of the US demography, due to the smaller pension population.

The Netherlands is an exception with regard to this relationship. The elasticity is virtually stable, because the slight increase in the number of unemployed is matched by a small increase in the benefit volume.

The elasticity of the participation of elderly men in relation to unemployment reduces somewhat in most countries, because after equalisation with US demography there are fewer men aged 50-64 years. This weighs more heavily than the higher unemployment that results from the larger labour force. In the Netherlands and Germany the number of elderly men increases due to the standardisation, however, so that the elasticity grows. In Germany this is due to the relatively small World War I cohorts who are still in the labour force at the start of the 1980s. In the US these cohorts were larger, therefore the simulation leads to more elderly in Germany.

The elasticity of the participation of women relative to unemployment shows hardly any change following the simulation, because the share of this group in the total population is virtually the same in all countries; Germany is the only exception, with a fall in the elasticity.

74 In the presentation of variants 2-4, the growth in the benefit volume has been related to a standardised base rate. This prevents the estimate of the growth – which is the central focus of hypothesis 2 – from being distorted if one country has a low starting level and another a high one (a proportionally equal change weighs more heavily in the former case than the latter).

75 In the US demography variant, a mutation was also assigned to Germany for 1992. This makes the number of observations in this variant the same as for the other countries.

76 These expected values reflect the application of the NAIRU in the initial unemployment rate and the unemployment trend between 1980 and 1999, and the altered effect of the unemployment variable on the benefit volume. In 1980 the NAIRU was well below the cyclical employment level in Great Britain, the USA and Belgium, and substantially higher in Germany and the Netherlands. In the first three countries this leads to a lower base rate for the benefit volume; in the latter two countries it leads to a higher initial level.

In the period 1980-1999 the structural unemployment rate increased strongly in most countries, with the exception of Denmark and the Netherlands (virtually constant) and the US, where it fell. However, the drop in US structural unemployment was less marked than the fall in cyclical unemployment, which *ceteris paribus* leads to a higher 1999 benefit volume. Similarly, in Germany and France the unemployment rate according to the NAIRU rose less strongly than on the basis of the economic cycle, implying less volume growth. In Denmark cyclical unemployment was lower in 1999 than in 1980, while structural unemployment rose. In Great Britain cyclical unemployment remained unchanged between these two measurement years, but the NAIRU increased.

The relationship of mutations in structural unemployment with the benefit volume has been assessed by estimating the effect of changes in the absolute number of structurally unemployed on the incidence of unemployment benefits, social assistance and employee dependency. The USA scores lower than the other countries in this respect (an unstandardised effect of 0.61 versus 0.69-0.79) because comparatively fewer unemployed are in receipt of unemployment benefit. If these coefficients are converted to elasticities, the unstandardised effect of the annual percentage changes in unemployment on the volume turns out to have decreased in the NAIRU variant (0.03-0.10, versus 0.09-0.18 in the US demography simulation); it is lowest in Sweden. Thus, the elimination of the cyclical unemployment component not only smoothes the peaks and troughs in the benefit volume trend, but also implies that changes in unemployment weigh less heavily in all countries.

Combining these factors, the increase of the benefit dependency growth which occurs in the USA and Great Britain in the final simulation mainly results from the combination of a lower base rate and a larger subsequent increase in unemployment; this is not fully compensated for by the reduced elasticity with the benefit volume. The decrease in the estimated growth in benefits in Sweden, Belgium and France mainly stems from the lower elasticity. In France this is reinforced by the smaller unemployment growth according to the NAIRU.

77 In Denmark the impact of the pension variable is somewhat smaller in this variant (+15%).

78 This is a slightly distorted impression, however, because Canada and Australia have not been included in the simulations. In the 1980s the average growth rate in Canada exceeded that of the Netherlands; and over the entire period Canada, France and Australia attain higher averages than the Netherlands.

79 The Danish strategy did not prove to be a recipe for success. Early exits grew strongly in Denmark and benefit dependency among 65 and 66 year-olds rose sharply over time, as indicated by the influence of the pension take-up variable in the baseline model. The strategy was therefore abandoned, and in 2004 the retirement age in Denmark was lowered to 65 years, and as in other countries more attention was given to curbing exits from the labour market below that age, among other things by converting the *Efterløn* into flexible pension arrangements (see e.g. Ebbinghaus, 2003).

80 In practice, the growing impact of the number of lone-parent families is mitigated to some extent by the reform of the American social assistance in the 1990s. This system break is left out of consideration in the fourth variant, however, for reasons of comparability.

81 Seen in absolute terms, the biggest part of the growth in disability benefits in Great Britain occurs with *Invalidity Benefit* and *Disability Assistance*. It should be noted that the latter has been included in the category 'social assistance' in the decomposition analysis in figure 5.6.

Chapter 6

1. The Poor Law Amendment Act of 1834 aroused heated public debate in England at the time. Interestingly enough, the same arguments were used to some extent as in present policy discussions, for example with regard to the positive and negative economic functions of social security (see §3.6.3) and the creation of poverty traps. The 1834 legislative amendment limited access to poor relief on the grounds of utilitarian principles. Largely based upon the work of Bentham (1948 [1789], 1962 [1838-1843]), the idea gained ground that treating the poor too generously would impose a burden on the collectivity, because the incentives for people to look for work, save money or start a business would become too weak. In line with this, the revised English Poor Law aimed to deter the poor from claiming relief. It stipulated that recipients were no longer allowed to live in family dwellings of their own; they were to be incarcerated in work houses, where the conditions should be less favourable than if people went to work for the lowest wage, and where men, women and older children were separated. The administration of poor relief was also revised. The previously autonomous parishes were allowed to work together in unions in order to raise funds to establish new work houses; but if they did, they came under the supervision of the national Poor Law Commission. This eventually led to a centralised bureaucracy, which supervised administration at the local level. The law was later relaxed, partly because the work houses did not offer a suitable solution for mass unemployment during periods of recession.

2. Until the Weimar Republic, social assistance in Germany was provided under the jurisdiction of the individual *Ländern*. The first formal regulation appeared in Bavaria in 1811 (*Allgemeine bayerische Verordnung, das Armenwesen betreffend*). The Prussian *Armenpflegegesetz* from 1842 was more extensive; among other things it stipulated that the state was required in the interests of public welfare to organise the provision of social assistance. The state imposed an obligation on organisations dealing with poverty to provide such help. These organisations, however, were not legally bound to support all poor individuals, as the latter had no right to social assistance. The first national provision in Germany was created in 1924, and consisted of the *Reichsfürsorgepflichtverordnung* and the *Reichsgrundsätze über die Voraussetzungen, Art und Maß der öffentlichen Fürsorge*. The present German law on *Sozialhilfe* dates from 1961, and was fairly radically overhauled in 2005. It still allows great freedom to the federal states (including with regard to the level of social assistance benefits), though coordination does take place on this.

3. Also compare: "Capability is [...] a set of vectors of functionings, reflecting the person's freedom to lead one type of life or another. Just as the so-called 'budget set' in the commodity space represents a person's freedom to buy commodity bundles, the 'capability set' in the functioning space reflects the person's freedom to choose from possible livings" (Sen, 1992: 40). Sen does stress that it is desirable from the point of view of evaluation to consider both aspects: "The evaluative focus of this 'capability approach' can be either on the *realized* functionings (what a person is actually able to do) or on the *capability set* of alternatives she has (her real alternatives). The two give different types of information – the former about the things a person does and the latter about the things a person is substantively free to do" (Sen, 1999: 75).

4. According to Sen, a low income is in itself not an indicator for poverty. In his view, the key is whether the income is inadequate, *given* the personal characteristics and the individual's circumstances: "To have inadequate income is not a matter of having an income level below an externally fixed poverty line, but to have an income below what is adequate for the person in question. In the income space, the relevant concept of poverty has to be *inadequacy* (for generating minimally acceptable capabilities) rather than *lowness* (independent of personal characteristics). A 'poverty line' that ignores individual characteristics altogether cannot do justice to our real concerns underlying poverty, viz. capability failure because of inadequate economic means. Often it will make sense to group individuals into certain categories (related to class, gender, occupational group, employment status, and so on)." (Sen, 1992: 111)

5. Sen (1999: 81-85) distinguishes three ways in which capabilities can be measured directly. In the case of a total comparison, all possible capability vectors are ranked in terms of a particular criterion (such as poverty or inequality). With a partial ranking, a selection of such vectors is ranked, without any attempt at completeness. In a distinguished capability comparison, the issue of ranking and weighting does not apply, because only one capability is considered. If capabilities (or functionings) have to be weighted, Sen (1999: 78-79) argues that the weights should be established via a democratic procedure, though he acknowledges that this can be "extremely messy" compared with a technocratic approach: "In arriving at an 'agreed' range for *social evaluation* (for example, in social studies of poverty), there has to be some kind of reasoned 'consensus' on weights, or at least on a range of weights. This is a 'social choice' exercise, and it requires public discussion and a democratic understanding and acceptance".

6. Nussbaum (2000: 78-80) presents the following list of 'central human functional capabilities': life (being able to live to the end of a human life of normal length; not dying prematurely, or before one's life is so reduced as to be not worth living); bodily health (including being adequately nourished and having adequate shelter); bodily integrity; senses, imagination and thought (including an adequate education); emotion; practical reason; affiliation (love and friendship); connection with other species (nature, animals); play; control over one's environment (including politi-

cal participation, being able to hold property). Nussbaum argues that these capabilities are mutually independent: they are separate components, and shortage of one cannot be compensated by a surplus of another. She also argues that the list of capabilities is universally applicable, a conclusion that she bases on a combination of Aristotelian ethics and her own comparison of the living conditions of women in the USA and India.

This list is not very discriminatory: it encompasses a great many things, and yet the author herself notes that her catalogue is not exhaustive (Nussbaum, 2000: 95). This implies that her interpretation of capabilities goes far beyond the basic deficits which are often associated with poverty or a socially acceptable minimum standard of living. In addition, by regarding them as intrinsically unrelated, she implicitly treats all capabilities as equally important. However, it is questionable whether one would want to give an aspect such as 'being able to laugh, to play, to enjoy recreational activities' (the 'play' capability) the same weight as the physical survival of individuals. Finally, even within prosperous Western societies the 'universal' nature of the list is contestable: a town-dweller who never leaves his city, a butcher, or someone with a phobia of dogs or an allergy to insect bites probably has a very specific interpretation of the capability to 'connect with other species'. As a result, Nussbaum's list is susceptible to the sectarism objection.

7   Dworkin argues in this connection that the 'capabilities' approach is not a 'Third Way', but is a variant of resourcism. He interprets Sen's ideas as follows: "Government should strive to insure that any differences in the degree to which people are not equally capable of realising happiness and other 'complex' achievements should be attributable to differences in their choices and personality and the choices and personality of other people, not to differences in the personal and impersonal resources they command. If we do understand equality of capabilities in that way, it is not an alternative to equality of resources but only the same set of ideals set out in a different vocabulary. Of course people want resources to improve their 'capabilities' for 'functionings' – that is, in order to improve their power to do what they want. But (on this reading of Sen's position) it is their personal and impersonal resources, not the happiness or well-being that they can achieve through their choices, that are matters of egalitarian concern." (Dworkin, 2000: 303). For this reason, Dworkin supports only two fundamentally different approaches in the 'Equality-of-what' discussion: welfarism and resourcism.

8   In the first edition of *A theory of justice* (Rawls, 1971), primary goods are interpreted as things which every rational person would wish to have, regardless of the life they aspire. Rawls was thinking mainly of goods that are distributed by the society in which people live; primary *social* goods, such as basic freedoms, equal opportunities, income and financial assets, and 'self-worth' (in so far as this is determined by social circumstances). 'Natural' primary goods are thus left out of consideration: things such as talents, disabilities, mental states, needs and 'conversion capacities' (i.e. the ability to convert primary goods into what actors want). In the second edition, Rawls opts for a broader definition: "Primary goods are now characterized as what persons need in their status as free and equal citizens, and as normal and fully cooperating members of society over a complete life. Interpersonal comparisons for purposes of political justice are to be made in terms of citizens' index of primary goods and these goods are seen as answering to their needs as citizens as opposed to their preferences and desires" (Rawls, 1999: xiii).

9   In the extensive literature on poverty the terms 'absolute' and 'relative' are used in different ways. In the sociological tradition, and also in the work of Sen, an absolute threshold is one where there is a link to minimal standards (in terms of necessities, capabilities, recourses), regardless of the level achieved by others; a relative poverty line is one where poverty is established relative to the position of a reference group (see e.g. Mack & Lansley, 1985: 16-20). This is the interpretation that is followed here.

In the economic tradition the distinction absolute/relative often refers to the way which a certain poverty line is adjusted over time (the indexation mechanism). A poverty line is then often regarded as relative if it follows the evolution in average prosperity, and as absolute if it does not; or, formulated more precisely: "A relative view is typically one in which the rules for identifying the poor change as (some) other economic conditions change. [...] An 'absolute' notion of poverty is fixed in terms of the relevant spaces at some point in time and, from that time on fixed in 'absolute' terms in some space. If the relevant space is real income, then an absolute view implies a poverty line that is fixed in real terms" (Jäntti & Danziger, 2000: 313).

10 This quotation is followed by a number of characteristic examples of the socio-historical variation in minimum standards (Smith, 1909 [1776]: 541-542): "A linen shirt, for example, is, strictly speaking, not a necessary of life. The Greeks and Romans lived, I suppose, very comfortably, though they had no linen. But in the present times, through the greater part of Europe, a creditable day-labourer would be ashamed to appear in public without a linen shirt, the want of which would be supposed to denote that disgraceful degree of poverty, which, it is presumed, no body can well fall into without extreme bad conduct. Custom, in the same manner, has rendered leather shoes a necessary of life in England. The poorest creditable person of either sex would be ashamed to appear in public without them. In Scotland, custom has rendered them a necessary of life to the lowest order of men; but not to the same order of women, who may, without any discredit, walk about bare-footed. In France, they are necessaries neither to men nor to women; the lowest rank of both sexes appearing there publicly, without any discredit, sometimes in wooden

shoes, and sometimes bare-footed. Under necessaries therefore, I comprehend, not only things which nature, but those things which the established rules of decency have rendered necessary to the lowest rank of people. All other things I call luxuries."

11 Elaborating the argument, Sen notes that a low relative income may be a possible cause of poverty. In wealthier societies, one's relative income position can determine the degree to which a person is able to realise capabilities at a minimum level: "*Relative* deprivation in the space of *incomes* can yield *absolute* deprivation in the space of *capabilities*. In a country that is generally rich, more income may be needed to buy enough commodities to achieve the *same social functioning*, such as 'appearing in public without shame'. The same applies to the capability of 'taking part in the life of the community'. These general social functionings impose commodity requirements that vary with what *others* in the community standardly have" (Sen, 1992: 115-116; see also Sen, 1985: 671).

12 Rawls' definition of the two principles was discussed more extensively in chapter 2.

13 This is not to be equated with freedom of choice in general. The capabilities approach is concerned with the freedom to be able to decide on things that are important for the life one wishes to live; cf. Sen (1992: 63-64): "Some types of choosing can be *valuable* parts of living, giving us reason to treasure them. But there are other choices that we may have no great reason to value, and the *obligatory* requirement to face and deal with them may impose on us losses of time and energy which we may have good reasons to resent. Thus the expansion of some types of choices can reduce our ability to choose life-styles that we might treasure. So the conflict here is not really between our freedom *tout court*, on the one hand, and our advantages, on the other, but primarily between different *types* of freedom – the freedom to exercise active choice over a range of (possibly trivial) options and the freedom to lead a leisured life without the nuisance of constantly having to make trivial choices."

14 This counter-argument was put forward in a different form as early as the 13th century by Thomas Aquinas. In the *Summa Theologica* he asks whether the imposition of taxes by a ruler can be described as robbery. The answer is 'no' as long as it is the collective interest that is being served and no excessive force is being used: "It is no robbery if princes exact from their subjects that which is due to them for the safe-guarding of the common good, even if they use violence in so doing: but if they extort something unduly by means of violence, it is robbery even as burglary is" (Aquinas, 1947 [1265-1274]: *Secunda secundae partis*, question 66, article 8).

15 As well as the more practical point that compensating for self-caused deficits by the government may create a perverse incentive, making it attractive to fall back on the collective provisions and pushing up the costs to high levels; the moral hazard problem (see chapter 3).

16 It is possible to stretch the argument even further: a condition that is considered fair may in fact lead to unfair results. For example, if it is felt that an unemployed benefit claimant should be willing to perform labour, a work test can be attached to benefit entitlements: the unemployed person must be willing to work, and must prove this by applying for sufficient jobs and accepting work offered to him by the benefits agency. Is this condition still fair if the imposed obligation means that unemployed people are forced to perform work in which they are exploited or abused, or which puts them in physical danger? Something similar also applies for the imposition of sanctions on people who do not meet certain conditions. Suppose an unemployed person has not applied for enough jobs, and that their benefit is cut as a result. Is that fair if the income reduction has very negative consequences for dependent family members, who cannot help it if their partner or father has behaved irresponsibly? It is possible to refine the conditions further in order to avoid such unfair outcomes (for example: people must accept work, but not if it threatens their physical or psychological health); however, this increases transaction costs and may well make the rules and their implementation more complex than one would wish.

17 Compare note 6 to this chapter.

18 In New Age metaphysics and its predecessors (theosophy, anthroposophy), dark-brown auras are considered to be indicative of egoism, cold-heartedness, dependence, illness and destruction.

19 In §2.7 it was argued that groups and communities are no collective actors; therefore they cannot act themselves, but only through their individual members. However, they are important as 'carriers' of informal rules: the values, norms, and conventions applying within a group or community. Groups are generally smaller than communities and are characterised by shared activities. Within a community, many groups may coexist.

20 *Quality of life* (QoL) is another notion somewhat related to poverty. Rapley (2003) presents a detailed summary of the various QoL approaches (see also e.g. Noll, 2000; Berger-Schmitt & Noll, 2000). In the objective tradition, the concept refers to the life situation in countries or communities. This is normally measured using general indicators such as life expectancy or leisure time use, or on the basis of specific indicators for fields in which the government can exert an influence (e.g. school dropout, crime rates). There are many examples of such 'states of society', such as the index used by SCP since 1974 to describe the life situation in the Netherlands (Boelhouwer & Roes, 2004; Roes, 2008: 107-113). The recent abundance of life situation indices at the local level (regions, municipalities, neighbourhoods), in which notions such as liveability and safety play a central role, also fits into this approach.

In a second tradition, QoL relates to the life situation that people subjectively perceive. The aggregate of individual opinions is then considered to be indicative for the well-being of the entire population. In the unidimensional variant, the degree of well-being is established by asking people whether they are happy or satisfied with their lives (see e.g. Hagerty & Veenhoven, 2003). The multidimensional variant looks at satisfaction with a large number of areas of life (work, family, relationships, housing, health, material possessions), with the answers being summarised in a general index score.

Theoretically the concept of QoL is much broader than poverty, and can refer to all kinds of areas of life. It is not so much concerned with deficits in terms of minimal necessities, but can also relate to an optimum or maximum. The relationship with the available resources remains indirect. In research practice, poverty is accordingly often treated as only one of the indicators for the broader QoL concept. In objective QoL indices, the poverty rate may then for example be included, while in multidimensional subjective QoL criteria people's satisfaction with their financial situation is taken into account.

Recently, approaches of this type have also become popular among economists; see e.g. Layard (2005). It seems as if these are not entirely aware of the long tradition of QoL research and the 'social indicator movement'. Van Praag & Ferrer-i-Carbonell (2004, 2006) focus the economic QoL approach on poverty. They distinguish a number of domains of subjective poverty, which they measure using satisfaction questions in survey research. In addition to 'financial satisfaction' they use indicators for 'non-monetary poverty': people's satisfaction with their job, their housing, their health, their leisure time use and their environment. These are in turn related to general satisfaction (a survey question about satisfaction or happiness) which can be used to determine poverty lines. In this interpretation, poverty is interpreted so broadly that it becomes synonymous with QoL.

In the approach advocated here, however, theoretically these are two different constructs. From a research perspective, it is more interesting to find suitable operationalisations for both concepts and to investigate their mutual relationships than to equate them with each other. A practical objection to regarding QoL aspects as an indicator for poverty is that people's satisfaction largely depends on their individual characteristics (age, personality, biological characteristics, physical illness, psychological disorders). Material circumstances influence these aspects to only a limited extent: above a certain level of prosperity, in empirical research the correlation between objective QoL criteria and subjective satisfaction indicators is generally weak. Cummins (2000: 62) ascribes this to a process of 'cognitive homeostasis': people have "the ability to maintain normal levels of subjective well-being in the presence of diverse environmental conditions. In other words, within a considerable range of objective living conditions it would be predicted that subjective well-being would be independent".

21 Poverty can also impact on the social differentiation within the community. This occurs whenever poor people are recognisable as a separate social category. Simmel (1971b [1908]) discussed this in some detail in his classic description of the poor as a 'social type' (alongside the stranger, the adventurer, the miser and the spendthrift).

22 This passage on social exclusion is taken in part from Jehoel-Gijsbers & Vrooman (2007); see also Jehoel-Gijsbers (2004).

23 Several other distinctions are mentioned in the literature as well (cf. Jehoel-Gijsbers & Vrooman, 2007). Sometimes poverty is conceived as something static (a given income situation), while social exclusion is regarded as dynamic (a process of lagging behind and a lack of future prospects). However, poverty may very well be analysed in a dynamic sense, as a process of impoverishment (Goodin et al., 1999; Jäntti & Danziger, 2000; Vrooman & Hoff, 2004). It also happens that poverty is considered as a micro-phenomenon (a lack of resources on the individual or household level), whereas social exclusion would derive from a lack of 'community resources', including an inadequate social infrastructure. The latter contextual aspect, however, can in principle also be included in multi-level analyses which relate poverty to various socio-cultural and structural conditions.

24 In this conceptualisation social exclusion is not a trait of certain communities, or, as in the French tradition, a process taking place in society at large. Jehoel-Gijsbers (2004: 33-39) and Jehoel-Gijsbers & Vrooman (2007) argue that such meso- and microlevel aspects better be regarded as context variables. These influence both the process of becoming socially excluded, and the state of social exclusion at the individual level.

25 Cultural non-integration, however, did not empirically scale in the same direction as the three other dimensions, and was therefore omitted from the general index; see also Jehoel-Gijsbers & Vrooman (2007).

26 In the *European Values Study* 1999, for example, respondents were asked whether a just society should guarantee that all citizens were assured that their basic needs would be met. In many European countries approximately 90% of the respondents concurred with this statement. Findings from the *Eurobarometer* 2001 survey point in the same direction for the elderly; 90-97% of respondents felt that every elderly citizen should have access to a guaranteed minimum pension.

Interesting results have also been obtained in experimental philosophy, a field which supplements traditional philosophical methods of contemplation and thought experiments with actual or quasi-experiments (cf. Knobe & Nichols,

2008). Thus, Frohlich et al. (1987) and Michelbach et al. (2003) investigated whether people actually adopt Rawlsian principles of distributive justice if they participate in experiments which simulate the 'original position' and the 'veil of ignorance'. The former authors conclude that the maximin strategy is not the most preferred one; people choose "what Rawls has called an 'intuitionistic' principle which attempts to take into account not only the position of the worst-off individual but the potential expected gain for the rest of society. The overwhelmingly preferred principle is maximizing the average income with a floor constraint" (Frohlich et al., 1987: 1). According to Michelbach et al. (2003: 523) the maximin principle is not widely upheld either: "a considerable minority prioritize [competing allocation principles] consistent with a Rawlsian maximin strategy". Both these experiments were conducted among groups of students, so it is not clear to what extent the results are representative of the views held by the general public.

27 It emerged from the *International Social Survey Programme* (ISSP) that the populations of the countries studied here attach great importance to protecting the elderly. In many countries, over 90% of respondents feel that the government should guarantee this group a decent standard of living. In two liberal welfare states, the USA and Australia, the figure is fractionally lower (87-91%), but here too there is massive support for government responsibility with regard to the living conditions of the elderly. The *Eurobarometer* 2001 survey suggests that the same applies for children: 80% or more believe that this group, too, should be assured of a decent standard of living. The picture is more differentiated when it comes to the unemployed: in most of the European countries studied here, 80-93% of respondents in the ISSP believe that the government should offer this group a decent standard of living; however, the figure is considerably lower in Australia and Canada (around 65%) and the US (48%).

28 Empirical research into the support for the conditioning of rights is scarce. To the extent that it is available, the phrasing of survey questions seems to influence the degree of support considerably. For example, both in the *Eurobarometer* (2001) and in the *European Values Study* (1999), respondents were asked whether unemployed people should have to accept jobs they were offered. In the first case the condition was imposed that the unemployed should have to accept work, even if this was beneath their educational qualifications; in the second case the sanction was mentioned that an unemployed person would lose their benefit entirely if they refused work. It is little surprise that the first formulation received more support in the countries studied here (two-thirds to over three-quarters of respondents) than the second (37-64%).

Perhaps telling is the fact that little support was found in Dutch research for income transfers to which *no conditions at all* are attached. In 2004 only 8% of the Dutch were in favour of such an unconditioned partial basic income (Vrooman et al., 2004: 336-338, 356). Here again, however, the phrasing plays a key role. A much less specific item in the *Eurobarometer* 2001 generated much more support; 68% of the Dutch respondents agreed with the general statement that "the government should provide everyone with a guaranteed basic income". Set against the outcomes of the national survey with detailed questions about the basic income, this is improbably high. It may be that it was made insufficiently clear to the respondents in the *Eurobarometer* precisely what the basic income comprises (e.g. the absence of a duty to apply for jobs), and that they confused it with the existing social safety net in social assistance and old-age pension systems. According to the periodic SCP study *Cultural Changes in the Netherlands*, the latter arrangements often receive a great deal of support (see for instance Roes, 2008: 115-116).

29 Ultimately, whether an operational criterion is a good translation of a theoretical concept cannot be established unambiguously: these are epistemic correlations which cannot be determined objectively. It can however be stipulated that any observable criterion should be a plausible and logical conversion of the intended theoretical concept, given the current status of the scientific debate. For this discussion, see e.g. Dessens & Jansen (1987).

30 Many empirical studies of 'the perception of poverty' do not focus on what meaning people attribute to the concept, but rather on the perceived causes of poverty among the population. Such 'lay attributions of poverty' may consist of laziness, misfortune, social injustice, government policy, the state of the economy, modernisation of society, etc. (see Van Oorschot & Halman, 2000; Gallie & Paugam, 2002; Larsen, 2006; Lepianka, 2007).

31 Over 80% of the Australian respondents felt that poverty is best described by statements such as "Not having enough to buy basics like food, housing or clothing", "Having to struggle to survive each and every day" and "Not having enough money to make ends meet". Only a minority supported a definition in terms of "Not having enough to be able to live decently", "Not having enough to buy what most others take for granted", "Having a lot less than everyone else" and "Not being able to afford any of the good things in life".

32 A fairly large residual group see poverty mainly as an imbalance between income and expenditure. This 'difficulty in making ends meet' category (13%) associates poverty with things such as "being short of money at the end of the month". Strictly speaking, such a criterion would imply that very wealthy households are also to be regarded as poor if they spend too much.

As a corollary to this, there is also a group who link poverty to specific financial problems, such as high fixed costs, problematic debts and payment arrears (2%).

There were also quite a number of respondents who did not give a personal opinion of what they understand by poverty, but referred to official criteria. The largest section of this group (9%) referred to policy norms and to groups that are identified using statutory criteria: people with an income below the minimum wage, single mothers on social security benefit, etc., are poor. A small group (1%) measure poverty using research-based definitions, such as those in the Dutch *Poverty Monitor* (Vrooman et al., 2007a).

There are only a small number of 'poverty deniers': just 2% of respondents believe that genuine poverty does not exist in the Netherlands, but is a phenomenon only to be found in distant countries (Africa is often cited as an example). A limited group (6%) were unable or unwilling to answer the survey question.

33 This classification is concerned with the operational poverty criteria with a scientific basis. It ignores policy-based or 'official' poverty lines, such as the threshold based on 105% of minimum benefits which sometimes is used in Dutch poverty research (see for a critical discussion: Vrooman & Snel, 1999).

34 It was pointed out earlier that in the economic literature on poverty the terms 'absolute' and 'relative' sometimes refer to the method of indexation of the poverty line (whether or not it is corrected for price inflation or the evolution of wealth).

35 Cf. Sen (1981: 26-28): "In identifying the poor for a given set of 'basic needs' it is possible to use at least two alternative methods. One is simply to check the set of people whose actual consumption baskets happen to leave some basic need unsatisfied. This we may call the 'direct method', and it does not involve the use of any income-notion, in particular not that of a poverty-line income. In contrast, in what may be called the 'income method', the first step is to calculate the minimum income π at which all the specified minimum needs are satisfied. The next step is to identify those whose actual income fall below that poverty line [...] The 'direct method' and the 'income method' are not, in fact, two alternative ways of measuring poverty, but represent two alternative *conceptions* of poverty. The direct method identifies those whose actual consumption fails to meet the accepted conventions of minimum needs, while the income method is after spotting those who do not have the ability to meet these needs within the behavioural constraints typical in that community. Both concepts are of some interest on their own in diagnosing poverty in a community, and while the latter is a bit more remote in being dependent on the existence of some typical behaviour pattern in the community, it is also a bit more refined in going beyond the observed choices into the notion of ability".

36 Poverty lines based on consumption or possession are especially useful when the information on the available resources cannot be measured reliably (e.g. because people refuse on a large scale to reveal their income and assets), where there is a large informal economy, a high level of home production, or extensive material support from the social network. In these circumstances, such criteria may be the most suitable proxy indicator for poverty.

37 The median income is the amount whereby one half of the population has a higher income and the other half a lower income. This criterion is more suitable than the average, since it is less susceptible to outliers (very high or very low incomes).

38 A variant of this approach, which is not often used in research, is based not only on the possession of such goods, but also on the ability to replace them if they are irreparably damaged. In this approach, households which possess a washing machine, television, etc., but would not be able to replace it are poor.

39 Townsend (1979: 273) also developed a 'deprivation standard in poverty', which derived from his relative deprivation index. This criterion classifies people as poor if their income is below the level at which deprivation begins to increase disproportionately. At the end of the 1960s, more than a quarter of the British population were identified as poor in this way.

40 Van Praag & Ferrer-i-Carbonell (2004: 295) illustrate this point by assuming that disposable income is distributed in a lognormal way. This is the case when the logarithms of the incomes are normally distributed. The original incomes do not then have the characteristic 'bell shape' of the normal distribution, but are skewed: a relatively large group of people with lower incomes, and a long tail with decreasing frequencies as income rises. Based on this rather common assumption, they show that the poverty rate depends exclusively on the standard deviation, which can be regarded as a measure for income inequality. In practice, incomes are not distributed in a precisely lognormal way; for example, there may be more peaks in the lower segment due to the various social assistance norms for different types of households. Often, however, the lognormal distribution provides a good approximation of the actual income distribution; for the Netherlands, see e.g. Pommer et al. (2003: 51). Neal & Rosen (2000) discuss the theoretical principles underlying the "characteristic skew of earnings distributions", and point out that "observed income distributions tend to have tails that are thicker and longer than the lognormal", and that the Pareto distribution often fits better for the higher incomes.

41 If average income is taken as a reference point instead of median income, this focus problem is greater. In that case the poverty line also moves upwards when the incomes of rich people rise in real terms while those at the lower end of the income distribution remain constant. Jäntti & Danziger (2000: 327) rightly observe that "it does not seem reasonable to let an increase in Queen Elizabeth's income raise the poverty line and our assessment of the extent of poverty in the UK".

42 In Ireland, GDP per head of the population rose by 61% between 1987 and 1997, while inflation during that period stood at 29%. Households at the lower end of the income distribution benefited rather less from economic growth than the higher income groups. The consequence was that relative poverty based on the 60%-norm *increased* - from 29% to 36% -, despite the substantial income gains for the bottom groups (cf. Layte et al., 2000).
In addition, there is a phasing problem with the relative income threshold. It is not necessarily the case that as soon as the median income rises, the poverty line should increase proportionally (and it is probably even less obvious that the poverty line should fall immediately when median income declines).

43 This occurs if there are no observations between 60-100% of median income. Empirically, this rarely occurs. However, it can be tempting for policymakers when using this criterion to keep the median incomes as low as possible and to fix the guaranteed minimum income by law at 61% of the median. This will limit the observed relative poverty rate and minimise social assistance expenditure. Of course, such an approach does not rule out the possibility that a large group of people with an income above the relative threshold lack the means to meet the expenses that are unavoidable within their community.

44 A possible alternative is to base the threshold on 60% of the median income across all EU member states. While this has the obvious advantage that poverty rates are measured by the same yardstick in all countries, it does not solve some of the other problems. Such a relative EU-wide poverty line is also 'fetishistic', because no link is made to the living standard people can actually attain with 60% of the median EU income. In the richest countries the threshold amount is likely to be low, thus leading to low poverty rates; but it may be that the amount is not sufficient to pay all the indispensable costs for a considerable part of the population. By contrast, in the less prosperous member states 60% of median EU income may imply a level which the middle classes find hard to attain, hence a very high poverty rate; but such a threshold could be well above the level that is actually needed for unavoidable expenses in these countries.
A further complication is that the poverty rate in each member state becomes dependent on prosperity growth elsewhere. If the income distribution remains constant in all countries, but Germany experiences a sharper increase in median income than the other EU member states, poverty rates in the latter will rise (this is exacerbated by Germany's large share in the total EU population). And if Turkey were to join the EU, the median income across member states would decline, leading to decreasing poverty rates.

45 For most of these 11 countries, all six measurement points in the ECHP or LIS were available, with the exception of Denmark and Belgium (no observations in the early 1980s) and Canada (no observation after 2000).

46 The researcher can attempt to resolve this by refining the questionnaire: a different formulation of the items (a hot meal rather than meat every other day), follow-up questions which assess whether people do not have things or are unable to perform certain activities as a result of their financial deficits. It cannot however be taken for granted that this will produce a more reliable picture; e.g., it may be that respondents who cannot afford certain items will state they prefer to do without, in order to hide their poverty. And however meticulous, honest and competent the researcher may be, discretionary elements will always remain in this approach.

47 This problem of establishing the threshold value also occurs when the index is not determined as a sum score of the individual items, but via factor analysis or an optimal scaling technique. A choice can then be made for a statistical criterion, e.g. by classing all respondents with a factor score with one standard deviation from the average as poor. Whilst such a limit may appear more sophisticated, it is still arbitrary. Only when it is demonstrated that people below that specific threshold value experience more material hardship (home evictions, etc.), feel poor *en masse*, etc., does it acquire any substantive meaning.

48 The 'get along-question' reads as follows: "What is the smallest amount of money a family of four (husband, wife, and two children) needs each week to get along in this community"?

49 The central idea with the subjective poverty line is that the answers to the MIQ correlate with actual income levels and household size: the greater these are, the higher the amount that respondents say they need. Goedhart et al. (1977: 514) assume that changes in income levels tend to spark off a process of adaptation. If someone has a relatively high income which falls, they will adjust downwards their norm for the required minimum in the MIQ as they become accustomed to the lower income. The reverse applies for someone with a lower income whose earnings increase: they begin seeing the newly attained standard of living as normal, and this will be reflected in a higher amount in response to the MIQ. There is however one point where this 'misperception' does not occur, and that indicates where the poverty line lies. This point can be interpreted as the level at which people generally feel that they are not able to make ends meet. Technically, this is estimated using the regression formula:

$$\log Y_{min} = \alpha_0 + \alpha_1 \log Y + \alpha_2 \log Fs$$

where Y_{min} is the answer to the MIQ, Y is the actual income and Fs is the size of the household. The amounts cited in response to the MIQ and the actual income are logarithmically transformed to obtain a linear relationship. By equating Y_{min} and Y, poverty lines are obtained for different household types (see e.g. Van den Bosch, 2001: 90-91). In a more elaborate variant, the SPL is calculated by also taking into account the average income and household composition in a reference group (Kapteyn et al., 1988; Van den Bosch, 2001).

50   The most frequently used version of the Income Evaluation Question is:
Please try to indicate what you consider to be an appropriate amount of money for each of the following cases. Under my (our) conditions I would call an after-tax income per week/month/year (please encircle the appropriate period) of:
about ... very bad
about ... bad
about ... insufficient
about ... sufficient
about ... good
about ... very good

These response categories are numerically mapped onto a scale ranging from 0 ('very bad') to 1 ('very good'). In the numerical transformation, the verbal qualifications are regarded as the midpoints of six intervals (0 - $^1/_6$, $^1/_6$ - $^2/_6$, etc.). 'Bad' thus corresponds with 0.250, 'insufficient' with 0.417, and 'sufficient' with 0.583 (see Van den Bosch, 2001: 93-98). A welfare level of 0.4 (between 'bad' and 'insufficient') or 0.5 (just below 'sufficient') is often regarded as indicative for a situation of poverty. The Leyden Poverty Line (LPL), like the SPL, is established by estimating a regression equation across all respondents, whereby the amounts corresponding to various welfare levels are related to the household composition and the actual income level.

51   There are two main variants of the Income Satisfaction Question. The first runs "With your current household income, how can you make ends meet?" and generally offers response categories ranging from 'very easy' to 'very difficult'. The second formulation is more general: "How do you feel about your standard of living/income?" and is generally evaluated on a 5 or 7-point scale (ranging from 'delighted' to 'terrible').

52   The Minimum Spending Question reads "In your opinion, how much would you have to spend each month (/year) in order to provide the basic necessities for your family? By basic necessities I mean barely adequate food, shelter, clothing and other essential items required for daily living". Another option is not to compare the poverty line obtained in this way against the actual outlays, but to set it against the income of the respondents. This produces a 'subjective budget method' which falls into the same category as the Subjective Poverty Line (SPL) and the Leyden Poverty Line (LPL). This approach is not ideal, however, because people can call on other sources to fund expenditure (for example, people may have put money aside in advance to cover school and tuition fees for their children). Garner & Short (2005: 6) accordingly conclude that, "comparing expenditure outlays is likely the appropriate resource measure to compare to a MSQ threshold".

53   As stated, when using the SPL and LPL methods, a correction is sometimes applied for reference group effects, for example by level of education. Although this introduces 'relative' elements into the assessment of poverty, that is different from deriving the threshold *in principle* from the subjectively required income deficit. The SPL and LPL indicate the absolute income level at which people have difficulty making ends meet or which they qualify as bad or insufficient; and the MIQ and IEQ do not ask about the income deficit of this group compared to others.

54   With the income ruler method, survey respondents are asked to estimate the incomes of a number of occupational groups and categories of benefit recipients, and then to indicate how high they believe those incomes should be. A similar question was included in several waves of the International Social Survey Programme (ISSP); it was used in §4.3 for the analysis of informal social security rules. The ratio between the average desirable income of the group with the lowest preferred level (usually social assistance benefit recipients) and that of a common occupation, such as a policeman or a self-employed plumber, can be used to define a means-based subjective-relative poverty line. For the Netherlands in the 1980s, Szirmai (1986: 107) arrived at a ratio of 0.40-0.46%, while according to Hermkens & Van Wijngaarden (1987: 102) the figure was 0.45-0.49%. To date, however, such a method has not been used to determine the percentage of poor people.

55   This is because in prosperous societies there is usually a strong correlation between the percentage of people who consider a good or service indispensable and the rates of possession and consumption. There are only a few exceptions to this rule. The percentage of people who are able to save is often substantially lower than the share who consider this necessary. The reverse occurs with the items "new, not second hand clothes" and "a roast meat joint or its equivalent once a week": the share of people who consider this necessary is much lower than the percentage who actually have it (Van den Bosch, 2001: 50-51, 58).

56   Apart from the issue of its validity, the Minimum Spending Question suffers from similar reliability problems as income-based survey methods. However, cognitive psychological research has shown that people are able to indicate fairly accurately which expenses are necessary for them, including situations where they have to economise. In this

sense, this type of method may be somewhat more reliable than subjective methods based on income assessments (Stinson, 1997, 1998). The strict nature of the question also means that the poverty rate measured via the MSQ is generally lower than via the MIQ.

57 Mack & Lansley's method based on consensual necessities has also been applied in a number of other countries; Van den Bosch (2001: 49-86) discusses studies from Denmark, Ireland and Belgium. The obvious advantage of this approach is that it seeks its basis in the perception of poverty among the population, even though the input (the list of goods and services that respondents have to assess) is provided by experts. Moreover, in all countries studied the same goods consistently turn out to be considered necessary by a majority, and there are no large 'vertical' differences between social groups in the assessment of the basic necessities: it is not the case that poor and rich people, taxpayers and benefit claimants have a completely different view of necessities – something which would make it difficult to construct a general criterion for measuring poverty using this method.

Yet here again operationalisation problems arise. In the first place, there is no clear empirical dividing line between goods that are indispensable and those that can be done without. Mack & Lansley posited a threshold where an item was defined as a consensual necessity if at least 50% of the respondents regarded it as indispensable. This 'democratic' threshold appears to be on the low side, however: in order to be able to speak of a consensus, more is probably required than a simple numerical majority. However, if a stricter threshold is taken (e.g. 85%), few consensual necessities remain, while with a lower threshold (15%) few items are considered superfluous. For the majority of the items, therefore, it is not possible to speak of an evident consensus.

Furthermore, even while there is no great variation between social strata, a number of 'horizontal' differences, between demographic groups, do occur. In most studies the evaluation of necessities varies between age groups and household types. This makes it difficult to construct a universally applicable consensual standard. Moreover, the correlations between the various necessities are not high: they do not form a clear and reliable scale. Van den Bosch (2001) does not consider the latter a problem; in his view no underlying dimension 'degree of indispensability' is assumed on which respondents must score consistently. Yet his final conclusion is negative: "there is not a well-defined public consensus on the minimum standard of living. The reason is not so much that there are strong disagreements about this matter, but rather that individuals are apparently uncertain about the necessity of a range of items for modern living. Secondly, depending on a person's circumstances and characteristics, perceptions of necessities differ, indicating that the minimum standard of living is composed of different items for different groups in society" (Van den Bosch, 2001: 83). These reliability issues make the method ill-suited for measuring poverty.

58 In principle, the direct measurement of an informed consensus makes the consensual budget method an interesting approach. Through the explication of meanings and the subsequent discussion, panel members agree on a shared conceptualisation of poverty and translate this into a joint operational poverty line. There are however also a number of disadvantages, as a result of which consensual budget standards have to date been used to only a limited extent. As with expert budget standards, this approach is very labour-intensive, and it is therefore difficult with this method, too, to develop and update the standard for a large number of different household types. In addition, the 'citizen's panel' should reflect the assessment of a wide cross-section of the population and contain more than just a small group of experts as in the traditional budget approach. But there are limits to this: the consensual method can never be based on as many observations as a traditional representative survey. This can cause the budget to become dependent on chance characteristics of the selected panel members – not only in terms of their moral opinions and cognitive frames, but also in terms of differences between the participants as regards their financial knowledge, budgeting skills and their ability to persuade others of their opinion. Finally, it is also possible that the interaction does not lead to a shared consensus (though it has to be said that in the studies carried out using this method to date that consensus has been fairly strong). In that case, it may be that there is no unanimity on the definition of poverty in the population at large, as already suggested by Walker (1987: 222): "failure to reach a consensus among a relatively small number of people must seriously call into question the likelihood of achieving consensus among the many". However, a lack of consensus in the citizen's panel may also be due to its coincidental composition, or rather accidental aspects of the interaction process. Because of these objections, it is questionable whether the consensual budget method in itself can generate a reliable poverty line, though at the very least it is an interesting supplementary indicator which deserves wider testing.

59 Minkman & Van Praag (1997) posit that the answers to the IEQ are 'calibrated', whereas those to the MIQ are not. They suppose that the precision in determining the poverty threshold is increased, because the respondents have to enter amounts for a number of hierarchically arranged verbal qualifications. In practice, however, it is found that pairs such as 'good/bad' and 'sufficient/insufficient' are not placed on a single dimension by everyone: "For some, these two scales ask very different questions: 'good/bad' is seen as a judgment about the quality of life, and 'sufficient/insufficient' as a judgment about what is absolutely necessary for survival. A 'very bad' income might yet be 'sufficient for survival' (Garner et al., 1998: 45).

60 Garner et al. (1998: 45) observe the following in this connection: "Original dollar estimates were often much too low, and some respondents had real trouble figuring out what would be sufficient for survival, especially if they never had experienced hardship. Some proved totally unable to generate dollar amounts, and others did so only in very gross terms, often in increments of $1,000. The process of determining expenses is not always dependent upon the income level or family structure of the respondent, but may hinge upon knowledge of the family's finances. If the respondent happened to be the designated bill payer in a household, lists of expenses and dollar estimates were likely to be different from those of family members who did not pay bills. In one family, for instance, the bill payer's estimate of monthly expenses was twice that of the spouse who did not pay the bills".

61 Van den Bosch (2001: 297-298) points out that in international comparative research generally various organisations are responsible for the fieldwork for surveys incorporating the MIQ and the IEQ. This leads to differences in questionnaire design and interview procedures and makes it difficult to ensure that the phrasing of the questions in the surveys is identical. The most important factor, however, are the language and cultural differences: "Assuming that 'making ends meet', 'de eindjes aan elkaar knopen' (Dutch) and 'joindre les deux bouts' (French) have the same meaning in standard-of-living terms seems rather heroic. Of course, they will mean roughly the same thing in all countries. The question is at which point roughly becomes too rough. The finding that in 1985 the SPL in The Netherlands was almost 20 percent below the Belgian SPL, even though median disposable household income in the Netherlands was higher, producing a 16 percent point difference in low income rates, suggests that that point sometimes is exceeded". For the SPL, this author reports an increase in the Italian poverty rate from 9% to 33% between 1979 and 1987, whereas in Belgium the poverty rate rose from 4% to 25% in the period 1979-1985. Based on the LPL, the poverty rate in the Netherlands increased from 16% in 1979 to 29% in 1985 and 36% in 1986, which "would seem to indicate an ongoing and accelerating social disaster [...] or a very strong rise in aspiration levels" (cf. Van den Bosch, 2001: 104, 106).

62 The LPL generally produces higher poverty rates than the SPL. Van den Bosch (2001: 157-158) reports on ten studies in which the SPL is compared with the LPL at a welfare level of 0.4 (cf. note 50 to this chapter). In eight cases, the poverty rate according to the SPL is lower (by more than 2% on average). Comparison with the LPL at a welfare level of 0.5, which logically detects more poverty, is possible for 12 countries. With two exceptions, the poverty rate according to the SPL is then lower than according to the LPL (by an average of 9%).

63 Booth (1902 [1889]) divided the population of London into eight groups based on the level and the regularity of their income, their labour market position, their living circumstances and their behaviour. He regarded the lowest four classes (according to his estimate 31% of the population) as poor, by which he meant that people were living "under a struggle to obtain the necessities of life and make both ends meet" or "in a state of chronic want" (Booth, 1902 [1889]: 33-62).

Seebohm Rowntree (1901: 86-118) defined a line for 'primary poverty' based on the necessary outlays for food, housing, clothing, lighting, fuel and other "minimum necessaries for the maintenance of merely physical efficiency". His threshold for 'secondary poverty' referred to people who in principle had sufficient income to realise the physical efficiency that was desirable for the factory workers of York, "were it not that some portion of it was absorbed by other expenditure, either useful or wasteful". Using this method – and based on one of the first ever large-scale empirical surveys (more than 11,000 households) – Seebohm Rowntree estimated that 28% of the population of York were poor, and that roughly a third of these people were living below the primary poverty line. He stressed that this criterion referred to a very frugal way of life, with no scope whatsoever for discretionary expenditure: "And let us clearly understand what 'merely physical efficiency' means. A family living upon the scale allowed for in this estimate must never spend a penny on railway fare or omnibus. They must never go into the country unless they walk. They must never purchase a halfpenny newspaper or spend a penny to buy a ticket for a popular concert. They must write no letters to absent children, for they cannot afford to pay the postage. They must never contribute anything to their church or chapel, or give any help to a neighbour which costs them money. They cannot save, nor can they join sick club or Trade Union, because they cannot pay the necessary subscriptions. The children must have no pocket money for dolls, marbles or sweets. The father must smoke no tobacco, and must drink no beer. The mother must never buy any pretty clothes for herself or for her children, the character of the family wardrobe as for the family diet being governed by the regulation, 'Nothing must be bought but that which is absolutely necessary for the maintenance of physical health, and what is bought must be of the plainest and most economical description'. Should a child fall ill, it must be attended by the parish doctor; should it die, it must be buried by the parish. Finally, the wage-earner must never be absent from his work for a single day. If any of these conditions are broken, the extra expenditure involved is met, *and can only be met*, by limiting the diet; or, in other words, by sacrificing physical efficiency" (Seebown Rowntree, 1901: 133-134).

64 Doyal & Gough (1991) developed a theory of universal human needs they considered to be objective. They posit that each actor has two universal basic needs: 'physical health' and 'personal autonomy'. This follows from their neo-

Kantian argumentation that individuals can only act (and in this sense 'exist') if they are physically and mentally capable of doing so. The former means that their physical survival must be guaranteed, the latter that people must have a degree of freedom to make choices: "since physical survival and personal autonomy are the preconditions for any individual action in any culture, they constitute the most basic human needs – those which must be satisfied to some degree before actors can effectively participate in their form of life to achieve any other valued goals" (Doyal & Gough, 1991: 54). In addition, they identify 11 'intermediate needs', which the actor must satisfy at least a minimal level in order to meet the two basic needs. The requirements for physical health are: adequate nutritional food and water; adequate protective housing; a non-hazardous work environment; a non-hazardous physical environment; and appropriate health care. And to ensure personal autonomy, six intermediate needs must be satisfied: security in childhood; significant primary relationships; physical security; economic security; safe birth control and child-bearing; and basic education. Doyal & Gough (1991: 210-212) regard poverty as an aspect of economic security. This would seem to be too narrow an interpretation: things such as enough food, suitable housing and the ability to afford basic healthcare and educational opportunities for children are things that prosperous societies will readily want to include in a definition of poverty. If actors really have to meet all these intermediate needs to a certain degree, it would be necessary to include the monetarisable part in the poverty line. There is then a clear risk that this will be on the high side.

65 According to Sarlo (2001: 9-10), the *non-sustainable subsistence level* refers to a living standard "which is unhealthy and will compromise long-term physical well-being. It will lead to illness and an early death. Non-sustainable subsistence implies having food that is just enough to keep one alive (for the time being), likely obtained from charitable sources (e.g. food bank or soup kitchen), and, if purchased, the least expensive foods at grocery stores (bread, rice, potatoes and reduced items). Shelter is likely to be inadequate, unhealthy, or non-existent. People who are intermittently or usually homeless would be in this category. Clothing and any other possessions are likely to be very limited, donated from charitable sources, and often inadequate for wide changes in weather". Sarlo estimates that a single Canadian in 2000 needed approximately CAD 2,000-4,000 per year for this (or the equivalent in donated goods).

At the *sustainable subsistence level* people can "survive day-to-day in a way that does not compromise their long-term physical health. The food would be nutritious and balanced and fulfil all requirements of healthy eating. Shelter may be Spartan, crowded, and inexpensive but not unhealthy. It may be a room in a house or in an institution or it may be accommodation shared with two or more people. Clothing, whether obtained from charitable sources or bough at a store, is just adequate to meet seasonal requirements". Some migrants can be placed in this group (new arrivals and illegal immigrants), but also people living in certain institutions (prisons and care homes, depending on their living circumstances) and members of religious orders who have taken a vow of poverty. It is estimated that this requires an amount of CAD 5,000-6,000 for a single person.

Sarlo regards the *basic needs level* as the central criterion for measuring poverty. This living standard "includes food providing a nutritious diet that satisfies all norms of energy, balance and palatability and that is purchased in groceries stores using no savings strategies; shelter that consists of apartment accommodation that is not subsidized and is appropriate in size for the family and includes all the usual furnishings and appliances; clothing purchased new at popular department stores; a telephone with a local telephone service; all necessary household supplies; household insurance; laundry requirements; public transportation; personal care; any out-of-pocket health care needs; and a small amount for school supplies and correspondence". Sarlo estimates the budget required by a single person at CAD 8,900 per year.

At the *comfort level*, items are also included which are not necessary at the minimum level but which are desirable. They include "a range of items that many consider to be amenities: recreation expenditures, long-distance telephone, ability to give gifts, travel, tobacco and alcohol, cable television, meals in restaurants, and expenses for pets". To achieve this level, a single person in 2000 needed CAD 12,000-16,000.

66 The prescriptive method discussed here needs to be distinguished from the descriptive method. The latter merely aims to describe the actual patterns of expenditure of different household types, of which many national statistics offices regularly publish summaries (based on household expenditure survey data). In the prescriptive method, empirical differences in expenditure patterns are taken into account, but it is ultimately the researcher who determines the budget standard. This normative character was one of the reasons for the American Bureau of Labor Statistics to stop compiling prescriptive budgets at the end of the 1980s, bringing to an end a time series that began in 1908/1909 (Johnson et al., 2001).

67 With poverty lines based on food ratios, the necessities are interpreted very narrowly: as long as the proportion of food remains constant, the poverty rate does not change, even if things such as rent or electricity prices rise sharply. In addition, preferences may distort the picture with this criterion: if people with a high income eat in expensive restaurants every day, they may be classed among the poor on the grounds of their high food ratio. The food ratio criterion can also prove to be unstable over time if large price changes occur (failed harvests, price falls due to the

elimination of import duties). Moreover, no allowance is made for changes in living standards. If the level of prosperity rises, the food ratio will fall, but the norm for what is the minimum necessary is also likely to increase. The food ratios threshold then leads to an overestimation of the decline in poverty because it takes no account of the changing nature of the necessities.

If the fixed costs ratio is taken as a basis, diseconomies of scale are a distorting factor. Single persons generally have high fixed costs because they cannot share them, and according to this criterion a comparatively large share of this group tends to be classed as poor. Here again, preferences can be problematic: if people on higher incomes voluntarily choose to live in expensive housing, their fixed costs ratio rises and they may end up below the poverty line.

A similar complication arises with the total expenses approach: households with very high incomes are regarded as poor in this approach as soon as they spend more than they earn. Moreover, the poverty rate depends on the financial behaviour of those concerned; if two people have the same means, but one of them does not mind being overdrawn while the other does everything in their power to ensure that they do not get into debt, the first person will be classed as poor while the second will not. This implies that a deteriorating payment morality will lead to an increase in the observed poverty using this criterion. Finally, dissaving need not always be an indication of poverty. There are for example pensioners who deliberately address the private assets they have built up. It appears far-fetched to regard such 'private dissavers' as poor, but not people who have built up assets via a pension fund and receive periodic payments from it.

This is not to say that the information provided by food ratios, fixed costs and total expenditure is not relevant, but only that these are not very suitable criteria for measuring poverty. Even so, if the aim is to map out the degree of poverty, it is for example useful to investigate when debts become precarious, and which types of debt are considered the most problematic from the perspective of poverty. In the Dutch *Poverty Monitor* (Vrooman & Hoff, 2004; Vrooman et al., 2007a) this is used as a supplementary indicator. Following the reasoning of Jehoel-Gijsbers (2005), the 'survival debts' (made in order to buy indispensable items) probably imply a greater underlying poverty problem than 'adaptation debts' (which occur when people experience a sudden income deterioration, e.g. because they lose their job or as a result of divorce), 'overspending debts' (due to the purchase of luxuries people cannot afford) or debts ensuing from 'handicapping tastes' (such as drug addiction).

68 Two types of budget are commonly used at international level. The first focuses on essential necessities, and is referred to as a 'low cost' or 'basic needs' budget. The second type is higher, but is still below the level at which public opinion regards people as living 'in luxury'. This is described using terms such as 'modest but adequate' or 'some comfort'. In 1909, the US Bureau of Labor Statistics introduced two (descriptive) budget standards based on a study of the living conditions of cotton-mill workers, which they named 'a minimum standard of bare essentials' and 'a fair standard of living'. The same Bureau published a 'modest but adequate' budget standard for an urban working family in 1947 (Johnson et al., 2001). More recent examples include the 'low cost but acceptable' and 'modest but adequate' budgets that are compiled on a regular basis by the Family Budget Unit of the University of York for various types of families (see http:// www.york.ac.uk/res/fbu/publications.htm). Sarlo (2001) notes the 'basic needs poverty line' that has been applied in Canada. In Australia, the Social Policy Research Centre developed both types of budget. Here, the 'low-cost budget standard' has been described as "a level of living which may mean frugal and careful management of resources but would still allow social and economic participation consistent with community standards and enable the individual to fulfil community expectations in the workplace, at home and in the community, corresponding to a standard of living which is achievable at about one-half of the median standard". The 'modest but adequate budget standard' is fairly high in this study, being defined as "one which affords full opportunity to participate in contemporary Australian society and the basic options it offers ... lying between the standards of survival and decency and those of luxury as these are commonly understood ... (falling) somewhere around the median standard of living experienced within the Australian community as a whole" (Saunders et al., 1998: 438). The Australian study also refers to budget approaches in the Scandinavian countries, Germany, New Zealand, Hong Kong and Malaysia. Often these are descriptive, and they are not always used for assessing poverty. In the Netherlands, the National Institute for Family Finance Information compiles similar budgets (Nibud, 2008); and for Belgium, see for instance Van den Bosch (1997).

69 Soede (2006: 65-71) also provides the reference budgets for couples with and without children. Since the implicit equivalence scales in the Nibud method are not the same as those published by Statistics Netherlands (Siermann et al., 2004), this leads to slightly different results. Soede also discusses a number of other reference budgets, which for example incorporate a more generous clothing allowance and the costs of smoking.

70 The indexation mechanism is derived from the recommendations by Citro & Michael (1995), but the initial threshold amounts and the equivalence scales are not. This does not alter the fact that the report by the US National Academy of Sciences has been an important source of inspiration for the SCP poverty line. The NAS report was compiled in a bid to find a solution to the shortcomings of the official poverty threshold used in the US, introduced at the end of the 1960s

as part of the 'War on Poverty' (see Fisher 1992, 1997). The US poverty threshold is based on the work of the economist Orshansky (1963, 1965). Budget research at the time had shown that families of three or more people spend roughly a third of the total household budget on food. Based on this fact, the poverty threshold was determined as a generalised food ratio: a sparse food budget for this family type was multiplied by a factor of three. To allow for diseconomies of scale, it was decided to use a slightly higher multiplier (3.7) for couples; and the poverty line for single persons was set at 80% of the budget for couples. Using this technique, Orshansky defined a large number (more than a hundred) of different poverty thresholds, which depended on the size and composition of the household.

One objection to the official American poverty line is that its basis has remained unchanged since the 1960s, whereas consumption patterns have changed considerably. In the middle of the 1990s, an average family was spending only a seventh of the total household budget on food, so that the multipliers were no longer correct. The question was also raised as to whether the costs of other necessary items (such as energy and housing) – the weight of which had logically increased over time relative to food – should not be taken into account when establishing the poverty threshold. This points to a more general problem: the trend in prosperity and changes in the composition and living circumstances of the population imply that the official statistic is probably no longer an accurate reflection of poverty in the US. This problem is all the more pressing because the entitlements of American citizens to grants and provisions under anti-poverty programmes often are linked to their distance from the official threshold. This may imply that the target groups of the poverty policy are no longer being adequately reached due to the 'fossilised' nature of the US poverty line. Citro & Michael (1995: 43) concluded: "it is dangerous to let a key social indicator become so frozen in place that, when societal conditions change, it can no longer adequately reflect what it was designed to measure".

Citro & Michal (1995) advocated monitoring the development of poverty over time by using the indexation mechanism that also has been adopted here (see main text). An important difference compared with the SCP method is however that the NAS evades the issue of the precise level of the initial poverty threshold somewhat. The authors state that in principle, the expenditure on "food, clothing and shelter (including utilities), plus a little more" should determine this level (Citro & Michael, 1995: 50-58). A general social consensus on the necessity of these three cost items is assumed: "We selected food, clothing and shelter because they represent basic living needs with which no one would quarrel. That is, people may quarrel about the need for specific kinds of food, clothing and housing – such as whether air conditioning is essential – but not about the need for food, housing and clothing in broad terms". The operational poverty line put forward by the NAS was however not drawn up in accordance with this principle. Based on an analysis of the norm amounts in a number of existing poverty thresholds, the NAS fairly arbitrarily opts for a poverty threshold of between USD 13,700 and USD 15,900 (1992 prices). The lowest amount is at the 30th percentile of expenditure on food, clothing and shelter in the US budget data, with a multiplier of 1.15 for the other necessary items. The highest amount corresponds to the 35th percentile in the expenditure distribution, with a multiplier of 1.25.

In practice, this makes the NAS threshold somewhat fetishistic: it is unclear which standard of living the initial threshold makes possible. Other differences compared with the method advocated here are that the NAS takes a different reference household as a starting point (a couple with two children) and applies a steeper equivalence scale. The method proposed by the NAS was elaborated for the USA in subsequent years (see e.g. Short et al., 1999; Short, 2005), but to date has not been implemented.

71 Obviously, the universalism/particularism dimension can also be given more weight than the scope, and in that case the institutionally determined poverty risk would theoretically be greater in the corporatist countries than the liberal group. This would for instance be plausible if among the representatives of this regime type, large groups were not covered by social insurance and had no access to social assistance. The fact that the levels for those who are covered (the 'insiders') are generous would then not be enough to prevent large-scale poverty.

72 In §6.1, reference was to the argument of neoclassical economics that redistribution via the social security system tends to reduce the level of prosperity. If this line of reasoning is taken further, one could posit that per capita GDP should be seen as an endogenous trait of the various regime types. From that point of view, the extensive social-democratic and corporatist regimes ultimately must combine flat income distributions with limited national wealth (and therefore low household incomes): small differences, but high levels of poverty. Similarly, the liberal regimes inevitably bring about larger income differentials and greater collective prosperity; and the latter will translate into low rates of poverty. It was argued in §3.6.3, however, that the influence of social security arrangements on the prosperity of a community is not theoretically fixed. Other factors (such as natural resources, the infrastructure, the education level of the population, developments in the world economy) can have a bigger impact on a country's level of wealth than the institutional setup. Whether an extensive welfare state holds back or promotes prosperity is an empirical matter, to which the available research was found not to provide a final answer. Furthermore, it should be noted that the collective prosperity in the countries studied here does not correlate directly with the regime type – at least not in the direction that would be expected on the grounds of the neoclassical theory. In 2000, per capita

GDP in the six countries with an extensive social-democratic or corporatist regime was 5% higher on average than in the four representatives of the liberal regime. The latter group includes both the USA, the second wealthiest of all the countries studied here (Norway has a higher per capita GDP) and Australia, the country with the lowest collective prosperity.

73 However, figure 6.1 also shows a number of corporatist observations with 'social-democratic' poverty rates, though no clear line or pattern can be discerned: Belgium in 1985 and 1998, Germany in 1981, 1989 and 2000, and France in 2002.

74 The analyses have been performed on the data of LIS wave 5, release 1. Poverty figures are based on the equivalised net disposable income as standardly calculated in the LIS project. The construction of this and a description of the underlying variables can be found at http://www.lisproject.org/techdoc.htm. The monetary value of some near cash benefits, such as food stamps, housing benefits and education benefits are taken into account. Non-cash benefits such as free school meals or medical care are however generally not included in net disposable income in the LIS.

In the variable used, the very high incomes have been removed in accordance with the standard LIS routine for top-coding. At the bottom end, a lower limit of EUR 2,000 of the equivalised net disposable income was applied. This eliminates negative and zero incomes, in particular.

In all countries, persons in households consisting of students living outside the parental home were left out of consideration. This group often has a high risk of poverty, but this is generally attributable to unobserved income components (student grants and loans, parental contributions, provisions in kind, such as student housing). Moreover, students generally have favourable future prospects, so their poverty tends to be temporary in nature. In the unweighted data sets, the proportion of persons living in such student households varied between 0.1% (Belgium) and 2.1% (Sweden).

Specific adjustments were made for two countries. In the Netherlands, households with incomplete sets of questionnaires were left out of consideration, as recommended by the LIS. The original data set of Australia does not include children aged younger than 15 years; normally these are taken into account via the weighting factor. Since the multivariate analyses performed here require physical records, for each Australian child a synthetic case has been compiled, based on information on the household composition. To this end, the record of the head of household was copied as many times as the number of children aged younger than 15. The position in the household was converted for these cases from head to child. Their age was taken as 8 years, the class average of the 0-14 year-olds. Gender was randomly assigned to the individual synthetic children, based on the proportion of 51.1% boys and 48.9% girls which applied for the Dutch population aged 0-14 years in 2000. The education level was set at 'in education', the labour market position at 'not in labour force'. The other person variables were set at missing for the Australian children. Detailed information on the LIS project and of the national data sets used is available at http://www.lisproject.org.

75 The Dutch norms for 2000 were converted for the other countries using the OECD purchasing power parities for actual individual consumption. In three countries, however, the data used did not relate to the year 2000. In the United Kingdom (1999) and Australia (2001) the norm amounts for 2000 were corrected by applying the index of expenditure on basic budget items according to the National Accounts. For the Netherlands (1999) the amounts given by Soede (2006) and Soede & Vrooman (2007, 2008b) were used.

76 There are also a number of other theoretical problems with the econometrically determined equivalence factors:
    - only equivalent incomes are considered; the welfare impact of time that is not spent on acquiring a market income is left out of consideration (leisure, care and household production);
    - it is not self-evident that all members of multiple-person households will experience the same welfare or utility from a given equivalised income;
    - only the equivalences in a given year are considered, whereas it may be more logical to look at spending patterns over a longer period and in relation to the phase of life.

77 Note that all persons younger than 18 years who are not the head of the household or a partner are regarded as children in these analyses, and the appropriate equivalence factor is accordingly applied. This differs from the practice followed by Eurostat, for example, with the 'modified OECD scale', where the age limit for children is set at 14 years. From the perspective of parental responsibility and the attainment of full legal capacity, this appears to be on the young side.

78 The steady increase in the poverty rates deviates from the outcomes generally obtained when a sensitivity analysis such as this is performed on the basis of a relative income threshold (e.g. 60% of the median). The pattern is then often non-linear, with the highest poverty rates at the two extreme parameter values chosen. Coulter et al. (1992) discuss three effects which underlie this. The first effect is that the poverty rate rises as the parameter values increase: because the threshold amounts for non-single households are higher, more observations fall below that threshold. In addition, the form of the income distribution below the poverty line changes with higher parameter values: the poverty deficits and the dispersion of those deficits tend to increase (effect 2). Thirdly, higher parameter values imply

that the median equivalised income falls, and the poverty line therefore also moves downwards. The latter works in the opposite direction to the first two effects, and explains the non-linear pattern often seen in a sensitivity analysis of equivalence scales with relative income thresholds: "A U-shaped curve ... will occur if the third effect outweighs the first two at some values of θ but not others" (Coulter et al., 1992: 1076). With the poverty line adopted here, the third effect does not occur: the threshold amount of the reference household does not change if the parameter values of the equivalence scale are increased. Theoretically, therefore, it would be expected that the headcount ratio gradually increases. If a composite poverty measure is used which is also sensitive to the deficits and the dispersion of those deficits, the increase will be even greater.

79 A similar sensitivity analysis was performed for the median deficits of poor households. This often is slightly non-linear: the low equivalence scales generate fairly high deficits, but at first these become smaller if higher parameters are chosen. From a certain point median deficits start to rise, and fairly sharply for variants 17 and 18.
Of all the countries studied, the variation in the median deficits when different equivalence scales are used is greatest in the Netherlands. This is probably due to the specific composition of the poor population, which in the Netherlands contains comparatively few single elderly persons. The number of households in which the income changes as a result of the standardisation is higher (compare the second effect of Coulter et al. (1992) discussed earlier). As a consequence, the position of the Netherlands in the ranking of median deficits is not stable. With the basic needs criterion, the Netherlands occupies first place (highest median deficit) according to the equivalence scale compiled by Statistics Netherlands, but fifth position according to the Oxford scale. Based on the modest but adequate variant, the Netherlands occupies second and eighth position, respectively. The positions of the other countries are more stable if these different equivalence scales are applied, with the exception of France according to the basic needs criterion (a drop of six places).

80 Sen (1976) and Jäntti & Danziger (2000) state that composite measures of poverty should preferably meet the following theoretical requirements:
(1) they should depend on poor incomes alone (*focus axiom*: if the income of non-poor persons changes, this should not affect the degree of poverty)
(2) they should be sensitive to the average income among the poor (*monotonicity axiom*: if poor people become less poor, or pass the poverty line, the degree of poverty should decrease)
(3) they should be sensitive to the distribution of income (*transfer axiom*: a transfer of a poor to a less poor person increases the degree of poverty)
(4) they should not be affected by a reordering of persons or households (*symmetry*)
(5) they should not be affected by an identical proportional increase in the number of units with each income level (*replication invariance*).

The composite measures used here are defined as:
  Intensity index: $H \cdot I$
  Sen index: $H \cdot ((I + (1-I)) \cdot G \cdot (q/q+1))$
  Shorrocks index: $H \cdot (I(2-H) + H(1-I) \cdot G)$

  where
  H = headcount ratio (= incidence, poverty rate)
  I = median income deficit of poor persons (as % of poverty threshold)
  G = Gini coefficient of income deficits
  q = number of observations

The intensity index only complies with axioms 1-3, the Sen index with 1-4. The Shorrocks index meets all five conditions. Zheng (1997) discusses a wider array of axioms and aggregate poverty measures.

81 In the subsamples used here (cf. below), there are between 55 and 292 poor people per country, a total of more than 1,700 observations. If a balanced design (the same number of observations in each country, as in the analysis of the poverty incidences) were used in such models, this figure would fall further, to just over 600 observations across 11 countries. A multi-level analysis of the country scores on the composite indices is hampered by the fact that the contributions of the individual cases to this macro-figure are unknown.

82 In version 10 of Stata, more hierarchical levels can be analysed, but this version was not available when the calculations were carried out on the LIS computer system. If it had been, there would still have been a weighting problem. In principle, multi-level weights are preferable in such an analysis (see e.g. Pfeffermann et al., 1998; Grilli & Pratesi, 2004). However, the sampling probabilities are not known in the LIS for all three levels (persons in households in

countries); and the available software needed to calculate these weights could only handle two hierarchical levels (cf. Chantala et al., 2006).
83 These 'physically weighted' subsamples were drawn as follows in each country:
    - all persons were first sorted on a random variable, implying households and their members were placed in an arbitrary order;
    - a stratified random sample was drawn from this, in proportion to the decile categories of the original weighting factor in the poor and non-poor groups. The number of sampled cases in each stratum was 4-5 times greater than was ultimately needed;
    - these sampled cases were then sorted by country, poor/not poor and household number;
    - in order to minimise the number of cases from one and the same household, a systematic random sample was then drawn, in which a case was selected from the sorted file every 4-5 persons. This meant that multiple persons from the same household could only be selected in case of very large households.

    The physically weighted subsamples replicated the poverty rates from the larger original weighted samples to an accuracy of between 0 and 0.2 percentage points. There were only 1% of households from which more than one household member was selected. If a multi-level analysis is performed with the household number as the second level (disregarding the country differences), the standard errors at the first level hardly increase and the conclusions remain the same. Skipping the household level from the multi-level analysis therefore has virtually no influence on the estimated results in this set of samples, because the number of respondents who are clustered in some way is now very small. In addition, the shares of the various categories of the independent variables (age, education, sex, etc.) in the physically weighted subsamples at no point deviate substantially from the original distributions. This is generally also the case with the poverty incidences for each of these categories, although there are some larger deviations at country level (for example, the poverty risk for families with lots of children is five percentage points lower in the physically weighted sub sample in Canada than in the original sample). This often has to do with the small numbers in the physically weighted subsamples, so that a difference of just a few poor observations in the constituent groups can weigh fairly heavily at the country level.
84 For three countries it was not possible to reproduce the ISCED classification accurately in the LIS data, and proxy variables were used instead. In the United Kingdom it was assumed that those who had left full-time education at age 15 or lower had achieved ISCED-levels 1 and 2. For Canada the group up to and including the level '11-13 years elementary and secondary school (but not graduated)' was selected. Australia was the most problematic. The only selection that could be made here was the group with no 'higher/bachelor degree' or 'other post-school qualifications'. This category with no additional qualifications probably also contains a number of people at ISCED-3 level. Set against the official data (OECD, 2006: 37), the proportion of low-educated people appears on the high side in the Danish LIS data set in particular. This also applies to a lesser extent for the United Kingdom and Australia, two countries with a proxy variable. In the Netherlands, by contrast, the proportion of low-educated people in the LIS data set is somewhat lower than according to the official figures.
85 The empirical correlation between GDP per capita and regime type is in fact limited within the group of countries studied here; see note 72 to this chapter.
86 The analysis was also performed with poverty according to the basic needs criterion as the dependent variable, using different physically weighted subsamples (because the poor/non-poor groups are not the same). This did lead to very similar conclusions. However, at level 1 the effect of the single-parent family is no longer significant. At level 2 the effects of all regime variables are fractionally weaker, but generally remain equally significant. The only exception to this is the effect of the dummy variable for the corporatist regime type in model 7, which is now only significant at p<.10 (formerly at p< .05).
87 In a multi-level logistical regression model no estimate is obtained of the explained variance, as is the case in a normal regression analysis. Here, the method proposed by Snijders & Bosker (1999: 225-229) was followed, an extension of the R^2 criterion put forward by McKelvey & Zavoina (1975). The underlying idea is that with a dichotomous classification, an explained proportion variance can be calculated if it is assumed that the contrast (here: poor/not poor) is the result of exceeding threshold values in an underlying continuous process. The explained variance across the two levels is equal to the variance of the linear predictor. In a logistical model, the level-1 variance is by definition equal to $\Pi^2/3$, or 3.29 (in a probit model the level-1 variance is equal to 1). The level-2 variance is estimated in the model.
88 In an extra model, in which only the level-1 determinants were incorporated, the proportion of unexplained variance was 0.36. Compared with the empty model 1 in table 6.6, the unexplained variance at level 1 logically falls. However, the unexplained variance at level 2 also reduces, from 7.5% to 4.0%. This is due to the correction for compositional differences between the countries in terms of the level-1 variables. The introduction of per capita GDP in model 2 leads to an additional reduction compared with the extra model in the unexplained variance at level 2 (from 4.0%

to 2.9%). The improvement in the fit (Δ −2 Log Likelihood, ΔWald χ^2) in model 2 compared with the model with only level-1 variables is statistically significant at p<0.10.
89 The likelihood ratio test can be used in a multi-level logistical model if the computer program is based on numerical integration, as here; see Snijders & Bosker (1999: 220).
90 Esping-Andersen's de-commodification scores were based on 12 characteristics of old age pensions, unemployment benefits and sick leave benefits. For each characteristic, the countries were classified into three levels (low/medium/high de-commodification), on the grounds of their standard deviation from the mean. The coded categories were then added up and weighted with the take-up rate of the pensions and, respectively, the coverage of the unemployment and sick leave benefits among the labour force.
91 When the constituent indices are added together directly (without a weighting factor), the threefold division between the regime types (cf. figure 6.3) remains clearly present. Individual countries do however move up or down in the rankings: Norway and France, for example, then have a higher poverty risk because the relatively good pension provisions weigh less heavily in the total; the reverse occurs in the United Kingdom. In principle, it seems better to apply the weighting factor; otherwise the same weight is for instance implicitly attached to survivor's benefits as to old-age pensions, whereas in practice the latter are important for a much larger group and are therefore theoretically much more influential determinants of the poverty risk.

Chapter 7

1. The summaries at the end of the individual chapters look in more depth at the questions raised in the Introduction.
2. No volume data were available for Northern Ireland. The volume growth in Great Britain was higher than expected, partly because of the sharp increase in the number of people on disability benefit, which does not fit in with the liberal regime type.
3. The labour market participation rate of elderly men fell in Sweden to a much lesser extent than in Belgium, Germany and France. In Denmark, the volume of early exit benefits grew strongly in the period studied, as it did in the corporatist group, but this was offset to some extent by the higher Danish statutory retirement age (67 years).
4. For variables with an even number of categories, an additional middle code was assigned for the generic hybrid.
5. Unlike in the analysis in chapter 4, where four characteristics were nominally scaled, all variables were quantified ordinally here. To obtain a consistent interpretation of the dimensions, the solution was rotated.
6. In latent profile modelling an estimate is made for each case of how great the likelihood is of falling within a given cluster. The technique also makes it possible to test whether the fit of various models differs (see also chapter 4). Due to the limited number of cases (n=15), models with four clusters or more could not be tested in the present analysis; these were not identified. A two-cluster latent profile model proved to fit the data significantly better than the baseline model, in which all empirical systems and ideal-types are placed in the same cluster. The fit of the three-cluster model is higher, but not to the extent that the difference becomes statistically significant (p=.15). Both the two-cluster and the three-cluster models produced virtually the same outcomes as the determinist hierarchical cluster analyses. Here again, a two-cluster solution reveals an opposition between liberal/non-liberal, while the three-cluster model (where the fit is not significantly better) confirms the distinction liberal/social-democratic/corporatist. The Netherlands once more scale with the social-democratic cluster, albeit with a lower likelihood of that classification than the Scandinavian countries. The only difference compared with the outcomes of the hierarchical cluster analysis is that in both latent profile models the generic hybrid ends up in the liberal group. The empirical systems are however consistently placed in the same cluster as their theoretical ideal-types, with a very high degree of probability (p > .90).

List of references

A

Aaron, H.J. (1982). *Economic effects of social security*. Washington: The Brookings Institution.

Abrahamson, P. (1999). "The welfare modelling business". In: *Social Policy & Administration* (33) 4, pp. 394-415.

Ackerman, B. (1980). *Social justice in the liberal state*. New Haven: Yale University Press.

Aghion, Ph., E. Caroli & C. García-Peñalosa (1999). "Inequality and economic growth: the perspective of the new growth theories". In: *Journal of Economic Literature* (37) 6, pp. 1615-1660.

Ajzen, I. & M. Fishbein (1980). *Understanding attitudes and predicting social behavior*. Englewood Cliffs: Prentice-Hall.

Algava, E. (2002). "Les familles monoparentales". In: *Population* (57) 4-5, pp. 733-758.

Alston L.J., Th. Eggertsson & D.C. North (1996). *Empirical studies in institutional change*. Cambridge: Cambridge University Press.

Aquinas, Th. (1947 [1265-1274]) *Summa Theologica*. Benziger Bros. edition, available through http://www.ccel.org/a/aquinas/summa/home.html.

Arbuckle, J.L. (2006). *Amos 7.0 User's Guide*. Chicago: SPSS Inc.

Arents, M., M.M. Cluitmans & M.A. van der Velde (2000). *Benefit dependency ratios; an analysis of nine European countries, Japan and the US*. The Hague: VUGA.

Arts, W. & J. Gelissen (2001). "Welfare states, solidarity and justice principles: does the type really matter?" In: *Acta Sociologica* (44) 4, pp. 283-299.

——— (2002). "Three worlds of welfare capitalism or more? A state-of-the-art report." In: *Journal of European Social Policy* (12) 2, pp. 137-158.

Atkinson, A.B. (1999). *The economic consequences of rolling back the welfare state* (Munich lectures in economics). Cambridge/London: MIT Press.

Atkinson, A.B. & Bourguignon, F. (eds) (2000). *Handbook of income distribution* (volume 1). Amsterdam: Elsevier.

Axelrod, R. (1981). "The emergence of cooperation among egoists". In: *The American Political Science Review* (75) 2, pp. 306-318.

——— (1984). *The evolution of cooperation*. New York: Basic Books.

B

Barr, N. (1992). "Economic theory and the welfare state: a survey and interpretation". In: *Journal of Economic Literature* (30) 6, pp. 741-803.

Beaujot, R. & J. Liu (2002). *Children, social assistance and outcomes: cross-national comparisons*. Syracuse: Maxwell School of citizenship and public affairs (Luxembourg Income Study Working Paper No 304).

Beck, U. & E. Beck-Gersheim (eds) (1994). *Riskante Freiheiten*. Frankfurt am Main: Suhrkamp Verlag.

Becker, G.S. (1993 [1964]). *Human capital; a theoretical and empirical analysis, with special reference to education*. Chicago: University of Chicago Press.

Becker, H. (1992). *Generaties en hun kansen*. Amsterdam: Meulenhoff.

de Beer, P.T. (2001). *Over werken in de postindustriële samenleving*. Den Haag: Sociaal en Cultureel Planbureau.

Benford, F. (1938). "The law of anomalous numbers". In: *Proceedings of the American Philosophical Society* (78) 4, pp. 551-572.

Bentham, J. (1948 [1789]). *An introduction to the principles of morals and legislation*. New York: Hafner Publishing Company.

——— (1962 [1838-1843]). "Tracts on poor laws and pauper management". In: J. Bowring (ed), *The works of Jeremy Bentham* (vol. 8). New York: Russell & Russell, Inc.

Bentler, P.M. & D.G. Bonnet (1980). "Significance tests and goodness of fit in the analysis of covariance structures. In: *Psychological Bulletin* (88) 3, pp. 588-606.

Berger, P.L. & Th. Luckmann (1966). *The social construction of reality; a treatise in the sociology of knowledge*. New York: Anchor.

Berger-Schmitt, R. & H.-H. Noll (2000). *Towards a European system of social reporting and welfare measurement*. Mannheim: Centre for survey research and methodology (ZUMA).

Berghman, J. (1986). *De onzichtbare sociale zekerheid*. Deventer: Kluwer.

——— (1990). *Defining social security*. Edinburgh: University of Edinburgh.

——— (1995). "Social exclusion in Europe: policy context and analytical framework". In: G. Room (ed), *Beyond the threshold: the measurement and analysis of social exclusion*. Bristol: The Policy Press.

Berghman, J., R. Muffels, A. de Vries & M. Vriens (1988). *Armoede, bestaansonzekerheid en relatieve deprivatie*. Tilburg: Katholieke Universiteit Brabant.

Berghman, J. & I. Verhalle (2003). "Gericht op de toekomst: sociale zekerheid en sociale cohesie". In: J. Berghman, A. Nagelkerke, K. Boos, R. Doeschot & G. Vink (eds), *Honderd jaar sociale zekerheid in Nederland*. Delft: Eburon.

Berting, J. (1978). "Sociale ongelijkheid". In: L. Rademaker (ed), *Sociologische Encyclopedie*. Utrecht/Antwerpen: Het Spectrum.

Beveridge, W.H. (1942). *Social insurance and allied services*. London: H.M. Stationary Office.
BiB (2003). *Wie haben die Familienstrukturen in Deutschland sich entwickelt?* Wiesbaden: Bundesinstitut für Bevölkerungsforschung.
Bingley, P., H.D. Gupta & P.J. Pedersen (2002). *The effect of pension programme incentives on retirement behaviour in Denmark*. Aarhus: Centre for Labour Market and Social Research.
Black, D. (1948). "On the rationale of group decision-making". In: *Journal of Political Economy* (56) 1, pp. 23-34.
――― (1987). *The theory of committees and elections*. Dordrecht: Kluwer Academic Publishers.
Blossfeld, H.-P. & Y. Shavit (1993). "Persisting barriers: changes in educational opportunities in thirteen countries". In: Y. Shavit & H.-P. Blossfeld (eds), *Persistent inequality – changing educational attainment in thirteen countries* (pp. 1-24). Boulder: Westview Press.
Boelhouwer, J. & Th. Roes (2004). "The social state of the Netherlands; a model based approach to describing living conditions and quality of life". In: W. Glatzer, S. von Below & M. Stoffregen (eds), *Challenges for Quality of Life in the contemporary world: advances in Qualities-of-life studies, theory and research*. Dordrecht: Kluwer Academic Publishers.
Bolívar, S. (1819). "Discurso ante el congreso de Angostura, 15 de Febrero de 1819". In: E. Mondolfi (ed), *Bolivar: ideas de un espíritu visionario (antología)* (pp. 49-75). Caracas: Biblioteca del Pensamiento Venezolano.
Bonoli, G. (1997). "Classifying welfare states: a two-dimension approach". In: *Journal of Social Policy* (26) 3, pp. 351-372.
――― (1999). "Public attitudes to social protection and political economy traditions in western Europe". In: *European Societies* (2) 4, pp. 431-452.
Booth, Ch. (1902 [1889]). *Life and labour of the people in London* (vol. 1, revised edition). London: MacMillan.
van den Bosch, K. (1997). *Wat heeft een gezin nodig om rond te komen? Budgetnormen voor drie typen gezinnen*. Antwerpen: UFSIA/Centrum voor Sociaal Beleid.
――― (2001). *Identifying the poor; using subjective and consensual measures*. Aldershot: Ashgate.
Bosker, R.J. (2002). "Veranderende onderwijskansen?". In: J.C. Vrooman (ed), *Sociale ongelijkheid: breuk of continuïteit?* Amsterdam: SISWO/Nederlandse Sociologische Vereniging.
Bourdieu, P. (1990). *In other words: essays towards a reflexive sociology*. Stanford: Stanford University Press.
Bradshaw, J. (ed) (1993). *Budget standards for the United Kingdom*. Aldershot: Avebury.
Bradshaw, J., J. Ditch, H. Holmes & P. Whiteford (1993). *Support for children: a comparison of arrangements in fifteen countries*. London: HMSO.
Bradshaw, J. & N. Finch (2002). *A comparison of child benefit packages in 22 countries*. London: Department for Work and Pensions.
Bradshaw, J., S. Middleton, A. Davis, N. Oldfield, N. Smith, L. Cusworth & J. Williams (2008). *A minimum income standard for Britain – what people think*. York: Joseph Rowntree Foundation/Loughborough University.
Brinton, M. & V. Nee (1998). *The new institutionalism in sociology*. New York: Russel Sage Foundation.
Brixy, U., R. Gilberg, D. Hess & H. Schröder (2002). "Wie nah am Arbeitsmarkt sind die Arbeitslosen?" In: Bundesanstalt für Arbeit, *IAB-Kurzbericht*, 21-1-2002.
van den Broek, A. (1996). *Politics and generations; cohort replacement and generation formation in political culture in the Netherlands*. Tilburg: Tilburg University Press.
Bunjes, A.M, L.M.H.J. van Geffen, T.M. Keuzenkamp, S.G. Lijftocht & W. Wijga (1977). *Inkomens op tafel; persoonlijke meningen over eigen en andermans salaris*. Alphen aan den Rijn/Brussel: Samson.
Burniaux, J.M., T.T. Dang, D. Fore, M.F. Förster, M. Mira d'Ercole & H. Oxley (1998). *Income distribution and poverty in selected OECD countries*. Paris: OECD.
Burricand, C. & N. Roth (2000). "Les parcours de fin de carrière des générations 1912-1941: l'impact du cadre institutionnel". In: *Économie et Statistique* (5) 335, pp. 63-79.
Burt, R. (1992). *Structural holes: the social structure of competition*. Cambridge (Mass.): Harvard University Press.

C
Carcillo, S. & D. Grubb (2006). *From incapacity to work: the role of active labour market policies*. Paris: Organisation for Economic Co-operation and Development (OECD Social, Employment and Migration Working Papers no 36).
Casati, R. & A. Varzi (2002). "Events". In: *The Stanford Encyclopedia of Philosophy* (Fall 2002 edition; http://plato.stanford.edu).
Castles, F.G. (1996). "Needs-based strategies of social protection in Australia and New Zealand". In: G. Esping-Andersen (ed), *Welfare states in transition: national adaptations in global economics*. London: Sage Publications.
――― (1998). *Comparative public policy: patterns of post-war transformation*. Cheltenham: Edward Elgar.
CBS/SCP (1999). *Het meten van armoede*. Voorburg/Heerlen: Centraal Bureau voor de Statistiek.

Chantala, K., D. Blanchette & C.M. Suchindran (2006). *Software to compute sampling weights for multilevel analysis.* Chapel Hill: Carolina Population Center, UNC. Available at http://www.cpc.unc.edu/ restools/data_analysis/ ml_sampling_ weights (version January 17, 2006).

Citro, C.F. & R.T. Michael (eds) (1995). *Measuring poverty: a new approach.* Washington DC: National Academy Press.

Coase, R.H. (1937). "The nature of the firm". In: *Economica* (4) 16, pp. 386-405.

――― (1960). "The problem of social cost". In: *Journal of Law and Economics* (3) 1, pp. 1-44.

Cohen, S.J.D. (1982). "Masada: literary tradition, archaeological remains, and the credibility of Josephus". In: *Journal of Jewish Studies* (33) 1-2, pp. 385-405.

Coleman, J.S. (1990). *Foundations of social theory.* Cambridge (Mass.): The Belknap Press of Harvard University Press.

Coleman, J.S., E.Q. Campbell, C.J. Hobson, J. McPartland, A.M. Mood, F.D. Weinfeld & R.L. York (1966). *Equality of educational opportunity.* Washington DC: U.S. Government Printing Office.

Collins, R. (1991). "A Marx for the twenty-first century?" In: *Society* (28) 1, pp. 85-87.

Coulter, F.A.E., F.A. Cowell & S.P. Jenkins (1992). "Equivalence scale relativities and the extent of inequality and poverty." In: *The Economic Journal* (102), September, pp. 1067-1082.

Cowell, F.A. & M. Mercader-Prats (1999). "Equivalence scales and inequality". In J. Silber (ed), *Handbook on income inequality measurement* (pp. 405-438). Deventer: Kluwer.

CPB/SCP (2003). *Social Europe; European Outlook 1.* The Hague: The Netherlands Bureau of Economic Policy Analysis/Social and Cultural Planning Office. (Also downloadable from http://www.scp.nl)

Cummins, R.A. (2000). "Objective and subjective quality of life". In: *Social Indicators Research* (52) 1, pp. 55-72.

D

Daniels, N. (1990). "Equality of what: welfare, resources, or capabilities?". In: *Philosophy and Phenomenological Research* (50) Fall/supplement, pp. 273-296.

Danziger, S., R. Haveman, & R. Plotnick (1981). "How income transfer programs affect work, savings, and the income distribution: a critical review". In: *Journal of Economic Literature* (19) 3, pp. 975-1028.

David, P.A. (1985). "Clio and the economics of QWERTY". In: *American Economic Review* (75) 2, pp. 332-337.

Davies, J.B. & A.F. Shorrocks (2000). "The distribution of wealth". In: A.B. Atkinson & F. Bourguignon (eds), *Handbook of income distribution (vol. 1)* (pp. 606-675). Amsterdam: Elsevier.

Dekker, P. & P. Ester (1995). "Political attitudes in a generational perspective: the Netherlands, 1970-1992". In: *Acta Politica* (30) 1, pp. 57-74.

Dekkers, H.P.J.M., R.J. Bosker, & G.W.J.M Driessen (2000). "Complex inequalities of educational opportunities. A large-scale longitudinal study on the relation between gender, social class, ethnicity and school success". In: *Educational Research and Evaluation* (6) 1, pp. 1-24.

Deleeck, H. (1991). *Zeven lessen over sociale zekerheid.* Leuven/Amersfoort: Acco.

Dessens, J.A.G. & W. Jansen (1987). *Operationaliseren: traditie en kritiek.* Utrecht: Drukkerij Elinkwijk (Thesis Utrecht University).

DHHS (1991). *Social security programs throughout the world.* Washington: US Department of Health & Human Services (Social Security Administration).

Don, F.J.H. & J.P. Verbruggen (2006). "Models and methods for economic policy: 60 years of evolution at CPB". In: *Statistica Neerlandica* (60) 2, pp. 145-170.

Douben, N.H. (1980). "Sociale zekerheid in de verzorgingsstaat". In: G.M.J. Veldkamp (ed), *De economie en het sociaal zekerheidsbeleid* (pp. 69-76). Deventer; Kluwer.

――― (1986). *Economie en sociale zekerheid.* Groningen: Wolters-Noordhoff.

Downs, A. (1957). *An economic theory of democracy.* New York: Harper Collins.

Doyal, L. & I. Gough (1991). *A theory of human need.* Houndsmill/Basingstoke: MacMillan.

Dronkers, J. & W.C. Ultee (1995). *Verschuivende ongelijkheid in Nederland – sociale gelaagdheid en mobiliteit.* Assen: Van Gorcum.

Durkheim, E. (1897). *Le suicide: étude de sociologie.* Paris: Félix Alcan.

――― (1901). *Les règles de la méthode sociologique.* Paris: Félix Alcan (2nd ed.).

――― (1922). *Éducation et sociologie.* Paris: Librairie Félix Alcan.

Dworkin, R. (2000). *Sovereign virtue; the theory and practice of equality.* Cambridge (Mass.): Harvard University Press.

E

Eardley, T., J. Bradshaw, J. Ditch, I. Gough & P. Whiteford (1996). *Social assistance in OECD countries.* (2 vols.). London: HMSO.

Ebbinghaus, B. (2003). *Exit from externalization; reversing early retirement in Europe, the USA and Japan.* Geneva: International Social Security Association.

EC (1990). *Comparative tables of the social security schemes in the member states of the European communities.* Brussels/Luxembourg: Commission of the European communities.
────── (2002). *Mutual information system on social protection in the EU member states and the EEA (MISSOC); comparative tables.* Brussels: European Commission.
────── (2006). *Adequate and sustainable pensions; synthesis report 2006.* Luxembourg: Office for Official Publications of the European Communities.
────── (2007). *Joint report on social protection and social inclusion; supporting document.* Brussels: European Commission.
van Echtelt, P. & S. Hoff (2008). *Wel of niet aan het werk; achtergronden van het onbenut arbeidspotentieel onder werkenden, werklozen en arbeidsongeschikten.* Den Haag: Sociaal en Cultureel Planbureau.
Eggertsson, Th. (1996). "A note on the economics of institutions". In: L.J. Alston, Th. Eggertsson & D.C. North, *Empirical studies in institutional change* (pp. 6-24). Cambridge: Cambridge University Press.
Einerhand, M.G.K., G. Knol, R. Prins & T.J. Veerman (1995). *Sickness and invalidity arrangements; facts and figures from six European countries.* The Hague: Ministry of Social Affairs and Employment/VUGA.
Einstein, A. (1934). "On the method of theoretical physics". In: *Philosophy of Science* (1) 2, pp. 163-169.
Eisenberg, Ph. & P.F. Lazarsfeld (1938). "The psychological effects of unemployment". In: *Psychological Bulletin* (35) 6, pp. 358-390.
Eisenstadt, S.M. (1968). "Social institutions". In: *International Encyclopedia of the Social Sciences* (pp. 409-429). New York: Macmillan.
Engbersen, G. (1989). "Culturen van langdurige werkloosheid". In: *Amsterdams Sociologisch Tijdschrift* (15) 4, pp. 545-575.
────── (1990). *Publieke bijstandsgeheimen; het ontstaan van een onderklasse in Nederland.* Leiden/ Antwerpen: Stenfert Kroese.
Engbersen, G., K. Schuyt, J. Timmer & F. van Waarden (1993). *Cultures of unemployment; a comparative look at long-term unemployment and urban poverty.* Boulder: Westview Press.
Engbersen, G. & R. Staring (2000). "De morele economie van lage-inkomensgroepen: armoede en informaliteit". In: G. Engbersen, J.C. Vrooman & E. Snel (eds), *Balans van het armoedebeleid; vijfde jaarrapport armoede en sociale uitsluiting* (pp. 76-100). Amsterdam: Amsterdam University Press.
Engelbrecht, H. J. (2003). "Human capital and economic growth: cross-section evidence for OECD countries". In: *Economic Record* (79) June (special issue), pp. 40-51.
Erikson, E. (1963). *Childhood and society.* New York: W.W. Norton & Company.
Ervik, R. (1998). "The redistributive aim of social policy; a comparative analysis of taxes, tax expenditure transfers and direct transfers in eight countries". In: *Luxembourg Income Study working paper series* (184). Syracuse (NY): Maxwell school of citizenship and public affairs.
Esping-Andersen, G. (1989). "The three political economies of the welfare state". In: *Canadian Review of Sociology and Anthropology* (26) 1, pp. 10-36.
────── (1990). *The three worlds of welfare capitalism.* Cambridge: Polity Press.
────── (ed) (1996). *Welfare states in transition: national adaptations in global economics.* London: Sage.
────── (1999). *Social foundations of postindustrial economics.* Oxford: Oxford University Press.
────── (2003). "Why no socialism anywhere? A reply to Alex Hicks and Lane Kenworthy". In: *Socio-Economic Review* (1) 1, pp. 63-70.
Etzioni, A. (1995). *The spirit of community.* London: Fontana Books.
Eurostat (2004a). "Pensions in Europe: expenditure and beneficiaries". In: *Statistics in Focus – Population and social conditions,* 8. Luxembourg: Eurostat.
────── (2004b). "Poverty and social exclusion in the EU". In: *Statistics in Focus – Population and social conditions,* 16. Luxembourg: Eurostat.
────── (2008). *ESSPROS Manual; the European System of integrated Social PROtection Statistics (ESSPROS).* Luxembourg: Office for Official Publications of the European Communities.

F
Feldstein, M. (ed) (1998). *Privatizing social security.* Chicago: University of Chicago Press.
Ferrarini, T. & K. Nelson (2002). "The impact of taxation on the equalising effect of social insurance to income inequality; a comparative analysis of ten welfare states". In: *Luxembourg Income Study working paper series* (327). Syracuse (NY): Maxwell school of citizenship and public affairs.
Fisher, G.M. (1992). "The development and history of poverty thresholds". In: *Social Security Bulletin* (55) 4, pp. 3-14.
────── (1997). *From Hunter to Orshansky: An overview of (unofficial) poverty lines in the United States from 1904 to 1965.* Washington DC: US Census Bureau (www.census.gov/hhes/poverty/ povmeas/papers/hstorsp4.html).

―― (2001). *Enough for a family to live on? Questions from members of the American public and new perspectives from British social scientists*. Washington DC: Paper 23th Annual Research Conference of the Association for Public Policy and Management.

―― (2007). *An overview of recent work on standard budgets in the United States and other Anglophone countries*. Washington: US Department of Health and Human Services (http://aspe.hhs.gov/ poverty/papers/ std-budgets/index.htm).

Flora, P. (ed) (1986). *Growth to limits; the Western European welfare states since World War II* (vol. I). Berlin/New York: Walter de Gruyter.

Förster, M & M. Mira d'Ercole (2005). *Income distribution and poverty in the OECD countries in the second half of the 1990s*. Paris: Organisation for Economic Co-operation and Development.

Frank, R.H. (1992). "Melding sociology and economics; James Coleman's Foundations of Social Theory" (review). In: *Journal of Economic Literature* (30) 3, pp.147-170.

Frankfurt, H.G. (1997 [1978]). "The problem of action". In: A.R. Mele (ed) (1997), *The philosophy of action*. Oxford: Oxford University Press (pp. 42-52) [reprint from *American Philosophical Quarterly* (15), pp. 157-162].

Frohlich, N., J.A. Oppenheimer & C.L. Eavey (1987). "Laboratory results on Rawls's distributive justice". In: *British Journal of Political Science* (17) 1, pp. 1-21.

Frijda. N.H. (1986). *The emotions*. Cambridge/Paris: Cambridge University Press/Édition de la Maison des Sciences de l'Homme.

―― (2007). *The laws of emotion*. Mahwah (NJ): Lawrence Erlbaum Associates.

G

Gaillard, J.-M. (1995). *L'ENA – Miroir de l'état, de 1945 à nos jours*. Bruxelles: Éditions Complexe.

le Gall, D & C. Martin (1987). *Les familles monoparentales; evolution et traitement social*. Paris: Les Éditions ESF.

Gallie, D. & S. Paugam (eds) (2000). *Welfare regimes and the experience of unemployment in Europe*. Oxford: Oxford University Press.

―― (2002). *Social precarity and social integration; report for the European Commission based on Eurobarometer 56.1*. Brussels: European Commission.

Garfinkel, H. (1967). *Studies in ethnomethodology*. Englewood Cliffs (NJ): Prentice Hall.

Garner, T.I., S. Shipp, D.M. Steiger & T. Manieri (1998). "Subjective assessments of economic well-being: cognitive research at the U.S. Bureau of Labor Statistics". In: *Focus: Revising the poverty measure* (19) 2, pp. 43-46.

Garner, T.I. & K. Short (2005). *Economic well-being based on income, consumer expenditures and personal assessments of minimum needs*. Washington DC: US Department of Labor.

Gauthier, A.H. & J. Hatzius (1997). "Family benefits and fertility: an econometric analysis". In: *Population Studies* (51) 3, pp. 295-306.

Geleijnse, L., J.C. Vrooman & R.J.A. Muffels (1993). *Tussen ministelsel en participatiemodel; een verkennende studie naar stelselvarianten in de sociale zekerheid*. Rijswijk/Den Haag: Sociaal en Cultureel Planbureau/VUGA.

Gelissen, J. (2002). *Worlds of welfare, worlds of consent? Public opinion on the welfare state*. Leiden/Boston: Brill. First edition (Gelissen 2002[1]): Amsterdam: Thela Thesis.

Geulen, D. (2002). "Die historische Entwicklung sozialisationstheoretischer Ansätze". In: K. Hurrelmann & D. Ulich (ed), *Handbuch der Sozialisationsforschung* (6th ed., pp. 21-54). Weinheim/Basel: Beltz Verlag.

Giddens, A. (1984). *The constitution of society; outline of the theory of structuration*. Cambridge: Polity Press.

Gifi, A. (1990). *Nonlinear multivariate analysis*. Wiley: Chichester.

Goedhart, Th., V. Halberstadt, A. Kapteyn & B.M.S. van Praag (1977). "The poverty line: concept and measurement". In: *The Journal of Human Resources* (12) 4, pp. 503-520.

Goldthorpe, J. H. (2000). *On sociology: numbers, narratives, and the integration of research and theory*. Oxford: Oxford University Press.

Goodin, R.E., B. Heady, R. Muffels & H.-J. Dirven (1999). *The real worlds of welfare capitalism*. Cambridge: Cambridge University Press.

Goodman, R. (1998). "The 'Japanese-style welfare state' and the delivery of personal social services". In: R. Goodman, G. White & H. Kwon (eds), *The East Asian welfare model: welfare orientalism and the state* (pp. 139-158). London: Routledge.

Gottschalk, P. & T. M. Smeeding (2000). "Empirical evidence on income inequality in industrial countries". In: A.B. Atkinson & F. Bourguignon (eds), *Handbook of income distribution* (vol. 1) (pp. 261-307). Amsterdam: Elsevier.

Gough, I. (2001). "Social assistance regimes: a cluster analysis". In: *Journal of European Social Policy* (11) 2, pp. 165-170.

Grilli, L. & M. Pratesi (2004). "Weighted estimation in multilevel ordinal and binary models in the presence of informative sampling designs". In: *Survey Methodology* (30) 1, pp. 93-103.

Graafland, J.J., R.A. de Mooij, A.G.H. Nibbelink & A. Nieuwenhuis (2001). MIMIcing tax policies and the labour market. Amsterdam: North-Holland.

de Grip, A. & R. Dekker (1993). "Winnaars en verliezers op de arbeidsmarkt in de jaren tachtig". In: *Tijdschrift voor Arbeidsvraagstukken*, (9) 3, pp. 220-229.

de Grip, A. & J. van Loo (2000). "Winnaars en verliezers op de arbeidsmarkt 1990-1995". In: *Tijdschrift voor Arbeidsvraagstukken*, (16) 1, pp. 6-17.

de Grip, A. & S. Dijksman (2004). "Winnaars en verliezers op de arbeidsmarkt 1995-2000: naar een kenniseconomie?". In: *Tijdschrift voor Arbeidsvraagstukken*, (20) 2, pp. 169-181.

——— (2008). "Winnaars en verliezers op de arbeidsmarkt 2000-2005". In: *Tijdschrift voor Arbeidsvraagstukken*, (24) 1, pp. 6-15.

Grubb, D., S. Singh & P. Tergeist (2009). *Activation policies in Ireland*. Paris: Organisation for Economic Co-operation and Development (OECD Social, Employment and Migration Working Papers no 75).

Gulliksen, H. & J.W. Tukey (1958). "Reliability for the law of comparative judgment". In: *Psychometrica* (23) 2, pp. 95-110.

Gundelach, P. (1994). "National value differences: modernisation or institutionalisation?". In: *International Journal of Comparative Sociology* (35) 1-2, pp. 37-58.

H

Habermas, J. (1981). *Theorie des kommunikativen Handelns; Band 2: Zur Kritik der funktionalistischen Vernunft*. Frankfurt am Main: Suhrkamp.

Hagenaars, A.J.M. (1985). *The perception of poverty*. Alblasserdam: Kanters (Thesis Leyden University).

Hagenaars, A.J.M., K. de Vos & B.M.S. van Praag (1987). *Arm en arm is twee; een empirische vergelijking van armoededefinities*. Den Haag: Ministerie van szw.

Hagenaars, A. & K. de Vos (1988). "The definition and measurement of poverty". In: *Journal of Human Resources* (23) 2, pp. 211-221.

Hagenaars, A., K. de Vos & M.A. Zaidi (1994). *Poverty statistics in the late 1980s: research based on micro-data*. Luxembourg: Office for Official Publications of the European Communities.

Hagerty, M. & R. Veenhoven (2003). "Wealth and happiness revisited. Growing wealth of nations does go with greater happiness". In: *Social Indicators Research* (64) 1, pp. 1-27.

Hagfors, R. & O. Kangas (2004). *Neural computation as a clustering method for comparative welfare state research*. Paper 2nd annual Espanet conference. Oxford: St. Antony's College.

Halberstadt, V. (1976). *Naar een economische theorie van de publieke sector*. Leiden: Universitaire Pers.

Hall, J.R. (1987). *Gone from the promised land; Jonestown in American cultural history*. New Brunswick: Transaction Books.

Hall, P.A. & R.C.R. Taylor (1996). "Political science and the three new institutionalisms". In: *Political Studies* (44) 5, pp. 936-957.

Hardin, G. (1968). "The tragedy of the commons". In: *Science* (162), 3859, pp. 1243-1248.

Härkönen, J. & J. Dronkers (2006). "Stability and change in the educational gradient of divorce; a comparison of seventeen countries". In: *European Sociological Review* (22) 5, pp. 501-517.

Harsanyi, J.C. (1976). *Essays on ethics, social behavior, and scientific explanation*. Dordrecht: Reidel.

Hart, H. (1982). *Essays on Bentham: studies in jurisprudence and political theory*. Oxford: Clarendon Press.

Hartmann, N. (1962 [1925]). *Ethik*. Berlin: Walter de Gruyter & Co.

Haskey, J. (1998). "One-parent families and their dependent children in Great Britain". In: Office for National Statistics, *Population Trends*, 1, pp. 5-14.

——— (2002). "One-parent families – and the dependent children living in them – in Great Britain". In: Office for National Statistics, *Population Trends*, 3, pp. 46-57.

Hayek, F. (1993 [1960]). *The constitution of liberty*. London: Routledge.

Hays, W.L. (1973). *Statistics for the social sciences*. London: Holt, Rinehart and Winston.

Hempel, C.G. (1966). "The theoretician's dilemma; a study in the logic of theory construction". In: C.G. Hempel, *Aspects of scientific explanation and other essays in the philosophy of science* (pp. 173-226). New York: The Free Press.

Hermkens, P.L.J. & P.J. van Wijngaarden (1987). *Rechtvaardigingscriteria en inkomensongelijkheid; onderzoek uit 1976 herhaald*. Den Haag: Ministerie van Sociale Zaken en Werkgelegenheid.

van den Heuvel, F.G. & J.C. Vrooman (1991). "Preventieve sociale zekerheid". In: F.G. van den Heuvel, J.C. Vrooman & P.J. van Wijngaarden, *Preventie van arbeidsongeschiktheid en werkloosheid*. Den Haag: VUGA/ Nederlands Genootschap voor Sociale Zekerheid.

Hicks, A. & L. Kenworthy (2003). "Varieties of welfare capitalism". In: *Socio-Economic Review* (1) 1, pp. 27-61.

Hill, T.P. (1996). "A statistical derivation of the significant-digit law". In: *Statistical Science* (10) 4, pp. 354-363.

Hills, J., J. Le Grand & D. Piachaud (eds) (2002). *Understanding social exclusion*. Oxford: Oxford University Press.

Hoebel, E.A. (1954). *The law of primitive man; a study in comparative legal dynamics*. Cambridge (Mass.): Harvard University Press.
Hoff, S. & C. Vrooman (2002). *Zelfbepaalde zekerheden; individuele keuzevrijheid in de sociale verzekeringen: draagvlak, benutting en determinanten*. Den Haag: Sociaal en Cultureel Planbureau.
Hoff, S. & G. Jehoel-Gijsbers (2003). *De uitkering van de baan; reïntegratie van uitkeringsontvangers in de periode 1992-2002*. Den Haag: Sociaal en Cultureel Planbureau.
Hohfeld, W.N. (1919). *Fundamental legal conceptions as applied in judicial reasoning*. New Haven: Yale University Press.
Huch, K.J. (1972). *Einübung in die Klassengesellschaft; über den Zusammenhang von Sozialstruktur und Sozialisation*. Frankfurt am Main: S. Fischer Verlag.
Hurrelmann, K. (2002). *Einführung in die Sozialisationstheorie* (8th ed.). Weinheim/Basel: Beltz Verlag.
Hurrelmann, K. & D. Ulich (eds) (2002). *Handbuch der Sozialisationsforschung* (6th ed.). Weinheim/Basel: Beltz Verlag.

I

ILO (1944). *Approaches to social security; an international survey*. Montreal: International Labour Office.
────── (various years). *Yearbook of Labour Statistics*. Geneva: International Labour Office.
────── (1992). *The cost of social security*. Geneva: International Labour Office.
Inglehart, R. (1977). *The silent revolution; changing values and political styles among Western publics*. Princeton: Princeton University Press.
Inglehart, R. (1990). *Culture shift in advanced industrial society*. Princeton: Princeton University Press.
Ingram, P. (1998). "Changing the rules: interests, organizations, and institutional change in the U.S. hospitality industry". In: M.C. Brinton & V. Nee, *The new institutionalism in sociology* (pp. 258-276). New York: Russel Sage.

J

Jahoda, M. (1982). *Employment and unemployment, a social-psychological analysis*. Cambridge: Cambridge University Press.
Jäntti, M. & S. Danziger (2000). "Income poverty in advanced countries". In: A.B. Atkinson & F. Bourguignon (eds), *Handbook of income distribution* (vol. 1) (pp. 309-378). Amsterdam: Elsevier.
Jehoel-Gijsbers, G. (2004). *Sociale uitsluiting in Nederland*. Den Haag: Sociaal en Cultureel Planbureau.
────── (2005). "Problematische schulden". In: C. Vrooman, H.-J. Dirven, A. Soede & R. Trimp (eds), *Armoedemonitor 2005* (pp. 53-102). Den Haag: Sociaal en Cultureel Planbureau.
Jehoel-Gijsbers, G. & C. Vrooman (2007). *Explaining social exclusion; a theoretical model tested in the Netherlands*. The Hague: The Netherlands Institute for Social Research | SCP.
────── (2008a). *Social exclusion of the elderly; a comparative study of EU member states*. Brussels: Centre for European Policy Studies (ENEPRI Research Report No 57). Available at http://www.ceps.eu.
────── (2008b). "Sociale uitsluiting in Nederland en Europa". In: SCP, *Betrekkelijke betrokkenheid; studies in sociale cohesie – Sociaal en Cultureel Rapport 2008*, pp. 234-258. Den Haag: Sociaal en Cultureel Planbureau.
Jenkins, S.P. & P.J. Lambert (1997). "Three 'I's of poverty curves, with an analysis of UK poverty trends". In: *Oxford Economic Papers* (49) 3, pp. 317-327.
Johnson, D.P. (1979). "Dilemmas of charismatic leadership: the case of the People's Temple". In: *Sociological Analysis* (40) 4, pp. 315-323.
Johnson, D.S., J.M. Rogers & L. Tan (2001). "A century of family budgets in the United States". In: *Monthly Labor Review* (124) 5, pp. 28-45.
Jones, A.J.I. & M. Sergot (1993). "On the characterisation of law and computer systems: the normative systems approach". In: J.-J. Meyer & R.J. Wieringa (eds), *Deontic logic in computer science* (pp. 275-307). Chichester: John Wiley and Sons.

K

de Kam, C.A., C.G.M. Sterks & G.M.J. Veldkamp (1989). *Schets van de leer van de sociale zekerheid*. Deventer: Kluwer.
Kangas, O.E. (1994). "The politics of social security: on regressions, qualitative comparisons, and cluster analysis". In: T. Janoski & A.M. Hicks (eds), *The comparative political economy of the welfare state* (pp. 346-364). Cambridge: Cambridge University Press.
Kapteyn, A., S. van de Geer & H. van der Stadt (1985). "The impact of changes in income and family composition on subjective measures of well-being". In: M. David & T. Smeeding (eds), *Horizontal equity, uncertainty and economic well-being* (pp. 35-64). Chicago: Chicago University Press.
Kapteyn, A., P. Kooreman & R. Willemse (1988). "Some methodological issues in the implementation of the subjective poverty line". In: *The Journal of Human Resources* (23) 2, pp. 222-242.
de Kemp, A.A.M. (1992). *Ouderen tussen pensioen en bijstand*. Rijswijk/Den Haag: Sociaal en Cultureel Planbureau/ VUGA.
Kerr, S. (1983). *Making ends meet; an investigation into the non-claiming of supplementary pensions*. London: Bedford Square Press.

van Kessel, J.G.F.M. (1985). *Sociale zekerheid en recht*. Deventer: Kluwer.
Klaassen, C.A.C. (1981). *Sociologie van de persoonlijkheidsontwikkeling*. Deventer: Van Loghum Slaterus.
Kline, R.B. (1998). *Principles and practice of structural equation modeling*. New York/London: The Guildford Press.
Kloosterman, R.C. (1987). *Achteraan in de rij; een onderzoek naar de factoren die (her)intreding van langdurig werklozen belemmeren*. Den Haag: Organisatie voor Strategisch Arbeidsmarktonderzoek.
Kluegel, J.R. & M. Miyano (1995). "Justice beliefs and support for the welfare state in advanced capitalism". In: J.R. Kluegel, D.S. Mason & B. Wegener (eds), *Social justice and political change: public opinion in capitalist and post-communist states* (pp. 81-105). New York: Aldine de Gruyter.
Knobe, J. (2008). "The concept of intentional action: a case study in the uses of folk psychology". In: J. Knobe & S. Nichols (eds), *Experimental philosophy*. New York: Oxford University Press.
Knobe, J & S. Nichols (eds) (2008). *Experimental philosophy*. New York: Oxford University Press.
Knuth, M. & Th. Kalina (2002). "Early exit from the labour force between exclusion and privilege; unemployment as a transition from employment to retirement in West Germany". In: *European Societies* (4) 4, pp. 398-418.
Kohli, M. (2002). "Lebenslauftheoretische Ansätze in der Sozialisationsforschung". In: K. Hurrelmann & D. Ulich (ed), *Handbuch der Sozialisationsforschung* (6th ed.; pp. 303-317). Weinheim/Basel: Beltz Verlag.
Kohn, M.L. (1983). "On the transmission of values in the family: a preliminary formulation". In: A.C. Kerckhoff (ed), *Research in sociology of education and socialization, a research annual; Personal change over the life course* (pp. 1-12). Greenwich (Conn.): JAI Press Inc.
Kollmann, G. (2000). *Social security: summary of major changes in the cash benefits program*. Washington: Social Security Administration.
Korpi, W. (2003). "Welfare-state regress in Western Europe: politics, institutions, globalization, and europeanization". In: *Annual Review of Sociology* (29), pp. 589-609.
Korpi, W. & J. Palme (1998). "The paradox of redistribution and strategies of equality: welfare institutions, inequality and poverty in the western countries". In: *American Sociological Review* (63) 3, pp. 661-687.
Kranendonk, H. & J. Verbruggen (2007). SAFFIER; *a multi-purpose model of the Dutch economy for short-term and medium-term analyses*. The Hague: The Netherlands Bureau for Economic Policy Analysis|CPB.
Kroft, H., G. Engbersen, K. Schuyt & F. van Waarden (1989). *Een tijd zonder werk; een onderzoek naar de levenswereld van langdurig werklozen*. Leiden/Antwerpen: Stenfert Kroese.
Kvist, J. (1999). "Welfare reform in the Nordic countries in the 1990s; using fuzzy-set theory to assess conformity to ideal types". In: *Journal of European Social Policy* (9) 3, pp. 231-252.

L

van Langendonck, J. (1992). "Het probleem van de preventie". In: P.J. van Wijngaarden, F.G. van den Heuvel & J.C. Vrooman (eds), *Preventie in de sociale zekerheid*. Den Haag: VUGA/Nederlands Genootschap voor Sociale Zekerheid.
Laroque, P. (1966). "Social security and social development". In: *Bulletin of I.S.S.A* (19) 3-4, pp. 83-90.
Larsen, C.A. (2006). *The institutional logic of welfare attitudes; how welfare regimes influence public support*. Aldershot: Ashgate.
Lay, M.G. (1992). *Ways of the world; a history of the world's roads and of the vehicles that used them*. New Brunswick (NJ): Rutgers University Press.
Layard, R. (2005). *Happiness; lessons from a new science*. London: Penguin Books Ltd.
Layard, R., S. Nickell & R. Jackman (1991). *Unemployment; macroeconomic performance and the labour market*. Oxford : Oxford University Press.
Layte, R., B. Nolan & C.T. Whelan (2000). "Targeting poverty; lessons from monitoring Ireland's national anti-poverty strategy". In: *Journal of Social Policy* (29) 4, pp. 553-575.
Lazarsfeld-Jahoda, M. & H. Zeisl (1933). *Die Arbeitslosen von Marienthal. Ein soziographischer Versuch über die Wirkungen langdauernder Arbeitslosigkeit*. Leipzig: S. Hirzel Verlag.
Lepianka, D.A. (2007). *Are the poor to be blamed or pitied? A comparative study of popular poverty attributions in Europe*. Tilburg: Tilburg University.
Leibfried, S. & S. Mau (2008). *Welfare states: construction, deconstruction, reconstruction*. London: Edward Elgar.
Levine, D. (1971). "Introduction", in: G. Simmel, *On individuality and social forms* (ed D. Levine), pp. ix-lxv. Chicago: The University of Chicago Press.
Lewbel, A. (1997). "Consumer demand systems and household equivalence scales". In: M.H. Pesaran & P. Schmidt (eds), *Handbook of applied econometrics, volume II: microeconomics*. Oxford: Blackwell Publishers.
Lewis, O. (1959). *Five families: Mexican case studies in the culture of poverty*. New York: Basic Books.
——— (1968). *A study of slum culture; backgrounds for La Vida*. New York: Random House.
——— (1969). "Cultures of poverty". In: P. Moynihan (ed), *On understanding poverty: perspectives from the social sciences*. New York: Basic Books.

Liebowitz, S.J. & S.E. Margolis (1990). "The fable of the keys". In: *Journal of Law & Economics* (33) 1, pp. 1-25.
Lindenberg, S. (1983). "Afbeelden en verklaren met modellen in de sociologie". In: S. Lindenberg & F.N. Stokman (eds), *Modellen in de sociologie*. Deventer: Van Loghum Slaterus.
Littlewood, P., I. Glorieux, S. Herkommer & I. Jönsson (eds) (1999). *Social Exclusion in Europe: Problems and paradigms*. Aldershot: Ashgate.
van Loo, L.F. (1987). *Den arme gegeven...; een beschrijving van armoede, armenzorg en sociale zekerheid in Nederland, 1784-1965*. Meppel: Boom.
―――― (1992). *Arm in Nederland 1815-1990*. Meppel: Boom.
Lucas, R.E. (1988). "On the mechanics of economic development". In: *Journal of Monetary Economics* (22) 1, pp. 3-42.

M

Mack, J.H. & S. Lansley (1985). *Poor Britain*. London: Allan & Unwin.
Malinowski, B. (1944). *A scientific theory of culture and other essays*. Chapel Hill: The University of North Carolina Press.
Mars, G., W. Arts, & R. Luijkx (2002). "Na de val van de muur; baanmobiliteit in een herenigd Duitsland". In: *Mens & Maatschappij* (77) 3, pp. 254-279.
Marx, K. & F. Engels (1848). *Manifest der kommunistischen Partei*. London: J.E. Burghard.
Mason, A. (2005). "Economic demography". In: D.L. Poston & M. Micklin, *Handbook of Population*. New York: Kluwer Academic/Plenum Publishers.
McConnell, T. (2002). "Moral dilemmas". In: *The Stanford Encyclopedia of Philosophy* (Spring 2002 edition; http://plato.stanford.edu).
McDonald, P. (2002). "Sustaining fertility through public policy: the range of options". In: *Population* (English edition) (57) 3, pp. 417-446.
McEwan, I. (1997). *Enduring love*. London: Jonathan Cape.
McKee-Ryan, F.M., Z. Song, C.R. Wanberg & A. J. Kinicki (2005). "Psychological and physical well-being during unemployment: a meta-analytic study". In: *Journal of Applied Psychology*, (90) 1, 53-76.
McKelvey, R.D. & W. Zavoina (1975). "A statistical model for the analysis of ordinal level dependent variables". In: *Journal of Mathematical Sociology* (4), pp. 103-120.
Mead, G.H. (1934). *Mind, self and society, from the standpoint of a social behaviorist* (ed C.W. Morris). Chicago/London: The University of Chicago Press.
―――― (1938). *The philosophy of the act* (ed C.W. Morris). Chicago/London: The University of Chicago Press.
Melai Committee (1980). *Adviescommissie Zedelijkheidswetgeving; eindrapport*. Den Haag: SDU.
Mele, A.R. (ed) (1997). *The philosophy of action*. Oxford: Oxford University Press.
Mele, A. (2003). "Intentional action: controversies, data and core hypotheses". In: *Philosophical Psychology* (16) 2, pp. 325-340.
Michelbach, P.A., J.T. Scott, R.E. Matland & B.H. Bornstein (2003)."Doing Rawls justice: an experimental study of income distribution norms". In: *American Journal of Political Science* (47) 3, pp. 523-539.
Middendorp, C.P. (1978). *Progressiveness and conservatism; the fundamental dimensions of ideological controversy and their relationship to social class*. Berlin/New York: Mouton-De Gruyter.
―――― (1991). *Ideology in Dutch politics; the democratic system reconsidered 1970-1985*. Assen/Maastricht: Van Gorcum.
Middleton, S. (2000). "Agreeing poverty lines: the development of consensual budget standards methodology". In: J. Bradshaw & R. Sainsbury (eds), *Researching Poverty* (pp. 59-76). Aldershot: Ashgate.
Milanovic, B. (2000). "The median voter hypothesis, income inequality and income redistribution: an empirical test with the required data". In: *Luxembourg Income Study working paper series* (184). Syracuse (NY): Maxwell school of citizenship and public affairs.
Mill, J.S. (1998 [1861]). *Utilitarianism* (ed R. Crisp). Oxford/New York: Oxford University Press.
Mincer, J. (1993 [1984]). "Human capital and economic growth". In: *Collected essays of Jacob Mincer, vol. 1: studies in human capital* (pp. 285-302). Aldershot: Elgar.
Minkman, M. & B.M.S. van Praag (1997). "Het begrip 'armoede': is het meetbaar?" In: G. Engbersen, J.C. Vrooman & E. Snel, *De kwetsbaren – tweede jaarrapport armoede en sociale uitsluiting*. Amsterdam: Amsterdam University Press.
Moffitt, R. (1992). "Incentive effects of the U.S. welfare system: a review". In: *Journal of Economic Literature* (30) 3, pp. 1-61.
Moor, I., I. Vossen & M. Arents (2002). *Benefit dependency ratios by gender; an international comparison* (final report). The Hague: Ministry of Social Affairs and Employment.
Muffels, R.J.A. (1993). *Welfare economic effects of social security; essays on poverty, social security and labour market: evidence from paneldata*. Tilburg: Katholieke Universiteit Brabant.
Murray, C. A. (1984). *Losing ground; American social policy, 1950-1980*. New York: Basic Books.
―――― (1997). *What it means to be a libertarian; a personal interpretation*. New York: Broadway Books.

N

Neal, D. & S. Rosen (2000). "Theories of the distribution of earnings". In: A.B. Atkinson & F. Bourguignon (eds), *Handbook of income distribution (vol. 1)*. Amsterdam: Elsevier (pp. 379-427).

Nibud (2006). *Minima effectrapportage gemeente X*. Utrecht: Nationaal Instituut voor Budgetvoorlichting. Available through www.nibud.nl

────── (2008). *Budgethandboek*. Utrecht: Nationaal Instituut voor Budgetvoorlichting.

Nickell, S.J. (1997). "Unemployment and labor market rigidities: Europe versus North America". In: *Journal of Economic Perspectives* (11) 3, pp. 55-74.

Nigrini, M.J. (1996). "A taxpayer compliance application of Benford's Law". In: *Journal of the American Taxation Association* (18) 1, pp. 72-91.

NIS (2001). *Bevolking en huishoudens: huishoudens en familiekernen*. Brussel: Nationaal Instituut voor de Statistiek.

Noll, H.-H. (2000). *Social indicators and social reporting: the international experience*. At: www.ccsd.ca/ noll1.html (downloaded October 7, 2005).

North, D.C. (1990). *Institutions, institutional change and economic performance*. Cambridge: Cambridge University Press.

────── (1998). "Economic performance through time". In: M.C. Brinton & V. Nee, *The new institutionalism in sociology* (pp. 247-257). New York: Russel Sage.

Northrop, F.S.C. (1947). *The logic of sciences and the humanities*. New York: Macmillan.

Nozick, R. (1974). *Anarchy, State, and Utopia*. New York: Basic Books.

Nussbaum, M. C. (2000). *Women and human development: the capabilities approach*. Cambridge: Cambridge University Press.

O

Obinger, H. & U. Wagschal (1998). "Das Stratifizierungskonzept in der clusteranalytischen Überprüfung". In: S. Lessenich & I. Ostner (eds), *Welten des Wohlfarhtskapitalismus – der Sozialstaat in vergleichender Perspektive* (pp. 109-135). Frankfurt am Main: Campus Verlag.

OECD (1982). *The OECD list of social indicators*. Paris: Organisation for Economic Co-operation and Development.

────── (1988). *Reforming public pensions*. Paris: Organisation for Economic Co-operation and Development.

────── (1993). *Employment Outlook*. Paris: Organisation for Economic Co-operation and Development.

────── (1994). *The OECD Jobs Study – evidence and explanations; Part II: the adjustment potential of the labour market*. Paris: Organisation for Economic Co-operation and Development.

────── (1995a). *The tax/benefit position of production workers*. Paris: Organisation for Economic Co-operation and Development.

────── (1995b). *Labour Force Statistics 1973-1993*. Paris: Organisation for Economic Co-operation and Development.

────── (1996). *Economic Outlook* (59) June 1996. Paris: Organisation for Economic Co-operation and Development.

────── (1997a). *Making work pay: taxation, benefits, employment and unemployment*. Paris: Organisation for Economic Co-operation and Development.

────── (1997b). *Employment Outlook*. Paris: Organisation for Economic Co-operation and Development.

────── (1998a). *The battle against exclusion – social assistance in Australia, Finland, Sweden and the United Kingdom*. Paris: Organisation for Economic Co-operation and Development.

────── (1998b). *The battle against exclusion (vol. 2) – social assistance in Belgium, the Czech Republic, the Netherlands and Norway*. Paris: Organisation for Economic Co-operation and Development.

────── (1999). *The battle against exclusion (vol. 3) – social assistance in Canada and Switzerland*. Paris: Organisation for Economic Co-operation and Development.

────── (2000). *Labour Force Statistics 1979-1999*. Paris: Organisation for Economic Co-operation and Development.

────── (2001). *Ageing and income – financial resources and retirement in 9 OECD countries*. Paris: Organisation for Economic Co-operation and Development.

────── (2002). *Benefits and wages – OECD indicators*. Paris: Organisation for Economic Co-operation and Development.

────── (2003a). *Employment Outlook – towards more and better jobs*. Paris: Organisation for Economic Co-operation and Development.

────── (2003b). *Labour Force Statistics 1982-2002*. Paris: Organisation for Economic Co-operation and Development.

────── (2004). *The labour force participation of older workers – the effects of pension and early retirement schemes*. Paris: Organisation for Economic Co-operation and Development.

────── (2006). *Education at a glance*. Paris: Organisation for Economic Co-operation and Development.

────── (2007). *Pensions at a glance; public policies across OECD countries*. Paris: Organisation for Economic Co-operation and Development.

────── (2008). *Growing unequal? Income distribution and poverty in OECD countries*. Paris: Organisation for Economic Co-operation and Development.

van Oorschot, W.J.H. (1994). *Take it or leave it – a study of non-takeup of social security benefits*. Tilburg: Tilburg University Press.
— (2000). "Who should get what, and why? On deservingness criteria and the conditionality of solidarity among the public". In: *Policy and Politics* (28) 1, pp. 33-48.
— (2005). *Immigrants, welfare and deservingness opinions in European welfare states*. Aalborg: CCWS.
van Oorschot, W. & L. Halman (2000). "Blame or fate, individual or social? An international comparison of popular explanations of poverty". In: *European Societies* (2) 1, pp. 1-28.
van Oorschot, W. & W. Arts (2005). "The social capital of European welfare states: the crowding out hypothesis revisited". In: *Journal of European Social Policy* (15) 1, pp. 5-26.
Orshansky, M. (1963). "Children of the poor". In: *Social Security Bulletin* (26) 7, pp. 3-13.
— (1965). "Counting the poor: another look at the poverty profile". In: *Social Security Bulletin* (28) 1, pp. 3-29.
Ostrom, C.W. (1990). *Time series analysis – regression techniques*. Newbury Park: Sage.

P
Papadakis, E. & C. Bean (1993). "Popular support for the welfare state: a comparison between institutional regimes". In: *Journal of Public Policy* (13) 3, pp. 227-254.
Pareto, V. (1935 [1916]). *The mind and society; a treatise on general sociology*. New York: Harcourt, Brace and Company. [*Trattato di sociologie generale*. Firenze: Barbera].
— (1968 [1901]). *The rise and fall of elites; an application of theoretical sociology*. Totowa (N.J.): The Bedminster Press. ["Un applicazione di teorie sociologiche". In: *Rivista Italiana de Sociologia*, pp. 402-456].
Parsons, T. (1951). *The social system*. New York: Free Press of Glencoe.
— (1964). *Social structure and personality*. New York: Free Press of Glencoe.
Paugam S. (1996). "La constitution d'un paradigme". In: S. Paugam (ed), *L'exclusion, l'état des savoirs* (pp. 7-19). Paris: La Découverte.
Pfau-Effinger, B. (2005). "Culture and welfare state policies: reflections on a complex interrelation". In: *Journal of Social Policy* (34) 1, pp. 3-20.
Pfeffermann, D., C.J. Skinner, D.J. Holmes, H. Goldstein & J. Rasbash (1998). "Weighting for unequal selection probabilities in multilevel models". In: *Journal of the Royal Statistical Society, Series B* (60) 1, pp. 23-56.
Piaget, J. & B. Inhelder (1969). *The psychology of the child*. New York: Basic Books.
Pitruzzello, S. (1999). *Decommodification and the worlds of welfare capitalism; a cluster analysis*. Florence: European University Institute (Schuman Centre/European Forum; seminar paper ws/90, 16 june 1999).
Pollak, R.A. & T.J. Wales (1979). "Welfare comparisons and equivalence scales". In: *American Economic Review* (69) 2, pp. 216-221.
Pommer, E., J. van Leeuwen & M. Ras (2003). *Inkomen verdeeld; trends in ongelijkheid, herverdeling en dynamiek*. Den Haag: Sociaal en Cultureel Planbureau.
Popper, K.R. (1968 [1959]). *The logic of scientific discovery*. New York: Harper & Row [first translated edition New York: Basic Books].
Posner, E.A. (2000). *Law and social norms*. Cambridge (Mass.)/London: Harvard University Press.
van Praag, B.M.S. (1971). "The individual welfare function in Belgium: an empirical investigation". In: *European Economic Review* (2) 3, pp. 337-369.
van Praag, B.M.S. & A. Kapteyn (1973). "Further evidence on the individual welfare function of income: an empirical investigation in the Netherlands". In: *European Economic Review* (4) 1, pp. 33-62.
van Praag, B.M.S., V. Halberstadt & H. Emanuel (1982). "De valkuil der sociale zekerheid". In: *Economisch Statistische Berichten* (67) 3378, pp. 1155-1159.
van Praag, B.M.S. & A. Ferrer-i-Carbonell (2004). *Happiness quantified; a satisfaction calculus approach*. Oxford: Oxford University Press.
— (2006). *A multi-dimensional approach to subjective poverty*. Amsterdam: University of Amsterdam.
Putnam, R. (2000). *Bowling alone*. New York: Simon & Schuster.

R
Ragin, C. (1994). "A qualitative comparative analysis of pension systems". In: T. Janoski & A.M. Hicks (eds), *The comparative political economy of the welfare state* (pp. 320-345). Cambridge: Cambridge University Press.
— (2000). *Fuzzy-set social science*. Chicago: The University of Chicago Press.
Rapley, M. (2003). *Quality of life research: a critical introduction*. London: Sage.
Ras, M., E. Pommer & J.M. Wildeboer Schut (2002). *Income on the move*. Brussels: European Commission.
Rawls, J. (1999 [1971]). *A theory of justice* (1999: revised edition). Harvard (MA): Harvard University Press.
— (1993). *Political liberalism*. New York: Columbia University Press.
Raz, J. (1986). *The morality of freedom*. Oxford: Clarendon Press.

van Rhijn Commission (1945/1946). *Sociale zekerheid; rapport van de Commissie, ingesteld bij beschikking van den minister van Sociale Zaken van 26 Maart 1943, met de opdracht algemeene richtlijnen vast te stellen voor de toekomstige ontwikkeling der sociale verzekering in Nederland* (3 vols. + annexes). Den Haag: Rijksuitgeverij.

Roebroek, J.M. & M. Hertogh (1998). *De beschavende invloed des tijds; twee eeuwen sociale politiek, verzorgingsstaat en sociale zekerheid in Nederland*. Den Haag: COSZ/VUGA.

Roemer, J.E. (1996). *Theories of distributive justice*. Cambridge (Mass.): Harvard University Press.

Roes, Th. (ed) (2008). *Facts and figures of the Netherlands; social and cultural trends 1995-2006*. The Hague: The Netherlands Institute for Social Research | SCP.

Room, G. (ed) (1995a). *Beyond the threshold: the measurement and analysis of social exclusion*. Bristol: The Policy Press.

——— (1995b). "Poverty in Europe. Competing paradigms of analysis". In: *Policy and Politics* (23) 2, pp. 103-113.

Ross, D. (2006). "Game Theory". In: *The Stanford Encyclopedia of Philosophy* (Spring 2008 edition; http://plato.stanford.edu).

Runciman, W.G. (1966). *Relative deprivation and social justice; a study of attitudes to social inequality in twentieth-century England*. London: Routledge & Kegan Paul.

S

Saint-Arnaud, S. & P. Bernard (2003). "Convergence or resilience? A hierarchical cluster analysis of welfare regimes in advanced countries". In: *Current Sociology* (51) 5, pp. 499-528.

Saraceno, C. (1997). "The importance of the concept of social exclusion". In: W. Beck, L. van der Maesen & A. Walker (eds), *The social quality of Europe* (pp. 157-164). The Hague: Kluwer.

——— (2001). *Social exclusion. Cultural roots and diversities of a popular concept*. Paper presented at the conference on 'Social exclusion and children', Institute for Child and Family Policy, Columbia University, 3-4 May.

Sarlo, C.A. (2001). *Measuring poverty in Canada*. Vancouver: The Fraser Institute.

Saunders, P. (2004). *Towards a credible poverty framework: from income poverty to deprivation*. Sydney: The Social Policy Research Centre.

Saunders, P., J. Chalmers, M. McHugh, C. Murray, M. Bittman & B. Bradbury (1998). *Development of indicative budget standards for Australia*. Canberra: Department of Social Security.

Scanlon, Th. (1998). *What we owe to each other*. Cambridge (Mass.): Harvard University Press.

Scherer, P. (2002). *Age of withdrawal from the labour market in OECD countries*. Paris: Organisation for Economic Co-operation and Development.

Schmidtz, D. (1995). *Rational choice and moral agency*. Princeton, N.J.: Princeton University Press.

SCP (1992). *Sociaal en Cultureel Rapport 1992*. Rijswijk/Den Haag: Sociaal en Cultureel Planbureau/VUGA.

——— (1998). *Sociaal en Cultureel Rapport 1998*. Rijswijk/Den Haag: Sociaal en Cultureel Planbureau /Elsevier bedrijfsinformatie.

——— (2001). *The Netherlands in a European perspective; Social & Cultural Report 2000*. The Hague: Social and Cultural Planning Office. (Also downloadable from http://www.scp.nl)

——— (2002). *De kwaliteit van de quartaire sector; Sociaal en Cultureel Rapport 2002*. Den Haag: Sociaal en Cultureel Planbureau.

Scruggs, L. & J. Allan (2006). "Welfare state decommodification in eighteen OECD countries: a replication and revision". In: *Journal of European Social Policy* (16) 1, pp. 55-72.

Searle, J.R. (1995). *The construction of social reality*. New York: The Free Press.

Seebohm Rowntree, B. (1901). *Poverty: a study of town life*. London: MacMillan and Co., Limited [facsimile edition; Bristol: The Policy Press, 2000].

Sen, A. (1976). "Poverty: an ordinal approach to measurement". In: *Econometrica* (44) 2, pp. 219-231.

——— (1980). "Equality of what?". In: S.M. McMurrin (ed), *Tanner lectures on human values*. Salt Lake City: University of Utah Press.

——— (1981). *Poverty and famines – an essay on entitlement and deprivation*. Oxford: Clarendon Press/Oxford University Press.

——— (1983). "Poor, relatively speaking". In: *Oxford Economic Papers* (35) 2, pp. 153-156.

——— (1985). "A sociological approach to the measurement of poverty; a reply to professor Peter Townsend". In: *Oxford Economic Papers* (37) 4, pp. 669-675.

——— (1992). *Inequality re-examined*. Cambridge (Mass.): Sage.

——— (1993). "Capability and well-being". In: M.C. Nussbaum & A. Sen (eds), *The quality of life*. Oxford: Oxford University Press.

——— (1999). *Development as freedom*. Oxford: Oxford University Press.

Seyfang, G. (2001). "Working for the Fenland Dollar: an evaluation of local exchange trading schemes as an informal employment strategy to tackle social exclusion". In: *Work, Employment and Society* (15) 3, pp. 581-593.

Shalev, M. (1996). *The privatization of social policy? Occupational welfare and the welfare state in America, Scandinavia and Japan.* London: McMillan. (Introduction, pp. 8-14)

―――― (2007). "Limits and alternatives to multiple regression in comparative research". In: *Comparative Social Research (Capitalisms considered)* (24) (yearbook), pp. 261-308.

Short, K.S. (2005). "Material and financial hardship and income-based poverty measures in the USA". In: *Journal of Social Policy* (34) 1, pp. 21-38.

Short, K., T. Garner, D. Johnson & P. Doyle (1999). *Experimental poverty measures: 1990-1997.* Washington DC: US Census Bureau.

Siaroff, A. (1994). "Work, welfare and gender equality: a new typology". In: D. Sainsbury (ed), *Gendering welfare states.* London: Sage Publications.

Siermann, C.L.J., P.J.J. van Teeffelen & L.J.M. Urlings (2004). *Equivalentiefactoren 1995-2000.* Voorburg: Centraal Bureau voor de Statistiek.

Simmel, G. (1971a [1908]). "The stranger". In: G. Simmel, *On individuality and social forms* (ed D. Levine; pp. 143-149). Chicago: The University of Chicago Press. ["Der Fremde". In: *Soziologie; Untersuchungen über die Formen der Vergesellschaftung* (pp. 685-691). München/Leipzig: Duncker & Humblot].

―――― (1971b [1908]). "The poor". In: G. Simmel, *On individuality and social forms* (ed D. Levine; pp. 150-178). Chicago: The University of Chicago Press. ["Der Arme". In: *Soziologie; Untersuchungen über die Formen der Vergesellschaftung* (pp. 345-374). München/Leipzig: Duncker & Humblot].

Simon, H. (1986). "Rationality in psychology and economics". In: *Journal of Business* (supplement) (59) 4, pp. S209-S224.

Small, M.L. & K. Newman (2001). "Urban poverty after the truly disadvantaged: the rediscovery of the family, the neighborhood, and culture". In: Annual Review of Sociology (27), pp. 23-45.

Smith, A. (1909 [1776]). *An inquiry into the nature and causes of the wealth of nations.* New York: Collier and Sons.

Snijders, T.A.B. (2001). "Methoden van netwerkanalyse". In: J.C. Vrooman (ed), *Netwerken en sociaal kapitaal* (pp. 23-42). Amsterdam: SISWO/Nederlandse Sociologische Vereniging.

Snijders, T.A.B. & R.J. Bosker (1999). *Multilevel analysis – an introduction to basic and advanced multilevel modelling.* London: Sage Publications.

Soede, A.J. (2006). *Naar een nieuwe armoedegrens?* Den Haag: Sociaal en Cultureel Planbureau.

Soede, A.J., J.C. Vrooman, P.M. Ferraresi & G. Segre (2004). *Unequal welfare states; distributive consequences of population ageing in six European countries.* The Hague: Social and Cultural Planning Office.

Soede, A. & C. Vrooman (2007). "Noodzakelijke bestedingen als armoedegrens". In: *Economisch Statistische Berichten* (92) 4510, pp. 296-299.

―――― (2008a). *A comparative typology of pension regimes.* Brussels: Centre for European Policy Studies (ENEPRI Research Report No 54). Available at http://www.ceps.eu.

―――― (2008b). *Beyond the breadline; a poverty threshold based on a generalised budget approach.* The Hague: The Netherlands Institute for Social Research | SCP.

Sorrentino, C. (2000). "International unemployment rates: how comparable are they?" In: *Monthly Labor Review* (123) 6, pp. 3-20.

Spade, P.V. (2006). "William of Ockham". In: *The Stanford Encyclopedia of Philosophy* (Fall 2006 edition); http://plato.stanford.edu/.

SSA (1986). *Disability History Report.* Washington: Social Security Administration.

SSA (2002). *Social security programs throughout the world.* Washington: Social Security Administration.

von Staden, H. (1996). " 'In a pure and holy way': personal and professional conduct in the Hippocratic Oath". In: *Journal of the History of Medicine and Allied Sciences* (51), pp. 406-408.

Statistisches Bundesamt (2002). *Leben und arbeiten in Deutschland.* Wiesbaden: Statistisches Bundesamt.

Stiglitz, J.E. (2006). *Making globalization work.* New York: W.W. Norton & Co.

Stinson, L.L. (1997). *The subjective assessment of income and expenses: cognitive test results (final report).* Washington: Bureau of Labor Statistics.

―――― (1998). *Subjective assessments of economic well-being: wave II – cognitive interviews (final report).* Washington: Bureau of Labor Statistics.

Stirner, M. (1971 [1845]). *Der Einzige und sein Eigentum.* Leipzig: Otto Wigand, 1845. English edition: *The ego and his own* (ed J. Carrol), London: Jonathan Cape.

Strengmann-Kuhn, W. (2004). *Poverty measurement with the European Community Household Panel.* Paper prepared for the ChangeQual Network Meeting in Paris. Frankfurt am Main: Goethe Universität.

Svallfors, S. (1997). "Worlds of welfare and attitudes to redistribution: a comparison of eight western nations". In: *European Sociological Review* (13) 3, pp. 283-304.

―――― (2003). "Welfare regimes and welfare opinions: a comparison of eight Western countries". In: J. Vogel (ed),

European welfare production – institutional configuration and distributional outcome (pp. 171-196). Dordrecht/Boston/London: Kluwer Academic Publishers.

de Swaan, A. (1988). *In care of the state; health care, education and welfare in Europe and the United States in the modern era.* Cambridge: Polity Press.

——— (1989). *De verzorging in het teken van het kapitaal.* Amsterdam: Stichting Dr J.M. den Uyl-lezing.

——— (2001). *Words of the world; the global language system.* Cambridge: Polity Press/Blackwell.

Szirmai, A. (1986). *Inequality observed: a study of attitudes towards income inequality.* Aldershot: Avebury.

T

Thijssen, J. & J.M. Wildeboer Schut (2005). "Armoede in hoofdlijnen". In: C. Vrooman, H.-J. Dirven, A. Soede & R. Trimp (eds), *Armoedemonitor 2005* (pp. 16-52). Den Haag: Sociaal en Cultureel Planbureau.

Thoenes, P. (1962). *De elite in de verzorgingsstaat; sociologische proeve van een terugkeer naar domineesland.* Leiden: Stenfert Kroese.

Thoreau, H.D. (1849). "Resistance to civil government (Civil disobedience)". In: *Aesthetic Papers* (pp. 179-211). Boston: The Editor (E.P. Peabody).

Thurow, L. (1975). *Generating inequality.* New York: Basic Books.

Titmuss, R.M. (1958). "The social division of welfare". In: R.M. Titmuss, *Essays on the welfare state.* London: Unwin University Books.

——— (1974). *Social policy: an introduction.* London: Allen & Unwin.

TK (1976/1977). *Rijksbegroting XV: Sociale Zaken.* Den Haag: Tweede Kamer der Staten-Generaal (vergaderjaar 1976/1977, 14100 No 2).

——— (1991/1992a). *Nota over de toestand van 's Rijks Financiën; tekstgedeelte van de Miljoennennota 1992.* Den Haag: Tweede Kamer der Staten-Generaal (vergaderjaar 1991/1992, 22300 No 1).

——— (1991/1992b). *Rijksbegroting XV: Sociale Zaken en Werkgelegenheid.* Den Haag: Tweede Kamer der Staten-Generaal (vergaderjaar 1976/1977, 22300 XV No 2).

——— (1996/1997). *Sociale nota 1997.* Tweede Kamer, vergaderjaar 1996/1997, 25002, nrs. 1-2.

Townsend, P. (1979). *Poverty in the United Kingdom – a survey of household resources and standards of living.* Harmondsworth: Penguin.

Turner, D., L. Boone, C. Giorno, M. Meacci, D. Rae & P. Richardson (2001). "Estimating the structural rate of unemployment for the OECD countries". In: *OECD Economic Studies* (33) pp. 171-216. Paris: Organisation for Economic Co-operation and Development.

U

UNDP (1995). *Human Development Report 1995.* New York/Oxford: United Nations Development Programme/Oxford University Press.

——— (2007). *Human Development Report 2007/2008.* New York/Houndmills, Basingstoke, Hampshire: United Nations Development Programme/Palgrave Macmillan.

V

van der Veen, R.J. (1990). *De sociale grenzen van beleid; een onderzoek naar de uitvoering en de effecten van het stelsel van sociale zekerheid.* Leiden: Stenfert Kroese.

Veldkamp, G.M.J. (1978). *Inleiding tot de sociale zekerheid en de toepassing ervan in Nederland en België, deel I: karakter en geschiedenis.* Deventer: Kluwer.

——— (1984). *Schets van de leer van de sociale zekerheid.* Deventer: Kluwer.

Verheul, J.M. (1989). *Fraude en misbruik in de sociale zekerheid.* Deventer: Kluwer.

Vermunt, J.K. & J. Magidson (2002). "Latent class cluster analysis". In: J.A. Hagenaars & A.L. McCutcheon (eds), *Applied latent class analysis* (pp. 89-106). Cambridge: Cambridge University Press.

Verschuren, P.J.M. (1991). *Structurele modellen tussen theorie en praktijk.* Utrecht: Het Spectrum.

Viaene, J., J. van Steenberge & D. Lahaye (1976). *Schade aan de mens, deel III: evaluatie van de gezondheidsschade.* Antwerpen/Amsterdam: Maarten Kluwer.

Viaene, J., J. Huys, M. Justaert, D. Lahaye, D. Simoens, & J. van Steenberge (1990). *Actuele uitdagingen voor de sociale zekerheid, deel III: Hervorming van de sociale zekerheid: vanuit een nieuw begrippenkader?* Brugge: Die Keure.

Vis, B. (2007). "States of welfare or states of workfare? Welfare state restructuring in 16 capitalist democracies, 1985-2002". In: *Policy and Politics* (35) 1, pp. 105-122.

Vogel, J. (2003) "Income and material living standards". In: J. Vogel (ed), *European welfare production: institutional configuration and distributional outcome* (pp. 113-145). Dordrecht: Kluwer.

de Voogd, J. & E. van Schooneveld (1991). *Gebruikersruimte in de volksverzekeringen; een verkennend onderzoek naar de AOW, AWW, AKW en AAW*. Den Haag: VUGA.

de Vos, K. (1991). *Micro-economic definitions of poverty*. Rotterdam: Erasmus Universiteit (Thesis).

Vrooman, J.C. (1994). "Preventieve sociale zekerheid: holle frase, toverspreuk of toekomstbeeld?" In: J. van Steenberge, S. Klosse & L.J.M. de Leede (eds), *Preventie: een solide basis voor sociale zekerheid?* (pp. 107-121). Antwerpen: MAKLU.

―――― (1995). "Sociale zekerheid". In: *Compendium voor Politiek en Samenleving in Nederland* (deel III, pp. 1-84). Houten: Bohn Stafleu Van Loghum.

―――― (ed) (1999). *Moderne sociale dilemma's*. Amsterdam: SISWO/Nederlandse Sociologische Vereniging.

―――― (2000). "Arme mensen". In: SCP, *Oud & nieuw 1999-2000* (pp. 4-8). Den Haag: Sociaal en Cultureel Planbureau.

―――― (2006). "Subjectieve definities van armoede". In: F. Otten, C. Vrooman, W. Bos & S. Hoff (eds), *Armoedebericht 2006* (pp. 58-61). Voorburg/Heerlen: CBS.

―――― (2007). "Slotbeschouwing". In: C.Vrooman, S. Hoff, F. Otten & W. Bos (eds), *Armoedemonitor 2007* (pp. 171-188). Den Haag: Sociaal en Cultureel Planbureau.

―――― (2008a). "In 1 Europa". In: P. Dekker, V. Veldheer & R. van den Brink (eds), *Alles kan korter* (pp. 14-15). Den Haag: Sociaal en Cultureel Planbureau/Éditions Dix sept juillet.)

―――― (ed) (2008b). *The elderly poor in the EU's New Member States*. Brussels: Centre for European Policy Studies (ENEPRI Research Report No 60). Available at http://www.ceps.eu.

Vrooman, J.C. & J. Dronkers (1986). "Changing educational attainment processes: some evidence from the Netherlands". In: *Sociology of Education* (59) 2, pp. 69-78.

Vrooman, J.C. & K.T.M. Asselberghs (1994). *De gemiste bescherming – niet-gebruik van sociale zekerheid door bestaansonzekere huishoudens*. Den Haag: Ministerie van Sociale Zaken en Werkgelegenheid/VUGA.

Vrooman, C. & E. Snel (1999). "Op zoek naar de 'echte armen'". In: G. Engbersen, J.C. Vrooman & E. Snel (ed), *Armoede en verzorgingsstaat – vierde jaarrapport armoede en sociale uitsluiting* (pp. 15-47). Amsterdam: Amsterdam University Press.

Vrooman, C. & S. Hoff (eds) (2004). *The poor side of the Netherlands; results from the Dutch 'Poverty monitor', 1997-2003*. The Hague: Social and Cultural Planning Office.

Vrooman, C., S. Hoff & A. Soede (2004). "Sociale zekerheid". In: SCP, *In het zicht van de toekomst; Sociaal en Cultureel Rapport 2004* (pp. 315-360). Den Haag: Sociaal en Cultureel Planbureau.

Vrooman, C., S. Hoff, F. Otten & W. Bos (eds) (2007a). *Armoedemonitor 2007*. Den Haag: Sociaal en Cultureel Planbureau.

Vrooman, C., M. Gesthuizen, S. Hoff, A. Soede & J.M. Wildeboer Schut (2007b). "Inkomen en werk". In: R. Bijl, J. Boelhouwer & E. Pommer (eds), *De sociale staat van Nederland 2007* (pp. 123-158). Den Haag: Sociaal en Cultureel Planbureau.

W

Walker, R. (1987). "Consensual approaches to the definition of poverty: towards an alternative methodology". In: *Journal of Social Policy* (16) 2, pp. 213-226.

Wasserman, S. & K. Faust (1994). *Social network analysis*. New York/Cambridge: Cambridge University Press.

Weber, M. (1905). "Die protestantische Ethik und der 'Geist' des Kapitalismus". In: *Archiv für Sozialwissenschaft und Sozialpolitik* (20/21).

―――― (1922). *Wirtschaft und Gesellschaft (Grundriss der Sozialökonomik, III. Abteilung)*. Tübingen: J.C.B. Mohr Verlag (Paul Siebeck). English translation: M. Weber (1968). *Economy and society (vol. 1)*; ed by G. Roth & C. Wittich. Berkeley/Los Angeles/London: University of California Press.

―――― (1988 [1922]). "Die 'Objektivität' sozialwissenschaftlicher und sozialpolitischer Erkenntnis". In: M. Weber, *Gesammelte Aufsätze zur Wissenschaftslehre* (pp. 146-214). Tübingen: J.C.B. Mohr (Paul Siebeck) (7. Auflage).

Wendel, W.B. (2002). "Mixed signals: rational choice theories of social norms and the pragmatics of explanation". In: *Indiana Law Journal* (77) 1, pp. 1-63.

White, G. (1977). *Socialisation*. London: Longman.

White, G. & R. Goodman. (1998). "Welfare orientalism and the search for an East Asian welfare model". In: R. Goodman, G. White & H. Kwon (eds), *The East Asian welfare model: welfare orientalism and the state* (pp. 3-24). London: Routledge.

White, S. (2004). "Social minimum". In: *The Stanford Encyclopedia of Philosophy* (Winter 2004 edition); http://plato.stanford.edu/.

Wildeboer Schut, J.M., J.C. Vrooman & P.T. de Beer (2001). *On worlds of welfare; institutions and their effects in eleven welfare states*. The Hague: Social and Cultural Planning Office. (Also downloadable from http://www.scp.nl)

Wildeboer Schut, J.M. & S. Hoff (2007). *Geld op de plank; niet-gebruik van inkomensvoorzieningen*. Den Haag: Sociaal en Cultureel Planbureau.

Wilensky, H.L. (1975). "Economic level, ideology, and social structure". In: H.L. Wilensky, *The welfare state and equality; structural and ideological roots of public expenditures* (pp. 15-49). Berkeley: University of California Press.

Williams, C. C., T. Aldridge, R. Lee, A. Leyshon, N. Thrift & J. Tooke (2001). "Bridges into work? An evaluation of local exchange and trading schemes (LETS)". In: *Policy Studies* (22) 2, pp. 119-132.

Williamson, O.E. (1985). *The economic institutions of capitalism*. New York: Free Press.
—— (1998). "The institutions of governance". In: *The American Economic Review* (88) 2, pp. 75-79.
Williamson, O.E. & S.G. Winter (eds) (1991). *The nature of the firm*. New York: Oxford University Press USA.
Wilson, W.J. (1987). *The truly disadvantaged: the inner city, the underclass, and public policy.* Chicago: University of Chicago Press.
—— (1997). *When work disappears; the world of the new urban poor*. New York: Alfred A. Knopf.
Winch, P. (1958). *The idea of a social science and its relation to philosophy*. London/Henley-on-Thames: Routledge & Kegan Paul.
Wittgenstein, L. (1953). *Philosophical investigations*. Oxford: Blackwell.
Wouters, Th. A. (1968). *Van bedeling naar verheffing. Evolutie in de verhouding tegenover de behoeftige mens te 's-Hertogenbosch, 1854-1912.* Tilburg: Stichting Zuidelijk Historisch Contact.
Wrong, D.H. (1961). "The oversocialized conception of man in modern sociology". In: *American Sociological Review* (26) 2, pp. 183-193.

Z

Zhang, J. & J. Zhang (2004). "How does social security affect economic growth? Evidence from cross-country data". In: *Journal of Population Economics* (17) 3, pp. 473-500.
Zheng, B. (1997). "Aggregate poverty measures". In: *Journal of Economic Surveys* (11) 2, pp. 123-162.
Zijderveld, A.C. (2000). *The institutional imperative – the interface of institutions and networks.* Amsterdam: Amsterdam University Press.